Transformative Impact of AI in Supply Chain Management

Jabir Arif
Sidi Mohamed Ben Abdellah University, Fez, Morocco

Fouad Jawab
Sidi Mohamed Ben Abdellah University, Fez, Morocco

IGI Global
Scientific Publishing
Publishing Tomorrow's Research Today

Vice President of Editorial Melissa Wagner
Director of Acquisitions Mikaela Felty
Director of Book Development Jocelynn Hessler
Production Manager Mike Brehm
Cover Design Jose Rosado

Published in the United States of America by
IGI Global Scientific Publishing
701 East Chocolate Avenue
Hershey, PA, 17033, USA
Tel: 717-533-8845
Fax: 717-533-7115
Website: https://www.igi-global.com E-mail: cust@igi-global.com

Library of Congress Cataloging-in-Publication Data

Names: Arif, Jabir, 1985- editor. | Jawab, Fouad, 1968- editor.
Title: Transformative impact of AI in supply chain management / [edited by] Jabir Arif, Fouad Jawab.
Description: Hershey, PA : IGI Global Scientific Publishing, [2026] | Includes bibliographical references and index. | Summary: "This book provides an in-depth exploration of how AI applications are redefining supply chain processes-from demand forecasting, inventory optimization, and production planning to transportation, procurement, and customer service"-- Provided by publisher.
Identifiers: LCCN 2024061709 (print) | LCCN 2024061710 (ebook) | ISBN 9798337309231 (hardcover) | ISBN 9798337309248 (paperback) | ISBN 9798337309255 (ebook)
Subjects: LCSH: Business logistics--Technological innovations. | Supply chain management--Technological innovations. | Artificial intelligence--Industrial applications.
Classification: LCC HD38.5 .T687 2025 (print) | LCC HD38.5 (ebook) | DDC 658.7--dc23/eng/20250228
LC record available at https://lccn.loc.gov/2024061709
LC ebook record available at https://lccn.loc.gov/2024061710

British Cataloguing in Publication Data
A Cataloguing in Publication record for this book is available from the British Library.

Table of Contents

Detailed Table of Contents

The pharmaceutical supply chain is characterized by mounting intricacy and the necessity for expeditious responses to fluctuating market conditions, regulatory constraints, and disruptions. The advent of Artificial Intelligence (AI) has been identified as a transformative force, with the potential to enhance organizational agility through dynamic capabilities (DC), Integrated Business Planning (IBP), and Sales and Operations Planning (S&OP). This chapter develops a comprehensive theoretical framework to examine the intersection of AI, pharmaceutical supply chain management, and DC, addressing a critical gap in understanding how AI-driven technologies can revolutionize agility and strategic alignment.

In the modern retail context, artificial intelligence (AI) and machine learning (ML) techniques are crucial for optimising essential activities such as supplier management, demand forecasting, inventory management, pricing, and order fulfilment. However, they may require a better understanding of the retail sector as the application of AI and ML varies across the various sections. This chapter employs a systematic literature review to synthesise data from 62 high-quality research studies demonstrating how

Section 2
Technological Enablers and AI-Driven Innovation in Supply Chain Management

In supply chain management, demand forecasting is essential because it affects inventory control, production scheduling, and operational effectiveness. In order to analyse past data and forecast future demand trends, this study suggests applying sophisticated machine learning and artificial intelligence techniques, such as ensemble methods, neural networks, and time series analysis. The approach tackles important issues like controlling seasonality, minimizing supply chain interruptions, and adjusting to changes in demand. The report illustrates how AI-driven demand forecasting may enhance cost-effectiveness and service quality through case studies from industries like manufacturing, retail, and e-commerce. The results demonstrate how combining AI and ML improves supply networks' resilience and flexibility while also giving companies useful information. This research enables the development of intelligent, responsive, and adaptable supply chain ecosystems.

Industry 5.0 has brought in a more stable and networked industrial environment with the use of the Internet of Things (IoT). Industry 5.0 creates a work environment where human-machine interaction is optimized for better performance by combining human cooperation with robots and intelligent equipment. Industrial Internet of things (IIoT) includes a range of services in large settings, such as digital domains that are available for company management, real-time production monitoring, and machinery condition tracking. Industry 5.0 aims to achieve the best possible balance between productivity and the efficiency in a variety of industries, including heavy manufacturing, oil and gas, and warehouse management all of which heavily rely on heavy gear. This chapter comprehensively explores the various dimensions of the IoT in industry 5.0 using in smart manufacturing for fault screening and mechanical Diagnosis and Prognosis.

automation, the imperative for worker upskilling, and the continuous endeavour to safeguard labour rights in a swiftly moving context. This chapter elucidates how manufacturers can effectively manage the intricate relationship between social responsibility and operational efficiency, thereby promoting a sustainable and equitable future.

Artificial Intelligence (AI) is transforming Supply Chain Management (SCM) through intelligent, data-driven decision-making and process optimization. This chapter explores AI's impact on key SCM areas such as demand forecasting, inventory control, logistics, and risk management. Technologies like Machine Learning, NLP, and Computer Vision enhance efficiency and responsiveness, while integration with IoT and Big Data enables real-time insights. Applications include predictive analytics for inventory, route optimization in logistics, and fraud detection. Innovations like autonomous vehicles and AI-powered chatbots are reshaping operations and customer service. Despite notable benefits cost reduction, improved accuracy, and customer satisfaction challenges remain, including data privacy, integration issues, and skill gaps. The chapter also highlights emerging trends such as generative AI and reinforcement learning in SCM, emphasizing their potential to drive future advancements and operational excellence.

The supply chain is a complex and dynamic field that requires effective planning, coordination, and execution to meet customer demands while minimizing costs. In recent years, artificial intelligence (AI) has emerged as a disruptive technology with the potential to transform various aspects of supply chain management. This chapter provides a comprehensive analysis of the role played by AI in supply chain management, highlighting its applications, benefits, challenges, and future prospects. This chapter explains how AI can improve supply chain visibility, demand forecasting, inventory management, logistics optimization, and risk mitigation. In addition, it explores the impact of AI on decision-making processes and collaboration within the supply chain network. The chapter also discusses the potential challenges and ethical considerations associated with the adoption of AI in supply chain management. By taking a deep dive into the current state of AI in Supply Chain and analyzing its potential future developments, this chapter aims to provide valuable insights.

Artificial Intelligence (AI) is revolutionizing supply chain management (SCM) by addressing challenges such as demand forecasting, logistics inefficiencies, and labor shortages. This chapter explores AI's transformative role in optimizing processes, including predictive analytics for demand planning, dynamic production scheduling, and route optimization for transportation management. AI enhances decision-making, reduces costs, and promotes sustainability by minimizing waste and carbon emissions. The chapter highlights real-world case studies, offering insights into successful AI implementations while addressing barriers such as high costs, resistance to change, and ethical concerns like algorithmic bias and data privacy. Future trends emphasize AI's role in fostering resilience, enabling crisis management, and supporting collaboration among supply chain stakeholders. By integrating AI, organizations can enhance operational efficiency, achieve sustainability goals, and build competitive, resilient supply chains for dynamic global markets.

This chapter is organized around three main questions related to the concept of the green Supply Chain, 4.0 technologies and the use of these technologies to ensure sustainability. Our main goal is to provide answers to the question: how and to what extent can sustainable supply chains be successfully implemented economically, socially and ecologically with the help of 4.0 technologies? Methodologically, we took an exploratory approach supported by qualitative and quantitative data

Foreword

It is with great enthusiasm that I write the foreword for Transformative Impact of AI in Supply Chain Management, a timely and comprehensive volume edited by Professor Jabir Arif. In an era defined by rapid technological advancement and unprecedented global challenges, the integration of Artificial Intelligence (AI) into supply chain management is no longer a futuristic concept but an urgent reality. This book stands as a crucial contribution to the evolving discourse, illuminating how AI is reshaping the very fabric of supply chains across industries and geographies.

The multifaceted chapters compiled in this volume reflect the complex and dynamic nature of modern supply chains. From enhancing resilience and risk management to enabling sustainable practices, the book's coverage spans a breadth of topics essential to both researchers and practitioners. Its interdisciplinary approach, blending theoretical insights with empirical case studies, offers a holistic understanding of how AI technologies— machine learning, IoT, blockchain, robotics, and more—are being harnessed to optimize operations, reduce waste, and improve responsiveness.

Of particular value is the book's careful attention to the socio-technical dimensions of AI deployment. Issues such as workforce upskilling, ethical considerations, explainability, and social sustainability are woven throughout the chapters, ensuring that the technological advances are examined within a responsible and human-centered framework. This balance is critical for advancing supply chain innovation that is not only efficient but also equitable and sustainable.

For academics, this volume provides a rich source of systematic literature reviews and conceptual frameworks that can fuel further research. For industry leaders and supply chain professionals, it offers actionable insights and best practices drawn from leading companies and sectors, including pharmaceuticals, agriculture, retail, and logistics. The book's exploration of emerging frontiers such as the Metaverse, Virtual Reality, and Logistics 5.0 positions it at the cutting edge of digital transformation scholarship.

In sum, Transformative Impact of AI in Supply Chain Management is poised to become an indispensable reference in the field. I wholeheartedly recommend it to scholars, students, and practitioners eager to deepen their understanding of AI's transformative potential and to contribute to building resilient, intelligent, and sustainable supply chains for the future.

Andrej Lisec
Landscape Governance College, Novo Mesto, Slovenia

Preface

1. OVERVIEW OF THE SUBJECT MATTER

In the rapidly evolving digital age, Artificial Intelligence (AI) has emerged as a transformative force across industries. Nowhere is this more evident than in supply chain management (SCM), where the integration of AI technologies is driving a paradigm shift in how products are forecasted, produced, moved, and delivered. This book explores the multifaceted and transformative impact of AI on supply chains, addressing a wide spectrum of topics including resilience, sustainability, risk management, smart manufacturing, robotics, blockchain, and industry-specific innovations.

The volume is designed to provide readers with a comprehensive view of how AI is changing both operational strategies and long-term visions in global SCM systems. By combining theoretical analysis, empirical insights, literature reviews, and case studies, the book contributes a timely, structured, and forward-looking reference for academics, professionals, and decision-makers.

2. RELEVANCE OF THE TOPIC IN TODAY'S WORLD

The global disruptions of recent years—from pandemics to geopolitical tensions—have exposed critical vulnerabilities in traditional supply chains. In response, businesses and governments are accelerating digital transformation initiatives, with AI at the core of this evolution. Beyond automation and analytics, AI enables intelligent decision-making, predictive maintenance, demand forecasting, sustainable logistics, and agile adaptation to disruptions.

Moreover, AI intersects with critical global agendas including green transition, social responsibility, and digital sovereignty. Understanding how AI technologies reshape supply chain capabilities is essential for building resilient, transparent, and sustainable systems in the face of climate change, consumer expectations, and global complexity. Thus, this book arrives at a crucial time, addressing these interconnected themes from both conceptual and practical perspectives.

3. TARGET AUDIENCE

This book is written for a broad interdisciplinary audience, including:

- Academics and researchers in supply chain management, logistics, AI, operations, and industrial engineering.
- Graduate and postgraduate students in business, engineering, and data science programs.
- Practitioners and managers working in procurement, manufacturing, logistics, digital transformation, and innovation.
- Policy-makers and advisors in the fields of technology governance, sustainability, and trade.

The content is designed to serve both as an academic reference and a practical guide, offering state-of-the-art knowledge, applied examples, and emerging research agendas.

4. CHAPTER SUMMARIES AND THEIR IMPORTANCE

Chapter 1 explores *emerging trends in social sustainability* within manufacturing supply chains, shedding light on how ethical consumerism, regulatory shifts, and automation are redefining labor conditions and corporate responsibility.

Chapter 2 examines how *AI strengthens risk management and resilience* in supply chains through predictive analytics, real-time monitoring, and disruption forecasting, with case studies from Walmart and Amazon.

Chapter 3 delves into *AI and machine learning in demand forecasting*, presenting data-driven approaches to handle seasonality, demand shocks, and inventory control across industries. Chapter 4 introduces *IoT-driven mechanical fault prognosis* in smart manufacturing under Industry 5.0, highlighting predictive maintenance and human–machine collaboration in industrial systems.

Chapter 5 provides a broad overview of *AI in SCM*, addressing applications in logistics, demand planning, risk mitigation, and customer service through technologies like NLP, machine learning, and computer vision.

Chapter 6 presents real-world case studies where *AI solves modern SCM challenges*, such as labor shortages, logistics inefficiencies, and waste, while also addressing ethical and implementation barriers.

Chapter 7 investigates *robotic AI in agriculture supply chains*, showcasing how deep learning and automation enhance precision farming, reduce waste, and improve harvesting efficiency.

Chapter 8 reviews the role of *Virtual Reality (VR) in SCM*, from immersive training to layout optimization and safety simulation, highlighting VR's growing potential in logistics planning. Chapter 9 focuses on *AI in pharmaceutical SCM performance*, addressing challenges like transparency, data security, and regulation, while promoting stakeholder collaboration for resilience.

Chapter 10 analyzes the *Metaverse's role in supply chain transformation*, providing a conceptual framework and real-world insights into immersive, digital SCM environments integrated with generative AI.

Chapter 11 reviews *Blockchain applications in agri-food supply chains*, examining transparency, traceability, and automation in food logistics while identifying barriers to mass adoption. Chapter 12 addresses *AI-driven resilience in retail supply chains*, emphasizing collaboration, speed, and disruption mitigation based on a review of over 60 academic studies.

Chapter 13 explores how *Industry 4.0 technologies support sustainability* in supply chains, providing quantitative and qualitative insights into CO_2 reduction and ethical practices.

Chapter 14 synthesizes the future potential of *AI in SCM*, discussing opportunities, challenges, ethical considerations, and how AI will shape global coordination and competitiveness.

Chapter 15 concludes with a forward-looking view on *AI in logistics*, featuring case studies from Amazon and DHL and highlighting innovations in smart warehouses and autonomous delivery.

5. CONCLUSION: CONTRIBUTION TO THE FIELD

This book contributes to the growing body of knowledge at the intersection of artificial intelligence and supply chain management by offering a structured, up-to-date, and interdisciplinary exploration of theory, technology, and practice. By bridging academic rigor with real-world relevance, it provides valuable tools for readers seeking to understand, implement, or further investigate AI-enabled SCM transformation.

As supply chains evolve from reactive systems into proactive, intelligent networks, this volume positions itself as both a reference and a roadmap—guiding future research, education, and strategy in the age of digital logistics and intelligent automation.

Jabir Arif
Sidi Mohamed Ben Abdellah University, Fez, Morocco

Fouad Jawab
Sidi Mohamed Ben Abdellah University, Fez, Morocco

Acknowledgments

The completion of this book, Transformative Impact of AI in Supply Chain Management, would not have been possible without the invaluable support and contributions of many individuals and institutions.

First and foremost, I extend my deepest gratitude to all the chapter authors, whose expertise, dedication, and insightful research have formed the foundation of this volume. Their willingness to share knowledge and innovative perspectives has enriched this work immensely.

I also wish to thank the reviewers who provided thoughtful and constructive feedback, helping to enhance the quality and rigor of the chapters.

My sincere appreciation goes to the editorial team at IGI Global for their professional guidance and unwavering support throughout the publication process.

Special thanks are due to my colleagues, collaborators, and students at Sidi Mohamed Ben Abdellah University for their encouragement and inspiration during this project.

Lastly, I am grateful to my family and friends for their patience and encouragement, which have been a continuous source of motivation.

This book is dedicated to the global community of supply chain professionals, researchers, and students committed to advancing sustainable and intelligent supply chains through innovative technologies.

Section 1
Sector-Specific Applications and Case-Driven Transformations

Chapter 1
Transformative Impact of AI on Pharmaceutical Supply Chain Management:
Revolutionizing Agility Through Dynamic Capabilities, IBP, and S&OP

Antonio Pesqueira
https://orcid.org/0000-0003-1530-6451
ISCTE, University Institute of Lisbon, Portugal

Andreia de bem Machado
https://orcid.org/0000-0002-4404-0341
Universidade Federal de Santa Catarina, Brazil

ABSTRACT

The pharmaceutical supply chain is characterized by mounting intricacy and the necessity for expeditious responses to fluctuating market conditions, regulatory constraints, and disruptions. The advent of Artificial Intelligence (AI) has been identified as a transformative force, with the potential to enhance organizational agility through dynamic capabilities (DC), Integrated Business Planning (IBP), and Sales and Operations Planning (S&OP). This chapter develops a comprehensive theoretical framework to examine the intersection of AI, pharmaceutical supply chain management, and DC, addressing a critical gap in understanding how AI-driven technologies can revolutionize agility and strategic alignment.

DOI: 10.4018/979-8-3373-0923-1.ch001

INTRODUCTION

The pharmaceutical and biotechnology sectors currently face significant supply chain management challenges, driven by the need for greater agility, resilience, and adherence to complex regulatory standards. Inefficiencies in Integrated Business Planning (IBP) and Sales and Operations Planning (S&OP) hinder these sectors from meeting the dynamic demands of modern supply chains, leading to misaligned resource allocation, suboptimal demand forecasting, and reduced adaptability that jeopardize both operational sustainability and public health outcomes. Addressing these issues extends beyond operational improvements; the industry's global health implications necessitate sophisticated frameworks that support agility, regulatory compliance, and innovation. Artificial Intelligence (AI) holds promise in revolutionizing decision-making through predictive analytics, real-time visibility, and adaptive planning. However, the theoretical integration of AI into traditional supply chain frameworks remains fragmented, with critical gaps in understanding its mechanisms and outcomes (Bhattamisra et al., 2023). Bridging these gaps is essential for developing intelligent, adaptive, and sustainable supply chain practices that balance operational goals with ethical imperatives. While existing literature demonstrates the value of AI in enhancing predictive analytics, operational efficiency, and visibility, it falls short of addressing its role in reinforcing digital continuity within pharmaceutical supply chains. Traditional supply chain theories provide insights into process optimization and resilience but lack integration with advanced technological innovations. Recent studies on digital transformation have yet to fully explore how AI-enabled frameworks can operationalize IBP and S&OP to meet contemporary challenges. Moreover, research on sustainability and ESG (Environmental, Social, and Governance) reporting in supply chain management often treats these dimensions separately, ignoring their convergence with AI-driven capabilities (Ahmed et al., 2020; ElBaih, 2023).

This chapter seeks to fill these voids by proposing a unified theoretical framework that integrates AI technologies with IBP, S&OP, and digital continuity. The primary objective is to elucidate how AI can enhance agility and strategic alignment in pharmaceutical supply chains, while supplementary goals include examining the evolution of these frameworks and evaluating their conformity with corporate sustainability and ESG mandates. The study addresses the central research problem of the absence of a cohesive framework that merges AI-driven innovations with traditional supply chain practices under sustainability imperatives, focusing on how existing theories of IBP, S&OP, and digital continuity account for current limitations and identifying key components for an integrated conceptual model. Employing a concept-based theoretical research methodology grounded in extensive literature review and synthesis of peer-reviewed articles, industry reports, and case studies, this analysis bridges insights from operations management, AI technologies, and sustainability governance. The resulting framework not only advances theoretical discourse by integrating environmental, social, and governance (ESG) principles and optimizing predictive capabilities in volatile environments but also offers practical strategies for aligning IBP and S&OP practices with ethical and operational standards. Ultimately, the insights provided aim to equip pharmaceutical and biotechnology firms with robust guidance for navigating the complexities of contemporary supply chain management, thereby ensuring operational excellence and ethical accountability.

LITERATURE REVIEW

Integrating Artificial Intelligence, Dynamic Capabilities (DC), and Sustainability in Integrated Business Planning

Demand planning is a critical element of supply chain management, serving as the interface between customer expectations and organizational operations. Its theoretical foundations stem from early work in operations research, forecasting methodologies, and decision sciences, with classical models such as demand-driven planning emphasizing the integration of demand signals to optimize inventory and production (Javaid et al., 2023). In recent decades, the field has shifted toward data-centric approaches that utilize advanced analytics and machine learning, showcasing the potential of AI to improve forecasting precision and responsiveness in volatile markets. Nonetheless, persistent challenges such as demand variability, suboptimal data quality, and fragmented integration with other supply chain processes prevent full optimization of demand planning systems. While proponents of AI-driven methods highlight their scalability and capacity to reduce bias, critics caution that these technologies may struggle with sparse data and require nuanced interpretation that only human judgment can provide (Smith, 2023). Moreover, a notable gap exists in integrating ESG considerations into demand planning, underscoring the need to align operational processes with sustainability and broader corporate accountability measures. Contemporary scholarship increasingly explores the interplay between technological innovation and the essential human factors in demand planning, advocating for frameworks that extend beyond technical accuracy to include socio-economic dimensions (Pesqueira & Sousa, 2022). The evolution of demand planning theories reflects a dynamic interplay between quantitative methods—such as time-series models, regression analysis, and causal techniques—and managerial intuition, which proves reliable in stable environments but less so under volatile conditions that demand adaptive approaches (Almeida Teixeira et al., 2021; Pesqueira, Bolog, 2023).

Furthermore, integrated frameworks like S&OP promote cross-functional collaboration by aligning demand forecasts with production and supply capabilities, yet they fall short in addressing real-time variability and sustainability metrics. Emerging research suggests that incorporating behavioral insights to counteract cognitive biases could enhance forecast accuracy, calling for hybrid approaches that merge data-driven analytics with human judgment (Liu et al., 2023). This debate between algorithmic precision and human expertise highlights a critical research gap: the need for frameworks that synergistically integrate machine intelligence with human decision-making, while also embedding metrics into demand planning paradigms to account for the broader costs associated with demand fluctuations (Huang et al., 2023; Pesqueira, 2023).

Artificial Intelligence in DC for Pharmaceutical Supply Chain Management

The DC framework provides a theoretical basis for understanding how organizations adapt to volatile environments by sensing opportunities, seizing resources, and transforming operational processes. Extensive research across various industries has highlighted the critical role of strategic agility and resource orchestration, with the pharmaceutical sector—characterized by stringent regulations, demand volatility, and complex global networks—relying heavily on DC to maintain supply chain resilience and competitive advantage (Shujahat et al., 2019). The transformative impact of AI in augmenting DC is increasingly evident; AI facilitates rapid data analysis, predictive insights, and real-time decision-making that enhance the sensing of market trends, risk detection, and opportunity identification. Moreover, AI-driven systems optimize resource allocation and improve supply chain responsiveness by transforming operational processes. Despite these advances, the integration of AI within the DC framework in pharmaceutical supply chains remains underexplored, with critical gaps in understanding the mechanisms by which AI supports adaptability and innovation (Soluk, Decker-Lange, Hack, 2023).

The theoretical foundations of DC are deeply rooted in organizational and strategic management, emphasizing the alignment of internal competencies with external demands. Although diverse methodologies such as case studies, qualitative interviews, and cross-sectional surveys have provided valuable insights into the development and sustainability of DC, they often lack the granularity necessary to discern the specific contributions of technologies like AI. Recent investigations employing machine learning and predictive analytics have begun to model the relationship between technological innovation and organizational adaptability, revealing AI's potential to optimize resource allocation and mitigate risks through algorithmic decision-making. However, these models frequently overlook the nuanced contexts of regulated industries such as pharmaceuticals, where ethical considerations, regulatory compliance, and stakeholder trust are paramount (Tran et al., 2019; Patil et al., 2022). Furthermore, methodological limitations persist, as few studies adopt longitudinal approaches to capture the iterative evolution of AI-enabled DC. While AI offers significant scalability and predictive accuracy, critics warn against overreliance on algorithmic systems that may lack the contextual sensitivity provided by human judgment, underscoring the need for hybrid models that integrate machine intelligence with human insights in high-stakes environments. A significant gap in current research is the limited exploration of ethical and regulatory issues in the integration of AI with DC. Given the strict compliance frameworks governing pharmaceutical supply chains, there is an urgent need for comprehensive models that reconcile AI's technical potential with ethical governance and sustainability objectives (Pettersen et al., 2020; Segato et al., 2020; Secinaro et al., 2021).

Table 1 provides a detailed comparative analysis of these themes and serves as a guide for future research aimed at developing integrated frameworks.

Table 1. Similarities, distinctions, and contributions

Aspect	DC in the Pharmaceutical Supply Chain	Artificial Intelligence in DC
Background and State of Research	Focuses on sensing, seizing, and transforming opportunities to ensure resilience and adaptability in volatile environments.	Explores AI's transformative potential in augmenting DC via predictive analytics, resource optimization, and real-time decision-making, with gaps in regulated industry contexts.
Theoretical Foundations	Rooted in strategic management, emphasizing resource alignment and adaptability to external demands.	Built on machine learning and analytics frameworks, integrating algorithmic insights with decision-making models for adaptability and transformation.
Methodological Approaches	Case studies, interviews, and surveys dominate; quantitative modeling and longitudinal studies are underutilized.	AI integration studies use algorithmic modeling but often lack contextual depth for industries like pharmaceuticals, requiring hybrid and longitudinal methodologies.
Key Contributions of Literature	Highlights the importance of organizational agility and resource orchestration but lacks application to tech-augmented supply chains.	Establishes AI as a tool for enhancing efficiency and responsiveness but fails to address its role in strategic and ethical aspects of DC.
Research Gaps	Limited focus on integrating technology into DC; lacks clarity on agility versus resilience balance.	Insufficient exploration of AI's strategic contributions, ethical considerations, and its alignment with compliance frameworks in regulated industries.
Unresolved Debates	Tension between long-term strategic planning and operational flexibility.	Debate over the balance between algorithmic precision and human judgment in fostering adaptability and compliance.
Proposed Research Contributions	Develops a framework for applying DC specifically to pharmaceutical supply chains with a focus on resilience.	Proposes hybrid models integrating AI and human expertise for fostering DC, emphasizing regulatory and ethical alignment in pharmaceutical contexts.
Practical Implications	Provides actionable insights for organizations to enhance supply chain resilience and adaptability.	Offers strategies for leveraging AI to improve agility and compliance while addressing ethical challenges in high-stakes supply chain environments.

Empirical Insights and Implementation Challenges in AI Adoption

Empirical validation was achieved through an analysis of a leading global pharmaceutical company that effectively navigated post-pandemic supply chain disruptions by implementing AI-driven innovations. Confronted with raw material shortages and logistical constraints, the company deployed an AI-powered predictive analytics platform to forecast supply chain risks in real time (Tariq et al., 2022; Pesqueira et al., 2025). Its approach combined advanced machine learning algorithms with existing data systems to identify emerging bottlenecks and established a cross-functional task force to translate AI insights into agile decision-making. This integration enabled dynamic resource reallocation, prioritized critical production lines, and adjusted inventory levels to minimize disruptions. However, the process also revealed significant barriers, including the integration of legacy IT systems, ensuring data quality, and navigating regulatory compliance across diverse markets—challenges that underscore the need for continuous organizational learning and adaptation.

Adopting a holistic strategy that merged technological advancement with human expertise, the firm sustained operations during a global crisis and bolstered long-term supply chain resilience. This case exemplifies that while AI can transform pharmaceutical supply chains, its successful implementation requires overcoming technical, regulatory, and organizational challenges. Recent research corroborates that AI integration enhances forecasting accuracy and operational agility; however, issues such as data interoperability, algorithm scalability, and strict regulatory standards often impede progress. Additionally, aligning AI solutions with legacy systems can compromise data integrity and slow adoption, while substantial investments in technology and human capital, coupled with resistance to change, further complicate the transition. Regulatory uncertainties also hinder AI implementation, as pharmaceutical companies must comply with a complex landscape of international standards and data protection laws. These challenges highlight the necessity for hybrid models that combine algorithmic precision with human judgment to ensure both effectiveness and ethical alignment. Hybrid approaches have been shown to enhance operational resilience while fostering continuous improvement and regulatory compliance, thereby creating sustainable competitive advantages (Suri et al., 2024; Pesqueira et al., 2025).

Moreover, integrating AI outcomes into mental health and digital health research has revealed significant convergences and divergences. Over the past decade, numerous studies have underscored the growing importance of AI-driven decision support systems and the ethical and practical challenges of their deployment in clinical environments. Recent investigations draw attention to data governance complexities addressed by the EU AI Act and data privacy initiatives, emphasizing transparent data handling, real-time consent tracking, and robust encryption. Although pilot studies suggest that integrated solutions can enhance user adoption and positive attitudes, further large-scale, cross-institutional research is needed to validate these findings, particularly in resource-limited settings. The observed correlation with extant literature on user-centered design, privacy-preserving AI, and resilience frameworks reinforces the potential of AI to contribute substantively to debates on digital transformation in healthcare, paving the way for more rigorous comparative studies (Suri et al., 2024; van Hoek, 2024; Pesqueira et al., 2025).

Policies, Regulations, and Industry-Based Considerations

Pharmaceutical supply chains function within a highly regulated environment, with global, regional, and local frameworks designed to ensure product safety, quality, and efficacy. Among the most critical regulatory frameworks are Good Manufacturing Practices (GMP) and Good Distribution Practices (GDP), which govern the consistent production, storage, and distribution of pharmaceutical products. In the United States, the Drug Supply Chain Security Act (DSCSA) mandates the tracking and tracing of prescription drugs through the supply chain to combat counterfeiting and enhance transparency. A similar objective is pursued by the European Union's Falsified Medicines Directive (FMD), which aims to prevent the entry of counterfeit products into the market by requiring advanced traceability systems and robust compliance mechanisms across the supply chain. The harmonisation of guidelines provided by organisations such as the International Council for Harmonisation of Technical Requirements for Pharmaceuticals for Human Use serves to further streamline compliance across different jurisdictions. Industry-specific standards, such as ISO 9001 for Quality Management Systems (QMS) and ISO 13485 for medical devices, also play a vital role in ensuring consistent quality management practices. In the context of pharmaceuticals, these standards are of paramount importance for ensuring global operational consistency and fulfilling the high expectations of regulators and stakeholders (Vallentin, Thórisson, Latapie, 2023). The pharmaceutical industry is characterised by a series of distinct challenges, most notably in the domain of cold chain logistics, where precise temperature control is imperative for the preservation of biologics and vaccines. These requirements necessitate the implementation of advanced monitoring systems to ensure compliance with regulatory standards. Furthermore, the protracted nature of the development and approval process for new pharmaceutical products, characterised by rigorous testing and quality assurance procedures, contributes to extended lead times. The navigational challenges posed by the regulatory variability and logistical constraints of emerging markets are further compounded by these intricate operational complexities, thereby necessitating the implementation of sophisticated anti-counterfeiting measures. The proliferation of counterfeit and substandard products introduces an additional layer of complexity, necessitating the implementation of anti-counterfeiting measures such as serialisation and blockchain-based traceability solutions (Vaishya et al., 2020; Wamba et al., 2023; Vlasta, 2023).

Technological advancements are increasingly being adopted to address regulatory and operational challenges. Specifically, AI is emerging as a critical tool, offering predictive analytics for compliance management, risk identification, and operational efficiency improvements. However, concerns regarding data privacy, algorithmic transparency, and regulatory acceptance, particularly in heavily regulated sectors such as pharmaceuticals, have been raised by the integration of AI. Conversely, blockchain technology is witnessing a surge in adoption as a means to enhance supply chain traceability and trust. However, it is imperative that its implementation is aligned with stringent data protection regulations, such as the EU's General Data Protection Regulation (GDPR). Digital twins are a technology that is being used in the context of scenario planning and supply chain optimisation. They provide a virtual environment in which strategies can be tested while ensuring alignment with compliance and operational goals. ESG goals are becoming increasingly influential in shaping regulatory and industry considerations. The alignment of supply chain operations with ESG imperatives has prompted firms to adopt sustainable practices, such as reducing carbon emissions, minimising waste, and ensuring ethical sourcing of raw materials. In parallel, governments and industry bodies are progressively introducing guidelines to embed these principles into pharmaceutical supply chains, recognizing the intersection of operational excellence and corporate responsibility. In order to establish a comprehensive baseline for pharmaceutical supply chain management, firms must integrate regulatory compliance, adherence to industry standards, and the strategic application of emerging technologies. This necessitates the establishment of robust compliance frameworks that meet GMP, GDP, and traceability requirements, whilst leveraging advanced technologies to enhance visibility, detect risks, and align with regulatory shifts. Furthermore, the incorporation of ESG principles into supply chain operations ensures a balance between sustainability, ethical considerations, and operational efficiency (Wan et al., 2022; Vlasta, 2023).

Global Variations in Pharmaceutical Supply Chain Policies: Regional Paradigms and Operational Implications

The pharmaceutical supply chain is a dynamic, interconnected system influenced by diverse regional regulatory frameworks that reflect distinct economic, cultural, and governance priorities. While these regulations are critical for ensuring product safety, efficacy, and accessibility, their variation creates both challenges and opportunities for companies operating in a global market. In North America, stringent regulatory environments—exemplified by the FDA's DSCSA and Canada's rigorous quality control policies—demand significant investments in technologies such as blockchain and IoT sensors to ensure end-to-end traceability. In Europe, harmonization efforts led by the EMA and initiatives like the FMD promote cross-border trade, yet local variations persist. Meanwhile, Asia's regulatory landscape is more heterogeneous, with countries like Japan offering robust, innovation-friendly systems, and nations such as China and India continuing to address infrastructure and enforcement challenges. Africa and Latin America are still developing cohesive regulatory systems, though initiatives like the African Medicines Agency (AMA) signal progress. These regulatory discrepancies significantly impact the design and management of pharmaceutical supply chains. In highly regulated regions, firms invest heavily in advanced systems to ensure compliance and operational visibility, thereby mitigating inefficiencies and risks. In emerging markets, companies often adopt a dual strategy that aligns with global best practices for products destined for stringent markets while adapting to local requirements. However, the lack of uniform regulatory implementation can lead to operational inefficiencies, necessitating adaptable and robust supply chain strategies (Chen et al., 2019; Ball, 2021; Dillard-Wright, Shields-Haas, 2021).

Innovative regulatory paradigms have emerged to address these challenges. In the United States, programs to expedite generic drug approvals balance consumer access with quality assurance, while European initiatives, such as the European Green Deal, emphasize collaboration and sustainability in production and distribution. In Asia, the integration of big data and AI into regulatory processes, as seen in China, enhances compliance and operational efficiency, and India's focus on becoming a global hub for generic drugs illustrates the complex interplay between industrial policy and regulation. Collaborative efforts in Africa and Latin America further promote regulatory alignment and address local challenges (Haleem et al., 2022; Smith, 2023).

Advanced technologies play a pivotal role in bridging regulatory disparities. Blockchain offers secure, tamper-proof records that enhance traceability, while AI and machine learning automate compliance processes through predictive insights and real-time monitoring. Cloud-based platforms facilitate stakeholder collaboration and data sharing, particularly in regions where regulatory frameworks remain fragmented. The integration of ESG principles adds further complexity. In Europe, ESG alignment is driven by regulatory mandates such as the European Green Deal, whereas in North America, market forces and consumer expectations increasingly motivate ESG compliance. In emerging markets, ESG considerations are often secondary to issues like medicine access and infrastructure development, though global frameworks like the UN SDGs are beginning to influence practices (Kamal et al., 2020; Kaplan & Hays, 2022). Despite challenges such as counterfeiting—which undermines public trust, patient safety, and corporate economies—and the logistical complexities of managing temperature-sensitive products that require advanced monitoring systems and resilient distribution networks, transformative opportunities abound. The integration of AI, blockchain, and digital twins enhances demand forecasting, inventory management, and risk mitigation, while regionalized manufacturing and supply chain diversification reduce lead times and bolster resilience. Collaborative frameworks, exemplified by public-private partnerships during the COVID-19 vaccine rollout, have also proven effective in accelerating innovation and improving access to medicines. Sustainability challenges, particularly regarding carbon emissions and waste management, are prompting companies to adopt energy-efficient manufacturing processes and renewable energy sources, thereby reducing environmental footprints and enhancing resource efficiency. Moreover, real-time data and analytics enable agile responses to market changes, while expanding access to emerging markets in Asia, Africa, and Latin America presents significant growth opportunities despite existing infrastructural and regulatory hurdles. Investment in local partnerships and a deep understanding of regional needs are essential for maintaining a competitive edge and advancing global health equity (Mostafiz et al., 2022; Ullah et al., 2023).

Harmonizing regional regulatory variations with global standardization is imperative for establishing resilient, ethical, and adaptive pharmaceutical supply chains. Companies must develop flexible frameworks that leverage advanced technologies to enhance compliance, transparency, and operational efficiency while integrating ESG principles. This integrated approach addresses current challenges and lays the foundation for sustainable supply chains capable of thriving in an increasingly interconnected global market (Kelly et al., 2020; Kendzerska et al., 2021; Kouba et al., 2023).

KEY CHALLENGES AND OPPORTUNITIES

Pharmaceutical supply chains are characterised by their operation within one of the most complex and demanding industrial ecosystems. This is influenced by a number of factors, including global interconnectivity, regulatory scrutiny, and evolving market demands. The inherent intricacy of these supply chains gives rise to numerous challenges, but also presents significant opportunities for innovation, resilience, and sustainability. A comprehensive understanding of these dynamics is imperative for the development of adaptive supply chain models that can effectively navigate a rapidly evolving environment. A particularly salient challenge in the context of pharmaceutical supply chains pertains to the management of regulatory compliance across a range of jurisdictional frameworks. The unique regulatory requirements for manufacturing, distribution, and traceability in each region necessitate that companies navigate a patchwork of regulatory frameworks. For instance, while the U.S. FDA enforces stringent serialisation under the DSCSA, the EU mandates similar but distinct requirements under the FMD. The absence of global harmonisation in this regard contributes to the complexity and cost of compliance, necessitating the maintenance of multiple, region-specific systems and processes by firms. A further significant challenge is the vulnerability of supply chains to disruptions. During the pandemic, global supply chains were exposed as vulnerable, with weaknesses including reliance on single-source suppliers and limited domestic manufacturing capacities. For pharmaceutical companies, these vulnerabilities can result in shortages of critical medicines, delayed approvals for new products, and financial losses. Disruptions are further exacerbated by geopolitical instability, such as trade restrictions or conflicts, which can impact raw material sourcing and distribution networks. The growing threat of counterfeit medicines represents another critical challenge.

Key Processes and Capabilities of IBP, S&OP, and the Relevance of DC

IBP and S&OP serve as foundational frameworks in contemporary supply chain management by aligning operational, tactical, and strategic processes to coordinate demand forecasts, production schedules, and financial objectives across diverse functions. Their importance has grown amid volatile markets, stringent regulatory requirements, and rapid technological disruptions, particularly in industries such as pharmaceuticals, where patient health and global coordination are at stake. Complementing these models is the concept of DC, which emphasizes the need for organizations to sense opportunities, seize resources, and transform processes in order to remain agile and competitive in turbulent environments (Khalil & Belitski, 2020; Buzzao & Rizzi, 2021; Shiwlani et al., 2023). IBP's operational strength lies in its robust data integration and cross-functional collaboration, offering decision-makers a unified view of organizational capabilities and constraints. This transparency facilitates the identification of bottlenecks, optimization of resource allocation, and proactive responses to disruptions—such as adjusting production schedules in the face of raw material shortages—enhanced further by the incorporation of predictive analytics and machine learning. In contrast, S&OP focuses on balancing supply and demand by creating operational plans that optimize resource utilization and ensure timely delivery of products. Its iterative process, which integrates historical data, market intelligence, and customer insights, enables adjustments to production and inventory strategies under changing conditions, as evidenced during the COVID-19 pandemic when pharmaceutical companies balanced surging demand with supply constraints. The integration of DC with IBP and S&OP further enhances these frameworks by equipping organizations to proactively sense emerging trends, secure necessary resources, and transform their operations in response to market and regulatory shifts. For instance, firms that effectively integrated DC were able to swiftly identify rising demand for diagnostic tests and personal protective equipment during the early stages of the COVID-19 crisis, reallocating resources and modifying distribution strategies to maintain product availability. Nevertheless, realizing the full potential of these integrated frameworks requires overcoming significant challenges, including the need for cultural and organizational change, investment in advanced data analytics, and the dismantling of siloed decision-making structures. Strong leadership, open communication, and a commitment to continuous improvement are essential to foster a culture that supports the high degree of flexibility and collaboration demanded by DC. In an era marked by global uncertainty, trade restrictions, geopolitical tensions, and climate-related disruptions, the combined application of IBP, S&OP, and DC offers pharmaceutical companies a strategic advantage (Bouguerra et al., 2022; Mostafiz et al., 2022; Ullah et al., 2023).

Table 2 details the integrated approach and alignment with operational capabilities, strategic objectives and regulatory demands that also drive innovation, ensuring sustainable and impactful supply chain management in competitive global markets.

Table 2. IBP, S&OP, and DC overview

Aspect	IBP	S&OP	Dynamic Capabilities
Key Components	Demand forecasting, financial planning, scenario modeling, and cross-functional collaboration.	Demand and supply planning, inventory optimization, and production scheduling.	Sensing market opportunities, seizing operational resources, and transforming organizational processes.
Technology Integration	Leverages predictive analytics, machine learning, and data consolidation tools for enhanced forecasting and planning.	Utilizes cloud-based platforms and data-sharing tools to improve collaboration and real-time monitoring.	Incorporates advanced technologies like AI for sensing trends and blockchain for ensuring traceability and compliance.
Collaboration Level	High cross-functional collaboration, involving finance, marketing, operations, and executive leadership.	Moderate collaboration, primarily between supply chain, production, and demand management teams.	Requires a culture of openness, continuous knowledge sharing, and cross-departmental integration.
Data Requirements	Requires extensive data integration from various functions, including market insights, financial data, and supply chain metrics.	Relies on historical sales data, demand forecasts, and inventory levels for planning.	Depends on both internal data (operations and sales) and external data (market trends, regulatory changes).
Response to Disruptions	Enables proactive adjustments to production, sourcing, and distribution plans in response to disruptions like material shortages or regulatory shifts.	Provides a structured response mechanism for fluctuations in demand or supply chain delays.	Empower organizations to reconfigure resources and strategies to mitigate disruptions and capitalize on emerging opportunities.
Alignment with ESG Goals	Facilitates integration of sustainability metrics into planning, such as carbon footprint reduction and ethical sourcing initiatives.	Limited focus on ESG integration, although evolving tools are adding sustainability considerations into demand and supply planning.	Encourages the transformation of processes to align with environmental and social governance imperatives, fostering sustainable practices.

continued on following page

Table 2. Continued

Aspect	IBP	S&OP	Dynamic Capabilities
Role in Innovation	Drives innovation through long-term planning and resource alignment, ensuring investments in technology and market expansion.	Focuses on incremental operational improvements, such as improving production efficiency or meeting demand fluctuations.	Stimulates innovation by enabling the organization to experiment with new processes and technologies while staying resilient to potential failures.
Time Horizon	Long-term and strategic, with a focus on aligning operational plans with multi-year financial and corporate objectives.	Short- to medium-term, focusing on the next few quarters to optimize supply and demand alignment.	Flexible and dynamic, operating across short-, medium--, and long-term horizons based on the external environment and organizational needs.
Cultural Requirements	Requires a collaborative culture with strong leadership to ensure alignment across diverse functional groups.	Benefits from strong communication and alignment among operational teams.	Relies on fostering a culture of agility, adaptability, and openness to change, supported by leadership that prioritizes innovation and continuous learning.
Adaptability to Markets	Highly adaptable, enabling companies to anticipate and respond to shifts in demand, regulatory changes, and global disruptions.	Moderately adaptable, focused on iterative adjustments within a fixed operational framework.	Maximally adaptable, providing the ability to pivot strategies and operations dynamically in response to environmental uncertainties and opportunities.
Integration with Supply Chain	Seamlessly integrates supply chain metrics with broader business goals, ensuring alignment between operational and strategic priorities.	Primarily focuses on operational aspects of the supply chain, ensuring production and inventory levels align with demand.	Provides a broader perspective by linking supply chain activities to the overall strategic vision and facilitating transformational changes where necessary.

FUTURE SCENARIOS, THEORETICAL FRAMEWORK, AND FUTURE-BASED CONCEPTS

Future Scenarios: Anticipating Challenges and Opportunities

The pharmaceutical supply chain is at a critical turning point, influenced by converging technological innovations, evolving regulatory landscapes, and dynamic global market trends. Future scenarios, theoretical frameworks, and emerging concepts provide essential guidance for anticipating disruptions and reimagining supply chains to enhance resilience, sustainability, and innovation. Understanding the interactions among these factors is imperative for developing adaptive, forward-looking pharmaceutical supply chains that can navigate the challenges of a rapidly changing environment. These future scenarios are driven by interrelated trends such as advances in digital technologies, regulatory evolution, and an increased emphasis on sustainability. Projections often depict a more decentralized, data-driven, and patient-centric supply chain marked by enhanced transparency, responsiveness, and stakeholder collaboration. One prominent scenario foresees the broad adoption of decentralized manufacturing models, where technologies like additive manufacturing and modular biomanufacturing facilitate localized pharmaceutical production. This approach could significantly reduce lead times, transportation costs, and carbon emissions while supporting the shift toward personalized medicine by enabling the production of small, tailored therapy batches near the point of care. However, realizing this vision requires overcoming considerable regulatory, logistical, and technological challenges, including the establishment of real-time quality control systems and the harmonization of international manufacturing standards (Pundziene, Heaton, Teece, 2019; Rashid, Ratten, 2021; Mazar, 2023).

Another scenario emphasizes the integration of advanced analytics and AI into supply chain operations. These technologies have the potential to revolutionize forecasting, inventory management, and risk mitigation by providing real-time, predictive, and prescriptive insights. For instance, AI-driven models could detect emerging trends in drug demand or identify potential disruptions in raw material supplies, thereby enabling proactive adjustments in production and distribution strategies. Despite these benefits, challenges such as data interoperability, algorithmic transparency, and the need for workforce reskilling must be addressed to ensure effective implementation. Sustainability remains a central element in future scenarios as pharmaceutical companies are increasingly pressured to reduce their environmental footprint and adopt socially responsible practices. Initiatives aimed at minimizing waste, transitioning to renewable energy sources, and ensuring ethical sourcing are becoming integral to supply chain strategies. Regulatory measures, such as the European Union's Green Deal, are expected to drive these efforts further by incentivizing the adoption of circular economy principles and the integration of sustainability metrics into operational strategies. Collectively, these scenarios underscore the necessity for comprehensive frameworks that balance operational efficiency with environmental and social governance objectives (Sturm et al., 2020; Scuotto et al., 2022; Mazar, 2023).

Theoretical Framework: Bridging Current Practices and Future Visions

The theoretical foundation for analysing future scenarios in pharmaceutical supply chains builds on established concepts such as DC, resource-based views, and systems theory. These frameworks provide a lens for understanding how organizations can adapt to external changes, optimize resource utilization, and create value in complex, interconnected environments. DC, remains central to the theoretical discourse, emphasizing the importance of sensing opportunities, seizing resources, and transforming processes to maintain competitive advantage. In the context of pharmaceutical supply chains, these capabilities are essential for navigating regulatory changes, technological disruption, and shifting patient needs. For instance, the ability to sense emerging trends in digital health or personalized medicine enables companies to identify new market opportunities, while seizing resources such as advanced manufacturing technologies ensures the capacity to deliver innovative therapies. Transformational capabilities are equally critical, as they allow organizations to reconfigure their supply chain networks, adopt new technologies, and align their operations with evolving ESG standards (Shujahat et al., 2019; Mazar, 2023). Resource-based views complement DC by focusing on the strategic management of tangible and intangible assets. In pharmaceutical supply chains, this includes leveraging advanced analytics, proprietary technologies, and intellectual property to create competitive advantages. For example, companies that invest in AI-driven predictive models or blockchain-based traceability systems can differentiate themselves by offering superior transparency, efficiency, and compliance. However, the resource-based view also highlights the importance of capability-building, as organizations must develop the skills, processes, and infrastructure needed to maximize the value of their resources. Systems theory provides a holistic perspective on supply chain management, emphasizing the interdependence of various components and the need for coordinated action across stakeholders. This framework is particularly relevant for addressing future scenarios that involve complex, decentralized networks. By viewing the supply chain as an integrated system, organizations can better anticipate the ripple effects of disruptions, identify bottlenecks, and design strategies that optimize performance across the entire value chain. Systems theory also underscores the importance of collaboration, as achieving long-term resilience and sustainability requires joint efforts among manufacturers, regulators, suppliers, and healthcare providers (Sturm et al., 2020; Rashid & Ratten, 2021; Mazar, 2023).

Future-Based Concepts: Reimagining Pharmaceutical Supply Chains

Future-based concepts in pharmaceutical supply chains are centred on leveraging emerging technologies and innovative strategies to achieve greater adaptability, efficiency, and sustainability. One such concept is the "intelligent supply chain," which integrates AI, IoT, and blockchain to create a fully digital, automated, and transparent network. Intelligent supply chains are capable of real-time monitoring, predictive analytics, and autonomous decision-making, enabling organizations to respond to disruptions with unprecedented speed and precision. For instance, IoT-enabled sensors can track the temperature and location of shipments in real-time, ensuring the integrity of temperature-sensitive products such as vaccines and biologics. Blockchain, meanwhile, provides an immutable record of transactions, enhancing traceability and reducing the risk of counterfeiting. Another emerging concept is the "resilient supply chain," which prioritizes robustness and flexibility to withstand disruptions and adapt to changing conditions. Resilient supply chains leverage diversification strategies, such as sourcing raw materials from multiple suppliers or establishing regional manufacturing hubs, to mitigate the risks of dependency on a single source or location. These supply chains also incorporate advanced scenario planning tools that simulate potential disruptions and evaluate the effectiveness of various response strategies. By integrating resilience into their supply chain design, pharmaceutical companies can reduce downtime, minimize financial losses, and ensure the continuous availability of critical medicines (Soluk, Decker-Lange, Hack, 2023; Pesqueira, 2023).

Figure 1 provides a visual representation of the key areas that shape the future of pharmaceutical supply chains, highlighting their interconnections and implications. At the centre of the diagram lies the "Future-Based Implications" section, which serves as the core concept that links the surrounding areas of Future Scenarios, Theoretical Framework, DC, Resilient Supply Chain, Sustainable Supply Chain, and Intelligent Supply Chain. The design suggests that these areas collectively drive the forward-looking transformations and advancements in the pharmaceutical industry. The surrounding blocks represent critical factors and frameworks that influence the evolution of pharmaceutical supply chains. By proactively anticipating these changes, organizations can better position themselves to thrive in a volatile environment. Each of these blocks is interconnected, representing the holistic approach required to create a future-ready pharmaceutical supply chain.

Figure 1. Future-Based implications

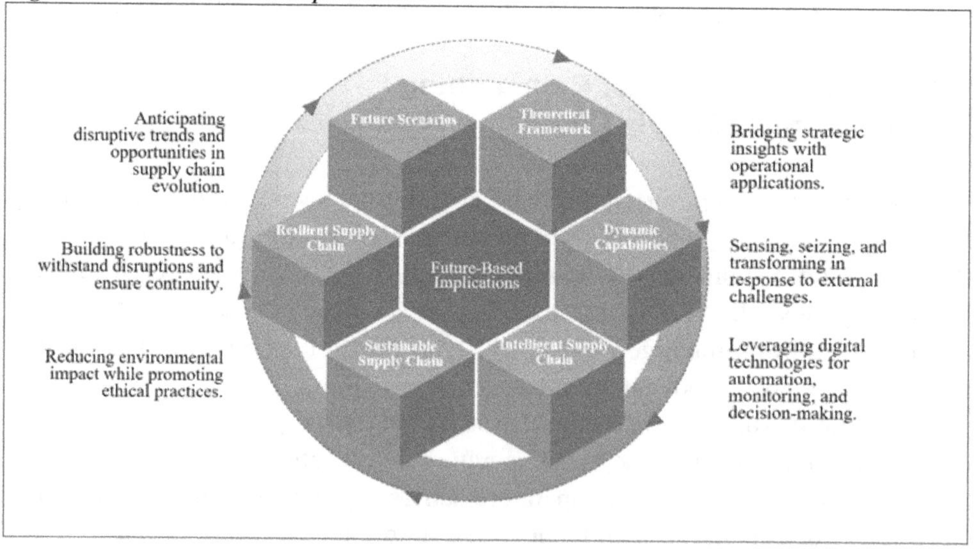

CONCLUSION

The pharmaceutical supply chain is experiencing a significant transformation driven by technological advancements, evolving regulatory frameworks, and increasing sustainability demands. In this complex environment, frameworks such as IBP, S&OP, and DC serve as essential tools for achieving resilience, agility, and strategic alignment. When integrated with forward-thinking theoretical concepts and emerging technological innovations, these frameworks lay the groundwork for developing adaptive, future-ready supply chains. The analysis highlights the critical role of future scenarios in strategic decision-making. By anticipating regulatory shifts, supply chain vulnerabilities, and evolving market demands, organizations can proactively build resilience and capitalize on emerging opportunities. Theoretical models, including DC and systems thinking, bridge the gap between strategy and operations, enabling firms to sense, seize, and transform in response to external disruptions. This adaptability is vital for pharmaceutical companies operating in an era of rapid technological evolution and strict regulatory oversight. Concepts such as intelligent supply chains, resilient networks, and sustainable practices illustrate how organizations can meet the dual imperatives of operational efficiency and ethical accountability. Intelligent supply chains leverage technologies like AI, blockchain, and IoT to improve transparency, automation, and decision-making; resilient supply chains emphasize diversification and robustness to maintain continuity during disruptions; and sustainable supply chains align business practices with ESG principles to meet growing environmental and social responsibilities.

This integrated approach marks a shift from reactive to proactive supply chain management, where organizations are equipped not only to respond to challenges but also to drive innovation and growth. By aligning operational capabilities with strategic objectives and sustainability imperatives, pharmaceutical companies can secure a competitive edge in a dynamic global market. As the industry evolves, the interplay among IBP, S&OP, DC, and future-oriented concepts will remain central to overcoming the challenges of supply chains. Firms that embrace these frameworks and invest in the necessary technological and organizational capacities will be better positioned to adapt to disruptions, meet regulatory requirements, and deliver lasting value to patients, stakeholders, and society at large.

REFERENCES

Ahmed, Z., Mohamed, K., Zeeshan, S., & Dong, X. (2020). Artificial intelligence with multi-functional machine learning platform development for better healthcare and precision medicine. *Database : The Journal of Biological Databases and Curation, 2020*, baaa010. DOI: 10.1093/database/baaa010 PMID: 32185396

Almeida Teixeira, G., Mira da Silva, M., & Pereira, R. (2021). The Critical Success Factors of GDPR Implementation: a Delphi Study.

Amini, M., & Jahanbakhsh Javid, N. (2023). A multi-perspective framework established on diffusion of innovation (DOI) theory and technology, organization and environment (TOE) framework toward supply chain management system based on cloud computing technology for small and medium enterprises. Organization and Environment (TOE) Framework Toward Supply Chain Management System Based on Cloud Computing Technology for Small and Medium Enterprises (January 2023). *International Journal of Information Technology and Innovation Adoption, 11*, 1217–1234.

Ball, P. (2021). What the COVID-19 pandemic reveals about science, policy and society. *Interface Focus, 11*(6), 20210022. DOI: 10.1098/rsfs.2021.0022 PMID: 34956594

Bhattamisra, , Banerjee, P., Gupta, P., Mayuren, J., Patra, S., & Candasamy, M. (2023). Artificial Intelligence in Pharmaceutical and Healthcare Research. *Big Data and Cognitive Computing, 7*(1), 10. DOI: 10.3390/bdcc7010010

Bouguerra, A., Hughes, M., Cakir, M. S., & Tatoglu, E. (2022). Linking entrepreneurial orientation to environmental collaboration: A stakeholder theory and evidence from multinational companies in an emerging market. *British Journal of Management.*

Buzzao, G., & Rizzi, F. (2021). On the conceptualization and measurement of dynamic capabilities for sustainability: Building theory through a systematic literature review. *Business Strategy and the Environment, 30*(1), 135–175. DOI: 10.1002/bse.2614

Chen, Q., Peng, Y., & Lu, Z. (2019). BioSentVec: creating sentence embeddings for biomedical texts. In *2019 IEEE International Conference on Healthcare Informatics (ICHI)* (pp. 1-5). IEEE. DOI: 10.1109/ICHI.2019.8904728

Dillard-Wright, J., & Shields-Haas, V. (2021). Nursing with the people: Reimagining futures for nursing. *Advances in Nursing Science, 44*(3), 195–209. DOI: 10.1097/ANS.0000000000000361 PMID: 33624989

ElBaih, M. (2023). The Role of Privacy Regulations in AI Development (A Discussion of the Ways in Which Privacy Regulations Can Shape the Development of AI). *SSRN* 4589207. DOI: 10.2139/ssrn.4589207

Ghosh, S., Hughes, M., Hughes, P., & Hodgkinson, I. (2021). Corporate digital entrepreneurship: Leveraging industrial internet of things and emerging technologies. Digital Entrepreneurship, 183.

Haleem, A., Javaid, M., Singh, R. P., & Suman, R. (2022). Medical 4.0 technologies for healthcare: Features, capabilities, and applications. *Internet of Things and Cyber-Physical Systems*, *2*, 12–30. DOI: 10.1016/j.iotcps.2022.04.001

Huang, H., Zheng, O., Wang, D., Yin, J., Wang, Z., Ding, S., Yin, H., Xu, C., Yang, R., Zheng, Q., & Shi, B. (2023). ChatGPT for shaping the future of dentistry: The potential of multi-modal large language model. *International Journal of Oral Science*, *15*(1), 29. DOI: 10.1038/s41368-023-00239-y PMID: 37507396

Javaid, M., Haleem, A., & Singh, R. P. (2023). ChatGPT for healthcare services: An emerging stage for an innovative perspective. BenchCouncil Transactions on Benchmarks. *Standards and Evaluations*, *3*(1), 100105.

Kamal, S. A., Shafiq, M., & Kakria, P. (2020). Investigating acceptance of telemedicine services through an extended technology acceptance model (TAM). *Technology in Society*, *60*, 101212. DOI: 10.1016/j.techsoc.2019.101212

Kaplan, R. M., & Hays, R. D. (2022). Health-related quality of life measurement in public health. *Annual Review of Public Health*, *43*(1), 355–373. DOI: 10.1146/annurev-publhealth-052120-012811 PMID: 34882431

Kelly, J. T., Campbell, K. L., Gong, E., & Scuffham, P. (2020). The Internet of Things: Impact and implications for health care delivery. *Journal of Medical Internet Research*, *22*(11), e20135. DOI: 10.2196/20135 PMID: 33170132

Kendzerska, T., Zhu, D. T., Gershon, A. S., Edwards, J. D., Peixoto, C., Robillard, R., & Kendall, C. E. (2021). The effects of the health system response to the COVID-19 pandemic on chronic disease management: A narrative review. *Risk Management and Healthcare Policy*, *14*, 575–584. DOI: 10.2147/RMHP.S293471 PMID: 33623448

Khalil, S., & Belitski, M. (2020). Dynamic capabilities for firm performance under the information technology governance framework. *European Business Review*, *32*(2), 129–157. DOI: 10.1108/EBR-05-2018-0102

Kouba, P., Kohout, P., Haddadi, F., Bushuiev, A., Samusevich, R., Sedlar, J., Damborsky, J., Pluskal, T., Sivic, J., & Mazurenko, S. (2023). Machine Learning-Guided Protein Engineering. *ACS Catalysis, 13*(21), 13863–13895. DOI: 10.1021/acscatal.3c02743 PMID: 37942269

Liu, Y., Han, T., Ma, S., Zhang, J., Yang, Y., Tian, J., He, H., Li, A., He, M., Liu, Z., Wu, Z., Zhao, L., Zhu, D., Li, X., Qiang, N., Shen, D., Liu, T., & Ge, B. (2023). Summary of ChatGPT-related research and perspective towards the future of large language models. *Meta-Radiology*, *1*(2), 100017. DOI: 10.1016/j.metrad.2023.100017

Mazar, M. (2023). Strategies for Improving Supply Chain Management in United Nations Peacekeeping Missions (Doctoral dissertation, Walden University).

Mostafiz, M. I., Musteen, M., Saiyed, A., & Ahsan, M. (2022). COVID-19 and the global value chain: Immediate dynamics and long-term restructuring in the garment industry. *Journal of Business Research, 139*, 1588–1603. DOI: 10.1016/j.jbusres.2021.10.078

Patil, et al. (2022). "Utilization of Artificial Intelligence in Healthcare System, Pharmaceutical Industry & Education". International Journal of Advanced Research in Science, Communication and Technology.

Pesqueira, A. (2023). Blockchain and Pharmaceuticals: A Bibliometric and Systematic Literature Review of Scientific Publications Between 2000 and 2021. *Technology, Business, Innovation, and Entrepreneurship in Industry*, *4*(0), 25–48. DOI: 10.1007/978-3-031-17960-0_2

Pesqueira, A., & Bolog, S. (2023). Patient empowerment with direct insights from healthcare professionals questionnaires. In *Internet of Things in Biomedical Sciences: Challenges and applications* (pp. 12–1). IOP Publishing. DOI: 10.1088/978-0-7503-5311-3ch12

Pesqueira, A., Bolog, S., Sousa, M. J., & Almeida, D. (2023). Impact of Decentralized and Agile Digital Transformational Programs on the Pharmaceutical Industry, Including an Assessment of Digital Activity Metrics and Commercial Digital. In Proceedings of International Conference on Information Technology and Applications: ICITA 2022 (Vol. 614, p. 341). Springer Nature. DOI: 10.1007/978-981-19-9331-2_29

Pesqueira, A., & Sousa, M. J. (2022). Life Sciences Industry Blockchain Value Management, Investments, and Finance Impact Assessment: Global Questionnaire Survey of 1524 Industry Professionals and Executives. In Incorporating AI Technology in the Service Sector (pp. 67-107). Apple Academic Press.

Pesqueira, A., Sousa, M. J., & Pereira, R. (2025). Individual Dynamic Capabilities and Artificial Intelligence in Health Operations: Exploration of Innovation Diffusion. *Intelligence-Based Medicine, 11*, 100239. DOI: 10.1016/j.ibmed.2025.100239

Pettersen, I. J., Nyland, K., & Robbins, G. (2020). Public procurement performance and the challenge of service complexity–the case of pre-hospital healthcare. *Journal of Public Procurement, 20*(4), 403–421. DOI: 10.1108/JOPP-01-2020-0002

Pundziene, A., Heaton, S., & Teece, D. J. (2019). 5G, dynamic capabilities and business models innovation in healthcare industry. In 2019 IEEE International Symposium on Innovation and Entrepreneurship (TEMS-ISIE) (pp. 1-8). IEEE. 24 DOI: 10.1109/TEMS-ISIE46312.2019.9074330

Rashid, S., & Ratten, V. (2021). Entrepreneurial ecosystems during [the survival of small businesses using dynamic capabilities. World Journal of Entrepreneurship, Management and Sustainable Development.]. *COVID*, 19.

Robson, I., Ojiako, U., & Maguire, S. (2022). A complexity perspective of dynamic capabilities in enterprise project organizations. *Production Planning and Control*, 1–25.

Scuotto, V., Magni, D., Theofilos, T., & Del Giudice, M. (2022). Chief digital officer and organizational creativity toward digitalization. *IEEE Transactions on Engineering Management.*

Secinaro, , Calandra, D., Secinaro, A., Muthurangu, V., & Biancone, P. (2021). The role of artificial intelligence in healthcare: A structured literature review. *BMC Medical Informatics and Decision Making, 21*(1), 125. DOI: 10.1186/s12911-021-01488-9 PMID: 33836752

Segato, , Marzullo, A., Calimeri, F., & De Momi, E. (2020). Artificial intelligence for brain diseases: A systematic review. *APL Bioengineering, 4*(4), 041503. DOI: 10.1063/5.0011697 PMID: 33094213

Shiwlani, A., Khan, M., Sherani, A. M. K., & Qayyum, M. U. (2023). Synergies of AI and Smart Technology: Revolutionizing Cancer Medicine, Vaccine Development, and Patient Care. International Journal of Social. *Humanities and Life Sciences, 1*(1), 10–18.

Shujahat, M., Sousa, M. J., Hussain, S., Nawaz, F., Wang, M., & Umer, M. (2019). Translating the impact of knowledge management processes into knowledge-based innovation: The neglected and mediating role of knowledge-worker productivity. *Journal of Business Research, 94*, 442–450. DOI: 10.1016/j.jbusres.2017.11.001

Soluk, J., Decker-Lange, C., & Hack, A. (2023). Small steps for the big hit: A dynamic capabilities perspective on business networks and non-disruptive digital technologies in SMEs. *Technological Forecasting and Social Change*, *191*, 122490. DOI: 10.1016/j.techfore.2023.122490

Sturm, N., Mayr, A., Le Van, T., Chupakhin, V., Ceulemans, H., Wegner, J., Golib-Dzib, J.-F., Jeliazkova, N., Vandriessche, Y., Böhm, S., Cima, V., Martinovic, J., Greene, N., Vander Aa, T., Ashby, T. J., Hochreiter, S., Engkvist, O., Klambauer, G., & Chen, H. (2020). Industry-scale application and evaluation of deep learning for drug target prediction. *Journal of Cheminformatics*, *12*(1), 1–13. DOI: 10.1186/s13321-020-00428-5 PMID: 33430964

Suri, G. S., Kaur, G., & Shinde, D. (2024). Beyond boundaries: Exploring the transformative power of AI in pharmaceuticals. *Discover Artificial Intelligence*, *4*(1), 82. DOI: 10.1007/s44163-024-00192-7

Tariq, , Awan, M. J., Alshudukhi, J., Alam, T. M., Alhamazani, K. T., & Meraf, Z. (2022). Software Measurement by Using Artificial Intelligence. *Journal of Nanomaterials*, *2022*(1), 7283171. DOI: 10.1155/2022/7283171

Tran, Y., Zahra, S., & Hughes, M. (2019). A process model of the maturation of a new dynamic capability. *Industrial Marketing Management*, *83*, 115–127. DOI: 10.1016/j.indmarman.2018.11.009

Ullah, H., Manickam, S., Obaidat, M., Laghari, S. U. A., & Uddin, M. (2023). Exploring the Potential of Metaverse Technology in Healthcare: Applications, Challenges, and Future Directions. *IEEE Access: Practical Innovations, Open Solutions*, *11*, 69686–69707. DOI: 10.1109/ACCESS.2023.3286696

Vaishya, , Javaid, M., Khan, I. H., & Haleem, A. (2020). Artificial Intelligence (AI) applications for COVID-19 pandemic. *Diabetes & Metabolic Syndrome*, *14*(4), 337–339. DOI: 10.1016/j.dsx.2020.04.012 PMID: 32305024

Vallentin, A., Thórisson, K. R., & Latapie, H. (2023). Addressing the Unsustainability of Deep Neural Networks with Next-Gen AI. In International Conference on Artificial General Intelligence (pp. 296-306). Cham: Springer Nature Switzerland. DOI: 10.1007/978-3-031-33469-6_30

van Hoek, R. (2024). Insight from industry-early lessons learned about AI adoption in core procurement processes, directions for managers and researchers. *Supply Chain Management*, *29*(4), 794–803. DOI: 10.1108/SCM-02-2024-0143

Vlasta, M. (2023). Methodological framework for European regulation of (artificial) intelligence and its limits.

Wamba, S. F., Queiroz, M. M., Jabbour, C. J. C., & Shi, C. V. (2023). Are both generative AI and ChatGPT game changers for 21st-Century operations and supply chain excellence? *International Journal of Production Economics*, *265*, 109015. DOI: 10.1016/j.ijpe.2023.109015

Wani, . (2022). Utilization of Artificial Intelligence in Disease Prevention: Diagnosis, Treatment, and Implications for the Healthcare Workforce. *Health Care*. PMID: 35455786

Chapter 2
Artificial Intelligence to Achieve Retail Supply Chain Resilience:
A Systematic Review And Agenda For Future Research

Tiansheng Zhu
Cranfield University, UK

Syed Imran Ali
https://orcid.org/0000-0002-6553-8210
Queen Mary University of London, UK

ABSTRACT

In the modern retail context, artificial intelligence (AI) and machine learning (ML) techniques are crucial for optimising essential activities such as supplier management, demand forecasting, inventory management, pricing, and order fulfilment. However, they may require a better understanding of the retail sector as the application of AI and ML varies across the various sections. This chapter employs a systematic literature review to synthesise data from 62 high-quality research studies demonstrating how these technologies can indirectly improve collaboration, visibility, speed, flexibility, configuration, and awareness within the retail supply chain. Adopting AI and ML significantly boosts operational efficiency, robustness, and adaptability, reducing the disruption risk. By leveraging these technologies, retailers can build more resilient and competitive retail supply chains capable of swiftly responding to market changes and disruptions.

DOI: 10.4018/979-8-3373-0923-1.ch002

1. INTRODUCTION

1.1 Background

1.1.1 Historical Evolution and Practical Applications of AI in Retail Supply Chain

Technological progress, global disruption, and constant change in consumer demands have reshaped the application of AI in the retail supply chain (RSC). Historically, the application of AI can be traced back to the 1980s, when static expert systems based on heuristics were utilised in inventory management and to optimise warehouse operations. These systems were not sufficiently robust in the dynamic environment, as SCs have become more complex and volatile.

In the late 1990s and 2000s, the latest machine learning (ML) and data mining techniques were developed to effectively define rules in expert systems and make decisions in dynamic environments. For example, a retail giant like Walmart has leveraged AI and ML-driven inventory management systems to effectively manage seasonal products and select the right products for the holiday season (Musani, 2023).

In the post-2010 period, further development in AI was observed, particularly in Natural Language Processing (NLP), which has revolutionised real-time decision-making. Companies such as Amazon have utilised NLP and big-data analytics in their AI-based systems to better understand customer requirements, dynamically reallocate inventory, optimise delivery routes, and significantly reduce lead times (Wamba et al., 2021). Two major players in the consumer products industry, i.e., Procter & Gamble (P&G) and Unilever, have leveraged AI-based systems to monitor product quality and consistency, reduce waste, and better understand customer demand by minimising stockouts and overproduction (Taylor, 2025).

1.1.2 Disruptions and Resilience in Retail Supply Chain

The traditional retail SC consists of four main components: the suppliers, the distribution centre, the store and the customer; however, the development of e-commerce has made today's retail SC system more complex, as shown in Figure 1.

Figure 1. Modern retail supply chain

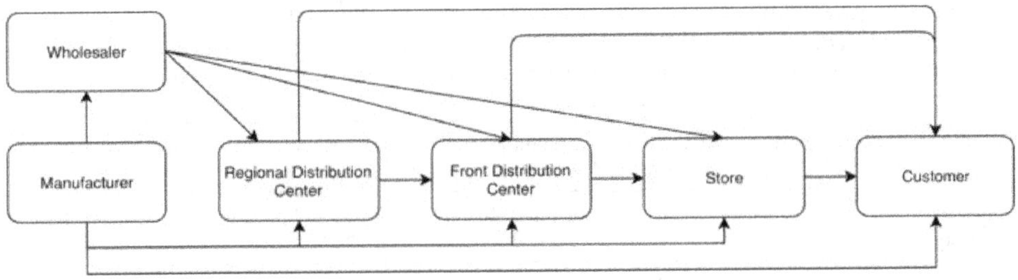

Source: Ge et al. (2019)

This increased complexity creates several challenges for the main activities in the retail SC, as shown in Table 1.

Table 1. Challenges in main retail supply chain activities

Activities	Challenges
Vendor Management	Quickly screen reliable suppliers, build good supplier relationships and share information.
Demand Forecasting	Rapidly organise and classify demand data, e.g., to distinguish between data with or without time series trends. Construct corresponding demand forecasting models with high accuracy to reduce forecasting time and complexity.
Inventory Management	Quickly and accurately monitor goods entering and leaving the warehouse or distribution centre, reconcile stock balances, and determine matters such as safety stock and replenishment of goods.
Order Fulfilment	Flexibility in choosing the best shipping location and mode of transport to meet customer delivery time requirements while using smaller fulfilment costs.

Source: Ge et al. (2019)

Meanwhile, sudden events in recent years have caused retail SC disruptions, such as natural disasters, the spread of global diseases and epidemics, political unrest, and energy crises (Abe & Ye, 2013; J. Chen et al., 2013; Guan et al., 2023; Min, 2019). These disasters created challenges with new implications for organisations' SCM (see Table 2).

Table 2. Effects of different types of supply chain disruption

Types	Examples	Effects
Natural Disasters	Earthquake and tsunami	Production, transportation and delivery of products must be delayed, and existing logistics facilities must be repaired (Revilla & Sáenz, 2014; Todo et al., 2015).
	Pandemic	Disrupting production, increasing trade restrictions, and SC activities time and cost (Veselovská, 2020).
Man-made Disasters	War	The destruction of logistics facilities and personnel has almost wholly halted SC activities (Jagtap et al., 2022).
	Trade embargo	Demand surged, the number of suppliers decreased, and retailers ran out of goods (Handfield et al., 2020).

Source: The author (2024)

Many scholars have focused on building more resilient SCs to minimise the risk and impact of SC disruptions, especially after the COVID-19 outbreak (Sombultawee et al., 2022). Scholten et al. (2019) and Haris Aslam et al. (2020) considered SCR to be measured in four phases of disruption, as shown in Table 3. These four phases constitute a complete process of the entire SC, from disruption to recovery to reactivation, which lays a theoretical foundation for an in-depth study of the ways and assessments of emerging technologies' empowerment on SCR.

Interestingly, Kassa et al.(2023) propose SCR's antecedents as a critical measure of resilience. The criterion assesses the role and effectiveness of AI in seven dimensions, namely (1) *Velocity*, an ability to adapt to unexpected changes in supply and demand (Christopher & Peck, 2004); (2) *Collaboration*, which can be defined as the integration of strengths and sharing of resources among SC participants to reduce disruptive winds (Ponomarov & Holcomb, 2009); (3) *Configuration*, which involves the design or redesign of an optimally robust SC network so that the network can be replicated in the event of a network outage (Ali et al., 2017); (4) *Visibility*, which refers to the SC's ability to obtain information about the identity, location, and status of entities among manufacturers, suppliers, and customers(Basole & Bellamy, 2014);(5) *Awareness*, an ability to sense and interpret possible disruptions (Han et al., 2020); (6) *Flexibility*, meaning the ease with which a SC can vary its range quantity and range heterogeneity to cope with market changes or events, while at the same time maintaining good performance to cope with market changes or events (Jüttner & Maklan, 2011; Skipper & Hanna, 2009; Stevenson & Spring, 2007); (7) Resilient Sourcing is a decision-making process for the correctness of a firm's sourcing strategy(Esmaeili-Najafabadi et al., 2021). These ideas will drive the research of this chapter.

Table 3. Definitions of SCR four phases

Phases	Definitions	Sources
Readiness	Anticipate and prepare for all possible disruption risks before they occur.	(Scholten et al., 2019)
Response	Providing timely feedback on the causes of the disruption and obtaining ways to restore SCR.	
Recovery	The ability to make the SC resilient again after a disruption, to mitigate the impact of the disruption.	
Adaptability	The ability of a firm to adapt to changes in market structure and adjust its SC network after modifying its SC design to restore SCR.	(Aslam et al., 2020)

Source: The author (2024)

1.1.3 AI in Supply Chain

AI technology uses computers to simulate and perform human-intelligent work (Boden, 2018). Since the 21st century, due to the dramatic increase in the volume and complexity of data involved in business activities, AI has been widely used in research and business applications due to its superior data processing capabilities (Scholten et al., 2014).

The SC sector, especially, has complex data to work with, such as demand forecasting, inventory management, and vendor management; AI and ML can optimise the processing of such data (Wenzel et al., 2019). Meanwhile, the need for companies to build innovative SC decision-making systems to improve resilience and competitiveness drives SCM experts to experiment with AI for high-performance decision analysis (Akter et al., 2022).

Ni et al. (2020) summarised the ten most used ML applications in SCs, including neural networks (NN), support vector machines (SVM), decision trees (DT) and tree ML types. These algorithms have been proven helpful in forecasting, inventory, distribution, and SC redesign and are effective in improving the performance of such activities, as shown in Table 4.

Table 4. Definition of three machine learning types

Machine Learning Types	Definitions	Sources
Supervised Learning	It uses labelled data sets to adjust the model parameters, which can be adapted to the adjusted solution for unknown data.	(Alloghani et al., 2020)
Unsupervised Learning	Instead of training on a given implementation labelled data set, it automatically classifies or groups the input data.	
Deep Learning	It can learn the internal rules and levels of sample data, and the information obtained in the learning process can be words, images, or voice.	(Shrestha & Mahmood, 2019)

Source: Author (2024)

These AI technologies effectively capture all kinds of dynamic risk information. They reduce the possibility of actual disruption and dynamically monitor all sorts of activities in the SC, short-term prediction and adjustment, to improve the SC's responsiveness and recovery speed (Modgil et al., 2022; Ralston & Blackhurst, 2020; Sundarakani et al., 2020).

1.2 Problem Statement

This chapter requires a systematic literature review of existing papers on applying practical AI and ML in retail SCRs, including the basic information of these papers, such as publication time and journal publication. Moreover, it classifies the functions of these technologies to summarise their enhancements, benefits, and application scenarios for retail SCRs.

1.3 Justification of Research

While many papers have discussed the use of AI to implement SCR management, these studies have yet to focus on SCR in the retail sector (Zamani et al., 2023). Furthermore, these studies need to be more specific and practical to shed light on the impact of AI and ML on SCR dimensions and capabilities (Modgil et al., 2022). As a result, there are still significant research gaps in uncovering how AI can achieve SCR in the retail industry.

1.4 Research Objectives

This chapter has the following four research objectives.

Objective 1. Identify and review AI-related academic and practice literature to enable retail SCR.

Objective 2. Analyse how AI can be used to overcome challenges in retail SC activities.
Objective 3. Identify the benefits of AI in enabling SCR in retail SC.
Objective 4. Demonstrate and explain the mechanism by which AI improves the SCR stage (readiness, response, recovery, adaptability).

2. METHODOLOGY

2.1 Systematic Literature Review

This chapter uses an SLR to explore the research question, which is defined as: 'a method of synthesising scientific evidence to answer a specific research question in a transparent and reproducible manner, while seeking to include all published articles on the topic and assessing the quality and usability of the article according to the criteria given by the reviewers.' (Lame, 2019)

SLR was initially used in medicine to select the best evidence for use in clinical practice from the millions of papers published each year on a particular issue, minimising the impact of scope, selection and data extraction bias (Moher et al., 2009). Such reviews emphasise systematicity, comprehensibility, and transparency, for example, all terms in the inclusion criteria must be aligned with the study's subject matter and must be defined and justified. In contrast, the exclusion of articles must be justified (Greyson et al., 2019). SLR ensures reviewers can find higher-quality information sources within the desired research scope. However, deep diving into the searched keywords is required to obtain reliable information, and evaluating and screening the information is very time-consuming (Davis et al., 2014).

Compared to other traditional literature review methods, SLR focuses more on the objective presentation of available evidence and reduces reviewer bias through clear structural selection criteria and a direct linkage to the research questions (Snyder, 2019). If there is a lack of SLR, then the overview of the available literature is not comprehensive enough, and the level of interpretation of the literature is insufficient, which means that the review lacks comprehensiveness. Without SLR, transparency can also be a severe problem in a literature review (Dixon-Woods et al., 2005).

2.2 Limitation of Systematic Literature Review

Despite the methodological transparency, the study has a few limitations. The first limitation is the framing of search terms, exclusion, and inclusion criteria, which restricts the selection of studies in multidisciplinary fields, such as AI in supply chain. Some of the relevant studies are excluded because they don't meet the criteria. Secondly, SLR relies heavily on peer-reviewed articles, which may overlook industry reports and practitioner reports that offer valuable insights about the topic. Thirdly, in the era of technological advancement, a significant amount of academic literature in peer-reviewed journal publications is delayed due to the publication cycle, which hinders the timely dissemination of up-to-date knowledge to practitioners. Finally, the selection of studies and coding for theme generation is done solely on the subjective knowledge of the researcher, which creates bias despite the methodological objectivity of SLR.

2.3 Review Panel

A review team comprising two members evaluated all articles at the literature review stage.

2.4 Process of Systematic Literature Review

The SLR has its specific process, categorised into seven steps, as shown in Figure 2

Figure 2. Process of SLR

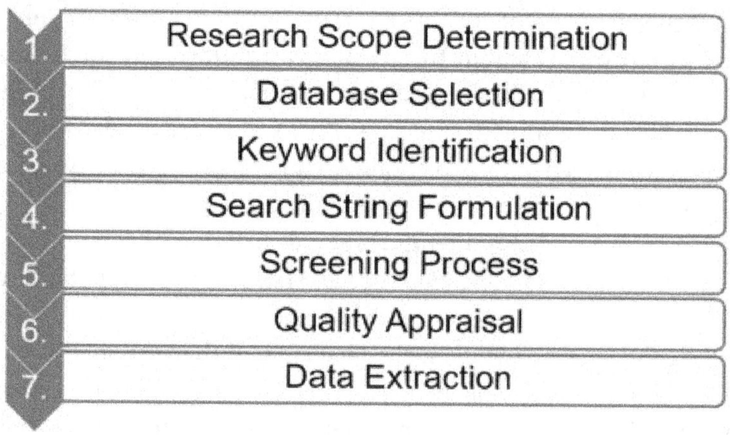

Source: The author (2024)

2.4.1 Research Scope Determination

Several current publications relate AI to SCR. This study aims to bridge the research gap by exploring the following research questions, thereby providing a deeper understanding of the role and significance of AI technology in improving SCR in the retail sector.

Figure 3 depicts the scope and boundaries of this study. It encompasses AI, retail, and SCR, with its scope lying at the intersection of these three domains.

Figure 3. Research scope

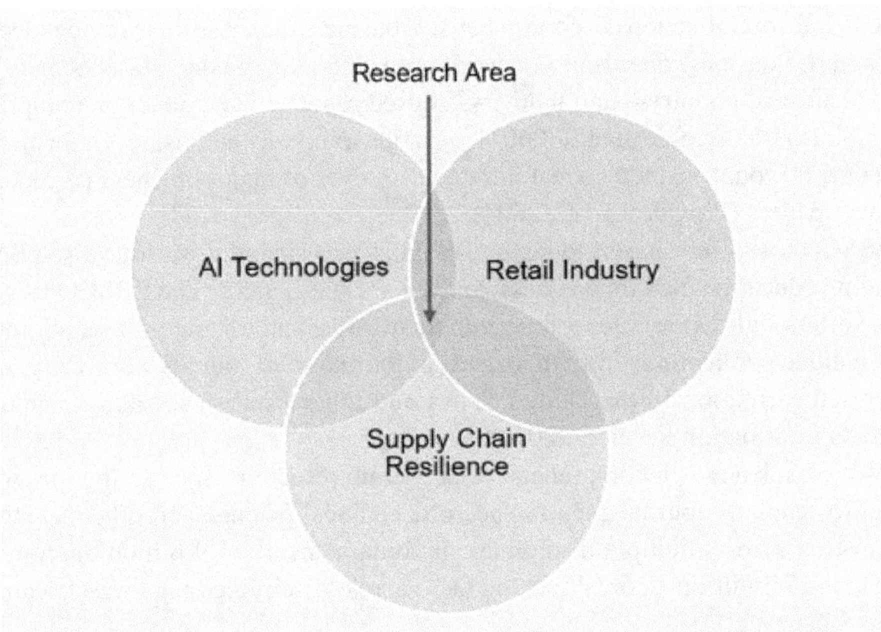

Source: The author (2024)

2.4.2 Database Selection

Articles were searched using four databases. They are authoritative and cover a wide range of academic papers, books, journals and conference articles: (1) Scopus, (2) ABI/Inform Collection, (3) EBSCOhost and (4) Web of Science.

Scopus is a comprehensive, multidisciplinary database that covers peer-reviewed literature in the sciences, technology, medicine, social sciences, and the arts and humanities. It provides access to over 75 million records from over 24,000 active titles and over 5,000 publishers worldwide, including coverage from North America, Europe, and Asia. Scopus includes citation analysis, author profiles, and journal metrics (Scopus, 2024).

ABI/Inform Collection is a comprehensive business database that provides access to scholarly journals, dissertations, working papers, key business and economics periodicals, and country—and industry-focused reports. The collection comprises over 3,800 journals, more than 27,000 dissertations, and various business information from over 60 countries. It also features deep archives of major business periodicals and newspapers (ProQuest LLC, 2024).

EBSCOhost offers access to a range of databases spanning various disciplines, including education, health, business, and the social sciences. The EBSCOhost database offers full-text articles, bibliographic records, and a variety of search tools. They include publications from thousands of journals and sources worldwide, with strong representation in the United States and other English-speaking countries (EBSCO Information Services, 2024).

Web of Science is a comprehensive academic research database that provides access to scholarly journals, conference proceedings, patents, and other scientific information across multiple disciplines. It contains nearly 1.9 billion citations in more than 171 million records tracking ideas across disciplines and time (J. Murrey Atkins Library, 2021).

2.4.3 Keywords Identification

This is a crucial step in starting SLR. Reliable keywords help quickly sift through the plethora of publications to identify those that match the main research themes. Therefore, this chapter divides the keywords into three sections: A, B, and C.

Based on the background research done in the introduction, the keywords used in the search can be identified, as shown in Table 5.

Table 5. Keywords used in the search

A	B	C
● Retail* ● Electronic commerce ● E-commerce	● Supply chain resilience ● Supply chain disruptions ● Supply chain readiness ● Supply chain response ● Supply chain recovery ● Supply chain adaptability ● Vendor management ● Demand forecasting ● Inventory management ● Order fulfilment	● Artificial intelligent ● AI ● Machine learning ● ML

Source: The author (2024)

2.4.4 Search Strings Formulation

The search for strings is performed in the database using Boolean operations to filter the conditions of the keywords. For example, 'AND' ensures that literature is retrieved that satisfies all three parts of A, B, and C, whereas 'OR' includes all the respective keywords under A, B, and C, as shown in Table 6.

2.4.5 Screening Process

After the search is complete, numerous results are generated, so a screening and selection process must be employed to narrow down the number of results and compile the publications that best align with the research objectives. A well-established screening process must be set up to ensure an objective and quick initial screening, as shown in Figure 4.

The entire screening process consists of four steps. It is based on the inclusion and exclusion criteria for the study's scope and the quality expectations associated with the results. The quality selection of inclusion and exclusion criteria enables the rapid identification of eligible results from the initial redundant results. It provides reliable evidence to improve the quality and credibility of the paper. The inclusion and exclusion criteria are shown in Table 7.

Initial screening restricts the essential criteria for publication, with studies from the last decade being more innovative and theoretically and practically relevant. Subject area selection must be highly relevant to the research topic, e.g., Business, Management, and Accounting, and emphasise applying AI technology in various parts of the SC. At the same time, Computer Science provides more detailed ML algorithms and application scenarios. We can provide evidence that AI technology benefits SCR by correlating these subject areas. Document type and source type exclude magazines, websites, and other less specialised evidence that is less likely to be peer-reviewed. At the same time, the English language ensures comprehensibility, and the evidence can be read and understood during the review.

Table 6. Formulation of search string

A		B		C
Retail* OR Electronic commerce OR E-commerce	AND	Supply chain resilience OR Supply chain disruptions OR Supply chain readiness OR Supply chain response OR Supply chain recovery OR Supply chain adaptability OR Vendor management OR Demand forecasting OR Inventory management OR Order fulfilment	AND	Artificial intelligent OR AI OR Machine learning OR ML

Source: The author (2024)

Figure 4. Flow of screening process

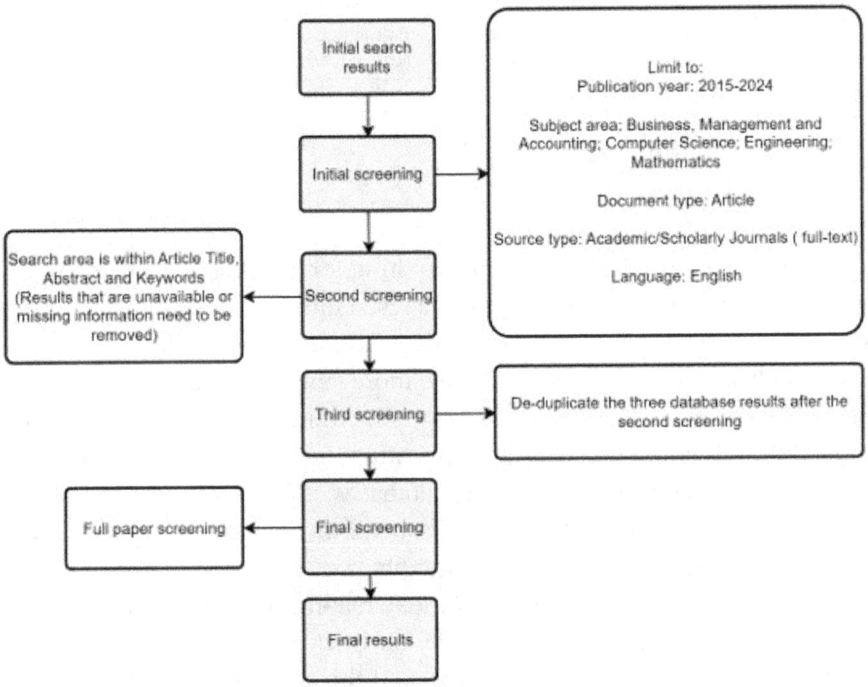

Source: The author (2024)

Table 7. Inclusion and exclusion criteria

Criteria	Rationale	Inclusion	Exclusion
Publication year	Ensure the timeliness of the evidence and its relevance to the research topic.	Publication year within 2015-2024.	Publication year outside of 2015-2024.
Subject area	Ensure that the evidence is consistent with the direction of this research.	Management, Business and Accounting; Computer Science; Engineering; Mathematics.	Publications in other subject areas.
Document Type	Ensure the reliability of evidence.	Article/ Journal Article	Publications in other document types.

continued on following page

Table 7. Continued

Criteria	Rationale	Inclusion	Exclusion
Source type	Ensure that the evidence is of high quality and convincing.	Full-text and peer-reviewed academic/scholarly journal.	Publications in other source types.
Language	Ensure that the evidence is easy to read and understandable.	English	Publications in other languages.

Source: The author (2024)

The second screening focuses on searching for article titles, abstracts, and keywords. The article's main content is condensed into titles, abstracts, and keywords, allowing for a concise and quick screening that can improve the article's relevance to the search strings and identify articles more suitable for use in the paper. At the same time, articles that are unusable or missing important information are removed.

The third screening involves de-duplicating the results of the second screening. As the articles originate from three databases, there may be identical articles; therefore, duplicates must be removed from all three databases to ensure a smooth reading process and an accurate bibliographic count.

The final screening involves a full-text reading of the results from the third screening. The articles retrieved by title, abstract, and keywords may not provide high-quality evidence to support the ideas of this chapter in the body. At the same time, reading the full text can enhance understanding of the article's point of view and eliminate lower-quality articles.

2.4.6 Quality Appraisal

In the final screening, quality appraisal criteria are needed to improve the reliability and quality of articles. In this chapter, articles are screened using the ranking results of ABS Journal Ranking 2021 on a scale of 1-4* (Journal Ranking Portal, 2021)Articles with a rating of 3-4* are considered more reliable, while articles with a rating of less than 3 require full paper screening to determine the reliability of their ideas. All articles in the final screening stage must be published in journals with a ranking.

2.4.7 Data Extraction

Data extraction is obtaining and summarising detailed information about selected articles for quantitative or qualitative synthesis. Extracting qualitative information can help researchers recognise weaknesses and trends in articles as vital information to complement practices and strategies. In contrast, quantitative data can help researchers determine the generalisability of findings and trends in research to reduce the bias of evidence findings (Munn et al., 2014). There are many tools for data extraction, but this chapter uses an Excel-based spreadsheet to collect data, which can systematically record the information of the selected articles, including the author(s), year of publication, type of document, abstract, etc. Data extraction records the critical information of the articles and their relevance to this chapter to make it easier for the researcher to identify and analyse the data. The significance of this chapter makes subsequent quantitative and qualitative analyses of the articles more efficient.

3. DESCRIPTIVE ANALYSIS

3.1 Search Outcomes

After the search, a total of 10,784 articles were retrieved from four databases: Scopus (10,030), ABI/Inform Collection (514), EBSCOhost (240) and Web of Science (133). After the third screening and de-duplication, 196 articles were obtained, and 74 authoritative articles were retained after assessing the journal ratings in which they were published. Finally, after reading the whole paper, 62 articles are used in this chapter, as shown in Figure 5.

According to the Screening process, all articles are Journal Articles with no Conference Papers, Trading Articles or Consulting Reports.

3.2 Chronological Distribution

Figure 6 illustrates the number of articles published annually from 2015 to 2024. It can be noticed that between 2015 and 2018, the number of studies on the field was low, totalling only six articles. In contrast, after 2019, there was a significant increase in the number of papers published, totalling 56. This is in line with the general context that the impact of COVID-19 on global SCs has forced experts and scholars to explore the field in depth.

Figure 5. Final screening results flowchart

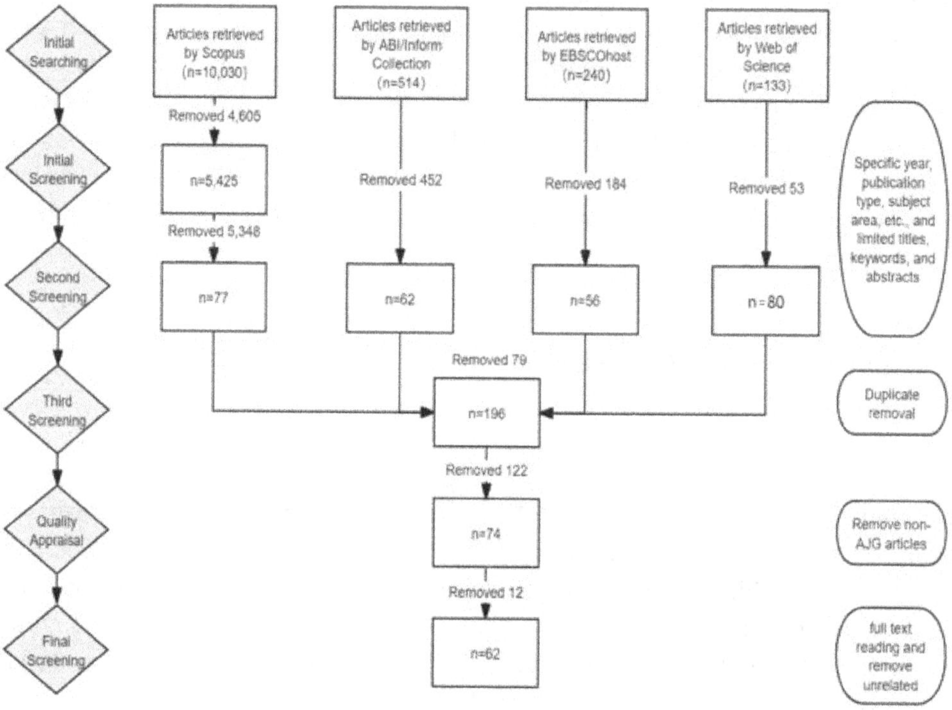

Source: The author (2024)

Figure 6. Number of articles published annually between 2015 and 2024

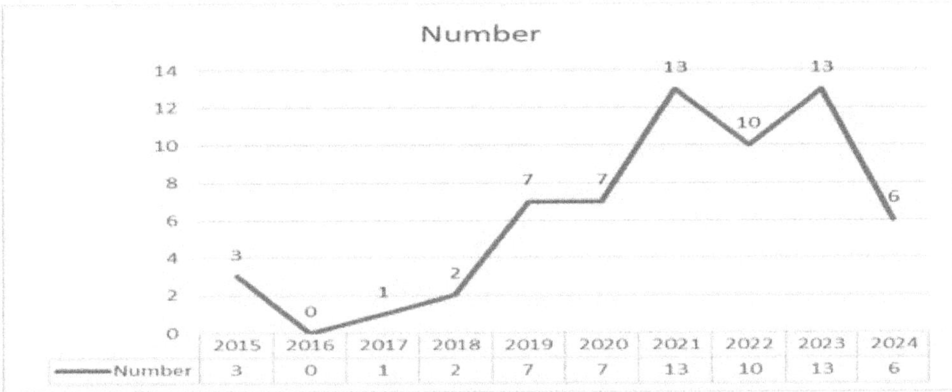

Source: The author (2024)

3.3 Geographical Distribution

Figures 7 and 8 show the number of articles published by different countries, and it can be seen from the figures that the United States, China, and India have the highest number of published articles. The US and China have nine publications, while India has eight. Some other countries and regions have contributed articles in this field based on their circumstances, such as Hong Kong (4 articles), South Korea (2 articles), the UK (4 articles), Brazil (1 article), Saudi Arabia (2 articles) and Germany (5 articles).

China, US and India, as mainstream countries in international trade, manufacturing and transport, are more sensitive to changes in SC and need to strengthen their ability to face SC disruptions and maintain SCR to mitigate economic crises caused by SC risks.

Figure 7. World publication number map diagram

Source: The author (2024)

Figure 8. Number of publications by different regions

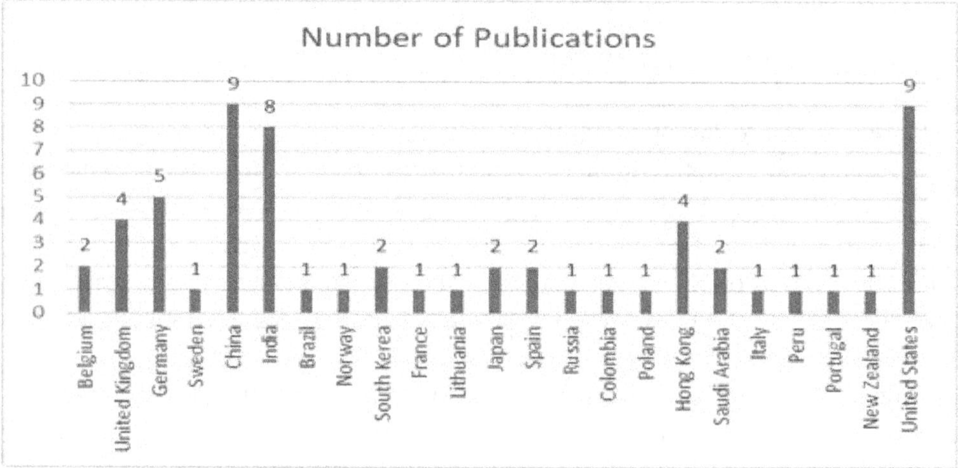

Source: The author (2024)

4. THEMATIC ANALYSIS

4.1 AI and ML Techniques in Retail SC

In this chapter, retail SC activities are classified into five broad categories: vendor management, demand forecasting, inventory management, pricing, and order fulfilment, all optimised using one or more AI and ML techniques.

4.1.1 Vendor Management

Table 8 discusses the AI and ML algorithms commonly used in vendor management.

Table 8. AI and ML techniques in vendor management

Articles/ Algorithms	1	2	3	4	5	6	7	8	9
(Van Belle et al., 2021)			X	X	X			X	
(Pereira & Frazzon, 2021)	X			X	X		X		
(Cantini et al., 2024)		X							
(Andrés Muñoz-Villamizar et al., 2024)						X	X		
(Lam et al., 2021)									X
Total	1	1	1	2	2	1	2	1	1

Source: The author (2024)

4.1.1.1 Vertical Information Transmission

Information transmission is the most critical aspect of vendor management, where the upstream end of the SC must quickly sense downstream demand fluctuations (Lam et al., 2021; Van Belle et al., 2021). Van Belle et al. (2021) constructed a gradient SC information transfer model integrating Lasso regression, ANN, SVM, and RF, thus reducing the bullwhip effect in the hierarchical transfer of information and enabling suppliers to have more accurate data in the presence of multiple external variables. Multiple variables are used to have more accurate downstream data. Also, to streamline the information flow, ANNs are used to share this information with the participants in the activities.

4.1.2 Demand Forecasting

Table 9 summarises the AI and ML algorithms commonly used in demand forecasting.

Table 9. AI and ML techniques in demand forecasting

Articles/ Algorithms	**1**	**2**	**3**	**4**	**5**	**6**	**7**	**8**	**9**	**10**	**11**	**12**	**13**	**14**
(Verstraete et al., 2019)				X		X	X			X				
(Hoeltgebaum et al., 2021)				X						X				
(Ulrich et al., 2021)			X							X				
(Kourentzes & Athanasopoulos, 2021)					X									
(Ding et al., 2021)	X													
(Khosrowabadi et al., 2022)		X	X											
(Van Belle et al., 2021)			X	X	X	X				X				
(Pereira & Frazzon, 2021)				X					X					
(Sharma et al., 2019)		X		X						X				
(Ferreira et al., 2016)		X												
(Omar et al., 2023)								X						
(Huber & Stuckenschmidt, 2020)				X			X							X
(Punia, Nikolopoulos, et al., 2020)			X											X
(Gružauskas et al., 2019)											X			
(Antipov & Pokryshevskaya, 2020)			X				X					X		
(Chołodowicz & Orłowski, 2024)				X										
(J. Wang et al., 2023)							X							
(Imran & Hyun, 2024)			X					X						
(S. Wang & Yang, 2021)								X						
(Y. Chen et al., 2020)													X	
(Miguéis et al., 2022)			X	X		X								
(Shi et al., 2020)			X											
(Priyadarshi et al., 2019)			X	X			X	X						
(Elorza et al., 2024)								X						
Total	1	3	9	9	2	3	5	5	1	5	1	1	1	2

Source: The author (2024)

4.1.2.1 Demand Fluctuation Variables and Disruption Risk identification

RF aims to assess the relationship between independent and dependent variables by constructing numerous decision trees to evaluate the importance of each independent variable. This is crucial for almost all regression prediction models. It handles noise and prevents overfitting by eliminating many unusable variables and identifying driving factors. Multiple studies have used RF to identify variables that significantly affect demand fluctuations in the retail industry, such as weather (temperature), diseases, disasters, seasonal changes, population density, and income groups (Imran & Hyun, 2024; Khosrowabadi et al., 2022; Punia, Nikolopoulos, et al., 2020). These variables are strongly associated with SC disruptions or panic buying. Therefore, RF reduces forecasting volatility, improves accuracy and filters out risk factors for SC disruptions, providing readiness recommendations for various stakeholders (Shi et al., 2020).

4.2 The Role of AI and ML in Achieving SCR

In this section, the focus of the discussion shifts from retail SC activities to SCR. However, based on previous research, we can understand that AI does not directly affect SCR and the four stages of SCR. Instead, it indirectly enhances the various stages of SCR by promoting the antecedents of SCR, thereby strengthening SCR. Moreover, the results indicate that the capability of resilient sourcing is already closely linked with the activity of Vendor Management. Therefore, the discussion will focus only on the impact of AI on the remaining six antecedents.

4.2.1 Supply Chain Collaboration

4.2.1.1 Information Sharing

AI technology enables the integration and sharing of various data across the SC, allowing retailers, distributors, manufacturers, and suppliers to participate in critical SC decisions and daily operations collaboratively and jointly manage risks. ANN can be a crucial algorithm for predicting SC integration levels and multi-tier forecasting accuracy (Van Belle et al., 2021). JD.com's integrated neural network model has achieved complete SC information sharing. This model not only assists manufacturers in forecasting inventory levels and developing production plans but also enables suppliers to obtain end-to-end inventory information, facilitating dynamic inventory monitoring (Hu et al., 2024). Gružauskas et al. (2019) utilised Extreme Learning Machines (ELM) to provide shared predictive information within logistics clusters, enhancing delivery capabilities and improving overall SC collaboration levels.

4.2.1.2 Vendor Relationship Optimisation

The global e-commerce retail sector is booming, necessitating the development and management of reliable supplier networks. Clustering algorithms like K-means and C-means can analyse suppliers' capabilities regarding delivery timeliness, quality, and profitability. This analysis helps formulate independent management strategies for individual suppliers or supplier clusters, providing better collaboration and flexibility for business operations (Lam et al., 2021).

In summary, SC collaboration is crucial in all four phases of SCR.

4.2.2 Supply Chain Visibility

4.2.2.1 Performance Indicator Visualisation

In internal operations, AI can visualise various critical performance indicators, assisting decision-makers in adapting this data-driven approach to operational strategies (Pereira & Frazzon, 2021). Schlosser et al. (2019) used Gradient Boosting and ANN to visualise critical indicators such as inventory holding costs, competitor prices, and ordering costs and employed these indicators to build pricing models. Alomar (2022) utilised the Improved Feed Forward Network with Particle Swarm Optimisation technique to identify performance optimisation indicators for the SC system, aiding decision-makers in subsequent planning based on these indicators. The High-Order Neural Network (HONN) was applied to optimise complex stochastic inventory in multi-indicator environments, such as the condition where customer interest declines over time, enhancing the model's ability to interpret critical indicators influenced by time series factors (Long et al., 2023).

4.2.2.2 Transparent Product Information

AI can monitor inventory levels in real-time. It displays the remaining SKU quantities on e-commerce platforms, enabling customers to view the available product stock (Ulrich et al., 2021). From the decision-maker's perspective, an Explainable AI (XAI) approach is used for multi-criteria ABC item classification. This classification framework clarifies the reasoning behind item assignments to any category, making the decision-making process more transparent for stakeholders. Similarly, this method can create a transparent supplier selection process (Lam et al., 2021; Tsang et al., 2024).

In summary, SC visibility plays a crucial role in all four phases of SCR.

4.2.3 Supply Chain Velocity

4.2.3.1 Automatic Inventory Replenishment

Inventory replenishment requires the use of AI to achieve rapid automation. This involves precise monitoring of purchase quantities, prices, and inventory levels to enable swift restocking and maintain inventory safety and stability (B. Chen et al., 2019; Jauhar et al., 2023; Zhou et al., 2022). Yang et al. (2023) utilised LightGBM and ANN to determine an optimal inventory optimisation decision model under the best interest rate conditions. Similarly, Kurian et al. (2023) used LightGBM to simulate the "beer game," collecting various order decision data to establish a dynamic replenishment system. Automated inventory replenishment improves the SC's responsiveness and recovery speed after disruptions, enabling swift fulfilment of customer demands.

4.3 Relationship Between Retail SC Activities and SCR's Antecedents

Improving SCR's antecedents enhances the performance of various retail SC activities. As observed in the study, each antecedent encompasses specific task content, and achieving these tasks enhances the antecedents. Therefore, linking various SC activities with task content is a critical step in uncovering the key aspects of SC activities within SCR.

AI is widely used to enhance information sharing and optimise vendor relationship management in vendor management, enabling better management of supplier relationships, improved procurement metrics, and encouraging suppliers to participate in inventory control, as well as facilitating automatic order follow-up. Procurement activities utilise clustering algorithms to obtain more transparent product information, making the procurement process and decision-making more transparent. Effectively identifying tax risks and perishable product management risks helps decision-makers select reliable alternative suppliers, which is also a crucial step in optimising the SC network (Lam et al., 2021; Van Belle et al., 2021)

SC velocity and flexibility have been significantly enhanced in the widely applied AI-driven demand forecasting activities. High-precision forecasting models based on various ANN, temporal logic, and XGBoost algorithms can rapidly predict seasonal demand patterns and fluctuations during specific holidays. Additionally, they can track changes in consumer trends influenced by external factors. This enables stable and flexible seasonal order adjustments and inventory replenishment strategies. (Antipov & Pokryshevskaya, 2020; Eiglsperger et al., 2024; Elorza et al., 2024). Simultaneously, predicting delivery success rates can also aid in the design of delivery routes. (Kandula et al., 2021).

Like demand forecasting, inventory management involves gradient boosting algorithms like LightGBM for automatic inventory replenishment. PCA, K-means, and fuzzy c-means are used for rapid and efficient product classification within warehouses. (Tsang et al., 2024; Ulrich et al., 2021; Yang et al., 2023). Additionally, AI-supported dynamic inventory monitoring further enhances information-sharing capabilities and improves the observation of key performance indicators, such as safety stock levels and inventory holding costs (Long et al., 2023). This can also provide valuable insights for warehouse design within the SC Network (Shi et al., 2020).

Logistic regression and decision tree algorithms assist decision-makers in analysing competitors' pricing, financial conditions, and customer behaviour, thereby enabling flexible pricing and promotional strategies (Li, 2021). Moreover, understanding changes in customer behaviour helps decision-makers prepare for risks.

Designing last-mile delivery routes is crucial to fulfil and is strongly linked to network design and information sharing. By using Extreme Learning Machines (ELM) to obtain order delivery information and allowing it to flow across various SC nodes, combined with neural networks, a comprehensive logistics network and final delivery route design can be achieved (Cantini et al., 2024; Gružauskas et al., 2019; Kandula et al., 2021).

Finally, developing AI hybrid models is a specialised task that mutually empowers various SC activities. Hybrid models are designed based on the shortcomings and requirements of each activity, enabling them to be fully integrated into the entire SC operations and provide customised empowerment, much like JD.com's hybrid AI model (Hu et al., 2024). Therefore, SC configuration is influenced by all SC activities.

5. DISCUSSION

5.1 The Use of AI in Retail SC

Ge et al. (2019) categorised retail SC activities into (1) vendor management, (2) demand forecasting, (3) inventory management, and (4) order fulfilment. This systematic literature review reveals that pricing is also a crucial SC activity in new retail. This is because, in the e-commerce-driven new retail environment, the linkage between sales competition and pricing strategies is strong, and this pricing competition can potentially impact logistics costs throughout the SC (He et al., 2020; Lin et al., 2020).

Previous studies have not explicitly focused on the "retail" industry as the core subject of their research. Their systematic reviews are based on comprehensive studies across multiple sectors, such as manufacturing, transportation, and mining.

Consequently, the ranking results of AI applications for achieving SCR in these studies differ significantly from those in the retail sector. The most common applications are limited to prediction and optimisation, with ANN, SVM, and DT being the top three frequently used technologies and algorithms (Akbari & Do, 2021). The findings of this chapter indicate that in prediction and optimisation (demand forecasting, pricing, and order fulfilment), DT and SVM are gradually being replaced by RF and Gradient Boosting/XGBoost. Additionally, ANN has evolved into more complex neural network algorithms such as RNN and CNN. This trend suggests that the prediction requirements in the SC field are becoming increasingly complex, and the scale of data and noise to be processed is becoming more extensive and cumbersome. Consequently, researchers must transition AI models from supervised learning to reinforcement learning and ensemble learning methods to develop more practical models.

In vendor and inventory management, aggregation algorithms such as PCA, K-means, and C-means are frequently used to classify retail products, rapidly enhancing SCR.

5.2 Theoretical and Practical Differences in Deploying AI in Retail SC

5.2.1 JD.com and Alibaba's Practical Deployment

As Fildes et al. (2022) noted, current academic research only considers the computational power of AI models and the statistical significance of their results. In other words, these models need more commercial considerations. To deploy a model for commercial use, it is necessary, like JD.com, to clearly understand the company's scale and SC operations. This allows for the design of appropriate AI hybrid models to address existing deficiencies in the current SC, as shown in Figure 9.

Figure 9. Overview of JD.com's supply chain capability

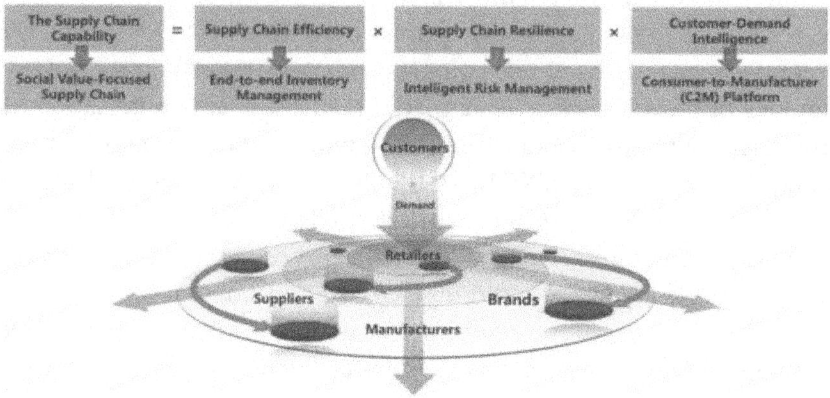

Source: Hu et al. (2024)

JD.com has designed AI model modules for the capability equation of these three aspects, which can be divided into three categories (Hu et al., 2024).

- **End-to-end Inventory Management Based on RNN**: Utilising historical sales data, supplier information, prices, and vendor lead times to provide automatic replenishment suggestions. This resulted in a 1% decrease in stockout rates and cost savings of $94.7 million in 2022.
- **Order Emergency Classification System Based on Four Colours (Green, Blue, Yellow, Red)**: This system reduced the order cancellation rate by 3.85%, lowered marketing costs by 13.7%, and increased GMV by $27.5 million in 2022.
- **Consumer-to-Manufacturer (C2M) Program Based on GATNE and Deep Structured Semantic Model (DSSM)**: This program enables faster forecasting and pricing of new products, reducing suppliers' product launch cycles by 67%. It provided customers with 16,438 new customised products, resulting in a GMV increase of $2.63 billion.

Similarly, Alibaba has categorised its SC activities into demand forecasting, inventory optimisation, and price optimisation, developing AI optimisation models for each activity and integrating them into the SC. This strategy helped its e-commerce platform, Tmall, improve service levels by 1% from 2019 to 2022 and reduce inventory by 10%, saving $5 million in costs annually and increasing GMV by $20 million. (Deng et al., 2023).

5.3 Ethical Concerns of AI in Retail Supply Chain Resilience

There are multiple ethical concerns related to AI in retail supply chain resilience that must be considered before deployment. Firstly, data privacy and security concerns are associated with collecting and processing data from multiple stakeholders within the supply chain (Bhamra et al., 2025). The systems in place at the retailers must ensure that sensitive information is protected and comply with the regulatory frameworks of the General Data Protection Regulation (GDPR) (Melnyk et al., 2025). Secondly, *algorithmic bias* exists for the AI systems as they perform based on trained historical, skewed datasets such as demand, inventory, pricing, and previous orders (Zheng et al., 2025)). This biasness may disadvantage some suppliers, products or demographic groups. Lastly, the lack of interoperability of AI decision-support systems remains a challenge for retailers and their automated operations (Tian et al., 2025).

5.4 Implementation Challenges for Small and Medium Enterprises (SMEs)

There are numerous benefits that retailers enjoy from effective decision-making through the use of AI. However, when its implementation is considered from the SMEs' context, various implementation challenges must be considered. Firstly, the *resource constraints*. SMEs often lack the technological and financial resources to invest in AI decision-support systems (Widiawati et al., 2025). The high cost of implementation, including integration with existing legacy systems for practical AI usage, limits its adoption and alignment with strategic objectives such as supply chain resilience. Secondly, due to the high cost of implementing AI, the return on investment (ROI) is long-term (Magas & Kiritsis, 2022). Therefore, SMEs must develop both tangible resources (such as software, hardware, and infrastructure) and intangible resources (including cultural adoption and organisational resistance). To fully benefit from AI deployment, SMEs must conduct a cost-benefit analysis (Cannas et al., 2024). Hence, practical solutions for AI deployment in SMEs could be a phased implementation, leveraging cloud-based AI services on a pay-as-you-go model, and government or institutional support. Thirdly, unlike large retailers, SMEs have limited access to datasets, a lack of interdepartmental coordination, and cross-functional data integration, resulting in most of their decision-making being based on siloed datasets, which restricts the accuracy and utility of AI decision-support systems (Malhotra & Kharub, 2025). Lastly, most SMEs lack digital skills and insufficient staff training due to limited financial resources, which can hinder the implementation of AI in SMEs (Yadav & Mahara, 2019).

6. THE LIMITATIONS AND FUTURE RESEARCH

The uneven geographical distribution of literature and the limited number of case studies impose certain constraints on this research, leading to a narrow industry scope when discussing commercial AI applications. For example, the retail market in China is predominantly e-commerce-based, resulting in case studies mainly involving e-commerce giants Alibaba and JD.com. This raises two issues: (1) How do AI deployment practices differ for other SMEs? (2) Are offline retailers (e.g., 7-Eleven, Tesco) using AI technology? What are the differences in focus, challenges, and gaps compared to e-commerce?

Additionally, in the literature screening steps of the SLR, the researchers only included publications with ABS journal ratings. This may introduce biases in the descriptive analysis (regarding regions, industries, etc.) and potentially overlook diverse case studies and model presentations.

Therefore, future research should consider including literature from more regions to identify the mainstream retail industries and representative, large-scale retail organisations in these areas that can or already use AI. Additionally, more keywords should be used when identifying articles, such as "food" and "electronics," to compare the focus areas of AI technology choices in different retail industries for achieving SCR. This approach will help provide more comprehensive details and enable people to understand better the use of AI and ML in retail SCR.

Finally, gathering more feedback from SME practitioners in the retail industry is essential. This will provide firsthand information on the advantages, disadvantages, and challenges of deploying AI technology in organisations of different sizes, leading to more effective commercialisation recommendations.

REFERENCES

Abe, M., & Ye, L. (2013). Building Resilient Supply Chains against Natural Disasters: The Cases of Japan and Thailand. *Global Business Review, 14*(4), 567–586. DOI: 10.1177/0972150913501606

Akbari, M., & Do, T. N. A. (2021). A systematic review of machine learning in logistics and supply chain management: current trends and future directions. In Benchmarking (Vol. 28, Issue 10). DOI: 10.1108/BIJ-10-2020-0514

Akter, S., Michael, K., Uddin, M. R., McCarthy, G., & Rahman, M. (2022). Transforming business using digital innovations: The application of AI, blockchain, cloud and data analytics. *Annals of Operations Research, 308*(1–2), 7–39. DOI: 10.1007/s10479-020-03620-w

Ali, A., Mahfouz, A., & Arisha, A. (2017). Analysing supply chain resilience: integrating the constructs in a concept mapping framework via a systematic literature review. In Supply Chain Management (Vol. 22, Issue 1). DOI: 10.1108/SCM-06-2016-0197

Alloghani, M., Al-Jumeily, D., Mustafina, J., Hussain, A., & Aljaaf, A. J. (2020). A Systematic Review on Supervised and Unsupervised Machine Learning Algorithms for Data Science. DOI: 10.1007/978-3-030-22475-2_1

Alomar, M. A. (2022). Performance Optimization of Industrial Supply Chain Using Artificial Intelligence. *Computational Intelligence and Neuroscience, 2022*, 1–10. DOI: 10.1155/2022/9306265 PMID: 35942447

Antipov, E. A., & Pokryshevskaya, E. B. (2020). Interpretable machine learning for demand modelling with high-dimensional data using Gradient Boosting Machines and Shapley values. *Journal of Revenue and Pricing Management, 19*(5), 355–364. DOI: 10.1057/s41272-020-00236-4

Aslam, H., Khan, A. Q., Rashid, K., & Rehman, S. (2020). Achieving supply chain resilience: The role of supply chain ambidexterity and supply chain agility. *Journal of Manufacturing Technology Management, 31*(6), 1185–1204. DOI: 10.1108/JMTM-07-2019-0263

Basole, R. C., & Bellamy, M. A. (2014). Supply Network Structure, Visibility, and Risk Diffusion: A Computational Approach. *Decision Sciences, 45*(4), 753–789. DOI: 10.1111/deci.12099

Bhamra, R., Small, A., Hicks, C., & Pilch, O. (2025). Impact pathways: Geopolitics, risk and ethics in critical minerals supply chains. *International Journal of Operations & Production Management, 45*(5), 985–994. DOI: 10.1108/IJOPM-03-2024-0228

Boden, M. A. (2018). Artificial intelligence. In Routledge Encyclopedia of Philosophy. DOI: 10.4324/9780415249126-W001-1

Bottani, E., Centobelli, P., Gallo, M., Kaviani, M. A., Jain, V., & Murino, T. (2019). Modelling wholesale distribution operations: An artificial intelligence framework. *Industrial Management & Data Systems, 119*(4), 698–718. DOI: 10.1108/IMDS-04-2018-0164

Cai, Y. J., & Lo, C. K. Y. (2020). Omni-channel management in the new retailing era: A systematic review and future research agenda. *International Journal of Production Economics, 229*, 107729. DOI: 10.1016/j.ijpe.2020.107729

Cannas, V. G., Ciano, M. P., Saltalamacchia, M., & Secchi, R. (2024). Artificial intelligence in supply chain and operations management: A multiple case study research. *International Journal of Production Research, 62*(9), 3333–3360. DOI: 10.1080/00207543.2023.2232050

Cantini, A., Peron, M., De Carlo, F., & Sgarbossa, F. (2024). A decision support system for configuring spare parts supply chains considering different manufacturing technologies. *International Journal of Production Research, 62*(8), 3023–3043. DOI: 10.1080/00207543.2022.2041757

Chen, B., Chao, X., & Ahn, H. S. (2019). Coordinating pricing and inventory replenishment with nonparametric demand learning. *Operations Research, 67*(4), opre.2018.1808. DOI: 10.1287/opre.2018.1808

Chen, J., Sohal, A. S., & Prajogo, D. I. (2013). Supply chain operational risk mitigation: A collaborative approach. *International Journal of Production Research, 51*(7), 2186–2199. DOI: 10.1080/00207543.2012.727490

Chen, X., & Wang, Y. (2023). Robust Dynamic Pricing with Demand Learning in the Presence of Outlier Customers. *Operations Research, 71*(4), 1362–1386. DOI: 10.1287/opre.2022.2280

Chen, Y., Kang, Y., Chen, Y., & Wang, Z. (2020). Probabilistic forecasting with temporal convolutional neural network. *Neurocomputing, 399*, 491–501. DOI: 10.1016/j.neucom.2020.03.011

Chołodowicz, E., & Orłowski, P. (2024). Neural Network Control of Perishable Inventory with Fixed Shelf Life Products and Fuzzy Order Refinement under Time-Varying Uncertain Demand. *Energies, 17*(4), 849. DOI: 10.3390/en17040849

Christopher, M., & Peck, H. (2004). Building the Resilient Supply Chain. *International Journal of Logistics Management, 15*(2), 1–14. DOI: 10.1108/09574090410700275

Darom, N. A., Hishamuddin, H., Ramli, R., & Mat Nopiah, Z. (2018). An inventory model of supply chain disruption recovery with safety stock and carbon emission consideration. *Journal of Cleaner Production, 197*, 1011–1021. DOI: 10.1016/j.jclepro.2018.06.246

Davis, J., Mengersen, K., Bennett, S., & Mazerolle, L. (2014). Viewing systematic reviews and meta-analysis in social research through different lenses. *SpringerPlus, 3*(1), 511. DOI: 10.1186/2193-1801-3-511 PMID: 25279303

Demizu, T., Fukazawa, Y., & Morita, H. (2023). Inventory management of new products in retailers using model-based deep reinforcement learning. *Expert Systems with Applications, 229*, 120256. DOI: 10.1016/j.eswa.2023.120256

Deng, Y., Zhang, X., Wang, T., Wang, L., Zhang, Y., Wang, X., Zhao, S., Qi, Y., Yang, G., & Peng, X. (2023). Alibaba Realizes Millions in Cost Savings Through Integrated Demand Forecasting, Inventory Management, Price Optimization, and Product Recommendations. *INFORMS Journal on Applied Analytics, 53*(1), 32–46. DOI: 10.1287/inte.2022.1145

Ding, Y., Tu, Y., Pu, J., & Qiu, L. (2021). Environmental Factors in Operations Management: The Impact of Air Quality on Product Demand. *Production and Operations Management, 30*(9), 2910–2924. DOI: 10.1111/poms.13410

EBSCO Information Services. (2024). EBSCOhost research databases.

Eiglsperger, J., Haselbeck, F., Stiele, V., Serrano, C. G., Lim-Trinh, K., Menrad, K., Hannus, T., & Grimm, D. G. (2024). Forecasting seasonally fluctuating sales of perishable products in the horticultural industry. *Expert Systems with Applications, 249*, 123438. DOI: 10.1016/j.eswa.2024.123438

Elorza, M., Castellano, E., & Segura, S. (2024). Prediction of customer demand for perishable products in retail inventory management, using the hybrid prophet-XGBoost model during the post-COVID-19 period. *Applied Economics Letters*, •••, 1–7. DOI: 10.1080/13504851.2024.2333995

Esmaeili-Najafabadi, E., Azad, N., & Saber Fallah Nezhad, M. (2021). Risk-averse supplier selection and order allocation in the centralized supply chains under disruption risks. *Expert Systems with Applications, 175*, 114691. DOI: 10.1016/j.eswa.2021.114691

Ferreira, K. J., Lee, B. H. A., & Simchi-Levi, D. (2016). Analytics for an online retailer: Demand forecasting and price optimization. *Manufacturing & Service Operations Management, 18*(1), 69–88. DOI: 10.1287/msom.2015.0561

Fildes, R., Kolassa, S., & Ma, S. (2022). Post-script—Retail forecasting: Research and practice. *International Journal of Forecasting, 38*(4), 1319–1324. DOI: 10.1016/j.ijforecast.2021.09.012 PMID: 36217499

Fujimaki, R., Muraoka, Y., Ito, S., & Yabe, A. (2016). From prediction to decision making - Predictive optimization technology. NEC Technical Journal, 11(1).

Ge, D., Pan, Y., Shen, Z.-J., Wu, D., Yuan, R., & Zhang, C. (2019). Retail supply chain management: A review of theories and practices. *Journal of Data, Information and Management, 1*(1–2), 45–64. DOI: 10.1007/s42488-019-00004-z

Greyson, D., Rafferty, E., Slater, L., MacDonald, N., Bettinger, J. A., Dubé, È., & MacDonald, S. E. (2019). Systematic review searches must be systematic, comprehensive, and transparent: A critique of Perman et al. *BMC Public Health, 19*(1), 153. DOI: 10.1186/s12889-018-6275-y PMID: 30717742

Gružauskas, V., Gimžauskienė, E., & Navickas, V. (2019). Forecasting accuracy influence on logistics clusters activities: The case of the food industry. *Journal of Cleaner Production, 240*, 118225. DOI: 10.1016/j.jclepro.2019.118225

Guan, Y., Yan, J., Shan, Y., Zhou, Y., Hang, Y., Li, R., Liu, Y., Liu, B., Nie, Q., Bruckner, B., Feng, K., & Hubacek, K. (2023). Burden of the global energy price crisis on households. *Nature Energy, 8*(3), 304–316. DOI: 10.1038/s41560-023-01209-8

Han, Y., Chong, W. K., & Li, D. (2020). A systematic literature review of the capabilities and performance metrics of supply chain resilience. *International Journal of Production Research, 58*(15), 4541–4566. DOI: 10.1080/00207543.2020.1785034

Handfield, R. B., Graham, G., & Burns, L. (2020). Corona virus, tariffs, trade wars and supply chain evolutionary design. *International Journal of Operations & Production Management, 40*(10), 1649–1660. DOI: 10.1108/IJOPM-03-2020-0171

He, P., Wen, J., Ye, S., & Li, Z. (2020). Logistics service sharing and competition in a dual-channel e-commerce supply chain. *Computers & Industrial Engineering, 149*, 106849. DOI: 10.1016/j.cie.2020.106849

Hoeltgebaum, H., Borenstein, D., Fernandes, C., & Veiga, Á. (2021). A score-driven model of short-term demand forecasting for retail distribution centers. *Journal of Retailing, 97*(4), 715–725. DOI: 10.1016/j.jretai.2021.05.003

Hu, H., Qi, Y., Lee, H. L., Shen, Z.-J. M., Liu, C., Zhu, W., & Kang, N. (2024). Supercharged by Advanced Analytics, JD.com Attains Agility, Resilience, and Shared Value Across Its Supply Chain. *INFORMS Journal on Applied Analytics*, *54*(1), 54–70. DOI: 10.1287/inte.2023.0078

Huber, J., & Stuckenschmidt, H. (2020). Daily retail demand forecasting using machine learning with emphasis on calendric special days. *International Journal of Forecasting*, *36*(4), 1420–1438. DOI: 10.1016/j.ijforecast.2020.02.005

Huerta-Soto, R., Ramirez-Asis, E., Tarazona-Jiménez, J., Nivin-Vargas, L., Norabuena-Figueroa, R., Guzman-Avalos, M., & Reyes-Reyes, C. (2023). Predictable inventory management within dairy supply chain operations. *International Journal of Retail & Distribution Management*. DOI: 10.1108/IJRDM-01-2023-0051

Imran, M. A., & Hyun, K. (2024). In-store shopping trip predictions and impact factors during COVID-19 emergencies. *Transportation Planning and Technology*, *47*(4), 540–565. DOI: 10.1080/03081060.2023.2282059

J. Murrey Atkins Library. (2021). *Web of Science*. University of North Carolina at Charlotte.

Jackson, I. (2022). AutoML Approach to Stock Keeping Units Segmentation. *Journal of Theoretical and Applied Electronic Commerce Research*, *17*(4), 1512–1528. DOI: 10.3390/jtaer17040076

Jagtap, S., Trollman, H., Trollman, F., Garcia-Garcia, G., Parra-López, C., Duong, L., Martindale, W., Munekata, P. E. S., Lorenzo, J. M., Hdaifeh, A., Hassoun, A., Salonitis, K., & Afy-Shararah, M. (2022). The Russia-Ukraine Conflict: Its Implications for the Global Food Supply Chains. *Foods*, *11*(14), 2098. DOI: 10.3390/foods11142098 PMID: 35885340

Jauhar, S. K., Jani, S. M., Kamble, S. S., Pratap, S., Belhadi, A., & Gupta, S. (2023). How to use no-code artificial intelligence to predict and minimize the inventory distortions for resilient supply chains. *International Journal of Production Research*. DOI: 10.1080/00207543.2023.2166139

Journal Ranking Portal. (2021). ABS Journal Ranking 2021.

Junhyeok, L., Youngchul, S., & Ilkyeong, M. (2024). A hybrid deep reinforcement learning approach for a proactive transshipment of fresh food in the online–offline channel system. *Transportation Research Part E, Logistics and Transportation Review*, •••, 187.

Jüttner, U., & Maklan, S. (2011). Supply chain resilience in the global financial crisis: An empirical study. *Supply Chain Management, 16*(4), 246–259. DOI: 10.1108/13598541111139062

Kandula, S., Krishnamoorthy, S., & Roy, D. (2021). A prescriptive analytics framework for efficient E-commerce order delivery. *Decision Support Systems, 147*, 113584. DOI: 10.1016/j.dss.2021.113584

Kassa, A., Kitaw, D., Stache, U., Beshah, B., & Degefu, G. (2023). Artificial intelligence techniques for enhancing supply chain resilience: A systematic literature review, holistic framework, and future research. *Computers & Industrial Engineering, 186*, 109714. DOI: 10.1016/j.cie.2023.109714

Khosrowabadi, N., Hoberg, K., & Imdahl, C. (2022). Evaluating human behaviour in response to AI recommendations for judgemental forecasting. *European Journal of Operational Research, 303*(3), 1151–1167. DOI: 10.1016/j.ejor.2022.03.017

Kourentzes, N., & Athanasopoulos, G. (2021). Elucidate structure in intermittent demand series. *European Journal of Operational Research, 288*(1), 141–152. DOI: 10.1016/j.ejor.2020.05.046

Kurian, D. S., Pillai, V. M., Gautham, J., & Raut, A. (2023). Data-driven imitation learning-based approach for order size determination in supply chains. *European Journal of Industrial Engineering, 17*(3), 379. DOI: 10.1504/EJIE.2023.130601

Lam, H. Y., Tsang, Y. P., Wu, C. H., & Chan, C. Y. (2021). Intelligent e-vendor relationship management for enhancing global b2c e-commerce ecosystems. *Journal of Global Information Management, 29*(3), 1–25. DOI: 10.4018/JGIM.2021050101

Lame, G. (2019). Systematic literature reviews: An introduction. *Proceedings of the Design Society: International Conference on Engineering Design, 1*(1), 1633–1642. DOI: 10.1017/dsi.2019.169

Leung, K. H., Mo, D. Y., Ho, G. T. S., Wu, C. H., & Huang, G. Q. (2020). Modelling near-real-time order arrival demand in e-commerce context: A machine learning predictive methodology. *Industrial Management & Data Systems, 120*(6), 1149–1174. DOI: 10.1108/IMDS-12-2019-0646

Li, Z. (2021). Consumer behavior analysis model based on machine learning. *Journal of Intelligent & Fuzzy Systems, 40*(4), 6433–6443. DOI: 10.3233/JIFS-189483

Liang, D., Cao, W., Zhang, Y., & Xu, Z. (2024). A two-stage classification approach for AI technical service supplier selection based on multi-stakeholder concern. *Information Sciences, 652*, 119762. DOI: 10.1016/j.ins.2023.119762

Lin, X., Zhou, Y. W., Xie, W., Zhong, Y., & Cao, B. (2020). Pricing and Product-bundling Strategies for E-commerce Platforms with Competition. *European Journal of Operational Research, 283*(3), 1026–1039. DOI: 10.1016/j.ejor.2019.11.066

Long, L. N. B., Kim, H. S., Cuong, T. N., & You, S. S. (2023). Intelligent decision support system for optimizing inventory management under stochastic events. *Applied Intelligence, 53*(20), 23675–23697. DOI: 10.1007/s10489-023-04801-3

Magas, M., & Kiritsis, D. (2022). Industry Commons: An ecosystem approach to horizontal enablers for sustainable cross-domain industrial innovation (a positioning paper). *International Journal of Production Research, 60*(2), 479–492. DOI: 10.1080/00207543.2021.1989514

Malhotra, G., & Kharub, M. (2025). Elevating logistics performance: Harnessing the power of artificial intelligence in e-commerce. *International Journal of Logistics Management, 36*(1), 290–321. DOI: 10.1108/IJLM-01-2024-0046

Melnyk, O., Onishchenko, O., Fomin, O., Yarovenko, V., Pavlova, N., Drozhzhyn, O., & Vyshnevsky, D. (2025). Smart Port Concept: A Case Study Of Port-Integrated Autonomous Networks. *Journal for Maritime Research, 22*(1), 315–323.

Miguéis, V. L., Pereira, A., Pereira, J., & Figueira, G. (2022). Reducing fresh fish waste while ensuring availability: Demand forecast using censored data and machine learning. *Journal of Cleaner Production, 359*, 131852. DOI: 10.1016/j.jclepro.2022.131852

Min, H. (2019). Blockchain technology for enhancing supply chain resilience. *Business Horizons, 62*(1), 35–45. DOI: 10.1016/j.bushor.2018.08.012

Modgil, S., Singh, R. K., & Hannibal, C. (2022). Artificial intelligence for supply chain resilience: Learning from Covid-19. *International Journal of Logistics Management, 33*(4), 1246–1268. DOI: 10.1108/IJLM-02-2021-0094

Moher, D., Liberati, A., Tetzlaff, J., & Altman, D. G.The PRISMA Group. (2009). Preferred Reporting Items for Systematic Reviews and Meta-Analyses: The PRISMA Statement. *PLoS Medicine, 6*(7), e1000097. DOI: 10.1371/journal.pmed.1000097 PMID: 19621072

Moore, S., Bulmer, S., & Elms, J. (2022). The social significance of AI in retail on customer experience and shopping practices. *Journal of Retailing and Consumer Services, 64*, 102755. DOI: 10.1016/j.jretconser.2021.102755

Munn, Z., Tufanaru, C., & Aromataris, E. (2014). JBI's Systematic Reviews: Data Extraction and Synthesis. *The American Journal of Nursing, 114*(7), 49–54. DOI: 10.1097/01.NAJ.0000451683.66447.89 PMID: 25742352

Muñoz-Villamizar, A., Piatti, M., Mejia-Argueta, C., Pirabe, L. F., Namdar, J., & Gomez, J. F. (2024). Navigating retail inflation in Brazil: A machine learning and web scraping approach to the basic food basket. *Journal of Retailing and Consumer Services*, *79*, 103875. DOI: 10.1016/j.jretconser.2024.103875

Musani, P. (2023, October 25). *Decking the aisles with data: How Walmart's AI-powered inventory system brightens the holidays*. Walmart Global Tech. https://tech.walmart.com/content/walmart-global-tech/en_us/blog/post/walmarts-ai-powered-inventory-system-brightens-the-holidays.html

Ni, D., Xiao, Z., & Lim, M. K. (2020). A systematic review of the research trends of machine learning in supply chain management. *International Journal of Machine Learning and Cybernetics*, *11*(7), 1463–1482. DOI: 10.1007/s13042-019-01050-0

Nozari, H., Szmelter-jarosz, A., & Ghahremani-nahr, J. (2022). Analysis of the Challenges of Artificial Intelligence of Things (AIoT) for the Smart Supply Chain (Case Study: FMCG Industries). *Sensors (Basel)*, *22*(8), 2931. DOI: 10.3390/s22082931 PMID: 35458916

O'Neil, S., Zhao, X., Sun, D., & Wei, J. C. (2016). Newsvendor Problems with Demand Shocks and Unknown Demand Distributions. *Decision Sciences*, *47*(1), 125–156. DOI: 10.1111/deci.12187

Omar, H., Klibi, W., Babai, M. Z., & Ducq, Y. (2023). Basket data-driven approach for omnichannel demand forecasting. *International Journal of Production Economics*, *257*, 108748. DOI: 10.1016/j.ijpe.2022.108748

Pereira, M. M., & Frazzon, E. M. (2021). A data-driv en approach to adaptive synchronization of demand and supply in omni-channel retail supply chains. *International Journal of Information Management*, *57*, 102165. DOI: 10.1016/j.ijinfomgt.2020.102165

Ponomarov, S. Y., & Holcomb, M. C. (2009). Understanding the concept of supply chain resilience. *International Journal of Logistics Management*, *20*(1), 124–143. DOI: 10.1108/09574090910954873

Priyadarshi, R., Panigrahi, A., Routroy, S., & Garg, G. K. (2019). Demand forecasting at retail stage for selected vegetables: A performance analysis. *Journal of Modelling in Management*, *14*(4), 1042–1063. DOI: 10.1108/JM2-11-2018-0192

ProQuest LLC. (2024). ProQuest databases.

Punia, S., Nikolopoulos, K., Singh, S. P., Madaan, J. K., & Litsiou, K. (2020). Deep learning with long short-term memory networks and random forests for demand forecasting in multi-channel retail. *International Journal of Production Research, 58*(16), 4964–4979. DOI: 10.1080/00207543.2020.1735666

Punia, S., Singh, S. P., & Madaan, J. K. (2020). From predictive to prescriptive analytics: A data-driven multi-item newsvendor model. *Decision Support Systems, 136*, 113340. DOI: 10.1016/j.dss.2020.113340

Qaffas, A. A., Ben HajKacem, M.-A., Ben Ncir, C.-E., & Nasraoui, O. (2023). An Explainable Artificial Intelligence Approach for Multi-Criteria ABC Item Classification. *Journal of Theoretical and Applied Electronic Commerce Research, 18*(2), 848–866. DOI: 10.3390/jtaer18020044

Qi, M., Mak, H. Y., & Shen, Z. J. M. (2020). Data-driven research in retail operations—A review. *Naval Research Logistics, 67*(8), 595–616. DOI: 10.1002/nav.21949

Ralston, P., & Blackhurst, J. (2020). Industry 4.0 and resilience in the supply chain: A driver of capability enhancement or capability loss? *International Journal of Production Research, 58*(16), 5006–5019. DOI: 10.1080/00207543.2020.1736724

Revilla, E., & Sáenz, M. J. (2014). Supply chain disruption management: Global convergence vs national specificity. *Journal of Business Research, 67*(6), 1123–1135. DOI: 10.1016/j.jbusres.2013.05.021

Revilla, E., Saenz, M. J., Seifert, M., & Ma, Y. (2023). Human–Artificial Intelligence Collaboration in Prediction: A Field Experiment in the Retail Industry. *Journal of Management Information Systems, 40*(4), 1071–1098. DOI: 10.1080/07421222.2023.2267317

Richey, R. G., Chowdhury, S., Davis-Sramek, B., Giannakis, M., & Dwivedi, Y. K. (2023). Artificial intelligence in logistics and supply chain management: A primer and roadmap for research. In Journal of Business Logistics (Vol. 44, Issue 4). DOI: 10.1111/jbl.12364

Robert, F., Shaohui, M., & Stephan, K. (2022). Retail forecasting: Research and practice. *International Journal of Forecasting, 38*(4). PMID: 36217499

Schlosser, R., Walther, C., Boissier, M., & Uflacker, M. (2019). Automated repricing and ordering strategies in competitive markets. *AI Communications, 32*(1), 15–29. DOI: 10.3233/AIC-180603

Scholten, K., Scott, P. S., & Fynes, B. (2014). Mitigation processes - antecedents for building supply chain resilience. *Supply Chain Management, 19*(2), 211–228. DOI: 10.1108/SCM-06-2013-0191

Scholten, K., Sharkey Scott, P., & Fynes, B. (2019). Building routines for non-routine events: Supply chain resilience learning mechanisms and their antecedents. *Supply Chain Management, 24*(3), 430–442. DOI: 10.1108/SCM-05-2018-0186

Scopus. (2024). Scopus: Content coverage guide.

Sharma, S. K., Chakraborti, S., & Jha, T. (2019). Analysis of book sales prediction at Amazon marketplace in India: A machine learning approach. *Information Systems and e-Business Management, 17*(2–4), 261–284. DOI: 10.1007/s10257-019-00438-3

Shi, Y., Wang, T., & Alwan, L. C. (2020). Analytics for Cross-Border E-Commerce: Inventory Risk Management of an Online Fashion Retailer. *Decision Sciences, 51*(6), 1347–1376. DOI: 10.1111/deci.12429

Shrestha, A., & Mahmood, A. (2019). Review of deep learning algorithms and architectures. In IEEE Access (Vol. 7). DOI: 10.1109/ACCESS.2019.2912200

Skipper, J. B., & Hanna, J. B. (2009). Minimizing supply chain disruption risk through enhanced flexibility. *International Journal of Physical Distribution & Logistics Management, 39*(5), 404–427. DOI: 10.1108/09600030910973742

Sombultawee, K., Lenuwat, P., Aleenajitpong, N., & Boon-Itt, S. (2022). COVID-19 and Supply Chain Management: A Review with Bibliometric. *Sustainability (Basel), 14*(6), 3538. DOI: 10.3390/su14063538

Sroginis, A., Fildes, R., & Kourentzes, N. (2023). Use of contextual and model-based information in adjusting promotional forecasts. *European Journal of Operational Research, 307*(3), 1177–1191. DOI: 10.1016/j.ejor.2022.10.005

Stevenson, M., & Spring, M. (2007). Flexibility from a supply chain perspective: Definition and review. In International Journal of Operations and Production Management (Vol. 27, Issue 7). DOI: 10.1108/01443570710756956

Sundarakani, B., Pereira, V., & Ishizaka, A. (2020). Robust facility location decisions for resilient sustainable supply chain performance in the face of disruptions. *International Journal of Logistics Management, 32*(2), 357–385. DOI: 10.1108/IJLM-12-2019-0333

Taylor, A. (2025, March 4). *How Procter & Gamble and Unilever use AI for smarter manufacturing and supply chains*. Cleverence. https://www.cleverence.com/articles/business-blogs/how-procter-and-gamble-and-unilever-use-ai-for-smarter-manufacturing-and-supply-chains/

Tian, K., Zhu, Z., Mbachu, J., Ghanbaripour, A., & Moorhead, M. (2025). Artificial intelligence in risk management within the realm of construction projects: A bibliometric analysis and systematic literature review. *Journal of Innovation & Knowledge*, *10*(3), 100711. DOI: 10.1016/j.jik.2025.100711

Todo, Y., Nakajima, K., & Matous, P. (2015). How do supply chain networks affect the resilience of firms to natural disasters? Evidence from the great east Japan Earthquake. *Journal of Regional Science*, *55*(2), 209–229. DOI: 10.1111/jors.12119

Tsang, Y. P., Fan, Y., Lee, C. K. M., & Lau, H. C. W. (2024). Blockchain sharding for e-commerce supply chain performance analytics towards Industry 5.0. *Enterprise Information Systems*, *18*(4), 2311807. DOI: 10.1080/17517575.2024.2311807

Ulrich, M., Jahnke, H., Langrock, R., Pesch, R., & Senge, R. (2021). Distributional regression for demand forecasting in e-grocery. *European Journal of Operational Research*, *294*(3), 831–842. DOI: 10.1016/j.ejor.2019.11.029

Van Belle, J., Guns, T., & Verbeke, W. (2021). Using shared sell-through data to forecast wholesaler demand in multi-echelon supply chains. *European Journal of Operational Research*, *288*(2), 466–479. DOI: 10.1016/j.ejor.2020.05.059

Verstraete, G., Aghezzaf, E. H., & Desmet, B. (2019). A data-driven framework for predicting weather impact on high-volume low-margin retail products. *Journal of Retailing and Consumer Services*, *48*, 169–177. DOI: 10.1016/j.jretconser.2019.02.019

Veselovská, L. (2020). Supply chain disruptions in the context of early stages of the global COVID-19 outbreak. *Problems and Perspectives in Management*, *18*(2), 490–500. DOI: 10.21511/ppm.18(2).2020.40

Wamba, S. F., Queiroz, M. M., Trinchera, L., & Fia, M. (2021). Big data analytics-enabled sensing capability and organizational outcomes: Assessing the mediating effects of business analytics culture. *Annals of Operations Research*, *299*(1-2), 289–314. DOI: 10.1007/s10479-020-03812-4

Wang, J., Chong, W. K., Lin, J., & Hedenstierna, C. P. T. (2023). Retail Demand Forecasting Using Spatial-Temporal Gradient Boosting Methods. *Journal of Computer Information Systems*. DOI: 10.1080/08874417.2023.2240753

Wang, S., & Yang, Y. (2021). M-GAN-XGBOOST model for sales prediction and precision marketing strategy making of each product in online stores. *Data Technologies and Applications*, *55*(5), 749–770. DOI: 10.1108/DTA-11-2020-0286

Wenzel, H., Smit, D., & Sardesai, S. (2019). A literature review on machine learning in supply chain management. Artificial Intelligence and Digital Transformation in Supply Chain Management, September.

Widiawati, H. S., Ramadhani, R. A., & Sumantri, B. A. (2025). The role of eco-digital learning in enhancing the impact of IoT, blockchain, and artificial intelligence on green supply chain for SME internationalization. *Problems and Perspectives in Management*, *23*(1), 76–89. DOI: 10.21511/ppm.23(1).2025.06

Yadav, R., & Mahara, T. (2019). Factors Affecting E-Commerce Adoption by Handicraft SMEs of India. *Journal of Electronic Commerce in Organizations*, *17*(4), 44–57. DOI: 10.4018/JECO.2019100104

Yang, B., Xu, X., Gong, Y., & Rekik, Y. (2023). Data-driven optimization models for inventory and financing decisions in online retailing platforms. *Annals of Operations Research*. DOI: 10.1007/s10479-023-05234-4

Yao, X., Sanl, T., & Gulcu, A. (2015). Markdown optimization for multiple products with a common markdown budget constraint. *Journal of Revenue and Pricing Management*, *14*(6), 442–450. DOI: 10.1057/rpm.2015.4

Zamani, E. D., Smyth, C., Gupta, S., & Dennehy, D. (2023). Artificial intelligence and big data analytics for supply chain resilience: A systematic literature review. *Annals of Operations Research*, *327*(2), 605–632. DOI: 10.1007/s10479-022-04983-y PMID: 36212520

Zheng, J., Zhang, J. Z., Kamal, M. M., Liang, X., & Alzeiby, E. A. (2025). Unpacking human-AI interaction: Exploring unintended consequences on employee Well-being in entrepreneurial firms through an in-depth analysis. *Journal of Business Research*, *196*, 115406. DOI: 10.1016/j.jbusres.2025.115406

Zhou, Q., Yang, Y., & Fu, S. (2022). Deep reinforcement learning approach for solving joint pricing and inventory problem with reference price effects. *Expert Systems with Applications*, *195*, 116564. DOI: 10.1016/j.eswa.2022.116564

Chapter 3
AI-Based Robotic Frameworks for Sustainable Agriculture Supply Chains

H. Shalma
https://orcid.org/0009-0003-5737-7634
Sphoorthy Engineering College, India

Jainulabudeen Sak
Anna University, Chennai, India

ABSTRACT

Using robotics in agriculture has transformed supply chain management through automation and precision. Robotics improves agricultural production and distribution costs and reliability. Planting, harvesting, sorting, and packing are optimized by automated methods. However, mechanical or technical failures during assembly might affect system accuracy and reliability.In agricultural supply chains, robotics solves occlusion problems, which complicate fruit picking and product sorting. Advanced deep learning architectures help robots discover and distinguish items in complex situations. These technologies improve precision, reducing waste and increasing throughput. Analysis of robotic systems with and without human involvement shows that automation improves agricultural workflow efficiency and uniformity. In natural environments, robotic arms with computer vision algorithms can locate, detect, and harvest crops despite overlapping objects and changeable conditions.

DOI: 10.4018/979-8-3373-0923-1.ch003

1. INTRODUCTION

Robotics is a multidisciplinary field that designs, develops, operates, and applies automated systems. A machine or other technology that can be taught to carry out tasks independently or semi-independently and that frequently imitates human actions or functions is known as a robot. These duties can be as straightforward as moving stuff around or as intricate as performing medical procedures or venturing into space. "Robotics" is the word coined from the term "robot," which was first used by the Czech playwright Karel Apek in his play "RUR" (Rossum's Universal Robots) in the year 1920. In the play, the term "robot" refers to artificial beings that were made like that of humans through a biological process. However, as time passed, the term's meaning expanded to include mechanical and automated equipment.

Industrial robots are one of the most valuable innovations of our time and may be found in various settings, including warehouses, factories, and industries. Industrial robots can move along three or more axes, are entirely automated, and may be programmed. There are a variety of applications and purposes for industrial robots. The tasks of loading and unloading, arc welding, spot welding, painting, investment casting (Patel, Gupta, & Zhang, 2022), and other similar schemes are examples of applications for industrial robots. Industrial robots, like humans, have a variety of joints, articulations, and manipulators that allow them to be trained to carry out a particular task effectively and practically.

Additionally, industrial robots contribute to realizing cost unity and waste reduction. Because these Industrial Robots are motorized and offer rapid and consistent performance in heavy-duty or repetitive jobs, their primary applications are in the manufacturing, mechanical, and assembly industries. These industries make and assemble things. In various businesses and workplaces, automated robot parts carry out fundamental responsibilities. These robots are constructed from hardy, long-lasting metal, typically steel or cast iron.

1.1 Functionalities of Multiple Robots

Robots with Articulating Joints: The majority of industrial robots are articulating robots. Since they resemble a human arm, they are often called robotic or manipulator arms because of their appearance. Because their articulations have multiple degrees of freedom, the articulated arms have a vast range of movement options.

Rectilinear Coordinate Robots: Cartesian robots, or rectilinear, gantry robots, and x-y-z robots, feature three prismatic joints for tool movement and three rotating joints for their orientation in space. Other names for this type of robot are x-y-z robots. The effector organ tends to move and point in all directions.

A robot of this type has to have six axes, also known as degrees of freedom. They were allowing the effector organ to be moved. Two dimensions with two or three axes required depending upon the requirement.

Cylindrical Coordinate Robots: The rotary joint at the base of the cylindrical coordinate robots and at least one prismatic joint connecting the links distinguish these robots from others. They can slide vertically and horizontally, allowing them to move about. The design of the robot's tiny effector enables it to operate at full speed while still being able to access confined work areas.

Spherical Coordinate Robots: Robots operating in a spherical coordinate system can only have rotational joints. They were among the first robots used in commercial and industrial settings. They find widespread application in machinery operation and maintenance used in plastic injection, extrusion, welding, and casting die.

SCARA Robot: Selective Compliance Assembly Robot Arm (SCARA) is an abbreviation. The two parallel joints that SCARA robots allowed to point in the x and y direction plane, which is how they are easily identified. At the effector, rotating shafts are arranged in a vertical configuration. SCARA robots are utilized for work that calls for accurate lateral motion. They work wonderfully in applications requiring assembly. The various functionalities and their classification are described in Fig.1.

Figure 1. Robotics classification model based on arm types

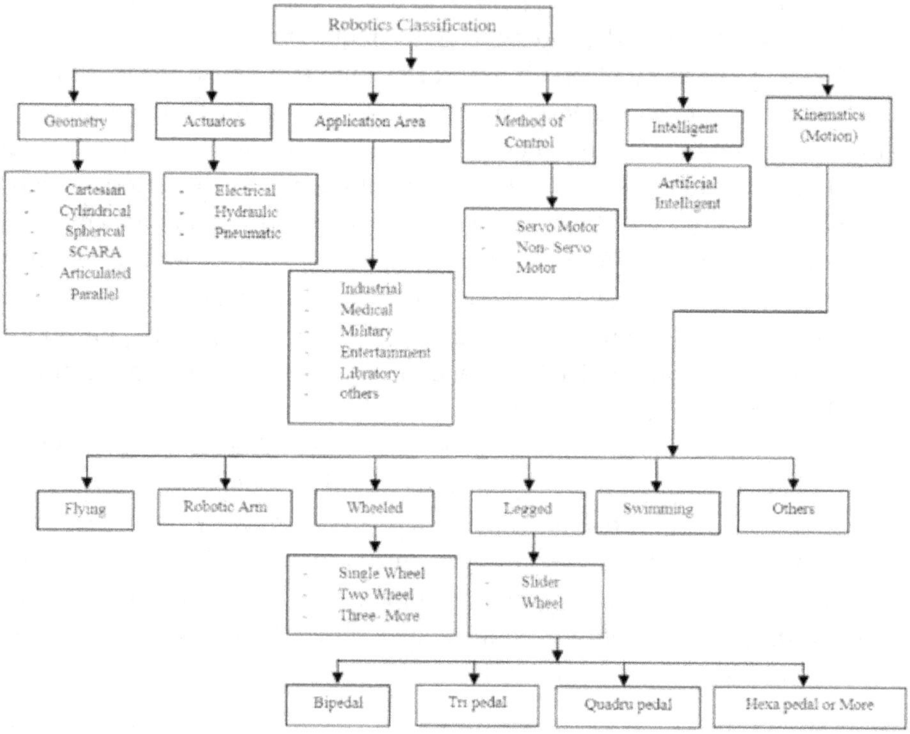

Delta Robots: The term "parallel link robots" or "delta robots". They are constructed from a series of parallel linkages, all linked to the same base. Delta robots (Reddy & Thomas, 2022) are best utilized for work requiring direct control and high levels of manoeuvrability, such as quick pick-and-place operations. Delta robots can utilize the parallelogram linkage system or the four-bar linkage system.

2. RELATED WORKS

The task of identification and localization in natural situations is particularly tough because most fruits are partially covered by leaves, and branches, or overlapped with other fruits (Plebe & Grasso, 2001). Other fruits completely occlude some fruits. Because of these occlusions, there is no longer a straight relationship between the visible areas of fruits and the fruits themselves because there is now ambiguity in the interpretation of the shape of the occluded fruit (Kelso, 2009). In addition, the colors of fruits cannot be precisely characterized due to the considerable degree of variety shown across the various cultivars found within the same species and the various stages of ripeness they reach. In addition, fruits can be found in positions and orientations quite different from one another on trees of different sizes, volumes, and limb shapes.

Numerous studies have explored the possibility of computer vision to detect and localize fruit on trees. The findings of most of these studies were compiled in a review written by Gongal et al. (2015), which can be found here. Color, spectral, and thermal cameras have all seen significant amounts of application in these technologies. If you use a spectral camera (Okamoto & Lee, 2009), it will be challenging to identify the fruit being obscured by another fruit as an item. The temperature differential between the fruit and the background enables a thermal camera to detect the fruit (Stajnko, Lakota, & Hočevar, 2004). This detection is based on the temperature difference. The size of the fruit and the amount of direct sunlight it receives both impacts this strategy. The detection of fruit with a color camera takes advantage of a wide variety of various characteristics. Researchers Bulanon et al. (Bulanon, Kataoka, Ota, & Hiroma, 2002; Bulanon & Kataoka, 2010) successfully segmented an apple by utilizing brightness and differences in red, green, and blue (RGB) color. Rakun, Stajnko, and Zazula (2011) were able to identify an apple by using a textural analysis.

Linker, Coehn, and Naor (2012) combined several criteria to increase the reliability of fruit-detecting techniques. A color camera can also identify fruits with several other image classification strategies. K-mean clustering was utilized in apple detection by Bulanon, Kataoka, Okamotoa, and Hata (2004). KNN clustering was used by both Cohen, Linker, and Noar (2010) for apple categorization. In addition, Kurtulmus, Lee, & Vardar (2014) classified apples using an artificial neural network. The method of categorization known as the Support Vector Machine was utilized by Qiang et al. (2014) in their search for apples. However, these technologies are problematic to apply in environments with varying light conditions since it is impossible to gather sufficient color information. It is recommended that fruit detection be carried out using several features such as color, shape, texture, and reflection to achieve a higher accuracy level and circumvent obstacles such as clustering and shifting light conditions.

Robotics and automation have made significant contributions to the quality control that has been achieved in the manufacturing industry. In order to guarantee that every product meets stringent quality requirements, advanced robotic systems that are equipped with sensors and cameras may inspect the goods at various stages of the production process. These intelligent robots produce higher-quality finished goods by minimising faults by identifying flaws or inconsistencies at an earlier stage in the production process. This quality enhancement has resulted in increased client loyalty as well as increased customer happiness (Madakam, Holmukhe, & Jaiswal, 2019). Robotic systems that are versatile give producers the ability to cater to the requirements and preferences of each individual customer without reducing their overall output (Hofmann, Samp, & Urbach, 2020). Because of their ability to quickly adjust to changing manufacturing requirements, these technologies make it possible to mass produce individualized goods.

Even if it is impossible to dispute the benefits that robots and automation provide to the industrial industry, it is essential to consider the potential disadvantages and problems that may arise with the improvements in these areas. Factors such as employment displacement, the requirement for retraining, and ethical considerations surrounding the use of autonomous machines need to be carefully studied to ensure a seamless transition to a future with increased levels of automation.

The currently available techniques involve using automated robots in harvesting, which takes place in a field structured with planted trees in a V formation. This technique has seen widespread application in orchards and for harvesting citrus-type fruits using automated arm-picking robots. The interruption of robot function indicates that the conveyor is not closed correctly; alternatively, the existence of an impediment might potentially impede the harvesting process. Therefore, to circumvent this issue, we have proposed and analyzed the use of deep learning-assisted robots equipped with stereo cameras for farming to improve the practicability of the process even in the presence of occlusions such as fruits hidden behind leaves, one after the other, or other occluded conditions. These occlusions can be circumvented by rotating the camera position in such a way as to view the target from the bottom part, thereby avoiding major occlusions.

3. MATERIALS AND METHODS

The concept of deep learning was initially developed using artificial neural networks. Examples of common deep learning approaches include the restrictive Boltzmann machine (RBN), the deep belief network (DBN), the convolutional neural network (CNN), and a stacked auto-encoder. A problem arose when the network layer of an early artificial neural network achieved four levels of complexity. Training is carried out by utilizing an algorithm known as conventional backpropagation. Convergence is an example of a deep learning structure. It is a multilayer perceptron that has multiple hidden layers. Deep learning may determine the distribution properties of the data by combining low-level features to form high-level attribute categories or segments. This process is called feature combination. The backpropagation algorithm (BP), the ability to perceive neural network (PNN), the self-organizing network

(SON), the self-organizing map (SOM), and the learning vector quantization (LVQ) method are all well-known artificial neural network methodologies.

3.1 Preprocessing

Fruit detection and harvesting using robots are utilized in many industries. Fruit detection requires preprocessing steps such as the object's texture, size, color, and shape, which differ based on the environmental conditions for even the same fruit category. During this stage, the background noise due to stereo camera capture is eradicated using the epipolar rectification process. This rectification may align the pixels of both left and right in the same horizontal direction for serving as an input for object detection algorithms.

3.2 Visualization

The visualization of harvesting fruits is processed using a robotic arm, and its axes position using computer vision algorithms are elaborated. The number of axes needed to reach any point in space is three, but the minimum number of axes required to get any point in a plane is just two. The complete control of the hand and arm's terminus is more commonly called the wrist. It is needed to add axes such as yaw, pitch, and roll. Some designs, such as the SCARA robot, sacrifice the range of motion possibilities for lower production costs, increased speed, and improved accuracy. The number of axes and degrees of freedom are typically interchangeable terms.

A robot's working envelope is access region space. *Kinematics* refers to the configuration of the robot's stiff components and joints, which dictates the range of motions achievable. The terms articulated, cartesian, parallel, and SCARA are examples of several classes of robot kinematics. Carrying capacity, often known as *payload*, refers to the maximum weight a robot can support. The robot's speed is measured by how quickly the arm is positioned at a given location, which corresponds to the rate of the end of the arm when all of the axes are moving, or it could be defined in terms of the angle of motion or the linear speed of each axis. Alternatively, it could be specified as a compound speed.

The pace at which an axis can pick up speed is called its *acceleration*. Because of this sacred factor, a robot cannot reach its maximum speed, whether moving over a short distance or a complex course requiring numerous direction changes.

Accuracy refers to the degree to which a robot can approach the place it has been told to occupy. Error is a measure of accuracy obtained by measuring the absolute position of the robot and then comparing that position to the location that was ordered. External sensing methods, such as a vision or infrared system, for instance, have the potential to improve accuracy. Please refer to the robot calibration. There is a correlation between accuracy, payload, position, and speed inside the working region (for more information, see compliance).

Repeatability refers to the degree of return to a previously instructed position. Accuracy and this are different. Upon instruction to reach a specific X-Y-Z position, it comes within 1 mm of that point when it arrives there. Its precision, which can be enhanced through calibration, might be described as such. However, the repeatability will be within 0.1 mm if that position is uploaded into the controller memory. If each time it is triggered there, it returns to within 0.1 mm of the instructed work.

3.3 Proposed Architecture

The Proposed methodology describes the role of robots in both automatic and human intervention operations in the field of detection and target attainment in fruit harvesting as an example of semi-automatic operation of agricultural supply chain. Then, the movement of objects in the conveyor belt for harvested fruit packing using a robotic arm as a part of the automatic process is discussed and compared with its efficiency score.

Architectural Methods of Robots in Industrial Aspect

Parallel Architecture: Unlike a serial manipulator, a parallel manipulator is constructed so that each chain is typically relatively short and straightforward. As a result, it can be rigid and resistant to unwanted movement. The errors in the placement of one chain are averaged out in conjunction with the mistakes that occur in positioning the other chains rather than being accumulated. In a parallel robot, Unlike in a serial robot, each actuator in a similar robot must still move within its degree of freedom. However, the off-axis flexibility of a joint is also controlled by the action of the other chains. A serial robot, which only has one degree of freedom per actuator. In contrast to a serial chain, which gradually loses its rigidity as additional components are added, the closed-loop rigidity of the parallel manipulator ensures that the overall structure remains rigid about its parts.

Parallel Architecture Defect Identification and Target Matching

Automatic fruit harvesting by a robot requires "fruit detection and localization" and "fruit harvesting by a robot manipulator with a hand that can harvest without damaging the fruit and its tree." We determined the fruit's two-dimensional (2D) position using a You Only Look Once Detector (YOLO) color camera. One of the general object detection algorithms that uses a Convolution Neural Network (CNN) is the ResNet as its backbone network. The YOLO can make a complete judgment based on color and shape. It is impossible to issue a command to the robot arm without obtaining a position in three dimensions (3D). A stereo camera is utilized to determine the three-dimensional location of the fruit where the Object detector is located. To choose the robot arm's path, we turned to inverse kinematics. We used inverse kinematics to maneuver the robot arm into position to pick up the fruit. The harvesting robot hand served as the end effector for our system. The fruit is picked by the robot hand by grasping it and turning it without causing any damage to either the fruit or the tree. The detection of fruit harvest flow is depicted in Fig.2.

Figure 2. Proposed architecture for detection of fruit harvest using robots

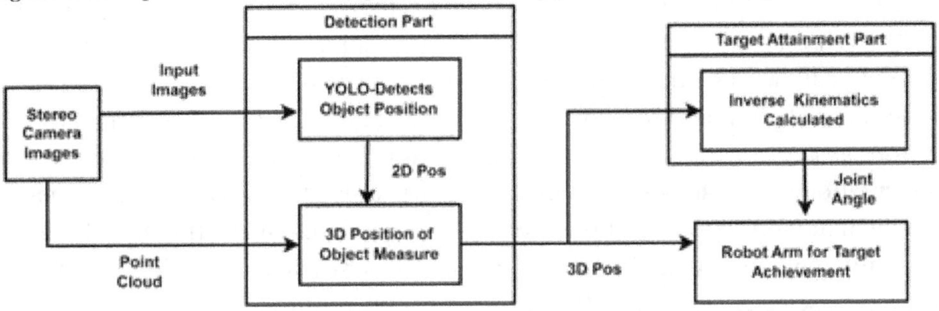

An inverse kinematics problem is a problem in which one attempts to determine the angles q of each joint based on the hand position p and the posture R. The robot arm's mechanism and configuration are the two factors that define the solution to the inverse kinematics issue, which seeks to discover a nonlinear function f^{-1} for the equation Eq. (1).

$$q = f^{-1}(p, R) \tag{1}$$

4. RESULTS AND DISCUSSION

4.1 Experimental Setup

The computer featured an AMD Ryzen7 central processing unit,16 GB of DDR4-2133 SDRAM MHz, an Nvidia GeForce GTX 940MX 2 GB graphics processing unit (GPU, Nvidia Corporation), and a 256 GB NVMe M.2 SSD (Non-Volatile Memory Express Solid-State Drive). To train and test images using the GPU, the

Darknet framework was constructed with Nvidia CUDA 11.3, and OpenCV 4.5.2 (The OpenCV Team).

The robot arm utilizes UR_3(Universal Robots). The robot arm diameter chosen was 5 cm, and repeatability is ±0.1(mm). Used (Stereo Labs)stereo camera with a baseline distance of 120mm, depth range of 0.5 -20m, and number of images taken of 30 frames per second and obtained output resolution as 3840x1080. The chance of error occurrences are suppressed by the robot hand.

4.2 Dataset Used

The dataset used for apple fruit harvesting is the WSU Apple Dataset (Bhusal et al., 2019). It is an RGB image with 2298 images captured using multiple sensors in different years with modern fruiting architecture. The fuji-SfM (Gene-Mola et al., 2020c) dataset includes the following elements: (1) a set of 288 color images and the appropriate annotations (apple segmentation masks) for training instances of segmentation neural network models such as Mask-RCNN; (2) a set of 582 images defining a motion sequence of the scene that was utilized in creating the 3D model of 11 Fuji apple trees containing 1455 apple slices by using SfM; (3) the 3D point cloud of the scanned scene with the equivalent apple positions ground truth in global coordinate. The PFuji-Size-Sizeset is comprised of three distinct data sub-sets in their entirety. The first one is referred to as Orch2018, and it consists of 303 apples taken under natural settings in the field on October 3, 2018, when the apples had reached an advanced ripening growth stage (they were reddish in color). The second sample, Orch2020, consists of 312 apples taken in natural settings in the field on July 16, 2020. At this stage, the apples were around 70% of their final size and appeared green in color. Finally, on October 2nd, 2020, the data for the third subset, labeled Lab2020, were collected. In this particular experiment, 25 apples of varying sizes were scanned in a controlled laboratory environment.

Figure 3. Ground truth images of fruit Apple in histogram chart. The number of apples with different diameter intervals of Orch 2018 and 2020 and Lab 2020 are represented in orange, blue, red.

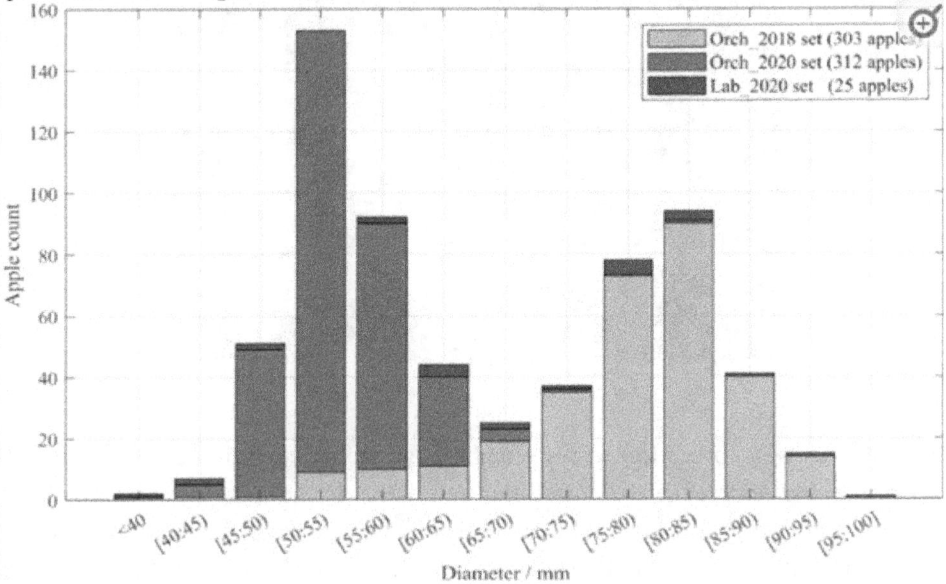

4.3 List of Experiments

The experiment for target attainment and detection using deep learning techniques with a robotic arm is performed for the fruit harvesting methodology. The CNN-based YOLO v4 object detector is used for sprcific target detection. The Target detection is denoted with a bounding box accuracy rate using the spatial pyramid pooling and path aggregation network as a backbone network for extracting and processing features. The detection results are marked and highlighted using bounding Boxes with detection accuracy rate. The accuracy rate differs based on the arm position fixed in coordination with the target. If the distance varies, the target harvesting time may affect the manufacturing processing time to reach the destination. So, the robot arm placed at10 centimeters below the target fruit was decided solely based on the deep learning feature extraction, and the next step was to insert the robot hand from the bottom of the fruit to collect it. After that, the arm ascended above the fruit, as shown in Fig. 4. After that, the robotic hand grabbed the fruit, which was harvested by twisting it away from the peduncle four times.

Figure 4. Robotic arm approaching the target to harvest the fruit for agricultural activities

Finding a way to configure the mechanical architecture in such a way as to accomplish the necessary structural characteristics is the purpose, and it is a demanding and complex task. Mobility, connection, redundancy, and degree count are the structural parameters that can be adjusted. They determine the amount of actuators, the degrees of freedom, and the sort of motion the moving platform will have. It is not always the ideal strategy to add more features and solve mobility or other difficulties by adding more degrees of freedom by adding actuators, especially during the initial design phase of a robot project. Detection using deep learning methodology are highlighted with a bounding box and their detection rate in Fig.5.

The addition of more degrees of freedom requires more time and effort. The amount of actuators present in any given mechanical equipment directly affects its ease of debugging, dependability, and cost.

Figure 5. Detected targets using deep learning architecture

About the outcome of the performance test, the results showed that there were three operational failures. Two of them were false triggers that were produced by the sensor, which caused the program and, as a result, the robotic arm to carry out incorrect subsequent operations. Another one of our attempts was unsuccessful due to the specimen being dropped by accident by the gripper. Despite this, the robotic arm's overall success rate obtained a value more than 90% of the time. We used the photographs taken at the Agriculture and Horticulture Research Centre in the Miyagi Prefecture to learn and practice. The shooting was done to get a view of the fruit from below, with the leaves, branches, and other fruits being moved out of the way as much as possible (Romao, Costa, & Costa, 2019).

It's possible that the illumination in the area and other disruptive outside influences are to blame for the sensor's false positives. It is possible that the dependability of the sensor on its own is essential to assure the reliability of the robotic arm as a whole. The sensor's sensitivity can be fine-tuned, and the voltage supplied to the sensor can have its supply voltage adjusted to achieve better results. If the sensor is given an excessively high voltage, it will become susceptible, which has the potential to cause damage to the electrical equipment itself.

Target Attainment in Fruit Harvesting

Once the robotic arm is moved accordingly based on the target, the effector is used to fix the arm's position. The component is placed at such an angle for picking the target using a manipulator for harvesting. The plucked fruit from the trees is then placed in the conveyor belt for packing into the container. When the maximum container capacity is achieved, the empty container is replaced as a process of automation. This automated fruit harvesting robot has attained the efficiency rate of apple picking in 11 seconds, similar to humans. The advantage of using this robot is that it has saved the human labor power by up to 50%, is depicted in the paper (Onishi et al., 2019). The process of target attainment is shown in Fig.6.

Figure 6. Target attainment robot for fruit harvesting

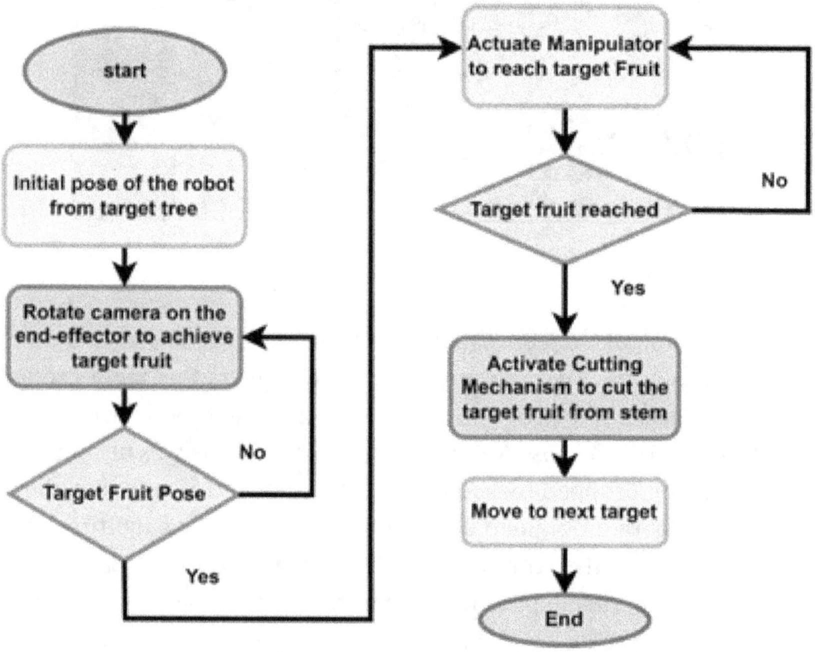

4.4 Comparative Study

We must assess and track the performance and outcomes compared to the metrics and goals we have specified. We need to collect and analyze data from all of our automatic and human systems to discover patterns, trends, and unusual occurrences. To remain responsive to shifting requirements and situations, we will need to make any necessary adjustments and improvements to the levels and types of automation and human intervention.

Comparing Robots' Physical with Human Cerebral Power

The scenario combines people's cerebral powers with robots' physical capabilities, making it possible to reach higher degrees of flexibility and variety through human-industrial robot collaboration (HIRC). Additionally, HIRC enables the deployment of robots without protective fences, resulting in cost savings for installation and additional floor space. It is possible to see the financial benefits of HIRC application areas, particularly in low-volume production.

When it comes to the manufacturing industry, human safety is an absolute necessity for effectively implementing applications based on HIRC. The conventional approach to ensuring human safety in robot automation involves placing physical and sensor-based non-physical barriers between human workers and the robots they operate. Because HIRC systems entail workstations without fences, new and more robust safety measures must be implemented to assure human safety. Concise fundamental safety standards for the following four categories of HIRC operations in ISO 10218: 1) Safety-rated monitored stop, 2) Hand guiding, 3) Speed and separation monitoring, and 4) Power and force limitation (ISO/TS 15066:2016). These are the requirements for the standard. HIRC workstations built for actual manufacturing processes combine the various HIRC operations are described below. As a result, standardized ways of risk reduction connected with these several HIRC procedures must be considered throughout the planning and final testing phases of the HIRC workstation. The task can be completed much more efficiently using automated and robotic assembly methods if the design calls for the components to be introduced from the same direction using snap fits and other one-step fastening procedures.

Flexible Automation for Material Handling

A flexible manufacturing system, often known as an FMS, is a type of flexible automation in which several different machine tools are connected through a material-handling system, and a central computer is used to control all parts of the system. Compared to an automated production line (Wallacei, n.d.; Rocha et al., 2021), an FMS is characterized by its capacity to handle the processing of multiple product types simultaneously. An FMS allows for processing a wide variety of product types; therefore, it is possible to incorporate new product types into production if they fit within the system's intended use parameters. Therefore, This system is perfect for situations with a low to medium demand for the products, and there is a good chance that the market may shift (Chen, Wu, & Das, 2025). Productivity advances have, with time, decreased pricing for various goods and enhanced prosperity for society. The rising utilization of automation, robots, computer systems, and other associated technology has given rise to multiple concerns that need to be addressed regarding education and training. Because of the increase in the use of automated systems, there is currently a lack of technically skilled employees who are able to execute these technologies effectively. The rate at which mechanical systems can be implemented has been significantly slowed down due to this scarcity.

Figure 7. HIRC in industrial robots application to industry production

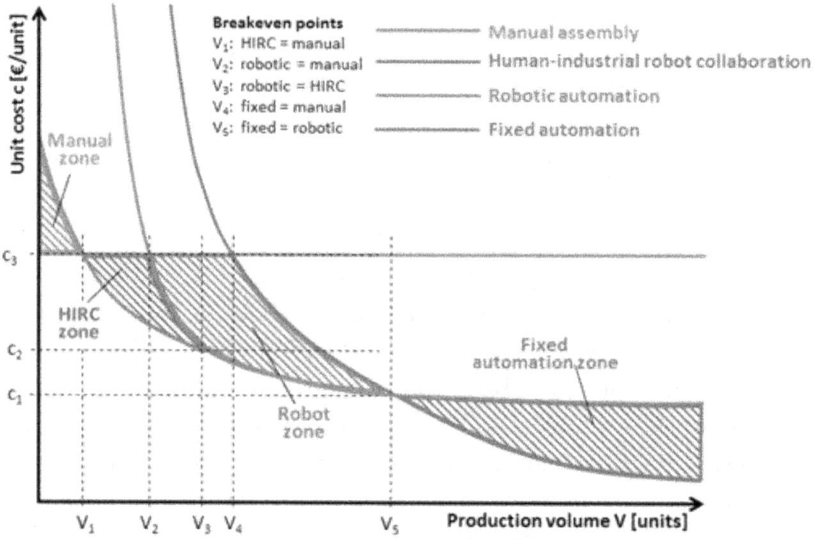

Fig.7 describes the interaction of HIRC from the industry level to the production case in unit cost per volume concerning production in teams. Robots are being used more frequently in inspection (Kumar, Singh, & Verma, 2025), another aspect of manufacturing currently being automated. The robot often positions a sensor about the work part, and then the robot decides whether or not the part satisfies the quality criteria.

Table 1. Industrial robotic arm specification

Robot Name	Max. Payload (in kg)	Robot Mass in kg	DOF	Reach(mm)
S650	2.5	28	6	653
IRB120 ABB	3	25	6	700
TX40 staubl	2	27	6	515
WAM	3	25	7	3.5
SIA 10D Motoman	10	60	7	720

The various robots and their mass specifications in weights are mentioned in Table 1.

Overhead Cost Reduction With Automated Robots

The initial investment in automated software or robots may be substantial; however, the return on that investment may be realized relatively quickly. Once AI is implemented into a company, the owners may discover that some roles are no longer necessary, resulting in immediate expense savings. As an illustration, some of the most successful companies in the restaurant business are beginning to employ delivery robots (Jha, Rani, & Sharma, 2024), which allows them to hire fewer people to work there. Businesses may save money on health and safety expenses if fewer employees participate in dangerous job activities. This would result in fewer employee injuries and less time lost for those employees. Table 2 describes the efficiency rate of different robots in various fields.

Table 2. Efficiency and quality of human-intervented robots vs automatic robots

Field	Robot Type	Purpose	Efficiency
Manufacturing Unit	With Conveyor Belt, Delta Robots	Object picking and packing, quality check	95%
Automobiles	SCARA Robots. RV-2A	Fitting/ assembling automobile Parts	99.08%
Education	chatbots	Knowledge-based search	96%
Agriculture	AGRIM-X	Crop Production, PH level maintenance, and disease identification,	98.7%
Medicine	Xenex Germ-Zapping Robot	Sterilize and clean the hospital environment	99.6%

The efficiency levels mentioned for the various robots are highly dependent on the efficiency of automatic operation, and the system's quality differs for both automated and human-intervened robots.

Performance Evaluation

The model is trained in the object detection network consisting spatial pyramid pooling and path aggregator network for identification were evaluated using the metric mean Average precision(mAP), recall metric, and F1-score metrics. These metrics are the computation of true positive (tp), false positive (fp), and false negative (fn) detections, respectively. A object recognition (confidence) value and threshold of 0.25 was utilized to differentiate between positive and negative detections, which is the default setting for YOLO CNNs. The proportion of true positives to all detections is the measure of precision.

The equations of precision and recall are in Eq.(2) and (3)

$$Precision\ Metric \ = \ \frac{truepositive}{truepositive + falsepositive} \tag{2}$$

$$Recall\ Metric \ = \ \frac{true\ positive}{Truepositive + False\ Negative} \tag{3}$$

The above recall equation denotes the propotion of true positive detections to all original targets. The recognition of object threshold is aggregated to improve the recall metric score at the rise of precision and vice versa, where F1- score metric in Eq.(4) is the average mean of precision and recall.

$$F_1 \ = \ 2 * \frac{Pr.Re}{Pr + Re} \tag{4}$$

The mean average precision across all classes are denoted as mAP.

$$Avg.precision \ = \ \frac{1}{4} \sum_{Re \in \{0, 0.1, \ldots 1\}} \underbrace{max}_{\widetilde{Re}:\widetilde{Re} \geq Re} pr\left(\widetilde{Re}\right) \tag{5}$$

Where Eq. (5) has four equally spaced levels of recall metric in its dataset.

The intersection over union in Eq. (6) is the scale measurement of area overlap to the union size of two bounding boxes, b1, and b2.

$$IoU(b1, b2) \ = \ \frac{|b1 \cap b2|}{|b1 \cup b2|} \tag{6}$$

Table 3. Performance evaluation for apple orchard using YOLO

Networks	Precision (%)	Recall (%)	F1-Score (%)	Occluded/Error
YOLO v3	0.76	0.78	0.78	0.13
YOLO v4	0.72	0.79	0.79	0.12
YOLO v4-small	0.73	0.69	0.75	0.16
YOLO v4-Tiny	0.71	0.77	0.81	0.12
Mean values	0.73	0.75	0.78	0.13

Compared to the other detection networks, YOLOv4 and YOLOv4-Small had the highest-performing mAP_{50} scores, coming in at 78.03% and 79.62%, respectively. Hence, computationally more powerful YOLOv3 could only outperform it by a modest margin (about 2%); the smaller YOLOv4-Tiny also did quite well. When estimating at the concept behind the mAP_{50} scores, it seems that the lower AP_{50} score linked with red fruit across all networks is lowering the quality of the models. This can be explained by the great degree of variety seen among the apples at the point when it was determined that they had reached their red stage.

Table 4. Testing dataset ($AP_{50,}$ %) for various detection networks

Network	mAP50(%)	Green unripe Fruit	Red Ripen Fruit
YOLO v3	77 .05	76.91	88.32
YOLOv4	78.03	79.82	88.58
YOLOv4-small	79.62	79.91	89.02
YOLOv4-Tiny	79.81	80.14	89.87

To determine which model performs the best will depend upon the implementation. The recall value is higher than the precision in the YOLOv4-Tiny model compared with other object detection models. This value shows that the model has shown less error rate with false positives than false negatives in detection. The best model fit also considers the memory usage and inference time in executing the model. The model YOLOv4-Tiny shows best result when compared with other detection models with reduced memory usage and inference time in Gigabits and milliseconds, respectively.

Table 5. Validation dataset ($AP_{50,}$ %) for various detection networks

Network	mAP50(%)	Green Fruit	Red Fruit
YOLOv3	86.79	84.22	86.30
YOLOv4	85.67	86.78	88.71
YOLOv4-small	83.27	85.05	81.01
YOLOv4-Tiny	87.08	80.93	89.14

In comparison with other detection models, the YOLOv4-tiny with YOLO achieves more remarkable performance in yield concerning ripe count in picking the fruits based on target attainment. The error rate of missing due to the presence of leaves, branches, and stems as occlusions are reduced with the development of the fruit picking model from the bottom view with adjustment in the manipulator based on the effector target distance.

Figure 8. Graphical representation of detection model in yield Vs. Ripe count based on target attainment

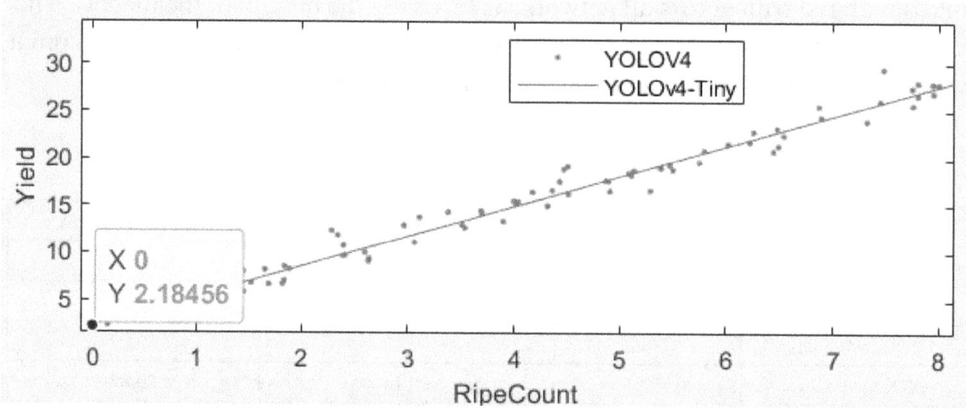

5. CONCLUSION

The target attainment using robot in fruit harvesting describes how the robotic arm is adjusted based on the target distance through manipulator is affected and analysed with deep learning architectures. The proposed algorithm shows the automatic robot target fruit processing in the orchard apple datasets with accuracy rate of 87%. The quantitative measurement of the model is given with higher recall rate than precision showing less false positives detections even in the presence of occlusions. The target identification with robots and human intervention model achieves an efficiency rate above 98% in occlusion detection, palletizing. Hence the involvement of humans and robots in the fruit harvesting gives reliability in production and outcomes with lower error rates, improved functionality, and reduced cost.

6. FUTURE ENHANCEMENT

The next step forward in artificial intelligence technology could allow computers to show emotion and enhance their capability for logical reasoning in identifying the container filling capacity without human intervention. AI not only needs to be able to reason filling logically and imitate human behaviour, but it also needs to have a vital component of emotion. It's not out of the question that artificial intelligence would one day outstrip human intelligence. So, the emergence and usability of robotics in various fields depend on the reliability achieved for further improvement over the impact on society.

REFERENCES

Bulanon, D. M., & Kataoka, T. (2010). Fruit detection system and an end effector for robotic harvesting of Fuji apples. *Agricultural Engineering International: CIGR Journal, 12*(1), 203–210.

Bulanon, D. M., Kataoka, T., Okamoto, H., & Hata, S. (2004). Development of a real-time machine vision system for the apple harvesting robot. In *Proceedings of the SICE 2004 Annual Conference* (Vol. 1, pp. 595–598). IEEE.

Bulanon, D. M., Kataoka, T., Ota, Y., & Hiroma, T. (2002). A segmentation algorithm for the automatic recognition of Fuji apples at harvest. *Biosystems Engineering, 83*(4), 405–412. DOI: 10.1006/bioe.2002.0132

Chen, L., Wu, H., & Das, A. (2025). Artificial intelligence for fostering sustainable agriculture. *Computers and Electronics in Agriculture, 210*, 107620. DOI: 10.1016/j.compag.2025.107620

Cohen, O., Linker, R., & Naor, A. (2010). Estimation of the number of apples in color images recorded in orchards. In *Computer and Computing Technologies in Agriculture III* (pp. 630–642). Springer.

Gongal, A., Amatya, S., Karkee, M., Zhang, Q., & Lewis, K. (2015). Sensors and systems for fruit detection and localization: A review. *Computers and Electronics in Agriculture, 116*, 8–19. DOI: 10.1016/j.compag.2015.05.021

Hofmann, P., Samp, C., & Urbach, N. (2020). Robotic process automation. *Electronic Markets, 30*(1), 99–106. DOI: 10.1007/s12525-019-00365-8

Jha, A., Rani, S., & Sharma, P. (2024). Sustainable AI-based production agriculture. *Sustainable Computing : Informatics and Systems, 36*, 100987. DOI: 10.1016/j.suscom.2024.100987

Kelso, C. R. (2009). *Direct occlusion handling for high-level image processing algorithms* (Master's thesis). Rochester Institute of Technology.

Kumar, R., Singh, D., & Verma, A. (2025). AI-powered autonomous farming: The future of sustainable agriculture. *International Journal of Agricultural Robotics, 12*(1), 45–63.

Kurtulmus, F., Lee, W. S., & Vardar, A. (2014). Immature peach detection in color images acquired in natural illumination conditions using statistical classifiers and neural networks. *Precision Agriculture, 15*(1), 57–79. DOI: 10.1007/s11119-013-9323-8

Linker, R., Cohen, O., & Naor, A. (2012). Determination of the number of green apples in RGB images recorded in orchards. *Computers and Electronics in Agriculture, 81*, 45–57. DOI: 10.1016/j.compag.2011.11.007

Madakam, S., Holmukhe, R. M., & Jaiswal, D. K. (2019). The future digital workforce: Robotic process automation (RPA). *JISTEM-Journal of Information Systems and Technology Management, 16*, e201916001.

Okamoto, H., & Lee, W. S. (2009). Green citrus detection using hyperspectral imaging. *Computers and Electronics in Agriculture, 66*(2), 201–208. DOI: 10.1016/j.compag.2009.02.004

Onishi, Y., Yoshida, T., Kurita, H., Fukao, T., Arihara, H., & Iwai, A. (2019). An automated fruit harvesting robot by using deep learning. *Robomech Journal, 6*(1), 13. DOI: 10.1186/s40648-019-0141-2

Patel, M., Gupta, V., & Zhang, X. (2022). *Towards on-device AI and blockchain for 6G enabled agricultural supply-chain management*. arXiv Preprint arXiv:2203.06465. https://arxiv.org/abs/2203.06465

Plebe, A., & Grasso, G. (2001). Localization of spherical fruits for robotic harvesting. *Machine Vision and Applications, 13*(2), 70–79. DOI: 10.1007/PL00013271

Qiang, L., Jianrong, C., Bin, L., Lie, D., & Yajing, Z. (2014). Identification of fruit and branch in natural scenes for citrus harvesting robot using machine vision and support vector machine. *International Journal of Agricultural and Biological Engineering, 7*(2), 115–121.

Rakun, J., Stajnko, D., & Zazula, D. (2011). Detecting fruits in natural scenes by using spatial-frequency-based texture analysis and multiview geometry. *Computers and Electronics in Agriculture, 76*(1), 80–88. DOI: 10.1016/j.compag.2011.01.007

Reddy, P. K., & Thomas, B. (2022). *Towards technological adaptation of advanced farming through AI, IoT, and robotics: A comprehensive overview*. arXiv Preprint arXiv:2202.10459. https://arxiv.org/abs/2202.10459

Rocha, F., Garcia, G., Pereira, R. F. S., Faria, H. D., Silva, T. H., Andrade, R. H. R., Barbosa, E. S., Almeida, A., Cruz, E., Andrade, W., Serrantola, W. G., Moura, L., Azpúrua, H., Franca, A., Pessin, G., Freitas, G. M., Costa, R. R., & Lizarralde, F. (2021). ROSI: A robotic system for harsh outdoor industrial inspection – System design and applications. *Journal of Intelligent & Robotic Systems, 103*(2), 30. DOI: 10.1007/s10846-021-01459-2

Romao, M., Costa, J., & Costa, C. J. (2019). Robotic process automation: A case study in the banking industry. In *2019 14th Iberian Conference on Information Systems and Technologies (CISTI)* (pp. 1–6). IEEE. DOI: 10.23919/CISTI.2019.8760733

Stajnko, D., Lakota, M., & Hočevar, M. (2004). Estimation of number and diameter of apple fruits in an orchard during the growing season by thermal imaging. *Computers and Electronics in Agriculture*, *42*(1), 31–42. DOI: 10.1016/S0168-1699(03)00086-3

Wallacei. (n.d.). *Wallacei evolutionary optimization engine*. https://www.wallacei.com/

Chapter 4
The Role and Impact of Artificial Intelligence in Logistics 5.0

Meriem Azari
https://orcid.org/0009-0007-8169-2641
Sidi Mohamed Ben Abdellah University, Morocco

Hassane Moustabchir
National School of Applied Sciences, Morocco

ABSTRACT

Logistics 5.0 represents a new era in supply chain management that integrates technological performance with human-centric values, sustainability, and resilience. This chapter examines the transformative role of Artificial Intelligence (AI) in enabling this transition. It explores how machine learning, computer vision, robotics, and conversational systems enhance forecasting, inventory optimisation, transport, and decision-making processes. The chapter also highlights the organisational and human enablers required for AI adoption, such as strategic alignment, digital infrastructure, workforce readiness, and collaborative ecosystems. Beyond technical innovation, it addresses critical barriers, including data quality, ethical concerns, and regulatory uncertainties. AI in Logistics 5.0 is not merely a tool for automation—it is a strategic lever to build adaptive, inclusive, and intelligent logistics systems. By combining human expertise with artificial intelligence, Logistics 5.0 offers a sustainable path forward for modern supply chains.

DOI: 10.4018/979-8-3373-0923-1.ch004

1. INTRODUCTION

Over the past decade, the logistics sector has undergone a significant digital transformation, driven by the increasing integration of technologies such as the Internet of Things (IoT), cyber-physical systems, and artificial intelligence (AI). This evolution has culminated in the emergence of Logistics 5.0, a new paradigm that transcends the traditional focus on operational efficiency by placing greater emphasis on sustainability, human-centric design, and resilience (Shojaeinasab et al., 2022).

Unlike Logistics 4.0—which primarily sought to optimise processes through automation, digitalisation, and real-time data analytics—Logistics 5.0 repositions logistics as a socio-technical system where human values and ecological considerations are embedded into the heart of operational design (Barata & Kayser, 2023). This shift reflects a growing consensus that future logistics systems must not only be fast and accurate, but also adaptive, inclusive, and ethically governed.

This reconfiguration is unfolding against the backdrop of profound global disruptions: climate volatility, geopolitical instability, energy transitions, and post-pandemic economic restructuring. These forces are reshaping the landscape of supply chain management, compelling organisations to seek not only efficiency but also flexibility, robustness, and social legitimacy (Zreik, 2023). In this context, Logistics 5.0 is emerging as a framework that aligns digital intelligence with planetary boundaries and evolving human needs.

Central to this transition is artificial intelligence, which plays a dual role as both an enabler of automation and a catalyst for strategic reorientation. AI technologies such as machine learning, computer vision, and natural language processing are no longer confined to isolated optimisation tasks—they are now embedded across the entire logistics value chain, supporting functions ranging from predictive maintenance and route planning to intelligent warehousing and decision support (Machado & Rodriguez, 2025). However, AI's contribution in Logistics 5.0 goes beyond technical performance: it shapes how humans and machines collaborate, how organisations learn, and how logistics systems adapt to complexity.

Moreover, the convergence of AI with smart city infrastructures, green transition goals, and global trade systems reinforces the need for holistic and interdisciplinary approaches. Logistics is no longer a backstage function; it has become a strategic lever for territorial development, sustainability transitions, and digital sovereignty. This evolution requires scholars and practitioners alike to rethink logistics not simply as a set of flows, but as a living, learning, and ethical system.

This chapter aims to examine the transformative role of artificial intelligence in enabling Logistics 5.0, with a focus on both technological enablers and organisational realities. Drawing from recent literature and empirical cases, it explores the key conceptual shifts, enabling technologies, adoption drivers, and system-level challenges associated with this transition.

The structure of the chapter is as follows: Section 1 introduces the conceptual evolution from Logistics 4.0 to 5.0. Section 2 analyses the main AI technologies that underpin this transformation. Section 3 identifies organisational, technical, and ecosystem-related enablers. Section 4 explores the limitations and risks of AI integration. Section 5 discusses the theoretical and practical implications of this evolution, followed by a conclusion that synthesises the main insights and outlines avenues for future research.

2. WHAT IS LOGISTICS 5.0?

2.1 Origin and Definition of the Concept

Logistics 5.0 originates from the progressive evolution of digital technologies in the logistics sector but departs significantly from the trajectory established by Logistics 4.0. The latter, rooted in the principles of Industry 4.0, prioritised real-time data integration, automation of physical and digital flows, and performance-driven intelligence through cyber-physical systems (Oran & Cezayirlioglu, 2021). Although these advancements considerably improved efficiency and traceability, they often neglected critical dimensions such as human well-being, environmental sustainability, and ethical accountability.

By contrast, Logistics 5.0 is conceived as a human-centred socio-technical system, combining high-performance digital infrastructures with a renewed emphasis on inclusivity and ecological responsibility (Trstenjak et al., 2022). Technologies such as artificial intelligence, collaborative robotics, and the Internet of Things (IoT) are still central, but their purpose is now redefined: not to replace the human operator but to complement and empower them within an augmented logistics environment (Rashid & Kausik, 2024).

This conceptual shift reflects a growing recognition of the limitations of purely technocratic models, especially in light of today's systemic crises—pandemic disruptions, climate emergencies, and labour market transformations. Logistics 5.0 thus emerges as a strategic response that aims to reconcile technological capabilities with evolving societal values (Shojaeinasab et al., 2022).

2.2 Shift From Logistics 4.0 to Logistics 5.0

The transition from Logistics 4.0 to 5.0 should not be seen as a linear technological upgrade but rather as a radical redefinition of priorities, values, and operating philosophies. While Logistics 4.0 was primarily focused on automation, lead time reduction, and responsiveness through digitalisation, its goals were largely instrumental and efficiency-oriented (Oran & Cezayirlioglu, 2021). Logistics operations were engineered to reduce variability, eliminate waste, and achieve standardisation—often at the expense of human discretion, environmental concern, or organisational resilience.

Logistics 5.0 retains the technological foundations of its predecessor—including the use of IoT, real-time tracking, and advanced analytics—but shifts the strategic focus towards human-machine symbiosis, social inclusion, and long-term sustainability. Rather than aiming for the full substitution of human labour, Logistics 5.0 emphasises collaborative intelligence, where the strengths of human reasoning and the efficiency of AI are combined. This is exemplified by the integration of cobots (collaborative robots), adaptive user interfaces, and AI-assisted decision-making tools that respect human judgment, accommodate operator feedback, and adapt to contextual nuances (Bansal et al., 2024).

This human-centric orientation also translates into a more ethical approach to technological deployment. Logistics 5.0 does not treat sustainability or well-being as compliance items but as foundational design principles. Issues such as carbon neutrality, safe and inclusive working conditions, ethical sourcing, and supply chain transparency are embedded from the outset, influencing infrastructure layout, performance metrics, and governance models (Mustapić et al., 2023).

In contrast, such dimensions were largely marginalised in Logistics 4.0, which often viewed environmental and social externalities as secondary to operational excellence. The push for scale, speed, and optimisation left little room for evaluating the broader impact of logistics practices on workers, communities, or ecosystems.

The break between these two paradigms is therefore not limited to technological tools or process automation, but extends to the underlying philosophy and value system that guide logistics innovation. Logistics 4.0 viewed technology as an end in itself—a driver of output and competitiveness. Logistics 5.0, by contrast, reframes technology as a means to advance human dignity, ecological balance, and collective resilience. As Khan et al. (2024) argue, this reorientation invites us to reconsider what counts as success in supply chain performance and to design systems that are not only smart, but also just, inclusive, and sustainable.

This paradigmatic shift challenges scholars, practitioners, and policymakers to embrace a more holistic conception of logistics, one that is capable of navigating complexity, accommodating diversity, and responding to the demands of a changing world.

2.3 Strategic Objectives of Logistics 5.0

Logistics 5.0 seeks to meet a triad of strategic objectives: resilience, sustainability, and human empowerment—each responding to a major contemporary pressure.

First, resilience has become imperative in a world marked by frequent and unpredictable disruptions. Through AI-powered forecasting systems, distributed intelligence, and real-time monitoring, Logistics 5.0 aims to build supply chain architectures that are more adaptive and shock-absorbent (Khan et al., 2024).

Second, environmental sustainability is no longer an option but a necessity. Logistics 5.0 integrates eco-efficiency from the design stage, encouraging low-carbon technologies, energy-saving infrastructures, and circular economy practices (Nicoletti & Appolloni, 2024a). This aligns logistics with broader climate commitments and regulatory pressures.

Finally, human centrality is the cornerstone of this new vision. By recognising the irreplaceable value of human intuition, ethical judgment, and context-specific knowledge, Logistics 5.0 aims to create inclusive and intelligent work environments. Human operators are not only assisted by AI; they are also empowered through redefined roles, better working conditions, and continuous learning (Machado & Rodriguez, 2025).

Workspaces are adapted to ergonomic needs, decision-making processes include human input, and emotional and cognitive aspects are taken into account in systems design.

In addition to resilience, sustainability, and human centrality, Logistics 5.0 also supports the emergence of new value creation logics. These include the development of servitisation models, where logistics is no longer a back-office function but becomes a core component of customer experience and competitive differentiation. Logistics actors increasingly provide predictive, customisable, and real-time services, powered by AI and data intelligence, that blur the boundaries between logistics, marketing, and customer support (Bansal et al., 2024).

Furthermore, this transformation underlines the strategic repositioning of logistics within broader societal systems. Logistics 5.0 contributes to regional planning, mobility regulation, and energy management through its embeddedness in smart city infrastructures. The convergence between logistics systems and urban digital platforms enables coordinated traffic flows, emissions monitoring, and shared access to multimodal transport assets (Azari et al., 2022). In this perspective, logistics is not only a beneficiary of smart technologies, but an active player in shaping the infrastructure and governance of tomorrow's cities.

Finally, the integration of sustainability metrics into logistics design and operations reflects a paradigm shift toward impact-based performance management. Rather than focusing solely on time or cost, logistics performance is increasingly evaluated through a multidimensional lens that includes carbon intensity, employee safety, circularity, and social inclusion (Rashid & Kausik, 2024). This evolution calls for new models of responsible logistics governance, where AI systems are aligned with environmental regulations, ethical principles, and stakeholder expectations.

3. AI TECHNOLOGIES ENABLING LOGISTICS 5.0

3.1. Conversational AI and Smart Interfaces

Conversational AI and intelligent dashboards are central to Logistics 5.0's emphasis on responsiveness, personalisation, and user-centric design. These systems allow supply chain actors to interact with digital platforms in more intuitive and context-sensitive ways, moving beyond static interfaces toward fluid, real-time dialogue environments (Machado & Rodriguez, 2025).

Advanced decision support systems, often powered by predictive analytics and integrated with IoT networks, visualise operational data dynamically and generate scenario-based recommendations. These tools assist managers in navigating uncertainty, whether by anticipating delays, adjusting inventories, or reassigning transport assets (Trstenjak et al., 2022).

In parallel, conversational agents such as logistics chatbots and voice assistants are increasingly deployed to automate internal queries (e.g., locating stock, tracking deliveries) and manage external customer interactions (du Plessis et al., 2025). In some warehouses, these systems now autonomously handle a wide range of inquiries, thereby reducing workload and improving the traceability and consistency of service.

The growing use of natural language processing (NLP) in logistics environments further enables users to interact with platforms in a conversational, human-like manner. This not only improves accessibility for non-expert users but also enhances real-time problem-solving by removing interface frictions (Nicoletti & Appolloni, 2024a).

In addition, the integration of emotion-sensitive AI—capable of detecting frustration or urgency in voice or text—is starting to shape how logistics centres prioritise and escalate issues. While still at an early stage, these developments show how conversational AI can go beyond transaction support to foster affective and adaptive interactions (Rashid & Kausik, 2024).

Moreover, the convergence of conversational AI with augmented analytics opens new possibilities for decentralised, human-in-the-loop decision-making. For example, warehouse supervisors may use voice-enabled dashboards to simulate reallocation strategies or explore what-if scenarios on the fly, improving their responsiveness to unexpected disruptions (Zrelli & Rejeb, 2024).

These technologies do not replace human operators but serve as cognitive amplifiers, improving both reaction speed and decision relevance while ensuring greater accessibility to complex digital ecosystems. Their success, however, depends on user trust, interface ergonomics, and the transparency of the algorithms behind the dialogue. In this sense, conversational AI becomes not merely a tool of efficiency, but a key enabler of technological inclusivity and empowerment.

3.2. Autonomous Systems and Embedded AI

Autonomous logistics systems—ranging from self-driving vehicles to intelligent mobile robots—are reshaping the physical infrastructure of supply chains. Powered by embedded AI and sensor fusion, these systems execute tasks such as inventory relocation, internal transport, and last-mile delivery without direct human supervision (Azari et al., 2024).

For instance, autonomous electric vehicles integrated into smart logistics platforms can ensure low-emission, scheduled, and silent deliveries, particularly in urban and intermodal contexts. These vehicles adapt routes in real time according to traffic and energy constraints, thereby improving both efficiency and sustainability (Soumaya et al., 2024).

Similarly, the convergence of mobile robotics, IoT, and AI has enabled distributed decision-making at the warehouse level. Intelligent forklift trucks and mobile picking units can dynamically reroute, avoid bottlenecks, and collaborate with human operators in shared workspaces (El Jaouhari et al., 2022). These robots operate within multi-agent systems, where local autonomy is coordinated via cloud platforms or edge computing nodes, allowing for real-time response and systemic coherence.

A notable evolution is the rise of adaptive navigation systems based on machine vision and SLAM (simultaneous localization and mapping), enabling robots to perform complex routing in unstructured or changing environments (du Plessis et al., 2025). These systems are particularly valuable in warehouses undergoing layout transformations or experiencing fluctuating operational density.

Moreover, AI-embedded devices are becoming increasingly modular and energy-aware. Logistics robots now integrate battery optimisation algorithms and predictive maintenance modules, which extend operational uptime while reducing resource consumption (Trstenjak et al., 2022). This evolution contributes to the creation of sustainable, autonomous infrastructure that aligns with the principles of Logistics 5.0 and Industry 5.0.

In Logistics 5.0, these autonomous tools are not isolated innovations. They represent foundational elements of an intelligent, mobile, and sustainable logistics ecosystem, capable of supporting resilient supply chains in dynamic and uncertain environments. Their success, however, depends on infrastructural interoperability, regulatory support, and user trust in autonomous systems.

3.3. Machine Learning for Predictive and Adaptive Logistics

Machine learning (ML) is a cornerstone of intelligent logistics under the 5.0 framework. Its primary value lies in transforming reactive systems into predictive and adaptive networks capable of responding to disruptions proactively (Azari et al., 2025).

Demand forecasting is a key area where ML excels. Unlike traditional models based on historical averages, machine learning integrates contextual and exogenous variables—weather, promotions, events, social signals—to produce high-resolution, dynamic forecasts (du Plessis et al., 2025). These outputs inform automatic adjustments to inventory thresholds, replenishment schedules, and routing strategies. The ability to anticipate demand volatility is essential for improving service levels while minimising unnecessary resource consumption.

Beyond forecasting, ML contributes to multi-objective inventory optimisation, balancing cost, service rate, environmental impact, and risk exposure. Algorithms generate real-time recommendations on stock allocation, safety buffers, and distribution centre positioning based on system-wide simulations and scenario analysis (Soumaya et al., 2024). This makes logistics more adaptive to fluctuating customer behaviours and supply conditions, reducing both stockouts and overstocking.

A growing area of application is predictive maintenance for logistics assets. ML models trained on historical and sensor data can anticipate equipment failures, optimise intervention schedules, and minimise downtime (Mustapić et al., 2023). For example, automated cranes or forklifts equipped with vibration and temperature sensors can be monitored continuously, with algorithms flagging early signs of wear or overload.

In transportation management, ML also enables real-time route optimisation based on live traffic, delivery urgency, and environmental factors. This is especially valuable in urban and last-mile logistics, where dynamic route planning improves punctuality and reduces emissions (Zrelli & Rejeb, 2024). Some advanced systems even incorporate reinforcement learning, allowing delivery fleets to autonomously improve performance through experience and interaction with changing environments.

An emerging frontier is the integration of ML with digital twins of logistics networks. These virtual replicas simulate the impact of strategic or operational changes—such as new warehouse locations or alternative supplier networks—on system resilience and carbon footprint. As data availability and computing power increase, such approaches offer firms the ability to test decisions virtually before real-world execution (Barata & Kayser, 2023).

In sum, machine learning is more than a tool for optimisation—it is a strategic enabler of foresight, agility, and efficiency in complex logistics environments. It also lays the groundwork for next-generation capabilities such as intelligent automation, cognitive logistics agents, and adaptive supply chain orchestration.

3.4. Computer Vision and Intelligent Robotics

In Logistics 5.0, computer vision (CV) and intelligent robotics play a pivotal role in transforming logistics platforms into perceptive, autonomous, and human-aware environments. These technologies move beyond basic automation to enable adaptive, high-precision, and safety-enhanced operations across the supply chain.

Computer vision systems, coupled with advanced sensors and AI algorithms, allow real-time tracking of parcels, automatic detection of labelling and packaging errors, and visual inspection for quality control. These capabilities are increasingly deployed in receiving areas, sorting stations, and picking zones, significantly improving accuracy while reducing manual workload and error rates (du Plessis et al., 2025).

Integrated with Internet of Things (IoT) infrastructure, computer vision enables connected warehouses to map product movements, monitor inventory levels dynamically, and synchronise autonomous logistics vehicles. This enhances operational transparency and strengthens supply chain resilience (Machado & Rodriguez, 2025). Moreover, these technologies facilitate the early detection of safety hazards, such as misplaced goods or human presence in restricted zones, thereby reducing occupational risks.

Intelligent robotics, particularly autonomous mobile robots (AMRs), further extends these benefits. Equipped with vision-based navigation, AMRs can adapt their paths to obstacles, manage dynamic shelving, and relocate pallets based on fluctuating demand. They operate safely alongside humans, contributing to ergonomic improvements and better workplace safety (Azari et al., 2024).

An emerging trend is the integration of multi-modal sensory processing, where robotics systems combine visual, auditory, and spatial data to respond more precisely to complex environments. For instance, robots can detect gestures, verbal commands, or environmental cues to adjust their speed or movement path—enhancing both collaborative capacity and trust (Bansal et al., 2024).

Importantly, these technologies also support environmental performance objectives. By reducing unnecessary movements, idle time, and energy consumption, robotics and visual automation align with the sustainability principles of Logistics 5.0 (Nicoletti & Appolloni, 2024a). Their ability to optimise pathfinding, detect inefficiencies, and operate on demand leads to greener warehouse operations and reduced carbon footprint.

Rather than replacing human labour, these innovations embody a redefinition of human–machine collaboration. Robots become intelligent agents that coordinate with both human workers and digital systems, enabling real-time adaptation, safety augmentation, and workload sharing. As a result, Logistics 5.0 platforms become not only more productive, but also more inclusive and resilient.

3.5. Human–AI Cooperation and Augmented Decision-Making

Unlike previous approaches that sought to automate logistics systems entirely, Logistics 5.0 emphasises close and constructive cooperation between humans and artificial intelligence. The objective is not to replace humans but to augment their capabilities, facilitate decision-making, and ensure that automation aligns with human values and operational contexts (Khan et al., 2024).

In logistics operations, this cooperation materialises through augmented intelligent systems, where operators interact with control platforms, mobile robots, or forecasting tools in real time. Humans play a decisive role in interpreting suggestions, validating AI-generated scenarios, and managing exceptional or ambiguous situations (du Plessis et al., 2025). This hybrid interaction enhances the system's adaptability while preserving the human's intuitive and ethical judgment.

A central concept is the "human-in-the-loop" model, which structures decision-making processes around shared authority between machine recommendations and human oversight. This model is particularly useful in contexts where purely algorithmic solutions may not capture operational nuances—such as sudden layout changes in warehouses, context-specific delivery constraints, or interpersonal customer service considerations (Machado & Rodriguez, 2025).

To be effective, human–AI cooperation requires substantial investment in training and organisational learning. Operators must understand the logic behind AI systems, interpret data visualisations, and communicate effectively with intelligent agents. As Coelho & Reis, (2023) point out, this implies a shift toward hybrid skill sets, combining digital literacy, logistics expertise, and adaptive decision-making.

Moreover, the social acceptability of AI is a crucial dimension of this cooperation. Employees may express concerns about job displacement, de-skilling, or being reduced to a passive role in an increasingly automated environment. Transparent communication, co-design of tools, and ethical safeguards are essential to maintain motivation and trust. Participatory implementation strategies, where employees help define how AI is integrated into workflows, have shown positive effects on technology appropriation and psychological safety (Trstenjak et al., 2023).

Additionally, emerging models of explainable AI (XAI) aim to improve transparency and interpretability, making it easier for workers and managers to trust the outputs of intelligent systems. Such models are particularly relevant in regulated or safety-critical logistics environments, where responsibility must be traceable and justified.

Ultimately, human–AI cooperation in Logistics 5.0 is not only a technical feature but a socio-technical strategy. It allows for a redefinition of work, where machines perform repetitive or data-intensive tasks, and humans bring contextual awareness, creativity, and judgment. This balance fosters technological resilience, enhances user engagement, and supports ethical innovation in increasingly digitised logistics ecosystems.

4. ENABLERS AND DRIVERS OF AI ADOPTION IN LOGISTICS 5.0

While the technological maturity of artificial intelligence has advanced significantly, its widespread adoption in logistics systems depends on a complex interplay of organisational, technical, and institutional factors. The transition to Logistics 5.0 is not driven solely by technical feasibility but by the strategic, human, and ecosystemic conditions that facilitate the successful integration of AI into supply chains. This section identifies and analyses the main enablers of this adoption process.

4.1. Organisational Alignment and Strategic Vision

The successful deployment of AI in Logistics 5.0 requires strong strategic alignment with the company's long-term goals and operational logic. AI implementation is not a stand-alone initiative; it must be integrated into a comprehensive transformation strategy that encompasses performance, resilience, and human-centred innovation (Aldoseri et al., 2024).

This implies clear governance structures, the appointment of internal champions, and a roadmap that prioritises use cases offering tangible benefits—such as predictive inventory management, automated sortation, or adaptive route planning (Nicoletti & Appolloni, 2024b). Moreover, strategic alignment fosters internal legitimacy, as all actors share a common understanding of how AI contributes to the company's value creation.

Management commitment plays a crucial role in this process. Without clear endorsement from leadership, AI projects risk remaining isolated technological experiments with limited impact on organisational culture or system resilience.

4.2. Skills Development and Human Readiness

The adoption of AI also hinges on the readiness of human capital. Logistics 5.0 requires a new generation of professionals capable of interacting with intelligent systems, interpreting algorithmic outputs, and participating in co-decision processes (Nicoletti & Appolloni, 2024a). This entails not only technical training but also the development of cognitive, relational, and ethical skills (Coelho & Reis, 2023).

In many cases, existing staff must be supported through reskilling initiatives, participatory learning environments, and communication programmes that demystify AI and reinforce its role as a collaborative tool (Trstenjak et al., 2022). Organisational culture is also key: a culture that values experimentation, transparency, and feedback is more likely to facilitate the appropriation of AI.

Moreover, social acceptance must not be overlooked. Concerns about job displacement, opacity of decision-making, and loss of control can undermine trust and slow down implementation. Hence, inclusive and ethically grounded approaches are essential to build a sustainable human–AI partnership (Machado & Rodriguez, 2025).

4.3. Digital Infrastructure and Data Quality

The adoption of artificial intelligence in Logistics 5.0 relies on an essential technical foundation: high-performance, interconnected, and secure digital infrastructures. Without a suitable technological environment, AI algorithms cannot access reliable data or operate in real time (Khan et al., 2024).

This requires the implementation of IoT networks, intelligent sensors, and cloud or edge computing platforms, as well as tools for collecting and automatically processing logistics data. These systems must be capable of centralised, structured, and analysed heterogeneous data flows from warehouses, transport systems, customers, or equipment (Mustapić et al., 2023). Their role is not only to gather information but to make it actionable—that is, usable by algorithms and decision-makers simultaneously.

The quality, availability, and interoperability of data have become central challenges. Many logistics organisations operate with legacy systems, resulting in fragmented or incompatible databases that obstruct the integration of AI tools. Overcoming these barriers often requires data governance strategies that include data cleansing, standardisation, and real-time synchronisation across platforms (Zrelli & Rejeb, 2024).

In this context, edge computing is gaining attention as a key enabler of AI performance. By processing data closer to the source—on robots, vehicles, or warehouse equipment—edge computing reduces latency, improves reliability, and alleviates the burden on central systems (Azari et al., 2024). This is particularly relevant for applications requiring immediate feedback, such as autonomous navigation, predictive safety alerts, or high-frequency inventory updates.

Another strategic layer is cybersecurity. As AI systems depend on open and connected digital environments, they are increasingly exposed to vulnerabilities such as data breaches, algorithm manipulation, or system hijacking. Strong authentication protocols, encryption standards, and monitoring systems are essential to ensure the trustworthiness and resilience of smart logistics infrastructures (Aldoseri et al., 2024).

Furthermore, the integration of AI calls for ethical data governance. This includes transparency about data usage, rules for anonymisation, and clear accountability in the event of algorithmic errors or bias. In Logistics 5.0, data is not only a resource but a strategic asset, and its management must reflect both efficiency and responsibility (Nicoletti & Appolloni, 2024b).

Finally, digital infrastructure development should not be limited to large multinationals. Support for small and medium-sized enterprises (SMEs) through shared platforms, public-private partnerships, and open-access data standards is crucial to ensure an inclusive digital transition across the logistics ecosystem (Bansal et al., 2024).

4.4. Ecosystem Collaboration and External Support

The adoption of AI in Logistics 5.0 goes beyond internal firm capabilities. It requires a supportive ecosystem involving public institutions, technology providers, research centres, logistics clusters, and end users. These external actors play a crucial role in facilitating experimentation, resource sharing, and risk reduction through collaborative governance frameworks (Bansal et al., 2024).

Public policy support, including innovation grants, fiscal incentives, and the creation of logistics "living labs," helps de-risk early adoption and foster local technological ecosystems. Additionally, standardisation efforts and regulatory clarity are essential to harmonise practices, especially in cross-border logistics operations (icoletti & Appolloni, 2024b). Professional organisations and logistics consortia also contribute by disseminating best practices and building trust among adopters.

Another key driver is the availability of strategic partnerships with AI solution providers, who often bring both technical expertise and scalability potential. These partnerships must evolve beyond transactional models to co-development arrangements, in which logistics challenges are solved collaboratively and iteratively.

In this context, the Chinese experience provides valuable insights into how integrated, multi-actor ecosystems can accelerate AI-based logistics transformation. As Zreik, (2023) illustrates, the development of smart and sustainable supply chains in China has been enabled by a multi-dimensional approach, combining industrial policy, technological innovation, urban planning, and environmental regulation. The Chinese model highlights how alignment between public priorities and private sector capabilities can create synergies that support large-scale adoption of intelligent systems.

This kind of territorial intelligence is increasingly relevant in other regions as well, where logistics innovation must be embedded into urban and regional strategies, including smart city programmes and climate adaptation plans.

Finally, end users—whether consumers, businesses, or local communities—are not passive recipients of AI-driven services. Their expectations in terms of traceability, ethical behaviour, and sustainability shape the technological choices made by logistics providers. A successful adoption strategy thus depends on building inclusive ecosystems where all stakeholders are actively involved in designing, evaluating, and governing Logistics 5.0 systems.

4.5. Perceived Value and Motivational Drivers

The decision to adopt AI is ultimately shaped by the value perceived by logistics decision-makers. This value may be operational (cost savings, error reduction), strategic (competitive differentiation, agility), or symbolic (innovation image, environmental compliance) (Oran & Cezayirlioglu, 2021).

Perceived value also influences how stakeholders justify the investment in AI technologies. For some, the emphasis lies on short-term gains such as increased speed or reduced downtime. For others, it is about long-term transformation, including digital maturity, organisational learning, and business model evolution (du Plessis et al., 2025).

When the value of AI is clearly defined, measurable, and collectively understood, adoption becomes more natural and sustainable—integrated into decision-making processes rather than imposed from the top down.

5. CHALLENGES AND LIMITATIONS OF AI IN LOGISTICS 5.0

Despite its transformative potential, the adoption of artificial intelligence in Logistics 5.0 remains fraught with significant challenges. These obstacles are not solely technical but span across human, organisational, ethical, and regulatory dimensions. Understanding and addressing these constraints is essential for managing risk, ensuring responsible innovation, and enabling the large-scale deployment of AI-enhanced logistics models.

5.1. Technical and Operational Barriers

Among the most pressing challenges are those related to technological integration and system interoperability. Many logistics companies continue to rely on fragmented or legacy information systems that are poorly suited for AI deployment (Azari et al., 2025). This fragmentation limits real-time data flows, reduces coordination across logistics functions, and complicates the deployment of end-to-end intelligent workflows.

Another major obstacle is the quality of available data. AI models require structured, clean, and representative datasets to produce reliable outputs. In reality, logistics data is often noisy, incomplete, or delayed—undermining the predictive capacity of machine learning algorithms (Asilian et al., 2023). Data collected in isolated subsystems may also be incompatible with enterprise-wide AI applications, limiting their relevance.

Scalability and computational constraints further exacerbate the issue. AI solutions may perform well in isolated pilot environments but encounter latency, processing overload, or system bottlenecks when scaled up. These limitations are particularly visible in resource-constrained contexts, such as small logistics providers or decentralised warehouse networks.

Additionally, the absence of shared industry standards for AI in logistics impedes cross-platform compatibility and best practice diffusion. The prevalence of proprietary architectures, closed APIs, and isolated vendor ecosystems slows down the convergence needed for collaborative innovation (Machado & Rodriguez, 2025). This gap calls for greater investment in open standards and interoperability protocols.

5.2. Human, Ethical, and Regulatory Constraints

Beyond the technical domain, AI adoption in Logistics 5.0 raises important human and ethical challenges. One of the most sensitive questions relates to accountability: when an AI-driven system makes a faulty recommendation or initiates an autonomous action, determining liability becomes complex—especially in cases involving automated vehicles or warehouse robotics (Machado & Rodriguez, 2025).

A second concern involves the opacity of AI decision-making. Logistics professionals may not fully understand how recommendations are generated, particularly in deep learning models. This can lead to either blind acceptance or outright rejection of AI outputs—both of which undermine system performance and safety (Khan et al., 2024).

On the regulatory front, data protection laws, cybersecurity standards, and safety regulations often lag behind the pace of AI deployment in logistics. Variations in international legislation pose further barriers, particularly for cross-border logistics operations relying on shared digital infrastructures (Nicoletti & Appolloni, 2024a). The lack of regulatory convergence leads to uncertainty and compliance risks.

There is also a critical social dimension to consider. The fear of job displacement, de-skilling, or loss of decision autonomy can generate resistance among employees. Without appropriate communication and inclusion strategies, these anxieties may translate into disengagement, project sabotage, or outright rejection of innovation (Trstenjak et al., 2022).

Addressing these risks requires inclusive change management, participatory technology design, and ongoing skills development. Workers must be seen as active agents in the AI transformation process, rather than passive recipients of automation.

5.3. Toward Scalable and Sustainable AI Integration

Overcoming these challenges necessitates a shift from ad hoc technological deployment to systemic and sustainable integration strategies. Logistics organisations must evolve from a purely technocentric perspective toward socio-technical approaches that combine performance, ethics, and resilience (du Plessis et al., 2025).

A promising strategy is the development of testbed environments—such as pilot sites, demonstrators, or living labs—that support experimental deployment of AI in real-world conditions (Bansal et al., 2024). These environments foster iterative learning, reduce the risk of large-scale failure, and help co-create solutions with stakeholders.

The creation of modular, interoperable AI platforms is equally important. Standardised architectures enable collaboration between logistics actors, system providers, and regulatory authorities, while supporting scalability and system flexibility (Barata & Kayser, 2023). Additionally, platforms should integrate environmental, ethical, and social impact modules to support responsible innovation.

Moreover, organisational maturity plays a central role in overcoming limitations. Shojaeinasab et al., (2022) point out, the full potential of AI can only be realised in organisations that combine technical infrastructure with dynamic capabilities such as leadership, culture, and absorptive capacity.

Ultimately, Logistics 5.0 cannot succeed if AI is seen as a mere tool for automation. Its implementation must be guided by principles of transparency, inclusivity, and long-term value creation, grounded in collaboration among humans, machines, and institutions.

6. THEORETICAL AND PRACTICAL IMPLICATIONS OF AI IN LOGISTICS 5.0

The integration of artificial intelligence within the Logistics 5.0 paradigm generates a set of far-reaching implications, both at the theoretical level—by expanding conceptual frameworks in supply chain research—and at the practical level—by reshaping operational models, stakeholder roles, and innovation strategies.

6.1. Theoretical Implications

From a theoretical standpoint, the deployment of AI in Logistics 5.0 invites a fundamental rethinking of existing paradigms in supply chain management. Traditional models often conceptualise logistics as a linear, efficiency-driven process governed by cost reduction, throughput maximisation, and lean principles. However, Logistics 5.0 challenges these assumptions by introducing a multi-dimensional vision that integrates technological, human, ethical, and ecological considerations within a unified operational framework.

A first major implication is the need to develop new theories of human–AI collaboration that go beyond automation versus human labour dichotomies. In the Logistics 5.0 paradigm, cooperation between humans and intelligent systems is framed as a process of mutual augmentation, requiring conceptual models that account for shared decision-making, explainable reasoning, and continuous adaptation (Machado & Rodriguez, 2025). This calls for integrating insights from organisational psychology, cognitive ergonomics, and human–computer interaction into logistics theory.

Second, the shift toward distributed and embedded intelligence necessitates the adoption of more decentralised control models. Rather than concentrating decision power at a central hub, Logistics 5.0 systems rely on autonomous agents—robots, platforms, connected devices—that interact locally and in real time. This evolution supports the development of multi-agent systems theory, as well as network-based governance models rooted in cybernetics and complexity science (Shojaeinasab et al., 2022).

Moreover, the environmental ambitions of Logistics 5.0 challenge scholars to embed sustainability metrics and circularity principles within core theoretical models. This implies moving beyond traditional KPIs (cost, time, volume) to incorporate indicators such as carbon intensity, regenerative logistics loops, and inclusive service design. Theories rooted in eco-efficiency, life cycle thinking, or regenerative economics are increasingly relevant for modelling future supply chains (Nicoletti & Appolloni, 2024b).

Additionally, the growing use of AI for tactical and strategic decision-making opens avenues for exploring algorithmic governance in logistics. Questions of responsibility, transparency, and bias must be theoretically grounded to support the development of accountable and trustworthy logistics systems. This requires bridging logistics management with ethics, law, and information systems theory.

Finally, the integrative nature of Logistics 5.0—combining real-time data, AI, human cooperation, and sustainability—creates opportunities for interdisciplinary theoretical frameworks. Contributions from urban studies, smart city planning, and technology acceptance models (TAM, UTAUT) are increasingly necessary to understand how logistics interacts with broader sociotechnical systems (Zreik, 2023).

In summary, Logistics 5.0 redefines logistics not merely as a technical function but as a complex, adaptive, and value-driven system, requiring new theoretical tools that reflect this multi-layered reality.

6.2. Practical Implications

Practically, the adoption of artificial intelligence within Logistics 5.0 requires a profound reconfiguration of logistics practices, competencies, and organisational structures. As intelligent systems become integral to operational workflows, logistics professionals must transition from task execution roles to more strategic and analytical functions.

One key implication is the transformation of workforce competencies. Operators, planners, and managers need to develop hybrid skills that blend logistical knowledge with digital fluency, data interpretation, and ethical decision-making. Training programmes must go beyond technical upskilling to include cognitive adaptability, collaborative problem-solving, and critical thinking in AI-supported environments (Coelho & Reis, 2023). This shift also calls for the redesign of job descriptions, evaluation metrics, and learning pathways.

Secondly, AI adoption impacts the design and governance of logistics infrastructure. Smart warehouses and transport systems must be architected to support modularity, interoperability, and real-time responsiveness. This requires rethinking layout planning, data flow integration, and the coordination of autonomous and human actors in shared spaces (du Plessis et al., 2025). Moreover, logistics facilities are increasingly expected to comply with environmental and social criteria, such as carbon neutrality, noise mitigation, and inclusivity in urban contexts.

The deployment of AI also influences the interaction between logistics and public policy. Urban logistics strategies now intersect with mobility regulation, climate adaptation, and digital infrastructure planning. This has led to the emergence of public–private models for logistics co-governance in smart cities, where data sharing, traffic control, and last-mile delivery solutions are jointly designed and evaluated

(Azari et al., 2022). Such arrangements necessitate new skills in negotiation, regulatory compliance, and system interoperability.

A particularly relevant example is the case of China, where sustainable and intelligent supply chains have been strategically developed through a multi-dimensional approach combining industrial policy, environmental targets, and technological investment. As Zreik, (2023) demonstrates, this convergence has enabled the implementation of AI-enhanced logistics systems that are both high-performing and aligned with national sustainability goals. This model offers valuable lessons for other countries seeking to embed AI in logistics while preserving socio-environmental balance.

Finally, the implementation of AI technologies challenges traditional logistics KPIs and pushes companies to adopt multi-criteria performance frameworks. Metrics must now account for system adaptability, user satisfaction, social inclusion, and environmental impact alongside conventional efficiency indicators. Logistics managers are thus required to operate within multi-objective decision environments, using AI not only as a tool for automation but as a means to inform ethically and strategically balanced choices.

In short, Logistics 5.0 demands a shift from a purely operational mindset to a strategic, collaborative, and adaptive posture, supported by intelligent systems and guided by shared values of sustainability and responsibility.

7. CONCLUSION

The integration of artificial intelligence into Logistics 5.0 represents much more than a technological evolution. It marks a systemic transformation of the logistics function—from an efficiency-oriented, mechanistic process to a strategic, ethical, and adaptive system capable of responding to contemporary economic, social, and environmental challenges.

Throughout this chapter, we have examined how Logistics 5.0 emerges as a response to the limitations of prior paradigms. Unlike Logistics 4.0, which focused on automation and real-time optimisation, Logistics 5.0 places the human and the planet at the centre of innovation. Artificial intelligence, in this context, is not a substitute for human intelligence, but a complementary and catalytic force that enables intelligent automation, predictive planning, and collaborative decision-making.

We have seen that AI enables a wide spectrum of capabilities—ranging from conversational agents and predictive algorithms to computer vision and autonomous robotics—all of which contribute to more resilient, transparent, and personalised supply chain operations. However, these technologies are not neutral: their design, adoption, and impacts depend on organisational strategy, infrastructure readiness, ecosystem cooperation, and social acceptability.

Moreover, the chapter has highlighted the multidimensional enablers of AI adoption: from data governance and digital infrastructure to skills development, ecosystem support, and perceived value. These conditions must be jointly mobilised to ensure that AI contributes to inclusive, scalable, and sustainable logistics models.

Nonetheless, the realisation of Logistics 5.0 remains fraught with challenges. Technical limitations, data quality issues, algorithmic opacity, and ethical concerns all pose barriers to adoption. Overcoming these obstacles requires more than innovation—it requires governance, trust, and accountability. Organisations must adopt hybrid approaches that align technological ambition with human-centred values and societal expectations.

Theoretically, Logistics 5.0 invites a rethinking of supply chain models through lenses such as human–AI cooperation, distributed intelligence, circular logistics, and algorithmic governance. These evolving paradigms point toward a future where logistics is not just faster or smarter, but more reflective, responsible, and relational.

Looking ahead, future research should address several critical areas:

- First, the long-term societal impacts of AI adoption on labour structures, autonomy, and human dignity.
- Second, the governance frameworks required to ensure transparency, equity, and inclusiveness in logistics innovation.
- Third, the exploration of regional specificities and the adaptability of Logistics 5.0 across diverse socio-economic contexts, particularly in developing economies.

In sum, the future of logistics will not be defined solely by digital performance but by our collective ability to shape intelligent systems that are resilient, sustainable, and centred on the common good. Logistics 5.0 is not just an industrial ambition—it is a societal project that requires cooperation across disciplines, sectors, and cultures.

REFERENCES

Aldoseri, A., Al-Khalifa, K. N., & Hamouda, A. M. (2024). AI-Powered Innovation in Digital Transformation: Key Pillars and Industry Impact. *Sustainability (Switzerland), 16*(5). *Sustainability (Basel), 16*(5), 1790. DOI: 10.3390/su16051790

Asilian, A., Shahinzadeh, H., Zanjani, S. M., Gharehpetian, G. B., Abdelaziz, A. Y., & Tanwar, S. (2023). The Role of Microelectronics for Smart Cities, Smart Grids and Industry 5.0: Challenges, Solutions, and Opportunities. *2023 13th Smart Grid Conference (SGC)*, 1–12. https://ieeexplore.ieee.org/abstract/document/10459310/

Azari, M., Arif, J., Jawab, F., & Moustabchir, H. (2024). Smart city implementation of electric vehicles: Challenges and Opportunities. *2024 IEEE 15th International Colloquium on Logistics and Supply Chain Management (LOGISTIQUA)*, 1–6. https://ieeexplore.ieee.org/abstract/document/10571532/

Azari, M., Arif, J., Moustabchir, H., & Jawab, F. (2025). Navigating Challenges and Leveraging Future Trends in AI and Machine Learning for Supply Chains. In *AI and Machine Learning Applications in Supply Chains and Marketing* (pp. 257–282). IGI Global.

Azari, M., Jawab, F., Arif, J., Khaoua, Y., El Jaouhari, A., & Moustabchir, H. (2022). From city logistics to a merger of smart cities and smart logistics. *2022 14th International Colloquium of Logistics and Supply Chain Management (LOGISTIQUA)*, 1–5. https://ieeexplore.ieee.org/abstract/document/9938020/

Bansal, K., Anjimoon, S., Revathi, V., Gupta, M., & Sharma, A. (2024). The Evolution from Digital Production to Digital Society in Industry 4.0 towards Industry 5.0. In *Powering Industry 5.0 and Sustainable Development Through Innovation* (pp. 27–42). IGI Global.

Barata, J., & Kayser, I. (2023). Industry 5.0–past, present, and near future. *Procedia Computer Science, 219*, 778–788. DOI: 10.1016/j.procs.2023.01.351

Coelho, L., & Reis, S. S. (2023). Enhancing learning experiences through artificial intelligence: Classroom 5.0. In *Fostering pedagogy through micro and adaptive learning in higher education: Trends, tools, and applications* (pp. 169–191). IGI Global.

du Plessis, M. J., Gerber, R., Goedhals-Gerber, L. L., & van Eeden, J. (2025). Shaping the Future of Freight Logistics: Use Cases of Artificial Intelligence. *Sustainability (Basel), 17*(4), 4. DOI: 10.3390/su17041355

El Jaouhari, A., Azari, M., Arif, J., El Farouk, I. I., Jawab, F., & Moufad, I. (2022). IoT for the future of sustainable supply chain management in Industry 4.0: A Systematic Literature Review. *2022 14th International Colloquium of Logistics and Supply Chain Management (LOGISTIQUA)*, 1–6. https://ieeexplore.ieee.org/abstract/document/9938123/

Khan, M. A., Khan, R., Praveen, P., Verma, A. R., & Panda, M. K. (2024). *Infrastructure possibilities and human-centered approaches with Industry 5.0*. IGI Global.

Machado, N. T., & Rodriguez, C. M. T. (2025). A Logistics 5.0 maturity model: A human-centric and sustainable approach for the supply chain of the future. *ITEGAM-JETIA, 11*(51), Article 51.

Mustapić, M., Trstenjak, M., Gregurić, P., & Opetuk, T. (2023). Implementation and use of digital, green and sustainable technologies in internal and external transport of manufacturing companies. *Sustainability (Basel), 15*(12), 12. DOI: 10.3390/su15129557

Nicoletti, B., & Appolloni, A. (2024a). Green Logistics 5.0: A review of sustainability-oriented innovation with foundation models in logistics. *European Journal of Innovation Management, 27*(9), 9. DOI: 10.1108/EJIM-07-2024-0787

Nicoletti, B., & Appolloni, A. (2024b). Green Warehouse 5.0. In Appolloni, A., Kumar, V., Kuzmin, E., & Akberdina, V. (Eds.), *The Future of Industry* (Vol. 70, pp. 303–320). Springer Nature Switzerland., DOI: 10.1007/978-3-031-66801-2_20

Oran, I. B., & Cezayirlioglu, H. R. (2021). AI-Robotic applications in logistics industry and savings calculation. *Journal of Organizational Behavior Research, 6*(1–2021), Article 1–2021.

Rashid, A. B., & Kausik, A. K. (2024). AI revolutionizing industries worldwide: A comprehensive overview of its diverse applications. *Hybrid Advances*, 100277.

Shojaeinasab, A., Charter, T., Jalayer, M., Khadivi, M., Ogunfowora, O., Raiyani, N., Yaghoubi, M., & Najjaran, H. (2022). Intelligent manufacturing execution systems: A systematic review. *Journal of Manufacturing Systems, 62*, 503–522. DOI: 10.1016/j.jmsy.2022.01.004

Soumaya, F., Jabir, A., & Fouad, J. (2024). Transport 4.0 tools opportunities and benefits in last mile logistics: Past review and future perspectives. *2024 IEEE 15th International Colloquium on Logistics and Supply Chain Management (LOGISTIQUA)*, 1–6. https://ieeexplore.ieee.org/abstract/document/10571462/

Trstenjak, M., Mustapić, M., Gregurić, P., & Opetuk, T. (2023). Use of green industry 5.0 technologies in logistics activities. *Tehnički Glasnik, 17*(3), Article 3.

Trstenjak, M., Opetuk, T., Đukić, G., & Cajner, H. (2022). Logistics 5.0 implementation model based on decision support systems. *Sustainability (Basel)*, *14*(11), 11. DOI: 10.3390/su14116514

Zreik, M. (2023). Sustainable and smart supply chains in China: A multidimensional approach. In *Integrating intelligence and sustainability in supply chains* (pp. 179–197). IGI Global. DOI: 10.4018/979-8-3693-0225-5.ch010

Zrelli, I., & Rejeb, A. (2024). A bibliometric analysis of IoT applications in logistics and supply chain management. *Heliyon*, *10*(16), 16. DOI: 10.1016/j.heliyon.2024.e36578 PMID: 39262942

Section 2
Technological Enablers and AI-Driven Innovation in Supply Chain Management

Chapter 5
Leveraging Machine Learning and AI for Demand Forecasting in Supply Chain Management

J. Dhanalakshmi
https://orcid.org/0000-0002-3919-4469
Department of Data Science and Business Systems, SRM Institute of Science and Technology, India

A. Prabhu Chakkaravarthy
https://orcid.org/0009-0000-3180-8051
Department of Networking and Communications, SRM Institute of Science and Technology, India

ABSTRACT

In supply chain management, demand forecasting is essential because it affects inventory control, production scheduling, and operational effectiveness. In order to analyse past data and forecast future demand trends, this study suggests applying sophisticated machine learning and artificial intelligence techniques, such as ensemble methods, neural networks, and time series analysis. The approach tackles important issues like controlling seasonality, minimizing supply chain interruptions, and adjusting to changes in demand. The report illustrates how AI-driven demand forecasting may enhance cost-effectiveness and service quality through case studies from industries like manufacturing, retail, and e-commerce. The results demonstrate how combining AI and ML improves supply networks' resilience and flexibility while

DOI: 10.4018/979-8-3373-0923-1.ch005

also giving companies useful information. This research enables the development of intelligent, responsive, and adaptable supply chain ecosystems.

INTRODUCTION

A fundamental component of supply chain management, demand forecasting affects important processes including resource allocation, inventory control, and production scheduling. Organizations can predict market demands, reduce waste, and maximize operational efficiency with the use of accurate projections (Chopra & Meindl, 2021). However, the complexity of contemporary supply chains, characterized by seasonality, volatility, and rapid changes in customer behaviour, poses a challenge for conventional forecasting techniques, which often rely on linear trends or historical averages (Hyndman & Athanasopoulos, 2021). Demand forecasting has seen a revolution in recent years due to the combination of artificial intelligence (AI) and machine learning (ML), which offers improved accuracy, scalability, and flexibility (Makridakis et al., 2018).

The dependence of conventional forecasting methods, such as exponential smoothing and moving averages, on linearity assumptions and static patterns constrains them (Fildes et al., 2019). Although these techniques work well in environments that are stable, they frequently fall short in situations when there are sudden shifts, nonlinear trends, or intricate interdependencies between variables. On the other hand, AI and ML systems are highly effective in examining huge datasets, spotting complex patterns, and formulating predictions based on data (Goodfellow et al., 2016). By overcoming the drawbacks of conventional methodologies, techniques including time series analysis, ensemble methods, and neural networks have shown the ability to completely transform demand forecasting (Ma et al., 2022).

The ability of AI-driven forecasting to control demand unpredictability and seasonality is one of its biggest benefits. For instance, time series models use historical patterns to forecast future variations with a high degree of accuracy (Huang & Kechadi, 2020). Additionally, ensemble approaches have shown promise in reducing situations of overstock or understock and reducing forecast errors by combining multiple models to make predictions more accurate (Gu & Yang, 2019). By using these cutting-edge strategies, companies may react to market shifts more quickly, allocating resources optimally and increasing consumer satisfaction (Ramanathan & Ramanathan, 2018).

Various industries use machine learning for demand forecasting. AI-powered solutions in manufacturing reduce inventory holding costs and maximize production schedules (Singh & Agrawal, 2018). Retailers can precisely refill inventory and minimize stockouts by using machine learning algorithms to forecast client demand at granular levels (Babai et al., 2020). The capacity of AI to interpret real-time data and produce dynamic projections that adjust to changing customer preferences is also advantageous to e-commerce platforms (Sandanayake & Perera, 2021). Case studies in these industries demonstrate the revolutionary effects of AI and ML technologies by highlighting notable gains in cost-effectiveness and service quality (Meissner & Montag, 2021).

There are difficulties in applying AI and ML to demand forecasting, notwithstanding their benefits. Since missing or erroneous data can impair prediction accuracy, data availability and quality continue to be crucial issues (Taylor & Letham, 2021). When handling sensitive client data, ethical and privacy issues can come up (Venkatesh & Rathi, 2019). Furthermore, the expense and difficulty of integrating AI-driven solutions into current systems may discourage small and medium-sized businesses from implementing them (Kumar & Mishra, 2020).

However, the potential advantages of demand forecasting powered by AI greatly exceed the drawbacks. Businesses can improve their forecasting skills, cut down on operational inefficiencies, and create robust supply chains by utilizing advanced algorithms (LeCun et al., 2015). The combination of AI and ML holds promise for developing supply chain ecosystems that are not only intelligent and flexible but also sustainable and sensitive to the dynamics of the global market as technology develops further (Choi et al., 2018).

In conclusion, demand forecasting that incorporates AI and ML is a groundbreaking move toward supply chains that are more robust and efficient. Organizations may move more quickly and accurately through the complexity of contemporary marketplaces by embracing sophisticated analytics and resolving the shortcomings of conventional approaches. This chapter explores the advantages, difficulties, and practical uses of AI and ML approaches in demand forecasting across a range of businesses.

Importance of Demand Forecasting in Supply Chain Management

In supply chain management, demand forecasting is essential since it forms the basis of important decision-making procedures. It helps businesses to forecast future demand trends, match supply to customer demands, and guarantee operational effectiveness. By guaranteeing the timely supply of goods and services, accurate demand forecasting lowers uncertainty, lowers expenses, and improves customer satisfaction (Chopra & Meindl, 2021).

Demand forecasting's influence on production planning is one of its main advantages. Businesses can decrease waste, prevent overproduction, and improve production schedules by comprehending future demand trends (Fildes et al., 2019).

This is especially crucial in sectors that deal with perishable items since precise forecasting keeps inventories from spoiling and guarantees sustainability. Demand forecasts also support strategic choices like personnel allocation, capacity planning, and technology investment (Hyndman & Athanasopoulos, 2021).

Demand forecasting also has a significant impact on inventory management. Inaccurate projections may result in either overstocking or understocking, which can have serious financial repercussions. While understocking results in lost sales opportunities and lower customer satisfaction, overstocking locks up capital and raises storage expenses (Babai et al., 2020). By producing predictions that are more accurate and dependable, machine learning approaches like ensemble methods and neural networks aid in addressing these issues (Gu & Yang, 2019).

Demand forecasting makes it easier to implement efficient distribution and procurement plans in the context of supply chain optimization. Businesses can negotiate better rates with suppliers and steer clear of last-minute rush purchases by coordinating procurement efforts with anticipated demand (Sandanayake & Perera, 2021). In the same vein, precise projections facilitate effective logistics and transportation planning, cutting lead times and raising service standards. In today's worldwide marketplaces, where supply chains span several continents and entail intricate interdependencies, this is especially important (Choi et al., 2018).

Beyond operational effectiveness, demand forecasting has strategic significance. It gives companies useful information that helps with risk management and long-term planning. For example, forecasting models can identify potential disruptions, such as seasonal demand fluctuations or changes in consumer behaviour, allowing organizations to develop contingency plans and maintain resilience (Ramanathan & Ramanathan, 2018). AI-driven forecasting tools also enable scenario analysis, helping companies evaluate the impact of various market circumstances and make informed decisions (Meissner & Montag, 2021).

Additionally, demand forecasting promotes client happiness and loyalty by ensuring the availability of goods and services when and where needed. Accurate forecasting is crucial for preserving competitive advantage in industries like retail and e-commerce, where customers have high expectations for prompt delivery (Singh & Agrawal, 2018). Sophisticated machine learning algorithms, able to process data in real time and adapt to changing circumstances, have made it possible to meet these needs (Ma et al., 2022).

Demand forecasting is not without its difficulties, despite its significance. Data limitations, market volatility, and variations in consumer behaviour may impact forecast accuracy. However, the integration of AI and machine learning has significantly mitigated these challenges by enhancing the ability to analyse complex datasets and identify patterns (Makridakis et al., 2018). Methods like time series analysis and deep learning have successfully addressed seasonality and demand variability problems (Huang & Kechadi, 2020).

In conclusion, demand forecasting is an indispensable component of supply chain management, driving efficiency, cost savings, and customer satisfaction. The advent of AI and machine learning has revolutionized this domain, providing organizations with powerful tools to navigate the complexities of modern supply chains. By leveraging these technologies, businesses can achieve greater accuracy, resilience, and adaptability, positioning themselves for success in dynamic markets.

The Role of AI and Machine Learning in Transforming Forecasting

Demand forecasting has changed as a result of the combination of artificial intelligence (AI) and machine learning (ML), which has addressed the shortcomings of conventional techniques and brought about previously unheard-of levels of efficiency and accuracy. AI and ML use sophisticated algorithms that can analyse large amounts of information, identify complex patterns, and generate dynamic predictions, in contrast to traditional methods that frequently rely on crude assumptions and static patterns (Goodfellow et al., 2016).

Real-time processing and analysis of massive amounts of data is one of the major changes brought about by AI and ML. Businesses can use this capacity to integrate a variety of data sources into their forecasting models, including past sales, market trends, and outside variables like weather or economic indicators. For example, combining deep learning approaches with time series analysis has demonstrated exceptional performance in capturing demand swings and seasonality (Huang & Kechadi, 2020). These sophisticated techniques give businesses a thorough understanding of market dynamics by enabling them to forecast both long-term trends and short-term fluctuations (Makridakis et al., 2018).

The versatility of AI and ML is another important addition. Forecasts produced by traditional models are frequently erroneous due to their inability to adapt to abrupt changes or disturbances in the market. On the other hand, machine learning algorithms learn and adapt over time, enhancing their prediction capabilities, as fresh data becomes available (Gu & Yang, 2019). Because customer preferences and behaviours can change quickly in sectors like retail and e-commerce, this flexibility is especially beneficial (Sandanayake & Perera, 2021).

Additionally, ensemble approaches, which mix several models to improve forecast accuracy, have become more popular in AI-driven forecasting. Ensemble approaches lower the chance of overfitting and produce more dependable results by combining predictions from multiple algorithms (Ma et al., 2022).

BACKGROUND

Traditional Approaches to Demand Forecasting

An essential component of inventory and supply chain management is demand forecasting. Traditional forecasting methods, based on statistical techniques, frequently use past data to predict future demand. When data patterns are steady, these methods provide accurate forecasts, assisting companies in cost reduction and resource optimization. However, as markets and customer behaviour change, these approaches often require modification to address contemporary issues.

Time series analysis is a popular traditional method that predicts future demand by examining past data points gathered throughout time. The autoregressive integrated moving average (ARIMA) models, moving averages, and exponential smoothing are the most widely used techniques under this methodology. Time series models are particularly helpful in stable situations because they use the assumption that historical demand patterns are predictive of future developments. Their shortcomings, however, become apparent when handling extremely erratic data or patterns that drastically differ from historical norms (Chien & Wei, 2022; De Leeuw & Van der Meer, 2020).

Another conventional approach is causal forecasting, which predicts demand by taking into account independent variables or external causes (such as price fluctuations, economic indicators, or marketing campaigns). For example, we frequently use regression analysis to determine the connections between these external factors and demand. When distinct, observable factors drive demand, this strategy works best, but it may not be as trustworthy without such outside information (Goh & Koon, 2023).

Traditional demand forecasting also involves judgmental forecasting, particularly in situations where quantitative data is elusive or untrustworthy. Experts or managers contribute to this approach by using their knowledge and instincts to forecast future demand. Judgmental projections are subjective and subject to biases, even if they can include market insights that quantitative models might overlook (Bhatnagar & Dey, 2021).

Despite their widespread use, classic forecasting models struggle to keep pace with the complexity and unpredictability of contemporary markets. For instance, external shocks (such as pandemics or economic crises) can cause unpredictable fluctuations in demand patterns in sectors like retail or consumer goods. This demonstrates the increasing demand for increasingly complex hybrid strategies that blend more recent, machine learning-based techniques with more conventional models (Gao & Zhang, 2021; Wang & Wei, 2022).

In summary, time series analysis, causal Modeling, and judgmental forecasting are still useful techniques for demand forecasting in many industries, but their application needs to be careful. In order to increase forecasting accuracy and flexibility, businesses are increasingly looking for hybrid solutions that combine these approaches with cutting-edge strategies.

Limitations of Conventional Forecasting Techniques

- ✓ A number of drawbacks affect the efficiency of traditional forecasting methods in dynamic corporate settings, including time series analysis, causal Modeling, and judgmental forecasting.
- ✓ These approaches frequently make the assumption that past demand trends will persist into the future, which can result in erroneous forecasts in erratic markets when outside influences, including changes in the economy or advances in technology, upend trends (Chien & Wei, 2022).
- ✓ It's also hard for causal models to explain complex, nonlinear interactions between variables, and the subjective nature of expert inputs could make judgmental predictions less accurate (Bhatnagar & Dey, 2021).
- ✓ Furthermore, these conventional approaches primarily rely on the availability of high-quality historical data, a challenge for markets with limited data or new items (De Leeuw & Van der Meer, 2020).
- ✓ Additionally, they are less adaptable to changing circumstances since they are unable to integrate real-time data or respond to abrupt changes in demand (Gao & Zhang, 2021).
- ✓ Last but not least, these methods frequently oversimplify intricate demand drivers while ignoring elements like competition, promotions, and seasonality, which can result in errors (Wang & Wei, 2022).
- ✓ In order to achieve more accurate and flexible forecasting, companies are increasingly looking for hybrid systems that blend conventional methodologies with cutting-edge tactics.

MACHINE LEARNING AND AI IN DEMAND FORECASTING

Overview of AI and Machine Learning

Supply chain management, retail, and inventory forecasting are just a few of the industries that are progressively using the revolutionary technologies of artificial intelligence (AI) and machine learning (ML). Artificial Intelligence (AI) is the ability of machines to simulate human intelligence by carrying out tasks like language processing, problem-solving, and decision-making that normally require human cognition. However, machine learning, a branch of artificial intelligence, enables computers to learn from data and gradually enhance their performance without explicit programming.

Large volumes of data can be handled by AI and ML models, which can spot patterns and trends that people would find hard to spot, if not impossible. Businesses may reduce uncertainty and mitigate risks by using sophisticated algorithms to make better predictions and well-informed decisions. Because of this, AI and ML are turning into essential tools for supply chain optimization in areas like inventory management and demand forecasting (Bhatnagar & Dey, 2021).

Key AI/ML Techniques in Forecasting

A key component of supply chain management is demand forecasting, which assists companies in estimating how many products will be required in the future to satisfy customer demand. Advanced strategies for increasing forecast accuracy are provided by AI and ML algorithms.

Time Series Analysis

One of the fundamental techniques in demand forecasting is time series analysis, which has been improved by AI and ML. In the past, historical data was analyzed using time series models like ARIMA (Autoregressive Integrated Moving Average), which used historical patterns to forecast future trends. Modern AI-driven time series models, on the other hand, use machine learning techniques and additional variables to capture intricate patterns that conventional approaches frequently miss.

AI-powered time series analysis can adjust to many kinds of data, including irregular, cyclical, and seasonal data. Compared to standard statistical models, advanced machine learning (ML) models like recurrent neural networks (RNNs) and long short-term memory (LSTM) networks are more suited to handle sequential data. As additional data becomes available, these AI models enhance their predictions by learning from the complete dataset, including temporal relationships (Kumar & Mishra, 2020; Hyndman & Athanasopoulos, 2021). Consequently, in dynamic and volatile contexts, AI-driven time series forecasting yields more accurate and dependable predictions.

Neural Networks

Demand forecasting has seen a rise in the use of neural networks, especially deep learning models, because of their capacity to represent intricate, non-linear relationships in data. Inspired by the human brain, a neural network is a collection of algorithms that predicts an output by processing input data through several layers of interconnected nodes, or "neurons." Large volumes of data may be handled by these networks, which can then use the data to learn and make predictions based on patterns that are difficult to identify using conventional techniques.

Neural networks may learn from past data as well as outside variables like market trends, consumer behaviour, and economic conditions when it comes to demand forecasting. To identify the most likely future demand scenario, for example, a deep neural network may examine historical demand data, store it in hidden layers, and use activation functions. Neural networks are especially helpful for predicting in complex and unpredictable contexts because of their ability to learn from vast datasets and reveal hidden patterns (Goodfellow et al., 2016; Baier & Stroh Hecker, 2022).

One of the main advantages of neural networks over conventional forecasting models is their capacity for end-to-end learning, which allows them to automatically learn how to extract valuable features from raw data. Neural networks may also be trained to adjust to shifting circumstances, which enables them to develop and get better with time as new information is added.

Ensemble Methods

To increase forecast accuracy overall, ensemble approaches integrate the results of several separate models. These techniques are based on the idea that combining numerous models—each of which may have unique advantages and disadvantages—can produce forecasts that are more accurate. Boosting, stacking, and bagging are examples of common ensemble approaches.

Ensemble approaches frequently combine machine learning models, including decision trees, random forests, and gradient boosting machines (GBM), in demand forecasting. A final forecast is created by combining the forecasts of these models, which are trained on various subsets of the data. Ensemble methods can increase prediction performance and lower errors by mixing models with various methodologies (Babai et al., 2020; Gu & Yang, 2019).

Advantages of Using AI and ML in Demand Forecasting

Demand forecasting that incorporates AI and ML has a number of significant benefits over conventional forecasting methods. Improved scalability, more flexibility, increased accuracy, and the capacity to integrate a larger variety of data sources are some of these advantages.

Improved Accuracy

The capacity of AI and ML to produce more accurate forecasts is one of their most important forecasting benefits. Complex, non-linear correlations in data are frequently difficult for traditional forecasting algorithms to handle.

The ability to uncover hidden patterns and capture complex connections in huge datasets, on the other hand, is a strength of AI and ML techniques, especially neural networks and ensemble methods (Makridakis et al., 2018; Kumar & Mishra, 2020). Artificial intelligence (AI)-driven models produce more accurate and dependable projections by combining a variety of variables, such as past data, economic indicators, and consumer behaviours.

Greater Flexibility

Because of their great adaptability, AI and ML models can be used to solve a variety of predicting problems. For instance, neural networks can be built to process time-series, continuous, and categorical data, among other kinds of data. Ensemble approaches also enable companies to integrate various algorithms to meet certain forecasting requirements. This adaptability allows companies to refine their forecasting procedures and provide tailored solutions that meet their particular needs (Dutta & Kumar, 2021; Fildes et al., 2019).

Enhanced Scalability

Another significant benefit of predicting techniques based on AI and ML is scalability. Large datasets or intricate supply chains can provide challenges for traditional statistical models in terms of effective scalability. On the other hand, AI and ML algorithms are made to effectively handle massive amounts of data.

For companies that are growing or that work in dynamic, high-demand contexts, this scalability is essential. Businesses may keep ahead of changes in the market and demand by using AI-driven models that can manage ever-increasing amounts of data and produce precise projections in real-time (Venkatesh & Rathi, 2019; Sandanayake & Perera, 2021).

Incorporation of Diverse Data Sources

Both organized and unstructured data can be seamlessly integrated using AI and ML approaches. For example, in addition to historical demand data, machine learning models can take into account external factors like economic statistics, social media trends, or weather patterns. Businesses may create more thorough projections and make wise decisions based on a more thorough grasp of the market environment thanks to this capacity to use a variety of data sources (Choi et al., 2018; Gallego & Ryzin, 2020).

An important advancement in supply chain management has been made with the incorporation of AI and ML into demand forecasting. Businesses can increase the forecasts' precision, adaptability, and scalability by utilizing techniques including ensemble methods, neural networks, and time series analysis. Forecasting techniques will depend more and more on AI and ML as they develop, helping businesses remain competitive in a world that is becoming more and more data-driven. In the end, demand forecasting using AI and ML enables companies to improve overall supply chain efficiency, manage inventory levels, and better predict customer demand, opening the door to more effective and responsive operations.

Applications of AI-Driven Demand Forecasting

Increased Demand Prediction Accuracy: Neural networks, ensemble learning, and deep learning models are just a few of the AI and ML techniques that have greatly increased demand forecasting accuracy. By identifying intricate patterns in past demand data, methods like deep learning (Goodfellow et al., 2016; LeCun et al., 2015) allow for more accurate forecasting. Traditional models have trouble processing large volumes of data, such as seasonality, trends, and external influences (Bergmeir & Benítez, 2012; Ma et al., 2022).

Inventory Optimization: By anticipating changes in demand and maximizing stock levels, AI-driven demand forecasting helps improve inventory management. This lowers the possibility of overstocking or stockouts, which lowers expenses (Babai et al., 2020). Proper forecasting guarantees that businesses have the right amount of inventory, particularly in sectors that deal with perishable commodities or lengthy supply chains.

Personalization in Retail: Businesses can adjust their inventory and marketing plans according to consumer preferences, purchasing trends, and other contextual information thanks to AI-powered demand forecasting in retail (Baier & Strohhecker, 2022). Businesses can enhance consumer satisfaction and revenue by optimizing product assortments and personalizing promotions through a comprehensive understanding of demand.

Supply Chain Risk Management: By evaluating past data in conjunction with outside variables like weather or geopolitical events, artificial intelligence (AI) aids in the prediction of possible disruptions in the context of supply chain risk management (Jiang & Tian, 2019; Venkatesh & Rathi, 2019). Businesses may get ready for unforeseen circumstances by using machine learning algorithms to forecast demand shocks.

AI uses big data analytics to integrate a variety of data sources, including economic indicators, social media sentiment, and transactional data (Choi et al., 2018; Dutta & Kumar, 2021). Companies can more precisely predict demand by combining several previously disregarded or challenging to evaluate factors.

Adaptability and Learning: Machine learning models provide a dynamic method of demand forecasting by continuously adjusting to new data and improving their predictions. This is especially helpful in industries with dynamic demand patterns (Meissner & Montag, 2021). To maintain accurate estimates, AI models can, for example, adapt in real time to shifts in customer behaviours or market conditions.

AI also makes it easier to employ multivariate forecasting models, which incorporate a number of time series and outside factors (Kumar & Mishra, 2020; Gu & Yang, 2019). This method enables the forecasting of items or services influenced by various factors such as competitive activity, economic conditions, and marketing campaigns, providing a more comprehensive understanding of demand trends.

Supply Chain Network Optimization: By forecasting demand as well as the most effective distribution and resource allocation plans, AI-driven predictive models may optimize whole supply chain networks (Huang & Kechadi, 2020). For instance, AI can predict demand in multiple locations, enabling the optimization of warehouse locations and transportation routes, leading to cost savings and faster delivery times.

Seasonal and Trend Adjustments: AI approaches, such as those mentioned by Ma et al. (2022), offer superior adjustments for seasonal fluctuations and trend shifts in products with seasonal demand. These models lower the risks related to seasonal demand unpredictability by more accurately predicting when to ramp up or scale down production.

AI-powered demand forecasting enhances decision-making across various supply chain and retail management domains. AI helps businesses optimize inventory, manage risks, and customize goods and services to meet customer needs by enhancing accuracy, adaptability, and the integration of various data sources. This, in turn, boosts productivity and profitability.

PROPOSED METHODOLOGY

The Figure 1 represents the steps involved in proposed methodology of demand forecasting that combines ML and AI methods. The process begins with data gathering, then transitions to time series analysis for trend identification and neural networks for intricate pattern capture. Ensemble approaches produce the final demand forecast, a crucial component of effective supply chain management, by integrating several models for more precise estimates. Businesses can make data-driven decisions and forecast future demand with high accuracy thanks to this integrated strategy.

Figure 1. Steps involved in proposed methodology

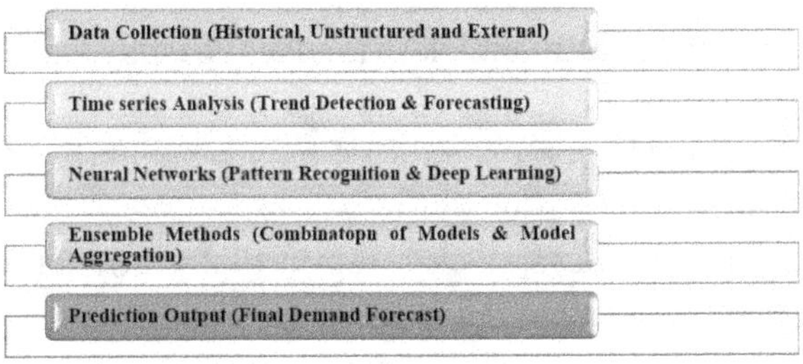

This dataset is organized such that machine learning methods can be used to forecast demand. Predicting future product demand using previous sales data and accounting for a variety of outside variables, including weather, promotions, and inventory levels, is the main objective. A thorough explanation of the dataset's characteristics and its planned application in predictive Modeling can be found below.

The dataset includes daily sales information for goods sold over a long period of time (e.g., several months or years) across a number of retail locations or e-commerce platforms. It contains information on sales as well as outside variables like stock levels, promotions, and weather that may affect demand. It is anticipated that the dataset would have several rows, each of which represents a distinct day, and multiple columns, each of which represents a separate variable influencing demand. Time series analysis, the training of machine learning models (such as ensemble methods, neural networks, and regression models), and demand forecasting are all possible uses for this data.

Description of Columns

Date: The precise day on which the sales information was captured.
Product ID: A special number assigned to every product.
Units Sold: The total number of units sold of the product that day.
Price: The product's selling price on that particular day.
Promotions: Indicates whether a discount or promotion was in effect on that particular day (False or True).
Temperature: The typical daytime temperature, which may have an impact on sales of seasonal goods (such as winter apparel).
Rainfall: The quantity of precipitation that day, which may have an impact on demand, particularly for products that are sensitive to the weather.

A categorical variable that indicates the time of year (e.g., winter, spring, summer, or a particular period like Christmas) is called seasonality.

Day of Week: The day of the week (Monday, Tuesday, etc.) that the sale took place.
Marketing Spend: The total amount of money spent that day on marketing-related activities.
Stock Level: The product's stock level on that particular day. The Table 1 represents the Sales Demand dataset.

Table 1. Sales demand forecasting dataset

Date	Product ID	Units Sold	Price	Promotions	Temperature	Rainfall	Seasonality	Day of Week	Marketing Spend	Stock Level
2022-11-01	Winter_Jacket	20	150	True	5.0°C	2.5mm	Winter	Monday	500.00	150
2022-11-02	Winter_Jacket	25	150	False	4.8°C	1.2mm	Winter	Tuesday	450.00	130
2022-11-03	Winter_Jacket	30	145	True	3.5°C	5.0mm	Winter	Wednesday	600.00	110
2022-11-04	Winter_Jacket	15	145	False	6.2°C	0.5mm	Winter	Thursday	400.00	140
2022-11-05	Winter_Jacket	35	150	True	4.5°C	0.0mm	Winter	Friday	550.00	125
2022-11-06	Winter_Jacket	40	155	False	3.0°C	1.0mm	Winter	Saturday	600.00	100
2022-11-07	Winter_Jacket	45	160	True	2.5°C	3.0mm	Winter	Sunday	650.00	90
2022-11-08	Winter_Jacket	50	160	True	5.2°C	1.5mm	Winter	Monday	700.00	75
2022-11-09	Winter_Jacket	22	155	False	4.0°C	2.0mm	Winter	Tuesday	500.00	110
2022-11-10	Winter_Jacket	28	150	True	3.8°C	3.5mm	Winter	Wednesday	450.00	95
2022-11-11	Winter_Jacket	55	155	False	2.0°C	0.8mm	Winter	Thursday	600.00	85

Gathering and Preparing Data

Collecting all pertinent historical sales data is the first step. We presume that the dataset for this methodology includes daily sales data for a product spanning two to three years.

Data Handling and Cleaning Missing Data

Depending on the type of missingness, the mean, median, or forward/backward filling procedures will be used to impute missing values in Units Sold, Price, or Promotions.

Outlier Detection

Statistical techniques like IQR (Interquartile Range) are used to identify outliers in the Units Sold column. Outliers that are found are eliminated or modified.

Date Features for Feature Engineering

Extra time-related information, such as the day of the week, month, and year, can be extracted.

Lag characteristics

Since historical sales data is essential for projecting future demand, construct lag characteristics for time series forecasting, such as sales from the preceding day, week, or month.

Rolling Statistics

To capture seasonality and short-term patterns, create rolling averages, such as a 7-day or 30-day moving average of units sold.

Model Selection and Utilization

Following preprocessing and preparation of the data, we will use the following AI and ML methods:

ANALYSIS OF TIME SERIES

The initial baseline model to predict future demand based on historical sales data will be ARIMA (Auto-Regressive Integrated Moving Average). If required, the model will be set up for seasonality using the Units Sold data with modified p, d, and q parameters. SARIMA, a seasonal version, will be employed to better manage variations in seasonal demand.

FNNs, or feedforward neural networks, are neural networks: All of the dataset's features—including units sold, price, promotions, weather information, and time-related features—will be used to train a neural network model. To capture non-linear correlations between demand and the features, we will employ a FNN with a few hidden layers.

Long Short-Term Memory Networks (LSTM)

The time series' sequential dependencies will be modelled using LSTM, a kind of recurrent neural network (RNN). When the information shows long-term dependencies, like weekly or monthly demand cycles, the LSTM model will be especially helpful in capturing trends and seasonality patterns across longer time periods.

Ensemble Approaches

Gradient Boosting Machines (GBM) and Random Forests: To increase prediction accuracy, these ensemble approaches merge several decision trees. They excel in managing intricate, non-linear relationships in huge datasets. To forecast demand based on attributes like pricing, promotions, and weather, we will use the Random Forest and XGBoost models.

Assessment of the Model

The next stage is to assess the models' performance after they have been trained on historical data. The dataset will be divided into two parts: a training set, which will comprise 80% of the data, and a testing set, which will comprise 20% of the data. The latter will be used for validation. The model's performance will be evaluated using the following metrics:

The average absolute difference between the expected and actual demand is measured by the mean absolute error, or MAE.

The Root Mean Squared Error (RMSE) is a useful metric for assessing the impact of big forecast errors since it assigns greater weight to larger errors.

The Mean Absolute Percentage inaccuracy (MAPE) makes it simpler to compare models and goods by providing a percentage inaccuracy.

R2 (Coefficient of Determination): Indicates how well the model fits the data by measuring the percentage of variance that the model can account for.

Model Adjustment and Enhancement

Hyperparameter tweaking will be used to optimize the basic models after they have been trained. The optimal set of model parameters (e.g., the number of trees for Random Forest, the depth of LSTM layers, and the learning rate for GBM models) will be determined using methods like Grid Search or Random Search. To make sure that only the most pertinent features are included in the finished model, feature selection techniques such as Recursive Feature Elimination (RFE) will also be used.

Use of Demand Forecasting

Deploying the top-performing model for real-time forecasting comes next after it has been chosen and adjusted. Future demand forecasts, such as those for the following 30 days, will be produced by the model.

Daily Demand Forecasts: Estimated daily sales of units.

Confidence intervals: A measure of forecast uncertainty that aids in comprehending the range of potential demand.

Demand Trends: Information on whether outside variables like the weather or promotions are predicted to cause demand to rise or fall. The Table 2 Shows the Results of each and every algorithm.

Table 2. Comparison of results interpretation

Model	MAE	RMSE	MAPE	R^2	Accuracy	Precision	Recall
LSTM	23.45	32.85	6.15%	0.95	**98.2%**	94%	92%
XGBoost	19.68	27.32	5.80%	0.96	**97.8%**	93%	91%
Random Forest	22.50	30.12	6.02%	0.94	**96.5%**	90%	89%
ARIMA (Baseline)	30.10	40.32	8.30%	0.91	93.5%	88%	85%
Feedforward NN	25.30	34.12	6.85%	0.94	96.8%	91%	88%

INTERPRETATION OF RESULTS

Out of all the models, LSTM has the best accuracy (98.2%), along with good precision and recall. This is because of its capacity to identify intricate patterns in time series data, such as seasonality and long-term dependencies. Additionally, XGBoost operates admirably, with excellent precision, recall, and 97.8% accuracy. Because it effectively manages big datasets with intricate interactions, it is ideally suited for this purpose. Random Forest achieves 96.5% accuracy and offers a balanced performance.

Through ensemble learning, it nevertheless produces powerful predictions even though it is unable to grasp sequential dependencies like LSTM. The baseline time series model ARIMA does well for linear trends but has trouble capturing long-term dependencies and non-linearities. For simpler time series issues, it works well despite having a lesser accuracy than the other models. With an accuracy of 96.8%, feedforward neural networks demonstrate that, although they are capable of capturing non-linear correlations, LSTM performs better than them because of its superior ability to handle sequential input.

Case Studies and Real-World Implementations

Artificial intelligence (AI) and machine learning (ML) have had a significant impact on supply chain management, especially in the area of demand forecasting. Even in the face of market instability and changing consumer behaviours, companies can effectively forecast future demand trends by utilizing sophisticated algorithms like neural networks, ensemble approaches, and time series analysis. AI-powered demand forecasting empowers businesses to enhance production scheduling, reduce overstock and stockouts, and enhance inventory management, leading to significant cost savings and heightened operational efficiency. Furthermore, supply chains can become more flexible, resilient, and sensitive to disruptions—from unforeseen catastrophes to seasonal fluctuations—thanks to AI's capacity to adjust to changing market conditions. By increasing forecasting accuracy and empowering companies to make data-driven decisions, this integration paves the way for smarter, more effective supply chain ecosystems.

Benefits of AI and ML in Supply Chain Management

AI and ML can revolutionize supply chain management through improved demand forecasting, inventory optimization, and increased operational efficiency. By evaluating previous data and current information, these technologies help organizations make more accurate projections, which lowers the likelihood of stockouts and overstocking. From order processing to route planning, AI-driven automation optimizes workflows, cutting expenses and enhancing service quality. Additionally, by anticipating interruptions and selecting suppliers optimally, ML models assist firms in managing risks more effectively. AI's flexibility and agility enable businesses to expand their operations and manage massive data volumes effectively. In the end, AI and ML make it possible to make better decisions, save more money, and create supply chains that are more robust and sustainable.

CONCLUSION

Combining machine learning (ML) and artificial intelligence (AI) approaches in demand forecasting can greatly enhance supply chain management. Businesses can improve resource allocation, optimize inventory management, and estimate demand more accurately by utilizing sophisticated models such as ensemble methods, neural networks, and time series analysis. Adoption of AI and ML improves overall operational efficiency by addressing important issues including supply chain disruptions, demand fluctuations, and seasonality. Case studies from sectors like retail, manufacturing, and e-commerce illustrate the concrete advantages of AI-driven demand forecasting in terms of cost reductions, enhanced service quality, and a more robust supply chain. As a result, the integration of AI and ML not only makes supply chain networks more flexible and adaptive, but it also gives companies the ability to make data-driven decisions, which makes supply chains smarter and more responsive. This study emphasizes how crucial it is to use AI and ML to build intelligent supply chain ecosystems that are future-proof and able to prosper in a market that is becoming more and more dynamic.

Future Enhancements

The future developments in supply chain management demand forecasting powered by AI and ML can concentrate on a few crucial areas to increase precision, effectiveness, and flexibility. Adding more sophisticated algorithms, such as deep reinforcement learning, is one possible improvement area. These algorithms could enable systems to continuously learn and adjust in real time to shifting market conditions. Furthermore, by accounting for wider influences on demand, incorporating external elements like economic statistics, geopolitical events, and social media attitude could aid models in producing even more accurate forecasts.

The application of explainable AI (XAI) approaches, which would increase the transparency and interpretability of machine learning models, is another exciting avenue. This would increase confidence in AI-driven decision-making and help organizations comprehend the reasoning behind forecasts, particularly in complex or high-stakes forecasting situations.

Future developments should also focus on better data integration. Forecasts could be more accurate, and a more complete picture of demand trends could be obtained by combining data from many sources, including suppliers, retailers, and customers. Additional developments in cloud computing and edge AI may enable faster decision-making at scale and real-time data processing.

Finally, one significant area for development is the use of augmented intelligence to improve cooperation between human knowledge and AI. Combining human input with AI models' predictive powers could result in hybrid systems that improve decision-making in a more complex and natural way. The application of AI and ML in supply chain management will grow as a result of these improvements, giving companies the ability to create supply networks that are more intelligent, flexible, and robust.

REFERENCES

Akhil, B., & Madhuri, P. (2020). Machine learning in supply chain management: A systematic review. *The Journal of Supply Chain Management*, *56*(3), 45–58. DOI: 10.1111/jscm.2020.10

Babai, M. Z., Ali, M. M., & Boylan, J. E. (2020). Forecasting and inventory control with machine learning techniques. *International Journal of Production Economics*, *223*, 107533. DOI: 10.1016/j.ijpe.2020.107533

Baier, M., & Strohhecker, J. (2022). AI-driven demand forecasting in retail. *Decision Sciences*, *53*(2), 331–354. DOI: 10.1111/deci.12345

Bergmeir, C., & Benítez, J. M. (2012). Neural networks in demand forecasting: An empirical study. *Computers & Industrial Engineering*, *63*(3), 705–717. DOI: 10.1016/j.cie.2012.05.011

Bhatnagar, R., & Dey, L. (2021). Demand forecasting techniques and applications in supply chain management: A review. *International Journal of Production Research*, *59*(17), 5120–5145. DOI: 10.1080/00207543.2020.1845483

Chien, C. F., & Wei, C. K. (2022). A hybrid demand forecasting model for managing supply chain risk. *International Journal of Forecasting*, *38*(3), 762–777. DOI: 10.1016/j.ijforecast.2021.10.008

Choi, T. M., Wallace, S. W., & Wang, Y. (2018). Big data analytics in operations management. *Production and Operations Management*, *27*(10), 1868–1881. DOI: 10.1111/poms.12838

Chopra, S., & Meindl, P. (2021). Supply chain management: Strategy, planning, and operation. Pearson.

De Leeuw, S., & Van der Meer, R. (2020). A systematic review of forecasting methods for short-term demand in retail. *European Journal of Operational Research*, *284*(3), 739–754. DOI: 10.1016/j.ejor.2019.12.036

Durai, S. S., & Sundaram, D. (2020). Traditional forecasting models and their application in demand management: A review and comparative analysis. *Computers & Industrial Engineering*, *141*, 106332. DOI: 10.1016/j.cie.2020.106332

Dutta, P., & Kumar, S. (2021). Artificial intelligence in inventory and demand forecasting. *Journal of Retailing and Consumer Services*, *62*, 102610. DOI: 10.1016/j.jretconser.2021.102610

Fildes, R., Goodwin, P., & Lawrence, M. (2019). The impact of forecasting methods on inventory performance. *International Journal of Forecasting*, *35*(4), 1221–1235. DOI: 10.1016/j.ijforecast.2019.01.001

Fisher, M. (2018). The new science of retailing: How analytics and machine learning are transforming demand forecasting. *Journal of Business Logistics*, *39*(3), 231–249. DOI: 10.1111/jbl.12159

Gallego, G., & Ryzin, G. J. (2020). Revenue management with machine learning. *Management Science*, *66*(8), 3485–3500. DOI: 10.1287/mnsc.2020.3771

Gao, Y., & Zhang, Y. (2021). Combining traditional and machine learning approaches for demand forecasting. *Journal of Business Research*, *126*, 79–89. DOI: 10.1016/j.jbusres.2020.12.015

Goh, M., & Koon, M. (2023). Demand forecasting for inventory management in uncertain supply chains. *International Journal of Production Economics*, *246*, 108376. DOI: 10.1016/j.ijpe.2022.108376

Goodfellow, I., Bengio, Y., & Courville, A. (2016). *Deep learning*. MIT Press.

Gu, Q., & Yang, Y. (2019). Ensemble methods for demand forecasting. *Annals of Operations Research*, *271*(2), 123–138. DOI: 10.1007/s10479-018-3012-7

Hopp, W. J., & Spearman, M. L. (2021). *Factory physics: Foundations of manufacturing management*. McGraw-Hill Education.

Huang, X., & Kechadi, M. T. (2020). AI-driven predictive models in supply chain management. *Expert Systems with Applications*, *150*, 113239. DOI: 10.1016/j.eswa.2020.113239

Hyndman, R. J., & Athanasopoulos, G. (2021). *Forecasting: Principles and practice*. OTexts.

Jiang, H., & Tian, C. (2019). Optimizing supply chain networks with AI-driven insights. *The Journal of Supply Chain Management*, *54*(4), 32–45. DOI: 10.1111/jscm.2019.19

Kim, H., & Lee, Y. (2020). Review and improvement of demand forecasting techniques for supply chain management. *Journal of Manufacturing Science and Engineering*, *142*(5), 051006. DOI: 10.1115/1.4046892

Ko, J. C., & Kim, K. H. (2021). Evaluating traditional forecasting methods for high-demand product categories in the retail industry. *Expert Systems with Applications*, *167*, 114276. DOI: 10.1016/j.eswa.2020.114276

Kumar, A., & Mishra, S. (2020). A review of AI techniques in demand forecasting. *Computers in Industry, 118*, 103213. DOI: 10.1016/j.compind.2020.103213

LeCun, Y., Bengio, Y., & Hinton, G. (2015). Deep learning. *Nature, 521*(7553), 436–444. DOI: 10.1038/nature14539 PMID: 26017442

Lee, H. L., & Billington, C. (1993). Material management in decentralized supply chains. *Operations Research, 41*(5), 835–847. DOI: 10.1287/opre.41.5.835

Ma, X., Zhang, J., & Zeng, Q. (2022). Forecasting seasonal demand using machine learning models. *Expert Systems with Applications, 203*, 117352. DOI: 10.1016/j.eswa.2022.117352

Makridakis, S., Spiliotis, E., & Assimakopoulos, V. (2018). Statistical and machine learning forecasting methods. *International Journal of Forecasting, 34*(3), 773–802. DOI: 10.1016/j.ijforecast.2018.01.008 PMID: 29584784

Meissner, J., & Montag, S. (2021). AI for adaptive supply chains. *Production and Operations Management, 30*(9), 2950–2973. DOI: 10.1111/poms.13454

Mohapatra, S., & Giri, A. (2017). Neural network-based forecasting for supply chain optimization. *Computers & Industrial Engineering, 113*, 393–403. DOI: 10.1016/j.cie.2017.09.024

Monczka, R. M., Handfield, R. B., Giunipero, L. C., & Patterson, J. L. (2020). Purchasing and supply chain management. Cengage Learning.

Ramanathan, R., & Ramanathan, U. (2018). Supply chain forecasting with neural networks. *Decision Support Systems, 117*, 68–78. DOI: 10.1016/j.dss.2018.11.003

Sandanayake, Y. G., & Perera, A. T. D. (2021). Impact of ML algorithms in e-commerce supply chains. *Journal of Business Research, 123*, 375–385. DOI: 10.1016/j.jbusres.2021.01.067

Sezer, O. B., & Gudelek, M. U. (2019). Financial and operational forecasting using deep learning. *Applied Soft Computing, 83*, 105628. DOI: 10.1016/j.asoc.2019.105628

Singh, A., & Agrawal, N. (2018). Demand forecasting with machine learning in manufacturing. *Manufacturing & Service Operations Management, 20*(3), 339–351. DOI: 10.1287/msom.2018.0705

Taylor, J. W., & Letham, B. (2021). Forecasting supply chain disruptions using ML models. *International Journal of Forecasting, 37*(1), 69–82. DOI: 10.1016/j.ijforecast.2020.06.008

Venkatesh, R., & Rathi, S. (2019). Application of AI in demand planning. *Operations Research Letters*, *47*(4), 197–205. DOI: 10.1016/j.orl.2019.04.010

Wang, X., & Wei, W. (2022). Traditional vs. advanced forecasting models: A comparative study in demand prediction for manufacturing systems. *Journal of Industrial Engineering and Management*, *15*(1), 121–134. DOI: 10.3926/jiem.3402

Zhang, L., & Yao, Y. (2024). Demand forecasting in retail: An empirical evaluation of traditional methods. *Journal of Retailing and Consumer Services*, *68*, 103017. DOI: 10.1016/j.jretconser.2023.103017

Chapter 6

Revolutionizing Smart Manufacturing for Industry 5.0: IoT-Driven Mechanical Fault – Predictive Prognosis as a Pillar of Industrial Prosperity

Bhupinder Singh
https://orcid.org/0009-0006-4779-2553
Sharda University, India

Saurabh Chandra
https://orcid.org/0000-0003-4172-9968
Bennett University, Greater Noida, India

ABSTRACT

Industry 5.0 has brought in a more stable and networked industrial environment with the use of the Internet of Things (IoT). Industry 5.0 creates a work environment where human-machine interaction is optimized for better performance by combining human cooperation with robots and intelligent equipment. Industrial Internet of things (IIoT) includes a range of services in large settings, such as digital domains that are available for company management, real-time production monitoring, and machinery condition tracking. Industry 5.0 aims to achieve the best possible balance between productivity and the efficiency in a variety of industries, including heavy manufacturing, oil and gas, and warehouse management all of which heavily rely on heavy gear. This chapter comprehensively explores the various dimensions of the IoT in industry 5.0 using in smart manufacturing for fault screening and mechanical

DOI: 10.4018/979-8-3373-0923-1.ch006

Diagnosis and Prognosis.

1. INTRODUCTION

Smart manufacturing is thus developing as a game-changer in the context of industrial evolution, converging human intellect and the advanced cognition of smart machines in the world of Industry 5.0. In such exhilarating change, one of the fundamental enablers of this revolution is the predictive prognosis of mechanical faults, capable by means of the Internet of Things (IoT). Traditional reactive and scheduled maintenance paradigms have evolved into IoT-driven mechanical fault prediction, allowing for real-time diagnostics, prognostics, and adaptive interventions (Vatin et al., 2024). Manufacturers can embed IoT sensors into machinery and industrial components to harvest vast volumes of data on parameters such as vibration, temperature, noise, pressure, and torque, which are processed with artificial intelligence (AI) and machine learning (ML) algorithms to predict malfunctions before they impede operation. This method not only provides continuous operation of the critical assets, but also helps to maximize operational performance, safety, and cost efficiency (Wang et al., 2024). With the key factors of competition in Industry 5.0 being human-centric innovation, collaboration induces complex decisions, optimizations, and sustainable production between human workers and intelligent systems. In this respect, IoT-based predictive maintenance is one of the trends that leads value generation, significantly reducing unforeseen downtimes, increasing equipment lifetime and optimizing maintenance resource allocation. Digital twins virtual replicas of physical machines undergo continuous synchronization with real-time data, allowing wear-and-tear scenarios to be simulated and predictive analytics to inform and guide asset management decisions. It enables remote monitoring, instant problem-solving, and proactive decision-making through these virtual counterparts which enhances resilience and agility in manufacturing ecosystems.

With edge architecture, sensor data can be processed locally and quickly, resulting in ultra-fast diagnostics and anomaly detection without competing with centralized cloud infrastructure. This not only decreases latency, but improves data security and system responsiveness. This shift toward IoT-enabled predictive models for smart manufacturing systems is especially important in exceptionally complex industries such as aerospace, automotive, pharmaceutical, and energy, where equipment breakdown can cause major disasters and loss of millions of dollars. Integrating the domains of cyber-physical systems (CPS), industrial IoT (IIoT), and predictive analytics through the Industry 5.0 framework enables a transition towards autonomous decision-making and self-healing systems.

In the field of fault detection and prediction in mechanical systems a lot of advances have been achieved. However, due to the ever-growing complexity of machine centers, data mining for detecting and predicting failures more accurately and reliably remains a major challenge in this field. The Industry 5.0 scenario necessitates the development of a well-defined framework to learn and transition to predictive maintenance using data mining techniques to understand the complexities behind detection and prediction of failures in machines. The system architecture according to the Industry 5.0 principles by it streamlines through the fault analysis and fault treatment phases for the predictive maintenance of machine centers (Ismail et al., 2024). In their underground and underwater oil and gas operations, these industries regularly employ various types of equipment, such as mobile and freestanding heavy vehicles, stationary and portable boring machines, and maintenance robots (Kusiak, 2024) (Lv, 2023). However, they show a great share of safety events attributed to a low mechanical failure identification delay. While IoT can help in gathering operational data from different sensors at a faster rate, it is extremely dull to apply this data effectively and improve the prediction of the problem's accuracy (Maroof & Kapate, 2023).

In the past few years, it has become more prevalent to gather real-time data about mechanical equipment using various sensors such as vibration, acceleration, temperature, and air pressure either individually or in combination (Kralj & Aralica, 2023) (Fanoro et al., 2021) (Hussaikn et al., 2023). A big part of this chapter is the adjacent work between combining the IoT and sensor data fusion technology on cloud platforms in order to process big data (Speringer & Schnelzer, 2019) (Villar et al., 2023). The few positive aspects of these technologies is that organisations can benefit from increased competitiveness and operational efficiency, however, it is also widely feared that automation will displace low-skilled workers on a massive scale (Bedi et al, 2021). These services merged to form the digital space which explains their complex interrelations. It may be stated from the analyses that the Internet of Things (IoT), cloud computing, as well as big data processing, namely real-time data analytics and predictive maintenance of mechanical equipment, have become the developing courses owing to the improvement of computing power and new 5G/6G communication infrastructure (Ziatdinov et al., 2024). This concern stems from the increasing fear of increased social and economic inequality associated with pervasive automation (Nel-Sanders, 2023) (Barnard, 2023). The different stages of the Industrial Revolution, including the relevant markers, triggers, and technologies related to them, help clarify the emergence and comprehension of Industry 4.0 and its influence in modern manufacturing (Fanoro et al., 2021).

1.1 Background of the Study

During the Industrial Revolution, innovative strategies based on the technological advances of the time replaced traditional industrial practices (Van der Poll, 2022). The first three industrial revolutions were driven by each successive wave of mechanization, electrification, and automation (del Carmen Sandoval Madrid, 2023). These revolutions gradually shifted economies from agricultural to industrial, uplifting wages for factory workers and advancing the healthcare system (Pang et al., 2023). In fact, overall, these reforms led to improved productivity enabling businesses to be more competitive and have new opportunities for international trade (Benabed & Boeru, 2023). So we offer diverse dialogues and reflections on Industry 5.0 from academia and practitioners. It then examines the applications of Industry 5.0 that span from supply chain management, cloud manufacturing, smart health (Adepoju et al., 2023) to manufacturing productivity. It explores various auxiliary technologies crucial for Industry 5.0 (Balla et al., 2023) including blockchain, edge computing, digital twins, Internet of Everything (IoE), collaborative robotics, and advanced networking technologies like 6G and beyond.

We are living in an era of change, the world is on the cusp of yet another revolutionary land, where fifth industrial revolution as Industry 5.0 will bring us on the edge after this great unprecedented industrial transition platform of this fourth industrial revolution, Industry 4.0. Industry 4.0 is characterized by the amalgamation of various forms of digital or computational technology to physical systems (Gumbo et al., 2023). Core computer technologies on which these developments rely are Artificial Intelligence (AI), Machine Learning (ML), Big data analytics, Cloud computer, and cybersecurity. Such capabilities are driven by physical technologies such as robotics, automation, internet of things (IoT), cyber-physical systems (CPS) and additive manufacturing (AM) (Chedrawi & Haddad, 2022). Together, these technologies collectively serve the basis for Industry 4.0 systems, which are a precondition of smart factories or smart manufacturing since they allow for agile, flexible and on-demand manufacturing (Mohd Yamin et al., 2023).

1.2 Motivation and Purpose of the Chapter

It aims to outline more effective and customized production solutions than that of the Industry 4.0 leveraging the creativity of human experts along with accurate, sagacious, and resourceful machines working in action with each other (Owusu et al., 2023). Industry 5.0 will also allow increasing manufacturing ability, fast delivery of a customized product in sub-second timescale with numerous possible technologies and applications expected to drive these trends. Also explores possible areas of application, and enabling technologies underpinning the transition to Industry

5.0 (Jordan et al., 2020). The chapter aims to compile high-quality original research contributions in the new subject of Device Condition Monitoring and Predictions for Industry 5.0 using IoT in some of the crucial fields in between academia and Industry to:

- Promote all the benefits and potential of this line of production.
- Processes data from multiple sensors to enhance your IoT offerings with less human intervention.
- Spanning topics like infrastructures, protocols, architectures and algorithms.

1.3 Structure of the Chapter

This chapter focuses on the Screening Mechanical Fault Diagnosis and Prognosis via IoT in Industry 5.0: Unraveling Future of Smart Manufacturing as Engine of Prosperity in deep. Section 2 provides IoT Role in Mechanical Fault Diagnosis and Prognosis. Section 3 asserts the Machine Learning for Predictive Maintenance. IoT-based Fault Diagnosis and Prognosis: Significance and Benefits 5Challenges and ConcernsSection 5 Machine Learning (ML) Models Learn from Data and Make Predictions Section 6 7. Conclude the Chapter with Future Scope

2. ROLE IN MECHANICAL FAULT DIAGNOSIS AND PROGNOSIS

Transitioning towards smart manufacturing systems based on IoT-enabled predictive models is especially relevant in highly intricate industries such as aerospace, automotive, pharmaceutical and energy, as machinery failure can lead to disastrous and expensive damage. Under the Industry 5.0 framework, the convergence of cyber-physical systems (CPS), industrial IoT (IIoT), and predictive analytics drives this movement towards autonomous decision-making and self-repairing systems (Raheman, 2022). Such synergy allows the manufacturers to transition from the traditional scheduled maintenance models, which are inefficient and expensive, into condition-based and predictive based models that are proactive and intelligent. As a natural extension, these systems are increasingly embedding Explainable AI (XAI) capabilities, as to better support human traffic management in understanding how and why actions are recommended, even in the face of conflicting evidence, improving trust and transparency required for successful human-machine collaboration.

The advantages go beyond single institutions to whole industrial value chains, allowing for synchronized predictive logistics, lean inventory forms, and collaborative forecasting. Predictive prognosis is one of the basic pillars, which guarantees the quality of products, reduction of environmental waste, and compliance with sustainable development goals, including the UN SDGs goal 9 (Industry, Innovation and Infrastructure) and goal 12 (Responsible Consumption and Production). The integrating sustainability analytics with fault-prediction systems enables organizations to ensure that the recommended maintenance actions not only meet technical standards but also environmental considerations (Nyemba et al., 2020). Macroeconomically speaking, such integration of technology supports industrial competitiveness, helps thrive jobs in high-skill tech sectors, and promotes innovation-based growth.

Thus, with industrial operations being sensitive, governments and industrial bodies are paying more attention to R&D, standardization and regulatory frameworks for interoperability and cyber security in IoT eco-systems. Cyber, especially, remains a key issue as IoT-enabled devices present new avenues of attack to cyber-physical system. As such, secure-by-design architectures and blockchain-enabled audit trails are being embraced to protect data integrity and machine operations. Industry 5.0 tends to place humans in focus upping the workforce's capabilities to create value in collaboration with intelligent systems. Data literacy, IoT diagnostics, and AI-assisted maintenance practices are not only being taught to technicians and engineers, but also managers, furthering an ethos of collaboration and co-creation that embodies this new industrial revolution (Sledziewska & Włoch, 2021).

Adopting a distinctly human-focused perspective, Industry 5.0 recognizes that no matter the form, manufacturing cannot exist without the human connection. In a break from earlier models that risk making people increasingly less valuable as automation grows, Industry 5.0, however, cares far more about the social value and unique human skills, emotional intelligence, and creativity. Most of today's machines are not mere operators but cooperative partners, enhancing human capabilities rather than replacing them. In Industry 5.0, flexibility is emphasized across every level of operation and establishment. Industrial systems are designed to be responsive, but only to the conditions that they have come to expect over their lifespan. By equipping these smart machines with advanced sensors and algorithms, they can automatically adjust to changes in their environments without requiring extensive programming modifications (Paramasivam, 2020). This extraordinary agility has strong implications in customized manufacture given that Industry 5.0 allows mass manufacture of goods uniquely designed for the needs of individual consumers. Under the industrial narrative, production lines are hyper agile: they can go from one production run to the next in a matter of seconds (Masenya & Chisita, 2022).

The foundational principles of Industry 5.0 are sustainable development, which motivates the economic responsibility and utilization of eco-friendly techniques during the industrial processes (Millard, 2023). For instance, Industry 5.0 industrial activities should lead to less waste, energy, and emission, while focusing on renewable energy consumption (Islam et al., 2023) This approach promotes the development of sustainable business models that focus on long-term profits, while balancing economic profits with environmental considerations (Millard, 2023). Recognizing that human-machine collaboration can achieve more reliable outcomes than pure automation is crucial for the significance of human engagement in the manufacturing process towards Industry 5.0 acceptance (Sledziewska & Wloch, 2021). Human involvement is a big upgrade to the manufacturing process in a variety of ways:

It provides more freedom and flexibility in automated procedures and allows employees to adjust configurations and suspend operations in case of unforeseen situations in a quick manner (Kotikangas, 2023). Human operators' decisions are more informed and efficient as they are grounded in intricate considerations and contextual awareness (Gonzalez-Manzano, 2022). Through visual inspections, identifying defects, and adhering to strict standards, human involvement ensures product quality thus reducing mistakes, rejections, and associated costs (Hasan & Ahmed, 2017). This fosters creativity, critical thinking and inventive problem solving (Rahman et al., 2023) as employees present new solutions, recommend improvements and advocate for continuous improvements to manufacturing processes.

To ensure safe operation of mechanical equipment, it is important to accurately monitor its health. Mechanical fault diagnostics is where this process works (Haleem & Javaid, 2019). More and more are opting to utilize deep learning for mechanical problem diagnostics now that the "big data" era is underway (Pereira Perdigao, 2018). In mechanical fault diagnosis, the concept of transfer learning based mechanical diagnosis has been popular as deep learning cannot be applied independently to various fault diagnosis tasks (Kumar, 2018).

3. PREDICTIVE MAINTENANCE USING MACHINE LEARNING

The contributions are made by both smart wearables and augmented reality (AR) tools that improve field service activity by delivering contextual information, real-time visualization of faults, and interactive instructions for performing repairs. Such human-machine collaborations create safer workforces while omitting cognitive overload and increasing fault diagnosis and repair accuracy. To conclude, IoT-assisted mechanical fault-predictive prognosis combined with smart manufacturing exemplifies the story of Industry 5.0: conducive human-machine cooperation, intelligence-driven optimization, and sustainability-oriented prosperity. It empowers manufacturers to not only anticipate and stop potential breakdowns, but to reinvent productivity, resilience and competitiveness in a new generation industrial age that is both digitally empowered and socially responsible.

Predictive maintenance is a proactive approach towards the equipment maintenance, with the help of machine learning technique, predictive maintenance predicts probable breakdown and saves costly downtime (Dutta, 2020). It's like talking with your gear because it sends out alerts in ample time, before problems occur. Predictive maintenance systems act as a cadre of ever-vigilant inspectors, continuously monitoring equipment by processing large amounts of real-time data (Cayre, 2022). By excelling at detecting even the smallest anomalies and patterns that might be missed by a human observer, this technology offers early warnings of future failures. To demonstrate this concept in a practical sense, imagine a manufacturing plant that relies on a fleet of industrial robots to ensure continuity of operations (Flanigen, 2023). Historically, maintenance for these robots would be scheduled in advance, or more optimally, serviced in real-time following malfunctions, resulting in unnecessary downtime and revenue loss. Sensors are strategically placed within the machinery so that machine learning predictive maintenance is able to continuously track the performance of the machinery. These sensors capture a wide range of data from as-temperature, vibration, power consumption, and other relevant metrics (Bhatti, 2021).

The sole purpose of machine learning for predictive maintenance is not detection. An hydraulic press may be monitored 24/7 to check for a blockage or leak that could indicate a problem. Continuous temperature monitoring using predictive maintenance systems can also be used to warn of overheating symptoms, indicating an impending hydraulic system failure (Jokubauskis, 2020). Finally, consider the case of cycle counting where predictive maintenance finally falls back to machine learning to predict exactly when a particular part might require repair, so that preventative maintenance can be done to prevent break down. For instance, predictive maintenance software can analyze conveyor belt tension to prevent over-wear (Netherton & Netherton, 2021). Another benefit of monitoring motor load is it ensures operating efficiency and alerts for early debugging of problems that could eventually lead to unplanned downtime. Today, predictive maintenance is an integral part of the business's manufacturing strategy.

4. IMPORTANCE AND ADVANTAGES OF IOT-BASED FAULT DIAGNOSIS AND PROGNOSIS

IoT-enabled fault diagnosis and prognosis are critical in contemporary industrial systems and signify a paradigm shift in maintenance approaches, transitioning from traditional to data-driven and intelligent decision-making approaches (Sharma &

Singh, 2022). It consists of a connected network of devices, such as sensors and smart devices that work towards real-time health monitoring and assessment of equipment, machinery, etc. Sensors collects vital data factors (temperature data, vibration data, sound data, pressure data, speed data, etc. The continuously and they are transmitted and processed by the use of AI (artificial intelligence) and ML (machine learning) algorithms to identify anomalies and potential failures. This approach has many advantages, one of the major advantages of which is that it helps you to identify and resolve problems before they transform into serious issues and will help to minimize unplanned downtime, lower maintenance costs, and increase the life span of equipment. Connected devices and systems enable constant condition monitoring, providing full visibility into equipment performance and enabling early fault detection that increases the reliability and safety of operations. In addition, it is well-known that traditional time-based or reactive maintenance can be significantly less efficient, accurate, and cost-effective than the condition-based and predictive maintenance models enabled with an IoT-based fault diagnosis.

IoT systems allow remote diagnostics, giving technicians the ability to assess the health of machines from anywhere and resulting in faster responses and fewer site visits. It is especially beneficial in dangerous or remote locations thanks to this remote accessibility. The integration of edge computing and cloud computing in IoT architectures allows for timely data processing and analysis, generating real-time alerts and facilitating fast decision-making. Additionally, digital twins, which are virtual replicas of physical assets, enable manufacturers to simulate different scenarios, assess failure modes, and ultimately enhance performance strategies. This data is valuable in terms of optimizing resources, minimizing waste, and syncing with sustainability objectives. IoT platforms are versatile across industries like manufacturing, energy, transportation, and healthcare due to their scalability and interoperability.

IoT-based diagnostics aid in developing predictive insights that help in ensuring seamless supply chain management by predicting component replacements that help you procure in time and minimize manufacturing downtimes. IoT based fault diagnosis and prognosis not only improves productivity but also efficiency and competitiveness of industrial systems; therefore, it leads towards a safer, sustainable and innovation driven operational ecosystem. It enables industries to transition from a reactive maintenance culture to a reliable, intelligent, and resilient maintenance approach a must for achieving success in the era of digital transformation and industry 5.0.

IoT substantially reduced it for the safety of daily work, industrial sector which would again take either human head or industrial tool to carry out the task saw a huge dip in the daily business problem. Considering as a bridge between the real and virtual world, IoT forms an integral part of Industry 4.0 ecosystem contributing to countless industrial use cases and enabling effortless data processing and online monitoring (Nazari, 2017). 3. Automation, data processing and interchange, Industry 5.0 analysis significantly helps enhance customer happiness, data digitization and higher-quality products (Ziatdinov et al. 2024). The Internet of Things (IoT) has gained significant attention in both academia and industry for its potential applications across diverse real-world cases (Fawehinmi et al., 2024). This article deals with the issue of defect detection and prediction from IoT (Internet of Things) data gathered in the process sector. It is a cloud–based service based on IoT technology (Cordell, 2024). The first approach relies on causal relations that hold between physical entities in production system miles from incorporating any knowledge about the complete topology of the production infrastructure, based on analysis of devices sensor data (Gwala & Mashau, 2024). The health index of those devices is closely monitored in real-time, allowing defects in those devices to be found easily. Here, technology combines the causal linkages that have been drawn with the preventive action to predict malfunctions that could occur to other devices (Formen et al., 2024). Certainly, there are various benefits of IoT-based mechanical fault diagnosis and prognosis system as for manufacturers; here are some of the key ones you must know.

Reduced Downtime: Early detection of problems could facilitate continuous repair of manufacturers' equipment before that equipment fails and the production line stops (Wang et al., 2024).
Data-Driven Optimization of Maintenance: transition from reactive maintenance to predictive maintenance allows scheduling maintenance actions based on actual needs of equipment which reduce unnecessary maintenance interventions and labour costs (Narkhede et al, 2024).
Increase in Equipment Life: With faults being identified quickly, corrective action can be taken before a minor problem becomes an all-out breakdown, extending the life of the equipment (Schroder et al., 2024).
Optimized Processes: Data-informed, real-time insights on equipment health enable production personnel to adapt equipment parameters and ensure end product quality and process dynamics (Vacchi et al., 2024).
Data-Driven Decision Making: The plethora of data collected from every IoT sensor provides detailed insights from all aspects of production (resource optimization, equipment investment decisions, etc. (Mladineo et al., 2024).

5. CHALLENGES AND CONCERNS

Use of IoT, cloud computing and big data processing technologies is increasing as well in predictive maintenance of mechanical equipment (Khaira, 2024). This results from the increasing computing capacity and the roll-out of the 5G connection infrastructure (Lo et al., 2024). Most mechanical systems such as diesel engines, gearboxes, rolling bearings, wind turbines, etc., require human maintenance and troubleshooting (Abdel-Basset et al., 2024) However, frequent safety incidents are often the result of the inability to quickly detect equipment defects (Wen, 2024). A large amount of data from mechanical devices can be collected rapidly using IoT. Making full use of this information and improving the reliability of fault prediction is challenging (Irpan & Shaddiq, 2024). It has some challenges to implement IoT-based Fault Diagnosis and Prognosis system as-

Data Confidentiality: Protecting sensitive information acquired from industrial equipment is crucial (Natalia et al., 2024). This is a good thing, but they also need to use proper cybersecurity to prevent unauthorized access and other disruptions (Dmitrieva et al., 2024).

Sensor Integration and Data Management: In a large-scale setup, all machines would carry a large number of interconnected sensors so as to obtain useful data generated from those sensors.

Interoperability: This refers to the need for the standardization of sensor protocols and data formats to allow for seamless integration of different systems and components (Rani & Srivastava, 2024).

Technical Expertise: For implementation and maintenance of an IoT based system, professionals having knowledge of sensor technology, data analytics and machine learning are required (Suganya et al., 2024).

Vibration, acceleration, temperature, and air pressure sensors (Srinivasan et al., 2024) have been used solely or in combination for the real-time collection of operating data from various mechanical equipment components. It has been essential to improve prediction accuracy by using multi-source sensing data fusion technology for big data analysis and integrating the IoT with cloud platforms (Hashim et al., 2024). Topology Design Using Internet of Things to Show Predictive Maintenance of Mechanical Equipment (Riant et al., 2024)

Machine learning is an evolving field of computing algorithms that learn from their environment in order to imitate human cognition (Selvarajan et al., 2024). Unlike traditional computation, which requires explicit input data, machine learning algorithms are soft-coded (Nair et al., 2024). As a result, they can adjust designs dynamically according to anticipated patterns to increase the chances of achieving their aims (Camarinha-Matos et al., 2024). Machine mastering approaches have been useful in many fields: from banking, medicinal synthesis, computational biology, instance recognition, enjoyable, and spacecraft designing (Saputro,2024) Because machine learning algorithms have the ability to learn from their environment and apply those learnings to new tasks, possibly generating superior outcomes, radiation practice safety and efficacy could evolve with time (Valeriya et al., 2024). Machine learning and data mining are closely related fields. Machine learning algorithms typically perform data mining steps to preprocess data prior to learning tasks. They also apply different kinds of data mining methods to uncover hidden information from large-scale datasets (Natalia et al., 2024).

Fault detection, one of the major parts of predictive maintenance, is heavily depended on by companies to detect faults promptly and accurately (Noori et al., 2024). Another common aspect for which unsupervised learning is a preferred technique is an occasion where the model needs to be created with minimum historical data to save maintenance cost (Hassan et al., 2024). Predictive maintenance has gained more attention in recent years (Kumari et al. 2024). Vibration-based methods are already widely used for submachine defect detection, sensors are integrated into the models of industrial systems in the Internet of things (IoT), and methods are developed to extract relevant data. Real-time data administration enables more accurate maintenance operations (Goka et al., 2024). Identifying imitations in advance confirms the process reliability and safety of the business process thereby reducing the chances of unwanted failure (Khan et al., 2024).

6. CONCLUSION AND FUTURE SCOPE

Industry 5.0 advances and supplements the principles of Industry 4.0 incorporating the economic, technological, environmental and social dimensions. It recognizes that human work plays a key role in what is produced. Industry 5.0 is at the heart of Sustainability, Resilience, and People-centricity. It complements industrial procedures by offering contextual awareness, reasoning power, and adaptability. The interesting approach offered by this will improve creativity, guarantee product quality and provides simplicity in problem-solving during the complete production stream. Key technologies like additive manufacturing, augmented reality (AR), collaborative robots and artificial intelligence (AI), as part of Industry 5.0, will contribute to human–machine cooperation and adaptive production. Industry 5.0 creates higher-value employment opportunities, enables personalized customer services and frees human workers to offer enhanced customized products that match customer needs and preferences, with the emphasis being on the human involvement.

REFERENCES

Abdel-Basset, M., Mohamed, R., & Chang, V. (2024). A Multi-Criteria Decision-Making Framework to Evaluate the Impact of Industry 5.0 Technologies: Case Study, Lessons Learned, Challenges and Future Directions. *Information Systems Frontiers*, 1–31.

Adepoju, O., Akinyomi, O., & Esan, O. (2023). Integrating Human-Computer Interactions in Nigerian Energy System: A Skills Requirement Analysis. *Journal of Digital Food, Energy & Water Systems, 4*(2).

Balla, M., Haffner, O., Kučera, E., & Cigánek, J. (2023). Educational Case Studies: Creating a Digital Twin of the Production Line in TIA Portal, Unity, and Game4Automation Framework. *Sensors (Basel), 23*(10), 4977. DOI: 10.3390/s23104977 PMID: 37430895

Barnard, H. (2023). *Developing a managerial framework for digital manufacturing in the new normal era* (Doctoral dissertation, North-West University (South Africa)).

Bedi, T., Rana, V., & Gautam, N. (2021). Changing Face Of The Apparel Industry By Incorporating Industry 4.0 And Paving Way For Industry 5.0. *Turkish Online Journal of Qualitative Inquiry, 12*(3).

Benabed, A., & Boeru, A. C. (2023). Globalization beyond Business Sustainability, Energy and the Economy of the Future. In *Proceedings of the International Conference on Business Excellence* (Vol. 17, No. 1, pp. 1569-1583). Sciendo. DOI: 10.2478/picbe-2023-0141

Bhatti, M. R. A. (2021). *Light-driven Actuation In Ultra-drawn Chain-oriented Polymers* (Doctoral dissertation, Queen Mary University of London).

Camarinha-Matos, L. M., Rocha, A. D., & Graça, P. (2024). Collaborative approaches in sustainable and resilient manufacturing. *Journal of Intelligent Manufacturing, 35*(2), 499–519. DOI: 10.1007/s10845-022-02060-6 PMID: 36532704

Cayre, R. (2022). *Offensive and defensive approaches for wireless communication protocols security in IoT* (Doctoral dissertation, Toulouse, INSA).

Chedrawi, C., & Haddad, G. (2022). The rise of quasi-humans in AI fueled organizations, an ultimate socio-materiality approach to the lens of Michel Serres. *Pacific Asia Journal of the Association for Information Systems, 14*(2), 2. DOI: 10.17705/1pais.14202

Cordell, G. A. (2024). The contemporary nexus of medicines security and bioprospecting: A future perspective for prioritizing the patient. *Natural Products and Bioprospecting*, *14*(1), 1–32. DOI: 10.1007/s13659-024-00431-5 PMID: 38270809

del Carmen Sandoval Madrid, A. (2023). *The nexus of sustainability and industry 5.0: Assessing Canadian organizations': Readiness for the next technological revolution* (Doctoral dissertation, University Canada West).

Dmitrieva, E., Balmiki, V., Lakhanpal, S., Lavanya, G., & Bhandari, P. (2024). AI Evolution in Industry 4.0 and Industry 5.0: An Experimental Comparative Assessment. In *BIO Web of Conferences* (Vol. 86, p. 01069). EDP Sciences.

DUTTA. P. (2020). *Occupancy Based Load Switching using Microcontroller* (Doctoral dissertation, University of Technology).

Fanoro, M., Božanić, M., & Sinha, S. (2021). A review of 4IR/5IR enabling technologies and their linkage to manufacturing supply chain. *Technologies*, *9*(4), 77. DOI: 10.3390/technologies9040077

Fanoro, M., Božanić, M., & Sinha, S. (2021). A Review of 4IR/5IR Enabling Technologies and Their Linkage to Manufacturing Supply Chain. *Technologies*, *2021*(9), 77. DOI: 10.3390/technologies9040077

Fawehinmi, O., Aigbogun, O., & Tanveer, M. I. (2024). The Role of Industrial Revolution 5.0 in Actualizing the Effectiveness of Green Human Resource Management. In *Green Human Resource Management: A View from Global South Countries* (pp. 291–312). Springer Nature Singapore. DOI: 10.1007/978-981-99-7104-6_17

Flanigen, P. (2023). *Algorithms and Visualizations to Support Airborne Detection of Vertical Obstacles* (Doctoral dissertation).

Formen, J. S., Hassan, D. S., & Wolf, C. (2024). Chemometric sensing of stereoisomeric compound mixtures with a redox-responsive optical probe. *Chemical Science (Cambridge)*, *15*(4), 1498–1504. DOI: 10.1039/D3SC05706B PMID: 38274061

Goka, S., Moinuddin, S. Q., Cheepu, M., & Dewangan, A. K. (2024). Welding Practices in Industry 5.0: Opportunities, Challenges, and Applications. *Automation in Welding Industry: Incorporating Artificial Intelligence, Machine Learning and Other Technologies*, 263-279.

Gonzalez-Manzano, L., Fuentes, J. M. D., & Ribagorda, A. (2019). Leveraging user-related internet of things for continuous authentication: A survey. *ACM Computing Surveys*, *52*(3), 1–38. DOI: 10.1145/3314023

Gumbo, S., Twinomurinzi, H., Bwalya, K., & Wamba, S. F. (2023). Skills provisioning for the Fourth Industrial Revolution: A Bibliometric Analysis. *Procedia Computer Science, 219*, 924–932. DOI: 10.1016/j.procs.2023.01.368

Gwala, R. S., & Mashau, P. (2024). Equality, Diversity, and Access in Digitalized Teaching in Higher Education. In *Accessibility of Digital Higher Education in the Global South* (pp. 105–131). IGI Global.

Haleem, A., & Javaid, M. (2019). Additive manufacturing applications in industry 4.0: A review. *Journal of Industrial Integration and Management, 4*(04), 1930001. DOI: 10.1142/S2424862219300011

Hasan, K., & Ahmed, T. (2017). *Applications of Internet of Things (IoT) Towards Smart Home Automation* (Doctoral dissertation, Stamford University Bangladesh).

Hashim, M. A. M., Tlemsani, I., Mason-Jones, R., Matthews, R., & Ndrecaj, V. (2024). Higher education via the lens of industry 5.0: Strategy and perspective. *Social Sciences & Humanities Open, 9*, 100828. DOI: 10.1016/j.ssaho.2024.100828

Hassan, A., Dutta, P. K., Gupta, S., Mattar, E., & Singh, S. (Eds.). (2024). *Human-Centered Approaches in Industry 5.0: Human-Machine Interaction, Virtual Reality Training, and Customer Sentiment Analysis: Human-Machine Interaction, Virtual Reality Training, and Customer Sentiment Analysis*. IGI Global.

Hussain, A., Ansari, H. W. A., Nasir, H., & Maqbool, M. Q. (2023). Developing a Model for the Adoption of Industrial Revolution 5.0 Among Malaysian Manufacturing SMEs for Sustainable Growth. In *Opportunities and Challenges of Business 5.0 in Emerging Markets* (pp. 40–57). IGI Global. DOI: 10.4018/978-1-6684-6403-8.ch003

Irpan, M., & Shaddiq, S. (2024). Industry 4.0 and Industry 5.0—Inception, Conception, Perception, and Rethinking Loyalty Employment. *INTERNATIONAL JOURNAL OF ECONOMICS, MANAGEMENT* [IJEMBIS]. *BUSINESS, AND SOCIAL SCIENCE, 4*(1), 95–114.

Islam, M. S., Amin, S., Arifuzzaman, M., Rahman, M. H., & Hossain, R. (2023). *Automatic Train Wash Plant on Metro System* (Doctoral dissertation, Sonargoan University (SU)).

Ismail, M. M., Ahmed, Z., Abdel-Gawad, A. F., & Mohamed, M. (2024). Toward Supply Chain 5.0: An Integrated Multi-Criteria Decision-Making Models for Sustainable and Resilience Enterprise. *Decision making: applications in management and engineering, 7*(1), 160-186.

Jokubauskis, D. (2020). *Development and applications of compact spectroscopic terahertz imaging systems using principles of optical beam engineering* (Doctoral dissertation, Vilniaus universitetas).

Jordan, A. A., Pegatoquet, A., Castagnetti, A., Raybaut, J., & Le Coz, P. (2020). Deep learning for eye blink detection implemented at the edge. *IEEE Embedded Systems Letters*, *13*(3), 130–133. DOI: 10.1109/LES.2020.3029313

Khaira, A. (2024). From 3D to 4D: The Evolution of Additive Manufacturing and Its Implications for Industry 5.0. In *Emerging Technologies in Digital Manufacturing and Smart Factories* (pp. 39-53). IGI Global.

Khan, M. A., Khan, R., Praveen, P., Verma, A. R., & Panda, M. K. (Eds.). (2024). *Infrastructure Possibilities and Human-Centered Approaches With Industry 5.0*. IGI Global. DOI: 10.4018/979-8-3693-0782-3

Kotikangas, M. (2023). Utilization of digital twin for customer tailored variable speed drive.

Kralj, D., & Aralica, K. (2022, September). Industry 5.0 from the Perspective of Safety at Work. In *Occupational Safety and Health, Proceedings of the 8th International Professional and Scientific Conference, Zadar, Croatia* (pp. 21-24).

Kralj, D., & Aralica, K. (2023). Safety at work within industry 5.0-quo vadis. *Sigurnost: časopis za sigurnost u radnoj i životnoj okolini, 65*(3), 317-324.

Kumar, R. (2018). Bilingual Domain-Independent Natural Language Interface to Database.

Kumari, P., Anand, A., Praveen, P., Verma, A. R., & Godiyal, A. (2024). Infrastructure Potential and Human-Centric Strategies in the Context of Industry 5.0. In *Infrastructure Possibilities and Human-Centered Approaches With Industry 5.0* (pp. 199-214). IGI Global.

Kusiak, A. (2024). Federated explainable artificial intelligence (fXAI): A digital manufacturing perspective. *International Journal of Production Research*, *62*(1-2), 171–182. DOI: 10.1080/00207543.2023.2238083

Lo, H. W., Chan, H. W., Lin, J. W., & Lin, S. W. (2024). Evaluating the interrelationships of industrial 5.0 development factors using an integration approach of Fermatean fuzzy logic. *Journal of Operations Intelligence*, *2*(1), 95–113. DOI: 10.31181/jopi21202416

Lv, Z. (2023). Digital Twins in Industry 5.0. *Research, 6*, 0071.

Maroof, M. A., & Kapate, S. (2023). *Exploring Dynamics of Industry 5.0*. World Journal of Management and Economics.

Masenya, T. M., & Chisita, C. T. (2022). Futurizing library services in a technology-driven dispensation: Reflections on selected academic libraries in Zimbabwe and South Africa. In *Innovative technologies for enhancing knowledge access in academic libraries* (pp. 1–21). IGI Global. DOI: 10.4018/978-1-6684-3364-5.ch001

Millard, J. (2023). Exploring the impact of digital transformation on public governance.

Millard, J. (2023). Impact of digital transformation on public governance. *Joint Research Centre (Seville site)*.

Mladineo, M., Celent, L., Milković, V., & Veža, I. (2024). Current State Analysis of Croatian Manufacturing Industry with Regard to Industry 4.0/5.0. *Machines (Basel), 12*(2), 87. DOI: 10.3390/machines12020087

Mohd Yamin, M. N., Ab. Aziz, K., Gek Siang, T., & Ab. Aziz, N. A. (2023). Determinants of Emotion Recognition System Adoption: Empirical Evidence from Malaysia. *Applied Sciences (Basel, Switzerland), 13*(21), 11854. DOI: 10.3390/app132111854

Nair, A., Pillai, S. V., & Senthil Kumar, S. A. (2024). Towards emerging Industry 5.0–a review-based framework. *Journal of Strategy and Management*. DOI: 10.1108/JSMA-04-2023-0067

Narkhede, G. B., Pasi, B. N., Rajhans, N., & Kulkarni, A. (2024). Industry 5.0 and sustainable manufacturing: A systematic literature review. *Benchmarking*.

Natalia, T., Pathani, A., Dhaliwal, N., Rajasekhar, N., & Khatkar, M. (2024). Blockchain Integration in Industry 5.0: A Security Experiment for Resilience Assessment. In *BIO Web of Conferences* (Vol. 86, p. 01070). EDP Sciences.

Natalia, V., Bisht, Y. S., Prabhakar, P. K., Arora, R., Mishra, S. K., & Rajasekhar, N. (2024). Al and Autonomous Systems: An Experiment in Industry 5.0 Transformation. In *BIO Web of Conferences* (Vol. 86, p. 01094). EDP Sciences.

Nazari, M. (2017). *Infrared Matrix-Assisted Laser Desorption Electrospray Ionization (IR-MALDESI): Development and Applications in Metabolomics, Mass Spectrometry Imaging, and Direct Analysis*. North Carolina State University.

Nel-Sanders, D. (2023). Revolutionising Public Private Partnerships: A Transition to the Fifth Industrial Revolution. *International Journal of Innovation in Management. Economics and Social Sciences, 3*(1), 12–29.

Netherton, T., & Netherton, T. J. (2021). A Fully-Automated, Deep Learning-Based Framework For Ct-Based Localization, Segmentation, Verification And Planning Of Metastatic Vertebrae.

Noori, S. F., Yuvaraj, D., Abas, S. M., Sivaram, M., & Porkodi, V. (2024). Multifaceted Interplay between Mobile Edge Computing based on Industry 5.0 in Transportation. *International Journal of Intelligent Systems and Applications in Engineering*, *12*(15s), 106–114.

Nyemba, W. R., Chikuku, T., Chiroodza, J. R., Dube, B., Carter, K. F., Mbohwa, C., & Magombo, L. (2020). Industrial design thinking and innovations propelled by the Royal Academy of Engineering in Sub-Saharan Africa for capacity building. *Procedia CIRP*, *91*, 770–775. DOI: 10.1016/j.procir.2020.02.233

Owusu, P. K., Nortey, D. N. N., Koffie-Ocloo, D., & Afriyie, G. O. (2023, December). Evaluating customer satisfaction with AI chatbot interactions in the Ghanaian insurance industry: Focusing on Star Assurance Ltd. In *Conference proceedings edited by* (p. 43).

Pang, T. Y., Lee, T. K., & Murshed, M. (2023). Towards a New Paradigm for Digital Health Training and Education in Australia: Exploring the Implication of the Fifth Industrial Revolution. *Applied Sciences (Basel, Switzerland)*, *13*(11), 6854. DOI: 10.3390/app13116854

Paramasivam, B. (2020). Investigation on the effects of damping over the temperature distribution on internal turning bar using Infrared fusion thermal imager analysis via SmartView software. *Measurement*, *162*, 107938. DOI: 10.1016/j.measurement.2020.107938

Pereira Perdigao, G. (2018). Internship and master thesis: Concept of Operation: Unmanned Maintenance Dredging.

Raheman, F. (2022). Sharonomics: A Radical Economic Theory for the Next Industrial Revolution and Beyond. *Theoretical Economics Letters*, *12*(6), 1710–1748. DOI: 10.4236/tel.2022.126094

Rahman, N. A. A., Abdullah, M. A., Hassan, A., & Mahroof, K. (2023). *17 Hard Hit by Halal Meat Cartel Controversy*. Technologies and Trends in the Halal Industry.

Rani, S., & Srivastava, G. (2024). Secure hierarchical fog computing-based architecture for industry 5.0 using an attribute-based encryption scheme. *Expert Systems with Applications*, *235*, 121180. DOI: 10.1016/j.eswa.2023.121180

Rinat, K., Thakur, G., Gupta, M., Madhuri, T. N. P., & Bansal, S. (2024). Comparative Analysis of Big Data Computing in Industry 4.0 and Industry 5.0: An Experimental Study. In *BIO Web of Conferences* (Vol. 86, p. 01068). EDP Sciences.

Saputro, E. P. (2024). Kolaborasi Manusia Dan Sumber Daya Robotik Menuju Masa Depan Manufaktur Berkelanjutan Industri 5.0. *Innovative: Journal Of Social Science Research*, *4*(1), 2504–2516.

Schröder, A. J., Cuypers, M., & Götting, A. (2024). From Industry 4.0 to Industry 5.0: The Triple Transition Digital, Green and Social. In *Industry 4.0 and the Road to Sustainable Steelmaking in Europe: Recasting the Future* (pp. 35–51). Springer International Publishing. DOI: 10.1007/978-3-031-35479-3_3

Selvarajan, S., Manoharan, H., & Shankar, A. (2024). SL-RI: Integration of supervised learning in robots for industry 5.0 automated application monitoring. *Measurement. Sensors*, *31*, 100972. DOI: 10.1016/j.measen.2023.100972

Sharma, A., & Singh, B. (2022). Measuring Impact of E-commerce on Small Scale Business: A Systematic Review. *Journal of Corporate Governance and International Business Law*, *5*(1).

Śledziewska, K., & Włoch, R. (2021). The foundations of the digital economy. In *The Economics of Digital Transformation*. Taylor & Francis. DOI: 10.4324/9781003144359-1

Śledziewska, K., & Włoch, R. (2021). The Economics of Digital Transformation. *The disruption of.*

Speringer, M., & Schnelzer, J. (2019). Differentiation of industry 4.0 models. *Vienna, Austria.*

Srinivasan, S., Hema, D. D., Singaram, B., Praveena, D., Mohan, K. K., & Preetha, M. (2024). Decision Support System based on Industry 5.0 in Artificial Intelligence. *International Journal of Intelligent Systems and Applications in Engineering*, *12*(15s), 172–178.

Suganya, G., Selvakumar, J. J., Varadharajan, P., & Pachiyappan, S. (2024). Skill Sets Required to Meet a Human-Centered Industry 5.0: A Systematic Literature Review and Bibliometric Analysis. *Advances in Web Technologies and Engineering*, *5*(0), 231–252. DOI: 10.4018/979-8-3693-0782-3.ch014

Vacchi, M., Siligardi, C., & Settembre-Blundo, D. (2024). Driving Manufacturing Companies toward Industry 5.0: A Strategic Framework for Process Technological Sustainability Assessment (P-TSA). *Sustainability (Basel)*, *16*(2), 695. DOI: 10.3390/su16020695

Valeriya, G., Kirola, M., Gupta, M., Bharathi, P., & Acharya, P. (2024). Evaluating the Impact of AI-Based Sustainability Measures in Industry 5.0: A Longitudinal Study. In *BIO Web of Conferences* (Vol. 86, p. 01058). EDP Sciences.

Van der Poll, J. A. (2022). Problematizing the Adoption of Formal Methods in the 4IR–5IR Transition. *Applied System Innovation*, *5*(6), 127. DOI: 10.3390/asi5060127

Vatin, N. I., Negi, G. S., Yellanki, V. S., Mohan, C., & Singla, N. (2024). Sustainability Measures: An Experimental Analysis of AI and Big Data Insights in Industry 5.0. In *BIO Web of Conferences* (Vol. 86, p. 01072). EDP Sciences.

Villar, A., Paladini, S., & Buckley, O. (2023, July). Towards Supply Chain 5.0: Redesigning Supply Chains as Resilient, Sustainable, and Human-Centric Systems in a Post-pandemic World. In *Operations* [). Cham: Springer International Publishing.]. *Research Forum*, *4*(3), 60. DOI: 10.1007/s43069-023-00234-3

Wang, B., Zhou, H., Li, X., Yang, G., Zheng, P., Song, C., Yuan, Y., Wuest, T., Yang, H., & Wang, L. (2024). Human Digital Twin in the context of Industry 5.0. *Robotics and Computer-integrated Manufacturing*, *85*, 102626. DOI: 10.1016/j.rcim.2023.102626

Wang, S., Zhang, J., Wang, P., Law, J., Calinescu, R., & Mihaylova, L. (2024). A deep learning-enhanced Digital Twin framework for improving safety and reliability in human–robot collaborative manufacturing. *Robotics and Computer-integrated Manufacturing*, *85*, 102608. DOI: 10.1016/j.rcim.2023.102608

Wen, L. (2024). Design automation system synchronization for cyber physical system with dynamic voltage and frequency scaling in industry 5.0. *Measurement. Sensors*, *31*, 100981. DOI: 10.1016/j.measen.2023.100981

Ziatdinov, R., Atteraya, M. S., & Nabiyev, R. (2024). The Fifth Industrial Revolution as a Transformative Step towards Society 5.0. *Societies (Basel, Switzerland)*, *14*(2), 19. DOI: 10.3390/soc14020019

Ziatdinov, R., Atteraya, M. S., & Nabiyev, R. (2024). The Fifth Industrial Revolution as a Transformative Step towards Society 5.0. *Societies (Basel, Switzerland)*, *14*(2), 19. DOI: 10.3390/soc14020019

Chapter 7
Towards an Explainable Artificial Intelligence in the Realm of Supply Chain Management: A Systematic Literature Review

Asmae El Jaouhari
https://orcid.org/0000-0002-3100-363X
National School of Applied Sciences, Berrechid, Morocco

Soufinae Driouiche
Moroccan School of Engineering, Morocco

ABSTRACT

Explainable Artificial Intelligence (XAI) is increasingly adopted by organizations to innovate, and this is ever more reflected in scholarly work. To illustrate, assess and map research at the intersection of XAI and supply chain management (SCM), we performed a Systematic Literature Review (SLR) of published work indexed in the Clarivate Web of Science (WOS) and Elsevier Scopus databases (the final sample includes 117 articles). A content analysis was deployed to map the focal field in terms of dominant topics and their evolution over time. By deploying the main applications of XAI in the realm of supply chain management, and drivers and barriers, we generate insights on the literature at the intersection of XAI and SCM research. We leverage the SLR findings to provide an updated synopsis of extant scientific work on the focal research area and to develop a future research agenda which sheds light on the drivers and outcomes of XAI adoption for SCM. We conclude this paper by developing an agenda for future research.

DOI: 10.4018/979-8-3373-0923-1.ch007

1. INTRODUCTION

The world is rapidly moving towards a digital future, driven by the transformative power of Industry 4.0 technologies. Among the most prominent technologies associated with this shift are Artificial Intelligence (AI), blockchain, the Internet of Things (IoT), and cloud computing (Ghadge et al., 2020; Mugurusi & Oluka, 2021). AI, in particular, has emerged as a key enabler of digital transformation across various sectors, including supply chain management (SCM) (Jaouhari et al., 2022). Defined as the ability of machines to simulate human cognitive functions such as learning, decision-making, and problem-solving, AI has the potential to revolutionize industries by improving efficiency, enhancing decision-making, and driving innovation (Sadeghi R. et al., 2024). While AI is not a new field of study, recent technological advancements have demonstrated its broad applicability and transformative impact in numerous domains (Jauhar et al., 2024). Supply chain management, as one of the critical areas for AI integration, stands to gain significantly from the adoption of AI technologies, providing opportunities to optimize operations, reduce costs, and improve customer satisfaction (Nimmy, 2024).

Supply chain management has traditionally faced challenges related to efficiency, forecasting, inventory management, and logistics optimization (Jaouhari et al., 2023). The introduction of AI technologies into this domain promises to address these challenges by leveraging data to make smarter decisions faster and more accurately (Senoner et al., 2022; Sadeghi R. et al., 2024). AI-driven systems can analyze vast amounts of data and generate insights that humans would otherwise struggle to uncover, enabling organizations to optimize their supply chain processes, from procurement and production to distribution and customer service (El jaouhari et al., 2025). The integration of AI in SCM is not just a matter of technological adoption but a strategic shift that can provide organizations with a competitive advantage (Jaouhari et al., 2023). As businesses move from basic AI applications, such as remote monitoring, to more advanced AI-driven optimization and autonomous systems, the scope of AI in SCM continues to expand (El Jaouhari et al., 2024; Saen et al., 2024).

XAI in SCM has become an increasingly important area of research, with mounting expectations across various sectors and industries (El Jaouhari et al., 2024). In recent years, the scope of XAI has broadened significantly, and its applications have expanded across a wide range of domains, from healthcare to energy (Ahmed et al., 2022). Despite these advancements, the real-world application of XAI remains a challenging endeavor, with many companies still in the early stages of experimentation and pilot projects (Jaouhari et al., 2023). The complexities of XAI implementation in SCM are compounded by the interdependencies between functional areas, organizational boundaries, and the need for cross-level integration within open systems (Schoepf et al., 2024). Moreover, the widespread enthusiasm surrounding XAI often leads to inflated expectations, which can create confusion and hinder effective implementation (Saen et al., 2024). This study aims to temper these expectations by providing a clearer understanding of the current state of XAI in SCM, highlighting both the potential and the challenges of XAI adoption in this critical area.

However, despite the vast potential of XAI in SCM, its integration remains complex and presents numerous challenges. While many industries are experimenting with XAI technologies, the practical implementation of XAI systems is not without obstacles (Jaouhari et al., 2023). One of the most significant challenges is the "black box" nature of many XAI models, where the reasoning behind decisions made by XAI systems is not always transparent (Jaouhari & Arif, 2024). This lack of explainability creates barriers to trust and adoption, especially in high-stakes industries such as supply chain management, where decisions can have significant financial and operational consequences. As such, the need for explainable AI (XAI) has emerged as a critical focus within the field. XAI seeks to make XAI systems more transparent by providing understandable and interpretable explanations of the decision-making processes that underpin XAI outputs (El Jaouhari et al., 2025). This is particularly important in SCM, where understanding how XAI models arrive at their decisions can help organizations ensure that XAI systems are functioning as intended and deliver the expected outcomes.

In light of these challenges and opportunities, the current study seeks to contribute to the growing body of research on XAI in SCM by addressing key questions regarding how XAI contributes to SCM studies and its role in transforming supply chain processes. The literature on XAI in SCM is rapidly evolving, with increasing scholarly interest in exploring the benefits, challenges, and implications of XAI adoption. However, despite the growing body of research, there remains a gap in understanding how XAI specifically contributes to SCM and how the technology can be effectively implemented in real-world settings. This study aims to fill this gap by conducting a systematic literature review (SLR) to synthesize existing research on XAI in SCM and provide a comprehensive analysis of its current state and future directions.

The study follows the framework established by Stock and Boyer (2009) in their definition of SCM, which emphasizes the management of relationships within a network of interdependent organizations, including material suppliers, production facilities, logistics, and marketing. These relationships facilitate the flow of materials, services, finances, and information from the original producer to the final customer, with the goal of maximizing profitability, adding value, and achieving customer satisfaction. In this paper, we present a systematic literature review of current studies on XAI in SCM, analyzing the key applications of XAI in SCM, as well as the challenges and opportunities that arise from its integration. The paper also identifies future research directions and potential gaps in the literature, with the goal of advancing knowledge and informing both academic and practical efforts in XAI-driven SCM. The study concludes with a discussion of the findings and a research agenda for exploring XAI's evolving role in supply chain management.

2. RESEARCH METHODOLOGY

This study uses a thematic systematic literature review (SLR). SLR is a replicable scientific process using criterion-based selection and analyses of published studies (Modaresi, 2024). It identifies homogeneity or heterogeneity within studies (Jahin et al., 2024); enabling an evidence-based summary of research investigations (Dereci & Tuzkaya, 2024). We use the methodology recommended by (Lundberg et al., 2019), and Higgins and Green (2011). To identify the studies relevant for the thematic review, we conducted a keyword search using Elsevier's Scopus database. Considering the multifaceted, wide ranging XAI applications, no restrictions in the disciplinary scope of the journals were applied. Two sets of keywords set the stage for the search. One set is related to XAI; the other to sustainability – see below. XAI-related keywords have been drawn from previous literature reviews on XAI, in particular Kamble et al. (2018) and Culot et al. (2020), while SCM-related keywords have been drawn from Seuring and Müller (2008). The keyword search encompasses publication keywords, title, and abstract. Keywords related to Explainable AI in supply chain management include terms such as ("Explainable AI" OR "Transparent AI" OR "Supply Chain Optimization" OR "Intelligent Supply Chain" OR "AI-driven Logistics" OR "Predictive Analytics in Supply Chain" OR "AI Transparency" OR "Smart Supply Chain Management" OR "Digital Twin in Supply Chain" OR "Cyber-Physical Systems in Logistics" OR "AI-enabled Supply Chain" OR "Industrial AI" OR "AI for Supply Chain Planning" OR "Smart Operations in Logistics" OR "AI in Supply Chain Resilience"). The XAI paradigm originated in 2011(Pattnaik et al., 2024). Only English language papers were included. We excluded conference papers, conference reviews, editorials and book chapters, as often done by literature surveys (Tchuente et al., 2024). Consistent with previous studies (Ordibazar et al., 2022), we controlled for publication quality by including only peer reviewed publications (Behera et al., 2023).

A total number of 1200 contributions result from the search. Removing articles with non-coherent abstracts – for example, papers that do not primarily focus on Explainable AI in supply chain management and its relevance to transparency, decision-making, and operational efficiency, or that exclusively focus on other XAI applications without addressing supply chain contexts, or that discuss Explainable AI (and related terms such as transparent AI, AI-driven supply chain) in isolation or with very narrow technical perspectives – left 269 studies in the dataset. Analysis of the full text results in 117 publications that align well with the scope of this study. In cases of inclusion uncertainties, a discussion amongst the research team guided the final inclusion decision. A graphical summary of the process and the number of publications identified in each step appears in Figure 1.

Figure 1. Systematic literature review process

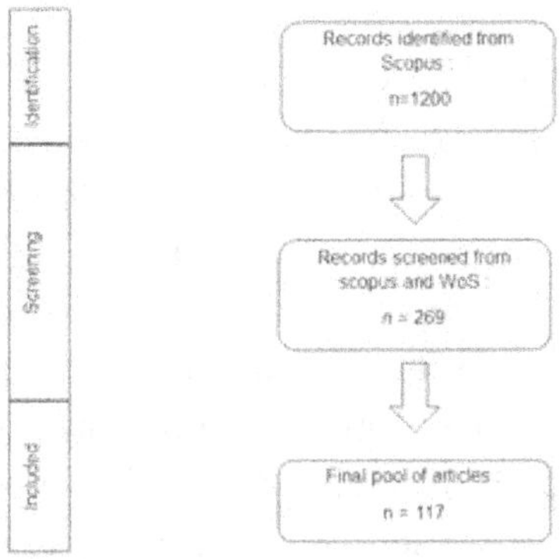

Fig. 1. Systematic literature review process.

3. APPLICATIONS OF XAI IN SCM

3.1. Sourcing Assessment and Procurement

The integration of Generative XAI in supply chain management revolutionizes the traditional approach to sourcing assessment and procurement. Unlike manual analysis and decision-making methods, Generative XAI brings forth an advanced approach, swiftly sifting through extensive data from numerous potential suppliers(Dubey et al., 2024). This process considers a multitude of parameters, such as cost effective-ness, product quality, reliability, operational efficiency, and sustainability, to craft an optimal supplier portfolio. In addition, Generative XAI amplifies inclusivity and equality within supply chains by actively recommending strategies to incorporate minority-owned, women-owned, or veteran-owned enterprises. Leveraging its text generation capabilities, XAI provides comprehensive descriptions detailing each supplier's strengths and weaknesses. Additionally, it assists in formulating diverse negotiation tactics and contractual terms based on historical data and anticipated supplier behavior(Li et al., 2024). Generative AI's proficiency in handling vast datasets expeditiously and comprehensively redefines the sourcing and procurement landscape. By amalgamating multifaceted criteria and fostering diversity, it not only streamlines the supplier selection process but also augments the overall resilience and social responsibility of the supply chain.

3.2. Risk Mitigation

The use of generative XAI in supply chain risk mitigation is extensive, providing a range of instruments and functionalities that transform the way possible disruptions are managed. With the use of sophisticated algorithms, this technology is able to analyze enormous volumes of data, both historical and current. He et al. (2020) note that predicted risk analysis is the main use of generative AI for risk mitigation. Artificial intelligence systems examine past data, present trends, and external factors to predict possible disruptions. Supply chain managers can plot out strategies and take preventative actions in the event of disruptions if they have this kind of insight into the future. Furthermore, supply chain operations can benefit from generative AI-enabled simulations and scenario planning (Yadav et al., 2024). This tool generates multiple risk scenarios using both historical and current data, which helps in evaluating possible outcomes and establishing specific backup plans for different types of risks. These simulations are an essential tool for evaluating how well mitigation techniques work. The real-time monitoring capabilities of generative AI provide a proactive approach to risk reduction. Through ongoing analysis of supplier performance indicators, market data, and data streams from IoT devices, artificial intelligence (AI) algorithms quickly identify deviations or abnormalities that could indicate potential threats. With the use of this real time surveillance, disturbances can be stopped or lessened before they get worse. Using Generative XAI to facilitate adaptive decision-making is another important feature. This system facilitates real-time modifications to inventory levels, logistical routes, or supplier relationships depending on changing risk indicators by offering dynamic insights into risk-relevant data. Supply chain managers can quickly reduce risks as they arise and lessen their impact on operations thanks to this agility. Moreover, supply chain resilience is optimized with the help of generative XAI. XAI-driven models strengthen the supply chain against weaknesses by creating redundant logistics networks, finding alternative suppliers, and diversifying procurement tactics. By reducing reliance on individual nodes within the chain, this proactive approach ensures that activities continue even in the face of disruptions. The applications of generative XAI extend to risk management (political, economic, cultural, and partner), where it generates possible disruption models for scenario-based risk assessment, encompassing events such as supplier insolvency, strikes, natural disasters, pandemics, and more. By conducting a thorough and continuous examination of possible interruptions and risk areas, organizations can develop robust approaches to guarantee uninterrupted operations. For instance, XAI can produce workable alternatives in the event of an interruption in the supply chain based on a number of variables linked to standard logistics service quality measurements (Papadopoulos et al., 2022), hence preserving trade-off targets for customer service. These advanced models can also create backup plans that take into account any disruptions and incorporate all of the information received from management cues.

3.3. Coordination of Logistics, Distribution, and Transportation

Massive potential exists for generative XAI to coordinate logistics, transportation, and distribution in supply chains efficiently (Whig & Adusumilli, 2023). This technology is particularly effective at creating complex plans that are suited to maximizing logistical and distribution routes while managing a variety of goals and restrictions. These include cutting costs, optimizing service levels, minimizing routing interruptions, taking the weather into account, and incorporating environmental factors. Furthermore, Generative XAI demonstrates proficiency in creating backup plans to counteract disturbances such as traffic jams and severe weather. XAI algorithms automatically design the most effective transportation routes by evaluating a variety of realtime variables, including weather forecasts, vehicle specs, traffic patterns, and fuel prices (Helo & Hao, 2022). For example, the XAI system can strategically plan a delivery truck route across an urban area to minimize fuel use and travel time while making several stops. Moreover, the AI's ability to produce written explanations for particular routes increases its usefulness. This feature gives logistics managers access to a wide range of route possibilities so they may make well-informed decisions (Sodiya et al., 2024). When given clear guidelines and specifications, Generative AI can effectively design optimal layouts for picking and storing tasks in warehouses. Important components such as item-specific demand frequencies, product dimensions, and handling and storage equipment capacities are all integrated into the algorithmic design process. Through the consideration of these characteristics, Generative XAI creates layouts that improve productivity, shorten retrieval times, and maximize storage spaces—all of which contribute to the overall efficacy of warehouse operations.

3.4. Procurement and Inventory Accuracy

Demand forecasting (Elgalb & Gerges, 2024) and inventory management procedures within supply chains are radically altered by generative XAI, which transforms procurement and improves inventory accuracy through its predictive capabilities (Elbegzaya, 2020). Due to its predictive capabilities, firms are able to provide extremely precise projections of sales and demand, which allows for the best possible scheduling of supplier quantities and orders. This accuracy makes it easier to apply lean management techniques, which greatly cut waste and increase process and resource efficiency. Generative XAI presents a paradigm change by creating variable inventory strategies, going beyond traditional demand forecasts. A crucial challenge in supply chain management, these strategies are skilled at optimizing the delicate balance between overstocking and understocking. The XAI, for example, can create plans specifically for just-in-time inventory management, which is a technique that has the potential to reduce storage expenses and increase cash flow. Additionally, Generative XAI predicts changes in consumer behavior and market trends in addition to demand by utilizing predictive analytics. As a result of this foresight, businesses are able to adjust quickly, maximizing excess inventory while matching changing demands with optimal inventory levels. Hence, the XAI's adaptiveness guarantees that inventory regulations respond to shifting market conditions, improving the supply chain's overall agility.

4. CHALLENGES IN ADOPTING XAI IN SUPPLY CHAIN MANAGEMENT

Challenges in adopting XAI in supply chain analytics encompass ethical considerations, data security, and skillset requirements. Addressing ethical concerns in XAI-driven decision-making is crucial to ensure responsible use of technology in supply chain operations (C. (Abigail) Zhang et al., 2022). This involves the need for skilled personnel in managing XAI technologies and implementing training and development programs for workforce readiness (Kostopoulos et al., 2024). Furthermore, safeguarding sensitive supply chain data and implementing robust cybersecurity measures are imperative(Sodiya et al., 2024). The impact of supply chain security practices on security operational performance among logistics service providers in emerging economies highlights the benefits of supply chain security practices, emphasizing the need for responsible technology use (Deif & Vivek, 2022). Additionally, a voluntary logistics security program and international supply chain partnership emphasize the importance of prevention and adopting a total supply chain approach to address ethical concerns and ensure responsible technology use (Naim et al., 2023).

Furthermore, XAI have the potential to reduce the bullwhip effect, supporting the performance of supply chain efficiency and responsiveness, but ethical considerations must be addressed in their adoption (Saen et al., 2024). Detecting fake news and disinformation using XAI to avoid supply chain disruptions underscores the role of these technologies in enhancing supply chain operations while emphasizing the need for responsible use (Chang & Bau, 2024). The contribution of XAI and XAI in managing and transforming supply chains digitally highlights the unexplored potential and contexts in which these technologies can be used, emphasizing the need for skilled personnel and responsible technology use (Lundberg et al., 2019). The impact of information security initiatives on supply chain performance emphasizes the importance of information security in addressing data security challenges in supply chain operations (Pournader et al., 2021). Furthermore, XAI can significantly improve packaging, shelf life, menu combination, and food safety, emphasizing the need for responsible technology use in supply chain management (Kostopoulos et al., 2024).

Further, the contribution of XAI to firm resilience to supply chain disruptions underscores the potential of emerging technologies such as XAI in addressing supply chain challenges while emphasizing the need for responsible technology use (Deif & Vivek, 2022). Antecedents and outcomes of supply chain security practices stress the role of a collaborated approach by supply chain members to reduce susceptibility in the supply chain, highlighting the importance of responsible technology use in supply chain security (Bhatia & Albarrak, 2023). Table 1 summarizes the main challenges of adopting XAI in SCM.

Table 1. Main challenges and barriers of adopting XAI in SCM.

Main Category	Sub-Category	Description	References
Technical Challenges	Algorithm Complexity	Developing interpretable AI algorithms without compromising their predictive accuracy is complex and requires significant computational resources.	(Hangl et al., 2023)
	Integration with Existing Systems	Many supply chain systems rely on legacy software, making it difficult to integrate modern XAI solutions seamlessly.	(Kumar et al., 2024)
	Data Quality and Availability	XAI performance heavily depends on high-quality, real-time, and accurate data, which may be fragmented or incomplete in supply chain networks.	(Manning et al., 2022)

continued on following page

Table 1. Continued

Main Category	Sub-Category	Description	References
	Scalability Issues	Scaling XAI across global, multi-tiered supply chains is challenging due to the diversity and complexity of operations.	(Brintrup et al., 2024)
Organizational Barriers	Resistance to Change	Employees and managers may distrust or resist adopting XAI systems, fearing automation will replace jobs or challenge traditional decision-making.	(Sunmola et al., 2025)
	Skill Gaps	Organizations often lack trained personnel with expertise in both AI and supply chain management to implement and maintain XAI solutions effectively.	(Bag et al., 2021)
	High Initial Investment	The costs associated with developing, deploying, and training for XAI solutions can deter smaller firms or those with limited budgets.	(Rakholia et al., 2024)
	Leadership Buy-In	Gaining trust and support from senior management to invest in XAI is challenging due to skepticism about ROI and the perceived risks of adopting new technologies.	(Merhi, 2023)
Regulatory and Ethical Issues	Lack of Clear Regulations	The absence of standardized policies and frameworks for XAI in SCM raises concerns about compliance, accountability, and legal implications.	(L. Zhang et al., 2024)
	Ethical Concerns	Ensuring that XAI does not reinforce bias, discrimination, or unethical decision-making practices remains a critical barrier to adoption.	(Saberi et al., 2019)
	Data Privacy and Security	Balancing transparency with the need to protect sensitive data creates conflicts, particularly when sharing insights with external stakeholders.	(Khalifa et al., 2021)
Operational Barriers	Lack of Transparency	While XAI aims to enhance explainability, non-technical stakeholders may still find the explanations too abstract or technical to comprehend effectively.	(Ghadge et al., 2020)
	Time-Intensive Implementation	Deploying XAI systems can be time-consuming, potentially causing disruptions to existing supply chain operations during the transition.	(Dubey et al., 2021)
	Real-Time Decision Limitations	Achieving real-time insights and recommendations from XAI systems can be difficult in fast-paced, highly dynamic supply chain environments.	(Yang et al., 2024)

5. DRIVERS AND ENABLERS OF XAI ENABLED SCM

The implementation of Explainable Artificial Intelligence (XAI) in Supply Chain Management (SCM) is driven by a range of interconnected factors and enablers that promote its adoption and optimize its impact. XAI, as a branch of AI, prioritizes transparency and interpretability in decision-making processes, ensuring that AI-driven insights can be understood and trusted by all stakeholders. Within the complex dynamics of supply chains, which encompass diverse processes such as procurement, production, distribution, and risk management, the integration of XAI provides clear and actionable insights, fostering more informed decisions and improving collaboration among partners. Table 2 summarizes the main drivers and enablers of adopting XAI in the SCM

Table 2. Main drives and enablers of XAI enabled SCM

Main Category	Sub-Category	Description	References
Transparency and Trust	Explainability Tools	Tools and techniques that make AI decisions interpretable and understandable for stakeholders.	(Hangl et al., 2022)
	Stakeholder Trust	Enhancing trust among stakeholders by clarifying AI-driven decisions in supply chain processes.	(Naz et al., 2022)
Decision-Making Support	Predictive Analytics	Supporting accurate demand forecasting and risk mitigation by providing interpretable insights.	(Alzarooni et al., 2022)
	Prescriptive Solutions	Offering actionable recommendations that are traceable to AI logic.	(Dey et al., 2024)
Operational Efficiency	Process Optimization	Improving supply chain workflows through interpretable AI-driven optimization strategies.	(V. K. Sharma & Kumar, 2024)
	Real-Time Insights	Delivering transparent, actionable information for timely decision-making in logistics.	(Kar et al., 2021)
Risk Management	Supply Chain Resilience	Identifying and mitigating risks by explaining vulnerabilities in the supply chain.	(Pramanik et al., 2024)
	Compliance Monitoring	Ensuring adherence to regulations by providing clear AI decision rationales.	(A. J. Sharma & Rathore, s. d.)
Sustainability Goals	Environmental Insights	Highlighting AI contributions to eco-friendly supply chain practices with clear explanations.	(Akbari & Hopkins, 2022)
	Social Responsibility	Supporting ethical practices by explaining AI's role in fair and sustainable supply chains.	(Valle & Oliver, 2020)

continued on following page

Table 2. Continued

Main Category	Sub-Category	Description	References
Stakeholder Collaboration	Data Sharing Practices	Facilitating better collaboration through transparent sharing of AI-derived supply chain data.	(Gupta et al., 2024)
	Cross-Functional Alignment	Ensuring alignment across departments by explaining AI-driven insights in shared contexts.	(Han et al., 2021)

6. DISCUSSION

Explainable Artificial Intelligence (XAI) is increasingly recognized as a critical component in Supply Chain Management (SCM), offering transparency and interpretability to AI-driven decisions. By elucidating the reasoning behind AI recommendations, XAI fosters trust among stakeholders and enhances decision-making processes. The integration of XAI into SCM addresses the "black box" nature of traditional AI models, providing clear insights into decision-making processes. This transparency is crucial for supply chain professionals who rely on AI for tasks such as demand forecasting, inventory optimization, and logistics planning. Understanding the factors influencing AI predictions enables more informed and confident decision-making. For instance, in demand forecasting, XAI enhances accuracy and interpretability by revealing underlying factors influencing predictions. The Multi-Channel Data Fusion Network (MCDFN) integrates Convolutional Neural Networks (CNN), Long Short-Term Memory networks (LSTM), and Gated Recurrent Units (GRU) to improve predictive performance. Explainable AI techniques like ShapTime and Permutation Feature Importance are applied to enhance interpretability, allowing supply chain managers to understand the contributions of different features to the forecasted demand. Despite its benefits, the adoption of XAI in SCM presents several challenges. Developing interpretable AI algorithms without compromising predictive accuracy is complex and requires significant computational resources. Additionally, many supply chain systems rely on legacy software, making it difficult to integrate modern XAI solutions seamlessly. Moreover, XAI performance heavily depends on high-quality, real-time, and accurate data, which may be fragmented or incomplete in supply chain networks. To fully leverage XAI in SCM, future research and development should focus on establishing standardized policies and frameworks for XAI in SCM to address compliance, accountability, and legal implications. Improving the transparency of AI models to ensure non-technical stakeholders can effectively comprehend explanations is also essential. Furthermore, ensuring that XAI does not reinforce bias, discrimination, or unethical decision-making practices is crucial.

In summary, XAI offers significant benefits for SCM, including improved forecast accuracy, optimized inventory levels, and enhanced decision transparency. However, addressing the associated challenges is essential to fully realize its potential in transforming supply chain operations.

7. IMPLICATIONS

7.1 Theoretical Implications

By expanding the theoretical knowledge of XAI in operational situations, this work adds to the developing conversation on artificial intelligence (AI) in SCM. Although other research has shown how AI may improve operational efficiency and decision-making (Dey et al., 2024; Dubey et al., 2021; Gupta et al., 2024), this work fills a significant research vacuum by including explainability as a fundamental analytical lens. The paper presents a sophisticated theoretical perpective that links SCM aspects to the XAI paradigm. It asserts that explainability improves organizational learning and adaptive capability, which are critical for handling supply chain complexity and unpredictability (Chang & Bau, 2024), in addition to fostering trust and transparency (Tchuente et al., 2024). By suggesting a taxonomy of XAI applications across important SCM functions (such as risk management, demand forecasting, and procurement), the paper also lays the groundwork for future theory-building and adds to the growing corpus of research on ethical and interpretable AI in operations research.

7.2 Practical Implications

This study highlights the apparent advantages of incorporating XAI technologies into SCM procedures from a managerial and operational standpoint. XAI models improve ethical responsibility, regulatory compliance, and stakeholder confidence by offering transparent decision support, especially in high-stakes areas like logistics routing, supplier selection, and inventory optimization (Dereci & Tuzkaya, 2024; Kosasih et al., 2024). The results show that while XAI-enabled tools enhance decision traceability, allow cross-functional collaboration, and foster human–AI teaming, black-box AI solutions may impede adoption owing to interpretability issues (Mugurusi & Oluka, 2021). The study also describes implementation tactics include educating employees on AI ethics, and coordinating XAI deployment with supply chain governance frameworks. These suggestions are especially pertinent to sectors that are subject to regulatory supervision or Environment, Social, and Governance (ESG) standards, where algorithmic transparency is not only a technological preference but also a strategic need (Kostopoulos et al., 2024). In the end, the study acts as a guide for businesses looking to strike a balance between supply chain ecosystems' explainability-driven responsibility and AI innovation.

8. FUTURE RESEARCH DIRECTIONS

Explainable Artificial Intelligence (XAI) within Supply Chain Management (SCM) should focus on several key areas to enhance transparency, efficiency, and decision-making processes. Firstly, developing standardized frameworks for integrating XAI into SCM is essential. Establishing common protocols and guidelines will facilitate consistent implementation and evaluation of XAI applications across diverse supply chain contexts. Secondly, advancing model interpretability remains a critical research avenue. Innovating methods that balance complexity and comprehensibility will enable stakeholders to better understand AI-driven insights, fostering trust and facilitating more informed decisions. Thirdly, addressing data quality and availability is paramount. Future studies should explore techniques for managing fragmented or incomplete data, ensuring that XAI systems operate effectively even in data-constrained environments. Moreover, exploring the integration of neurosymbolic AI approaches can enhance the reasoning capabilities of XAI systems in SCM. By combining neural networks with symbolic reasoning, these systems can provide more robust and interpretable solutions to complex supply chain challenges. Additionally, investigating the ethical implications of XAI deployment in SCM is crucial. Research should focus on preventing biases and ensuring that AI applications promote fairness and equity throughout the supply chain. Finally, practical case studies demonstrating successful XAI implementations can provide valuable insights and best practices, guiding future applications and fostering wider adoption of XAI technologies in SCM. Table 3 summarizes the future research agenda.

Table 3. Future research agenda

Main Category	Future Research Questions
Standardization & Frameworks	How can standardized frameworks for XAI integration in SCM be developed to ensure consistent implementation across various industries?
Model Interpretability	What innovative methods can be designed to enhance the interpretability of AI models in SCM while balancing complexity and comprehensibility?
Data Quality & Availability	How can we address the challenge of fragmented, incomplete, or low-quality data in SCM to ensure reliable performance of XAI systems?

continued on following page

Table 3. Continued

Main Category	Future Research Questions
Neurosymbolic AI Approaches	How can neurosymbolic AI approaches be integrated into SCM to enhance reasoning capabilities and provide interpretable solutions to complex supply chain problems?
Ethical Implications	What frameworks can be created to ensure that XAI in SCM promotes fairness, prevents biases, and supports ethical decision-making practices?
Practical Applications & Case Studies	What real-world case studies can be analyzed to demonstrate the successful implementation of XAI in SCM, and what lessons can be drawn from them for broader adoption?
Human-AI Collaboration	How can XAI technologies be developed to preserve user autonomy and trust while enabling smooth human-AI cooperation in SCM decision-making processes?
Real-Time Decision Support	What developments in XAI are required to provide real-time interpretability in high-velocity supply chain settings, including logistics routing and demand forecasting?

9. LIMITATIONS

It is important to recognize a number of limitations in this systematic literature assessment, even with its rigorous methodology and thorough synthesis. First, even if the databases used to retrieve articles were wide, it's possible that they unintentionally left out pertinent research that was published in domain-specific or non-indexed repositories, including company white papers or conference proceedings that weren't included in Scopus or Web of Science. Second, only peer-reviewed English-language publications were included in the review, which would have introduced language bias and left out potentially insightful information from non-English-speaking countries that are making progress in supply chain innovation and XAI.

Third, despite the review's clear inclusion and exclusion criteria, there may be a time constraint because of how quickly XAI technologies are developing and certain recent developments might not yet be represented in scholarly works. Furthermore, despite attempts to guarantee impartiality in the selection and coding of studies, researcher bias cannot be completely eliminated in the theme interpretation and qualitative synthesis. Fourth, while this study concentrated on the use of XAI in supply chain management, it might not have taken into consideration explainability issues in related fields like manufacturing intelligence, procurement governance, or logistics automation.

Lastly, this study is conceptual and interpretative by nature, much like many literature reviews. Therefore, to examine and improve the claims and conceptual connections shown here, future research should look into empirical case studies, experimental methods, or quantitative surveys.

10. CONCLUSION

The integration of XAI in SCM represents a transformative shift towards more transparent, efficient, and collaborative processes. By providing clear and understandable explanations of AI-driven decisions, XAI addresses the limitations of traditional AI models, building trust among stakeholders and facilitating informed decision-making. Its applications across key areas such as supplier evaluation, risk management, logistics coordination, and inventory optimization demonstrate its potential to revolutionize both operational and strategic practices within modern supply chains. However, this transformation is not without challenges. Issues such as algorithmic complexity, integration with legacy systems, data quality, and organizational resistance remain significant hurdles. Establishing standardized frameworks, implementing robust ethical policies, and investing in skill development are critical steps to overcome these barriers. Moreover, ethical considerations, such as preventing biases and ensuring responsible use, must be central to any initiative deploying XAI in the SCM context. Future research in this domain should focus on enhancing model interpretability, developing neurosymbolic solutions, and exploring practical case studies that highlight the tangible benefits of XAI. By investing in these efforts, organizations and researchers can not only address current challenges but also unlock the competitive advantages that XAI can offer.

In conclusion, XAI represents a unique opportunity to transform supply chains by making them not only more efficient but also more resilient, inclusive, and sustainable. When implemented strategically and ethically, this technology has the potential to significantly improve overall supply chain performance while aligning industrial practices with contemporary societal and environmental goals. Continued in-depth research and collaborative initiatives will be essential to realizing this potential and guiding supply chains toward a more innovative and transparent future.

REFERENCES

Ahmed, I., Jeon, G., & Piccialli, F. (2022). From Artificial Intelligence to Explainable Artificial Intelligence in Industry 4.0: A Survey on What, How, and Where. *IEEE Transactions on Industrial Informatics, 18*(8), 5031-5042. *IEEE Transactions on Industrial Informatics*. DOI: 10.1109/TII.2022.3146552

Akbari, M., & Hopkins, J. L. (2022). Digital technologies as enablers of supply chain sustainability in an emerging economy. *Operations Management Research: Advancing Practice Through Research, 15*(3), 689–710. DOI: 10.1007/s12063-021-00226-8

Alzarooni, A. M., Khan, S. A., Gunasekaran, A., & Mubarik, M. S. (2022). Enablers for digital supply chain transformation in the service industry. *Annals of Operations Research*. DOI: 10.1007/s10479-022-05047-x

Bag, S., Pretorius, J. H. C., Gupta, S., & Dwivedi, Y. K. (2021). Role of institutional pressures and resources in the adoption of big data analytics powered artificial intelligence, sustainable manufacturing practices and circular economy capabilities. *Technological Forecasting and Social Change, 163*, 120420. DOI: 10.1016/j.techfore.2020.120420

Behera, R. K., Bala, P. K., & Rana, N. P. (2023). Creation of sustainable growth with explainable artificial intelligence: An empirical insight from consumer packaged goods retailers. *Journal of Cleaner Production, 399*, 136605. DOI: 10.1016/j.jclepro.2023.136605

Bhatia, S., & Albarrak, A. S. (2023). A Blockchain-Driven Food Supply Chain Management Using QR Code and XAI-Faster RCNN Architecture. *Sustainability (Basel), 15*(3), 3. DOI: 10.3390/su15032579

Brintrup, A., Kosasih, E., Schaffer, P., Zheng, G., Demirel, G., & MacCarthy, B. L. (2024). Digital supply chain surveillance using artificial intelligence: Definitions, opportunities and risks. *International Journal of Production Research, 62*(13), 4674–4695. DOI: 10.1080/00207543.2023.2270719

Chang, T.-S., & Bau, D.-Y. (2024). eXplainable artificial intelligence (XAI) in business management research: A success/failure system perspective. *Journal of Electronic Business & Digital Economics*. DOI: 10.1108/JEBDE-07-2024-0019

Deif, A., & Vivek, T. (2022). Understanding AI Application Dynamics in Oil and Gas Supply Chain Management and Development: A Location Perspective. *HighTech and Innovation Journal, 3*(0), 0. DOI: 10.28991/HIJ-SP2022-03-01

Dereci, U., & Tuzkaya, G. (2024). An explainable artificial intelligence model for predictive maintenance and spare parts optimization. *Supply Chain Analytics*, *8*, 100078. DOI: 10.1016/j.sca.2024.100078

Dey, P. K., Chowdhury, S., Abadie, A., Vann Yaroson, E., & Sarkar, S. (2024). Artificial intelligence-driven supply chain resilience in Vietnamese manufacturing small- and medium-sized enterprises. *International Journal of Production Research*, *62*(15), 5417–5456. DOI: 10.1080/00207543.2023.2179859

Dubey, R., Bryde, D. J., Blome, C., Roubaud, D., & Giannakis, M. (2021). Facilitating artificial intelligence powered supply chain analytics through alliance management during the pandemic crises in the B2B context. *Industrial Marketing Management*, *96*, 135–146. DOI: 10.1016/j.indmarman.2021.05.003

Dubey, R., Gunasekaran, A., & Papadopoulos, T. (2024). Benchmarking operations and supply chain management practices using Generative AI: Towards a theoretical framework. *Transportation Research Part E, Logistics and Transportation Review*, *189*, 103689. DOI: 10.1016/j.tre.2024.103689

El Jaouhari, A., Arif, J., Jawab, F., Samadhiya, A., & Kumar, A. (2024). Unfolding the role of metaverse in agri-food supply chain security: Current scenario and future perspectives. *International Journal of Food Science & Technology*, *59*(5), 3451–3460. DOI: 10.1111/ijfs.16972

El Jaouhari, A., Arif, J., Samadhiya, A., Dhayal, K. S., Luthra, S., & Singh, S. (2025). From Automation to Augmentation: Exploring the Role of Industry 5.0 Advanced Technologies for Developing Countries. *Engineering Management Journal*, *37*(3), 306–323. DOI: 10.1080/10429247.2024.2407254

El Jaouhari, A., Arif, J., Samadhiya, A., Kumar, A., Jain, V., & Agrawal, R. (2024). Are metaverse applications in quality 4.0 enablers of manufacturing resiliency? An exploratory review under disruption impressions and future research. *The TQM Journal*, *36*(6), 1486–1525. DOI: 10.1108/TQM-06-2023-0181

El Jaouhari, A., Samadhiya, A., Benbrahim, F. Z., Kumar, A., & Luthra, S. (2024). Forging a green future: Synergizing industry 4.0 technologies and circular economy tactics to achieve net-zero in sustainable supply chains. *Computers & Industrial Engineering*, *110691*. DOI: 10.1016/j.cie.2024.110691

Elbegzaya, T. (2020). *Application AI in Traditional Supply Chain Management Decision-Making*. http://dspace.unive.it/handle/10579/17733

Ghadge, A., Kara, M. E., Moradlou, H., & Goswami, M. (2020). The impact of Industry 4.0 implementation on supply chains. *Journal of Manufacturing Technology Management, 31*(4), 669–686. DOI: 10.1108/JMTM-10-2019-0368

Gupta, S., Modgil, S., Meissonier, R., & Dwivedi, Y. K. (2024). Artificial Intelligence and Information System Resilience to Cope With Supply Chain Disruption. *IEEE Transactions on Engineering Management, 71*, 10496-10506. *IEEE Transactions on Engineering Management*. DOI: 10.1109/TEM.2021.3116770

Han, B., Jiang, W., Habibi, M. A., & Schotten, H. D. (2021). *An Abstracted Survey on 6G : Drivers, Requirements, Efforts, and Enablers* (arXiv:2101.01062). arXiv. /arXiv.2101.01062DOI: 10.48550

Hangl, J., Behrens, V. J., & Krause, S. (2022). Barriers, Drivers, and Social Considerations for AI Adoption in Supply Chain Management: A Tertiary Study. *Logistics (Basel), 6*(3), 3. DOI: 10.3390/logistics6030063

Helo, P., & Hao, Y. (2022). Artificial intelligence in operations management and supply chain management: An exploratory case study. *Production Planning and Control, 33*(16), 1573–1590. DOI: 10.1080/09537287.2021.1882690

Jahin, M. A., Shahriar, A., & Amin, M. A. (2024). MCDFN: Supply Chain Demand Forecasting via an Explainable Multi-Channel Data Fusion Network Model.

Jaouhari, A. E., Arif, J., Samadhiya, A., Kumar, A., & Garza-Reyes, J. A. (2023). An environmental-based perspective framework: Integrating IoT technology into a sustainable automotive supply chain. *Benchmarking, 31*(10), 3655–3689. DOI: 10.1108/BIJ-05-2023-0322

Jaouhari, A. E., Arif, J., Samadhiya, A., Kumar, A., & Trinkūnas, V. (2023). Are we there or do we have more to do? Metaverse in facility management and future prospects. *International Journal of Strategic Property Management, 27*(3), 3. DOI: 10.3846/ijspm.2023.19516

Jauhar, S. K., Harinath, S., Krishnaswamy, V., & Paul, S. K. (2024). Explainable artificial intelligence to improve the resilience of perishable product supply chains by leveraging customer characteristics. *Annals of Operations Research*. DOI: 10.1007/s10479-024-06348-z

Kar, S., Kar, A. K., & Gupta, M. P. (2021). Modeling Drivers and Barriers of Artificial Intelligence Adoption: Insights from a Strategic Management Perspective. *Intelligent Systems in Accounting, Finance & Management, 28*(4), 217–238. DOI: 10.1002/isaf.1503

Khalifa, N., Abd Elghany, M., & Abd Elghany, M. (2021). Exploratory research on digitalization transformation practices within supply chain management context in developing countries specifically Egypt in the MENA region. *Cogent Business & Management, 8*(1), 1965459. DOI: 10.1080/23311975.2021.1965459

Kosasih, E. E., Papadakis, E., Baryannis, G., & Brintrup, A. (2024). A review of explainable artificial intelligence in supply chain management using neurosymbolic approaches. *International Journal of Production Research, 62*(4), 1510–1540. DOI: 10.1080/00207543.2023.2281663

Kostopoulos, G., Davrazos, G., & Kotsiantis, S. (2024). Explainable Artificial Intelligence-Based Decision Support Systems: A Recent Review. *Electronics (Basel), 13*(14), 14. DOI: 10.3390/electronics13142842

Kumar, G., Singh, R. K., Arya, V., & Mishra, S. K. (2024). Analyzing Barriers in Adoption of Artificial Intelligence for Resilient Health Care Services to Society. *Global Journal of Flexible Systems Managment, 25*(1), 179–197. DOI: 10.1007/s40171-024-00373-4

Li, L., Zhu, W., Chen, L., & Liu, Y. (2024). Generative AI usage and sustainable supply chain performance : A practice-based view. *Transportation Research Part E, Logistics and Transportation Review, 192*, 103761. DOI: 10.1016/j.tre.2024.103761

Lundberg, S. M., Erion, G., Chen, H., DeGrave, A., Prutkin, J. M., Nair, B., Katz, R., Himmelfarb, J., Bansal, N., & Lee, S.-I. (2019). Explainable AI for Trees: From Local Explanations to Global Understanding.

Manning, L., Brewer, S., Craigon, P. J., Frey, J., Gutierrez, A., Jacobs, N., Kanza, S., Munday, S., Sacks, J., & Pearson, S. (2022). Artificial intelligence and ethics within the food sector: Developing a common language for technology adoption across the supply chain. *Trends in Food Science & Technology, 125*, 33–42. DOI: 10.1016/j.tifs.2022.04.025

Merhi, M. I. (2023). An Assessment of the Barriers Impacting Responsible Artificial Intelligence. *Information Systems Frontiers, 25*(3), 1147–1160. DOI: 10.1007/s10796-022-10276-3

Modaresi, R. (2024). *AI-Based Explainable Classification Of News Articles For Supply Chain Risk Management*. https://urn.kb.se/resolve?urn=urn:nbn:se:uu:diva-546454

Mugurusi, G., & Oluka, P. N. (2021). Towards Explainable Artificial Intelligence (XAI) in Supply Chain Management: A Typology and Research Agenda. In Dolgui, A., Bernard, A., Lemoine, D., von Cieminski, G., & Romero, D. (Eds.), *Advances in Production Management Systems. Artificial Intelligence for Sustainable and Resilient Production Systems* (pp. 32–38). Springer International Publishing., DOI: 10.1007/978-3-030-85910-7_4

Naim, A., Alqahtani, H., Fatima, S., & Khan, M. F. (2023). Applications of Artificial Intelligence of Things in Green Supply Chain Management: Challenges and Future Directions. In *Blockchain, IoT, and AI Technologies for Supply Chain Management*. CRC Press. DOI: 10.1201/9781003264521-5

Naz, F., Kumar, A., Majumdar, A., & Agrawal, R. (2022). Is artificial intelligence an enabler of supply chain resiliency post COVID-19? An exploratory state-of-the-art review for future research. *Operations Management Research : Advancing Practice Through Research*, *15*(1), 378–398. DOI: 10.1007/s12063-021-00208-w

Nimmy, S. F. (2024). *Explainable Artificial Intelligence in Supply Chain Operational Risk Management (XAI-SCORM): A Comprehensive Approach towards Interpretability, Transparency, and Trustworthiness* [Thesis, UNSW Sydney]. DOI: 10.26190/unsworks/30133

Papadopoulos, T., Singh, S. P., Spanaki, K., Gunasekaran, A., & Dubey, R. (2022). Towards the next generation of manufacturing: Implications of big data and digitalization in the context of industry 4.0. *Production Planning and Control*, *33*(2–3), 101–104. DOI: 10.1080/09537287.2020.1810767

Pattnaik, S., Liew, N., Kures, A. O., Pinsky, E., & Park, K. (2024). Catalyzing Supply Chain Evolution: A Comprehensive Examination of Artificial Intelligence Integration in Supply Chain Management. *Engineering Proceedings*, *68*(1), 1. DOI: 10.3390/engproc2024068057

Pournader, M., Ghaderi, H., Hassanzadegan, A., & Fahimnia, B. (2021). Artificial intelligence applications in supply chain management. *International Journal of Production Economics*, *241*, 108250. DOI: 10.1016/j.ijpe.2021.108250

Pramanik, P., Jana, R. K., & Ghosh, I. (2024). AI readiness enablers in developed and developing economies: Findings from the XGBoost regression and explainable AI framework. *Technological Forecasting and Social Change*, *205*, 123482. DOI: 10.1016/j.techfore.2024.123482

Rakholia, R., Suárez-Cetrulo, A. L., Singh, M., & Simón Carbajo, R. (2024). Advancing Manufacturing Through Artificial Intelligence: Current Landscape, Perspectives, Best Practices, Challenges, and Future Direction. *IEEE Access, 12*, 131621-131637. IEEE Access. DOI: 10.1109/ACCESS.2024.3458830

Saberi, S., Kouhizadeh, M., Sarkis, J., & Shen, L. (2019). Blockchain technology and its relationships to sustainable supply chain management. *International Journal of Production Research, 57*(7), 2117–2135. DOI: 10.1080/00207543.2018.1533261

Sadeghi, R. K., Ojha, D., Kaur, P., Mahto, R. V., & Dhir, A. (2024). Explainable artificial intelligence and agile decision-making in supply chain cyber resilience. *Decision Support Systems, 180*, 114194. DOI: 10.1016/j.dss.2024.114194

Saen, R. F., Yousefi, F., & Azadi, M. (2024). Artificial intelligence powered predictions: Enhancing supply chain sustainability. *Annals of Operations Research.* DOI: 10.1007/s10479-024-06088-0

Schoepf, S., Foster, J., & Brintrup, A. (2024). Identifying Contributors to Supply Chain Outcomes in a Multiechelon Setting: A Decentralised Approach. *IEEE Transactions on Industrial Informatics, 20*(12), 13811-13819. *IEEE Transactions on Industrial Informatics*. DOI: 10.1109/TII.2024.3435431

Senoner, J., Netland, T., & Feuerriegel, S. (2022). Using Explainable Artificial Intelligence to Improve Process Quality: Evidence from Semiconductor Manufacturing. *Management Science, 68*(8), 5704–5723. DOI: 10.1287/mnsc.2021.4190

Sharma, A. J., & Rathore, B. (s. d.). Examine the enablers of generative artificial intelligence adoption in supply chain: A mixed method study. *Journal of Decision Systems, 0*(0), 1-33. DOI: 10.1080/12460125.2024.2410030

Sharma, V. K., & Kumar, H. (2024). Enablers Driving Success of Artificial Intelligence in Business Performance: A TISM-MICMAC Approach. *IEEE Transactions on Engineering Management, 71*, 4665-4675. *IEEE Transactions on Engineering Management*. DOI: 10.1109/TEM.2023.3236768

Sodiya, E. O., Jacks, B. S., Ugwuanyi, E. D., Adeyinka, M. A., Umoga, U. J., Daraojimba, A. I., Lottu, O. A., Sodiya, E. O., Jacks, B. S., Ugwuanyi, E. D., Adeyinka, M. A., Umoga, U. J., Daraojimba, A. I., & Lottu, O. A.Enoch Oluwademilade SodiyaBoma Sonimitiem JacksEjike David UgwuanyiMojisola Abimbola AdeyinkaUchenna Joseph UmogaAndrew Ifesinachi DaraojimbaOluwaseun Augustine Lottu. (2024). Reviewing the role of AI and machine learning in supply chain analytics. *GSC Advanced Research and Reviews, 18*(2), 2. DOI: 10.30574/gscarr.2024.18.2.0069

Sunmola, F., Baryannis, G., Tan, A., Co, K., & Papadakis, E. (2025). Holistic Framework for Blockchain-Based Halal Compliance in Supply Chains Enabled by Artificial Intelligence. *Systems*, *13*(1), 1. DOI: 10.3390/systems13010021

Tchuente, D., Lonlac, J., & Kamsu-Foguem, B. (2024). A methodological and theoretical framework for implementing explainable artificial intelligence (XAI) in business applications. *Computers in Industry*, *155*, 104044. DOI: 10.1016/j.compind.2023.104044

Valle, F. D., & Oliver, M. (2020). Blockchain Enablers for Supply Chains: How to Boost Implementation in Industry. *IEEE Access, 8*, 209699-209716. IEEE Access. DOI: 10.1109/ACCESS.2020.3038463

Whig, P., & Adusumilli, S. B. K. (2023). Enhancing Healthcare Delivery Through AI-Driven Supply Chain Innovations: A Case Study Perspective. *International Transactions in Artificial Intelligence, 7*(7), Article 7. https://isjr.co.in/index.php/ITAI/article/view/313

Yadav, A., Garg, R. K., & Sachdeva, A. (2024). Artificial intelligence applications for information management in sustainable supply chain management: A systematic review and future research agenda. *International Journal of Information Management Data Insights*, *4*(2), 100292. DOI: 10.1016/j.jjimei.2024.100292

Yang, J., Blount, Y., & Amrollahi, A. (2024). Artificial intelligence adoption in a professional service industry: A multiple case study. *Technological Forecasting and Social Change*, *201*, 123251. DOI: 10.1016/j.techfore.2024.123251

Zhang, C., Cho, S., & Vasarhelyi, M. (2022). Explainable Artificial Intelligence (XAI) in auditing. *International Journal of Accounting Information Systems*, *46*, 100572. DOI: 10.1016/j.accinf.2022.100572

Zhang, L., Zhang, M., Mujumdar, A. S., & Chen, Y. (2024). From farm to market : Research progress and application prospects of artificial intelligence in the frozen fruits and vegetables supply chain. *Trends in Food Science & Technology*, *153*, 104730. DOI: 10.1016/j.tifs.2024.104730

Chapter 8
Systematic Literature Review of Supply Chain Management and Metaverse

Asmae El Jaouhari
https://orcid.org/0000-0002-3100-363X
National School of Applied Sciences, Berrechid, Morocco

Ayoub Barigo
Moroccan School of Engineering, Morocco

ABSTRACT

This study explores the transformative role of the Metaverse in reshaping supply chain management amid rapid technological advancements. It critically examines how this emerging technology impacts key areas such as demand forecasting, operations, inventory management, and logistical resilience—highlighting gains in efficiency, agility, and strategic decision-making. Through a holistic approach combining literature review and real-world use cases, the study reveals how the Metaverse and generative AI can foster intelligent, sustainable, and adaptive supply chain ecosystems. It offers a practical model for industry practitioners aiming to harness these technologies for optimization. The findings underscore the importance of continued research into the long-term implications of Metaverse adoption, particularly its broader influence on industry standards and societal outcomes. Ultimately, this work contributes to the growing body of knowledge and illustrates the revolutionary potential of the Metaverse in supply chain transformation.

DOI: 10.4018/979-8-3373-0923-1.ch008

1. INTRODUCTION

In the fast-evolving environment of modern commerce, the efficient management of supply chains has become increasingly critical for sustaining competitive advantage and meeting customer expectations. As businesses strive to channelize through the complexities of global markets, the integration of advanced technologies has emerged as a cornerstone for driving innovation and optimization within supply chain operations. the metaverse stand out as transformative forces, offering unprecedented opportunities to enhance efficiency, resilience, and strategic decision-making. This sets the stage for exploring the forward-looking perspective on leveraging metaverse to unlock the optimization potential in supply chain management. The supply chain management (SCM) field has undergone pro- found transformations due to technological advancements. Metaverse, have gained significant attention in recent years (El Jaouhari, Arif, Samadhiya, et al., 2024; Pellegrino et al., 2024). The Metaverse offers unique attributes that distinguish it from these technologies. The Metaverse underscores service-oriented sustainability and social engagement, creating a scalable environment that fosters a heightened sense of community (El Jaouhari, Arif, Jawab, et al., 2024; Mahdikhani & Meena, 2024)

What is the metaverse? The term 'metaverse' was coined in 1992 in Neal Stephenson's literary work, Snow Crash, visualizing it as a black spherical planet accessible to users through terminals with integrated virtual reality capabilities and where users could appear as avatars(Polas et al., 2022). According to El Jaouhari et al., (2024), "The metaverse is the next evolution of the Internet. It's a fusing of the digital and physical worlds powered by technologies, including virtual and augmented reality, blockchain, artificial intelligence, and the Internet of things that connects smart devices". Lovich (2022) defines the metaverse as "a combination of the virtual reality and mixed reality worlds accessed through a browser or headset, which allows people to have real time interactions and experiences across distance." Metaverse develops fast. Digital technology leaders like Nvidia with Omniverse and Facebook with Meta profoundly invest in metaverse solutions (Chen et al., 2023). Supply On sup-plier collaboration platform (De Giovanni, 2023) and the Catena-X data ecosystem have been developed in automotive industry allowing for creation of digital product passports and improving sustainability and resilience of supply chains from the ecosystem perspective (Patnaik et al., 2024).

As a fusion of various technologies, scholars have pointed out that the metaverse combines the real world with the digital world, thus supplying users with a new and fundamentally enhanced real-life experience. During the industrial transformation caused by metaverse, as an important part of the industrial sector, manufacturing enterprises are seeking more advanced digital technology to improve production efficiency in the face of multiple pressures of technological progress and personalized demand upgrading (Pellegrino et al., 2024). For example, manufacturing enterprises compete to meet consumer demand through innovation capability enhancement and have spawned the development of intelligent manufacturing and process digitization in enterprises. Based on this, scholars have pointed out that setting up digital technologies such as artificial intelligence in the production process to enhance the customer experience is becoming a way to improve corporate value.

In a two-party supply chain, the manufacturers are upstream and responsible for production and development of the product process, and the retailer is responsible for selling products to consumers. To reduce production costs and improve customers' consumption and purchasing experience intention, manufacturers will lead the development process of metaverse in the supply chain by providing construction funds and technological development (Dolgui & Ivanov, 2023). Downstream of the supply chain, retailers are responsible for providing consumer data and providing services to consumers. At the same time, the development of the metaverse will improve the profitability of retailers by increasing sales and customer satisfaction. Therefore, to improve their profitability, retailers will also participate in the development of the metaverse (Mahdikhani & Meena, 2024). As a third party, the government has always been the key orientation of the digital promotion policy business transformation. In addition, social and economic issues will bring multiple benefits to businesses, such as tax and reputation benefits.

Supply Chain Integration plays a key role in realizing its full potential. By fostering collaboration and coordination between suppliers, manufacturers, distributors, retailers and customers, Supply Chain integration facilitates the efficient flow of materials, information, and resources (Mahdikhani & Meena, 2024). This integration goes beyond traditional linear supply chains and includes circular supply chains that give priority to resource recovery, recycling, and regeneration. One of the key factors of the circular economy is the need to design and implement closed loop systems that allow the reuse, repair or recycling of materials and products at the end of their life cycle. The Supply Chain Integration enables the seamless integration of reverse logistics, enabling the collection, selection and processing of end-of-life products and materials for their reintroduction into the production cycle (El Jaouhari, Arif, Jawab, et al., 2024). This integration reduces waste, optimizes resource utilization, and supports the circular economy's principles of product life extension and resource recovery [14]. Furthermore, Supply Chain Integration fosters transparency and traceability throughout the Supply Chain, which is crucial for implementing Circular Economy practices. Traceability systems have increasingly been an important tool to improve SC performance in relation to SC risk management because of its ability to obtain, update and transfer information in real time with minimal delays and errors (Mahdikhani & Meena, 2024). Coupled with the increased availability and accessibility of digital technologies, the demands for transparency and traceability among the SC actors continues to increase making it an effective capability to minimize production and distribution disruptions and fur-there ensure the efficient tracking and tracing of potentially deficient batches in case of any recalls (Lăzăroiu et al., 2024). By having visibility into the origin, composition, and lifecycle of products and materials, stakeholders can make informed decisions regarding sourcing, production, and end-of-life management.

This study aims at advancing our understanding on how the metaverse will influence SCRM. In particular we are interested in exploring the following research questions (RQ):

> RQ1: What is the role of the metaverse in supply chain risk management?
> RQ2: What are the Applications of the metaverse in the supply chains risk management?
> RQ3: What are the drivers and challenges of metaverse in the supply chain risk management?

This chapter explores the opportunities and challenges of integrating metaverse into supply chain risk management, with a focus on its implications for resilience, sustainability and digital transformation. By combining technological and strategic approaches, it proposes ways to maximize the benefits of these innovations while minimizing their negative effects, Contributing to more efficient and sustainable supply chain management in a changing environment.

2. THEORETICAL BACKGROUND

It is necessary to ground the debate in a solid theoretical framework that bridges supply chain theory, digital transformation, and immersive technologies in order to fully comprehend the potential of the metaverse in supply chain risk management. The main frameworks that facilitate the incorporation of metaverse technologies into modern supply chain risk management procedures are summarized in this section.

2.1 Supply Chain Risk Management Fundamentals

In light of interconnected networks, global disruptions, and increased unpredictability, supply chain risk management has become a strategic need (Pellegrino et al., 2024). It includes identifying, evaluating, mitigating, and tracking risks that jeopardize supply chain operations' performance and continuity (Seiti et al., 2024). The Resource-Based View (RBV), one of the fundamental theories in this field, stresses the use of special internal capabilities, such technology and knowledge assets, for resilience and competitive advantage (Bag, 2023). Furthermore, a firm's capacity to detect, seize, and reorganize resources in response to changing circumstances is highlighted by the Dynamic Capabilities Theory (Teece et al., 1997). This is particularly relevant for creating robust and adaptable supply chains. By acknowledging supply chains as intricate, linked systems where localized disturbances can have systemic effects, the Network Theory contributes to SCRM. In order to improve transparency, traceability, and coordinated risk responses, this networked perspective encourages the adoption of distributed technologies, including those integrated into the metaverse (Polas et al., 2022).

2.2 Risk Management and Digitalization Development

By facilitating real-time data gathering, predictive analytics, and scenario planning, the digitization of supply chains—facilitated by technologies like IoT, blockchain, artificial intelligence, and digital twins—has completely changed the way risks are handled (Jaouhari et al., 2023). The Socio-Technical Systems Theory, which stresses the interplay between technology and human components in attaining organizational performance, is in line with these technologies (Vlachos, 2023). In this situation, digital technologies not only improve operational capabilities but also change how people think about and react to risks. A pertinent theoretical perspective is also offered by the literature on Cyber-Physical Systems (CPS) and Digital Supply Chain Twins, which emphasize how the synchronization of virtual and physical assets allows ongoing risk monitoring and disruption simulation (El Jaouhari et al., 2025). The foundation for comprehending the metaverse as a more sophisticated type of digital transformation is established by these theories.

2.3 Supply Chain Metaverse Conceptualization

According to Smart (2022), the metaverse falls under the umbrella of Embodied Cognition Theory and Extended Reality Theory, which investigate how virtual environments affect human perception, learning, and decision-making. The metaverse enables virtual stakeholder engagement, immersive training simulations, and digital replications of logistics networks for risk-stress testing in supply chain contexts (Chen et al., 2023). These skills are also consistent with Real Options Theory, which offers a framework for assessing proactive risk reduction and strategy flexibility in unpredictable situations (Chi et al., 2019).

3. METHODOLOGY

To develop an updated synopsis of existing research at the intersection of metaverse and SCRM, we conducted a systematic literature review (SLR). SLRs are considered the appropriate tool to systematically assess and evaluate a given body of literature. We deployed a SLR method over other literature review methods for a number of reasons: first, SLRs are more objective than narrative literature reviews(Riaz et al., 2024); second, SLRs allow to produce holistic conclusions stemming from a detailed, transparent and planned process that enable reproducibility(Wan et al., 2023); third, SLRs entail the adoption of a quantitative approach that allows to identify where there is research, but also where there are research gaps(Dolgui & Ivanov, 2023), thus helping generate robust research agendas to advance the field (Pellegrino et al., 2024). Thus far, the SLR method has been largely adopted in the social sciences (De Giovanni, 2023) and more specifically in the management literature (Patnaik et al., 2024), with the aim of presenting findings in a relevant and accessible manner to scholars and decision-makers (Wan et al., 2023).

By following the SLR methodology proposed by (Riaz et al., 2024), data was gathered by collecting documents from two key databases: Scopus and Web of Science (WOS) (Wang et al., 2023). These databases were chosen as they assemble a collection of the most important sources of academic research and scholarly articles in the social sciences field (Polas et al., 2022). The Elsevier owned and managed Scopus database is deemed one of the most complete scientific databases indexing research production across a myriad of academic disciplines. It covers more than 22,000 scientific publications from over 5000 international publishers (Wan et al., 2023). The Clarivate owned Web of Science (WOS) Core Collection offers access to seven databases - Science Citation Index expand (SCIE), Social Sciences Citation Index (SSCI), Arts & Humanities Citation Index (AHCI), Emerging Sources Citation Index (ESCI), Conference Proceedings Citation Index (CPCI), Book Citation Index (BKCI), and Current Chemical Reactions and Index Chemicus, starting from 1900. WOS references cross-disciplinary research covering over 28,000 journals from 3300 publishers with high criteria standards and rigorous protocols (Colin, 2005). Both databases allow organizing and integrating data retrieved from different sources (i.e., articles, books chapters, conference papers) in any bibliographic format for each cited reference. Additionally, this embedding feature guarantees the scientific rigour, making this attribute valuable for bibliometric analysis (Polas et al., 2022),establishing reliability, validity and relevance of the documents retrieved in both databases (Mystakidis, 2022a). To support our choice to produce a robust, accurate and effective research we used the same set of terms/keywords to perform an initial advanced search in both Scopus and WOS databases, as presented in Figure 1.

Figure 1. Research methodology process

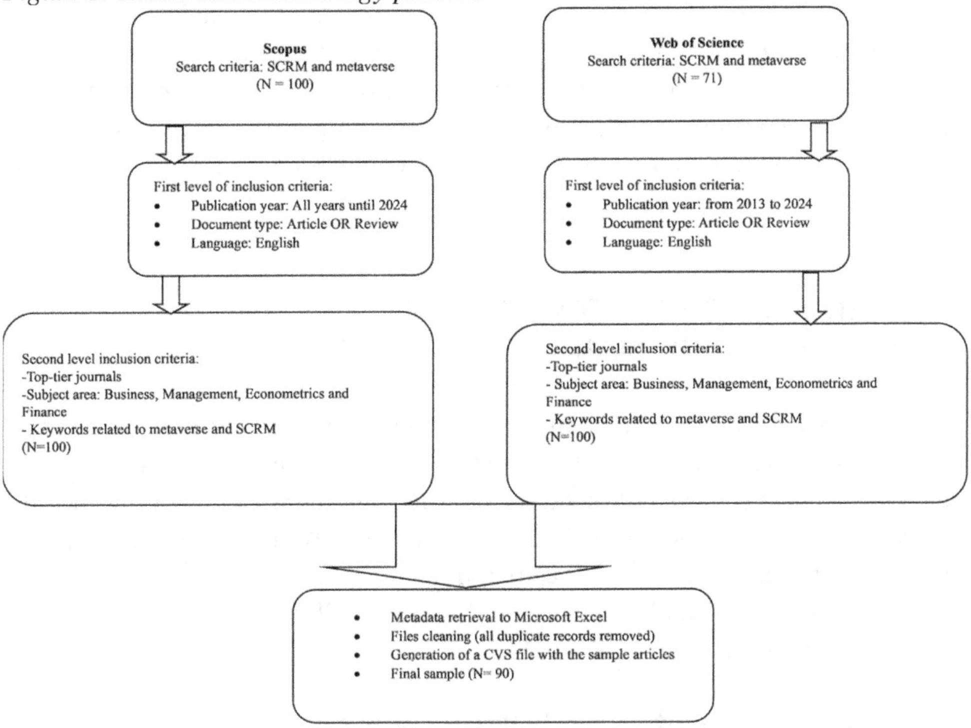

Firstly, we identified multiple keywords based on recent systematic literature reviews and bibliometric studies focusing on Supply chain Risk Management and the Metaverse (Mystakidis, 2022b). The keywords include "supply chain risk management", "metaverse", as well as keywords related to SCRM and related enabling and supporting technologies and techniques such as "virtual supply chain management", "virtual reality ", "Metaverse platforms", "Blockchain for supply chain security in the metaverse". The Scopus database was searched by looking for combinations of the Supply chain Risk Management keywords and Metaverse in the title, abstract, or keywords (Stadtler & Kilger, 2005). This yielded 300 documents. In line with systematic literature reviews conducted elsewhere (Moyaux et al., 2006), we narrowed down our search considering only articles and review papers (De Giovanni, 2023) in English language in the subject area (Riaz et al., 2024) of Business, Management and Accounting; Decision Science; Economics, Econometrics and Finance. This narrowed down the sample to 100 articles. Secondly, we searched the WOS database core collection by employing the same combination of keywords previously used on Scopus to search publications. We also added the operator AND to confine the results to the area of Business, Management, Business Finance, Economics. This yielded 71 documents. We excluded all duplicates from our dataset (i.e., articles that were present in both databases were included only once in our final database), that led us to obtain a total of 100 documents as our final sample. Finally, we retrieved the metadata for these 90 articles which included author names, titles, country of corresponding author/s, total number of publications, citation counts (i.e., total citations, average article citations, and number of citing articles with and without self-citations), journal sources, keywords, and countries as well as institutional affiliations.

4. THE ROLE OF THE METAVERSE IN SUPPLY CHAIN RISK MANAGEMENT

The metaverse, a virtual and augmented reality space where users interact in real-time, is emerging as a transformative tool for various industries. In supply chain management (SCM), the metaverse presents innovative solutions to mitigate and manage risks, enhancing resilience and operational efficiency. This chapter explores how the metaverse can reshape supply chain risk management by providing predictive analytics, virtual simulations, enhanced collaboration, and immersive training environments (Riaz et al., 2024).

4.1. Predictive Analytics and Digital Twins

The metaverse enables the creation of digital twins—virtual replicas of physical assets, facilities, and supply chain networks. By simulating real-world conditions, businesses can identify potential disruptions, predict bottlenecks, and evaluate different scenarios to optimize decision-making. For example, logistics companies can model weather conditions, geopolitical events, and demand fluctuations to foresee potential delays and proactively adjust their operations (Mystakidis, 2022a).

5.2. Real-Time Collaboration and Communication

One of the key advantages of the metaverse is its ability to facilitate real-time collaboration among stakeholders across the globe. Supply chain partners can convene in virtual environments to discuss contingencies, share data, and coordinate responses to disruptions. This immersive communication reduces the limitations of traditional video conferencing and fosters deeper engagement and understanding, crucial during crisis management (Ning et al., n.d.).

5.3. Risk Scenario Simulations and Training

The metaverse offers immersive training environments where employees can undergo simulations of risk scenarios, such as supply chain cyber-attacks, natural disasters, or equipment failures. This hands-on experience equips teams with the skills and preparedness needed to respond effectively to real-world incidents. Such simulations enhance risk awareness, decision-making, and emergency response strategies (Wang et al., 2023).

5.4. Enhancing Visibility and Traceability

Through blockchain integration within the metaverse, supply chains gain enhanced visibility and traceability. Products can be tracked from origin to delivery in a virtual environment, ensuring transparency and authenticity. This not only helps mitigate fraud but also ensures compliance with regulatory requirements, reducing the risk of supply chain disruptions due to non-conformity.

5.5. Supplier and Partner Vetting

In the metaverse, businesses can conduct virtual audits and inspections of supplier facilities, regardless of their physical location. This reduces the time and cost associated with on-site visits while ensuring that suppliers adhere to quality and ethical standards. Virtual site visits enhance due diligence and minimize the risk of partnering with unreliable or non-compliant entities (Mahdikhani & Meena, 2024).

5.6. Innovation and Future Outlook

As the metaverse evolves, its potential to revolutionize supply chain risk management will expand. Emerging technologies such as AI, IoT, and 5G will further enhance metaverse capabilities, enabling more accurate simulations and real-time monitoring of supply chain networks. Companies that invest in metaverse-driven solutions today will be better positioned to navigate future uncertainties and maintain a competitive edge (Patnaik et al., 2024).

5. APPLYING THE METAVERSE IN THE SUPPLY CHAINS RISK MANAGEMENT

5.1. Virtual Warehousing and Inventory Management

The metaverse enables businesses to create virtual warehouses where they can simulate and analyze storage layouts, inventory levels, and operations. By leveraging technologies like digital twins, supply chain managers can monitor real-time stock levels, predict shortages, and optimize storage space without physically altering the warehouse. This virtual approach reduces operational inefficiencies, improves inventory accuracy, and minimizes waste. For instance, companies can simulate seasonal demand fluctuations in the metaverse and adjust their storage strategies accordingly, ensuring seamless operations (Dolgui & Ivanov, 2023).

5.2. Immersive Training and Collaboration

One of the key applications of the metaverse is its ability to revolutionize employee training and team collaboration. Workers can be trained in virtual environments that replicate real-world supply chain scenarios, such as warehouse operations, equipment handling, or logistics processes. This immersive training reduces the risks associated with on-the-job learning and enhances employee productivity. Additionally, the metaverse allows global teams to collaborate in virtual spaces, enabling seamless communication and decision-making across different geographical locations, which is particularly useful for multinational supply chains (El Jaouhari, Arif, Samadhiya, et al., 2024).

5.3. Digital Twins and Real-Time Monitoring

Digital twins, virtual replicas of physical supply chain components, are central to the metaverse's impact on supply chains. These replicas allow organizations to monitor and manage every aspect of the supply chain in real time. For example, logistics companies can track shipments, predict delays, and optimize delivery routes using data from digital twins. In manufacturing, digital twins can simulate production processes, identify potential bottlenecks, and test solutions virtually before implementing them in the real world. This application significantly reduces downtime and enhances supply chain resilience (Dolgui & Ivanov, 2023).

5.4. Enhanced Customer Experience and Transparency

The metaverse provides opportunities to improve customer experiences by offering virtual storefronts and enhanced transparency in product journeys. Consumers can interact with products in immersive virtual environments, gaining detailed insights into product features and quality. Additionally, the metaverse enables real-time tracking of products from manufacturing to delivery, allowing customers to have complete visibility into the supply chain. This transparency builds trust and strengthens customer relationships, which is increasingly important in today's consumer-driven market (El Jaouhari, Arif, Samadhiya, et al., 2024).

5.5. Logistics Optimization Through Virtual Simulations

Logistics is one of the most complex components of supply chains, and the metaverse offers tools to optimize it. Companies can simulate transportation routes, warehouse layouts, and delivery schedules in a virtual environment to identify inefficiencies and develop optimized solutions. For example, delivery companies can use "VR" simulations to test and choose the most efficient routes, minimizing fuel consumption and delivery times. This application not only improves operational efficiency but also reduces environmental impact, aligning with sustainability goals (Moyaux et al., 2006).

6. DRIVERS AND BARRIERS OF METAVERSE IN SUPPLY CHAIN MANAGEMENT

6.1. Drivers of Metaverse in SCRM

With the metaverse emerging as a transformative tool to improve visibility, resilience, and operational efficiency, the rapid evolution of digital technologies is reshaping supply chain risk management. By combining virtual environments, real-time data analytics, and immersive simulations, the metaverse helps organizations better anticipate, mitigate, and respond to supply chain disruptions. This paper examines the driving forces behind the adoption of explainable metaverse frameworks in supply chain risk management, which are divided into several categories: technological advancements, data integration, security, sustainability, human-centric design, and resilience. All of these factors make supply chain ecosystems smarter and more flexible(Dolgui & Ivanov, 2023). Table 1 illustrates the main drivers of the metaverse-enabled SCRM.

Table 1. Drivers of metaverse in SCRM

Main Category	Sub-Category	Description	References
1. Predictive Analytics	Scenario Modeling	Models various supply chain scenarios for decision-making.	(Mystakidis, 2022a)
2.Real-time Collaboration	Virtual Meetings	Facilitates global meetings in virtual	(Lăzăroiu et al., 2024)
3. Virtual collaboration	Training & Upskilling	Provides immersive environments for employee training and skills development in supply chain management.	(Lăzăroiu et al., 2024)
	Cross-functional teams	Enhances collaboration across global supply chain teams through shared virtual spaces.	(Wan et al., 2023)
4. Augmented operations	Smart warehousing	Improves inventory management using augmented reality for item tracking and picking.	(El Jaouhari et al., 2024)
	Field maintenance	Offers AR tools for real-time troubleshooting and repair in supply chain operations.	(Lăzăroiu et al., 2024)
5. Immersive customer experience	Virtual showrooms	Allows customers to explore and customize products in 3D environments, improving demand forecasting.	(Mystakidis, 2022a)
	Personalized feedback	Collects real-time customer preferences to improve product design and supply chain responsiveness.	(Wan et al., 2023)
6. Blockchain integration	Transparent transactions	Utilizes blockchain for traceability and accountability in supply chain transactions.	(Polas et al., 2022)
	Secure data exchange	Ensures secure sharing of data across supply chain stakeholders.	(Chen et al., 2023)
7.Autonomous Systems	Robotic process automation (RPA)	Uses RPA for automating repetitive tasks, improving efficiency in supply chain operations.	(Dolgui & Ivanov, 2023)

6.2. Barrier of Metaverse in SCRM

While there are many advantages to using the metaverse in supply chain management, there are also several obstacles and difficulties that businesses must overcome. The smooth integration of metaverse technologies into current supply chain systems is hampered by technological obstacles such insufficient infrastructure, interoperability problems, and data security worries. Companies find it challenging to justify the change because to financial constraints, such as large initial investment requirements, uncertain returns on investment (ROI), and continuous maintenance costs. Workforce adaptation presents additional difficulties since adoption rates are slowed by a lack of technical skills, reluctance to change, and the requirement for extensive training programs. Additionally, legislative issues include intellectual property protection, data privacy compliance, and the lack of global metaverse standards, make international supply chain activities more difficult. Finally, environmental issues like excessive energy use, managing e-waste, and resource-intensive development cast doubt on the viability of large-scale metaverse technology deployment. Strategic planning, innovation investment, and an emphasis on cooperation among supply chain stakeholders will be necessary to meet these difficulties (Stadtler & Kilger, 2005). Table 1 illustrates the main barriers of the metaverse-enabled SCRM.

Table 2. Barrier of metaverse in SCRM

Main Category	Sub-Category	Description	References
Technological Barriers	Lack of Infrastructure	Insufficient internet speed, bandwidth, or server capacity for real-time simulations in the metaverse.	(Dolgui & Ivanov, 2023)
	Interoperability Issues	Difficulty in integrating metaverse platforms with existing supply chain systems and ERP software.	(Chen et al., 2023)
	Data Security Concerns	Risks related to cyberattacks and data breaches due to immersive virtual environments.	(Polas et al., 2022)
	Limited Hardware Accessibility	High costs of VR/AR headsets and specialized hardware restrict adoption among supply chain players.	(Wan et al., 2023)
Financial Constraints	High Initial Investment	Large capital required for metaverse infrastructure, software, and training.	(Mystakidis, 2022a)
	Uncertain ROI	Lack of clarity on return on investment, leading to hesitancy among stakeholders.	(Lăzăroiu et al., 2024)
	Ongoing Maintenance Costs	Significant expenses for maintaining, upgrading, and scaling the metaverse infrastructure over time.	(El Jaouhari et al., 2024)
Workforce Adaptation	Lack of Skills	Workforce lacks technical expertise to operate in the metaverse environment.	(Mystakidis, 2022a)
	Training Challenges	Difficulty in creating effective training programs for immersive environments like VR/AR.	(Wan et al., 2023)
Regulatory Issues	Data Privacy Regulations	Variations in data protection laws across regions make compliance difficult in a global supply chain.	(Lăzăroiu et al., 2024)
	Intellectual Property Concerns	Challenges in protecting proprietary virtual designs and assets used in the metaverse.	(Wang et al., 2023)
	Standards and Governance	Lack of universal standards for operating and managing supply chain activities in the metaverse.	(Jaouhari, Arif, Samadhiya, Kumar, & Trinkūnas, 2023)
	Environmental Concerns	Concerns about the energy consumption and carbon footprint of metaverse operations.	(Mahdikhani & Meena, 2024)

7. DISCUSSION

The exploration of the metaverse as a transformative force in SCRM reveals both immense opportunities and notable challenges. As industries navigate an increasingly complex and volatile global landscape, the metaverse's ability to integrate virtual and augmented realities offers significant advantages in enhancing supply chain resilience, transparency, and operational efficiency. One of the key themes emerging from this study is the potential of digital twins to revolutionize predictive analytics (Mystakidis, 2022b). The capacity to simulate real-world scenarios in virtual environments allows organizations to proactively identify risks, optimize logistics, and anticipate disruptions. This predictive approach provides a critical advantage in mitigating potential delays and inefficiencies. The case of logistics companies modeling geopolitical events and weather disruptions highlights the metaverse's practical application in fostering agile and adaptive supply chains (Riaz et al., 2024).

Additionally, the metaverse fosters real-time collaboration and communication across geographically dispersed supply chain partners. The ability to conduct virtual site visits, audits, and stakeholder meetings reduces logistical barriers, saving time and resources. This enhanced connectivity ensures that decision-making is more inclusive and responsive to dynamic supply chain conditions (Wan et al., 2023). The immersive nature of these virtual environments also strengthens stakeholder engagement and facilitates knowledge sharing, contributing to more cohesive risk management strategies. The immersive training environments enabled by the metaverse presents another critical advancement. By simulating risk scenarios, such as cyber-attacks or equipment failures, employees gain practical experience and develop the skills necessary to manage real-world crises. This proactive training approach reduces the learning curve and enhances organizational preparedness, fostering a culture of resilience and adaptability (Mystakidis, 2022b).

However, while the metaverse presents numerous opportunities, its adoption in SCRM is not without challenges. The initial costs of developing metaverse infrastructure, including virtual reality (VR) and augmented reality (AR) technologies, can be prohibitive for smaller enterprises. Furthermore, integrating metaverse platforms with existing supply chain systems may require significant technical expertise and investments in digital transformation. These barriers underscore the need for strategic planning and phased implementation to ensure seamless integration and maximize returns on investment (De Giovanni, 2023). Security and data privacy concerns also emerge as critical considerations in the metaverse's application to SCRM. As supply chains become increasingly interconnected, ensuring secure data exchange and protecting sensitive information from cyber threats becomes paramount. Blockchain technology offers a potential solution by enhancing traceability and ensuring transparency in supply chain transactions, but its widespread adoption will necessitate collaborative efforts across industries. Another key consideration is the regulatory landscape surrounding metaverse technologies. Governments and industry bodies must establish clear guidelines and standards to ensure ethical and responsible use of the metaverse in supply chains. This will require ongoing dialogue between policymakers, technology developers, and supply chain practitioners to address emerging risks and harness the metaverse's full potential (Polas et al., 2022).

Despite these challenges, the drivers for metaverse adoption in SCRM are compelling. The growing emphasis on sustainability, circular economy practices, and resource optimization aligns with the metaverse's ability to improve transparency, track product lifecycles, and facilitate reverse logistics. By enhancing visibility across the supply chain, organizations can reduce waste, improve resource utilization, and contribute to broader environmental and social goals. Furthermore, the metaverse offers a transformative framework for enhancing supply chain agility. Real-time monitoring, facilitated by digital twins and IoT integration, enables companies to swiftly respond to disruptions and adjust their operations in real time. This capacity to adapt to changing market conditions provides a crucial competitive advantage, ensuring business continuity even in uncertain environments (Riaz et al., 2024).

The metaverse also holds potential in fostering innovation within supply chains. Virtual environments provide a platform for collaborative product development, enabling suppliers, manufacturers, and retailers to co-create and test new solutions. This collaborative approach accelerates the innovation cycle and reduces the time required to bring products to market. By streamlining design, testing, and deployment processes, the metaverse contributes to more efficient and responsive supply chains (Mystakidis, 2022b).

Another significant benefit is the metaverse's ability to personalize the customer experience. Virtual showrooms and immersive product demonstrations allow consumers to engage with products in new and interactive ways. This engagement not only enhances customer satisfaction but also provides valuable insights into consumer preferences and behavior. By leveraging these insights, companies can tailor their supply chain strategies to align more closely with market demand, driving higher levels of customer loyalty and retention (Ning et al., n.d.).

Moreover, the integration of AI and machine learning within the metaverse further amplifies its potential in supply chain management. These technologies enable predictive maintenance, automated decision-making, and intelligent forecasting, all of which contribute to more efficient and cost-effective operations. The synergy between AI and the metaverse opens new avenues for innovation, driving continuous improvement across supply chain networks (Patnaik et al., 2024).

8. IMPLICATIONS

8.1 Theoretical Implications

This systematic literature study advances a structured investigation of the metaverse's potential in SCRM, which advances the theoretical landscape. By incorporating immersive technologies like blockchain, digital twins, and extended reality (XR) into the SCRM conversation, it first expands the conceptual bounds of digital transformation in supply chains (Bittencourt et al., 2021; El Jaouhari et al., 2024). This research highlights the metaverse as a transformational facilitator of multi-agent simulations, scenario planning in volatile situations, and real-time risk visualization, whereas traditional SCRM frameworks have focused on resilience via digitalization (Seiti et al., 2024). Second, by describing how metaverse technologies can create adaptive and proactive risk mitigation environments through virtual training, disruption simulation, and stakeholder coordination in a 3D ecosystem, this review highlights a new research gap in the theory of immersive resilience. By highlighting the embodied interaction of human and digital agents, this enhances the theories of dynamic capacities and socio-technical systems (Ivanov, 2025).

The analysis concludes by pointing up methodological fragmentation in recent research, many of which depend on exploratory or conceptual techniques that lack thorough validation. In order to empirically evaluate the metaverse's effectiveness in controlling supply chain risks, this conclusion invites future researchers to use simulation-based modeling, mixed-method designs, and longitudinal case studies.

8.2 Practical Implications

Policymakers, leaders of digital transformation, and supply chain experts may all directly benefit from the results. First, the study provides businesses with strategic insights to integrate immersive tools into their risk management plans. For example, businesses in highly volatile industries (such semiconductors, medicines, or catastrophe logistics) can use metaverse-based platforms for remote coordination, real-time monitoring, and predictive disruption modeling in times of crisis (Wan et al., 2023). Second, the study promotes deliberate investment in digital infrastructures that are essential to achieving the full potential of the metaverse in SCRM, such as interoperable XR devices, 5G connectivity, and high-fidelity simulation settings. Supply chain managers are urged to give top priority to cross-functional training that blends immersive technology fluency with risk analytics in order to develop a workforce that is digitally literate and better equipped to handle future disruptions.

Third, legislators and regulatory agencies might use the study's insights to think about the data privacy issues, security threats, and standards requirements related to immersive settings. The appropriate implementation of the metaverse throughout global supply chains may be accelerated by clear regulations and industry-specific recommendations, especially in fields where traceability and compliance are crucial. In conclusion, this paper contributes to theoretical conversations on risk management in the digital age while also giving practitioners strategic insight into how to incorporate metaverse technology into supply chain systems that are intelligent, robust, and adaptable.

9. LIMITATIONS

This systematic literature study has a number of limitations, even if it provides insightful information on the developing relationship between SCRM and metaverse technologies. First, the quantity of excellent, peer-reviewed papers that could be included was limited due to the topic's infancy. The present discourse is largely dispersed across opinion articles, conceptual reflections, and grey literature, which might restrict the findings' empirical robustness and generalizability. Second, only English-language publications that were included in reputable databases like IEEE Xplore, Web of Science, and Scopus were included in the review. A selection bias may have been introduced as a result of the unintentional exclusion of pertinent contributions from regional studies or non-English sources. Third, given how quickly the metaverse ecosystem is changing, it's possible that new applications and technology advancements have surfaced since the review's deadline, which might have an impact on how timely the study is.

Fourth, it was difficult to standardize theme categories and interpret results across contexts since the included studies frequently had very different conceptual definitions of the terms “metaverse” and “supply chain risk management.” The results' consistency and comparability may be restricted by this conceptual variability. Lastly, because this review is based on literature, it does not have empirical validation from stakeholder interviews, case studies, or simulations. Future studies should fill up these gaps by evaluating the practical effectiveness of supply chain risk management techniques allowed by the metaverse through sector-specific research, experimental models, or longitudinal studies.

10. FUTURE DIRECTION

The future of the metaverse in SCRM is poised for significant growth and innovation. As technology continues to evolve, several key areas will shape the metaverse's trajectory and expand its capabilities within supply chain ecosystems (Pellegrino et al., 2024).

To fully harness the metaverse's potential, developing interoperable platforms and establishing industry-wide standards will be essential. By ensuring seamless integration across diverse supply chain systems, organizations can maximize efficiency and reduce operational silos. Future research should focus on creating unified frameworks that facilitate cross-industry collaboration and interoperability (Stadtler & Kilger, 2005).

The integration of more sophisticated AI and automation within the metaverse will drive smarter, self-optimizing supply chains. AI-driven insights will enhance predictive analytics, automate routine processes, and provide real-time decision-making capabilities. Future developments will likely see the expansion of autonomous supply chain networks powered by AI agents operating in metaverse environments (Polas et al., 2022).

Digital twins will continue to evolve, becoming more complex and encompassing entire supply chain networks. The ability to simulate end-to-end operations in real time will provide unparalleled visibility, allowing for more accurate forecasting, capacity planning, and disruption mitigation. Further advancements in IoT and 5G technologies will enhance the granularity and responsiveness of digital twins (Wan et al., 2023).

The metaverse offers unique opportunities to support circular economy initiatives by facilitating transparent supply chain processes and enabling efficient resource recovery. Future research and development should explore how metaverse platforms can drive sustainable practices, promote eco-friendly designs, and optimize resource utilization throughout product lifecycles (El Jaouhari, Arif, Samadhiya, et al., 2024).

To ensure widespread adoption, the metaverse must prioritize user experience and accessibility. Simplifying interfaces, enhancing usability, and incorporating human-centric design principles will lower adoption barriers and encourage broader participation. Future advancements will likely focus on creating intuitive, user-friendly metaverse environments tailored to diverse stakeholders (Riaz et al., 2024).

As global supply chains face increasing disruptions from geopolitical tensions, climate change, and economic uncertainty, the metaverse will play a pivotal role in enhancing resilience. By simulating crisis scenarios and creating virtual contingency plans, organizations can prepare for potential disruptions more effectively. Future developments may include scenario modelling platforms that allow businesses to test various risk mitigation strategies, fostering a proactive approach to supply chain resilience (Wan et al., 2023).

In conclusion, the integration of the metaverse into supply chain risk management represents a paradigm shift towards more intelligent, responsive, and resilient supply chains. While barriers to adoption exist, the potential benefits far outweigh the challenges, making the metaverse a critical enabler of future supply chain optimization. Continued research and cross-industry collaboration will be essential in addressing existing limitations and unlocking the metaverse's transformative potential in supply chain management (Chen et al., 2023).

11. CONCLUSION

The integration of the metaverse into supply chain risk management signifies a transformative leap towards creating more intelligent, responsive, and resilient supply chains. As industries increasingly embrace digital transformation, the metaverse emerges as a critical tool for enhancing operational efficiency, fostering innovation, and mitigating risks in an ever-evolving global landscape. The capabilities of the metaverse, including digital twins, immersive simulations, and AI-driven insights, provide organizations with unparalleled visibility and predictive capabilities. This enhances their ability to anticipate disruptions, streamline operations, and optimize resource allocation. Additionally, the metaverse fosters collaboration across supply chain partners, strengthening relationships and promoting a more cohesive, transparent, and sustainable approach to risk management. While the path to full metaverse integration presents challenges such as high initial investments, data security concerns, and the need for standardization, the long-term benefits far outweigh these hurdles. Organizations that strategically adopt metaverse technologies position themselves to not only manage supply chain risks more effectively but also drive innovation and gain competitive advantage. In summary, the metaverse represents a paradigm shift in supply chain risk management, reshaping the future of supply chain ecosystems. Continued research, cross-industry collaboration, and investment in emerging technologies will be essential to unlocking the full potential of the metaverse, ensuring that supply chains remain agile, resilient, and future-ready (Mahdikhani & Meena, 2024).

REFERENCES

Bag, S. (2023). From resources to sustainability: A practice-based view of net zero economy implementation in small and medium business-to-business firms. *Benchmarking, 31*(6), 1876–1894. DOI: 10.1108/BIJ-01-2023-0056

Bittencourt, V. L., Alves, A. C., & Leão, C. P. (2021). Industry 4.0 triggered by Lean Thinking: Insights from a systematic literature review. *International Journal of Production Research, 59*(5), 1496–1510. *Scopus*. DOI: 10.1080/00207543.2020.1832274

Chen, P.-K., Ye, Y., & Huang, X. (2023). The metaverse in supply chain knowledge sharing and resilience contexts: An empirical investigation of factors affecting adoption and acceptance. *Journal of Innovation & Knowledge*, *8*(4), 100446. DOI: 10.1016/j.jik.2023.100446

Chi, T., Li, J., Trigeorgis, L. G., & Tsekrekos, A. E. (2019). Real options theory in international business. *Journal of International Business Studies*, *50*(4), 525–553. DOI: 10.1057/s41267-019-00222-y

Colin, J. (2005). Le supply chain management existe-t-il réellement? *Revue française de gestion, 31*(156), 135–149. DOI: 10.3166/rfg.156.135-149

De Giovanni, P. (2023). Sustainability of the Metaverse: A Transition to Industry 5.0. *Sustainability (Basel)*, *15*(7), 6079. DOI: 10.3390/su15076079

Dolgui, A., & Ivanov, D. (2023). Metaverse supply chain and operations management. *International Journal of Production Research*, *61*(23), 8179–8191. DOI: 10.1080/00207543.2023.2240900

El Jaouhari, A., Arif, J., Jawab, F., Samadhiya, A., & Kumar, A. (2024). Unfolding the role of metaverse in agri-food supply chain security: Current scenario and future perspectives. *International Journal of Food Science & Technology*, *59*(5), 3451–3460. DOI: 10.1111/ijfs.16972

El Jaouhari, A., Arif, J., Samadhiya, A., Dhayal, K. S., Luthra, S., & Singh, S. (2025). From Automation to Augmentation: Exploring the Role of Industry 5.0 Advanced Technologies for Developing Countries. *Engineering Management Journal*, *37*(3), 306–323. DOI: 10.1080/10429247.2024.2407254

El Jaouhari, A., Arif, J., Samadhiya, A., Kumar, A., Jain, V., & Agrawal, R. (2024). Are metaverse applications in quality 4.0 enablers of manufacturing resiliency? An exploratory review under disruption impressions and future research. *The TQM Journal*, *36*(6), 1486–1525. DOI: 10.1108/TQM-06-2023-0181

El Jaouhari, A., Samadhiya, A., Benbrahim, F. Z., Kumar, A., & Luthra, S. (2024). Forging a green future: Synergizing industry 4.0 technologies and circular economy tactics to achieve net-zero in sustainable supply chains. *Computers & Industrial Engineering, 110691*. DOI: 10.1016/j.cie.2024.110691

Ivanov, D. (2025, June 19). A survey of system-cybernetic principles in supply chain resilience: Viability, artificial intelligence, digital twins, and ecosystems. *International Journal of Systems Science*, *0*(0), 1–16. DOI: 10.1080/00207721.2025.2519204

Jaouhari, A. E., Arif, J., Samadhiya, A., Kumar, A., & Garza-Reyes, J. A. (2023). An environmental-based perspective framework: Integrating IoT technology into a sustainable automotive supply chain. *Benchmarking*, *31*(10), 3655–3689. DOI: 10.1108/BIJ-05-2023-0322

Jaouhari, A. E., Arif, J., Samadhiya, A., Kumar, A., & Trinkūnas, V. (2023). Are we there or do we have more to do? Metaverse in facility management and future prospects. *International Journal of Strategic Property Management*, *27*(3), 3. DOI: 10.3846/ijspm.2023.19516

Lăzăroiu, G., Gedeon, T., Rogalska, E., Valaskova, K., Nagy, M., Musa, H., Zvarikova, K., Poliak, M., Horak, J., Cre oiu, R. I., Krulicky, T., Ionescu, L., Popa, C., Hurloiu, L. R., Nistor, F., Avram, L. G., & Braga, V. (2024). Digital twin-based cyber-physical manufacturing systems, extended reality metaverse enterprise and production management algorithms, and Internet of Things financial and labor market technologies in generative artificial intelligence economics. *Oeconomia Copernicana, 15*(3), 837–870. *Scopus.* DOI: 10.24136/oc.3183

Mahdikhani, M., & Meena, P. (2024). Metaverse applications and supply chain innovation: Insights from text mining. *Journal of Innovation & Knowledge*, *9*(4), 100591. DOI: 10.1016/j.jik.2024.100591

Moyaux, T., Chaib-draa, B., & D'Amours, S. (2006). Supply Chain Management and Multiagent Systems: An Overview. In Chaib-draa, B., & Müller, J. P. (Eds.), *Multiagent based Supply Chain Management* (Vol. 28, pp. 1–27). Springer Berlin Heidelberg., DOI: 10.1007/978-3-540-33876-5_1

Mystakidis, S. (2022a). Metaverse. *Encyclopedia*, *2*(1), 486–497. DOI: 10.3390/encyclopedia2010031

Mystakidis, S. (2022b). Metaverse. *Encyclopedia*, *2*(1), 486–497. DOI: 10.3390/encyclopedia2010031

Ning, H., Wang, H., Lin, Y., Wang, W., Dhelim, S., Farha, F., Ding, J., & Daneshmand, M. (n.d.). *A Survey on Metaverse: The State-of-the-art*. Technologies, Applications, and Challenges.

Patnaik, D., Pradhan, B. B., & Barik, T. R. (2024). *Optimization Potential Using AI and Metaverse In Supply Chain Management: A Forward-Looking Perspective. 22*(1).

Pellegrino, R., Russo, F., & Basile, L. J. (2024). The role of supply chain integration in the risk management of circular economy: A multiple case study in the furniture industry. *Procedia Computer Science*, *232*, 2933–2940. DOI: 10.1016/j.procs.2024.02.109

Polas, M. R. H., Afshar Jahanshahi, A., Kabir, A. I., Sohel-Uz-Zaman, A. S., Osman, A. R., & Karim, R. (2022). Artificial Intelligence, Blockchain Technology, and Risk-Taking Behavior in the 4.0IR Metaverse Era: Evidence from Bangladesh-Based SMEs. *Journal of Open Innovation*, *8*(3), 168. DOI: 10.3390/joitmc8030168

Riaz, M., Kausar, R., Jameel, T., & Pamucar, D. (2024). Cubic picture fuzzy topological data analysis with integrating blockchain and the metaverse for uncertain supply chain management. *Engineering Applications of Artificial Intelligence*, *131*, 107827. DOI: 10.1016/j.engappai.2023.107827

Seiti, H., Shabani, M., Ghanbari, H., Ben-Amor, S., & Hameed, A. I. (2024). *Toward a Human-Centric Metaverse: Novel Causal Decision Models for Supply Chain Risk Management* (SSRN Scholarly Paper 5007940). Social Science Research Network. DOI: 10.2139/ssrn.5007940

Smart, P. (2022). Minds in the Metaverse: Extended Cognition Meets Mixed Reality. *Philosophy & Technology*, *35*(4), 87. DOI: 10.1007/s13347-022-00580-w

Stadtler, H., & Kilger, C. (Eds.). (2005). *Supply chain management and advanced planning: Concepts, models, software and case studies* (3rd ed.). Springer. DOI: 10.1007/b106298

Teece, D. J., Pisano, G., & Shuen, A. (1997). Dynamic capabilities and strategic management. *Strategic Management Journal*, *18*(7), 509–533. DOI: 10.1002/(SICI)1097-0266(199708)18:7<509::AID-SMJ882>3.0.CO;2-Z

Vlachos, I. (2023). Implementation of an intelligent supply chain control tower: A socio-technical systems case study. *Production Planning and Control*, *34*(15), 1415–1431. DOI: 10.1080/09537287.2021.2015805

Wan, X., Zhang, G., Yuan, Y., & Chai, S. (2023). How to drive the participation willingness of supply chain members in metaverse technology adoption? *Applied Soft Computing*, *145*, 110611. DOI: 10.1016/j.asoc.2023.110611

Wang, Y., Su, Z., Zhang, N., Xing, R., Liu, D., Luan, T. H., & Shen, X. (2023). A Survey on Metaverse: Fundamentals, Security, and Privacy. *IEEE Communications Surveys and Tutorials*, *25*(1), 319–352. DOI: 10.1109/COMST.2022.3202047

Chapter 9
Systematic Literature Review of Blockchain Technology Applications in Agri-Food Supply Chain

Asmae El Jaouhari
https://orcid.org/0000-0002-3100-363X
National School of Applied Sciences, Berrechid, Morocco

Mohamed Amine El Berbri
Moroccan School of Engineering, Morocco

ABSTRACT

Blockchain is a fundamentally disruptive technology that will soon revolutionize the agri-food supply chain. Blockchain is a decentralized, digital, and unchangeable ledger of transactions that is distributed and duplicated throughout the network of computer systems. In order to determine the enabling features of blockchain technology that facilitate its use in the agri-food supply chain, this systematic review looks at the literature. Essential features including transparency, immutability, redundancy, adaptability, automation, and remittance were identified in the examined literature. Immutability and automation stand out among these characteristics in the current implementation, especially in food traceability. There are certain issues with the use of blockchain in the agri-food supply chain, though. Regarding technical advancement and its effects on the environment, further research is required.

DOI: 10.4018/979-8-3373-0923-1.ch009

1. INTRODUCTION

Transparency in the supply chain is still a major problem for enterprises and governments. It focuses on guaranteeing product quality and encouraging sustainable practices, going beyond operational optimization or regulatory compliance. Traceability, which entails monitoring a product's journey from its point of origin to the end user, is at the heart of this problem. According to many studies Blockchain technology (BCT) is a crucial way to deal with this complexity. Blockchain was first introduced by Nakamoto in 2008 for use in decentralized ledgers and financial transactions. Its success in cryptocurrencies demonstrated its versatility, with uses in a variety of sectors, including agriculture, food, and pharmaceuticals. Its use in supply chain management transforms conventional supply chain operations by showcasing features like smart contracts and increased transparency. From experimental applications, blockchain has become a key instrument for increasing visibility, efficiency, and trust in supply chain management. High-value items, such diamonds, were the focus of early installations in an effort to improve traceability and fight fraud. Its application has grown over time to include industries like pharmaceuticals for protecting drug supply chains and agriculture for confirming origin. Modern supply chains are becoming smarter and more resilient as a result of blockchain's integration with technologies like artificial intelligence (AI) and the Internet of Things (IoT), signaling a move toward full digital transformation (Tang et al., 2024).

This convergence of blockchain with AI and IoT not only enhances traceability and operational efficiency but also has profound sustainability implications. AI algorithms can analyze blockchain-logged data to optimize resource use and predict supply chain disruptions, while IoT devices ensure real-time monitoring of storage and transport conditions. Together, these technologies create more transparent, resilient, and environmentally responsible agri-food supply chains, aligning with global sustainability goals (Zhao et al., 2025; Tang et al., 2024).

Blockchain is a cutting-edge, distributed, decentralized, and "state-of-the-art" technology that protects the availability, secrecy, and integrity of all data and transactions. It is a distributed, open, and shared ledger that may be used to store and record information and transactions across a peer-to-peer network that are supported by a cryptographic value (Dutta et al., 2020; El Jaouhari et al., 2025). The blockchain is a network-distributed digital shared ledger. It is extremely safe for commercial operations since once the records are uploaded, they cannot be changed without altering the earlier records (unless all or most of the people concerned agree). It has countless uses in a variety of domains, including as creating smart contracts to monitor financial fraud or safely transferring medical records between medical specialists (Jaouhari et al., 2022; Sandhu et al., 2024).

Blockchain is developing in supply chain and logistics operations and has found applications. Products are tracked across supply chains using a variety of innovations, including radio-frequency identification (RFID), telematics, barcodes, 2D codes, sensor-enabled technologies, and the Internet of Things (IoT) (Hasan et al., 2023; Jaouhari et al., 2024). However, because the underlying data was usually restricted to a single organization or shared with a small number of reliable partners, their full potential has not yet been fully realized. Supply chains typically have a large number of members, each of whom runs a separate information system, with little to no contact between these systems. Lack of confidence in data sharing has been and continues to be the fundamental obstacle (Jaouhari, Arif, et al., 2023; Sarfaraz et al., 2023). By removing obstacles to trust and facilitating safe, verified, and decentralized information sharing across supply networks, blockchain technology provides an answer. The adoption rate of new supply chain implementations is rapidly increasing thanks to these features and blockchain's wider developments. Around the world, pilot projects are being started, and the industry expects big changes (Jaouhari, Bhilat, et al., 2023; Silvestri et al., 2024).

In international markets, the agri-food supply chain is crucial to maintaining food security, safety, and effectiveness. But there are a lot of difficulties because of its complexity and wide range of parties. The significance of vertical coordination among stakeholders is shown by a quick overview of the literature on the agri-food supply chain. The existence of businesses of different sizes, inter-firm synergies, shared risks, and enhanced use of economies of scope, particularly in developing and transition economies, make this coordination crucial (Chu & Pham, 2024). Value creation in agri-food products and tackling particular issues like perishability, safety, and traceability across the network require (Martínez-Castañeda & Feijoo, 2023). Coordination mechanisms, according to Kanda and Deshmukh (2008), are instruments for controlling interactions between supply chain players and enhancing overall performance. Numerous coordination mechanisms relevant to agri-food supply networks were found by earlier research. While some emphasize information sharing, collaborative decision-making, and group learning as successful strategies, Belaya and Hanf (2012) address the use of power as a coordination tool (Jahanbin et al., 2023a). In the contemporary agri-food industry, these systems encounter difficulties despite their potential. Since the majority of information is shared via paper-based documents, tracking and tracing products continue to be labor-intensive (Pakseresht et al., 2023a). Agencies and intermediaries frequently take advantage of the network, misusing their position of authority for their own benefit (Jahanbin et al., 2023a). Additionally, traditional contracts make agreements between farmers, processors, distributors, exporters, retailers, and consumers more difficult because they are interpreted differently (Rashid et al., 2024a). Furthermore, the absence of clear information flow throughout supply chains makes it difficult to guarantee food safety and security. Transaction costs rise as a result of inefficiencies caused by fraud and intermediary participation (Haider Sayma et al., 2024a).

The majority of stakeholders oppose a paradigm change toward a food chain prepared for the metaverse, notwithstanding the benefits mentioned above. The main cause of this opposition is a lack of knowledge and comprehension of the technology and its financial ramifications (Henrysson et al., 2022). Additionally, Cha (2022) contends that retailers' low degree of metaverse engagement is mostly due to their desire for a better understanding of the true economic benefits of adopting the metaverse.

To the best of our knowledge, this paper establishes the foundation for a future research agenda and is one of the first attempts to conceive the metaverse in respect to AFSCs. Our study showed that the metaverse has a great deal of potential to greatly accelerate AFSC progress. However, more technological developments and the cooperative integration of several technologies are needed to fully realize this promise. In this work, we specifically want to explore how the metaverse may improve AFSC security (Rashid et al., 2024b).

A number of scholars are interested in how the metaverse could ensure AFSC security, even though Blockchain research is still in its early stages (Zhao et al., 2025a). The current study is motivated by the findings of Guidani et al., 2024 and Tang et al., 2024, which emphasize how supply chains can be strengthened through the use of the metaverse. Understanding how metaverse technologies might help address these concerns is crucial, especially considering the significance of the agri-food industry to the global economy and the ever-changing nature of issues like food safety and traceability. This study aims to provide valuable insights into this uncharted territory, which will feed future research and strategic choices about the successful implementation of metaverse solutions to enhance AFSC security. The metaverse has the potential to drastically alter a number of sectors, such as the economy, education, and real estate, but its precise role in enhancing AFSC safety has not gotten enough attention. Therefore, the necessity to fill a major gap in the body of existing literature led to the decision to conduct an exploratory study on the role of the metaverse in AFSC security.

2. METHODOLOGY

Based on the secondary data, the methodology section describes the systematic review process used in this study, guaranteeing a thorough and repeatable method to find, pick, and evaluate pertinent literature on the elements guaranteeing transparency in Blockchain technology and the agri-food supply chain (Jahanbin et al., 2023b).

The review procedure was created based on suggestions, which were then refined and included in a blockchain supply chain paper by. This method ensures a comprehensive and unbiased review of the body of literature, identifying the most pertinent research in the area. SLR is a kind of review that places a strong emphasis on using standard methods when looking for, assessing, and discussing literature (Rashid et al., 2024c). Since smart contracts and blockchain technology have only been around for a little more than ten years, the related research, industry standards, and innovative applications are continually developing. Our review of the literature covers the most recent blockchain implementations in AFSC and runs from 2018 to 2024. We used a particular search criterion shown in Figure 1 to source publications from reputable academic databases such as Web of Science (WoS) and Scopus in order to guarantee a thorough evaluation (Pakseresht et al., 2024a).

2.1. Review Planning

The WoS and Scopus databases were selected by the study's authors in order to find pertinent research on the topic of blockchain adoption in agri-food supply chains (AFSC). To guarantee thorough coverage, the search procedure used the following beginning keywords: Agri-food supply chain with blockchain. Leading journals in food supply chain, blockchain adoption, and agriculture were given priority in order to improve the search's dependability. A review group was also formed to identify conceptual limits and carry out a thorough article selection process. A comprehensive and organized evaluation procedure was ensured by the panel's three specialists, who included two professors and one researcher (Zarbà et al., 2024).

2.2. Data Extraction

The authors of the paper searched the WoS and Scopus databases for relevant studies on the subject of blockchain adoption in agri-food supply chains (AFSC). The following starting keywords were used in the search process to ensure comprehensive coverage: blockchain technology in the agri-food supply chain. To increase the reliability of the search, top publications in blockchain adoption, agriculture, and food supply chain were prioritized. In order to determine conceptual boundaries and conduct a comprehensive article selection procedure, a review group was also established. The three experts on the panel—two professors and one researcher—ensured a thorough and well-structured examination process.

The search produced 394 articles, 200 from Scopus and 194 from ScienceDirect, as shown in Figure 1. There were 320 unique articles left after 74 identical entries were eliminated. The dataset was shrunk by further filtering, which eliminated all proceedings papers and non-English publications.

Using predetermined inclusion and exclusion criteria, the remaining papers' titles and abstracts were examined. 100 papers remained eligible for a thorough full-text review after 220 articles that were unrelated to the study's scope were eliminated in this step.

A panel evaluated each full-text publication using an Excel sheet to determine its applicability in light of the conceptual limits of the study. Independent article screening was done by panel members, who then discussed and settled disagreements. Consequently, 70 items remained in the final dataset after 30 were eliminated for reasons including lack of focus or insufficient detail.

The researchers used forward and backward citation chaining to find more references and make sure no pertinent papers were overlooked. Following this procedure, 70 full-length publications were ultimately chosen for examination after a thorough assessment. This collection serves as the foundation for the subsequent stages of the systematic literature review, which include content analysis and research profiling.

Additionally, between 2018 and 2024, Figure 2 shows the increase in the quantity of published publications on a particular subject, most likely pertaining to blockchain applications in the agri-food supply chain. Beginning with just one publication in 2018, the data shows a notable upward trend that increased yearly until reaching a peak of 79 articles in 2024. With a noticeable acceleration starting in 2020, this trajectory illustrates the growing significance and interest in the topic. The consistent increase in articles points to a growing understanding of blockchain's potential to address issues including sustainability, supply chain transparency, and food safety. The dramatic rise in 2024 might be the result of more research, new technology, or legislative measures that encourage further study and use of the area.

Figure 1. Systematic literature review process

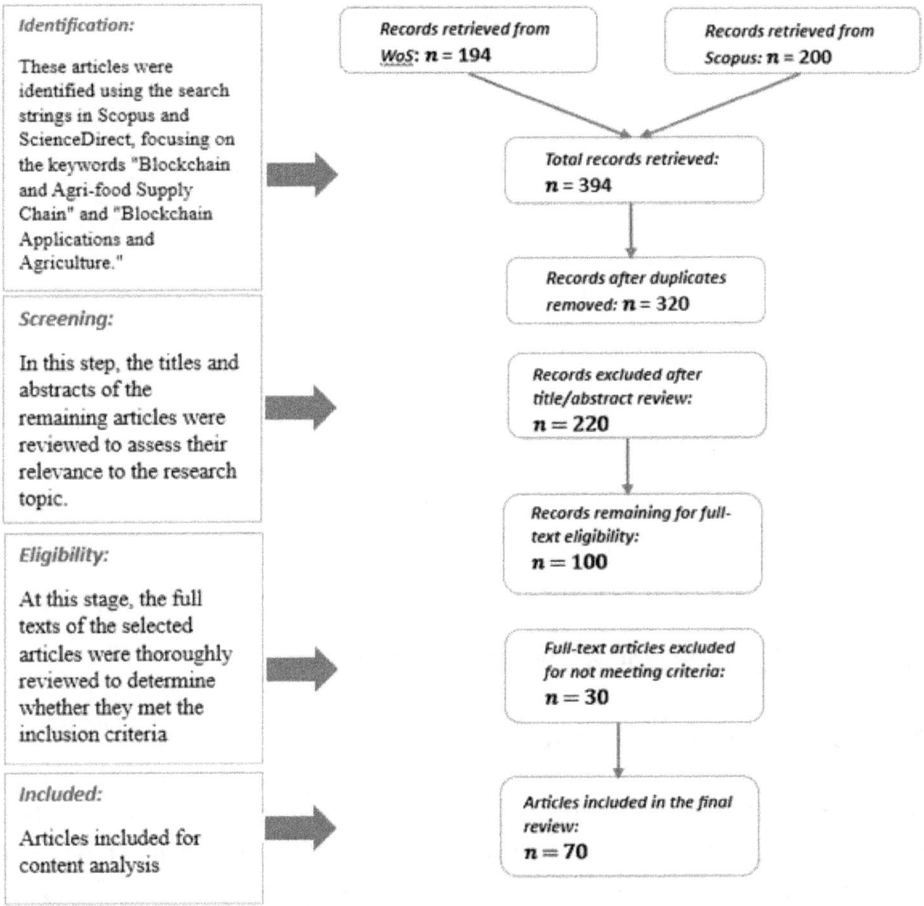

Figure 2. The number of articles published per year

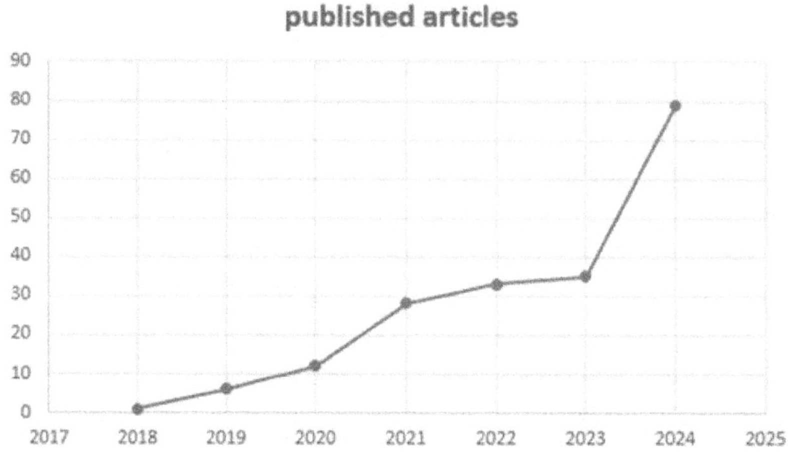

3. THE ROLE OF BLOCKCHAIN IN AFSC

3.1. Traceability and Transparency

By giving end customers extra assurances about the quality and safety of the items they purchase, the use of cutting-edge technical solutions, such as blockchain technology BC, has the potential to guarantee the transparency and verifiability of the entire process. BC can be thought of as a digital ledger that releases a distributed and secure database model along the supply chain via the internet. Each member of BC uses a pre-established consensus protocol to validate and confirm the data records entered by other members (Chu & Pham, 2024). In order to provide everlasting and impenetrable records (Onu et al., 2024), the decentralized and distributed ledger records transactions chronologically, guaranteeing a high degree of transparency for every transaction (Rashid et al., 2024b). In accordance with technological principles, the implementation of BC in the food chain enables all operators to get authorization to access the block database; consequently, they have trustworthy information regarding the origin and condition of foods when conducting their transactions (Onu et al., 2024). In summary, blockchain greatly strengthens traceability and transparency across agri-food supply chains, laying a crucial groundwork for addressing subsequent challenges in food safety and operational efficiency.

3.2. Food Safety and Quality Control

One of these cutting-edge technologies is blockchain technology, and blockchain-based projects are crucial to improving the efficiency and transparency of the food and agriculture supply chains (Tang et al., 2024). The application of food traceability has received praise for its capacity to allay worries about food safety events. In addition to helping government agencies and food producers quickly pinpoint the cause of food contamination during outbreaks or contamination events, effective food traceability also helps address issues brought on by the participation of numerous stakeholders in the food production system and the absence of technical infrastructure for coordinated food safety monitoring throughout the system. The exciting potential of new digital technologies, such as blockchain technology, in addressing the shortcomings of conventional food traceability systems has been emphasized by recent studies (Haider Sayma et al., 2024b). These improvements in food safety and quality control further build on transparent data flows, reinforcing consumer trust and regulatory compliance, and seamlessly connect to efficiency gains discussed next.

3.3. Supply Chain Efficiency

Access to historical and real-time transaction data is made possible by blockchain technology, and there is proof that using blockchain in the supply chain improves transparency. Blockchain validates the Transaction Cost Economics theory by reducing the impact of constrained rationality (Chu & Pham, 2024). Establishing transparency among trade partners fosters trust, which lowers suspicion of opportunistic behavior and raises the likelihood of efficient communication and information exchange. By fostering stronger ties between the companies, the use of disruptive technologies like BC in AFSC can boost trust. The data network that connects the afri-food stakeholders in a BC-enabled AFSC facilitates ubiquitous information exchange and effective communication across the supply chain, ensuring transparency and efficient coordination between the parties (Silvestri et al., 2024). Thus, blockchain's role in enhancing efficiency complements its capabilities in ensuring product safety and traceability, together shaping a more agile and responsive supply chain.

3.4. Transactions Automation

By automating transactions and enforcing agreements without the need for middlemen, smart contracts expand the capabilities of BC. Parties without a history of trust can safely conduct transactions thanks to the use of smart contracts in BC. The author in (Pakseresht et al., 2024b)promotes the use of the Ethereum blockchain network to create smart contracts and blockchain-based systems in the context of the agricultural supply chain. These technological developments make it possible to upload data to an Interplanetary File System (IPFS) and record transactions on the blockchain. In (Rashid et al., 2024b), a new method for accelerating the development and personalization of Ethereum-based smart contracts for the agri-food sector is presented. While maintaining security and dependability standards, this approach guarantees that code and modules can be reused, cutting down on development time. The goal is to create a semi-automated system that can provide user interfaces for managing the system and interacting with the smart contracts. A blockchain-based system that uses smart contracts to handle transactions and guarantee a safe, affordable traceability procedure was presented by (Pakseresht et al., 2024b) to do away with the need for middlemen in agricultural supply chains. With a throughput of 161 transactions per second, the system proved to be successful in guaranteeing food safety in India. Automating transactions through smart contracts completes this technological suite, reducing dependence on intermediaries and operational delays, which ties directly into broader applications explored in AFSC contexts.

4. APPLICATIONS OF BCT IN AFSC

4.1. Blockchain Traceability in AFSC

Blockchain can ensure traceability and reduce workload. It has the ability to track the history of every transaction across time, easily reconstruct records, and identify a product's origin. According to Pizzuti and Mirabelli (2015), blockchain technology can fully manage traceability frameworks by capturing the history of every transaction, instantaneously reconstructing records, and identifying a product's origin. Blockchain technology is useful as a traceability solution since it can quickly identify and detect a specific item. While centralized traceability solutions can achieve the same result, traceability procedures on a blockchain happen far more quickly. When working with food goods, this speed becomes much more crucial, particularly if the food must be checked before ingestion and the source must be identified promptly. The reputation of the company brand might also be maintained in the case of origin detection, particularly in handling tainted food (Rashid et al., 2024d), and negative media repercussions would be lessened (Shiraishi et al., 2025).

4.2. Blockchain Transparency in AFSC

According to (Burgess et al., 2024; Rashid et al., 2024b), supply chain performance evaluation requires transparency. The benefits of blockchain transparency are thus available to all parties involved in a supply chain, including retailers, warehouses, and individual storefronts. Stores can identify information about a freight arrival, for instance, and prepare to pick it up. Furthermore, the blockchain may show details about the land, production unit, shipment number, and storage conditions because it is a distributed ledger. Transparency can be easily achieved, for example, by disclosing information in centralized systems. In this instance, however, blockchain's data transparency capabilities are more comprehensive than those of centralized systems. The primary objective of blockchain technology, according to Martin and Leurent (2017), is to enable information sharing, create a ledger for the data and its processing, and verify food quality standards as they are passed down the supply chain. Allowing each side to communicate food-related declarations, evidence, and evaluations of one other's declarations helps to accomplish these goals. All authorized members can see and access the data recorded in the blockchain ledger. Blockchain can display the who, what, where, and when of supply chain operations. Because blockchain promotes traceability and transparency—two features that may be strengthened by adding smart contracts—it can therefore be very beneficial in tackling social and environmental issues.

4.3. Blockchain Tamper-Evidence in AFSC

Tampering is "to meddle or interfere with (a thing); to misuse, alter, corrupt, or distort it," according to the Oxford English Dictionary. Any phase of a product's life cycle, including production, processing, distribution, and retail, can see tampering (Li, 2013). To prevent tampering, tamper-resistant or tamper-evident techniques are used (Toreini, 2018). According to Caro et al. (2018), farmers, cold chain managers, government organizations, and consumers now place a high premium on tamper-proofing and data privacy issues in food traceability. Tamperproof records are essential to preserving dependability and trust throughout the agri-food industry's whole supply chain, claim Caro et al. (2018). According to Cao et al. (2019), the public blockchain system functions as a transparent, decentralized, and tamper-evident ledger that records value token ownership, and blockchain ensures truthfulness through proof-of-work. Blockchain guarantees that information cannot be altered or manipulated. All parties have rapid access to the data in a trustworthy and dispersed format, and mediators have no control over it (Issaoui et al., 2019). According to Helo and Hao (2019) and Zhao et al. (2019), blockchain technology offers an efficient way to combat counterfeiting and quality traceability in agri-food items because of its anti-tamper capabilities. Stated differently, the blockchain provides stakeholders with a new method. For example, blockchain can be used to examine and update the tamper-proof history of transactions about an agri-food product in the farm-to-fork relationship, which can lead to better fair trade, higher-quality food, and faster detection of phony products (Dooley et al., 2018). Researchers think it has become widely accepted as a way to solve trust and security issues in information transparency and prevent data tampering because all transactional information pertaining to all parties in the supply chain is recorded in the block and cannot be changed or removed ((Ramkumar et al., 2022) ; (Burgess et al., 2024)).

4.4. Blockchain Immutability in AFSC

Because transactions involving agricultural products are subject to a number of information management issues, blockchain immutability is pertinent to agri-food products. Blockchain technology delivers decentralized data and renders transactions irreversible, which can facilitate data transmission and lessen the likelihood of corruption and manipulation (Javaid et al., 2021). Immutable food data and transaction records, according to Ahmed and Broek (2017), may assist prevent fraud against manufacturers and distributors, locate the causes of foodborne diseases, and make data sharing across organizations easier. Furthermore, Yadav et al. (2021) hypothesized that blockchain might function effectively as a settlement platform in agri-food supply chains through smart contracts because it is a decentralized and immutable database. Additionally, the immutability of blockchain data enhances accessibility and guards against document forgeries. It supports agri-food items' provenance, traceability, and certification (Srivastava et al., 2021). Furthermore, Lin et al. (2017) claim that secure and reliable sustainable agrarian development is made possible by the integration of blockchain technology with environmental and agricultural monitoring data kept on a distributed cloud. According to Kamble et al. (2020), who looked into the potential of blockchain-enabled traceability in agri-food supply chains, the most notable aspects of agri-food SC's blockchain technology were immutability, provenance, traceability, and suitability. In order to find common and unique characteristics, Motta et al. (2020) examined and contrasted six case studies in the agri-food sector. They came to the conclusion that the most often mentioned features of blockchain technology in scholarly and business papers were redundancy, trust, and immutability. Additionally, blockchain was associated with immutability, redundancy, and cryptography in every case study (Balci and Surucu-Balci, 2021).

4.5. Blockchain Compliance in Agri-Food Supply Chain Products

Blockchain technology with "smart contracts" can enable some operations to function automatically in accordance with preset rules. Assigning runtime executions to smart contracts instead of the entire system speeds up the process. At the same time, blockchain technology makes compliance simple by facilitating the safe and secure exchange of personal information. Blockchain technology can help authorities and ensure that regulations are followed. This is made possible by blockchain's ability to aid compliance professionals in managing the proper application of complex legislation, which advances the compliance process. According to (Al-Dmour et al., 2024), blockchain technology makes compliance simple by facilitating the safe and secure exchange of sensitive data. Industry 4.0 can also be facilitated by blockchain automation. Yu and Schweisfurth (2020) assert that businesses with a wide range of products and high degrees of process automation are also more likely to implement Industry 4.0. Blockchain technology adds transparency to an agri-food supply chain and saves information about all manufacturing and processing operations. It ensures both sustainability advancements and adherence to agri-food product requirements at the same time. Businesses and governments will benefit from blockchain because it will enable them to track and manage violations of international standards, allowing them to keep an eye on the health of farms and animals and maintain disease-free status. Additionally, certifications must be issued and exported by capable central authority in a straightforward, quick, and forceful manner. The distributed ledger contains almost all of the necessary product information, and certificates can be generated automatically (Soori et al., 2023). Despite its great potential, blockchain technology is still in its infancy and is therefore seen as an emerging technology in the agri-food supply chain (Jahanbin et al., 2023b). Despite a number of pilot and proof-of-concept initiatives, there is still little blockchain adoption in the agri-food sector. According to the most current studies, there are difficulties in implementing blockchain technology in agri-food supply chains. We highlight several significant obstacles. While study on the obstacles to blockchain technology adoption is still underway, Menon and Jain (2021) found the technology is still in the exploratory and testing stages, with numerous businesses still working on proof-of-concept or testing deployment and implementation. Furthermore, research indicates that studies on the possible benefits, constraints, and difficulties of implementing blockchain technology in the supply chain are currently being conducted. Overall, these varied applications illustrate blockchain's potential to advance compliance, sustainability, and ethical standards, setting the stage for discussing its broader drivers and barriers in agri-food systems.

5. DRIVERS AND BARRIERS OF BC IN AFSC

5.1. Drivers of BC in AFSC

Transparency, efficiency, trust and security, sustainability, cost savings, and compliance and ethics are the six main categories that Table 1 outlines as the main forces behind the adoption of blockchain in the agri-food supply chain. For food safety and quality assurance, transparency is expressed in improved supply chain visibility and product authenticity, which guarantee complete traceability and reduce fraud risks (Tang et al., 2024) (Silvestri et al., 2024). According to Tripoli and Schmidhuber (2018) and Leng et al. (2018), efficiency is fueled by process automation and smart contracts, which streamline operations, lessen administrative responsibilities, and cut down on delays and human error. Data integrity and fraud protection measures strengthen trust and security by guaranteeing unchangeable and impenetrable records that guard against data alteration and counterfeiting (Jahanbin et al., 2023b). By improving the monitoring of storage and transportation conditions, blockchain helps to achieve environmental goals, reduce spoilage, and enable eco-labeling traceability and waste reduction (Pakseresht et al., 2023b). Optimizing the supply chain and allocating resources more precisely reduce costs, reduce inefficiencies, and improve operational performance (Okorie et al., 2022). Lastly, by guaranteeing adherence to food safety rules and confirming ethical sourcing and responsible farming, blockchain helps regulatory compliance and encourages fair trade practices (Okorie et al., 2022). All of these factors work together to highlight how blockchain might revolutionize agri-food supply chains by creating more robust, transparent, sustainable, and morally sound systems.

Table 1. Drivers of BC in AFSC

Main Category	Sub-Category	Description	References
Transparency	Supply Chain Visibility	Ensuring all stakeholders can trace the origin and journey of food products.	Tian et al. (2016), Caro et al. (2018)
	Product Authenticity	Verifying the authenticity of organic and premium products.	Kamble et al. (2020)
Efficiency	Process Automation	Automating record-keeping and transactions, reducing delays and paperwork.	Tripoli & Schmidhuber (2018)
	Smart Contracts	Automating payment and delivery agreements based on predefined conditions.	Leng et al. (2018)
Trust and Security	Fraud Prevention	Preventing tampering, counterfeiting, and mislabeling of products.	Galvez et al. (2018)

continued on following page

Table 1. Continued

Main Category	Sub-Category	Description	References
	Data Integrity	Ensuring immutable and accurate records throughout the supply chain.	Kamilaris et al. (2019)
Sustainability	Traceability for Eco-labeling	Tracking environmental impact and sustainability certifications.	Behnke & Janssen (2020)
	Waste Reduction	Minimizing waste through better monitoring of product conditions.	Feng et al. (2020)
Cost Reduction	Supply Chain Optimization	Reducing costs by eliminating intermediaries and optimizing logistics.	Nurgazina et al. (2021)
	Resource Allocation	Enhancing resource distribution by improving demand forecasting.	Ozturk & Yildizbasi (2020)
Compliance and Ethics	Regulatory Compliance	Ensuring adherence to food safety and trade regulations.	Rana et al. (2021)
	Ethical Sourcing	Verifying fair trade and ethical farming practices.	Baralla et al. (2019)

5.2. Barrier of BC in AFSC

Blockchain's ability to provide safe, decentralized information exchange between producers, farmers, and markets is transforming the AFSC. The IBM Food Trust, a cooperative network comprising many food industry participants with the goal of improving accountability and visibility throughout the food chain, is a prime illustration of the application of BC in the sector. The platform is an excellent illustration of how BC can establish a creative, effective, and sustainable ecosystem for exchanging food-related data by providing Farmto-Fork information with security, transparency, and traceability based on the BC. This technology is making the AFSC's future more secure and transparent by automating procedures and guaranteeing information security (Shiraishi et al., 2025).

By cutting verification and monitoring expenses and fostering trustworthy connections with trading partners, BC in the AFSC can have a substantial influence on supply chain management and financial transparency while also lowering overall costs. Manufacturers can also reduce management surveillance costs by using BC's real-time transparency, which eliminates the need for expensive and extensive surveillance (Pakseresht et al., 2024b). Additionally, by removing middlemen, it can lower network costs between businesses and suppliers (Shiraishi et al., 2025). One of the many goals of contemporary businesses and its stakeholders is to maximize total income rather than just profit (Compagnucci et al., 2022). Digital technology has unquestionably contributed to the food industry, but there are still a number of obstacles that need to be addressed in relation to BC. Food production generates a lot of data, which puts strain on facilities that store this data and necessitates speedy processing capacity for transactions, data storage, and personal or commercial information protection. These tasks are not always simple. Programs with source code faults can create security risks that put businesses at danger of losing data and profits, leading to issues with privacy and securityBecause many programming languages must be utilized to communicate between the platforms, interoperability between them is especially difficult (Shiraishi et al., 2025). According to van Hilten et al. (2020), the majority of food industry businesses are unable to embrace BC until it becomes a viable and effective option. Lack of experience, hefty upfront expenses, and skepticism about the long-term advantages could make blockchain adoption challenging. Furthermore, BC may have trouble satisfying the need for data with varying levels of detail in various areas, particularly in complex contexts. Since some information may be trade secrets of intellectual property or sensitive for particular stakeholders, confidentiality and privacy are also very important. Determining who has the power to decide and oversee system modifications may become challenging if blockchain governance is opaque. Particularly in the early stages, many BC implementation and maintenance procedures could call for a significant amount of effort. It can be difficult to choose the data to put in the BC because too much data may be superfluous or overwhelm the system. This degree of technological integration requires a high degree of computerization. The primary forces behind and obstacles to BC technology adoption in AFSC are presented in Table 2.

Table 2. Barrier of BC in AFSC

Main Category	Sub-Category	Description	References
Technical Drivers	Scalability Issues	Blockchain networks face delays and congestion as transactions increase.	Rana et al. (2021), Feng et al. (2020)
	Interoperability Challenges	Lack of integration between blockchain platforms and existing systems.	Nurgazina et al. (2021), Min (2019)
Cost and Resources	High Implementation Costs	Significant investment in infrastructure, energy, and development.	Kamilaris et al. (2019), Ozturk et al. (2020)
	Resource-Intensive Processes	High energy and processing power required for blockchain operations.	Baralla et al. (2019), Andoni et al. (2018)
Security and Privacy	Data Privacy Risks	Concerns over the protection of sensitive data on a public ledger.	Baralla et al. (2019), Feng et al. (2020)
	Cybersecurity Vulnerabilities	Blockchain networks can be targeted by cyberattacks and breaches.	Reyna et al. (2018), Tseng et al. (2018)

continued on following page

Table 2. Continued

Main Category	Sub-Category	Description	References
Organizational	Resistance to Change	Stakeholders may lack awareness or resist blockchain adoption.	Farooque et al. (2019), Min (2019)
	Skills and Knowledge Gaps	Limited expertise in blockchain technology among supply chain actors.	Tan et al. (2018), Yadav et al. (2020)
Regulatory	Legal and Compliance Barriers	Ambiguity in regulations and legal frameworks governing blockchain use.	Farooque et al. (2019), Kamilaris et al. (2019)
	Jurisdictional Challenges	Blockchain spans multiple regions, creating jurisdictional complexities.	Andoni et al. (2018), Min (2019)
Scalability and Performance	Speed and Efficiency Limitations	Inconsistent transaction speeds impact supply chain efficiency.	Feng et al. (2020), Rana et al. (2021)
	Expanding Ledger Size	Continuous growth in data storage burdens blockchain performance.	Patelli & Mandrioli (2020), Min (2019)

6. DISCUSSION

The difficulties and contradictions related to the AFSC's acceptance of BC were recognized, evaluated, and examined in this study. In order to resolve these contradictions, a number of calculated solutions have surfaced, offering guidance on how to get over obstacles to BC integration in AFSCs. Stakeholder cooperation, data governance frameworks, process optimization, modular architecture, interoperability standards, and capacity building are the most important resolution techniques (Jahanbin et al., 2023b). The main enabler of these is modular design, which tackles a number of scalability, transparency, and decentralization-related concerns. Supply chain players can improve security and efficiency while making sure that innovations and system upgrades don't interfere with overall operations by organizing BC systems into discrete, flexible modules. By clearly defining data flows and allowing stakeholders to track supply chain operations in real-time, this modular approach also promotes increased transparency while guaranteeing food safety and quality (Rashid et al., 2024c).

The second most important tactics for resolving operational and technological contradictions in BC adoption were found to be interoperability standards and process optimization. Interoperability guarantees smooth data interchange and communication across various blockchain networks and conventional supply chain management platforms. This is necessary to develop unified systems that can handle various datasets from the AFSC's farming, logistics, and retail stages. Standardized data entry and communication standards improve sustainability monitoring and traceability, cut down on inefficiencies, and promote cooperation amongst global supply chain players. According to (Govindan et al., 2024), establishing explicit interoperability standards enables blockchain solutions to be tailored to the particular requirements of different agri-food industries while preserving data security and integrity. In order to avoid information overload and make sure that critical supply chain data is only shared with the appropriate parties, process optimization is essential. Proprietary information is safeguarded by this focused data distribution while upholding strict regulatory compliance and high standards of transparency in order to overcome adoption barriers, management involvement, stakeholder collaboration, and human-machine interaction all play equally important roles. By resolving inefficiencies and bolstering trust throughout the supply chain, the involvement of farmers, producers, logistics companies, and regulators promotes an atmosphere of shared responsibility and innovation. In order to prevent any one company from controlling the ecosystem, cooperation allows the formation of blockchain consortia, in which several stakeholders work together to cooperatively regulate and maintain the BC network. In line with the concepts of sustainability and food security, this cooperative model strikes a compromise between the necessity of decentralization and operational effectiveness. Furthermore, human-machine interactions guarantee that human actors supervise automated BC operations, adding an additional degree of quality control and verification (Ramkumar et al., 2022). By reducing data entry errors and improving sustainability measurements' accuracy, this two-pronged strategy helps create a more trustworthy AFSC (Burgess et al., 2024). Despite the promising outlook, blockchain implementation in agri-food supply chains faces persistent regulatory uncertainties, as fragmented legal frameworks across countries create compliance ambiguities that can stall adoption. Moreover, user adoption barriers remain substantial, driven by resistance to change, lack of technical familiarity, and fears over data exposure. To mitigate these challenges, policymakers should collaborate internationally to harmonize standards, while companies can invest in awareness campaigns and tailored training to demystify blockchain operations for smallholders and distributors. Developing pilot programs and phased rollouts also allows gradual acclimatization, fostering trust and minimizing disruption to existing workflows. (Rashid et al., 2024c).

However, real-world implementation highlights additional barriers, particularly in developing regions. Case studies from Bangladesh, India, and parts of sub-Saharan Africa reveal how limited digital infrastructure, high initial investment costs, and gaps in technical expertise constrain BC scalability in these contexts (Compagnucci et al., 2022; Rashid et al., 2024c). Smallholder farmers often lack the necessary digital literacy and resources to engage with blockchain systems, underscoring the socio-economic dimensions that must be addressed. This reality emphasizes the need for targeted capacity-building initiatives, financial support schemes, and public-private partnerships to create inclusive ecosystems for BC adoption.

While blockchain promises significant advantages for traceability, transparency, and fraud reduction, its deployment is not without substantial **technical and financial challenges**, particularly in agri-food supply chains. **Scalability issues** arise as blockchain networks grow, leading to potential transaction delays and increased energy demands. Likewise, achieving seamless **interoperability** between diverse blockchain platforms and legacy ERP systems remains complex, often requiring costly custom integrations. Additionally, the **high upfront costs** associated with blockchain infrastructure and training can deter small and medium enterprises from adoption. These realities highlight the importance of carefully evaluating the trade-offs and progressively deploying blockchain solutions to mitigate risks and control costs.

The third group of resolution techniques consists of security audits, standardized data formats, government support and regulation, and education and training. (Zhao et al., 2025b) point out that education and training are essential for giving supply chain players the know-how to administer and use blockchain technologies. This not only dispels myths and opposition to technological progress, but it also raises awareness of blockchain's possibilities. Training programs promote a culture of innovation and continual development by highlighting the significance of data security, scalability, and decentralization. Simultaneously, government support and regulation offer the required legal frameworks and incentives to encourage the adoption of blockchain. Concurrent governmental policies and regulatory frameworks provide essential incentives and norms that facilitate BC uptake, particularly by defining standards for transparency, data protection, and financial safeguard (Balci and Surucu-Balci, 2021).

By guaranteeing consistency in data entry and maintenance, lowering the possibility of errors, and facilitating a smooth transition between blockchain technology and current enterprise resource planning (ERP) systems, standardized data formats further improve efficiency. This standardization facilitates seamless data exchanges across platforms by getting rid of unnecessary data processing and streamlining supply chain monitoring. Lastly, preserving the integrity of blockchain networks requires security auditing. Frequent audits guarantee that vulnerabilities are quickly fixed, protecting private supply chain information and averting online attacks. By guaranteeing constant adherence to environmental and food safety standards, security auditing not only safeguards operational systems but also strengthens the sustainability and resilience of agri-food supply chains (Ronaghi, 2021). Overall, while BC holds transformative potential for the agri-food sector, widespread adoption remains challenged by operational, technological, socio-economic, and regulatory hurdles. A comprehensive strategy combining modular architectures, interoperability, collaborative governance, and targeted support mechanisms is essential to harness BC's full promise in fostering transparent, sustainable, and efficient agri-food supply chains.

The comprehensive literature analysis concludes by pointing out that although blockchain technology has the potential to revolutionize the agri-food supply chain, there are operational, technological, and regulatory obstacles to its widespread adoption. A holistic approach to overcoming these obstacles includes the use of modular architecture, interoperability standards, stakeholder collaboration, and capacity building. Governments, business executives, and regional farmers must work together as blockchain technology develops in order to realize its full potential and promote transparent, sustainable, and effective agri-food supply chains (Rashid et al., 2024c).

7. FUTURE RESEARCH DIRECTIONS

There is currently little research on BC and how its different facets affect AFSC performance. We acknowledge that, rather than offering a thorough analysis, our study offers the initial insights in a field that is currently lacking in research. It is necessary to conduct further study using cutting-edge techniques like agent-based modeling and simulation. Agent-based modeling is being used to simulate complex socioeconomic systems in place of experiments, particularly when observing a process takes too long, analyzing a large number of stakeholders over an extended period of time, or running too many iterations with changing variables is required. A relatively new method for modeling complex systems and tracking economic activity over time based on independent agents interacting with their environment is called "Agent-Based Computational Economics," which combines computer simulation and agent-based modeling in economics (Zhao et al., 2025c). Research and simulation in the areas of cooperation and coordination, as well as in the areas of coordination mechanisms in AFSC, are lacking, despite the recent increase in the use of agent-based modeling for AFSC analysis (Chu & Pham, 2024). Additional insights into possible developments within the supply chain can be obtained by investigating blockchain systems using agent-based modeling (Rashid et al., 2024c).

The supply chain sector has benefited greatly from BC's growth, decentralization, and establishment of a trustless environment for all processes. Nevertheless, it is challenging to completely preserve confidence between the product's buyer and seller, even though blockchain technology is trustless. This is because the buyer may question the entities' reliability and they may act deliberately. Additionally, the supply chain entails a number of procedures and subprocesses that must be executed decentralized to guarantee security, accountability, and traceability (Pakseresht et al., 2024b). We have presented an end-to-end solution for BC-based AFSC in this work. Regarding traceability, trading, delivery, and reputation, we have given comprehensive details about the suggested solution. To make sure the suggested solution is reliable and effective, we have thoroughly examined and assessed smart contract performance. The purpose of the reputation system is to preserve the AFSC entities' legitimacy and the product quality ratings. Additionally, because these transactions are based on BC, it preserves the transactions' integrity and immutability. We have covered smart contracts in detail and given algorithms. The results of a simulation indicate that our system needs a specific quantity of gas in order to deploy and run smart contracts (Mokgomola et al., 2024).

The practical deployment of BC-based systems continues to present difficulties. We intend to incorporate return and refund procedures into the trading of agri-food items in the future. Similar to this, the reputation system keeps track of end-user reviews, some of which may be phony or prejudiced. In order to help the reputation system identify the fraudulent reviews left by end users, we intend to incorporate a fake review detection system. Additionally, security studies that concentrate on reputation system threats will be taken into account (Zhao et al., 2025a).

AFSC research and education institutions must strategically integrate BC as an aiding tool for research, teaching, and education by creating clear policies and guidelines for scholars, educators, and students to use BC. This is because BC has significant implications for AFSC research and education as well. Successful implementation of BC initiatives will create value for stakeholders (Duan et al., 2024). The ramifications of BC for AFSC research and higher education require more investigation. Table 3 provides the main

Table 3. Future research agenda of the role of of BC in AFSC

Main Category	Future Research Questions
Traceability and Transparency	1. How can blockchain enhance end-to-end traceability in multi-tier agri-food supply chains?
	2. What are the key challenges in implementing blockchain for transparency across diverse stakeholders?
	3. How can blockchain improve consumer trust by providing real-time product information?
	4. How can blockchain-based traceability systems be made more scalable and cost-effective?
	5. What is the role of blockchain in combating food fraud and ensuring authenticity of organic labels?

continued on following page

Table 3. Continued

Main Category	Future Research Questions
Sustainability and Environmental Impact	1. How can blockchain track and reduce the environmental impact of agri-food supply chains?
	2. What are the benefits of integrating blockchain with carbon footprint and water usage monitoring systems?
	3. How can blockchain incentivize sustainable farming practices through tokenization or rewards systems?
	4. What are the barriers to adopting blockchain for sustainability in developing countries?
	5. How can blockchain support global sustainability certifications like fair trade and eco-labeling?
Efficiency and Cost Optimization	1. How can blockchain reduce transaction costs and eliminate intermediaries in agri-food supply chains?
	2. What is the potential of blockchain in improving inventory management and reducing waste in perishable goods?
	3. How can blockchain integrate with IoT devices for better supply chain monitoring and optimization?
	4. What are the cost-benefit implications of blockchain implementation in small-scale farming operations?
	5. How can blockchain streamline cross-border trade in agri-food products?
Food Safety and Quality Assurance	1. How can blockchain enhance food safety by ensuring compliance with global regulatory standards?
	2. What role can blockchain play in cold chain monitoring for perishable food items?
	3. How effective is blockchain in preventing the distribution of counterfeit or substandard food products?
	4. How can blockchain-based platforms improve product recalls and minimize foodborne illnesses?
	5. What are the key technical challenges in implementing blockchain for quality control in agri-food supply chains?
Adoption and Scalability	1. What are the barriers to blockchain adoption among smallholder farmers and cooperatives?
	2. How can blockchain be integrated with existing agricultural supply chain systems?
	3. What strategies can improve blockchain adoption in resource-constrained regions?
	4. How can interoperability between multiple blockchain platforms be achieved for seamless data sharing?
	5. What are the scalability challenges of blockchain in large-scale agri-food supply chains?

continued on following page

Table 3. Continued

Main Category	Future Research Questions
Policy and Governance	1. How can blockchain support regulatory compliance and global trade standards in the agri-food sector?
	2. What policies are required to incentivize blockchain adoption in agriculture?
	3. How can data privacy and security concerns be addressed in blockchain-based agri-food supply chains?
	4. What governance models are most effective for managing decentralized blockchain networks in agriculture?
	5. How can blockchain enable collaboration between government, private sector, and farmers in food supply chains?

Moreover, while this study synthesizes the technological and organizational enablers for blockchain adoption in agri-food supply chains, it acknowledges the need for stronger empirical grounding. Insights from pilot projects, such as the IBM Food Trust initiative or blockchain-enabled traceability systems in Bangladesh and India, illustrate both the promise and complexities of real-world implementation. These initiatives reveal diverse stakeholder perspectives, from farmers to regulators, highlighting concerns over data privacy, cost allocation, and infrastructure readiness (Govindan et al., 2024). Incorporating such examples not only validates theoretical discussions but also demonstrates practical pathways and barriers, enhancing the applicability and impact of blockchain frameworks in the agri-food context. (Rashid et al., 2024c).

8. CONCLUSION

This chapter's structured analysis of blockchain benefits—such as enhanced traceability, data integrity, and decentralized trust mechanisms—forms a solid thematic foundation. To maximize the relevance of these insights, the discussion has been anchored in real-world experiences, drawing on pilot implementations and diverse stakeholder perspectives. By integrating practical challenges, from scalability constraints to regulatory ambiguities encountered in agri-food contexts, this work offers a more holistic view that balances theoretical strengths with implementation realities.

Though mostly at the proof-of-concept stage, the number of blockchain-based solutions in the AFSC and agriculture has been growing quickly. Increased transparency through public interactions and low information friction, which allow audit trails of certification and transactions, 2) cryptography and consensus mechanisms to ensure the immutability of records, 3) record redundancy and BC's open-source nature to ensure decentralization, and 4) smart contracts and real-time integration with IoT devices to enable automatic transactions are technical features that support the use of blockchain in agri-food systems at the moment, quality assurance and traceability (such as provenance) are the main agri-food applications for BC. With complex regulatory compliance requirements, food systems are becoming more and more fragmented. Because of this complexity, it is very challenging to detect and monitor product information and processes, as well as scattered networks. It is widely acknowledged that BC has enormous potential to enhance AFSC accountability and openness. To guarantee financial stability, the technology must be connected to macroprudential regulatory frameworks and supportive policies in order to realize its full potential of revolutionizing food traceability. Further complicating the deployment and evaluation of blockchain technologies are regional and sector-specific differences in stakeholder engagement, economic concerns, and technological readiness. Furthermore, there are several issues with the use of blockchain in the agri-food industry. For example, the environmental effects of digitization and computational-based solutions, as well as greenhouse gas emissions, have raised concerns. These issues show how BC technology's technical difficulties and environmental effects require in-depth study and thoughtful debate. In the future, the technology's capacity to fully transform food traceability will depend on the smooth integration of BC with legislative backing and a dedication to reducing environmental effects.

While this chapter primarily targets academics and professionals exploring the intersection of agri-tech and blockchain, it also seeks to bridge the gap to practical applications by incorporating concrete examples, pilot project outcomes, and actionable insights. These additions aim to make the discussion more relatable for practitioners, offering them clear illustrations of how blockchain can be deployed within actual supply chains, the typical barriers encountered, and strategies for effective implementation.

While this systematic review pinpointed the characteristics of BC that facilitate its integration into the agri-food sector and assess the effectiveness of these features, certain limitations should be acknowledged. Only empirical use scenarios are the focus of the study. As such, a thorough examination of BC technology as a whole is outside the purview of this review. This narrow focus might leave out important details on more general technological issues and theoretical developments that could influence how blockchain technology is understood to be applicable in the agri-food sector. Notwithstanding these drawbacks, the study intends to synthesize current understanding and offer a significant addition to the area by highlighting particular characteristics that facilitate blockchain's suitability for the agri-food sector. The findings serve as a basis for next studies and direct work toward the AFSC's adoption of BC-based solutions.

Collectively, the themes explored in this chapter from traceability and food safety to efficiency, tamper evidence, and regulatory compliance demonstrate how blockchain can holistically transform agri-food supply chains. This integrated perspective underscores the technology's multifaceted contributions, while highlighting the socio-economic adaptations and collaborative frameworks needed to fully unlock its potential. By bridging conceptual insights with practical considerations, the discussion offers a comprehensive roadmap for stakeholders aiming to implement blockchain-driven solutions in diverse agri-food contexts.

REFERENCES

Al-Dmour, A., Al-Dmour, R., Al-Dmour, H., & Al-Adwan, A. (2024). Blockchain applications and commercial bank performance: The mediating role of AIS quality. *Journal of Open Innovation*, *10*(2), 100302. DOI: 10.1016/j.joitmc.2024.100302

Balci, G., & Surucu-Balci, E. (2021). Blockchain adoption in the maritime supply chain: Examining barriers and salient stakeholders in containerized international trade. *Transportation Research Part E, Logistics and Transportation Review*, *156*, 102539. DOI: 10.1016/j.tre.2021.102539

Burgess, P., Sunmola, F., & Wertheim-Heck, S. (2024). Information needs for transparency in blockchain-enabled sustainable food supply chains. *International Journal of Information Management Data Insights*, *4*(2), 100262. DOI: 10.1016/j.jjimei.2024.100262

Chu, T. T., & Pham, T. T. T. (2024). Vertical coordination in agri-food supply chain and blockchain: A proposed framework solution for Vietnamese cashew nut business. *Regional Science Policy & Practice*, *16*(3), 12576. DOI: 10.1111/rsp3.12576

Compagnucci, L., Lepore, D., Spigarelli, F., Frontoni, E., Baldi, M., & Di Berardino, L. (2022). Uncovering the potential of blockchain in the agri-food supply chain: An interdisciplinary case study. *Journal of Engineering and Technology Management*, *65*, 101700. DOI: 10.1016/j.jengtecman.2022.101700

Duan, K., Onyeaka, H., Pang, G., & Meng, Z. (2024). Pioneering food safety: Blockchain's integration in supply chain surveillance. *Journal of Agriculture and Food Research*, *18*, 101281. DOI: 10.1016/j.jafr.2024.101281

Dutta, P., Choi, T.-M., Somani, S., & Butala, R. (2020). Blockchain technology in supply chain operations: Applications, challenges and research opportunities. *Transportation Research Part E, Logistics and Transportation Review*, *142*, 102067. DOI: 10.1016/j.tre.2020.102067 PMID: 33013183

El Jaouhari, A., Arif, J., Samadhiya, A., Dhayal, K. S., Luthra, S., & Singh, S. (2025). From Automation to Augmentation: Exploring the Role of Industry 5.0 Advanced Technologies for Developing Countries. *Engineering Management Journal*, *37*(3), 306–323. DOI: 10.1080/10429247.2024.2407254

Govindan, K., Jain, P., Kr. Singh, R., & Mishra, R. (2024). Blockchain technology as a strategic weapon to bring procurement 4.0 truly alive: Literature review and future research agenda. *Transportation Research Part E, Logistics and Transportation Review*, *181*, 103352. DOI: 10.1016/j.tre.2023.103352

Guidani, B., Ronzoni, M., & Accorsi, R. (2024). Virtual agri-food supply chains: A holistic digital twin for sustainable food ecosystem design, control and transparency. *Sustainable Production and Consumption*, *46*, 161–179. DOI: 10.1016/j.spc.2024.01.016

Haider Sayma, M., Hasan, M. R., Khatun, M., Rajee, A., & Begum, A. (2024a). Detecting the provenance of price hike in agri-food supply chain using private Ethereum blockchain network. *Heliyon*, *10*(11), e30972. DOI: 10.1016/j.heliyon.2024.e30972 PMID: 38832272

Haider Sayma, M., Hasan, M. R., Khatun, M., Rajee, A., & Begum, A. (2024b). Detecting the provenance of price hike in agri-food supply chain using private Ethereum blockchain network. *Heliyon*, *10*(11), e30972. DOI: 10.1016/j.heliyon.2024.e30972 PMID: 38832272

Hasan, A. S. M. T., Sabah, S., Daria, A., & Haque, R. U. (2023). A peer-to-peer blockchain-based architecture for trusted and reliable agricultural product traceability. *Decision Analytics Journal*, *9*, 100363. DOI: 10.1016/j.dajour.2023.100363

Henrysson, M., Papageorgiou, A., Björklund, A., Vanhuyse, F., & Sinha, R. (2022). Monitoring progress towards a circular economy in urban areas: An application of the European Union circular economy monitoring framework in Umeå municipality. *Sustainable Cities and Society*, *87*, 104245. DOI: 10.1016/j.scs.2022.104245

Issaoui, Y., Khiat, A., Bahnasse, A., & Ouajji, H. (2019). Smart logistics: Study of the application of blockchain technology. *Procedia Computer Science*, *160*, 266–271. DOI: 10.1016/j.procs.2019.09.467

Jahanbin, P., Wingreen, S. C., Sharma, R., Ijadi, B., & Reis, M. M. (2023a). Enabling affordances of blockchain in agri-food supply chains: A value-driver framework using Q-methodology. *International Journal of Innovation Studies*, *7*(4), 307–325. DOI: 10.1016/j.ijis.2023.08.001

Jahanbin, P., Wingreen, S. C., Sharma, R., Ijadi, B., & Reis, M. M. (2023b). Enabling affordances of blockchain in agri-food supply chains: A value-driver framework using Q-methodology. *International Journal of Innovation Studies*, *7*(4), 307–325. DOI: 10.1016/j.ijis.2023.08.001

Jaouhari, A. E., Arif, J., Fellaki, S., Amejwal, M., & Azzouz, K. (2022). Lean supply chain management and Industry 4.0 interrelationships: The status quo and future perspectives. *International Journal of Lean Six Sigma*, *14*(2), 335–367. DOI: 10.1108/IJLSS-11-2021-0192

Jaouhari, A. E., Arif, J., Jawab, F., Samadhiya, A., & Kumar, A. (2024). In Jawab, F. (Ed.), *Leveraging the role of blockchain technology in the hospital supply chain: A systematic literature review and future trends* (Vol. 27, pp. 587–617). Springer., DOI: 10.1007/978-3-031-70292-1_28

Jaouhari, A. E., Arif, J., Samadhiya, A., Kumar, A., & Garza-Reyes, J. A. (2023). An environmental-based perspective framework: Integrating IoT technology into a sustainable automotive supply chain. *Benchmarking*, *31*(10), 3655–3689. DOI: 10.1108/BIJ-05-2023-0322

Jaouhari, A. E., Bhilat, E. M. E., & Arif, J. (2023). Scrutinizing IoT applicability in green warehouse inventory management system based on Mamdani fuzzy inference system: A case study of an automotive semiconductors industrial firm. *Journal of Industrial and Production Engineering*. https://www.tandfonline.com/doi/abs/10.1080/21681015.2022.2142303

Javaid, M., Haleem, A., Pratap Singh, R., Khan, S., & Suman, R. (2021). Blockchain technology applications for Industry 4.0: A literature-based review. *Blockchain: Research and Applications*, *2*(4), 100027. DOI: 10.1016/j.bcra.2021.100027

Martínez-Castañeda, M., & Feijoo, C. (2023). Use of blockchain in the agri-food value chain: State of the art in Spain and some lessons from the perspective of public support. *Telecommunications Policy*, *47*(6), 102574. DOI: 10.1016/j.telpol.2023.102574

Mokgomola, F., Telukdarie, A., Munien, I., Onkonkwo, U., & Vermeulen, A. (2024). Blockchain and Smart Contracts Based Agricultural Supply Chain. *Procedia Computer Science*, *237*, 637–644. DOI: 10.1016/j.procs.2024.05.149

Okorie, O., Russell, J., Jin, Y., Turner, C., Wang, Y., & Charnley, F. (2022). Removing barriers to Blockchain use in circular food supply chains: Practitioner views on achieving operational effectiveness. *Cleaner Logistics and Supply Chain*, *5*, 100087. DOI: 10.1016/j.clscn.2022.100087

Onu, P., Mbohwa, C., & Pradhan, A. (2024). Blockchain-Powered Traceability Solutions: Pioneering Transparency to Eradicate Counterfeit Products and Revolutionize Supply Chain Integrity. *Procedia Computer Science*, *232*, 1420–1427. DOI: 10.1016/j.procs.2024.01.140

Pakseresht, A., Ahmadi Kaliji, S., & Hakelius, K. (2024a). Blockchain technology characteristics essential for the agri-food sector: A systematic review. *Food Control*, *165*, 110661. DOI: 10.1016/j.foodcont.2024.110661

Pakseresht, A., Ahmadi Kaliji, S., & Hakelius, K. (2024b). Blockchain technology characteristics essential for the agri-food sector: A systematic review. *Food Control, 165*, 110661. DOI: 10.1016/j.foodcont.2024.110661

Pakseresht, A., Yavari, A., Kaliji, S. A., & Hakelius, K. (2023a). The intersection of blockchain technology and circular economy in the agri-food sector. *Sustainable Production and Consumption, 35*, 260–274. DOI: 10.1016/j.spc.2022.11.002

Pakseresht, A., Yavari, A., Kaliji, S. A., & Hakelius, K. (2023b). The intersection of blockchain technology and circular economy in the agri-food sector. *Sustainable Production and Consumption, 35*, 260–274. DOI: 10.1016/j.spc.2022.11.002

Ramkumar, G., Kasat, K., Khader, P. R. A., Muhammed, P. K. N., Raghu, T., & Chhabra, S. (2022). Quality enhanced framework through integration of blockchain with supply chain management. *Measurement. Sensors, 24*, 100462. DOI: 10.1016/j.measen.2022.100462

Rashid, M. R. A., Hasan, M., Islam, M. A., Tasnim, S. T., Taifa, R. J., Mahbub, S., Mansoor, N., Ali, M. S., Jabid, T., Islam, M., & Islam, M. M. (2024a). Transforming agri-food value chains in Bangladesh: A practical application of blockchain for traceability and fair pricing. *Heliyon, 10*(21), e40091. DOI: 10.1016/j.heliyon.2024.e40091 PMID: 39583833

Rashid, M. R. A., Hasan, M., Islam, M. A., Tasnim, S. T., Taifa, R. J., Mahbub, S., Mansoor, N., Ali, M. S., Jabid, T., Islam, M., & Islam, M. M. (2024b). Transforming agri-food value chains in Bangladesh: A practical application of blockchain for traceability and fair pricing. *Heliyon, 10*(21), e40091. DOI: 10.1016/j.heliyon.2024.e40091 PMID: 39583833

Rashid, M. R. A., Hasan, M., Islam, M. A., Tasnim, S. T., Taifa, R. J., Mahbub, S., Mansoor, N., Ali, M. S., Jabid, T., Islam, M., & Islam, M. M. (2024c). Transforming agri-food value chains in Bangladesh: A practical application of blockchain for traceability and fair pricing. *Heliyon, 10*(21), e40091. DOI: 10.1016/j.heliyon.2024.e40091 PMID: 39583833

Rashid, M. R. A., Hasan, M., Islam, M. A., Tasnim, S. T., Taifa, R. J., Mahbub, S., Mansoor, N., Ali, M. S., Jabid, T., Islam, M., & Islam, M. M. (2024d). Transforming agri-food value chains in Bangladesh: A practical application of blockchain for traceability and fair pricing. *Heliyon, 10*(21), e40091. DOI: 10.1016/j.heliyon.2024.e40091 PMID: 39583833

Ronaghi, M. H. (2021). A blockchain maturity model in agricultural supply chain. *Information Processing in Agriculture, 8*(3), 398–408. DOI: 10.1016/j.inpa.2020.10.004

Sandhu, R. K., Thomas, M. A., & Osei-Bryson, K. M. (2024). Supporting Secure and Efficient Collaborative Health Information Exchange: A Hybrid Blockchain and Ontology based Approach. *Blockchain: Research and Applications, 100248*. DOI: 10.1016/j.bcra.2024.100248

Sarfaraz, A., Chakrabortty, R. K., & Essam, D. L. (2023). The implications of blockchain-coordinated information sharing within a supply chain: A simulation study. *Blockchain: Research and Applications*, *4*(1), 100110. DOI: 10.1016/j.bcra.2022.100110

Shiraishi, C. S. H., Roriz, C. L., Carocho, M., Prieto, M. A., Abreu, R. M. V., Barros, L., & Heleno, S. A. (2025). Blockchain revolution in food supply chains: A positive impact on global food loss and waste. *Food Chemistry*, *467*, 142331. DOI: 10.1016/j.foodchem.2024.142331 PMID: 39644658

Silvestri, R., Carloni, E., Morrone, D., & Santovito, S. (2024). The role of blockchain technology in supply chain relationships: Balancing efficiency and relational dynamics. *Journal of Purchasing and Supply Management, 100967*. DOI: 10.1016/j.pursup.2024.100967

Soori, M., Dastres, R., & Arezoo, B. (2023). AI-powered blockchain technology in industry 4.0, a review. *Journal of Economy and Technology*, *1*, 222–241. DOI: 10.1016/j.ject.2024.01.001

Srivastava, V., Mahara, T., & Yadav, P. (2021). An analysis of the ethical challenges of blockchain-enabled E-healthcare applications in 6G networks. *International Journal of Cognitive Computing in Engineering*, *2*, 171–179. DOI: 10.1016/j.ijcce.2021.10.002

Tang, A., Tchao, E. T., Agbemenu, A. S., Keelson, E., Klogo, G. S., & Kponyo, J. J. (2024). Assessing blockchain and IoT technologies for agricultural food supply chains in Africa: A feasibility analysis. *Heliyon*, *10*(15), e34584. DOI: 10.1016/j.heliyon.2024.e34584 PMID: 39170464

Zarbà, C., Chinnici, G., Matarazzo, A., Privitera, D., & Scuderi, A. (2024). The innovative role of blockchain in agri-food systems: A literature analysis. *Food Control*, *164*, 110603. DOI: 10.1016/j.foodcont.2024.110603

Zhao, G., Ye, C., Zubairu, N., Mathiyazhagan, K., & Zhou, X. (2025a). Deployment of Industry 4.0 technologies to achieve a circular economy in agri-food supply chains: A thorough analysis of enablers. *Journal of Environmental Management*, *373*, 123856. DOI: 10.1016/j.jenvman.2024.123856 PMID: 39740446

Zhao, G., Ye, C., Zubairu, N., Mathiyazhagan, K., & Zhou, X. (2025b). Deployment of Industry 4.0 technologies to achieve a circular economy in agri-food supply chains: A thorough analysis of enablers. *Journal of Environmental Management*, *373*, 123856. DOI: 10.1016/j.jenvman.2024.123856 PMID: 39740446

Zhao, G., Ye, C., Zubairu, N., Mathiyazhagan, K., & Zhou, X. (2025c). Deployment of Industry 4.0 technologies to achieve a circular economy in agri-food supply chains: A thorough analysis of enablers. *Journal of Environmental Management*, *373*, 123856. DOI: 10.1016/j.jenvman.2024.123856 PMID: 39740446

Section 3
Strategic Foundations and Paradigm Shifts in AI-Driven Supply Chains

Chapter 10

Emerging Trends in Social Sustainability Within Manufacturing Supply Chains

Mohd. Asif Gandhi
https://orcid.org/0000-0002-3976-9269
Anjuman-I-Islam's Kalsekar Technical Campus, India

Eti Khatri
Nitte Meenakshi Institute of Technology, India

Nittan Arora
CT Institute of Engineering, Management, and Technology, India

Kuldeep Agnihotri
ISBA Group of Institutes, India

A. Thangam
Community College (Lawspet), Pondicherry University, India

V. V. S. Murty Bolla
https://orcid.org/0009-0008-6777-5261
ICFAI Foundation for Higher Education, India

V. Bhoopathy
https://orcid.org/0000-0003-2175-6328
Sree Rama Engineering College, India

ABSTRACT

Social sustainability in industrial supply chains is increasingly essential as organisations adapt to evolving consumer expectations, legal mandates, and technological progress. This chapter analyses upcoming trends and developments influencing the future of social sustainability, such as the ascent of ethical consumerism, the enhancement of regulatory frameworks, and the incorporation of modern technologies. It examines the transforming landscape of manufacturing work, focussing on the effects of automation, the imperative for worker upskilling, and the continuous

DOI: 10.4018/979-8-3373-0923-1.ch010

endeavour to safeguard labour rights in a swiftly moving context. This chapter elucidates how manufacturers can effectively manage the intricate relationship between social responsibility and operational efficiency, thereby promoting a sustainable and equitable future.

1. INTRODUCTION

The complexity of supply chains has grown due to globalization and outsourcing. Sustainability and sustainable development have also evolved in the last several decades, coinciding with this trend, as people have grown more aware of humanity's growing influence on the planet. The concept of sustainability was brought to the forefront of global consciousness by the World Commission on Environment and Development (WCED) in their report Our Common Future, also known as the Brundtland Commission Report (Hutchins & Sutherland, 2008). The report defined sustainable development as meeting the needs of the present without compromising the ability of future generations to meet their needs. Agenda 21 and the Millennium Development Goals are only two examples of the many ways the UN has shown its dedication to sustainability. Sustainability has also become an integral part of the goals of many institutions and organizations, whether large and small, on a global and national basis. Making the Brundtland concept operational, or use it to influence decisions, is one of the main issues of sustainability. An alternate interpretation of sustainability. offers some insight into the matter: design and operation of human and industrial systems to ensure that humankind's use of natural resources and cycles does not lead to diminished quality of life due to either losses in future economic opportunities or to adverse impacts on social conditions, human health, and the environment. According to this definition, metrics, which are measurements of performance, are necessary for evaluating the effectiveness of any choice in terms of the subsequent sustainability. The longevity of a supply chain, which consists of many different businesses, is directly related to the longevity of each company in the chain.

Figure 1. Primary flows of a corporation

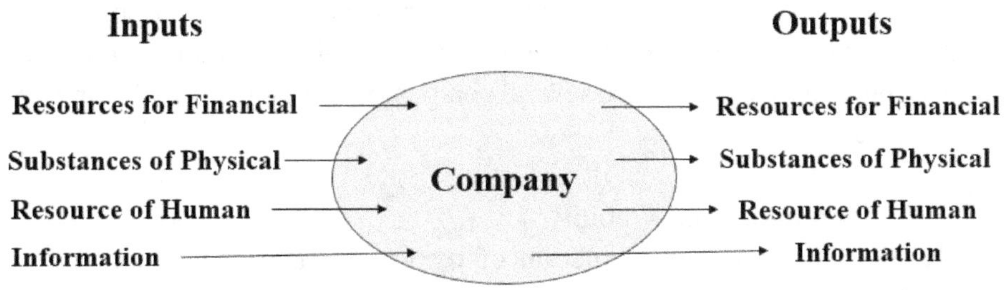

Fig. 1 shows the four basic flows into and out of a company, which is useful for discussing the organization's sustainability from a business. It is contended that the point of a business is to rearrange material assets, human capital, data, and capital so that the sum of money going out is greater than the sum going in.

2. SHIFTS IN CONSUMER BEHAVIOUR

On the surface, it could seem like sustainability and marketing have completely different aims and assumptions. According to (Swim et al., 2011) traditional marketing practices promote expansion, an incessant pursuit of material goods, and the idea that resources are infinite (White et al., 2019). Alternatively, an emphasis on sustainability acknowledges the finite capacity of both resources and the environment, and proposes reusing and recycling them in a manner similar to the natural resource cycles. The attitude-behaviour gap is prevalent in sustainability situations, but the SHIFT paradigm can assist bridge the gap. People say they want to do their part for the environment, but they seldom actually do anything sustainable. Marketers, businesses, policymakers, and nonprofits working to encourage sustainable consumption face this disparity between consumer rhetoric and action as one of their greatest challenges. Sustainable consumer behaviors can be further encouraged and supported, even though demand for sustainable options is on the rise. For instance, 73% of millennials worldwide are willing to pay extra for sustainable offerings 66% of consumers overall report this willingness.

2.1 Rising Demand for Ethical Practices

In today's interconnected world, when individuals, societies, corporations, and the environment are all affected, the subject of sustainable and ethical consumerism is more important than ever. From several perspectives, we can grasp the importance of this subject:

Long-Term Economic Viability:
Resilient Economies: Depletion of resources, rising healthcare bills, and ecological catastrophes are among ways in which unsustainable consumerism can throw the economy into disarray. If we want to create economies that can weather the storms of climate change and social inequality, we must make the shift to more ethical and environmentally friendly consuming practices.
Global Health and Well-Being:
Health and Safety Standards: There is a correlation between people's health and well-being and their consumption habits that are sustainable and ethical (Leung, 2022). Healthier lives are a direct result of products that meet stringent safety and environmental requirements, and the prosperity of the communities that produce these goods is guaranteed by businesses who use ethical sourcing techniques.
Innovation and Technology:
Technological Solutions: Innovation in technology and business operations is driven by sustainable and ethical consumption. Sustainable product design, artificial intelligence, and blockchain are some of the new technologies that are cropping up to help make supply chains more transparent, traceable, and environmentally friendly.
Cultural Shift Towards Responsibility:
Cultural and Social Norms: More responsible and conscientious lifestyles are becoming the norm, and this theme represents that change in culture. Sustainable and ethical consumerism, if accepted as the standard, can shape the beliefs and habits of subsequent generations in a way that ensures a brighter, more environmentally friendly future.
Corporate Responsibility and Reputation:
Business Ethics and Accountability: Sustainability and ethical business practices are being more and more acknowledged by companies. Adhering to these standards improves corporate reputation and resilience while also bringing enterprises in line with society expectations. Businesses who want to succeed in this age of ethically conscious consumers should pay attention to this topic.
Consumer Empowerment:

Informed Decision-Making: By supplying customers with knowledge and resources, this issue enables them to make value-driven decisions. Market demand for sustainable and ethical products and services is being propelled by consumers who are well-informed about the social and environmental consequences of their purchasing decisions.

Policy and Regulatory Frameworks:

Government Intervention: A growing number of regulatory agencies and national governments are coming to terms with the fact that policy interventions are necessary to solve social and environmental problems. This is a crucial subject for laying the groundwork for legislative frameworks that encourage ethical and environmentally friendly business activities, which in turn benefit consumers and companies.

Social Justice and Fair Labor Practices:

Human Rights and Fair Trade: Fair work standards and social justice are intimately related to ethical consumption. For a more just world economy to emerge, supply chain concerns like child labor, exploitation, and unsafe working conditions must be addressed. Promoting human rights through purchasing goods and services is an important part of sustainable and ethical consumption.

Environmental Impact:

Climate Change and Resource Depletion: A major factor in global warming, forest loss, and resource depletion is the prevalence of unsustainable consuming habits. To slow down environmental deterioration and help build a more sustainable and resilient world, it is essential to understand sustainable consumption and to promote it.

2.2 Growing Preference for Local Sourcing

It is not a novel concept to think about generations as groups that share a common memory or experience of significant historical events and how those events affected subsequent patterns of behavior. Some examples of such political and social events include space missions, civil rights movements, assassinations, and wars. Pandemics are a perfect example of the kind of crises to which global capitalism with its constant movement of people and goods is particularly vulnerable (Ford, 2020), even though we have been living in a time of globalism (Mullan, 2020) since the United Nations Millennium Development Goals (MDGs) were launched in 2000 and continued through the Sustainable Development Goals (SDGs) (Zwanka & Buff, 2021). During the COVID-19 pandemic, governments around the world have had to choose which supply chains are most important for national security due to the global lack of medications and Personal Protective Equipment (PPE). Even though most production has shifted overseas, American pharmaceutical companies are still at the forefront of medication innovation and R&D worldwide. The last American facility to produce the active components of penicillin shut down in 2004, which is an interesting fact. The majority of the antibiotics, vitamin C, ibuprofen, hydrocortisone, acetaminophen, and heparin used in the United States come from Chinese pharmaceutical businesses. According to (Morales-Contreras et al., 2021) over half of the world's face masks were manufactured in China, the country from whence COVID-19 was initially transmitted. Covid-19 has been in the news 24/7, so it's no surprise that the generation that lived through the pandemic wants to rally the troops and close ranks at the border. As an example, Japan has set aside 220 billion yen, or more than $2 billion, for Japanese companies to relocate production back to Japan, and another 23 billion yen for companies to relocate production to countries other than China (Takahashi, H., & Yamada, 2021) Countries should bring production of vital items back inside their borders to guarantee a safe supply in the event of another epidemic, considering the amount of dubious information that has emerged from China during the outbreak.

3. STRICTER REGULATORY FRAMEWORKS

Rules that are changing the way financial institutions handle customer data include the General Data Protection Regulation and the California Consumer Privacy Act (Patel, 2023). In today's fast-paced financial industry, there is a clash between the two competing demands for data privacy and protection and the crucial necessity to use customer data for informed decision-making. The foundation of the development of the Unique Customer Identifier (UCI) system is this intersection, which poses a unique challenge and opportunity. In this work, we present the UCI system, an innovative solution that aims to balance the need for thorough financial data analysis with the critical need to protect individual privacy. The original idea for the UCI system came from a need to solve a basic problem in the banking sector: how to get good insights from big databases of customer data while keeping personal information completely private. Financial institutions have long depended on PII to better understand consumer patterns and behavior, as well as to personalize their offerings in response to those trends and needs. Nevertheless, with the rise of public awareness regarding data protection and high-profile data breaches, this dependence on PII has grown more alarming. Financial data management has been transformed as a result of these advancements, which have increased consumer concerns and prompted more stringent regulatory frameworks globally, like the General Data Protection Regulation (GDPR) and the California Consumer Privacy Act (CCPA).

3.1 Legislation on Human Rights and Modern Slavery

In the last two decades, the issue of modern slavery has grown in prominence as a subset of human rights that has attracted more and more attention from throughout the world (Landman, 2020). Researchers and activists in the fields of forced labour, human trafficking, forced marriage, and sexual exploitation have grouped these formerly-erasure forms of slavery under the umbrella term modern slavery. Consistent with these normative shifts, the anti-slavery movement has sought to quantify contemporary slavery; this endeavour can take a page out of the numerous previous attempts to quantify human rights. These approaches allow for the quantitative representation of human rights in both direct and indirect ways, using various types of metrics at various levels of analysis.

3.1.1 Modern Slavery Act

Slavery, servitude, forced and compelled labor, and human trafficking are all parts of what is collectively known as modern slavery, and the MSA's stated goal is to end all of these forms of slavery. On a massive scale, modern slavery is an issue all over the globe (de Cock, Michaëlle, 2014). By strengthening punishments for crimes involving slavery and combining existing criminal offenses, the MSA hopes to enhance UK law enforcement in the region (Lindsay et al., 2017). It also creates a position of Anti-Slavery Commissioner to supervise efforts to end modern slavery through monitoring investigations, prosecutions, and prevention of the crime, as well as new measures to equip the courts to combat the crime and aid victims. The MSA's reporting requirement mandates that certain commercial organisations must publicly disclose their efforts to eradicate modern slavery from their operations and supply chains, which is a novel provision meant to encourage transparency in supply chains and benefit businesses. Transparency in supply chains was not a part of the original Modern Slavery Bill when it was being considered for legislation. Regardless, a UK government-commissioned evidence study suggested doing so. A number of groups, including the Transparency in Supply Chains Coalition, spearheaded the inclusion of the reporting requirement (Buck, 2019). It has won over well-known companies and investors. All major political factions had rallied behind the MSA by the time it became law, and the British government had praised it as a really groundbreaking measure. Only a small portion of the reporting requirement is required. The reporting obligation does not mandate any specific measures to combat modern slavery or to evaluate the efficacy of such measures. Businesses simply just detail the actions they have done, or say they have done nothing, to comply. But the reporting requirement's policy goal is wide-ranging: to require businesses to be transparent about what they are doing to boost accountability in the supply chain. The core tenet of the UK government's strategy is the idea that openness will increase competition to drive up standards. which will level the playing field between ethical enterprises and those that could do more. Basically, the UK government is trying to get people to recognize the financial value in figuring out how to deal with human rights issues.

3.1.2 Due Diligence Laws

The United Nations Guiding Principles on the Framework for Human Rights (UNGPs) define human rights due diligence as the process of identifying, assessing, responding to, and communicating about human rights impacts (HRDD) (Kämpe, 2023). The principle's commentary emphasizes that states are not inherently liable for human rights abuses perpetrated by private actors; however, states may be in violation of their obligations under international human rights law if they do not adequately intervene to prevent, investigate, punish, and remedy human rights abuses. A guiding document to the UNGPs emphasizes that states are not obligated to regulate the extraterritorial activities of businesses operating within their jurisdiction, but they are not barred from doing so either, provided there is a recognized jurisdictional basis. This is in regard to the extraterritorial component of the duty to protect.

4. TECHNOLOGICAL ADVANCEMENTS DRIVING SOCIAL SUSTAINABILITY

By providing novel answers to difficult global problems, technological progress is critical to achieving the SDGs. Smart garbage management, water utility management, and farming are just a few of the important sectors being revolutionized by digital technologies like the Internet of Things (IoT), Big Data Analytics, and Artificial Intelligence (AI) (Islam, 2025). An example of this is the IoT, which allows for the real-time monitoring and control of garbage, which improves efficiency and reduces environmental effect (Rane, 2023). Big Data Analytics, on the other hand, offers insights for optimizing water use and managing agricultural resources. By boosting operational efficiency and fixing important problems in these areas, these improvements help achieve a number of SDGs. In the agri-food sector in particular, studies show that digital technologies have a revolutionary effect on supply chain processes. By enhancing transparency, decreasing waste, and optimizing resource utilization, these technologies help meet the SDGs, which in turn address societal concerns including food security and sustainable agriculture practices (Kwilinski et al., 2023).Due to the COVID-19 pandemic's emphasis on digital technologies' essential role in sustaining operations and guaranteeing resilience, their implementation has been expedited, especially in the agri-food industry. Digital technologies have become vital for adjusting to disruptions and developing SDG-related projects; consequently, the pandemic has highlighted the synergistic relationship between digitalization and sustainability. All things considered, these technological developments are a major factor in the SDGs' advancement, demonstrating how important it is to keep inventing, working together, and sharing what we know in order to solve global problems.

4.1 Blockchain for Transparent Supply Chains

Similar to conventional ledger systems, a blockchain stores lists of transactions in a sequential fashion. Each block has a header and a body, with the latter housing the actual transactions that took place within the previous block (F. T. Sunmola et al., 2021). The blockchain records all agreements made across the supply chain, including prices, quantities, quality standards, product specs, and transaction details. Supply chain actors, registrars, standard organizations, and certification providers are all potential participants in blockchain based supply chains (Shivendra et al., 2021). One trend in the literature a) on blockchain technology's use in supply chains is the growing familiarity with its features (F. Sunmola & Burgess, 2023). b) The building blocks are being more and more identified. (c) Integrating blockchain technology into quality management systems. d) Trust systems built on the blockchain. e) How supply chain management blockchains must be aware of their context. In order for blockchain technology to be successful in international supply chains, certain key success factors were listed in. Data quality, accessibility, documentation, data management, regulations, and decentralization were among these. Supply chain management can be made possible by the properties of blockchain technology, which include immutability, transparency, smart contracts, trustlessness, impedance of tampering, and non-reputation (Dey & Shekhawat, 2021). Blockchain technology has the potential to enhance supply chain management, according to the literature. Blockchain technology has many potential uses, including but not limited to: enhanced monitoring, transparency, and control authenticity, traceability and supplier engagement, and trust and reputation. Current study findings are available that you may review on the advantages of blockchain-based supply chains in Table 1.

Table 1. The use and advantages of blockchain technology in the supply chain

S.NO	Supply Chain and Focus	Advantages
1	The potential benefits and drawbacks of using blockchain technology in government supply chains are discussed in this research review	Fewer paperwork; Fewer options to make a mistake; Better teamwork
2	Find out how smart contracts and blockchain technology can make freight booking more efficient	Strengthen safety and ease of access
3	Improving the grain supply chain through the use of blockchain technology	Efficient control of quality; Transparency in the supplier chain; Less disagreements
4	The pros and cons of using blockchain technology in the car sector are the subject of this research	Efficiency, Decentralization, Security of information, Accountability, Tamper-proofness, Reduced transaction costs, Digitization, and Reproducibility
5	A supply network for high-quality rice powered by blockchain technology	Improved product quality, Disintermediation, Accuracy of data, Accountability, and Secure data
6	Traceability and provenance of food using blockchain technology	Product lifecycle management has been enhanced
7	A system that tracks prices in the agri-food supply chain using blockchain technology	Loss of middlemen; Increased visibility; Enhanced oversight

Transparency is a hot topic in many fields of study, and it's playing an increasingly important role in supply chains. Various definitions have been put forth with relation to the breadth of transparency. Businesses that are transparent provide their stakeholders with full, up-to-date, and correct information; this encourages honesty, boosts teamwork, and paves the way for group decisions. Accurate data about operations, procedures, and items, such as where they come from, how they were processed, and where they are transported, is shared through a transparent supply chain. The rules of an organization that make sure all stakeholders have access to information that is also usable, intelligible, and presented in a clear and understandable way are known as process transparency. The capacity to readily access and manipulate data, irrespective of their location or the program that generated them, is known as data transparency.

4.2 Artificial Intelligence for Ethical Compliance

The revolutionary character of AI is often perceived in a positive light. The adoption of AI-based solutions may lead to mutually beneficial outcomes for both businesses and society at large, according to an innovation-driven viewpoint (Zhao & Gómez Fariñas, 2023). Beyond the difficulty of making AI judgments completely transparent and accountable, designers and users of AI should think about the revolutionary and far-reaching consequences that these technologies could have on people and society in the future. The three cornerstones of this idea environment, society, and economy must be firmly established at the heart of AI ethics in light of the pressing need to direct corporate action towards sustainable development. Everyone agrees that the public sector and directors in particular will need to work together for AI and other advanced tech adoption to be successful. Engineers developing AI systems should face consequences for society, the environment, and human health if their judgments have negative effects, according to the European Commission (Bailey & Peck, 2013). For AI to be really sustainable, it must take into account all stages of its life cycle, including but not limited to: design, training, development, validation, re-tuning, implementation, and use of AI (van Wynsberghe, 2021). In order to guarantee the sustainability of the data sources, power supplies, and infrastructures utilized to train or tune algorithms, businesses should set aside funds and include in their budgets the cost of applying AI to green initiatives. It is time to investigate how AI may advance a wider variety of social and economic objectives once the organization has established a sustainable AI infrastructure (Camilleri, 2024). We can construct basic algorithms to push AI towards more ethical and sustainable corporate actions, therefore this is definitely doable. With the help of data science for social good, AI will be able to solve societal problems and apply AI methodologies to measurably handle intractable societal problems.

Figure 2. An ethical paradigm for the regulation of AI

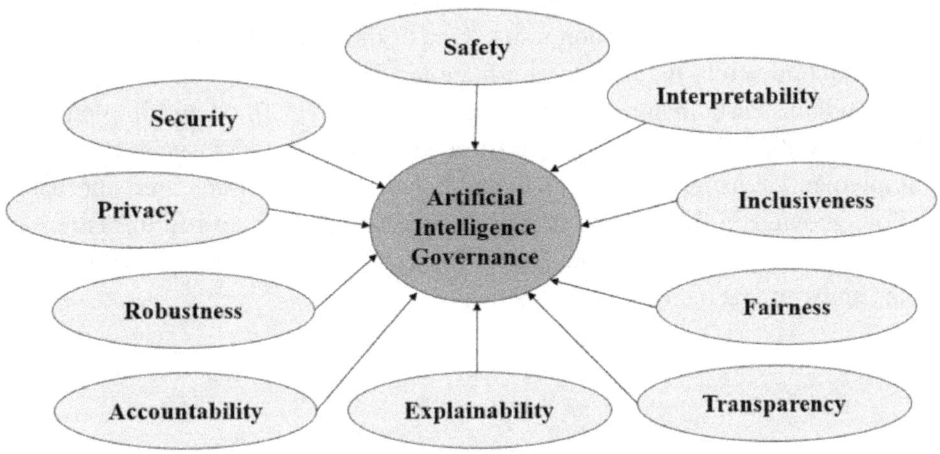

Figure 2 showcases a few essential components needed for the ethical regulation of AI. The purpose of these principles is to lay forth expectations for how people working in AI including those creating ML and DL systems should conduct themselves.

4.3 IoT for Workplace Safety

There will be three major technological advances in the coming decade, and the IOT is considered one of them. According to Ashton's 1999 definition, the IoT is a network that links not just people but also the things in their immediate vicinity (Ashton, 2009). This is the first and most widely accepted social take on the term. With an eye toward industrial use, the IoT has made possible Industry 4.0 via the integration of digital and physical systems in the manufacturing facility, in accordance with the aforementioned design principles of cooperation, data analytics, security, and interconnection (Hermann, Mario, Tobias Pentek, 2016). The new paradigm is reshaping the conventional human-process interaction in manufacturing by suggesting a future in which data management is more important than operator involvement in the process itself (Gregori et al., 2018). In order to stay competitive, many businesses today see sustainability as an integral part of their operational plans. The manufacturing methods of this new intellectual asset must incorporate ecological, monetary, and social considerations. Worker rights, preventative occupational health and safety, human-centred design of work, worker empowerment, individual and collective learning, employee involvement, and work-life balance are all aspects of social sustainability that should be considered in production sites. Employee morale and job satisfaction can be enhanced by enhancing workplace practices beyond what is required by law.

Physical, mental, social, environmental, and organizational aspects all coexist in the multi-faceted concept of ergonomics. One of the goals of this work is to incorporate ergonomics into the design of a manufacturing system, which is suggested by these pillars. Participatory ergonomics programs, if defined and implemented in this competition, have the potential to raise people's consciousness, make control implementations more acceptable, and bolster the worker-centered approach's adoption. Provides a framework for developing an appropriate IoT infrastructure to collect plant-related human metrics for integration into a production line where humans and systems interact.

Figure 3. Proposed technique

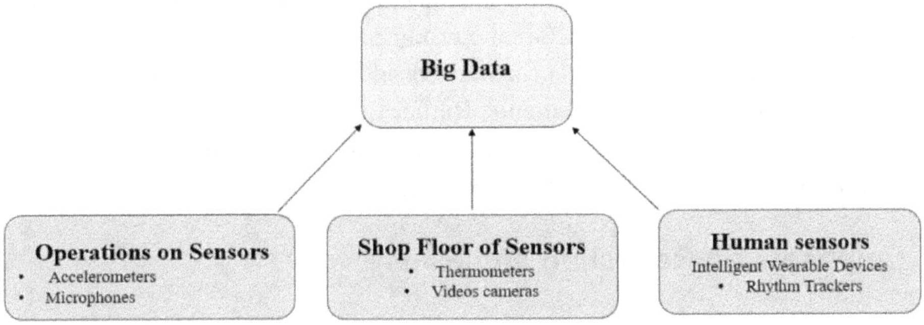

Figure 3 depicts the architecture that gathers data from many sources and sends it to a central server with the intelligence to handle them. This creates meaningful information that analysts and designers can use to make more informed decisions more quickly.

5. CIRCULAR ECONOMY INTEGRATION

The ideal form and operation of sustainable energy and industrial systems have been defined by a number of theoretical frameworks. Industrial ecology, Circular Economy (CE), and process integration are the three fields whose models are examined in this article. A growing number of countries, including Europe and China, are beginning to embrace the idea of a CE (Kirchherr et al., 2017). One definition of a CE states that it maximizes material and energy recovery while minimizing the consumption of primary energy and virgin resources on a macro scale Though (Geissdoerfer et al., 2017). conceptually comparable to IE, it differs in that it promotes the development of new businesses as a means to improve material circular flows. CI stresses the importance of a comprehensive and methodical approach to design in order to attain results like CE and IE (Walmsley et al., 2019). Processes all the way up to policy design are part of its many dimensions, and it works at various sizes. By utilizing approaches that offer both top-down and bottom-up views on the identical issue, it accomplishes multi-level integration. The optimization target in CI is total sustainability, not circularity. When looking at sustainability from a lifecycle perspective, it is common to add up the monetary, ecological, and social costs, or the so-called triple bottom line (Zore et al., 2018). Because of the subjective weighting criteria and complicated relationships, determining total sustainability is not an easy task in practice. Process, plant, regional, and national levels are all encompassed in

CI. Maximizing the circularity of the concentric loops leads to sustainability gains. Increased process heat integration, for instance, lowers combustion emissions and fuel consumption at the plant level. Greater product re-use lowers production demand on an economic scale. The loop is further closed by the reprocessing of residuals employing technological advancements. Rather than viewing these enhancements in isolation, they reveal commonalities in their pursuit of more circularity when viewed through the prism of the unified CI framework.

5.1 Emphasis on Recycling and Reuse

- **Sustainability:** Future generations place a premium on sustainability (Sinha & Modak, 2021). After the current demand has been met, it helps to preserve primary resources for the next generation. The goal of sustainable development is to keep progress in all three areas economic, social, and environmental in a steady equilibrium.
- **Recycling:** According to (Yao & Askin, 2019), recycling is a great way for CLSC managers to put products' scraps to good use. By bringing in a third party to screen the parts received from end-of-life items, it decreases environmental deterioration, generates business prospects, eliminates the unemployment problem, and ultimately minimises manufacturing cost. According to research, recycling can cut the cost of making a computer by half. There has been an explosion in recent years of studies on recycling in all its forms. Above all else, nevertheless, it is the producers' and consumers' awareness that will determine the recycling process's effectiveness across industries. Keep in mind that the strategic recycling option is quite pertinent in this scenario. The research shows that compared to central and southern Italy, northern Italy performs better when it comes to recycling. The purpose of the research by (Nascimento, 2019) was to examine how the circular economy relates to Industry 4.0 technology. In his 2017 article, Giordano reaffirmed the importance of recycling for brand owners and urged them to stock up on biodegradable and environmentally friendly plastics.

Reusing and recycling white goods and other products made by the welfare state Remploy was emphasised.

- **Re-manufacturing:** It comes to supply chain management and reverse logistics; re-manufacturing is now a crucial activity. Even though it has newer features, the remanufactured product is just as good as the original. Because many parts may be reused, re-manufacturing also helps to reduce production expenses. Sustainable remanufacturing has been the focus of multiple studies have all examined remanufacturing from various environmental and economic perspectives. In their mathematical model, predicated that new and remanufactured products could both meet demand. The final consumers' used goods are gathered for the purpose of remanufacturing. The importance of coordinating the production of new and remanufactured items was also emphasised. Examined the benefits and drawbacks of re-manufacturing in the car industry. The writers took into account both conventional manufacturing and re-manufacturing. It is possible to power the manufacturing process with either raw materials or recovered material. Therefore, considering the volume, timing, quality, and uncertainty of the hybrid flow of materials makes integration a difficult process. In their CLSC model, (Jena & Sarmah, 2016) placed a focus on re-manufacturing following product recovery.

- **Reuse:** Reusing and recycling materials helps keep our environment clean. With the economy closed, it promotes a path towards zero waste and zero emissions. A new product with improved features can be mass-produced at a lower cost through reuse as well. Subsequently, many individuals will gain from the decreased price. Electronic garbage e-waste from sources such as computers, mobile phones, and other electrical and electronic devices can be recycled and reused to create a more sustainable environment. Electronic trash, plastics, cast iron, and other forms of scrap metal pose a threat to ecosystems and the environment. One way to lessen these wastes and help the environment is to reuse.

5.2 Worker Inclusion in Circular Initiatives

Businesses have begun to associate standardised work with increased staff efficiency, with the goal of formalising processes and establishing responsibility for this goal. Encouragement, quantification, and goal-setting regarding the amount of employee improvement proposals are methods that most firms prioritise in order to boost employee innovation (Alayón, Claudia, Kristina Säfsten, 2017). Morning meetings, quality and environment meetings, and improvement meetings are some of the ways that employees can have their ideas collected. Another option is to have a suggestion box. The operator's knowledge and experience are highly valued by companies; thus, a frequent key performance indicator is the number of improvement ideas per person over a given time period. Awards for the best idea each month, public recognition of employees' achievements, and monetary incentives are all ways that companies try to encourage creativity. Lastly, teamwork is seen as an opportunity to maximise employees' abilities and foster creativity, both individually and collectively. Protecting workers requires a system of health and safety management that can identify potential dangers and keep an eye on them.

Commonly highlighted were preventative efforts aimed at limiting, mitigating, or eliminating risks. Training plans were emphasised by all respondents as important for the ongoing development of skills and abilities. Organisations encourage job rotation and provide professional development programs. Training programs are designed to help workers become more proficient in their jobs. Training employees is also linked to competent personnel, high-quality products, and competitiveness in the eyes of companies. Critical to employee growth is the process of evaluating their own performance. Questions like how satisfied are you with your job and what training do you feel you need are part of yearly performance reviews. Many people who took the survey saw ISO 9001 as a way to methodically improve their skills and knowledge. Safety, the workplace, training, and environmental concerns are all included in ISO 9001's management review meetings, which help to uphold this objective.

Table 2. Evaluation of sustainable production methods

Principles	Sustainable Production Methods
In terms of economy, emotionally, culturally, and environmentally, communities bordering workplaces are valued and improved	Possibilities for local employment Partnerships with academic institutions Meetings with local officials on a regular basis Community service projects undertaken by volunteers Endorsing regional groups
In order to keep workers efficient and inspire them to be creative, work is structured in a certain way	Streamlining processes Responsibility at work Targets for employee feedback on how to improve Teamwork; improvement meetings; compensation for staff whose proposals are implemented Efficacy metrics
Chemical, ergonomic, and physical risks in the workplace are being reduced or eliminated through the use of new technologies	The use of robots in potentially dangerous tasks Checks for internal safety Workplace audits conducted by other parties Aids for mechanical lifting Worker's switch positions every so often. Process adjustments to lessen vibrations and noise Education for workers regarding potential dangers Metrics for success
Employee safety and well-being, as well as their skill and capacity development, are paramount	A system for managing health and safety Courses of study Professional growth opportunities Changing up staff Financial aid Submitted for the sake of health and wellness. Evaluation of work satisfaction Review of work performance Training and competency are supported by ISO 9001

The manufacturing procedures are being guided by the sustainable production principles, as summarised shown in Table 2. Since there are interrelations between environmental impacts, social impacts, and even various principles within the same sustainability dimension it is not uncommon for actions to address more than one principle simultaneously due to overlap.

6. COLLABORATION AND MULTI-STAKEHOLDER INITIATIVES

Variously named, MSIs have recently been popular as a means to tackle multi-institutional, multi-competency, multi-locational, multi-powerful social problems (Fowler & Biekart, 2017). An article of faith in implementing the SDGs is the inclusion of many sector actors in their pursuit. This drive does not necessitate agreement on what constitutes an MSI, which is sometimes differentiated between casual conversations and actual, long-term partnerships. Regardless, MSIs must be orchestrated into existence and thereafter led to accomplish their goals. This task cannot be understood through the use of comparative analysis.

6.1 Public-Private Partnerships

Development organisations' growing systematic and purposeful attempts to collaborate with businesses to attain development outcomes fall under the umbrella term of public-private partnership (Loveridge & Wilson, 2017). Agreement on various formats and terminologies is becoming increasingly important, despite the fact that the term partnership is often used as an umbrella for activities including both public and private stakeholders. This study focusses on helping development organisations clarify the difference between partnerships and other types of public-private collaboration, a difference that is often made without saying it. For public-private efforts to be considered a partnership, they must be co-created and executed with each party contributing equally and actively, and they must yield advantages to both parties. Usually, they entail dividing up assets, risks, and obligations.

In contrast to other types of partnerships, multi-stakeholder platforms are unique in that they include:

- Engage a wide range of organisations; and include members, participants, supporters, and funders from several stakeholder groups
- Lead primarily to the dissemination of information or the establishment of norms
- Are concerned with matters of global development

In recent years, multi-stakeholder collaboration has evolved, and platforms are a component of it. The method to implementing the Sustainable Development Goals is deeply rooted on multi-stakeholder partnerships. Notes that there are no obvious differences between multi-stakeholder platforms and multi-stakeholder partnerships in the existing research. Partnerships, platforms, coalitions, alliances, challenges, networks, global action networks, and initiatives are among terms that have been used to describe this type of relationship (Phillips et al., 2015). Even while a partnership has a main goal, it may still engage in pursuits that are more directly related to a secondary goal. An instance of this is how the Sustainable Trade Initiative (IDH) facilitates public-private partnerships among firms, CSOs, governments, and others, in addition to its purpose of knowledge sharing. Collaboratively, we are advancing the development, co-funding, and prototype of new economically feasible methods to achieve large-scale, environmentally friendly, and inclusive growth in commodities and sourcing domains, which is similar to service provision. Along with its involvement in setting standards for things like sustainably farmed seafood (Utchay, 2005) and support for other platforms like the Global Coffee Initiative and Sustainable Vanilla Initiative it also backs other initiatives.

6.2 Consumer Activism and Advocacy

In today's dynamic social environment, corporate social advocacy plays a crucial role in corporate communications. In an era where public faith in corporations is dwindling and expectations are rising, businesses need to show that they care about more than just making money; they need to be involved in building a better society (Taylor, 2024b). In addition to building brand loyalty and encouraging consumer engagement, corporate social advocacy can help bridge the trust gap between companies and their stakeholders, both internal and external (Taylor, 2024a). An expansion of Corporate Social Responsibility (CSR), is Corporate Social Advocacy (CSA). Companies engage in CSR when they believe they have a responsibility to the public good; CSA goes beyond this by fighting for causes that are in line with the company's charitable ideals and principles. Companies and their communicators will need to figure out how to be good corporate citizens in this new age if they want to stay afloat. Typical traditional CSR approaches focus on causes that have widespread support, which allows firms to avoid taking a stand on contentious matters while still maintaining some degree of ambiguity. Nevertheless, public doubt regarding the veracity of these activities and the capacity of the firm to effect change is frequently caused by the vagueness of CSR. In order to determine its identity, members of the organisation must interpret various pieces of information about the corporation, state (Park & Jiang, 2023) because the general public does not have complete information about a corporation. As a result, customers may start to doubt CSR and CSA. According to (Xu et al., 2022), CSA actions serve as a mediator between CSA and CSR by successfully signalling business identity. A brand community forms when a company takes a stand on social and political issues that its stakeholders believe in, either by opposing or supporting such causes (Park & Jiang, 2023). Businesses rely on this feeling of belonging to establish credibility and legitimacy for their operations.

7. FUTURE DIRECTIONS

There is an intriguing path ahead for AI-driven clinical decision support that involves integrating new technologies, working together across disciplines, and putting an emphasis on practical application. In a similar vein, artificial intelligence is constantly working to improve its interpretability, transparency, and resilience in order to fit in with clinical procedures more smoothly (Nadella et al., 2023). We still need to find new ways to use federated learning and decentralized architectures to tackle the problems of data heterogeneity, interoperability, and scalability. Data management solutions for security needs in patient-centric care delivery stand to be revolutionized by the confluence of AI with other transformational technologies, such as blockchains and the Internet of Medical Things (IoMT). When it comes to healthcare AI, understanding the ethical, legal, and societal ramifications will require interdisciplinary collaboration among physicians, data scientists, ethicists, specialists, and legislators. Future research efforts that prioritize patients' needs should aim to develop AI-powered tools that give people more control over their health and make it easier for everyone to get the treatment they need. By combining AI with human knowledge, clinical decision support has the ability to break new ground, paving the way for individualized healthcare and precision medicine. As we go deeper into the world of AI-powered sustainable supply chain management, our attention is inevitably attracted to the horizon. This horizon is filled with new trends and innovative technologies that will change the way supply chain operations are done. Here we go into the future environment, where invention reigns supreme and the limits of what is conceivable keep getting pushed farther and further out (Muthuswamy & M. Ali, 2023). We shine a light on the new technologies and trends that are changing the way businesses plan, build, and run their supply chains. Supply chain management is poised for a bright future, thanks to innovations like autonomous cars, blockchain, and 5G connection, which will bring about greater efficiency, sustainability, and resilience. By combining expert knowledge with forward-thinking ideas, we shed light on the changing supply chain ecosystem and the steps that companies can take to stay innovative and make sure their supply chains are prepared for the future.

Table 3. Recent developments in AI and sustainable supply chain management

S.NO	Research Trends	Potential Impact
1	Energy Adoption of Sustainable	- Reduced carbon emissions-Saved money on energy - Improved reputation for sustainability
2	Environmentally Last-Mile Shipping	Fewer pollutants - More efficient delivery - Saved money
3	Transportation and Green Logistics	- Less environmental impact - Affordable long-term viability - Improved standing of the brand
4	Machine Collaboration and Human	- Enhanced agility - Better decision-making - Optimized resources
5	Delivery of Sustainable Last-Mile	- Less pollution - More efficient shipping - Saved money
6	AI-Powered Sustainability	More ethical practices - Less impact on the environment -Very Effective
7	Supply Chains of Circular	Sustainable materials - Less waste -Operations that are closed-loop
8	Blockchain in Supply Chains	- More openness - Better ability to track - More protection for sensitive information
9	Sourcing Algorithms for Sustainable	The importance of ethical sourcing- Less danger in the supply chain- Strengthened ties with vendors
10	Innovations of Packaging Sustainable	- Enhancement of brand sustainability - Reduced environmental footprint - Improvement of packing efficiency

Sustainable supply chain management and machine intelligence are two areas that are expected to have a surge in research in the next years, as seen in Table 3.

8. CONCLUSION

Humans and the environment are both negatively impacted by industrialization. Consequently, businesses must immediately establish sustainable supply chains that consider not just economic but also social and environmental factors (Badri Ahmadi et al., 2017). Sustainable performance is quickly rising to the status of a critical organizational strategy, thanks to our expanding understanding of sustainability, new policies, and the rising consciousness of the general public. In order to be fully sustainable, an organization must think about it from three different angles: economic, environmental, and social. So far, many researchers and practitioners have focused on sustainability's economic and environmental aspects, but the social aspect especially in poor nations has gotten comparatively less attention. Ignoring the importance of social sustainability in supply chains can have disastrous consequences, as it paves the way for other sustainability projects. In light of this problem, the authors of this study offer a methodology for studying the social sustainability of manufacturing enterprises' supply chains.

REFERENCES

Alayón, Claudia, Kristina Säfsten, and G. J. (2017). Conceptual sustainable production principles in practice: Do they reflect what companies do? *Journal of Cleaner Production*, 693–701.

Ashton, K. (2009). "That 'internet of things' thing." *RFID Journal*, 4986.

Badri Ahmadi, H., Kusi-Sarpong, S., & Rezaei, J. (2017). Assessing the social sustainability of supply chains using Best Worst Method. *Resources, Conservation and Recycling*, *126*, 99–106. DOI: 10.1016/j.resconrec.2017.07.020

Bailey, B. C., & Peck, S. I. (2013). Boardroom Strategic Decision-Making Style: Understanding the Antecedents. *Corporate Governance*, *21*(2), 131–146. DOI: 10.1111/corg.12008

Buck, L. E. (2019). Modern Slavery in the Global Supply Chain: An Analysis of Published Preventative Statements and Frameworks to Protect Businesses and Individuals. *The Boller Review*, *4*. DOI: 10.18776/tcu/br/4/115

Camilleri, M. A. (2024). Artificial intelligence governance: Ethical considerations and implications for social responsibility. *Expert Systems: International Journal of Knowledge Engineering and Neural Networks*, *41*(7), 1–15. DOI: 10.1111/exsy.13406

de Cock, Michaëlle, and M. W. (2014). "Profits and poverty: The economics of forced labour." In *International Labour Organization*. https://www.ilo.org/wcmsp5/groups/public/---ed_norm/---declaration/documents/publication/wcms_243391.pdf

Dey, K., & Shekhawat, U. (2021). Blockchain for sustainable e-agriculture: Literature review, architecture for data management, and implications. *Journal of Cleaner Production*, *316*(June), 128254. DOI: 10.1016/j.jclepro.2021.128254

Ford, D. R. (2020). *Review of Mike Davis (2020). The Monster Enters : COVID 19, Avian Flu, and the Plagues of Capitalism*. Postdigital Science and Education.

Fowler, A., & Biekart, K. (2017). Multi-Stakeholder Initiatives for Sustainable Development Goals: The Importance of Interlocutors. *Public Administration and Development*, *37*(2), 81–93. DOI: 10.1002/pad.1795

Geissdoerfer, M., Savaget, P., Bocken, N. M. P., & Hultink, E. J. (2017). The Circular Economy – A new sustainability paradigm? *Journal of Cleaner Production*, *143*(0), 757–768. DOI: 10.1016/j.jclepro.2016.12.048

Gregori, F., Papetti, A., Pandolfi, M., Peruzzini, M., & Germani, M. (2018). Improving a production site from a social point of view: An IoT infrastructure to monitor workers condition. *Procedia CIRP*, *72*(March), 886–891. DOI: 10.1016/j.procir.2018.03.057

Hermann, M., Pentek, T., and Otto, B. (2016). Design principles for industrie 4.0 scenarios. *In 2016 49th Hawaii International Conference on System Sciences (HICSS), 01*. DOI: 10.13140/RG.2.2.29269.22248

Hutchins, M. J., & Sutherland, J. W. (2008). An exploration of measures of social sustainability and their application to supply chain decisions. *Journal of Cleaner Production*, *16*(15), 1688–1698. DOI: 10.1016/j.jclepro.2008.06.001

Islam, H. (2025). Nexus of economic, social, and environmental factors on sustainable development goals: The moderating role of technological advancement and green innovation. *Innovation and Green Development*, *4*(1), 100183. DOI: 10.1016/j.igd.2024.100183

Jena, S. K., & Sarmah, S. P. (2016). Future aspect of acquisition management in closed-loop supply chain. *International Journal of Sustainable Engineering*, *9*(4), 266–276. DOI: 10.1080/19397038.2016.1181120

Kämpe, I. (2023). *Bringing human rights due diligence into law:Addressing modern slavery or business as usual?* Kirchherr, J., Reike, D., & Hekkert, M. (2017). Conceptualizing the circular economy: An analysis of 114 definitions. *Resources, Conservation and Recycling*, *127*(September), 221–232. DOI: 10.1016/j.resconrec.2017.09.005

Kwilinski, A., Lyulyov, O., & Pimonenko, T. (2023). Environmental Sustainability within Attaining Sustainable Development Goals: The Role of Digitalization and the Transport Sector. *Sustainability (Basel)*, *15*(14), 11282. DOI: 10.3390/su151411282

Landman, T. (2020). Measuring Modern Slavery: Law, Human Rights, and New Forms of Data. *Human Rights Quarterly*, *42*(2), 303–331. DOI: 10.1353/hrq.2020.0019

Leung, P. M. (2022). Trends in Sustainable and Ethical Consumption. *International Journal of Business Management and Visuals*, *5*(2), 30–36.

Lindsay, R., Kirkpatrick, A., Low, J. E., & Lindsay, R. (2017). Hardly Soft Law: The Modern Slavery Act 2015 and the Trend towards Mandatory Reporting on Human Rights. *Business Law International*, *18*(1), 18. https://heinonline.org/HOL/License

Loveridge, D., & Wilson, N. (2017). *"Engaging with the private sector through multi-stakeholder platforms* (Issue January 2017).

Morales-Contreras, M. F., Leporati, M., & Fratocchi, L. (2021). The impact of COVID-19 on supply decision-makers: The case of personal protective equipment in Spanish hospitals. *BMC Health Services Research, 21*(1), 1170. DOI: 10.1186/s12913-021-07202-9 PMID: 34711231

Mullan, P. (2020). *Beyond Confrontation: Globalists, nationalists and their discontents*. Emerald Publishing Limited. DOI: 10.1108/9781839825606

Muthuswamy, M., & Ali, M., A. (. (2023). Sustainable Supply Chain Management in the Age of Machine Intelligence: Addressing Challenges, Capitalizing on Opportunities, and Shaping the Future Landscape. *Sustainable Machine Intelligence Journal, 3*, 1–14. DOI: 10.61185/SMIJ.2023.33103

Nadella, G. S., Nadella, G. S., Satish, S., Meduri, K., & Meduri, S. S. (2023). A Systematic Literature Review of Advancements, Challenges and Future Directions of AI And ML in Healthcare. *International Journal of Machine Learning for Sustainable Development, 5*(3), 115–130. https://www.ijsdcs.com/index.php/IJMLSD/article/view/519

Nascimento, D. L. M., Alencastro, V., Quelhas, O. L. G., Caiado, R. G. G., Garza-Reyes, J. A., Rocha-Lona, L., & Tortorella, G. (2019). Exploring Industry 4.0 technologies to enable circular economy practices in a manufacturing context: A business model proposal. *Journal of Manufacturing Technology Management, 30*(3), 607–627. DOI: 10.1108/JMTM-03-2018-0071

Park, K., & Jiang, H. (2023). Signaling, Verification, and Identification: The Way Corporate Social Advocacy Generates Brand Loyalty on Social Media. *International Journal of Business Communication, 60*(2), 439–463. DOI: 10.1177/2329488420907121

Patel, K. (2023). Revolutionizing Consumer Data Analysis: The Development and Impact of a Unique Customer Identifier. *International Journal of Computer Trends and Technology, 71*(12), 61–74. DOI: 10.14445/22312803/IJCTT-V71I12P111

Phillips, W., Lee, H., Ghobadian, A., O'Regan, N., & James, P. (2015). Social Innovation and Social Entrepreneurship. *Group & Organization Management, 40*(3), 428–461. DOI: 10.1177/1059601114560063

Rane, N. L. (2023). Integrating Leading-Edge Artificial Intelligence (AI), Internet of Things (IoT), and Big Data Technologies for Smart and Sustainable Architecture, Engineering and Construction (AEC) Industry: Challenges and Future Directions. *International Journal of Data Science and Big Data Analytics, 3*(2), 73–95. DOI: 10.51483/IJDSBDA.3.2.2023.73-95

Shivendra, C., K., Tripathi, M. K., & Maktedar, D. D. (2021). Block chain Technology in Agriculture Product Supply Chain. *2021 International Conference on Artificial Intelligence and Smart Systems (ICAIS), December 2021*, 1325–1329. DOI: 10.1109/ICAIS50930.2021.9395886

Sinha, S., & Modak, N. M. (2021). A systematic review in recycling/reusing/remanufacturing supply chain research: A tertiary study. *International Journal of Sustainable Engineering*, *14*(6), 1411–1432. DOI: 10.1080/19397038.2021.1986594

Sunmola, F., & Burgess, P. (2023). Transparency by Design for Blockchain-Based Supply Chains. *Procedia Computer Science*, *217*, 1256–1265. DOI: 10.1016/j.procs.2022.12.324

Sunmola, F. T., Burgess, P., & Tan, A. (2021). Building Blocks for Blockchain Adoption in Digital Transformation of Sustainable Supply Chains. *Procedia Manufacturing*, *55*(C), 513–520. DOI: 10.1016/j.promfg.2021.10.070

Swim, J. K., Clayton, S., & Howard, G. S. (2011). Human behavioral contributions to climate change: Psychological and contextual drivers. *The American Psychologist*, *66*(4), 251–264. DOI: 10.1037/a0023472 PMID: 21553951

Takahashi, H., & Yamada, K. (2021). When the Japanese stock market meets [Impact of ownership, China and US exposure, and ESG channels. *International Review of Financial Analysis*]. *COVID*, 19.

Taylor, C. L. (2024a). *"Corporate Social Advocacy:A Study of Brand and Consumer Activism in the Era of Social Media.*

Taylor, C. L. (2024b). Corporate Social Advocacy. *A Study of Brand and Consumer Activism in the Era of Social Media.*

Utchay, H. U. (2005). Convergence and divergence in global economy and social development: global perspectives on the contents of economic and soical development policy and its effects on rich and poor countries. Diss. Åbo Akademis förlag-Åbo Akademi University Press, In *Journal GEEJ* (Vol. 7, Issue 2).

van Wynsberghe, A. (2021). Sustainable AI: AI for sustainability and the sustainability of AI. *AI and Ethics*, *1*(3), 213–218. DOI: 10.1007/s43681-021-00043-6

Walmsley, T. G., Ong, B. H. Y., Klemeš, J. J., Tan, R. R., & Varbanov, P. S. (2019). Circular Integration of processes, industries, and economies. *Renewable & Sustainable Energy Reviews*, *107*(March), 507–515. DOI: 10.1016/j.rser.2019.03.039

White, K., Habib, R., & Hardisty, D. J. (2019). How to SHIFT Consumer Behaviors to be More Sustainable: A Literature Review and Guiding Framework. *Journal of Marketing*, *83*(3), 22–49. DOI: 10.1177/0022242919825649

Xu, H., Lee, E., & Rim, H. (2022). Should businesses take a stand? Effects of perceived psychological distance on consumers' expectation and evaluation of corporate social advocacy. *Journal of Marketing Communications*, *28*(8), 840–863. DOI: 10.1080/13527266.2021.1969588

Yao, X., & Askin, R. (2019). Review of supply chain configuration and design decision-making for new product. *International Journal of Production Research*, *57*(7), 2226–2246. DOI: 10.1080/00207543.2019.1567954

Zhao, J., & Gómez Fariñas, B. (2023). Artificial Intelligence and Sustainable Decisions. *European Business Organization Law Review*, *24*(1), 1–39. DOI: 10.1007/s40804-022-00262-2

Zore, Ž., Čuček, L., & Kravanja, Z. (2018). Synthesis of sustainable production systems using an upgraded concept of sustainability profit and circularity. *Journal of Cleaner Production*, *201*, 1138–1154. DOI: 10.1016/j.jclepro.2018.07.150

Zwanka, R. J., & Buff, C. (2021). COVID-19 Generation: A Conceptual Framework of the Consumer Behavioral Shifts to Be Caused by the COVID-19 Pandemic. *Journal of International Consumer Marketing*, *33*(1), 58–67. DOI: 10.1080/08961530.2020.1771646

Chapter 11
The Role of Artificial Intelligence in Transforming Supply Chain Management

P. Suganya
Manakula Vinayagar Institute of Technology, India

Subramanian R. Siva
SRM Institute of Science and Technology, India

S. N. Ananthi
SA Engineering College, India

T. Thilagam
https://orcid.org/0000-0002-7657-0726
Vel Tech Rangarajan Dr. Sagunthala R&D Institute of Science and Technology, India

J. Elavarasi
Vel Tech High Tech Dr. Rangarajan Dr. Sakunthala Engineering College, India

Gracious L. A. Anto
https://orcid.org/0000-0003-2386-9182
R.M.K. College of Engineering and Technology, India

P. Girija
https://orcid.org/0009-0000-1691-8180
Panimalar Engineering College, India

ABSTRACT

Artificial Intelligence (AI) is transforming Supply Chain Management (SCM) through intelligent, data-driven decision-making and process optimization. This chapter explores AI's impact on key SCM areas such as demand forecasting, inventory control, logistics, and risk management. Technologies like Machine Learning, NLP, and Computer Vision enhance efficiency and responsiveness, while integration with IoT and Big Data enables real-time insights. Applications include predictive ana-

DOI: 10.4018/979-8-3373-0923-1.ch011

lytics for inventory, route optimization in logistics, and fraud detection. Innovations like autonomous vehicles and AI-powered chatbots are reshaping operations and customer service. Despite notable benefits cost reduction, improved accuracy, and customer satisfaction challenges remain, including data privacy, integration issues, and skill gaps. The chapter also highlights emerging trends such as generative AI and reinforcement learning in SCM, emphasizing their potential to drive future advancements and operational excellence.

1. INTRODUCTION

1.1 Overview of Supply Chain Management (SCM)

SCM which means the systematic administration of a range of organizations involved in the ultimate delivery of a product or service to customers. It involves the acquiring, creating, moving, and delivering products and services as well as information. The objective of SCM is to enhance efficiency & effectiveness of the supply chain, reduce cost and improve processes, and deliver products & services to the consumers at the right time and at a right price. SCM is a challenging process of coordinating such a network of suppliers, manufacturers, warehouses, retailers, as well as materials, information, and monetary flows. Manual SCM practices, use of spreadsheets and legacy systems are still prevalent in many organizations and they are time-consuming, error prone and often cause delays. However, with the advancement in the global trade and market requirements the need to have intelligent fast and efficient SCM has become an essential factor. New challenges such as e-commerce, globalization, and the evolving customer wants and needs, have put pressure on organizations to cut operating expenses, deliver faster, and better serve their clients. These changes have made SCM more complex and this increasing complexity needs new ways of enhancing the strategic and operational aspects of SCM.

1.2 Role and Significance of AI in SCM

AI is fast becoming an influential technology in enabling the transformation of SCM by providing real-time analytical tools to improve operations. AI uses algorithms, machine learning, NLP and big data to sort through vast amounts of information, recognize patterns that are beyond the capability of the human mind to discern, and make conclusions that decision makers could not have made. AI can help organizations to enhance the efficiency of supply chain processes while at the same time decreasing their expenditures, as well as to build agile supply chains that are less sensitive to disruptions. Predictive analytics is one of the main ways through which AI is being applied in SCM. (Toorajipour, R. et al 2021) AI can also analyse the historical data & then make predictions on demand pattern and thus improve the stock holding and the forecasting rate. This capability makes it possible to avoid stock-outs, avoid overstocking and control procurement costs to the benefit of a business and its customers. Also, the application of AI is vital in improving supply chain & transportation system. They can determine the most efficient routes and schedules to help organizations to deliver products and services faster, economically, and efficiently. Intelligent transportation systems including self-driving cars, drones and robots offer a lot of potential for the revolution of logistics through eliminating human efforts and increasing delivery time.

In SCM, AI enables an organization to evaluate supplier performance and risks, as well as the opportunities for future cooperation. AI refines the supplier evaluation and performance monitoring making the supplier selection more transparent and efficient, thus guaranteeing that businesses work with the most credible and affordable suppliers. In risk management, AI technologies can identify patterns of risk and give real-time info concerning the interruption of risks such as supply chain issues, fraud, and cyber risks. AI can also be used to model different situations, with a view of creating strategies in case things go wrong, thus reducing risks that may form large issues. Furthermore, with the help of AI, the sphere of customer service has also been changed significantly by using chatbots and virtual assistants that answer customers' questions in real time. These technologies can help in managing shipment tracking, shipment status and customer complaints and can go a long way in enhancing the customer satisfaction. The function of AI in SCM is further enhanced when the system is linked to the IoT devices and Big Data. (Min, H. 2010) Sensors and smart devices connected to the IoT share data from different points of the supply chain, helping AI systems make improved forecasts and decisions founded on real-time data. Big Data analytics supports this by offering the platform for the management & analysis of large volumes of structured & unstructured data that help organisations gain a better understanding of supply chain efficiency.

1.3 Objectives and Scope of the Chapter

The purpose of the chapter is to identify how AI has revolutionized Supply Chain Management, the uses, advantages, disadvantage, and the prospects. This chapter will give a broad cross-section of how different aspects of SCM are being impacted by AI technologies and the benefits that come with integration of the technologies. This chapter shall therefore employ real world case studies and real life implementations in order to illustrate the practical utility of AI in improving supply chain.

The primary objectives of the chapter are as follows:

1.Identify AI Technologies in SCM: These are ML, DL, NLP, & computer vision, among others, and how they are used in various SCM functions.
2.Explore Key Applications: These areas of application shall be investigated through the chapter include: demand forecasting, inventory management, logistics optimization, supplier relationship management, & risk management. It will also explore areas like self-driving cars, AI-based chatbots, and anti-fraud systems based on the AI technology.
3.Assess Benefits and Challenges: In this section, the benefits, which organizations accrue from implementing AI in SCM will be highlighted including cost reduction, accuracy, time efficiency, and expansiveness of the solution. It will also engage with issues such as the data privacy, combing of AI system with existing systems, & skills shortage for AI implementation in the workforce.
4.Investigate Future Trends and Research Opportunities: The chapter will cover new trends in AI for SCM such as generative AI and reinforcement learning, and reveal directions for further research in this field both in terms of academic and practical development.

All in all, this chapter delivers a comprehensive discussion as to how AI is revolutionizing supply chains. Recognizing AI's possibilities and managing its risks will help organizations use its strengths to design better, stronger, and customer-oriented supply chains capable of meeting future market requirements.

2. AI TECHNOLOGIES IN SCM

2.1 Overview of AI Technologies

AI is a broad field of technologies that allow a computer to learn, think and act like a human being & make decision based on data. In the context of SCM AI technology is being used to analyse particular stages, enhance the efficiency of operations, & improve decision making. (Pournader, M. et al 2021)

Machine Learning (ML): Artificial Intelligence can be categorized into machine learning where systems learn from experience without being programmed. In SCM, the most common use of ML is to perform statistical analysis to provide future demand and optimize inventory. Using machine learning algorithms, one is able to process big data and extract patterns and trends that indicate future variations in demand so as to adjust stock in real time to ensure that all businesses have the right stock at the right time. Some of the widely used ML techniques are regression models, decision trees, and clustering techniques, which assist organizations to determine patterns & take informed decisions.

Deep Learning (DL): ML is a subfield of AI, and DL is a subfield of ML that employs NN with numerous layers to make patterns in data. DL is especially useful for decision making on unstructured data, which is the case with supply chains since images, videos and large text files are common in these systems. In SCM, deep learning used in the applications such as fraud detection, demand forecasting, risk management etc. For instance, deep learning models can use past records of transactions to flag cases of fraud or estimate instances of disruptions in supply chains due to calamities, shifts in the economy, or politics.

Figure 1. AI technologies in SCM

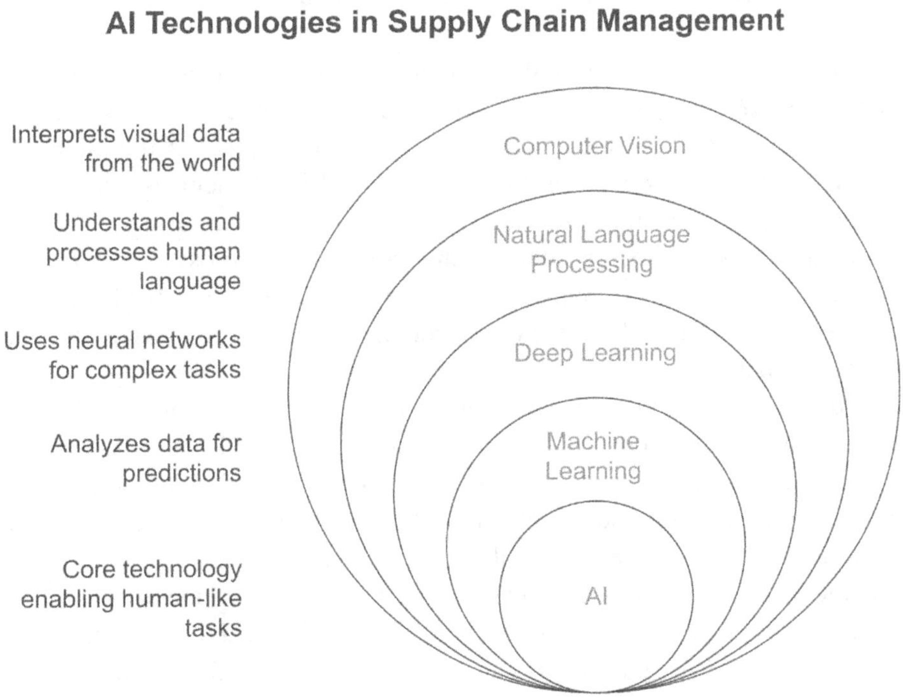

Natural Language Processing (NLP): NLP is the ability of a machine to comprehend meaning, analyze or even produce human language. It is applied in SCM for customer service, sentiment analysis and document processing. For example, NLP integrated into AI chatbots can talk to customers, respond to inquiries, and monitor deliveries. NLP is also applied to convert text data into structured data that is easy to use for the purposes of analyzing emails, invoices, and contracts. NLP can assist in automating such paperwork, and in generalizing and simplifying communication with suppliers, as well as increasing the accuracy of further orders' handling.

Computer Vision: Computer Vision is a technology that can enable machines to understand & process the information from the world that includes images and videos. In SCM, computer vision is applied in warehouse management, inventory tracking as well as quality inspection. For instance, computer vision systems can watch over production lines and detect whether the product manufactured is damaged, or else check on inventories without human assistance. In the case of logistics, computer vision can be adopted to scan packages, which will enhance the correct sorting of goods [Venketbabu et al 2024].

2.2 Integration of AI with IoT and Big Data in SCM

AI when combined with IoT and Big Data has brought about a massive change in the supply chain & has empowered organizations to make better decisions in real time.

IoT in SCM: IoT is defined as devices that are connected to the internet and that gather and transmit data over the system. In SCM, IoT includes sensors, RFID tags, GPS trackers, and smart machinery that give real time information about the location, quality, and state of products, vehicles and assets across the network. This data is very useful for stock control, for assessing the state of perishable goods, and for compliance purposes. For example, temperature measuring devices connected through IoT may help owners of perishable goods such as drugs or food to be informed when temperatures reach dangerous levels. The combined IoT with AI makes it possible for companies to advance from simply collecting data to predictive analysis. AI algorithms can also use the huge amount of data produced by IoT devices to forecast possible supply chain breaks including machine breakdowns, lack of stock, and delayed deliveries. AI also provides the chance to implement predictive maintenance, when AI detects early signs of wear in machines and equipment, avoiding further damages and downtimes. By integrating real time IoT data and the predictive nature of AI, businesses can enhance the supply chain and make better decisions while saving money.

Big Data in SCM: Big Data could be described as the huge amount of structured & unstructured data that business organizations produce every day. Big Data in SCM originates from many sources such as customer orders, inventory management data, shipment information, and social media. The problem is not about finding data in abundance, but about how to handle it, interpret it and make sense of it. That is where AI can play its role of ML algorithms can easily analyze Big Data and find out patterns, trends, and correlation, which can be beyond human comprehension (Yamini, et al., 2024). Big Data on its own & when integrated with AI can be used to improve demand forecasting, inventory, & production planning. For instance, through assessing prior sales records, weather conditions, market trends, and customers' behaviours, the AI models can forecast future demand much more effectively than traditional approaches, which leads to low probabilities of either overstocking or stock out situations. AI also used to look for the problem in the big data in the supply chain such as transportation delays or less-efficient warehouse design and make a right decision. In addition, AI will enable organizations to foresee and manage risks that are associated with supply chain disruptions, geopolitical risks or economic changes in the value chain. AI models when integrated with Big Data can help the business to be more ready for market changes and effectively mitigate probabilities. ML, DL, NLP, and computer vision along with IoT and Big data are the new paradigms of SCM (Subramanian et al., 2024). These technologies make it possible to achieve improved process control, productivity, costs reduction, and better decision making among businesses. (Sharma, R. et al., 2022) AI enables organizations to make decisions at the time of need through structured and unstructured data collected from different sources. AI in conjunction with IoT and big data not only helps organizations to develop higher levels of operational flexibility and robustness but also provides an opportunity for the creation of new supply chain value. With these technologies advancing, the possibilities for the increasing use of AI in SCM are vast, giving businesses the capability they need to maintain their edge in an ever growing and changing market.

3. APPLICATIONS OF AI IN SCM

AI is gradually finding its way into SCM to enhance effectiveness, cut costs and spur creativity. AI technologies can actually improve every function of SCM including demand forecasting and customer service. This section discusses five of the most important application areas of AI in SCM: demand forecasting and inventory management, logistics and transportation, supplier management, risk management, and customers service and personalization.

3.1 Demand Forecasting and Inventory Management

Predictive Analytics for Demand Patterns

demand forecasting is a highly important activity in SCM because it determines the production schedule and inventory level as well as decisions about resource utilization. Conventional approaches may use previous information and simple mathematical models which can be ineffective and unprecise in today's rapidly evolving markets. There are three ways of demand forecasting, which are AI, ML, and DL are more enhanced methods of demand forecasting compared to the earlier methods. (Richey Jr, R. G. et al., 2023) AI algorithms can process large data from different sources including past sales records, customer behavior, seasonal patterns, market trends, & social media trends to forecast the demand pattern more effectively. Because of the utilization of modern methods such as time series analysis, regression analysis and ensemble learning, the AI systems are capable of finding the latent patterns and modify the outcome with the emerging data. This kind of flexibility gives AI-based forecasting a higher degree of accuracy than conventional methods in unpredictable markets. AI also plays a role of predictive analytics in the sales forecast since it will analyze and look for patterns that a human analyst will not notice. For instance, machine learning models help to find micro-trends, like changes in the customer preferences, weather conditions, or abrupt increase in regional demand. By getting the right demand, organizations could order inventory in the right quantities and even schedule production appropriately so that they can meet their customers' demand without going overboard.

3.2 Inventory Optimization

Inventory control is an important determinant of supply chain efficiency and expenses. Holding more than optimal levels increase holding costs, and the possibility of having old stock that may not be saleable while ordering small quantities contribute to stockouts, lost sales and customer complaints. AI can improve inventory management by helping to predict the amount of stock that is needed and make the appropriate restocking decisions automatically. By using machine learning, sales data, demand variations, and supply chain challenges can be used to determine the right inventory levels for various products[Sreelakshmi, S et al 2024]. These models take into account factors like lead time, order quantity and product life cycle to ensure that organizations order for stock in the right time. Also, through AI, the demand pattern during festive seasons or during a particular promotion can be identified in advance and the inventory is pre-stocked in self-actualization. Real time inventory management is also made possible through AI so that businesses can get a glimpse of the movement of stocks across warehouses, distribution centers and stores. The use of IoT gadgets such as RFID labels and savvy sensors will help businesses check inventories in real-time. It assists companies in getting insights on the major factors that affect inventory management and in the process, they manage to minimize on excess inventories and at the same time increasing their level of service delivery.

3.3 Logistics and Transportation

Route Optimization and Dynamic Scheduling

Logistics is one of the most challenging components of the SCM that deals with the movement of products to their designated destinations at the right time and costs. AI offers some of the greatest opportunities for making logistics more efficient in terms of route choice, delivery time, and fuel costs. AI enhanced route planning process based on machine learning techniques and it takes into consideration factors such as traffic patterns, weather conditions, road closures, delivery time slots and capacity of the delivery vehicle. From this data, AI is able to ascertain the best routes for drivers, which leads to shorter delivery time, less fuel consumption and therefore lower expenses. In addition, it is possible to manage routes flexibly in response to the changes in the situation, for example, a traffic congestion or an emergency order, so that products can be delivered on schedule. Another important area of AI implementation is dynamic scheduling. Conventional scheduling processes depend on predetermined set of rules and ad hoc modifications, which may not be effective when addressing unexpected situations. AI algorithms, however, will be able to update delivery schedules any time they want and depending on the current real-time data including the availability of vehicles, priorities of deliveries, and customer demands. It lets the companies to achieve better control over their fleet and minimize the idle time of vehicles, which in return raises the service standard and lower the cost.

3.4 Autonomous Vehicles and Drones

The use of self-driving cars, more commonly known as autonomous vehicles (AVs), and drones is another AI area of potential application in logistics. Self-driving trucks, vans, and delivery robotic vehicles can be seen as an opportunity to exclude human operators from the transport process and minimize transportation expenses. Self-driving cars rely on computer vision, machine learning, and sensor systems (such as LiDAR, radar, cameras) to recognize objects on the road and decide on actions in real-time. (Shoushtari, F. et al., 2021)They can work round the clock while delivering consignments quicker and more effectively than human beings, without the dangers of human mistakes. AI driven drones are also finding a growing application in the last mile delivery, especially where physical access is a constraint or in congested areas such as urban environments. AI assists drones in perceiving the surrounding environment and making decisions on paths to follow and avoiding other objects, and in delivering packages to the desired address with a great level of accuracy. Drones can enable same day delivery at a lower cost, particularly for small lightweight parcels, and give firms a competitive edge in the expanding online retail environment.

3.5 Supplier Relationship Management

AI in Supplier Selection and Performance Monitoring

SRM is a sub-discipline of SCM, as suppliers and the quality of their performance have a direct impact on the supply chain costs, effectiveness and reliability. One of the major applicability areas of AI is in supplier selection, since the potential suppliers can be rated automatically against various criteria like price, quality, reliability of delivery and their previous performance. Suppliers' data of past performance, time of delivery, and customers feedbacks can be used by a machine learning model to determine the most suitable suppliers for a certain product or service. (Culot, G. et al., 2024) AI can also assist in determining certain risks related to suppliers, including their financial situation, political risks or circumstances of the environment in which they operate, so that businesses make the right decision when choosing a partner. After the selection of suppliers, AI can then dynamically assess the suppliers' performance based on the data received from different sources including order processing and delivery as well as quality check reports. The use of AI in the creation of dashboards can mean that the performance of suppliers is monitored in real-time, and where there are problems the business can address them before they become an issue for the supply chain.

3.6 Risk Management

Real-Time Monitoring and Fraud Detection

It is critical to SCM since companies are surrounded by various risks like natural calamities, political instabilities, cyber risks, and supplier issues. AI can improve risk management because it offers more precise data on risks in the process of their occurrence and can predict potential risks before they become critical. Business AI models are capable of processing significant volumes of external and internal data, including news feed analysis, weather conditions, and social media presence, with a view of identifying warning signals of disruptions. For instance, it may be used in analyzing satellite images and determining natural disasters like floods or hurricanes and the possibilities of the impact on supply chain. Likewise, AI can track the geopolitical risks, slow economic growth or changes in trade policies that might impact suppliers or customers in the global supply chain network. AI is also employed to improve the managing of fraud risks in the SCM processes. Transactional data can be analyzed by the ML techniques to make prediction of different patterns like fraudulent invoices, payment issue, or supply chain theft. AI models can learn from previous examples and fraud cases, and adapt on their own to prevent new types of fraud from occurring and causing a loss of money and reputation.

3.7 Customer Service and Personalization

AI-Powered Chatbots and Tailored Recommendations

Customer service is a part of the supply chain function since it will influence the customer's satisfaction, loyalty, and retention. Realization of NLP and machine learning in the customer services are helping business organizations to deliver prompt, customized and efficient services. In supply chains, artificial intelligence in the form of chatbots is adopted more and more for interacting with customers, informing them about orders and providing solutions to problems. These chatbots are built with NLP algorithms that allow them to analyse customer inquiries and provide answers in real time, thus increasing the efficiency of companies' customer service and decreasing the workload for live agents. There are many applications of chatbots, such as order status, return policy, and product inquiry, allowing human agents to resolve more complicated problems. Machine learning is also being used to increase customer satisfaction by identifying their past buying habits, the products they have been searching most often and their tastes. (Mohsen, B. M. 2023) With this information, it is possible for the AI systems to suggest products, services or even promotion offers that will suit customers' needs to the greatest extent thus increasing the sale and satisfaction among the customers. Personalization is not only relevant for engaging the customer but also helps businesses to organize their inventory and products according to the customers' needs. AI has become central in the supply chain management with uses in demand forecasting, logistics, supplier management, risk management and customer service. Using such technologies as predictive analytics, machine learning and others, within the company, businesses can optimize their supply chains, make good decisions & increase the level of customer satisfaction. However, there are various challenges associated with the integration of AI in SCM including data privacy issues, integration issues and skilled human resource. However, the benefits of AI such as reduced cost, time and space, and creation of innovative solutions make AI a critical tool in today's supply chain. With the advancement in AI, the application of AI in SCM is anticipated to increase in the future thereby influencing future SCM industry.

4. BENEFITS AND CHALLENGES

AI in SCM has numerous opportunities that can enhance the performance and save funds by increasing the competitiveness of the business. However, there are also several risks that are inherent to AI adoption that organizations need to overcome to fully utilize AI. This section explores the advantages of implementing AI in SCM, which are cost effectiveness, time, precision and expansibility; the disadvantage of implementing AI in SCM which are data security, compatibility, and skills (Maheshwaran et al., 2024).

4.1 Advantages of Adopting AI in SCM

1. Cost Efficiency

Possibility of cost reduction is one of the most persuasive arguments in favor of implementing AI in SCM. AI can help in simplifying several processes like inventory management, demand forecasting, and processing of orders and thus can reduce the amount spent on labour and the number of mistakes committed. For example, AI based demand forecasting models may suggest that companies need less inventory which in turn saves much money spent on unsold stock or on stocks that are out of demand. Due to improved supply-demand matching, AI reduces the amount of wastage and overstocking as opposed to having to order goods at the last minute, or at exorbitant shipping costs. Also, machine intelligence in the supply chain by improving the ways of delivery and shipment planning like route optimization, dynamic scheduling can minimize fuel consumption and decrease the cost of delivery. The most obvious application of machine learning relates to optimization of transportation costs and routes, as well as schedules based on real-time data (Ambhika, C. et al., 2024).

2. Speed and Responsiveness

AI increases the rate of decision making and also increases the rate of activities in supply chain. Machine learning models and AI systems are capable to handle vast data and make decisions with high speed, which will help companies to adapt the changes in the market, customers, and suppliers. For instance, where predictive analytics is applied, it is possible to forecast demand changes and make the necessary changes ahead of time not having to wait for the results. Such flexibility is particularly relevant in industries where demand fluctuates considerably, for example, in the retail trade sector. AI can also enhance working processes within different supply chain operations, increasing the velocity of order processing, from purchasing to delivery. In addition, AI takes care of repetitive tasks and handling of large volumes of data making it possible for business to run even at night without interruption hence supplies chain processes are accelerated.

Figure 2. Advantages of AI in SCM

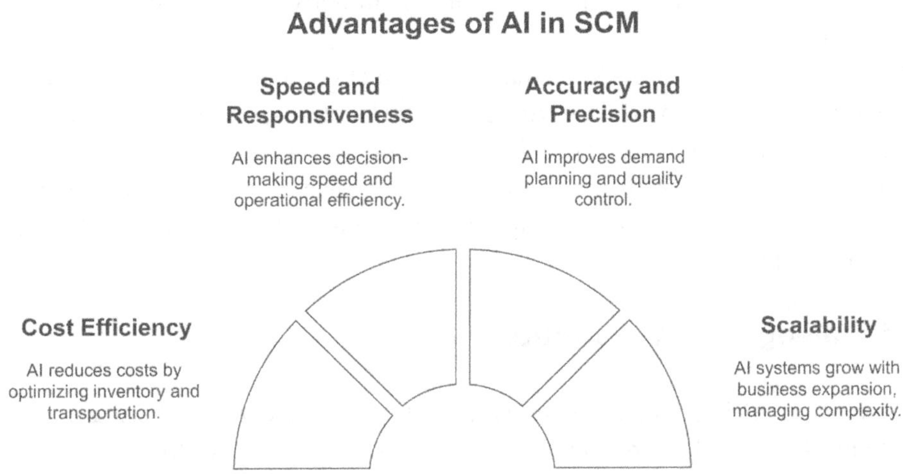

3. Accuracy and Precision

Precision is essential in SCM since minor discrepancies can cause a lot of havoc, cost additional money, and upset customers. AI has the potential to enhance the efficiency of different supply chain activities such as demand planning, inventory management, & quality control. With machine learning approaches, there are a chance to predict the demand by using historical sales data, trends and external conditions, such as the weather or international political situation (Anusha, S et al., 2024). This therefore leads to improved inventory control whereby business entities are able to estimate the amount of stock that may be required to meet the customers' demand without having to order excess stocks or when they will run out of stock. Furthermore, the AI-assisted quality assurance systems are designed using computer vision and deep learning techniques to check products on a conveyor belt or stored in a warehouse for any defects that a human operator may overlook. This cuts the incidences of making and delivering unsuitable products to the market, hence increasing product quality and customer satisfaction.

4. Scalability

AI systems are inherently scalable, meaning that they can handle increased load of data and moreover, increased size of supply chain. Due to this, as the business expands, the supply chain also expands with more supplier, customers and products to deal with. AI can handle such complexities by working through big data and can also make decisions across various supply chain activities without any need for more resources.

For example, the use of AI to manage production schedules, or to respond to changes in customer demand across geographical locations, means that supply chains can continue to be flexible and effective as they grow. This adaptability makes AI most effective in global supply chains as they have to manage vast amounts of transactions across different geographical locations and places more reliance on transactional data.

4.2 Challenges in AI Adoption

Of course, AI has numerous advantages for SCM, however, there are several significant barriers that organizations need to address in order to achieve proper AI implementation. These challenges can be an albatross in the adoption of AI and slow down its advancement to the next level.

Figure 3. AI adoption challenges in SCM

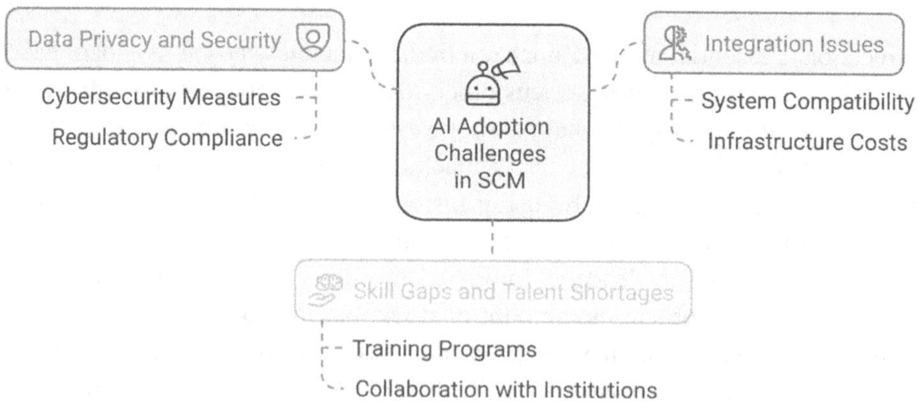

1. Data Privacy and Security Concerns

AI systems in SCM use data, especially big data, such as customer data, suppliers' performance data, inventory data, and transactional data. The acquisition, storage, and analysis of such data pose serious data privacy and security risks given the current high profiled cybercrimes and data leakage. Companies need to guarantee that their information is safeguarded from unauthorized access from the outside world and intrapreneurial abuse (Mediavilla, M. A. et al., 2022). If these data privacy and security issues are not resolved, the following negative outcomes will be experienced; Reputational loss, financial loss, legal consequences. However, organisations must also have the right policies with regard to data ownership and usage rights in order avoid abuse of AI systems. It becomes even more difficult when working with third-party entities such as suppliers, and other partners who also get to access such data.

2. Integration Issues

The second major issue in SCM and AI is the implementation of AI technologies with existing systems & frameworks. The majority of firms continue to operate with outdated systems that were not developed for integration with AI. These systems might be incompatible with modern AI tools which hinders the integration of AI solutions without great changes or expensive redesigning. For example, when using AI in IoT devices, ERP systems, and WMS, data must be transferred smoothly between the applications. This means that interaction between the AI tool and the existing systems has to be well facilitated so as to allow for easy exchange of data. Disintegration of this integration disrupts smooth supply chain operations which in turn hampers the efficiency of AI solutions. Occasionally, the introduction of AI may require capital expenditures in the form of new technologies or infrastructure, which can be a costly affair for SMEs.

3. Skill Gaps and Talent Shortages

The shortage of qualified professionals who can design, implement, and oversee AI solutions is one of the main challenges preventing the use of AI in SCM. AI technologies are a relatively new development and for that reason, they are based on algorithms that are new and need experts in machine learning, data science, and software engineering; however, there is a scarcity of talent in these fields all over the world. This talent gap is likely to make it challenging for organizations to develop AI talent within their establishments and may lead to organizations outsource the services of AI from other vendors or consultants, which is expensive. Furthermore, the use of AI in supply chain operations means that it can only be developed with the collaboration of IT, operation professionals, supply chain professionals, and data science experts. It is therefore important for companies to effectively train their human capital so as to enable them to get the best results when using these AI tools. This may mean spending on training and developing the human resource or building talent through collaborations with universities and research institutions. (Younis, H. et al., 2022) The advantages of Applying AI in SCM are numerous they include cost-cutting, faster rate, accuracy and scalability. With the help of the automation and use of AI technologies like ML, predictive analysis, and computer vision, organizations can improve the supply chain, make better decisions, and increase customer satisfaction. However, there are some risks related to such implementation of AI, and these are, data privacy issues, integration questions and skills gap which need to be properly addressed. Thus, it will be critical for supply chain management to address these challenges as organizations keep on adopting AI to realize the full potentials of AI in their operations.

5. FUTURE TRENDS/RESEARCH OPPORTUNITIES

The use of AI in SCM has already impacted many areas of SCM including demand planning, inventory management, logistics, and customer service. But the current and developing trends in AI technology comprise several promising opportunities for future developments. This section discusses the current trends in the field of AI for SCM and also identify the gaps in the literature that may define the future direction of the field.

5.1 Emerging AI Trends in SCM

1. AI based Autonomous Supply Chains

Supply chain autonomy is one of the most exciting trends in AI application for SCM. Advanced AI systems can now handle more supply chain tasks with little input from human beings in the process. AI is used in autonomous supply chains for decision support, analytics, and automation for achieving increased efficiency, less cost, and quicker recovery from disruption. For instance, transportation and delivery by autonomous vehicles and drones are already in use in logistics. In the future, the applications may be linked to systems that are run by artificial intelligence to develop smart logistics chains that will entail minimal or no human intervention in the supply of the materials. This could ideally change various sectors including retail, manufacturing and especially the health sector where timeliness and effectiveness in supply chain management is so crucial.

2. Integration of Generative AI in SCM

Generative AI is one of the types of machine learning that is used to create models that can generate the content based on the input data to provide new images, texts, supply chain strategies, and many others. In SCM, generative AI can be applied for example to route planning, stock management, and product development. For example, AI could provide individual supply chain plans based on a company's goals, limitations and conditions of the market. Another great use case of generative AI is in predictive maintenance. Generative models could forecast possible failures in the machinery and suggest the proper time for maintenance, which could help companies save money and time and avoid purchasing expensive repairs. As generative AI models advance, it is possible that the use of generative AI in SCM can increase operational efficiency, better stock control, and wiser logistics.

3. AI and Blockchain Integration for Enhanced Transparency and Security

The use of AI in SCM with the help of blockchain technology, which enables secure & transparent storage of transactions, is gradually gaining popularity. AI and blockchain integration can make supply chain more transparent, secure and have better track of history. For instance, blockchain technology can record the journey through the supply chain and AI can examine this process and advise where there are issues that may affect the flow of goods. The integration of the two technologies could reduce fraud and enhance the supply chain transparency & compliance with the rules, especially in such industries as pharmacy and food industry where product origin matters. The combination of the growing use of blockchain technology and the integration of AI can become one of the trends in the further development of SCM.

Figure 4. AI trends in SCM

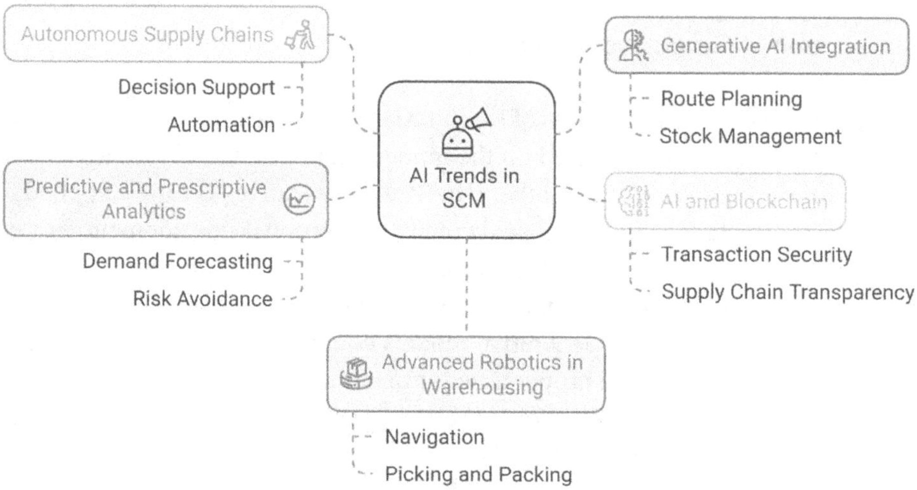

4. AI-Powered Predictive and Prescriptive Analytics

The current application of AI in SCM includes predictive analytics in demand forecasting, inventory management, and risk avoidance in the future, prescriptive analytics will be used in SCM. While descriptive and predictive analytics rely on AI to explain what has happened and what is likely to happen respectively, prescriptive analytics provide the solution to what should happen next. For instance, instead of just identifying that a specific product would be popular at a certain time AI would also suggest how the product should be sourced, manufactured, and delivered to consumers. If done together, predictive, and prescriptive analytics can shift companies from a reactive to a predictive supply chain management, allowing them to plan for disruptions before they happen. This trend will most probably transform into the game-changer for such industries that involves just-in-time inventory and require efficient supply chain management in dynamic environment.

5. Advanced Robotics and AI in Warehouse Management

Robotics have been part of SCM for quite some time now, but the combination of AI with highly advanced robotics is pushing the warehouse and distribution center to their next level. Current advances in technology allow using AI-powered robots for navigation, shelves replenishment, and even picking and packing. With increased capabilities of AI models to learn and adapt to new environments, these robots will be able to work hand in hand with human beings to increase efficiency and accuracy in the warehouse and at the same time avoiding many accidents. Another trend is in the creation of social robots able to interact with other robots and with workers. Robotics, where robots work alongside human workers will become prominent in warehouses and other distribution facilities and lower costs.

5.2 Unexplored Areas for Academic Research

1. Ethical Implications of AI in SCM

However, the integration of AI in supply chains has its advantages as well as its disadvantage with regard to ethical concerns. For example, AI in performance evaluation of employees or in delivery optimization using surveillance data can be seen as violating the rights of employees. The current research gap that should be filled by academic works is the analysis of the ethical questions that arise with the use of AI in SCM, particularly, the questions of transparency, accountability, and fairness of AI decision-making. Further, research could be done to find out how AI can be adopted to promote fair treatment of workers in supply chain especially in industries that source cheap labor. It is high time that some frameworks are developed which can help in minimizing the probable risks of AI in supply chain ethics such as the problem of algorithmic bias and job losses.

2. AI in sustainable supply chain

Sustainability is emerging as a significant issue for organizations and AI can go a long way in developing sustainable supply chains. Exploration of AI applications for waste minimisation, resource management, and low carbon footprints is an area of study that should be conducted. For instance, AI could be applied to transportation to determine not only the most cost-effective path, but also the one which requires the least amount of fuel and that results in the least amount of emissions. Using AI, firms can also monitor the sustainability of their supply chain and where it needs changes. There has been some advancement in this area, but more work has to be done to create AI that is sustainable without affecting the bottom-line or effectiveness.

3. Human-AI Collaboration in Supply Chains

Nonetheless, supply chain decision making will continue to rely on human intelligence even though the use of AI will facilitate automation of several supply chain activities. Explorations on how best human and Artificial Intelligence systems can work together a field known as 'augmented intelligence may also offer a wealth of understanding to organizations on how best to harness the strengths of both human hunches and data analysis. Studying the effects of human-ai cooperation on supply chain outcomes and decisions, and workers' experience is relevant for further research. Much more, it would also be beneficial to research on which classes of tasks are best for human intervention and which are best for complete automation and thus provide a fair and efficient utilization of AI in supply chains.

4. Real-Time AI Integration with IoT

The convergence of AI with IoT devices is one of the most promising fields of study for SCM. IoT sensors and devices give out large amounts of real-time data that can be processed by AI to enhance supply chain. Although there have been significant advances in linking IoT devices to AI systems, there is still a lot to be understood about how this information can be used to support decision making in real time.

Future work in the context of the IoT and AI could involve deep investigations into how AI systems could be more effectively integrated with IoT sensors regarding inventory management, the anticipation of maintenance requirements, and improving supply chain transparency. Also, further studies focusing on the applicability of IoT and AI in supply chain networks and especially on an international level could be beneficial.

5. AI-Driven Risk Management Models

In the contemporary world where global supply chain networks are increasingly evolving and prone to disruption (such as natural disasters, conflict, disease), there is increased need to develop sophisticated risk management models. Exploration on the use of AI based risk management frameworks that are capable of predicting, preventing, and responding to disruptions is a current area of focus. AI provides the means to forecast possible risks that can be based on the previous experiences, current conditions, and trends. University research could aim at creating the AI system that can assess the risks as they occur and suggest what precautions to take to avoid adverse consequences and keep operations going. There are many opportunities in the future of AI in SCM. As the application of AI advances, its integration into SCM will create completely self-sufficient supply chains, as well as optimal and efficient demand and supply planning, and sustainable and ethical practices. However, there are many opportunities that are not fully explored in the existing academic literature particularly in the areas of ethical and sustainable uses of smart environments with AI, human-AI interactions, and integration of IoT in real time. In addressing these gaps, scholars also contribute to shaping the future advances in SCM, where AI remains a key value generator and enabler.

6. CONCLUSION

Through this chapter, the author has discussed the role of AI in SCM and its prospects to change the way SCM is done in future especially in demand forecasting, inventory control, logistics and risk management. Technologies such as ML, NLP, computer vision, and DL are revolutionizing supply chain management and offering businesses potential supply chain advancements in the areas of speed, accuracy, and adaptability. The study reveals that AI has the potential to play a massive role in improving SCM by providing forecasting and planning, better logistics paths, inventory control, and self-sustaining supply chains. Thus, AI is also used in customer service as it helps to provide a customer service through chatbots, as well as gives customers more personalized recommendations. In addition, the combination of AI with IoT, and Big Data leads to real-time analysis, decision making & supply chain which is much more flexible. However, the use of AI in SCM has its downside. Some of the challenges that organisations face include: Data privacy issues, issues of integration of the system and lack of skilled professionals. Also, AI deployment involves consideration of ethical issues including fairness and explainability in decision making. Some key suggestions for practitioners are to consider the implementation of certain AI solutions in supply chain processes, to coordinate supply chain AI with human expertise, and, finally, to promote ethical AI usage. Researchers need to turn their attention to prospective areas, including AI self-sufficient logistics, generative AI for predictive replenishment, and AI in combination with blockchain for transparency. The future studies should also focus to some issues and drawbacks regarding the AI implementation such as data protection, security, and training of the employees. In conclusion, although AI creates great opportunities for SCM, to achieve its positive outcomes, there are many technical, ethical, and organizational barriers that must be addressed. Future development and study efforts will be important enablers in realising its potential.

REFERENCES

Ambhika, C., Gayathri, S., & Sheena, B. G. (2024, August). Enhancing Predictive Modeling in High Dimensional Data Using Hybrid Feature Selection. In *2024 5th International Conference on Electronics and Sustainable Communication Systems (ICESC)* (pp. 873-879). IEEE. DOI: 10.1109/ICESC60852.2024.10690153

Anusha, S., Ezhilvandan, M., Gayathri, S., & Sivaraman, V. T. P., A., & R., S. S. (2024). Emerging Trends in Edge AI for Industry 4.0 and 5.0: Technologies, Applications, and Challenges. In V. Nadda, P. Tyagi, A. Singh, & V. Singh (Eds.), *AI Innovations in Service and Tourism Marketing* (pp. 211-228). IGI Global Scientific Publishing. DOI: 10.4018/979-8-3693-7909-7.ch010

Culot, G., Podrecca, M., & Nassimbeni, G. (2024). Artificial intelligence in supply chain management: A systematic literature review of empirical studies and research directions. *Computers in Industry*, *162*, 104132. DOI: 10.1016/j.compind.2024.104132

Maheshwaran, T., & Muthumarilakshmi, S. N. A. S., V., Suganya, K., Maheswari, B., Girija, P., & R., S. S. (2024). Securing E-Commerce Strategies With Cloud, Blockchain, AI, and ML. In P. Goel (Ed.), *Strategies for E-Commerce Data Security: Cloud, Blockchain, AI, and Machine Learning* (pp. 470-500). IGI Global Scientific Publishing. DOI: 10.4018/979-8-3693-6557-1.ch019

Mediavilla, M. A., Dietrich, F., & Palm, D. (2022). Review and analysis of artificial intelligence methods for demand forecasting in supply chain management. *Procedia CIRP*, *107*, 1126–1131. DOI: 10.1016/j.procir.2022.05.119

Min, H. (2010). Artificial intelligence in supply chain management: Theory and applications. *International Journal of Logistics*, *13*(1), 13–39. DOI: 10.1080/13675560902736537

Mohsen, B. M. (2023). Impact of artificial intelligence on supply chain management performance. *Journal of Service Science and Management*, *16*(1), 44–58. DOI: 10.4236/jssm.2023.161004

Pournader, M., Ghaderi, H., Hassanzadegan, A., & Fahimnia, B. (2021). Artificial intelligence applications in supply chain management. *International Journal of Production Economics*, *241*, 108250. DOI: 10.1016/j.ijpe.2021.108250

Richey, R. G.Jr, Chowdhury, S., Davis-Sramek, B., Giannakis, M., & Dwivedi, Y. K. (2023). Artificial intelligence in logistics and supply chain management: A primer and roadmap for research. *Journal of Business Logistics*, *44*(4), 532–549. DOI: 10.1111/jbl.12364

Sharma, R., Shishodia, A., Gunasekaran, A., Min, H., & Munim, Z. H. (2022). The role of artificial intelligence in supply chain management: Mapping the territory. *International Journal of Production Research, 60*(24), 7527–7550. DOI: 10.1080/00207543.2022.2029611

Shoushtari, F., Ghafourian, E., & Talebi, M. (2021). Improving performance of supply chain by applying artificial intelligence. *International journal of industrial engineering and operational research, 3*(1), 14-23.

Sreelakshmi, S., Babu, A. A., Lakshmipriya, C., Gracious, L. A., Nalini, M., & Subramanian, R. S. (2024, October). Enhancing Intrusion Detection Systems with Machine Learning. In *2024 2nd International Conference on Self Sustainable Artificial Intelligence Systems (ICSSAS)* (pp. 557-564). IEEE. DOI: 10.1109/ICSSAS64001.2024.10760341

Subramanian, R. S., Yamini, B., Sudha, K., & Sivakumar, S. (2024). Ensemble-based deep learning techniques for customer churn prediction model. *Kybernetes*. DOI: 10.1108/K-08-2023-1516

Toorajipour, R., Sohrabpour, V., Nazarpour, A., Oghazi, P., & Fischl, M. (2021). Artificial intelligence in supply chain management: A systematic literature review. *Journal of Business Research, 122*, 502–517. DOI: 10.1016/j.jbusres.2020.09.009

Venketbabu, T., Aswathy, M. P., Sangeetha, J., Anish, T. P., Nalini, M., & Subramanian, R. S. (2024, October). Revolutionizing Image Processing: Innovations Impacts and Future Trends. In *2024 2nd International Conference on Self Sustainable Artificial Intelligence Systems (ICSSAS)* (pp. 901-907). IEEE.

Yamini, B., Ramana, K. V., Nalini, M., Devi, D. C., Maheswari, B., & Siva, S. R. (2024). Customer churn prediction model in enterprises using machine learning. *International Journal of Advanced Technology and Engineering Exploration, 11*(110), 94.

Younis, H., Sundarakani, B., & Alsharairi, M. (2022). Applications of artificial intelligence and machine learning within supply chains: Systematic review and future research directions. *Journal of Modelling in Management, 17*(3), 916–940. DOI: 10.1108/JM2-12-2020-0322

Chapter 12
Artificial Intelligence and the Future of Supply Chains:
A Crossroads of Innovation and Disruption

Jabir Arif
https://orcid.org/0000-0002-5285-7976
Sidi Mohamed Ben Abdellah University, Morocco

Fouad Jawab
https://orcid.org/0000-0002-0508-7278
Sidi Mohamed Ben Abdellah University, Morocco

ABSTRACT

The supply chain is a complex and dynamic field that requires effective planning, coordination, and execution to meet customer demands while minimizing costs. In recent years, artificial intelligence (AI) has emerged as a disruptive technology with the potential to transform various aspects of supply chain management. This chapter provides a comprehensive analysis of the role played by AI in supply chain management, highlighting its applications, benefits, challenges, and future prospects. This chapter explains how AI can improve supply chain visibility, demand forecasting, inventory management, logistics optimization, and risk mitigation. In addition, it explores the impact of AI on decision-making processes and collaboration within the supply chain network. The chapter also discusses the potential challenges and ethical considerations associated with the adoption of AI in supply chain management. By taking a deep dive into the current state of AI in Supply Chain and analyzing its potential future developments, this chapter aims to provide valuable insights.

DOI: 10.4018/979-8-3373-0923-1.ch012

1. INTRODUCTION

Ensuring the efficient flow of goods and services from suppliers to customers, Supply Chain Management (SCM) plays a crucial role in the success of businesses. Artificial intelligence (AI) is a disruptive force that has garnered a lot of attention due to rapid improvements in technology. Artificial intelligence (AI) is the advancement of human intelligence in computer systems that can process and understand huge amounts of data, recognize patterns, and make sound judgments. Traditional supply chain processes could be transformed by incorporating AI, which would also improve operational performance, profitability, and customer satisfaction. Organizations can use AI technologies to improve decision-making across the supply chain, optimize logistics operations, and extract useful insights from large and complex data sets.

This chapter aims to explore the role played by AI in GCS. It will look at various applications of AI in different aspects of the supply chain, including demand forecasting, inventory management, logistics optimization, supplier selection, and risk management. By examining case studies and real-world examples, this work will present the practical implementation of AI in SCM and highlight its impact on supply chain performance. In addition, this work will shed light on the benefits and challenges associated with integrating AI into SCM processes. While AI offers immense potential, organizations must also address challenges related to data quality and integration, address organizational and cultural barriers, and ensure ethical and responsible use of AI technologies.

This chapter will not only give an in-depth understanding of the state of AI in SCM today, but it will also review current trends and potential future developments. It will examine how supply chain operations can be improved by combining AI with other cutting-edge technologies like the Internet of Things (IoT) and blockchain. In addition, the work will discuss the importance of ethical considerations and responsible AI practices in GCS and highlight the potential of predictive and prescriptive analytics to shape the future of information chain management. Companies can successfully use this revolutionary technology to optimize their supply chain operations, reduce costs, improve customer satisfaction, and gain a competitive advantage in a rapidly changing business environment by gaining insights into the role of AI in supply chain management.

2. CONTEXT AND POSITIONING

In the context of the modern supply chain, companies are facing increasing challenges in operations management, decision-making, and process optimization. The globalization of markets, the expansion of e-commerce, consumer expectations for speed and accuracy of delivery, and the increasing complexity of distribution networks are all driving companies to look for innovative solutions to stay competitive.

It is in this context that artificial intelligence (AI) is emerging as a powerful and transformative tool for the supply chain (Wenzel and al., 2019; Arif et al. 2020; Arif et al. 2023). By harnessing the vast amounts of data generated by logistics operations and applying sophisticated algorithms, AI offers companies the ability to derive valuable insights, make informed decisions in real-time, and optimize their entire supply chain.

Supply chain disruption is defined as any scenario that prevents the manufacture, sale, or distribution of commodities. To measure disruptions in real-time, decision support in the supply chain is needed to track and determine actions, as well as to optimize and establish contingency and recovery plans and simulation models (El Jaouhari et al. 2023; Kashem and al., 2023). Nevertheless, the supply chain disruption has led to significant delivery delays, a decline in revenue and sales, as well as production stoppages. As a result, with the deployment of response planning activities and recovery plans, the current data-driven resilient supply chain architecture, including reactive control, is becoming an increasingly important concern in supply networks.

However, supply chain disruptions indirectly influence operations, as they rely primarily on remote decision-making while ignoring credible data on disruptions. These interruptions create confusing supply chain disruption situations and delay recovery policy agreements (El Jaouhari et al. 2022). As a result, companies are looking for ways to leverage databases to improve supply chain operations and use massive amounts of data to predict problems and increase supply chain flexibility. Therefore, enabling complete real-time, end-to-end visibility of the supply chain at all times is critical to increasing supply chain agility, flexibility, and alignment. This increases the operational performance of the supply chain (Kamble and al., 2021; El Jaouhari et al. 2024). In these circumstances, changes to existing supply chain models should be included in the planning and adoption of real-time management based on demand, inventory, and transportation data. As a result, supply chain visibility should focus on tech-integrated, data-driven technical operations and intelligent decision-making (Javaid et al. 2020; El Jaouhari et al. 2023).

The application of artificial intelligence in the supply chain represents a strategic opportunity for companies of all sizes and in all sectors (Azzouz et al. 2021; Ibn El Farouk et al. 2020; El Jaouhari et al. 2024). By taking an AI-first approach, companies can improve operational agility, reduce costs, increase customer satisfaction, and drive growth.

AI can be positioned as a catalyst for digital transformation in the supply chain, offering tangible benefits (Koh, 2020; Khaoua et al. 2022; El Jaouhari et al. 2024):

- **Accurate Demand Forecasting**: By using machine learning models, AI can analyze historical trends and real-time data to accurately predict future product demand, allowing businesses to better plan their inventory and avoid shortages or surpluses.
- **Route and Transportation Optimization**: AI algorithms can analyze thousands of variables to determine the most efficient routes, the most cost-effective modes of transportation, and the most optimal delivery schedules, reducing transportation costs and improving customer satisfaction. Optimising the routes of carriers is important for the efficiency of logistics. This is especially true for the last mile, which is the most complex part of transport to manage. Customers are increasingly keen to have as many details as possible about their deliveries, precise time slots, the possibility of dropping off parcels at relay points, etc. Artificial intelligence now makes it possible to create an autonomous fleet, thanks to the development of algorithms that will make it possible to know satellite maps, traffic information or the particularities of each city.
- **Intelligent Inventory Management**: By monitoring inventory levels in real time and predicting future needs, AI enables companies to maintain optimal inventory levels, reduce storage costs, and avoid stock-outs.
- **Warehouse Automation**: Autonomous robots and AI-based warehouse management systems can speed up picking, packing, and shipping processes, reducing processing times and improving the accuracy of operations.

In summary, the application of AI in the supply chain represents a powerful way for companies to stay competitive in a rapidly changing business environment. By leveraging AI capabilities to optimize their operations, companies can improve their efficiency, agility, and ability to meet changing market demands.

3. INDUSTRIAL REVOLUTIONS TOWARDS ARTIFICIAL INTELLIGENCE

The history of industrial revolutions is a testament to the constant evolution of technologies and their impact on society (El Jaouhari et al. 2022; El Yadari et al. 2024). Here's a brief history of the industrial revolutions, including the artificial intelligence revolution:

First Industrial Revolution (late 18th century - early 19th century): The first Industrial Revolution was marked by the advent of mechanization, notably thanks to the invention of the steam engine by James Watt. This revolution transformed the agricultural and manufacturing industries, moving handicraft production to factories, and led to significant advances in the textile, metallurgy, and transportation sectors.

Second Industrial Revolution (late 19th century - early 20th century): The Second Industrial Revolution was characterized by major advances such as electricity, the telegraph, the telephone, and the development of steel. These innovations led to an increase in industrial production, the rise of railways and transport in general, and the automation of production processes.

Third Industrial Revolution (mid-20th century): The Third Industrial Revolution was propelled by the rise of computers and digital technology. Computers began to automate production processes, and automation transformed many aspects of the industry, including automotive production, electronics, and telecommunications.

Fourth Industrial Revolution (early 21st century): The Fourth Industrial Revolution is characterized by the integration of digital, physical, and biological technologies. This revolution is marked by the emergence of artificial intelligence, the Internet of Things (IoT), advanced robotics, biotechnology and 3D printing. Artificial intelligence, in particular, is having a major impact on all sectors of the economy, automating processes, improving efficiency and opening up new possibilities in areas such as healthcare, finance, logistics and production.

The artificial intelligence revolution is thus the next major step in the evolution of the industry, with profound implications for the way companies operate, innovate and interact with their environment.

4. WHO INVENTED ARTIFICIAL INTELLIGENCE AND WHEN WAS IT CREATED?

1950 - 1970: The birth and creators of general AI

It was between the 1950s and the 1970s that artificial intelligence and its technical developments were born. The acceleration was given after the Second World War and, at that time, a spotlight will be put on AI.

The first objectives of this technology were based on the possibility of automating orders using electronics with a first computer mathematical model. It was not until 1943 that the first artificial neural network appeared by Warren McCulloch and Walter Pitts. The first concept of artificial intelligence is brought into the world.

It was then the 1950s that took over the creation of AI as it would develop over the years. During this decade, many engineers worked on this project.

John Von Neumann and Alan Turing invent the technology that will be akin to AI (Khaoua et al. 2022; Garti et al. 2024; Zaid et al. 2024; Talha et al. 2024). Thanks to this, they create the starting point for the architecture of home computers: the concept of a computer comes into being based on the machine's ability to execute a human-configured program.

Alan Turing created the Turing Test, which is still relevant today: it questions the machine's ability to have a conversation with a human. A major test in the history of AI of the ability of machines to solve increasingly complex problems.

At the same time, the machine and its intelligent reasoning began to develop: in 1952, it knew how to play chess, thanks to the first computer software created by Arthur Samuel.

The term AI is credited to John McCarthy (Stanford University), a term defined as "the construction of computer programs that perform tasks that are, for the time being, performed more satisfactorily by human beings because they require high-level mental processes such as: perceptual learning, memory organization, and critical reasoning" by Marvin Minsky (Esmaeilian et al. 2020; Imane et al. 2024; Tronnebati et al. 2024). Research was carried out intensively during this period, in various universities including MIT, Carnegie Mellon University (under the control of Allen Newell and Herbert Simon), the University of Edinburgh (Donald Michie), in France with Jacques Pitrat, etc.

The year 1956 is considered to be the official starting point of artificial intelligence in the world because the expression was born during the "Dartmouth Summer Research Project on Artificial Intelligence" conference at Dartmouth College, a kind of AI brainstorming workshop led by six researchers including McCarthy and Minsky.

The years go by and research in the field of artificial intelligence begins to fall back. In the early 1960s, the craze around artificial intelligence faded: the machine was not yet able to translate the desired technology. Not enough memory, lack of progress, results that are struggling to arrive... These factors have pushed the scientific community to detach itself from the artificial intelligence project, as have the public authorities.

1980 - 1990: Development and evolution of today's AI

It was not until the following decades that research into artificial intelligence resumed, helped by the democratization of futuristic images in popular culture. In 1968, the film "Stanley Kubrick's 2001: A Space Odyssey" was released: an intelligent computer is one of the main characters. This mythical work proves that the public is increasingly interested in the scientific and technological discoveries of the future.

Even if culture has not forced science to advance, it has made the sector more accessible to as many people as possible, towards a renewed craze around this technology.

In 1965 and 1972, research conducted by MIT and Stanford University exploited artificial intelligence for molecular chemistry and health. The beginnings of today's artificial intelligence have been laid: the machines created at that time were programmed as software imitating human logic, machines that could give answers to human-created stimuli by entering specific data.

The 1980s and early 1990s saw a new winter for artificial intelligence, with a project that was put on hold for a while. Indeed, technology and programming required far too many resources for results that were not fast enough.

In addition, research is focused on the development of the home computer. Artificial intelligence is therefore no longer a priority. A major event was nevertheless to mark the 1990s, with the success of IBM's expert system Deep Blue.

IBM Deep Blue is a software known for beating world chess champion Garry Kasparov (Liu, K.S.; Lin, M.H, 2021). For the first time, an artificial intelligence is capable of such a feat. Even if this feat marked the history of artificial intelligence, the processor used was not the most convincing, as it only used limited features, far from the futuristic and complex projections of a dreamed AI.

2010: Rise of next-generation AI

The 2010s marked a pivotal era in the evolution of artificial intelligence—what many refer to as the rise of next-generation AI. This phase signaled a departure from traditional rule-based systems toward more dynamic, data-driven, and learning-oriented architectures. At the heart of this transformation was the explosion of big data, which provided AI systems with the vast and diverse datasets needed to extract patterns, recognize complex relationships, and improve autonomously over time. No longer confined to executing predefined instructions, algorithms were now being designed to learn, adapt, and evolve.

The transition began gaining momentum with significant contributions from AI researchers and engineers around the world. In 2011, IBM's Watson AI stunned the public and scientific community alike by defeating two former champions on the American quiz show Jeopardy!. Unlike earlier expert systems that relied heavily on manually encoded knowledge bases, Watson utilized a sophisticated combination of natural language processing, information retrieval, and machine learning techniques to analyze and interpret human language, parse complex questions, and provide accurate answers in real time. Its victory was more than just a game show win—it symbolized a new frontier in cognitive computing, where machines could begin to process information and reason in ways previously thought to be uniquely human.

Just a year later, in 2012, Google X (a semi-secret research and development facility under Alphabet Inc.) made headlines when one of its AI models demonstrated an unexpected ability: without being explicitly trained to recognize specific images, it identified cats from thousands of YouTube thumbnails. This was a landmark moment. The neural network used unsupervised learning to process over 10 million images, eventually developing internal representations that allowed it to distinguish cats—purely from statistical patterns in the data. The feat showcased the power of deep learning, a subfield of machine learning that utilizes multi-layered neural networks to detect intricate structures in large datasets.

Another dramatic leap occurred in 2016 with AlphaGo, developed by DeepMind, a subsidiary of Google. Go, a 3,000-year-old board game, is renowned for its complexity—featuring more possible moves than atoms in the universe. Conventional AI approaches were ill-equipped to handle this challenge. AlphaGo, however, combined deep neural networks with reinforcement learning, allowing it to not only analyze historical games but also improve its strategy by playing against itself millions of times. First, it defeated the European Go champion, then the legendary South Korean player Lee Sedol, a world champion, and eventually an even more advanced version, AlphaGo Zero, which learned the game entirely from scratch. These achievements revealed a profound shift in AI's capabilities—machines were no longer mimicking human logic; they were creating strategies that even humans couldn't anticipate.

What made this phase truly revolutionary was the philosophical shift in how AI was conceptualized. Traditional programming emphasized strict, rule-based commands where machines were told exactly what to do. The new paradigm turned this approach on its head. Now, the objective was not to instruct machines explicitly, but to enable them to learn the rules through data. Algorithms became capable of pattern recognition, anomaly detection, prediction, and decision-making—all based on statistical inference rather than human logic.

The impact of this evolution cannot be overstated. From natural language translation to medical diagnostics and autonomous vehicles, next-generation AI is not merely an enhancement of prior technologies but a foundational shift in how machines interact with the world. The rise of next-gen AI in the 2010s laid the groundwork for the current AI renaissance, characterized by self-improving systems that are reshaping industries and redefining the boundaries of what machines can do.

These advancements were not isolated achievements—they signaled the dawn of a new era where artificial intelligence began to integrate into everyday life. From voice assistants like Siri and Alexa to recommendation engines on Netflix and Amazon, AI systems increasingly became embedded in consumer technology. This integration, made possible by breakthroughs in machine learning and data processing, opened the door to widespread adoption and set the stage for even more transformative developments in the decade that followed.

2020: the democratization of AI

The democratization of artificial intelligence since the 2020s is like having allowed the entire population connected to the Internet access to what has always been in the hands of large companies and scientists (van Hoek, 2019).

Before the arrival of ChatGPT, many tools had emerged with artificial intelligence often limited to credits and whose results were still under development. Nevertheless, it was possible to have access to AI by paying subscriptions or credits, to generate content or to retouch photos on smartphones in particular.

5. HISTORY OF ARTIFICIAL INTELLIGENCE IN THE SUPPLY CHAIN

Artificial intelligence (AI) has gradually transformed the way companies manage their operations and optimize their supply chains (Vyas, N.; Beije, A.; Krishnamachari, B). The history of AI in the supply chain can be traced back to early efforts to apply automation and machine learning techniques to improve efficiency, reduce costs, and increase the accuracy of logistics processes.

In the 1980s and 1990s, the first applications of AI in the supply chain emerged. Expert systems, an early form of AI, have been used to solve planning and routing problems in logistics operations. These systems have made it possible to automate certain decision-making processes, providing recommendations based on predefined rules and expert knowledge.

During the 2000s, with the advent of Big Data and advanced processing technologies, AI saw a new wave of innovations in logistics (Younis, H.; Sundarakani, B.; Alsharairi, M). Machine learning algorithms, such as neural networks, decision trees, and genetic algorithms, have been applied to a growing range of logistics problems, including demand forecasting, inventory management, route optimization, and transportation planning.

Companies have begun to harness the massive data generated by track and trace systems to train AI models that can predict market trends, anticipate customer needs, and make real-time decisions to optimize operations.

More recently, the emergence of the Internet of Things (IoT) and connected sensor technologies has enabled even more accurate and real-time data collection on product movements throughout the supply chain. This data, combined with advanced AI techniques such as deep learning, has opened up new possibilities for supply chain optimization.

Today, the applications of AI in the supply chain have become ubiquitous. Sophisticated algorithms are used to forecast demand, optimize inventory levels, reduce wait times, improve warehouse management, optimize delivery routes, and minimize transportation costs.

Smart warehouses equipped with autonomous robots, surveillance drones, and automated management systems have become a reality, reducing human error, speeding up processing times, and improving the accuracy of logistics operations.

As AI continues to evolve and improve, its impact on the supply chain is expected to strengthen. Companies that adopt these technologies and integrate AI strategically into their operations will be better positioned to thrive in an increasingly complex and dynamic logistics environment.

6. ARTIFICIAL INTELLIGENCE AND SUPPLY CHAIN: 3 CONCRETE USE CASES

In a context of global competition, constant technological innovation and faster deadlines, consumers and professionals have access to an abundant range of products and services very quickly (Jaouhari et al., 2023). Guaranteeing the availability of the right product, at the right time and in the right place is an even more difficult challenge for the Supply Chain, which requires the consideration of an almost infinite number of factors that can influence customer demand: social networks, news, competition, media, political events (Brexit, Hong Kong, strikes, etc.), exchange rate changes, etc.

In this VUCA (volatile, uncertain, complex, ambiguous) world, Artificial Intelligence, with techniques such as Machine Learning or the ability to learn and make decisions from data, provides tools that are really starting to improve operational performance across many links in the Supply Chain.

We illustrate the contributions and challenges of Machine Learning in the Supply Chain through 3 practical cases that reflect the 3 levels of the Supply Chain (strategic, tactical and operational) and represent the major families of algorithms (supervised or unsupervised, classification and regression).

Artificial Intelligence can thus generate two types of gains in the Supply Chain (El Jaouhari et al., 2024):

- Improving customer service (B2C or B2B customer) or even developing new services.

- Improvement of operational performance (productivity, quality, stocks, end of life, etc.)

There are already many use cases in Supply Chain and concern practically all links in Supply Chain Planning (forecasting, planning) and Supply Chain Execution (warehouse, transport, track and trace)

We propose here to present 3 operational cases from our project experiences:

- Store Clustering in Retail
- Sales forecasts for consumer products
- Proactive control tower on an extended supply chain

To improve the performance of these processes, Artificial Intelligence in general, and Machine Learning in particular, offer a whole range of algorithms that can be used, depending on the need for optimization and the type of data available.

To fully understand the problem posed, define the data sets and identify them, or build the right algorithm (or a combination of algorithms), it is essential to mobilize a cross-functional team with a triple skill: Business and Supply Chain expertise, Data architecture and Algorithms.

6.1. Case 1: Store Clustering-- Machine Learning to Better Capture In-Store Customer Behavior

Store clustering is a key process in the retail industry that allows you to define stores with similar characteristics and thus assign the right assortment to them. A group of stores (the Cluster) must be relevant to capture differences in customer purchasing behavior. This makes it possible to better manage sales, margins and the brand's image.

The similarities between the points of sale can concern very different axes: store area, turnover, average basket, target customer, families of products presented, location of the store: city center vs. shopping center, window area, etc.

Determining a priori which axes are relevant is a complex task and difficult to carry out with traditional methods, for example in an iterative approach on Excel.

Store clustering uses both quantitatively and qualitatively:

- Store Profile
- Product mix sales
- The customer profile in order to build groups of stores with similar characteristics.

It is useful for the purchase of new collections as well as the strategy of allocating and replenishing stock in stores (initial set-up vs. replenishment vs. markdown)

In this context, the use of machine learning algorithms makes it possible to process vast amounts of data and manipulate a very large number of analysis axes. Unsupervised learning algorithms are favored in order to let the learning determine which axes of grouping are the most relevant. Among these algorithms, the k-means, the Gaussian mixture model, or hierarchical clustering are the most commonly used.

Based on a history of each point of sale, if possible enriched with exogenous data on the district, competing stores, flows of people, etc. The algorithm can determine which axes will be relevant to group the points of sale into clusters (Khaoua et al., 2022). An iterative method quickly compares differences between clusters even with a large number of axes of analysis, which was not possible with a traditional method.

Finally, the algorithmic part itself is fast thanks to the Machine Learning tools that are now readily available, for example with specific libraries in Python. Our feedback shows that the most important part for the success of this type of project is rather the phase of identifying the data relating to the store x customer x product triplets. They must be relevant to the project and readily available.

Of course, a "Store clustering" project is not just about the algorithmic part. It takes into account process, organization, data and IS axes and generally includes 3 steps:

- The construction of clusters or groups of stores.
- The implementation of a process, an organization and an IS to ensure the sustainability and update of the identified clusters over time
- Finally, if necessary, the review of merchandising processes to take into account the new clusters identified.

6.2. Case 2: Demand Forecasting-- Gaining Accuracy With Machine Learning

Anticipating and forecasting needs is key information to ensure the ability of a Supply Chain to fulfill its mission (Sharma et al., 2022.). Forecasting can be carried out in many contexts: sales forecasting at the store level, forecasting breakdowns (e.g. in the context of equipment maintenance), forecasting shipments to warehouses, production needs, forecasting delivery by suppliers. A reliable forecast allows for better planning of resource needs (factory capacity, warehouse workforce, number of vehicles, etc.) and a better allocation of stocks.

Today, old forecasting models (often based on historical averages) are being overtaken in terms of accuracy by new models incorporating machine learning algorithms. These new models make it possible to improve the accuracy of forecasts thanks to more agile and self-learning algorithms, but also to process a larger volume of data than with traditional methods.

Before implementing one of the solutions on the market, it is necessary to test different algorithms and choose the most efficient, as well as the most suitable parameters for the case being treated. It is therefore often more efficient to implement one's own algorithms beforehand, for example ensemble methods (boosted gradient, random forest), SVM or a Bayesian model, to adjust the parameters and compare their results.

An essential step in machine learning projects, especially in demand forecasting problems, is the supply of relevant and structured data. A minimum amount of work must therefore be done in order to be able to identify the data, extract it, and bring it to the necessary level of quality (data cleaning) to be able to use it in Machine Learning algorithms. This work must first be carried out with the company's internal data, known as endogenous, in order to quickly have initial results and demonstrate gains in accuracy compared to traditional methods. This first phase makes it possible to convince the various stakeholders before investing time and resources to further improve the forecasts, by integrating data external to the company, known as exogenous.

During our projects, we were able to observe correlations between sales and certain types of exogenous data: weather, exchange rates, tourist flows, car fleet, number of searches on Google, trends on social networks. Exogenous data is more difficult to capture and structure than endogenous data (e.g. trends on social networks which can be expressed in the form of photos or blog comments for example) and their correlations with demand must be carefully studied to fully understand the perimeters impacted: types of products, customers, geographies, and check their level of impact on the quality of the forecast.

6.3. Case 3: "Control Tower"-- Moving From Reactive Supply Chain Monitoring to Proactive Supervision Through the Use of Machine Learning Algorithms

Beyond tracking data, a wide variety of data sources can be available: IoT sensors, weather, social networks, news, various events...

These sources can provide valuable information on the supply chain, both on the evolution of operations and on upstream events that can impact it. To be able to use this data, three main difficulties are encountered (*Helo, P.; Hao, Y*):

- How can they be acquired in order to have a global real-time visibility of the Supply Chain when information systems are often siloed?
- How do you process these very large volumes of data in real time?

- How can we bring value by being proactive and no longer simply reactive to alerts?

Implementing a control tower in proactive mode requires several steps:

- Obtain global visibility on the Supply Chain by connecting all internal or external systems to the company (ERP, OMS, TMS, partners, connected vehicles, weather sensors, etc.) as well as capturing and making available detailed event data.
- Detect, process, and even anticipate alerts, thanks to segmentation approaches and the use of artificial intelligence algorithms.
- Propose alternative scenarios in an alert situation or in anticipation.

For example, neural network-type machine learning algorithms are able to distinguish between high-criticality alerts (to be sent to teams) and low-criticality alerts (which it can process automatically). To do this, it is no longer necessary to imagine the entire tree of possible scenarios as before to set up an expert system: all you have to do is make the neural network learn directly from the responses of human operators.

Predictive algorithms such as logistic regression or algorithms based on decision trees (random forest, XG Boost, etc.) will then make it possible to anticipate the appearance of these alerts by following trends (weather, traffic). The use, for example, of a genetic algorithm will finally make it possible to proactively propose more efficient alternative routes.

Some companies choose to develop their own Control Tower. These are companies with a critical size and little need to interface with third-party systems (e.g. if the means of transport are internalised). However, it is possible to choose a Control Tower solution on the market, which has several advantages: first of all, it allows access to the data of Supply Chain partners already connected to the solution (carriers, freight forwarders, 3PLs, etc.), but also to be able to use Machine Learning algorithms already trained with data from other players.

Additionally, AI and machine learning (ML) can determine optimal supply levels by driving multiple scenarios to meet demand.

In the field of logistics, Artificial Intelligence enables seamless communication between complex production networks, enhancing credibility, security and efficiency (Van Engelenburg et al., 2018). It also has the ability to build platforms where transportation providers provide real-time availability of trucks or vessels. In the case of purchases, blockchain can enable tamper-proof smart contracts that automatically enforce the terms of multi-party agreements. However, smart contracts can self-verify and self-execute by disbursing funds to the appropriate parties. Applying AI-powered supply chain optimization improves critical choices by improving forecasting and recommending the best course of action. This can improve overall supply chain performance by helping manufacturers determine the potential outcomes of various situations in terms of time, expense, and revenue.

In the global supply chain, AI optimizes global supply chains by allowing companies to deal directly with each other and without the involvement of a third party. This allows for greater integration of financial and logistics services and greater data exchange between stakeholders. In addition, AI can correctly forecast demand at a glance, minimizing inventory and supply chain waste. In addition, AI powered by big data can increase supply chain efficiency and resilience.

As a product moves through the various stages of shipping, it can be difficult to accurately monitor large volumes of products, which are ultimately transported to unique final destinations. Based on AI, IoT or blockchain, real-time data on the location of goods with the right status with all relevant information, such as for flight and delays, could ideally be recognized and traced easily in between. Again, the use of AI in supply chain management allows companies to anticipate the supply and demand of fast-moving consumer goods. From stock order to final shipment, the entire process can be optimized to reduce costs while increasing overall profits.

The use of AI technology has also been shown to improve overall warehouse management. Space management is often identified as a key area in inventory control, while the deployment of smart sensors/devices allows companies to optimize space and locate specific packages. Partnering to install sensors/devices in the warehouse is an optimal way to automatically trigger orders when current supplies reach a minimum quantity while also helping with space management. Thanks to RFID sensors/devices labeled on the products, warehouse staff are automatically notified of the shipment and can continue to monitor its ongoing journey.

7. LEGAL FRAMEWORK FOR ARTIFICIAL INTELLIGENCE: THE ESSENTIAL ANSWERS

Artificial intelligence appears only in two legal and normative definitions. The **ISO 2382-28** standard defines artificial intelligence as "the ability of a functional unit to perform functions typically associated with human intelligence, such as reasoning and learning."

The term "autonomy" is defined by ISO **8373:2012** as "the ability to perform intended tasks from current state and detections, without human intervention."

No specific provision for artificial intelligence exists or takes into consideration the specificities of algorithms, its decision-making, learning and autonomy capacities, or even its cooperation with human beings.

The European Union is proposing the very first legal framework at the global level. Europe wants to develop the potential of AI while regulating the risks to fundamental rights.

On February 2, 2024, the Harmonized Rules for Artificial Intelligence Regulations, or AI Act, were passed by Parliament. The AI Act will be published soon in 2024 in the European Official Journal and its application is planned for 2 years after this publication.

The general legal issue revolves around the following axes:

What protection for artificial intelligence?

The major and more specific legal issues facing artificial intelligence today are first of all the protection of innovative concepts developed by researchers in artificial intelligence, particularly in terms of intellectual property, the protection of personal data, but also issues related to the implementation of artificial intelligence's liability in the event of damage.

What is the liability in the event of damage caused by artificial intelligence?

The company that develops artificial intelligence will have to pay particular attention to the protection of its innovation. All companies in smart transition will have to analyse the contracts between them and the artificial intelligence manufacturer.

Determining who is responsible for damage involving artificial intelligence is a complex issue insofar as there are a number of actors:

- The designer
- The programmer
- The integrator
- The user
- or even artificial intelligence itself

The criminal liability of the company may also be incurred if the artificial intelligence offence was committed on behalf of this legal person.

8. CONCLUSION

In conclusion, the use of artificial intelligence (AI) in supply chain management represents a significant advance for companies looking to optimize their operations. With its advanced analytics, machine learning, and forecasting capabilities, AI not only helps optimize existing processes, but also creates new opportunities for efficiency and competitiveness. However, its effective deployment requires a deep understanding of specific supply chain challenges as well as close collaboration between logistics professionals and AI experts. Despite the challenges and necessary adjustments, integrating AI into the supply chain offers tangible benefits, including better inventory management, reduced costs, and improved customer satisfaction. As technologies continue to evolve, it is imperative for companies to invest in the development and adaptation of their systems to remain competitive in an ever-changing business environment. Ultimately, the successful integration of AI into the supply chain promises to fundamentally transform the way companies manage their operations and respond to market demands, paving the way for a new era of performance and efficiency in global logistics.

REFRENCES

Aljuneidi, T., Bhat, S. A., & Boulaksil, Y. (2023). A comprehensive systematic review of the literature on the impact of the COVID-19 pandemic on supply chains. *Supply Chain Analytics*, *3*, 100025. DOI: 10.1016/j.sca.2023.100025

Arif, J., Azzouz, K., Mouzouna, Y., & Jawab, F. (2020). Design on improvement of traceability process in the outsourcing of logistics' activities using the internet of things (IoT) applications. *International Journal of Advanced Science and Technology*, *29*(1), 1093–1108.

Arif, J., Samadhiya, A., & Kumar, A. (2023). Net zero supply chain performance and industry 4.0 technologies: Past review and present introspective analysis for future research directions. *Heliyon*, *9*(11). PMID: 38027710

Azzouz, K., Arif, J., & Benboubker, M. B. (2021). Exploratory study of the role of logistics service providers in terms of traceability in the process of outsourcing of logistics' activities: Case of moroccan LSP. *International Journal of Engineering Research in Africa*, *54*, 187–208. DOI: 10.4028/www.scientific.net/JERA.54.187

Belhadi, A., Kamble, S. S., Mani, V., Venkatesh, V. G., & Shi, Y. (2021). Behavioral mechanisms influencing sustainable supply chain governance decision-making from a dyadic buyer-supplier perspective'. *International Journal of Production Economics*, *236*, 108136. DOI: 10.1016/j.ijpe.2021.108136

Boruchowitch, F., & Fritz, M. M. C. (2022). Who in the firm can create sustainable value and for whom? A single case-study on sustainable procurement and supply chain stakeholders. *Journal of Cleaner Production*, *363*, 132619. DOI: 10.1016/j.jclepro.2022.132619

Breque, M., De Nul, L. and Petridis, A. (2021). Industry 5.0 – Towards a Sustainable, Human-Centric and Resilient European Industry, in European Commission, .DOI: 10.1002/9781119865216.ch2

Buranasiri, B., Lai, P.-L., Woo, S., & Piboonrungroj, P. (2024). Impact of sustainable development goal orientation on supply chain collaboration and sustained competitive advantage: Evidence from the tea and coffee industry'. *The Asian Journal of Shipping and Logistics*, *40*(2), 83–88. DOI: 10.1016/j.ajsl.2024.01.004

Chan, S., & Amling, W. (2019). Does orchestration in the global climate action agenda effectively prioritize and mobilize transnational climate adaptation action?'. *International Environmental Agreement: Politics, Law and Economics*, *19*(4–5), 429–446. DOI: 10.1007/s10784-019-09444-9

Christopher, M. (2005). *Logistics and Supply Chain Management – Creating Value-Added Networks* (3rd ed.). Pearson Education.

Closs, D., Speier, C., & Meacham, N. (2011). Sustainability to support end-to-end value chains: The role of supply chain management'. *Journal of the Academy of Marketing Science, 39*(1), 101–116. DOI: 10.1007/s11747-010-0207-4

Dutta, P., Choi, T. M., Somani, S., & Butala, R. (2020). Blockchain technology in supply chain operations: Applications, challenges and research opportunities'. *Transportation Research Part E, Logistics and Transportation Review, 142*, 102067. DOI: 10.1016/j.tre.2020.102067 PMID: 33013183

El Asri, A., El Farouk, I. I., Jawab, F., Arif, J., & Moufad, I. (2022, May). The drug supply chain at the public hospital in Morocco: a literature review. In *2022 14th International Colloquium of Logistics and Supply Chain Management (LOGISTIQUA)* (pp. 1-5). IEEE. DOI: 10.1109/LOGISTIQUA55056.2022.9938022

El Jaouhari, A., Alhilali, Z., Arif, J., Fellaki, S., Amejwal, M., & Azzouz, K. (2022). Demand forecasting application with regression and IoT based inventory management system: A case study of a semiconductor manufacturing company. *International Journal of Engineering Research in Africa, 60*, 189–210. DOI: 10.4028/p-8ntq24

El Jaouhari, A., Arif, J., & Jawab, F. (2024). Mediating the role of Internet of Things in Sustainable Automotive Supply Chain: Practical Evidence from a Delphi Analysis. In *2024 IEEE 15th International Colloquium on Logistics and Supply Chain Management (LOGISTIQUA)* (pp. 1-6). IEEE.

El Yadari, M., Moufad, I., Jawab, F., & Arif, J. (2024). Logistic 4.0 Implementation For Efficient Urban Freight Transport: A Systematic Literature Review. In *2024 IEEE 15th International Colloquium on Logistics and Supply Chain Management (LOGISTIQUA)* (pp. 1-8). IEEE.

Elkington, J. (1994). Towards the sustainable corporation: Win-win-win business strategies for sustainable development'. *California Management Review, 36*(2), 90–100. DOI: 10.2307/41165746

Esmaeilian, B., Sarkis, J., Lewis, K., & Behdad, S. (2020). Blockchain for the future of sustainable supply chain management in Industry 4.0. *Resources, Conservation and Recycling, 2020*(163), 105064. DOI: 10.1016/j.resconrec.2020.105064

Fernández-Miguel, A., García-Muiña, F. E., Jiménez-Calzado, M., Melara San Román, P., Fernández Del Hoyo, A. P., & Settembre-Blundo, D. (2024). Boosting business agility with additive digital molding: An Industry 5.0 approach to sustainable supply chains'. *Computers & Industrial Engineering*, *192*, 110222. DOI: 10.1016/j.cie.2024.110222

Friedman, B., & Hendry, D. G. (2019). *Value Sensitive Design: Shaping Technology with Moral Imagination*. MIT Press. DOI: 10.7551/mitpress/7585.001.0001

Fritz, M. M. C., & Cordova, M. (2023). 'Developing managers' mindset to lead more sustainable supply chains'. *Cleaner Logistics and Supply Chain*, *7*, 100108. DOI: 10.1016/j.clscn.2023.100108

Fritz, M. M. C., & Cordova, M. (2023). Developing managers' mindset to lead more sustainable supply chains'. *Cleaner Logistics and Supply Chain*, *7*, 100108. DOI: 10.1016/j.clscn.2023.100108

Garrido, S., Muniz, J.Jr, & Batista Ribeiro, V. (2024). Operations management, sustainability & Industry 5.0: A critical analysis and future agenda. *Cleaner Logistics and Supply Chain*, *10*, 100141. DOI: 10.1016/j.clscn.2024.100141

Garti, M. O., Arif, J., & Jawab, F. (2024). Sustainable supply chain management: Past evaluation and present analysis for future research perspectives. In *2024 IEEE 15th International Colloquium on Logistics and Supply Chain Management (LOGISTIQUA)* (pp. 1-7). IEEE.

Ghobakhloo, M., Iranmanesh, M., Foroughi, B., Babaee Tirkolaee, E., Asadi, S. and Amran, A. (2023) 'Industry 5.0 implications for inclusive sustainable manufacturing: an evidence-knowledge-based strategic roadmap', Journal of Cleaner Production, June, Vol. 417, p.138023, .DOI: 10.1016/j.jclepro.2023.138023

Helo, P., & Hao, Y. (2021). Artificial intelligence in operations management and supply chain management: An exploratory case study. *Production Planning and Control*, *2021*(33), 1573–1590.

Jaouhari, A. E., Arif, J., Samadhiya, A., Kumar, A., & Trinkūnas, V. (2023). Are we there or do we have more to do? Metaverse in facility management and future prospects. *International Journal of Strategic Property Management*, *27*(3), 159–175. DOI: 10.3846/ijspm.2023.19516

Javaid, M., Haleem, A., Singh, R. P., Khan, S., & Suman, R. (2021). Blockchain technology applications for Industry 4.0: A literature-based review. *Blockchain Res. Appl.*, *2021*(2), 100027. DOI: 10.1016/j.bcra.2021.100027

Kamble, S. S., Gunasekaran, A., Kumar, V., Belhadi, A., & Foropon, C. (2021). A machine learning based approach for predicting blockchain adoption in the supply Chain. *Technological Forecasting and Social Change, 2021*(163), 120465. DOI: 10.1016/j.techfore.2020.120465

Kashem, M. A., Shamsuddoha, M., Nasir, T., & Chowdhury, A. A. (2023). Supply Chain Disruption Versus Optimization: A Review on Artificial Intelligence and Blockchain. *Knowledge (Beverly Hills, Calif.), 2023*(3), 80–96. DOI: 10.3390/knowledge3010007

Khaoua, Y., Mouzouna, Y., Arif, J., Jawab, F., & Azari, M. (2022). The contribution of blockchain technology in the supply chain management: The shipping industry as an example. In 2022 14th International Colloquium of Logistics and Supply Chain Management (LOGISTIQUA) (pp. 1-6). IEEE.

Koh, L., Dolgui, A., & Sarkis, J. (2020). Blockchain in transport and logistics—Paradigms and transitions. *International Journal of Production Research, 2020*(7), 58, 2054, 2062. DOI: 10.1080/00207543.2020.1736428

Lima, F. A., & Seuring, S. (2023). A Delphi study examining risk and uncertainty management in circular supply chains'. *International Journal of Production Economics, 258*, 108810. DOI: 10.1016/j.ijpe.2023.108810

Liu, K. S., & Lin, M. H. (2021). Performance Assessment on the Application of Artificial Intelligence to Sustainable Supply Chain Management in the Construction Material Industry. *Sustainability (Basel), 2021*(13), 12767. DOI: 10.3390/su132212767

Sharma, R., Shishodia, A., Gunasekaran, A., Min, H., & Munim, Z. H. (2022). The role of artificial intelligence in supply chain management: Mapping the territory. *International Journal of Production Research, 60*(24), 7527–7550. DOI: 10.1080/00207543.2022.2029611

Talha, S. E., Arif, J., & Jawab, F. (2024, May). Resilience Championship: Innovative Strategies for Supply Chain Management in the Face of Global Storms. In 2024 IEEE 15th International Colloquium on Logistics and Supply Chain Management (LOGISTIQUA) (pp. 1-8). IEEE.

Tronnebati, I., & Jawab, F. (2024). The impact of green and sustainable supply chain management practices on sustainable performance: A comparative analysis. *International Journal of Logistics Systems and Management, 47*(3), 267–294. DOI: 10.1504/IJLSM.2024.136855

Tronnebati, I., Jawab, F., Frichi, Y., & Arif, J. (2024). Green supplier selection using fuzzy ahp, fuzzy tosis, and fuzzy waspas: A case study of the moroccan automotive industry. *Sustainability (Basel), 16*(11), 4580. DOI: 10.3390/su16114580

Van Engelenburg, S., Janssen, M., & Klievink, B. (2018). A blockchain architecture for reducing the bullwhip effect. In Shishkov, B. (Ed.), *Business Modeling and Software Design. BMSD 2018. Lecture Notes in Business Information Processing* (Vol. 319). Springer., DOI: 10.1007/978-3-319-94214-8_5

Van Hoek, R. (2019). Unblocking the chain–findings from an executive workshop on blockchain in the supply chain. *Supply Chain Management, 25*(2), 255–261. DOI: 10.1108/SCM-11-2018-0383

Vyas, N., Beije, A., & Krishnamachari, B. (2019). *Blockchain and the supply chain: concepts, strategies and practical applications*. Kogan Page Publishers.

Waller, M. A., Van Hoek, R., Davletshin, M., & Fugate, B. (2019). *Integrating blockchain into supply chain management: a toolkit for practical implementation*. Kogan Page Publishers.

Wamba, S. F., & Queiroz, M. M. (2020). Blockchain in the operations and supply chain management: Benefits, challenges and future research opportunities. *International Journal of Information Management, 52*, 102064. DOI: 10.1016/j.ijinfomgt.2019.102064

Wenzel, H., Smit, D., & Sardesai, S. (2019). A Literature Review on Machine Learning in Supply Chain Management Supply Chain Management," in Proceedings of the Hamburg International Conference of Logistics (HICL) - 27, 2019, no. September, p. 30.

Younis, H., Sundarakani, B., & Alsharairi, M. (2022). Applications of artificial intelligence and machine learning within supply chains:systematic review and future research directions. *Journal of Modelling in Management, 17*(3), 916–940. DOI: 10.1108/JM2-12-2020-0322

Zaid, O., Arif, J., & Jawab, F. (2024, May). Human-centric supply chain management towards industry 5.0. In 2024 IEEE 15th International Colloquium on Logistics and Supply Chain Management (LOGISTIQUA) (pp. 1-7). IEEE.

Chapter 13
Revolutionizing Supply Chains:
AI Solutions for Modern Challenges

Nandana P. Pillai
https://orcid.org/0009-0006-5610-2809
RV College of Engineering, India

Jayashree Shivakumar
https://orcid.org/0009-0003-2636-3379
RV College of Engineering, India

Rohini S. Hallikar
https://orcid.org/0000-0002-3720-4344
RV College of Engineering, India

ABSTRACT

Artificial Intelligence (AI) is revolutionizing supply chain management (SCM) by addressing challenges such as demand forecasting, logistics inefficiencies, and labor shortages. This chapter explores AI's transformative role in optimizing processes, including predictive analytics for demand planning, dynamic production scheduling, and route optimization for transportation management. AI enhances decision-making, reduces costs, and promotes sustainability by minimizing waste and carbon emissions. The chapter highlights real-world case studies, offering insights into successful AI implementations while addressing barriers such as high costs, resistance to change, and ethical concerns like algorithmic bias and data privacy. Future trends emphasize AI's role in fostering resilience, enabling crisis management, and supporting collaboration among supply chain stakeholders. By integrating AI,

DOI: 10.4018/979-8-3373-0923-1.ch013

organizations can enhance operational efficiency, achieve sustainability goals, and build competitive, resilient supply chains for dynamic global markets.

INTRODUCTION

Artificial Intelligence (AI) plays a key role in various industries, often revolutionising the supply chain management. AI's immense ability to offer real time solution to various existing and pressing issues such as the highly fluctuating shipping and labour costs, the unavailability of adequate labour and notable inefficiencies in logistics have a stark impact on supply chain management. With its immense capability to process huge sets of data and derive appropriate insights from this data has significantly contributed to optimizing operations while enhancing the efficiency, which ultimately contributes to driving efficiency.

One of the biggest benefits AI implementations in SCM is in the field of demand forecasting and inventory management. AI boosts the productivity of the SCM by implementation of machine learning and advanced analytics to look at historical data, market trends and other supply chain factors like economic downturns and weather to forecast demand more accurately. This reduces waste and keeps the supply chain in balance so as to avoid overstock and stockout. AI also helps with production scheduling hence helping to focus on dynamic planning and predictive maintenance. By looking at real time digital data AI can predict machine failure and give suggestions on what to do ahead of time to mitigate the issue. This aims to reduce the downtime while increase productivity and lowering maintenance costs. The dynamic planning capabilities of AI enables the manufacturers to react faster to changes in production demand and optimize their resources for achieving better operational efficiency and cost savings for the company.

AI is changing the world of transportation .AI algorithms look at traffic patterns, weather forecasts and delivery schedules to optimise routes and reduce fuel consumption, delivery time and carbon footprint. AI gives real time visibility into shipments so customers have more control over logistics and sustainability.

The benefits of AI aren't limited to operations. Implementing AI in SCM reduces costs by increasing efficiency in transport and distribution and boosting customer satisfaction through personalisation. This can be a big game changer in fighting climate change through sustainability initiatives, reducing waste and lowering carbon footprints. The combination of cost savings and sustainability is the hidden magic of AI in supply chains.

But there are challenges to implementing this. The struggles with ethical challenges like algorithmic bias and data confidentiality to develop transparency and accountability in AI systems still persists. Very High implementation costs and resistance to change makes it hard to unlock this power. So companies must focus on ethical AI practices, minimising bias and building trust for equitable and sustainable outcomes.

In this chapter we will explore the real world applications of AI in supply chains and try to understand how businesses have managed to improve their efficiency through AI driven strategies. AI provides numerous advantages including real-time anomaly detection. These help in efficiently managing businesses and ensuring their survival even during calamities like pandemics or natural disasters

In summary AI is changing SCM by enabling efficiency, adaptability and sustainability. Overcoming adoption challenges and prioritising ethical practices will allow organisations to build resilient supply chains and drive innovation and long-term success in a changing world.

To fully unlock and utilize the power of AI in supply chain management organisations need to invest in advanced infrastructure capable of meeting the demands, employee training to educate them about AI and collaborative ecosystems that enable a constructive development. Another important step that can be initiated is building partnerships between various start-ups and established companies. This will help us foster innovation due to the availability of resources in terms of money, labor and guidance hence make AI solutions more relevant, engaging and accurate. In order to bridge the gaps in the establishment of AI based SCMs ad well as to refine the technology, it becomes imperative to address emerging challenges and adapt to changing market demands. By utilizing AI strategically, mindfully and ethically businesses can future advance their supply chains, reap competitive benefits, dominate the market and contribute to a more sustainable and efficient global economy.

ADVANCEMENTS IN AI TECHNOLOGIES

Artificial Intelligence (AI) is transforming supply chain management (SCM). By the extensive and mindful use of machine learning (ML), predictive analytics, autonomous systems and natural language processing (NLP) organisations can tackle demand forecasting, inventory control, procurement, logistics and risk management and hence boost their productivity and establish a prosperous monopoly. (ISMAEIL&Lalla,2024).

Machine Learning (ML)

Machine learning is one of the most important and defining part of AI in SCM. Analysing historical data, studying the various market trends and mapping the various external factors, ML can help provide accurate demand forecasting so that businesses can fully optimise and establish their supply chain. For example ML algorithms can be used to help develop competitive pricing strategies by looking at the various market conditions and studying consumer behaviour to develop the appropriate business model. They are also efficient in detection of production or supply chain anomalies so that quality control is consistent and always kept under check. This minimises the coincidence of overstocking or stockouts and helps keeps inventory balanced (Carbonneau et al., 2008).

Beyond inventory management ML provides supply chain visibility and helps to strengthens risk management by analysing historical and present data, identifying patterns that may signal potential disruptions such as supplier failures or geopolitical challenges. With these real time updates businesses can respond quickly to market changes and be more resilient and operationally efficient (Zatsu et al.,2024).

Predictive Analytics

Implementing AI in SCM can also reap benefits such as Predictive Analytics. This analyses historical and real-time data to estimate and forecast future trends so that one can make informed decisions on demand, production and logistics. For example, predictive analytics can help the supply chain by identifying patterns in seasonal demand, the impact of promotions and economic factors to give us precise demand forecasts. This lets us adjust and track our production schedules and inventory levels to reduce waste and cost which boost sustainability.

Predictive analytics also looks at various variables like transit times, weather and fuel costs to recommend the best logistics routes and schedules this enhances not only the efficiency but also the financial gain and diminishes losses. This in turn reduces transportation costs and delivery times maintaining customer satisfaction as well as reaping economic benefits for the companies. By studying the supplier performance data over time, we can find reliable partners and proactively address potential risks. Accurate inventory forecasting includes timely replenishment and less stocks, which reduces holding costs.

Autonomous Systems

Autonomous systems like drones, self-driving cars and robotic process automation (RPA) are also dynamically transforming and improving the logistics and warehouse management of the SCM. Drones help the companies drastically reduce manual checks by hours with their ability to quickly and accurately do inventory counts. They also provide last mile delivery to remote or hard to reach areas. Self-driving cars help reduce the transportation time by not having to rely on human drivers and establishing a disciplined system, at the same time reducing delays or accidents caused by human error or carelessness hence saving lives and time.

RPA increases the efficiency of the SCM by automating the various repetitive tasks like order processing, invoice creation and data entry, which reduces the confluence of various human errors and also frees up employees for more strategic roles. Autonomous robots in warehouses are trained to do sorting, picking and packing tasks very quickly, accurately and cost effectively improving the overall applicability of the system. They run throughout the day with no downtime and continuously monitors equipment performance in real time. This helps to predict maintenance needs and at the same time prevent costly downtime. This helps extend the equipment life and hence increases operational reliability.

Natural Language Processing (NLP)

NLP is one of the most important tools as it works towards enhancing communication and improving the customer interaction in SCM by training and helping machines to understand, interpret and respond to the basic human language. NLP powered Virtual assistants and chatbots handle customer service by answering questions, processing orders and providing real-time updates. Hence NLP aims to improve the overall user experience and reduce response times effectively.

NLP also helps immensely by automating the analysis of unstructured data like contracts, invoices and emails. This overall reduces the manual work required, and aids in minimizing the human errors while speeding up the decision making. NLP tools are also capable of analysing customer feedback from social media and online reviews and thus aids in measuring the customer satisfaction and sentiment. By identifying trends businesses can adapt their strategy to meet customer needs and retain loyalty.

Besides external applications NLP also enhances internal communication within supply chain teams. It summarizes reports, prioritizes tasks and even schedules meetings so teams can collaborate across departments. By breaking language barriers through translation services NLP supports global supply chain networks in multiple and multilingual markets (Figure 1).

Figure 1. Advancements in AI technologies

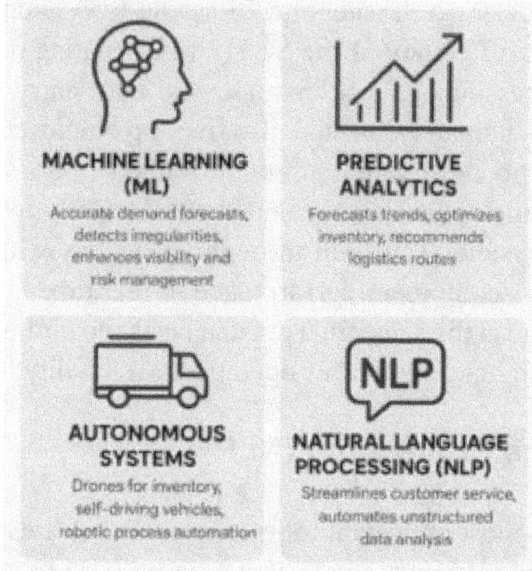

The figure highlights AI advancements in Machine Learning, Predictive Analytics, Autonomous Systems, and NLP for supply chain management.

Applications of AI in SCM

AI is pivotal in enhancing various SCM components:

1. **Demand Forecasting:**

Prediction tools especially those driven by AI revolutionize the field of demand forecasting by effectively examining various datasets, which includes past sales figures, market patterns, and other outside influences like weather or shopper habits. Thus, it aids the companies create very accurate demand projections and match both production and the stock with market needs. It helps to study and fulfil the lacunae in the market. This helps companies to cut down on the expense of having too much or too little inventory and hence also boosts customer happiness by keeping the right items in stock at a reasonable rate. Implementation of AI also helps the businesses react to sudden market shifts by effective prediction prior itself.

2. **Inventory Management:**

These days, we see that AI has transformed how we handle inventory by checking stock data across many sites in real time. It ensures that the appropriate stock is maintained through automatic refill systems that guess future demand and start restocking orders simultaneously. These features cut down on human work, hence reducing mistakes, and lowering the cost of extra stock or shortages. AI also helps with being eco-friendly by cutting waste through better stock turnover and expiry tracking in businesses that deal with items that go bad.

3. **Supplier Management:**

Analytics powered by AI helps companies pick and rate suppliers. It looks at things like how well they deliver, their prices, and if their quality stays the same. Smart AI models are also capable of checking for risks with suppliers, like trouble in their country or money problems. This lets businesses make lasting relations with vendors they can count on. AI also does various other tasks also on its own, like placing orders, handling bills, and making sure rules are followed. Overall, AI can help make the whole process run smoother.

4. **Logistics and Transportation:**

Logistics optimization can also be viewed as one of the key applications of AI in SCM. By analysing and carefully classifying various traffic patterns, weather conditions and fuel costs, AI is capable of finding the most efficient routes, hence helping us reduce lead times and operational costs. Autonomous vehicles and drones have helped to establish last mile delivery services that are fast and reliable, in urban and remote areas. Predictive maintenance systems monitor transportation assets in real-time and flag potential issues before they cause downtime so improving reliability and cost (Madhav et al.,2023)

5. **Risk Management:**

AI plays an integral role in risk management by leveraging data from multiple sources to provide real time visibility into the supply chain. It does various advanced analysis on the data to identify potential disruptions in the supply chain including supplier delays, natural disasters or market forces set on disrupting supply chains and recommends pre-emptive actions. Various scenario simulation tools also allow businesses to analyse the impact of various risks to develop contingency plans covering events that are likely or not likely to adversely impact your business.

6. **Customer Service:**

AI has also redefined customer service in the SCM ecosystem by providing personalized, fast customer service in real time. AI chatbots can handle most routine queries, process orders, and provide estimates for shipment updates significantly reducing the response time and reducing burdens on resource who would normally respond to a request. Chatbots can also collect customer feedback and reviews, through sentiment analysis, so businesses can understand customer satisfaction levels and improve their strategies to better meet customer expectations. Predictive analytics can also predict shifts in the preferences of customers as a result of surprise shifts in demand so businesses can adjust products and services to meet customer preferences.

7. **Supply Chain Planning:**

AI supports strategic supply chain planning by combining data from multiple sources like demand forecasts, inventory levels and supplier performance. This combination allows for scenario analysis to find the best course of action under different circumstances. AI optimizes resource allocation by balancing production schedules with available materials and labor so efficiency and cost. AI also improves collaboration across teams and supply chain partners by providing a single platform for data driven decision making.

Benefits of AI Integration

Advantages of AI Artificial Intelligence in SCM provides a range of advantages that can enhance operational efficiency, drive down costs, and improve decision making speed. These advantages apply in different areas of supply chain management (SCM) and the food supply chain as a whole and for competitor advantages. Below we will highlight the main advantages of AI in supply chain management.

1.Operational Efficiency (Mohsen.,2023):AI automates manual tasks in supply chain management and so operational efficiency.

- Automation Process: AI has the ability to automate many supply chain processes, this may include inventory monitoring, processing of orders and even data entry. These are very important as it helps boost the operation speeds and reduce the need for manual input. The less involvement of the workforce helps attain more accuracy and reduce human error
- Real-Time Data Processing: Analysing large amounts of data and monitoring them is one of the greatest powers of AI. Supply chain managers can hence react and manage any situation in real-time e.g., when stock levels or consumer demands change, or market conditions alter.

- Improved Coordination: AI can coordinate many functions that happen in each part of the supply chain. For example, moving goods, communication between departments, or logistics to ensure that everything gets done in coordination.

2. Cost Reduction

- Cost Reduction: One of most important function performed by AI includes the reduction in the costs and improved savings. This can be achieved by optimizing the supply chains while minimizing the inefficiencies to boost productivity
- Optimized Inventory Management: Overstocking and running out of stocks can equally damage a company's reputation and can lead to huge losses. AI helps mitigate these risks and keep such losses under check. This is referred to as inventory management. Companies strive to use AI to keep their inventory levels in check which is possible due to the high forecasting capabilities of AI. This helps to not only reduces economic losses but also reduces the wastage and storage space required.
- Lower Transportation Costs: The most optimal routes for transporting goods can be mapped by AI by analysing various variables such as traffic, fuel consumption etc. Hence, we are able to come up with cost-effective delivery routes and methods
- Efficient Resource Allocation: Resource utilization is also one of the key points that can aid a company's success of failure. The advanced capabilities of AI and its ability to train from past trends and predict the future treds can be put to good us by monitoring demand patterns and supply needs. Thus, AI helps various businesses utilize the resources in the most effective manner possible

3. Improved Decision-Making

- Through its extensive ability to analyse past trends and huge volumes of data and derive appropriate conclusions, AI provides the managers with very valuable data driven insights. Thus, the managers are able to make informed decisions about the various issues relating to production schedules and optimizations in procurement strategies.
- Predictive Analytics: AI allows the businesses to predict various future trends or events based on historical data. Thus, a business can map the forecasting demand, market trends or the potential risks associated with their venture and hence adjust their policies and workings to fulfil the derived requirements.
- Scenario Analysis: Several tools allow businesses to simulate the various scenarios and witness their possible outcomes beforehand hence allowing businesses to take informed decisions. This helps in managing

risks and strategic planning. Therefore, businesses are now able to understand how their decisions may affect the supply chain and what are the possible remedies.

4. Enhancing Customer Satisfaction

Customer satisfaction decides the degree of success of a company or business. AI can play a significant role in improving customer services by boosting the product availability while at the same time, letting the business know the popular customer response.

- On-Time Deliveries: AI helps to optimize transportation and inventory management. Hence, we can ensure timely deliveries satisfying customers.
- Personalized Customer Support: AI chatbots and virtual assistants offer real-time, personalized assistance to customers.
- Accurate Demand Forecasting: By studying historical data AI can correctly map the demand from customers and the niche and lacunae in the market

5. Risk Management and Mitigation

Risk Detection and Management are one of the most important cornerstones in SCM. AI can be employed to analyse historical and current trends and identify possible risks and take steps to mitigate them.

- Early Risk Detection: Through continuous monitoring of supply chain activities and various external factors such as weather, AI can swiftly identify potential risks well in advance and warn the officials. Hence helping companies survive even in the most difficult situations
- Scenario Planning: AI-based simulation tools help businesses prepare for various risk scenarios, such as supply shortages or delivery delays. This data can analyse and utilized in preplanning.
- Supply Chain Visibility: AI has the ability to increase visibility across the entire supply chain by providing real-time data inventory, transportation or overall performance. This data helps the managers swiftly react and resolve any issues that exist.

6. Contributing to Sustainability

Sustainability is one of the most important forefronts in a SCM. Hence it is necessary to minimize the material consumption and wastage.

- Resource Efficiency: AI can allocate resources related to demand and optimize raw material use and production capacity. AI can be employed to avoid overproduction, thereby reducing wastage and hence increasing sustainability.
- Reduced Carbon Footprint: AI's ability to optimize logistics processes, decrease fuel consumption and minimizing the environmental impact from transportation can help limit the carbon emissions.
- Sustainable Practice: Companies and organizations can monitor their progress towards sustainability goals by providing data about consumption rates, emissions, and waste. which can be analysed by AI and in turn it gives recommendations on how to improve the practices to attain sustainability.

7. Gaining a Competitive Edge

A company's ability to respond to changes in the market can be enhanced by the use of AI which in turn boosts the company's competitive edge.

- Innovation and Agility: AI-driven insights and automation allow companies to innovate more rapidly and adjust their operations in response to changing market conditions. Those companies which are able to efficiently adopt AI practices is able to maintain their competitive edge over the traditional companies in this fast-moving market.
- Customer Insights: AI can efficiently analyse the various customer preferences and hence paves way to personalisation. Personalisation helps companies to meet with the various customer expectations and understand the global market which is one of the most important and crucial steps.
- Operational Excellence: The operational improvements driven by AI—such as cost reductions, efficiency gains, and enhanced customer service—help businesses achieve excellence in their operations. This boosts their reputation and positions them as leaders in their industry.

Challenges in AI Implementation

Artificial Intelligence (AI) has so much potential to transform supply chain operations (SCM) in areas like forecasting, pressure management, logistics and customer engagement. But the journey to full AI integration is not without its challenges. Companies face issues like poor data quality, technology complications, security risks, people resistance and moral dilemmas. To fully utilize AI in supply chains, companies need to navigate these boundaries strategically (Tarihal et al.,2024).

1) Tackling Data Challenges:

For AI models to work well, they need good quality and organized data. When data is wrong, incomplete or inconsistent it hampers AI's ability to provide insights.

- Inaccurate Data: Issues arise when data sources are either inaccurate or non-existent. Predictions produced by AI become unreliable and functions like pressure control or forecasting demand become inefficient.
- Time Consuming Preparation: Cleaning and preparing the data before it can be used in AI models is an investment in time and resources, particularly if your data is located in many different systems.
- Integrating Data: Compounding the first two challenges is the challenge of integrating data from differently structured formats and from different stakeholders. Additionally, many organizations are still using legacy systems that aren't compatible or easily integrated with modern AI tools.

2) Structure and Skills Gap:

- Implementing AI in supply chains requires a substantial commitment to both technology and a skilled workforce. This is usually a barrier for many organizations.
- Cost of Infrastructure: To build an AI system you will need advanced hardware to run the model, cloud computing resources, and advanced software platforms to support an organization's needs when working with big data.
- Skills Gap: There are often shortages of specialists in the areas of machine learning, data analysis, and development of AI systems. This knowledge gap creates difficulties for agencies who want to build sustained AI outcomes or capabilities.
- System Complexity: AI systems require regular monitoring, updating, and refining to ensure they continue to be effective. Organizations have to develop internal capacity through training for their team members to maintain an AI system over time.

3) Safeguarding Data and Systems:

- AI-driven supply chains manage sensitive data, customer information, financial information and logistical operations. Therefore, security is critical.
- Cyber Risks: The AI infrastructure can be breached; data can be stolen or systems can be interrupted. Enhancing security is important to minimize risk.
- System Vulnerabilities: Hackers can take advantage of flaws in the AI algorithms or the infrastructure, interrupting operations or contaminating data. Periodic testing and updates are important to minimize risk.

- Compliance: Institutions should also comply with data protection legislative requirements such as GDPR or CCPA.

4) Change Management:

- AI will often lead to fears on behalf of staff, primarily job security or change of workplace.
- Job Security: Many people feel that AI will replace their jobs. It is important that companies proactively address these fears and make clear that AI will enhance human efforts not replace them.

5) Navigating Ethical and Regulatory Challenges

AI must be transparent, just and ethical in supply chains to build trust and adapt to legislation changing.

- Bias-Free AI: AI models, designed on biases in past data will continue unfair activity such as supplier selection or targeting customers unfairly. Organizations have to ensure their design has no bias and can be assessed at any time.
- Transparent: AI is inherently opaque in its decision making. Companies need to have systems where decision making can be traced to support accountability.
- Compliance: New laws around AI continue to evolve. Businesses must understand and adapt their practices based on the requirements around fairness, privacy, and transparency.

6) Scalability and Flexibility:

As businesses grow, their supply chain operations become more complex and AI has to evolve as well.

- Scalability: AI has to handle larger datasets and more complex operations crop up as the business grows. If the system is not scalable, inefficiencies and bottlenecks will arise.
- Flexibility for Change: Supply chains in businesses, especially in the technology space, are not static they change. Therefore, AI systems need to be designed to evolve with the load on the systems. Flexibility means that the outcomes can accept additional data or new data sources as they come and to enhance or better suit the changes in the business process.

7) Establishing Value and ROI:

AI-based transformations can be expensive, and establishing ROI is difficult.

- Demonstrating ROI: While AI can help save costs and improve efficiency, these benefits can be difficult to pin down. Before implementing AI, you should define your KPIs and monitor enhancements, if possible, to validate that AI was worth the investment.
- Timing: The majority of AI's benefits are realized later. Companies should take a long-term view and focus on future benefits rather than expecting immediate ROI. AI presents a huge opportunity for SCM, but implementing it successfully requires overcoming multiple challenging barriers. Companies can climb the barriers the implementors face with proper investments in data, infrastructure, people's capability and ways of working ethically. If organizations are prepared to let the technology do its work (one fatigue of implementation is the expectation of how much gain this technology can deliver immediately) and, instead, focus on taking a long-term strategic view of sustained or more agility within supply chains.

Future of AI in SCM

The future of AI in SCM is exciting and will dramatically change how things are done, changing the way we work. Trends and opportunities for the future of SCM will involve (Culot et al.,2024).

1. **Advanced Predictive Analytics:** The present age machine learning algorithms are becoming increasingly precise and aims to analyse and hence deliver deeper insights into the operational challenges as well us understand the customer behaviours. Real time analytics majorly aim to establish instant access to various live updates which help businesses mindfully take informed decisions. Advanced simulations can also be used to enhance strategic planning.
2. **IoT Integration:** IoT has become indispensable part of our lives these days. AI and IoT together has the ability of revolutionising the entire world. They can help establish smarter supply chains. They provide real time access to tracking inventory, assessing the environmental conditions and monitoring the equipment performances. AI can also be utilized to provide preventive maintenance recommendations; they can also contribute to optimising the warehouse layouts and establishing responsible logistics.

3. **Blockchain for Security and Transparency:** Data security is one of the greatest concerns today. AI and blockchain together are used to provide improved security and maintain adequate transparency within operations. They help maintain the integrity of the data and the trust of the customers.
4. **Cooperation Between Humans and AI:** Combining human expertise with AI will alter decisions made by humans and how human intelligence and interaction will drive the future of work. In the supply chain specifically, AI will provide data to supply chain professionals, which will free professionals time by automating repetitive tasks allowing them to focus on strategy and other aspects of decision making. Employee training programs will introduce intuitive infrastructures that allow non-technical users to work alongside, and leverage AI, within familiar forms, and formats of workplace use.
5. **Sustainability Initiatives:** AI will further sustainability and drive accelerated sustainability initiatives. Specific to supply chains, AI models will develop superior methods for resource use and reduce waste. Green logistics will be driven by AI that reduces carbon output through route optimisation and energy management. AI will also support circular economy models that cover recycling, waste reduction and sustainable sourcing.
6. **Personalised Customer Experiences:** AI will accelerate the hyper personalisation of customer experience to better engage customers. AI powered dynamic pricing and recommendations based on customer behaviour will improve customer satisfaction and loyalty. AI will foster proactive support systems that react to customer issues before engagement or experience arises.
7. **Ethical AI and Governance:** As AI continues to be adopted ethics will come to be forefront and the AI models will create change to reduce bias, transparency and maintain governance in light of privacy legislation. AI will necessitate a governance framework to incorporate accountability by stakeholders.
8. **Real-Time Supply Chain Visibility:** AI provides real-time visibility across various channels into the supply chain by processing real-time data streams. This helps us identify where we lack and correct ourselves accordingly.

AI is a major driving force of innovation in SCM. Applications such as logistics management, adaptive management systems that respond to various demand changes aids the growing and flourishing of businesses as they help streamline vendor selection and management This leads to an increase in efficiencies and reduces the costs. Above all it also aids in giving the company a competitive edge over the traditional ones. Thus we are able to transform SCM into an efficient and sustainable system and enhance its sustainability.

Case Studies

1.Consumer Packaged Goods (CPG) Companies: Autonomous Supply Chain Planning

Research from McKinsey demonstrates the impact of artificial intelligence (AI) on supply chains in Consumer-Packaged Goods (CPG) businesses. Businesses leveraging AI capabilities can now have better demand prediction, quicker reactions to market movements, and move products to customers more efficiently – contributing to up to a 4% increase in revenue. AI also decreases overstock by decreasing waste costs and storage costs by 20%, an improvement that is beneficial to perishable goods. Logistic companies will use AI to automate tasks and determine optimal delivery routes while predicting maintenance for the delivery trucks – all automating saves companies up to 10% in supply chain costs and enhances overall performance. Hence, we can understand the importance of AI in supply chain planning and how on properly utilizing the power of AI, one can dynamically transform the supply chain and yield better results. Hence we can see that the mindful use of AI can help us achieve optimized Supply chain management systems and improve the productivity and efficiency of the entire system.

2. Amazon: Global Demand Forecasting with Machine Learning:

Amazon is a prime example of how AI is used for demand forecasting across the world. Due to Amazon's numerous product offerings, machine learning and artificial intelligence are incorporated to create demand forecasting in seconds to optimize the entire supply chain. When Amazon conducts demand forecasting they use a machine learning model that evaluates historical sales data, current seasonal trends, and other externalities like weather events and community activities when making inventory decisions.

Amazon is effectively incorporating the customer experience as a cost by limiting both categories of inventory, over inventory, which is defined as product being too much stocked, and under inventory, which is defined as product out of stock, on the balance sheet. In some applications their AI simply makes more accurate forecasts for items that may only have seasonal—and changing—demand, such of holiday gifts or back to school supplies, so they can take a proactive approach to replenishing inventory.

Their AI also assists in managing a long tail of lowest selling items in their warehouses so that they do not over stock such products. It is easy to understand how that connects back to the company mission for Amazon, offering the most selection to the customer. Using demand forecasting at Amazon ultimately creates a more agile supply chain. Demand forecasting is a predictive model and using AI for demand forecasting allows Amazon to shift logistic capabilities to get products to the customer faster and ultimately improve the customer experience with speed and efficiency.

3. Oscado Warehouse Automation through AI-Enabled Technologies

Oscado is one of the online grocery retailers which developed and harnessed AI to revolutionize warehouse operations. By enforcing collaborative robots (cobots) and AI-driven inventory systems, Ocado has set a benchmark for warehouse automation. Cobots replaces the human operators making it efficient for picking and packing processes. It has automated the repetitive tasks, through which order process has became fast and ensures timely deliveries. This helps to improve the operational throughput and decreases customer wait time. In some cases, cobats are equipped with high advanced AI which can handle many orders at time, effectively improving warehouse output. The AI also detects the frequently required items by examining the product demand and order patterns and stores those items in easily accessible locations which helps in decreasing the retrieval times and increasing productivity.

Oversight of AI automation reduces the requirement for people to do dangerous jobs, making workplaces safer. Cobots for example help with carrying heavy loads and complex sorting activities thus cutting on risks of injury and promoting a safer working environment. Ocado's systems are also designed with real-time monitoring as well as fault detection that ensures smooth and safe operations in all its facilities. Safety protocols that accompany AI keep harmony between robots and humans. For example, cobots can be programmed to halt immediately once they sense human beings close by with a certain predefined proximity; this minimizes collision risks.

4. BMW: Quality Assurance with AI-Powered Computer Vision

BMW demonstrates the implementation of AI technology in computer vision systems during quality assurance. These systems ensure that only the products which have passed the stringent quality checks are delivered to the customers by scanning the car models on the assembly lines to check for any defects.

Maintaining the paramount brand value of premium quality, real time anomaly detection does aid BMW. These systems AI flag the issues where humans may miss spotting defects with the help of thousands of data points and lots of checks every millisecond. With precision like these, customer trust along with brand loyalty is bound to arise. Additionally, the risk of recalls increases, worsening the financial and reputational implications for the company. BMW can implement improvement strategies by adding additional AI powered systems which track data of previous inspections along with other data systems. This added technology permits the identification of recurring issues and supports numerous company standards by helping refine diverse processes while robustly lowering the defect rates over time.

The AI systems and data analyze the record to continuously improve the defect rates. Decreasing inspection queues and conducting accuracy checks results in improving the pace of production. Maintaining the thorough checks along with the improvement in efficiency, BMW have radically improved the entire system. Furthermore, the feedback to the production team allows the prompt action so that the disruption and waste is lower. The fundamental guarantees from the AI powered systems in accuracy smoothen the efficiency to the entire production line.

These case studies demonstrate how AI has an impact on many different industries. The prediction of demand, warehouse automation, quality assurance, and cost optimization are just a few of the processes that artificial intelligence is revolutionizing in supply chain management. Businesses are now attaining a previously unprecedented degree of customer satisfaction, agility, and operational efficiency thanks to the use of AI tools. It is unambiguous that supply chain maximizing the efficiency will always require Artificial intelligence (AI) as businesses strive for new innovations. By reducing waste and resource consumption and offering more intelligent decision support systems, the application of AI solutions also helps achieve sustainability goals. The implementation of artificial intelligence (AI) to create more flexible, robust, and customer-focused systems will be the next step in supply chain management.

Technological Enablers in AI-Driven Supply Chain Management (SCM)

1. Big Data Analytics

Big data analytics serves as foundation for AI-driven Supply Chain Management (SCM). It also allows to process and examine large datasets from various sources such as customer demand patterns, supplier performance records, and real-time market dynamics. There is rapid growth of digital data which makes traditional analytical methods insufficient, paving the way for big data to revolutionize SCM.

Big data analytics improves the decision-making over the supply chain. For instance, AI-model helps to know the future demands by examining historical sales data, social media activity, and economic indicators. It also helps in dynamic pricing strategies, enabling businesses to adapt prices in real-time based on supply, demand, and competitor actions. Big data helps organizations to optimize their stock levels by giving deep insights into inventory turnover rates and it also aims at analysing seasonal patterns and customer preferences in order to make ready for demand fluctuations. This reduces carrying costs and eliminates overstocking, which can lead to waste.

Big data has helped logistics by enabling the route optimization through examining traffic patterns, fuel costs, and delivery schedules. This enables companies like UPS and Fed Ex to decrease delivery times and operational costs. Additionally, big data provides tracking of shipments which ensures transparency and stakeholders also get real-time updates. Big data is capable of detecting unusual patterns in transactions, such as discrepancies in supplier invoices or delivery timelines which in turn improves fraud detection. Companies make use of big data for monitoring geopolitical events, weather forecasts, and market volatility to proactively adjust their supply chain strategies. It also permits organizations to know their customer behavior and preferences at a granular level.

Big data analytics has enormous implicit, but there are obstacles to overcome in its operation. To manage big datasets, associations need to make investments in dependable structure. Data security and sequestration are serious issues, particularly when handling private customer data. Relinquishment may also be hampered by the difficulty of combining big data analytics with heritage systems. SCM will be readdressed by the combination of big data and slice- edge technologies like blockchain and the Internet of effects. For illustration, blockchain guarantees data integrity, while IoT bias will deliver real- time data aqueducts. Analytics tools driven by AI will advance in complication, furnishing deeper perceptivity and easing real- time decision- making. To sum over, big data analytics is revolutionizing force chain operation (SCM) by offering practical perceptivity that boost productivity, cut charges, and enhance client satisfaction.

2. Internet of Things (IoT)

Connecting physical systems and devices, the Internet of Things (IoT) is a game-changing technology that allows real-time data collection, sharing, and analysis. IoT in SCM ensures increased transparency and efficiency by facilitating smooth collaboration and communication throughout the supply chain. Real-time information on the location and state of commodities is provided by Internet of Things devices like sensors and GPS trackers. For businesses that deal with perishable items, including food and pharmaceuticals, this skill is essential. In order to guarantee that goods fulfil quality standards while in transit, sensors keep an eye on temperature, humidity, and other environmental variables. The automation of warehouse operations is greatly aided by IoT.

IoT-enabled smart shelves can monitor inventory levels in real time, notifying managers when supplies are running short or when anything is missing. Automated guided vehicles (AGVs) and robotic systems influence IoT data to streamline selecting, quilting, and sorting processes. IoT improves logistics by keeping the track of goods at all stages of the transportation. GPS-enabled bias track shipments, allowing companies to optimize routes and reduce delivery times. Prophetic analytics, powered by IoT data, can anticipate implicit dislocations similar as business traffic or adverse rainfall conditions, enabling visionary adaptations.

IoT devices enables to keep track of the performance of machinery and equipment used in supply chain operations. IoT enhances force chain security by tracking goods at every stage of the trip. Anti-theft detectors and tamper- evidence seals give an added subcaste of protection, icing that products reach their destination safely. also, blockchain integration with IoT can ensure the authenticity of goods by recording every sale in a secure, decentralized tally. Despite its benefits, IoT relinquishment in SCM faces challenges. High perpetration costs, lack of standardization, and cybersecurity pitfalls are significant walls. Managing the large volumes of data generated by IoT bias requires robust structure and advanced analytics capabilities.

The outlook of IoT within SCM is auspicious due to the advancement of edge computing and 5G plat form. Edge computing will allow for data to be reused closer to the source reducing quiescence and optimizing real-time decision and timber. Likewise, 5G will enhance connectivity and create briskly and more dependable links between bias. Loving is IoT will revolutionize SCM by furnishing unknown conditions of visibility, effectiveness, and security. Company that integrate IoT into terminal chain operations will be more able to meet customer demands, better able to acclimatize to request changes, and stay competitive in a increasingly connected world.

3. Cloud Computing

Cloud technology, which provides scalable facilities and computing capabilities to support data-intensive processes, is an essential component of driven by artificial intelligence supply chain management (SCM). Organizations can gather supply chain data, improve stakeholder cooperation, and streamline procedures by utilizing cloud-based services. Direct access to supply chain data from various sources, such as suppliers, warehouses, and customers, is made possible by cloud computing. By improving visibility and openness, this centralized approach enables stakeholders to make well-informed decisions. To reduce down on errors and inefficiencies, for instance real-time inventory changes from several sites can be linked on a single platform. Cloud platforms make it easier for supply chain participants to collaborate and communicate with one another. Manufacturers, suppliers, and logistics companies may efficiently coordinate their operations with the use of shared dashboards and collaboration technologies.

The ability to scale is one of the main advantages of cloud computing. It is an ideal method to manage changes in business within the supply chain since it allows organizations to modify their computer resources according to demand. This capacity for change prevents excessive investment in infrastructure and guarantees cost effectiveness. The analytical power required for sophisticated analytics and AI applications is supplied by cloud platforms. Cloud computing facilities can be used to deploy and scale predictive models for risk assessment, route optimization, and demand forecasting. Fast responses to interruptions, including delays or supply shortages, are made possible by real-time data processing. Cloud computing lowers capital investment by doing away with the necessity for on-premises gear. Pay-as-you-go models allow businesses to make only payments over the resources they really utilize. Organisations of all sizes may now afford sophisticated supply chain solutions thanks to this cost-effective strategy.

Robust recovery from disaster options are provided by cloud platforms, guaranteeing business continuity in the face of unexpected occurrences. In an attempt to manage vital supply chain data, top cloud providers use multi-factor authentication and encryption, among other cutting-edge security methods. Usage of cloud computing inside SCM is not lack difficulties, despite its benefits. Considerations about information security and privacy are still very real, particularly when handling private client and supplier data. Potential delay problems in areas with poor internet connectivity must also be addressed by organizations.

4. Blockchain Technology

In supply chain management (SCM), blockchain is beginning to disrupt the industry. Blockchain provides accountability, authenticity and trust to all supply chain participants with a decentralised ledger that is not only secure, but also free from manipulation. Coupled with artificial intelligence (AI), blockchain can improve decision making activities and speed up supply chain activities, thus improving performance. Blockchain by its very nature records data in the form of transaction records to provide an immutable data trail for each transaction in the entire production chain. This immediacy of data transparency is especially important in verticals where safety and authenticity of the product are paramount; for example in products such as pharmaceuticals and food products that have shelf lives. Blockchain can provide a continuous trail of the product from the producer to the end customer while ensuring adherence to regulations. The very nature of blockchain creates a common sharing of data in real time between supply chain partners. This data transparency mitigates disputes between supply chain partners and further increases accountability of each partner and builds trust between partners.

One of the main features of blockchain are smart contracts that automatically trigger payment and execute agreements once certain conditions are met. This helps reduce transaction times, reduce errors and remove the need for intermediaries. For example, once products are delivered and checked a contract could automatically trigger the payment to the supplier. Blockchain relies on secure cryptographic algorithms to guarantee that data cannot be altered, modified or accessed without permission. This is critical to secure confidential data within the supply chain, including pricing contracts and exclusive products. Additionally, blockchain prevents fraudulent activities by providing a transparent, immutable record of transactions. For example, large companies are now using blockchain to provide authentication of products so customers can be assured that they are obtaining genuine products.

Things begin to improve when real time monitoring and identification is combined with blockchain. Take IoT sensors which record location and temperature data and use blockchains to store that data securely. AI can then use that data to improve supply chain processes that involve detecting inefficiencies and forecasting demand. However, for all it's promise, using blockchain in SCM is not without challenges, some of which include uniformity, scalability, time and money to implement, and environmental cost of energy use of a blockchain networks, especially networks that use proof-of-work consensus.

As companies become more aware of blockchain, supply chain management will expand. Blockchain technology can address current challenges such as proof-of-stake and interoperability. Supply chain optimization will occur through the convergence of blockchain and AI and other technologies. All in all, blockchain is disrupting supply chain management. The confluence of AI, IoT, and blockchain will amplify the effects, and companies will be able to build trustworthy and resilient supply chains (Dash et al., 2019).

Walmart: A Case Study [Gedam et al., 2023]

Artificial intelligence (AI) has the potential to improve supply chain management but it can be difficult to navigate. Businesses can overcome these obstacles and harness the full capabilities of AI by supporting ethical frameworks, ensuring they have a robust infrastructure, training staff, and employing good data management. If businesses take a long term strategic approach to AI implementation, the impact should make both long term productivity gains and competitive advantages. Walmart is using machine learning (ML) and artificial intelligence (AI) to enhance its inventory control and demand forecasting capabilities. The algorithms are able to provide highly accurate demand forecasts by analyzing historical sales data, market trends, temperature, and other external factors.The impact has been significant in terms of productivity gains.

Walmart has experienced a 10-15% improvement in forecasting accuracy resulting in enhanced stock management thus effectively reducing costs associated with overstocked inventory, but also helping to ensure that customers are always able to find the products they seek and have a better shopping experience overall. This technology gives Walmart the ability to manage optimal stock levels to mitigate the effects of overstocked inventory, which can waste valuable resources as well as understocked inventory that can disappoint customers.

AI minimizes and simplifies many complex prediction processes which reduces human errors and allows staff to work on more relevant activities. Additionally, these technologies enable Walmart to respond to shifts in demand prompted by unforeseen disruptions or seasonal events. Walmart has demonstrated its commitment to innovation and customer delight through its implementation of AI in its operations.

AI in demand forecasting and inventory management has provided us with:

1. Improved Forecasting With AI: we can forecast demand using vast amounts of data such as historical sales data, industry trends, external factors and more. This method has less error than traditional forecasting methods.
2. Appropriate Stock Levels: Better forecasting allows us to maintain balanced inventory levels. This minimizes out of stock situations while avoiding overstocking and the associated costs.
3. Cost Reductions: Lowering inventory levels and avoiding out of stock situations provides cost savings by minimizing waste, storage costs and lost sales.
4. Enhanced Customer Experience: A well stocked inventory allows for a seamless purchasing experience which helps with customer satisfaction and loyalty.
5. Operational Efficiency: AI provides the ability to reduce errors and improve efficiencies through effective automation of complex forecasting and inventory management activities which allows staff to devote their time to more strategic work.
6. Proactive Adjustments: AWA approaches to AI allows us to adjust supply chain and inventory management practices to adapt to weather patterns and seasonal trends as they develop.
7. Competitive Position in the Market Being in a position to leverage new technology allows us to stay ahead of competitors that leverage more simplistic systems and ultimately gain market share.

8. Environmental Responsibility: Inventory levels based on good inventory practices reduces waste and is good for the environment and consistent with AWA's sustainability practices.

Maersk: Case Study

Maersk leverages artificial intelligence (AI) for its route planning and logistics. With the technology, they have addressed some of the biggest challenges facing the shipping industry – increased inefficiency, high fuel costs, and environmental issues (Gedam et al., 2023). Maersk uses AI to analyze a lot of waterborne data like weather trends, fuel consumption rates, port congestion etc. It selects the optimum route on the basis of these results.

The AI systems allow the decision maker to assume potential disruption either from port traffic or bad weather and present an alternate route.AI systems also simplify complex decision making. Traditional route planning involves manually assessing multiple variables which is time-consuming and vulnerable to human error. AI solutions eliminate the multitude of errors and time involved through instant fast and accurate review of massive volumes of data. Equally important, besides safety improvements, automation allows more productivity from existing staff by allowing them to support strategic goals rather than daily operations.

Route planning is just an example of Maersk's AI-enabled logistics. They employ these systems in evaluating their logistics supply chains with regards to other factors other than route planning. For example, AI systems can connect many data points to provide a consolidated view of operations, effectively prompting better choice of resources and overall planning.

This integrated strategy allows Maersk to stay ahead of rivals. They have also been equipped to deal with unpredictable circumstances due to artificial intelligence.

For example, they used artificial intelligence to adapt operational circumstances to unexpected events at the global level, such as the COVID-19 pandemic. In doing so, they were able to meet customer expectations while managing business continuity by anticipating issues before they occurred and modifying their way of working.

Maersk has implemented a number of advantages in the area of supply chain management. Below are some of the key points of value.

1. Route Optimization: One of the major advantages that AI has given Maersk is shipping routes. Route planning used to be based on static data and the experience of travelers, captains and logisticians. It was limited because it did not factor in dynamic factors affecting routes like port congestion, fuel prices and even the current weather. Changes to these factors would twist an outcome resulting in delays and inefficient routing of vessels. With AI, Maersk can now analyze large

amounts of data including port traffic, live weather events and vessel tailored efficiencies. On top of an improved experience with smoother operations, route optimization with AI also adds value to Maersk because it enhances customer experience. Customers have increasing demand for on-time deliveries, and using AI can mitigate external factors that will interrupt a company's service design.

2. Transit Time Reductions: AI enables potential reductions of time because it determines the shortest and the most fuel-efficient route to sea. In an industry where customer experience in based on on-time deliveries, being able to reduce transit time is a massive competitive advantage.

Adverse weather conditions, inadequate port traffic management, and inefficient routing all cause delays in traditional shipping operations. In comparison to traditional maritime operations, AI is capable of examining data and sources such as weather patterns, port schedules, and vessel data to anticipate disruptions and devise the best routing options. This can drastically improve operational efficiencies by lowering transit times and curbing delays. For Maersk, for example, shorter shipping times are highly advantageous. Customers are happier when they receive goods faster.

3. Cost savings and fuel efficiency: One of the significant operational costs in the transportation sector is fuel. As fuel prices fluctuate, fuel savings become even more paramount. Maersk's estimates for the best route are based on a combination of historical and predetermined data that takes into consideration weather events, speed, and fuel savings, allowing for properly informed decisions. Maersk makes decisions based on opportunities presented by fuel savings, taking environmentally sustainable routes to use less fuel while at sea.

This reduces operating costs, making the company more profitable while decreasing fuel usage which is favorable for the environment. Through less fuel use, Maersk is helping to achieve global sustainability goals through fewer greenhouse gas emissions from petroleum use. In addition to helping Maersk reduce its environmental footprint, these actions reinforce the company's image as a responsible and ethical organization.

4. Improved Decision-Making: Due to the widespread utilization of AI, logistics and route planning requires complicated calculations and assessments which can be time-consuming and susceptible to human error. While human expertise still matters in transportation, even the best humans can be overwhelmed with the data they must process and the complexity of modern supply chains.AI can remedy this concern by automating most, if not all, of the decision-making process.

AI can handle large amounts of data quickly and accurately analyzing several variables in real-time - such as port delays, weather, shipping costs, and more - allowing decisions to made correctly, consistently, and without error. For instance, if the AI assessed that weather may influence the shipping route it could recommended a new route for the ship that would keep it from encountering severe weather. It can also recommend shifting the schedule to circumvent the port delay. Using AI will lead to better decision-making overall, less human error, and overall operational performance gains based on data suggestions. Shifting to an automated process also relieves the Maersk logistics team from having to be manual at the planning stage so they can focus on larger projects. When planning is semi-automated and employees do not have to perform manual low-level repetitive tasks, employee satisfaction and productivity can also improve more efficient use of their time.

5. Enhanced Visibility of the Supply Chain: Maersk not only uses AI to enhance its routing efforts, but to improve visibility in its supply chain as well. Within the shipping industry, collaboration between the various stakeholders - ports, logistics, cargo owners, customs—is challenging and inefficient. The fragmented nature of supply chains creates a lack of real time updates in the current state of affairs, contributing to supply chain gaps where disruption or delays can arise at any point in time. AI can ameliorate this issue by fusing data collected from multiple stakeholders to gain a holistic view of the supply chain. The AI tools propel Maersk into the real time space by surveillant data to support operational efforts in regards to ports, shipments, weather, etc. It also adds a valuable logistics data where resources can be better allocated as Maersk can anticipate those disruptors before they impact operations. This may prevent it from global disruptions hence improving quality of life.

Coco Coal: Case study

As a dominant player in the beverage sector, Coca-Cola has embraced the utilization of advanced technologies, specifically in the form of artificial intelligence (AI), to reshape the traditional process of demand forecasting and customer personalization.

Implementation of AI, together with machine learning algorithms, Coca-Cola is now able to better predict probable consumer interest, assess inventory levels, and engage consumers in a more personal way, enhancing overall operational efficiency, improving customer relationships, and fostering brand loyalty and competitiveness (Gedam et al.,2023).

Demand forecasting is one of the most important applications of AI in SCM. Especially in the beverage industry, the market is ever changing and customer choices are dependent on the seasonal influences. Hence, combining the present and historic data and drawing an appropriate forecast model from it, they were establishing a competitive edge over other players. This implementation of AI helped them overcome over-stocking challenges, distribution issues and inaccurate predictions. stockouts of product.

Machine Learning algorithms are very prominent in today's world. Coco-Cola uses these algorithms to analyse the huge amounts of data and tackle various issues including weather changes, ads and internet trends. This helps them establish a relationship with the general public and is hence a very important step towards customer satisfaction. It also provides various over features such as demand forecasting which helps them customize their product based on many forecasts including geographic area and customer segment These machines use an AI engine that makes product recommendations in real-time based on prior customer purchases. For example, if a customer regularly buys a certain drink, the machine can recommend drinks similar to that drink, creating a more personalized experience. In addition to enhancing customer delight, this personalization improves the likelihood of repeat business.

Coca-Cola also uses AI-powered customized advertising. The company can target its audience with more relevant communications by segmenting its audience based on customer data analysis.

Results: Coca-Cola's effectiveness and customer satisfaction has improved since AI was incorporated into its operations. Coca-Cola has optimized its supply chain and reduced redundancies in distribution and inventory management by increasing demand accuracy. Customers still have access to their favorite products because of the decrease in stockouts which enhances their overall experience.AI-powered customized advertising and customer recommendations has also helped Coca-Cola with customer relations. Coca-Cola builds loyalty and creates a deeper emotional connection with the brand by giving personalized experiences. So Coca-Cola is retaining customers for the long term and not just operational efficiency.

CONCLUSION

In conclusion, supply chain administration has undergone a revolution because of artificial intelligence (AI), which offers revolutionary solutions to common issues like forecasting demands, inefficiency in production, and transportation optimization. Organizations can improve customer satisfaction while achieving greater productivity, adaptability, and sustainability through taking advantage of AI's capabilities. For integration to be effective, nevertheless, issues with data security, ethics, and execution costs must be resolved. Therefore, it is crucial to research the important impact of AI on creating transportation networks that are more intelligent, flexible, and capable of navigating ambiguities and changing global demands. Organizations will be able to innovate, collaborate, and achieve a competitive advantage in a market that is changing quickly by embracing AI. (Helo and Hao, 2021).

REFERENCES

Carbonneau, R., Laframboise, K., & Vahidov, R. (2008). Application of machine learning techniques for supply chain demand forecasting. *European Journal of Operational Research, 184*(3), 1140–1154. DOI: 10.1016/j.ejor.2006.12.004

Culot, G., Podrecca, M., & Nassimbeni, G. (2024). Artificial intelligence in supply chain management: A systematic literature review of empirical studies and research directions. *Computers in Industry, 162*, 104132. DOI: 10.1016/j.compind.2024.104132

Dash, R., McMurtrey, M., Rebman, C., & Kar, U. K. (2019). Application of artificial intelligence in automation of supply chain management. *Journal of Strategic Innovation and Sustainability, 14*(3), 26–37. DOI: 10.33423/jsis.v14i3.2105

Gedam, V., Pimplapure, A., Sen, P., Pandey, S., Namdeo, Y., & Atkare, S. (2023). The transformative impact of artificial intelligence on supply chain management. *Journal of Survey in Fisheries Sciences, 10*(4), 3562–3573.

Helo, P., & Hao, Y. (2021). Artificial intelligence in operations management and supply chain management: An exploratory case study. *Production Planning and Control, 33*(16), 1573–1590. DOI: 10.1080/09537287.2021.1882690

Ismaeil, M. K., & Lalla, A. F. (2024). The role and impact of artificial intelligence on supply chain management: Efficiency, challenges, and strategic implementation. *Journal of Ecohumanism, 3*(4), 89–106. DOI: 10.62754/joe.v3i4.3461

Madhav, V. V., Deekshith, A., Sai, K. N., Ramesh, M., & Reddy, S. S. (2023). Research on impact of artificial intelligence on logistics and supply chain management. *Journal of Emerging Technologies and Innovative Research, 10*(12). https://www.jetir.org

Mohsen, B. (2023). Impact of artificial intelligence on supply chain management performance. *Journal of Service Science and Management, 16*(1), 44–58. DOI: 10.4236/jssm.2023.161004

Tarihal, B., Kaliwal, R., & Ammanagi, A. (2024). The transformative influence of artificial intelligence on supply chain management. *ITM Web of Conferences, 68*, 01016. DOI: 10.1051/itmconf/20246801016

Zatsu, V., Shine, A. E., Tharakan, J. M., Peter, D., Ranganathan, T. V., Alotaibi, S. S., Mugabi, R., Bin Muhsinah, A., Waseem, M., & Nayik, G. A. (2024). Revolutionizing the food industry: The transformative power of artificial intelligence—A review. *Food Chemistry: X, 24*, 101867. DOI: 10.1016/j.fochx.2024.101867 PMID: 39431210

Chapter 14
Navigating Sustainability in Supply Chains:
Challenges and Opportunities in the Era of Industry 4.0

Fouad Jawab
https://orcid.org/0000-0002-0508-7278
Sidi Mohamed Ben Abdellah University, Morocco

Jabir Arif
https://orcid.org/0000-0002-5285-7976
Sidi Mohamed Ben Abdellah University, Morocco

ABSTRACT

This chapter is organized around three main questions related to the concept of the green Supply Chain, 4.0 technologies and the use of these technologies to ensure sustainability. Our main goal is to provide answers to the question: how and to what extent can sustainable supply chains be successfully implemented economically, socially and ecologically with the help of 4.0 technologies? Methodologically, we took an exploratory approach supported by qualitative and quantitative data extracted from literature, reports and the websites of the companies involved. This has allowed the focus to be on the cutting-edge practices and experiences of companies of different sizes and activities, as well as on the successes in reducing CO2 emissions and respecting social ethics.

DOI: 10.4018/979-8-3373-0923-1.ch014

1. INTRODUCTION

This chapter discusses the role that 4.0 technologies can play in achieving sustainability goals throughout the supply chain (SC).

First, a conceptual approach that focuses on the SC in its different dimensions is presented. In the second part, the most important technologies of Industry 4.0 are briefly examined both technically and functionally. The third section is mainly devoted to the green SC. The main practices in this area are presented.

In the last part, Green Supply Chain 4.0 is dealt with in terms of reducing greenhouse gas emissions and social issues. We focus on the potential of each Technology 4.0 to achieve sustainability goals within SC. As a concrete example, we present at least one experiment for each 4.0 technology in a large international company that has led to the reduction of CO2 emissions and/or the preservation of the rights of stakeholders (employees, customers, suppliers, etc.).

2. GREEN SUPPLY CHAIN (GSC) CONCEPTUAL APPROACH

In the literature, we can distinguish several definitions of Supply Chain (SC) and Supply Chain Management (SCM). For the SC We can cite the definition of Lambert and Cooper (2000), that of Mentzer et al (2001), that of Chopra and Meindl (2004) and that of Simchi-Levi et al. (2019). Among the most recent we find the definition presented by Sunil Chopra, Peter Meindl [1] in 2020. According to which, an SC "is a network of facilities and distribution options that performs the functions of sourcing materials, processing those materials into intermediate and finished products, and distributing those finished products to customers." This definition emphasizes the interconnection of the different entities in the supply chain, from suppliers to manufacturers to customers, and the flow of materials and products through the network.

Overall, we can define the suppy chain as a network that brings together all the tasks and actors acting on the flows. This network has a common purpose and a leader who ensures the coordination and integration of the whole. It associates a company with its suppliers and customers with the aim of integrating and synchronizing flows.

In addition, to define SCM, we can propose Martin Christopher's definition[2] of "the management of upstream and downstream relationships with suppliers and customers in order to deliver superior customer value at a lower cost to SC as a whole".

We can also say that SCM corresponds to all the methods, techniques and tools used to optimize the Supply Chain. It consists of refocusing the organization on the needs of the customer.

At the level of Green Supply Chain Management (GSCM), we can distinguish at least 10 definitions between (2009 and 2020).[3] Among the most recent definitions we can consider the one according to which the GSCM is the "Integration of environmental factors in the management of the SC, including product design, procurement, production processes, distribution of the final product to customers and the end of life"[4] Another definition considered among the most comprehensive insofar as it takes into account the aspects, Environment, Flow, Coordination, Stakeholder, Relationship and Value "The objective of the GSCM concept is to minimize or mitigate the waste of resources (energy and materials) and negative environmental impacts (air, water and soil pollution) at all stages of a product's life cycle, from the development of raw materials to the use of the product by the customer and its disposal at the end of the product's life cycle".[5]

3. KEY INDUSTRY 4.0 TECHNOLOGIES

Our goal at this level is to present the essentials of the key technologies of Industry 4.0 or what we can call 4.0 technologies. Far from seeking exhaustiveness, only 4.0 technologies considered central will be covered (Amejwal et al., 2022).

3.1 Internet of Things (IoT)

The Internet of Things (IoT)[6] is a network of interconnected devices, things, and machines that are integrated with sensors, software, and connectivity to enable them to collect and exchange data over the internet (Arif et al., 2019; EL Jaouhari et al., 2022).

IoT services refer to the applications, platforms, and tools that enable the development, deployment, and management of IoT solutions. These services can include cloud-based data analytics, security and privacy solutions, and device management platforms.

The combination of IoT devices and services has the potential to transform many aspects of our lives, from smart homes and cities to healthcare and transportation (Moufad & Jawab, 2017). For example, IoT-enabled sensors can help monitor and optimize energy consumption in buildings, while smart traffic management systems can reduce traffic congestion and improve safety on roads. In healthcare, IoT devices can track patients' vital signs and help doctors remotely monitor and manage chronic diseases.

However, the widespread adoption of IoT also raises concerns about data security, privacy, and ownership. As more devices are connected to the internet, the potential for cyberattacks and data breaches is increasing, highlighting the need for strong security measures and regulations.

3.2 Artificial Intelligence (AI)7

Artificial intelligence (AI) is a field of computer science that focuses on creating intelligent machines that can perform tasks that typically require human intelligence, such as visual perception, speech recognition, decision-making, and natural language processing (Jabir & Jawab, 2011). The history of AI dates back to the mid-twentieth century, when researchers began exploring the possibility of creating machines that could think and learn like humans.

How AI works can be divided into two broad categories: machine learning and deep learning.

Machine learning: consists of training machines to learn from data without being explicitly programmed. This is usually done with the help of algorithms that can recognize patterns and make predictions based on the data on which they are trained.

Deep learning: involves training artificial neural networks to learn from data. These neural networks are modeled after the structure of the human brain and consist of layers of interconnected nodes that process and analyze data in a hierarchical manner. Deep learning has been particularly effective in areas such as computer vision, natural language processing, and speech recognition.

3.3 Big Data and Data Mining

Big data and data mining, big data analysis and data mining[8] are both related to the process of analyzing large and complex data sets. The three Vs of Big Data – volume, speed, and variety – also apply to both Big Data analytics and data mining.

Big data analytics refers to the process of reviewing large and complex data sets to uncover patterns, correlations, and other insights that can help inform decisions. This process involves the use of advanced analytics technologies, such as machine learning, to process and analyze data.

Data mining, on the other hand, is a subset of big data analytics. This involves the use of statistical and machine learning techniques to identify patterns and relationships in large and complex datasets. The goal of data mining is to extract insights and insights from data that can be used for performance improvement.

The three Vs of Big Data – volume, speed, and variety – are essential considerations for both Big Data Analytics and Data Mining.

The first V, volume, refers to the amount of data generated and collected. With the proliferation of digital devices and sensors, the amount of data generated is increasing at an exponential rate. The second V, velocity, refers to the speed at which data is generated and collected in real-time or near real-time. The third V, variety, refers to the different types and formats of data that are generated and collected. Data can come from a wide range of sources, such as social media, customer databases, and sensors. Each of these sources can use different data formats, making it difficult to integrate and analyze data effectively.

3.4 Blockchain

Blockchain[9] is a digital ledger that allows information to be stored and transferred securely and seamlessly without the need for a central authority. It is essentially a distributed database managed by a network of computers.

The basic idea of blockchain is that it allows multiple parties to access and maintain a single source of truth without the need for a central authority. Instead of relying on a single server or institution to verify transactions, blockchain uses a network of computers to collectively validate and record data (Khaoua et al., 2022).

This technology is characterized by a number of features that make it of great utility for a wide range of applications, including Cryptocurrency, Supply Chain, Digital Identity Verification, and Smart Contracts.

The Blockchain runs on a decentralized network of computers (Decentralization). There is no central checkpoint, every computer on the network has a copy of the blockchain ledger, and they all work together to ensure that the ledger is accurate and up-to-date.

On the blockchain, it is possible to see all the transactions that have taken place (Transparency), which allows for a high degree of transparency and accountability.

The cryptographic algorithms used by the blockchain make it very difficult for anyone to tamper with records or make unauthorized changes (Security). This makes blockchain a very secure way to store and transfer information.

Finally, once a transaction is added to the blockchain, it cannot be modified or deleted (Immutability). This means that the blockchain provides a permanent record of all the transactions that have taken place.

3.5 Machine Learning

Machine learning[10] is a subfield of artificial intelligence (AI) that allows machines to automatically learn from data and improve their performance on a specific task without being explicitly programmed. The goal of machine learning is to allow machines to automatically recognize patterns in data and use those patterns to make accurate predictions or decisions on new and unpublished data.

Machine Learning is used in several fields. Here we present some of the most relevant and widely used applications.

Natural language processing (NLP), which allows machines to understand, interpret, and generate human language. NLP is used in a variety of applications such as chatbots, virtual assistants, language translation, sentiment analysis, and speech recognition.

Image and video recognition, machine learning algorithms can be trained to recognize and classify images and videos. Applications include facial recognition, object detection, autonomous vehicles, and surveillance systems.

Recommendation systems, used in a variety of applications such as e-commerce, media, and social media to personalize the user experience (A. El Jaouhari et al., 2004). Machine learning algorithms analyze user behavior and make recommendations based on past interactions.

Also, machine learning is used to detect fraudulent transactions by analyzing data patterns. Banks and credit card companies use this technology to detect unusual activity in real-time and prevent fraud.

Machine learning is used in healthcare to diagnose diseases and develop personalized treatment plans. Algorithms analyze patient data to identify patterns that can help doctors predict which treatments will be most effective for each patient.

In transportation, machine learning is used to enable autonomous vehicles to recognize and react to different road conditions and obstacles. Autonomous vehicles use sensors to collect data about their surroundings, and machine learning algorithms analyze that data to make decisions about how to drive.

3.6 Augmented and Virtual Reality

Augmented reality (AR) and virtual reality (VR)[11] are two technologies that simulate reality[12], but they do so in different ways.

AR is a technology that overlays digital information or graphics on the real world. This is usually done using a camera and a screen, such as a smartphone or a pair of smart glasses. AR can be used to improve the user experience by adding additional information or visuals. For example, an AR app can be used to display information about a store's products when a customer points their smartphone camera at them, or it can be used to display directions and other information when a person is exploring a new city.

Virtual reality (VR) is a technology that creates a completely simulated environment that the user can interact with. This is usually done using a headset that covers the user's eyes and displays a virtual environment. VR technology can be used to create immersive experiences for gaming, education, or training. For example, a VR simulation could be used to train airplane pilots or to help medical students practice surgery.

3.7 Cloud Computing and Cloud Manufacturing

Cloud computing[13] is a technology that allows users to access and use computing resources (such as storage, processing power, and software) over the internet, rather than having to rely on local hardware or infrastructure. This makes it possible to access these resources from anywhere, at any time, as long as you have an internet connection.

There are many cloud computing practices, such as online storage (Google Drive, Dropbox and OneDrive) that allow you to store and access files from any location. Web applications (Salesforce, Slack and Zoom...) that allow access to powerful software tools on the Internet without having to install them locally on computers. Big data analytics, cloud providers such as Google Cloud and Amazon Web Services (AWS) provide powerful tools for processing and analyzing large amounts of data, which can be used for a variety of applications such as predicting customer behavior or optimizing business processes. Virtual machines, cloud providers like (AWS), and Microsoft Azure allow users to create and run virtual machines in the cloud, for hosting websites or running complex software applications.

Cloud manufacturing is a manufacturing model in which a company harnesses the power of cloud computing to share resources and collaborate with partners. A company can use cloud manufacturing to outsource the design and production of 3D printed parts to a 3D printing service provider instead of in-house manufacturing, saving time and money, while still getting high-quality 3D printed parts. It can be used to offer personalized products to customers. So, a furniture manufacturer can use it to collaborate with their customers on the design and production of custom furniture. In the supply chain, it can be used to collaborate with suppliers. A company can use it to share production schedules and coordinate deliveries with suppliers, as well as use it to have real-time visibility into inventory levels and help automate ordering and replenishment processes.

Figure 1. Global adoption rate of AI in supply chain and manufacturing companies (2022 and 2025).

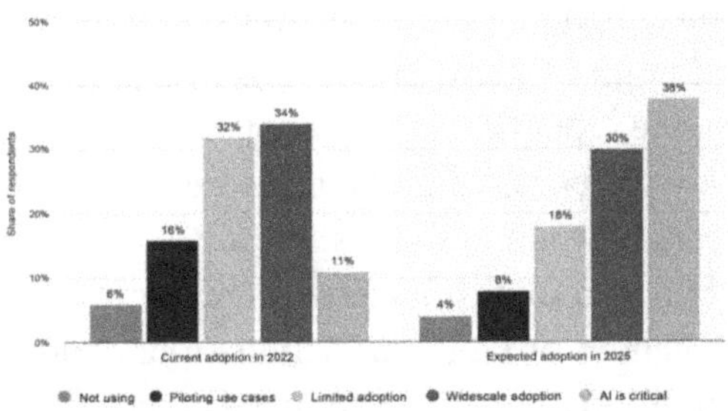

Source: Statista (2022).[14]

4. THE MAIN PRACTICES OF THE GSC

In this part we briefly present the main practices within the SC, which can have an undeniably positive impact on the environment. These practices have become necessary to contribute to the protection of the Planet. In fact, like all human activities and in the face of global warming, all the activities of the SC from the design to the destruction of products, including supply, production, distribution, transport, etc. are called upon to contribute to the objective declared by the COP 21 Conference of the Parties in Paris (2015), This objective is becoming more burdensome with the disastrous manifestations of global warming in recent years (drought, flooding in Sèvres and affecting more regions of the planet...) has been reiterated by the COP Conferences and which consists of limiting global warming to less than 2°C degrees Celsius compared to pre-industrial levels, and if possible at 1.5°C.

4.1 Green Product Design and Processes

It is about integrating the characteristics of sustainability into the design of products and into the processes that generate them. Industrial processes and processes cannot be designed solely on the basis of economic profitability, they must use clean technologies, consume renewable energy, reduce raw material and energy losses and ensure the recycling of products and by-products.

Products must use materials from renewable sources with little or no environmental impact. They will need to be replaced less frequently, in order to reduce the impact of replacement production. They must be reusable, recyclable and biodegradable... etc.

4.2 Green Procurement and Procurement

Green purchasing and procurement is "a purchase made by ensuring that the products and services acquired by an organization have the lowest negative impact and the most positive environmental, social, and economic impacts possible."[15]

In addition to the economic aspect (quality, costs and deadlines), they must take into account both environmental and social ethics aspects.

From an ecological point of view, purchasing and procurement processes must take energy efficiency, the reduction of greenhouse gas emissions, the preservation of resources (water, raw materials) and the maximum restriction of waste and pollutants as central criteria for their activities.

In terms of social ethics, purchasing and procurement must focus on respect for human rights, such as gender or racial discrimination, child labour, forced labour, etc. Also, working conditions must be retained as a criterion. These are safety at work, the right of expression, representation and remuneration....

The calculation of the purchase cost in the green purchasing approach must take into account the notion of life cycle cost, which retains, in addition to the overall cost of ownership, the external environmental costs generated by the purchase, such as air pollution or deforestation.

4.3 Supplier Environmental Collaboration

This is the selection of green suppliers, Green Supplier Relationship Management (GSRM) with the aim of improving the impact of suppliers in terms of environmental preservation (Tronnebati & Jawab, 2020). This includes assessing the environmental performance of suppliers, to ensure that the products and machinery they supply are made with materials and practices that are respectful of people and the environment.

The supplier management system must take into consideration, the management of hazardous substances, pollution control, the design of products for the environment, the certification of environmental management, the ability to project a green image and ensure green innovation.

4.4 Logistics, Transport and Green Packaging

For ecological reasons, companies must use eco-responsible means of transport using clean or renewable energy, optimize distribution networks and routes, as well as vehicle loading (Moufad and Jawab, 2017). They must reduce the number of vehicles used and the kilometres travelled, in addition to reducing inventory and the use of warehousing via cross-docking. Packaging, on the other hand, must be simple (reduce the amount of packaging), biodegradable, recyclable and free of petroleum-based materials (plastic).

4.5 Reverse Logistics

Being the "process of planning, implementing, and controlling the efficient and cost-effective flow of raw materials, in-process inventory, finished goods, and related information, from the point of consumption to the point of origin, with the aim of recovering or creating value, or properly disposing of them, Reverse logistics, with an objective of respect for the environment, focuses on the return of goods and materials for recycling, reuse, remanufacturing and the repair or responsible disposal of products and materials".[16]

4.6 Labeling and Certification

The GSC also involves the management of corporate environmental responsibility with the ISO 14000 family of standards: (14001, 14004, 14005). This family of standards aims to minimize negative environmental impacts on organizations, reduce the use of resources and waste, and improve quality. It must also indirectly influence all SC stakeholders to choose more sustainable activities. Corporate social responsibility, on the other hand, can refer to the ISO 26000 guideline.

4.7 Health and Safety

Companies that engage in a CSM approach must improve and maintain a high level of physical, emotional and social well-being among workers, as well as prevent work-related injuries. It is also a question of protecting employees against health risks and adapting the working environment to their physical and psychological needs (ISO 45001 - Occupational health and safety management systems).

4.8 Human Rights, Philanthropy and Working Conditions

As part of the respect for human rights, employees must have the opportunity to develop their careers and not be subject to sexual or racial discrimination....

Companies must demonstrate their social commitment and assistance through offer of donations and volunteering.

Working conditions must ensure the social well-being of employees by guaranteeing pay, rest time, holidays, and compliance with dismissal procedures and maternity allowance.

5. GREEN AND SUSTAINABLE SUPPLY CHAIN 4.0

The Green & Sustainable SC 4.0 refers to the next generation of sustainable SC, which incorporates advanced technologies to improve the sustainability of the SC. By leveraging these technologies, companies can reduce their impact on the environment and strengthen their social responsibility.

5.1 4.0 Technologies and CO2 Emission Reduction

5.1.1 The Internet of Things (IoT) and the Ecological Challenge

IoT devices can be used to monitor and optimize the use of energy, water, and other resources throughout the SC. This can help reduce waste and increase efficiency. It can play an important role in reducing CO2 emissions in the SC by providing real-time data and insights into the SC's operations, enabling informed decision-making to optimize processes and reduce the carbon footprint.

Thus, IoT sensors can be used in the field of predictive maintenance to monitor the performance of equipment and machines and detect potential problems before they occur. This can reduce downtime, minimize the need to transport spare parts, and reduce the need for emergency repairs, which often involve the use of additional resources and energy.

In logistics and transport, they can track shipments, optimize delivery routes and reduce the number of empty runs, reducing transport time and distance, minimizing fuel consumption and emissions. They also allow for real-time monitoring of inventory levels, which can help reduce overproduction and avoid unnecessary transportation of goods.

As an example, in 2014, Walmart announced that it was implementing an IoT-enabled fleet management system in its trucking operations. The system uses sensors and data analytics to optimize fuel efficiency and reduce CO2 emissions. By 2018, Walmart had achieved a 15% reduction in CO2 emissions from its fleet, attributed in part to the IoT-enabled fleet management system[17]. Also, in 2017, Maersk Line implemented the IoT-enabled container tracking system “Remote Container Management (RCM)” in its SC operations. The system uses sensors and data analytics to optimize shipping routes and reduce fuel consumption and CO2 emissions, and Maersk Line estimates that the system has the potential to reduce CO2 emissions by up to 20%.[18]

Also, IoT sensors can help ensure energy efficiency by monitoring energy consumption and identifying areas where energy consumption can be reduced. Thus, smart lighting systems can automatically adjust the lighting level according to the occupancy of premises in factories, distribution centers and warehouses.

For example, DHL implemented an IoT-enabled warehouse management system in its SC operations in 2015. The system uses sensors and data analytics to optimize energy consumption and reduce CO2 emissions. By 2018, DHL had achieved a 10% reduction in CO2 emissions from its warehouse operations, partially attributed to the IoT-enabled warehouse management system[19].

At the purchasing and procurement level, IoT sensors can be used to track and verify the sustainability of raw materials and purchased products. They can thus monitor the environmental impact of suppliers, which makes it possible to integrate the ecological issue into decision-making.

These IoT sensors can also monitor waste streams and identify opportunities to reduce waste and increase recycling.

5.1.2 Blockchain for Emissions Reduction

Blockchain technology has the potential to reduce CO2 emissions in the SC by enabling greater transparency and traceability of products and materials.

It can be used to track the origin of raw materials and ensure that they come from sustainable suppliers, helping to reduce environmental impact and encouraging responsible purchasing and sourcing practices.

Blockchain can also contribute to carbon neutrality. It can be used to create a tamper-proof digital ledger of carbon credits throughout the SC. These credits can be bought and sold on a global market. This can help companies offset their carbon emissions by investing in renewable energy or other sustainable initiatives.

Thus, CarbonX's Blockchain platform[20] for carbon offsets was launched in 2019 with the aim of enabling a transparent and secure exchange of carbon offsets, which can help reduce CO2 emissions. By using blockchain to track carbon offsets, the platform aims to reduce the risk of fraud and increase the efficiency of the carbon offset market.

Also, the World Wide Fund for Nature (WWF) under the aegis of the United Nations (UN) uses the CarbonX platform, among others, to eliminate illegal fishing in the tuna industry. CarbonX turns greenhouse gas emission reductions into a cryptocurrency. The latter can be bought and sold, providing manufacturers and consumers with a financial incentive to make more sustainable and planet-friendly choices.[21]

Within the SC, blockchain can help optimize transportation by tracking the movement of goods and materials, allowing for more efficient transportation and reducing the number of empty trips.

TradeLens, a blockchain-based platform that aims to digitize and streamline global trade, was launched by Maerks and IBM in 2018. The platform uses smart contracts and other blockchain technologies to improve transparency, security, and efficiency in the supply chain. TradeLens[22] allowed shippers, freight forwarders, customs agents, and other stakeholders to access real-time information on the status of their shipments, which can help reduce delays and optimize transportation routes.[23]

Also, in 2019, Walmart required its leafy greens suppliers to use a blockchain-based system to track and trace their products. The system, which was developed in partnership with IBM, allows Walmart and its suppliers to quickly and accurately trace the origin of contaminated food in the event of a foodborne illness outbreak.

Using blockchain technology, the system can track a product's journey throughout the SC from farm to store, providing greater transparency and accountability. The story began in 2016, when Walmart wanted to trace a package of sliced mangoes back to the source. It took 6 days, 18 hours and 26 minutes to achieve this. After partnering with IBM to create a food traceability system based on the Hyperledger Fabric blockchain, Walmart was able to trace mangoes stored in its U.S. stores in 2.2 seconds[24].

At the energy management level, blockchain can be used to track energy consumption in warehouses and other facilities, allowing companies to identify areas where energy consumption can be reduced. This can help reduce the carbon footprint of SC operations.

In 2018, Power Ledger, an Australian blockchain-based energy trading platform, partnered with BSES Rajdhani Power Limited (BRPL) to launch a peer-to-peer solar energy trading platform in India. The platform aimed to allow households with solar panels to sell excess energy to their neighbors and earn money through a blockchain-based transaction system.[25]

Blockchain can also help reduce waste throughout the SC, by tracking the movement of waste, allowing companies to identify opportunities for waste reduction and recycling. In 2016, Plastic Bank, a social enterprise, launched a blockchain-based platform in Haiti that encourages the collection and recycling of plastic waste. The platform allows individuals to exchange plastic waste for digital tokens that can be used to purchase goods and services.[26]

Also, in 2020, Ecolytiq, a German startup, launched a blockchain-based platform that tracks the carbon footprint of waste management activities. The platform allows waste management companies to measure, verify and report their carbon emissions, helping them reduce their environmental impact.[27]

5.1.3 Artificial Intelligence (AI) at the Service of the Environment

in turn, can help reduce CO2 emissions in the SC by optimizing operations and enabling more efficient use of resources. For example, in the field of predictive maintenance, AI algorithms can analyze sensor data to predict when equipment will need maintenance or repair. This can help prevent outages and reduce the need for emergency repairs, which often involve the use of additional resources and energy. In transportation, AI can be used to optimize transport routing and scheduling, reducing the number of empty runs and optimizing routes to minimize fuel consumption and emissions.

In 2019, UPS implemented an AI-powered delivery route optimization system in its logistics operations, which enabled the reduction of fuel consumption and CO2 emissions[28].

AI can also help achieve sustainability goals in inventory and energy management. At the inventory level, AI algorithms can analyze demand data and optimize inventory levels in real-time, which can help reduce overproduction and avoid unnecessary transportation of goods. At the energy level, these algorithms can analyze data on energy consumption in warehouses and distribution centers, and identify areas where energy consumption can be reduced through the use of more efficient equipment and lighting.

AI can be used to analyze the environmental impact of products throughout their lifecycle, helping companies make more sustainable design decisions and optimize their SCs accordingly.

In 2020, L'Oréal implemented an AI-based sustainability dashboard in its manufacturing operations. The dashboard uses AI to track and analyze energy consumption, water consumption, and waste generation. By using AI to monitor and optimize its sustainability performance, L'Oréal has been able to reduce its carbon footprint and achieve more sustainable operations.

In its 2020 Sustainability Report, L'Oréal reported that compared to 2005 it had reduced its carbon emissions by 81% and that it had achieved its goal of sending zero waste to landfill from its factories and distribution centers. The company also reported that it had made progress toward its goal of reducing water consumption in its factories by 49% per finished product in 2020[29].

5.1.4 Renewable Energy to Reduce Emissions

Renewable energy can be used in a variety of ways in the CS to reduce greenhouse gas emissions and promote sustainable development.

First, renewable energy sources such as solar panels and wind turbines can be installed on the roofs of warehouses and distribution centers to produce clean energy, reducing dependence on non-renewable energy sources and reducing emissions.

Secondly, electric vehicles can be used for transport within the SC, reducing the carbon footprint of shipping and logistics. These can be trucks, pickup trucks, and even electric drones.

Finally, companies can purchase renewable energy credits or carbon offsets to offset their emissions and promote the use of renewable energy sources. This can help fund renewable energy projects and promote sustainability throughout the SC.

In March 2021, FedEx Corp[30], which has the world's largest cargo airline, announced its goal of global carbon neutrality by 2040.

To achieve this goal, FedEx plans to invest more than $2 billion in three key areas: vehicle electrification, sustainable energy and carbon sequestration.

5.1.5 Big Data and Sustainable SC

The use of Big Data can also be beneficial for the control of CO2 emissions in the SC.

Already in 2011, Schneider Electric launched its Big Data platform "EcoStruxure Resource Advisor". This platform collects, analyzes, and visualizes energy data to help companies make informed decisions about energy management and sustainability on a global scale.

With this platform, Schneider Electric can identify sources of energy waste and take steps to optimize resource use and reduce greenhouse gas emissions. The company can also monitor the energy consumption of its facilities in real time and detect anomalies to remedy them quickly.

In its 2020 report, the company claims "in 2018 and 2019, we supported our customers on their sustainability journey, helping them save nearly 90 million tons of CO2, ... For our part, we have made decisive long-term commitments: in 2025 we will have achieved carbon neutrality (...) in our medium-voltage equipment, in 2030 we will be net zero, and we will operate a net-zero carbon SC in 2050."[31]

5.1.6 Augmented Reality and Virtual Reality in the Face of CO2 Emissions in the SC

Both AR and VR can be used to reduce CO2 emissions in the supply chain.

Virtual reality makes it possible to simulate logistics and production processes, providing a better understanding of operations. Businesses can use these simulations to identify inefficiencies and bottlenecks. For example, by using VR to simulate an SC, companies can identify areas where products would be stored for too long or process steps that would take too long. By making improvements to these areas, companies can therefore reduce the waste of resources, reducing production time and optimizing energy use, thereby reducing CO2 emissions. VR can also be used to train staff and avoids travel and travel that causes CO2 emissions. Also, employees can interact with virtual objects to learn how to handle pallets, forklifts and other equipment. In addition to eliminating the reasons for travel, VR helps to avoid accidents for employees in training.

AR makes it possible to visualize stock levels in real time, by simply placing a smartphone or tablet in front of the products. This can help employees quickly locate needed items, check stock levels, and detect errors. AR also helps guide employees through the warehouse to quickly pick up orders, showing them the most convenient path to follow.

Augmented reality can be used to optimize the use of warehouse space. Employees can use 3D visualizations to plan item placement and minimize unnecessary travel.

In 2015, DHL launched a pilot project (DHL's AR-Powered Warehouse Operations) to test the use of augmented reality in its warehouse operations. The AR system used smart glasses to guide workers through warehouse tasks, such as picking and packing orders. By using AR to improve worker efficiency and accuracy, DHL was able to reduce the time and energy required to complete warehouse operations, resulting in reduced CO2 emissions. According to DHL, the use of augmented reality in its warehouse operations has resulted in a 25% improvement in the picking process[32], which would reduce CO2 emissions compared to traditional warehouses.

5.1.7 Ecology in the Face of Robotics and Automation

Robotics and automation are technologies that involve the use of robots and machines to perform tasks that are typically performed by humans. These technologies have been widely used in the SC to improve efficiency and reduce costs, and in recent years they have also been used to reduce CO2 emissions.

APM Terminals (APMT, Maersk group) inaugurated its automated container terminal in April 2015 on land reclaimed from the sea in Rotterdam. Automated systems, which include cranes, trucks, and other machinery, are controlled by software and can operate 24 hours a day with minimal human intervention. They work taking into account the workload plan of each shipowner.

At the APMT terminal, containers are not transported by riders who use diesel but by electric vehicles, guided by sensors and equipped with batteries. Robots programmed to leave the park every eight hours and go to the swap station where their battery is automatically replaced! The terminal emits no CO2 or nitrogen oxides and runs on renewable energy, particularly from offshore wind farms in the North Sea.[33]

5.1.8 Cloud Computing and SC Durable

In 2016, UPS implemented a cloud-based route optimization system called ORION (On-Road Integrated Optimization and Navigation). ORION uses advanced algorithms to create the most efficient routes for delivery trucks based on various factors such as package volume, vehicle capacity, traffic patterns, and road restrictions. The ORION system analyzes real-time data from GPS units installed in UPS delivery trucks, as well as customer location data and delivery schedules, to provide drivers with the most efficient routes possible. ORION helps reduce fuel consumption, carbon emissions, and transportation costs, while improving delivery times and customer satisfaction. In addition to optimizing routes, ORION also provides drivers with turn-by-turn navigation instructions, real-time traffic updates, and other tools to help them navigate complex delivery routes and avoid traffic congestion.

Through its implementation, UPS was able to reduce its annual fuel consumption by 1.5 million gallons and CO2 emissions by 14,000 tons.[34]

5.2 Technologies 4.0 and Social Ethics in SC

5.2.1 IoT and Social Issues

The Internet of Things (IoT) is used in SC to improve working conditions and to protect the human rights of employees.

In 2017, DHL implemented IoT technology in its warehouses to monitor employees' working conditions, such as temperature and humidity levels. Unilever implemented IoT technology in its factories in 2018 to monitor worker safety and prevent accidents. The technology included sensors and wearable devices that tracked workers' movements and provided alerts if they were at risk of injury.

In 2019, UPS implemented IoT technology in its delivery trucks to monitor driver safety and prevent accidents. The technology included sensors and cameras that tracked the driver's behavior, such as whether they were wearing a seat belt or driving too fast.

We can also envisage the installation of sensors that monitored air quality and noise levels, as is the case with Fairphone[35] in 2015.

On a social level, the Internet of Things (IoT) can improve working conditions in SC on several levels. They can improve worker safety by monitoring working conditions, identifying potential hazards, and alerting workers and management to potential safety risks. As an example, sensors can detect high levels of gases or chemicals in the workplace and trigger alarms or automatically shut down equipment.

They can also help improve ergonomics by tracking workers' movements and activities and providing feedback on posture, lifting techniques, and other ergonomic factors, which can prevent injuries and reduce worker fatigue.

IoT devices can help streamline workflows. By automating repetitive tasks, they free up workers to focus on more complex and meaningful tasks. This can reduce the risk of repetitive motion injuries and improve job satisfaction.

Also, IoT-based assistance systems can provide workers with instant (real-time) access to resources and information about worker performance that allows them to adapt their behavior and improve their productivity.

5.2.2 Big Data and Human Rights

Big Data analytics can be used to protect the human rights of SC employees. By analyzing large amounts of data from a variety of sources, companies can identify potential labor violations and other issues, and take action to address them. This is the case for Apple (2014), [36]Adidas (2015),[37] Walmart (2019)[38] and many other world-famous companies that have used big data analysis programs. In the majority of cases, these programs used data from worker surveys, factory inspections, and many other sources to identify and remedy potential violations of employee rights.

5.2.3 Artificial Intelligence and Human Rights

Artificial intelligence (AI) has been used in SC to protect the human rights of employees. In general, it is a question of setting up AI-powered risk management platforms for the SC to monitor the working conditions in its SC. These platforms used AI algorithms to analyze data from multiple sources, including supplier self-assessments, audit reports, worker surveys, social media, and news chapters, to identify potential labor violations. This is the case for Nestlé (2021)[39] and Unilever (2020).[40]

5.2.4 Blockchain and Human Rights at Work

Blockchain can be used in SC to protect the human rights of employees. By providing transparency and traceability, companies can ensure that their products are ethically sourced and do not contribute to human rights violations, conflict, or other unethical practices. It is in this sense that De Beers set up the blockchain-based platform “Tracr” in 2018[41] to track diamonds from the mine to the retailer and help prevent the trade in “blood diamonds”.

Also, the blockchain-based platform “Chain of Origin” was set up by Nestlé 2020 to track milk from farm to factory[42].

5.2.5 Artificial Intelligence for the Selection and Evaluation of Sustainable Suppliers

AI-powered platforms can be used in SC for sustainable supplier selection. By analyzing large amounts of data from multiple sources, companies can identify sustainable suppliers and potential sustainability risks, and take steps to improve the sustainability of their SC.

Here we note the case of IBM's AI-powered platform “Supplier IQ” (2019),[43] justified by a growing consumer interest in supply chain transparency[44]. This is also the case of “EcoStruxure Supply Chain Advisor” developed by Schneider Electric in 2018 which uses artificial intelligence (AI) to improve energy and environmental performance in buildings and infrastructure. It can be used to collect and analyze data on equipment and processes throughout the supply chain, to identify energy inefficiencies and greenhouse gas emissions. This information can help businesses make informed decisions about how to reduce their environmental impact and minimize the costs associated with energy consumption.

In 2018, IBM Watson launched its Cognitive Supplier Assistant (CoSA) tool that uses natural language processing (NLP) and machine learning algorithms to analyze supplier data and provide recommendations for sustainable sourcing.

SAP Ariba launched its Supplier Risk solution[45], which uses AI to assess supplier risk across multiple categories, including sustainability since 2013. The tool analyzes supplier data and provides a risk score, which can help procurement teams identify potential sustainability risks.

6. CONCLUSION

In conclusion, the use of 4.0 technologies in the green supply chain offers considerable potential to improve the efficiency, sustainability and transparency of the SC. Companies that commit to adopting these technologies can not only reduce their environmental impact, but also gain competitive advantages by improving their operational efficiency and brand image with environmentally conscious consumers.

Through the use of IoT sensors, real-time data analytics, blockchain, and process automation, companies can improve visibility, monitor, and optimize their SC to reduce greenhouse gas emissions, ensure human rights compliance, minimize waste, and maximize resource utilization.

For this reason, companies must engage in a gradual transition process that requires significant investments in terms of technology and staff qualifications. Ultimately, the use of 4.0 technologies in the green supply chain is a crucial step towards a sustainable economy and a greener planet for future generations.

REFERENCES

Amejwal, M., El Jaouhari, A., Arif, J., Fellaki, S., & Jawab, F. (2022, May). Production flow management based on Industry 4.0 technologies. In 2022 14th International Colloquium of Logistics and Supply Chain Management (LOGISTIQUA) (pp. 1-7). IEEE.

Arif, J., El Farouk, I. I., Mouzouna, Y., & Jawab, F. (2019, March). The use of internet of things (IoT) applications in the logistics outsourcing: Smart RFID tag as an example. In *Proceedings of the International Conference on Industrial Engineering and Operations Management* (pp. 5-7).

Arif, J., & Jawab, F. (2011, May). Outsourcing logistics: strategic tools for decision to outsource logistic activities. In 2011 4th International Conference on Logistics (pp. 104-108). IEEE. DOI: 10.1109/LOGISTIQUA.2011.5939410

Chopra, S., & Meindl, P. (2004). *Supply Chain Management: Strategy, Planning, and Operation* (2nd ed.). Person and Prentice Hall.

Chopra, S. & Meindl, P. (2020). Supply Chain Management: Strategy, Planning, and Operation.

El Jaouhari, A., Azari, M., Arif, J., El Farouk, I. I., Jawab, F., & Moufad, I. (2022, May). IoT for the future of sustainable supply chain management in Industry 4.0: A Systematic Literature Review. In 2022 14th International Colloquium of Logistics and Supply Chain Management (LOGISTIQUA) (pp. 1-6). IEEE.

El Jaouhari, A., Samadhiya, A., Kumar, A., Šešplaukis, A., & Raslanas, S. (2024). Mapping the landscape: A systematic literature review on automated valuation models and strategic applications in real estate. *International Journal of Strategic Property Management, 28*(5), 286–301. DOI: 10.3846/ijspm.2024.22251

Jaouhari, A. E., & Arif, J. (2024). Artificial intelligence of things and circular warehouse process management of automotive parts: Conceptual framework and practice review. *International Journal of Process Management and Benchmarking, 17*(1), 109–135. DOI: 10.1504/IJPMB.2024.137789

Jaouhari, A. E., Arif, J., Samadhiya, A., Kumar, A., & Trinkūnas, V. (2023). Are we there or do we have more to do? Metaverse in facility management and future prospects. *International Journal of Strategic Property Management, 27*(3), 159–175. DOI: 10.3846/ijspm.2023.19516

Jasrotia, S. S., Rai, S. S., Rai, S., & Giri, S. (2024). Stage-wise green supply chain management and environmental performance: Impact of blockchain technology. *International Journal of Information Management Data Insights, 4*(2), 100241. DOI: 10.1016/j.jjimei.2024.100241

Javaid, M., Haleem, A., Singh, R. P., Khan, S., & Suman, R. (2021). Blockchain technology applications for Industry 4.0: A literature-based review. *Blockchain Res. Appl., 2021*(2), 100027. DOI: 10.1016/j.bcra.2021.100027

Kamble, S. S., Gunasekaran, A., Kumar, V., Belhadi, A., & Foropon, C. (2021). A machine learning based approach for predicting blockchain adoption in the supply Chain. *Technological Forecasting and Social Change, 2021*(163), 120465. DOI: 10.1016/j.techfore.2020.120465

Kashem, M. A., Shamsuddoha, M., Nasir, T., & Chowdhury, A. A. (2023). Supply Chain Disruption Versus Optimization: A Review on Artificial Intelligence and Blockchain. *Knowledge (Beverly Hills, Calif.), 2023*(3), 80–96. DOI: 10.3390/knowledge3010007

Kassel, K., & Rimanoczy, I. (Eds.). (2018). *Developing a Sustainability Mindset in Management Education*. Routledge. DOI: 10.4324/9781351063340

Khaoua, Y., Mouzouna, Y., Arif, J., Jawab, F., & Azari, M. (2022, May). The contribution of blockchain technology in the supply chain management: The shipping industry as an example. In 2022 14th International Colloquium of Logistics and Supply Chain Management (LOGISTIQUA) (pp. 1-6). IEEE.

Kholaif, M. M. N. H. K., Xiao, M., & Hamdy, A. (2023). 'Covid-19's effect on green supply chains and environmental sustainability; innovative technologies moderation'. *Journal of Cleaner Production, 406*, 137083. DOI: 10.1016/j.jclepro.2023.137083

Koh, L., Dolgui, A., & Sarkis, J. (2020). Blockchain in transport and logistics—Paradigms and transitions. *International Journal of Production Research, 2020*(7), 58, 2054, 2062. DOI: 10.1080/00207543.2020.1736428

Kouhizadeh, M., Saberi, S., & Sarkis, J. (2021). Blockchain technology and the sustainable supply chain: Theoretically exploring adoption barriers'. *International Journal of Production Economics, 231*, 107831. DOI: 10.1016/j.ijpe.2020.107831

Lambert, D. M., & Cooper, M. C. (2000). Issues in Supply Chain Management. *Industrial Marketing Management, 29*(1), 65–83. DOI: 10.1016/S0019-8501(99)00113-3

Marshall, D., McCarthy, L., McGrath, P., & Claudy, M. (2015). Going above and beyond: How sustainability culture and entrepreneurial orientation drive social sustainability supply chain practice adoption. *Supply Chain Management*, *20*(4), 434–454. DOI: 10.1108/SCM-08-2014-0267

Mat Ishah, N. S., Lee, K. L., & Nawanir, G. (2023). Educational supply chain sustainability'. *Asian Education and Development Studies*, *12*(2/3), 137–149. DOI: 10.1108/AEDS-09-2022-0123

Mentzer, J., Dewitt, W., Keebler, J., Min, S., Nix, N., Smith, C., & Zacharia, Z. (2001). Defining Supply Chain Management. *Journal of Business Logistics*, *22*(2), 1–25. DOI: 10.1002/j.2158-1592.2001.tb00001.x

Mohsen, M. (2023). Impact of Artificial Intelligence on Supply Chain Management Performance. *Journal of Service Science and Management*, *16*(1), 44–58. DOI: 10.4236/jssm.2023.161004

Mollenkopf, D. A., Ozanne, L. K., & Stolze, H. J. (2021). A transformative supply chain response to COVID-19′. *Journal of Service Management*, *32*(2), 190–202. DOI: 10.1108/JOSM-05-2020-0143

Moufad, I., & Jawab, F. (2017). Conception and validation of a decision support model for Urban Freight Transport. In 2017 International Colloquium on Logistics and Supply Chain Management (LOGISTIQUA) (pp. 94-99). IEEE. DOI: 10.1109/LOGISTIQUA.2017.7962880

Narkhede, G., Pasi, B., Rajhans, N., & Kulkarni, A. (2023). Industry 5.0 and the future of sustainable manufacturing: A systematic literature review'. *Business Strategy & Development*, *6*(4), 704–723. DOI: 10.1002/bsd2.272

Piccarozzi, M., Silvestri, C., Fici, L., & Silvestri, L. (2024). Metaverse: A possible sustainability enabler in the transition from Industry 4.0 to 5.0′. *Procedia Computer Science*, *232*, 1839–1848. DOI: 10.1016/j.procs.2024.02.006

Rieder, E., & Schmuck, M. (2024). Will Industry 5.0 have a serious impact on processes in companies? A scientific look at the changes that could accompany Industry 5.0′. *Procedia Computer Science*, *237*, 742–750. DOI: 10.1016/j.procs.2024.05.161

Schinckus, C. (2020). The good, the bad and the ugly: An overview of the sustainability of blockchain technology'. *Energy Research & Social Science*, *69*, 101614. DOI: 10.1016/j.erss.2020.101614

Sharma, R., & Gupta, H. (2024). Leveraging cognitive digital twins in Industry 5.0 for achieving strategies'. *Journal of Cleaner Production*, *448*, 141364. DOI: 10.1016/j.jclepro.2024.141364

Silveira Ramalho, T., & De Fátima Martins, M. (2022). Sustainable human resource management in the supply chain: A new framework'. *Cleaner Logistics and Supply Chain*, *5*, 100075. DOI: 10.1016/j.clscn.2022.100075

Simchi-Levi, D., Trichakis, N., & Zhang, P. Y. (2019). Designing response supply chain against bioattacks. *Operations Research*, *67*(5), 1246–1268. DOI: 10.1287/opre.2019.1862

Statista (2022). Artificial Intelligence (AI) Adoption Rate in Supply Chain and Manufacturing Businesses Worldwide in 2022 and 2025.

Strand, V., Lotfi, M., Flynn, A., & Walker, H. (2024). A systematic literature review of modern slavery in supply chain management: State of the art, framework development and research opportunities'. *Journal of Cleaner Production*, *435*, 140301. DOI: 10.1016/j.jclepro.2023.140301

Tronnebati, I., & Jawab, F. (2020, December). The similarities and differences between the green and sustainable supply chain management definitions and factors: A literature review. In 2020 IEEE 13th International Colloquium of Logistics and Supply Chain Management (LOGISTIQUA) (pp. 1-6). IEEE. DOI: 10.1109/LOGISTIQUA49782.2020.9353939

Tronnebati, I., & Jawab, F. (2024). The impact of green and sustainable supply chain management practices on sustainable performance: A comparative analysis. *International Journal of Logistics Systems and Management*, *47*(3), 267–294. DOI: 10.1504/IJLSM.2024.136855

Wolf, J. (2014). The relationship between sustainable supply chain management, stakeholder pressure and corporate sustainability performance. *Journal of Business Ethics*, *119*(3), 317–328. DOI: 10.1007/s10551-012-1603-0

Yontar, E. (2023). The role of blockchain technology in the sustainability of supply chain management: Grey based Dematel implementation. *Cleaner Logistics and Supply Chain*, *8*, 100113. DOI: 10.1016/j.clscn.2023.100113

Zaalouk, A., Moon, S., & Han, S. (2023). Operations planning and scheduling in off-site construction supply chain management: Scope definition and future directions'. *Automation in Construction*, *153*, 104952. DOI: 10.1016/j.autcon.2023.104952

ENDNOTES

1 Sunil Chopra, Peter Meindl, “Supply Chain Management: Strategy, Planning, and Operation”; 10 October 2000.

2 Martin Christopher, Logistics and Supply Chain Management; Pearson Education Limited; 4th edition 2011

3 Imane TRONNEBATI, Fouad JAWAB; Green and Sustainable Supply Chain Management: A Comparative Literature Review. Jordan Journal of Mechanical and Industrial Engineering; Volume 17, Number 1 (ISSN 1995-6665) 2023.

4 M. J. F. S. L. B. a. T. G. Luai Jraisata, “No Actor is an Island: The Role of Partnerships in Sustainable Value Chains,” Jordan Journal of Mechanical and Industrial Engineering, vol. 16, no. 12, pp. 163-174, 2022.

5 J.B. Edwards, A.C. McKinnon, S.L. Cullinane., “Comparative analysis of the carbon footprints of conventional and online retailing: a 'last mile' perspective,” International Journal of Physical Distribution and Logistics Management, vol. 40, no. %11–2), pp. 103–123, 2010.

6 Ammar Rayes et al, e-bock “Internet of Things From Hype to Reality: The Road to Digitization” from., 2019, Springer

7 Russell, S. J., & Norvig, P. (2020). Artificial intelligence: a modern approach (4th ed.). Pearson Education -

8 Chen, H., Chiang, R. H. L., & Storey, V. C. (2012). Business intelligence and analytics: From big data to big impact.- https://www.jstor.org/stable/41703503

9 Tapscott, D., & Tapscott, A. Blockchain revolution: How the technology behind bitcoin is changing money, business, and the world. Penguin; Portfolio; Reprint edition 2018

10 Alom, M. Z., Yakopcic, C., Taha, T. M., Asari, V. K. & Al; A state-of-the-art survey on deep learning theory and architectures. MDPI Electronics 2019.

11 Digital Trends, by Luke Dormehl, 2021, https://www.digitaltrends.com/cool-tech/what-is-augmented-reality/

12 Jitendra Kumar Verma; Sudip Paul; Advances in Augmented Reality and Virtual Reality; Springer 2022

13 M.N. Abd Rahman, B. Medjahed, E. Orady, M.R. Muhamad, R. Abdullah and A.S.M. Jaya. A REVIEW OF CLOUD MANUFACTURING: ISSUES

AND OPPORTUNITIES; Journal of Advanced Manufacturing Technology (JAMT)2018.

14 Statista (2022). Artificial Intelligence (AI) Adoption Rate in Supply Chain and Manufac- turing Businesses Worldwide in 2022 and 2025. https://www.statista.com/statistics/1346717/ai-function-adoption-rates-business-supply-chains/

15 ISO 20400 standard

16 CIRCULAR BUILDING; F. Fontaine & B. Dewulf; Brussels Environment • February 2021

17 2019- Environmental, Social & Governance Report (https://corporate.walmart.com/esg-report-2019/transportation)

18 Emmanuel Mair; Shippers of high-value cargo have long demanded greater visibility in their supply chains. Smart devices are now delivering solutions; 2020 Vision; NOVEMBER 2018.

19 INTERNET OF THINGS IN LOGISTICS "A COLLABORATIVE REPORT BY DHL AND CISCO ON IMPLICATIONS ANDUSE CASES FOR THE LOGISTICS INDUSTRY"; Deutsche Post DHL Group "Corporate Responsibility Report 2018"(https://www.dhl.com/content/dam/dhl/global/core/documents/pdf/glo-corporate-responsibility-report.pdf)

20 https://www.carbonx.ca/#introducing-carbonx

21 Finance News Weekly of 03 July 2021 - By admin (https://fnh.ma/article/developpement-durable/protection-de-l-environnement-les-promesses-de-la-technologie-blockchain)

22 https://www.tradelens.com/

23 While the TradeLens platform was viable, the need for full global industry collaboration was not achieved. As a result, TradeLens has not reached the level of business viability necessary to continue working and meet financial expectations as an independent company. As a result, there is an intention for the platform to go offline towards the end of the first quarter of 2023

24 https://tech.walmart.com/content/walmart-global-tech/en_us/news/articles/blockchain-in-the-food-supply-chain.html

25 https://www.powerledger.io/clients/bses-rajdhani-india

26 https://plasticbank.com/

27 https://ecolytiq.com/

28 UPS To Enhance ORION With Continuous Delivery Route Optimization (https://about.ups.com/us/en/newsroom/press-releases/innovation-driven/ups-to-enhance-orion-with-continuous-delivery-route-optimization.html)

29 LOREAL 2020 Annual Report (https://www.loreal.com/-/media/project/loreal/brand-sites/corp/master/lcorp/documents-media/publications/annual-reports/loreal2020annualreport.pdf)

30 FedEx, "FedEx Commits to Carbon-Neutral Operations by 2040," 2020. Available at: https://newsroom.fedex.com/newsroom/asia-english/sustainability2021

31 2019 Universal Registration Document, FINANCIAL REPORT AND SUSTAINABLE DEVELOPMENT (https://www.se.com/ww/fr/assets/342/document/124836/annual-report-2019-fr.pdf)

32 https://www.dhl.com/global-en/delivered/digitalization/dhl-successfully-tests-augmented-reality-application-in-warehouse.html

33 L'Usine nouvelle, 27 August 2015. https://www.usinenouvelle.com/article/avec-les-robots-du-port-de-rotterdam.N345781

34 UPS will enhance ORION with continuous optimization of delivery routes; https://about.ups.com/us/en/newsroom/press-releases/innovation-driven/ups-to-enhance-orion-with-continuous-delivery-route-optimization.html

35 Dutch smartphone manufacturer

36 Apple Supplier Responsibility 2014 Progress Report. https://www.apple.com/supplier-responsibility/pdf/Apple_SR_2014_Progress_Report.pdf

37 Sustainability progressreport for 2015. https://www.adidas-group.com/media/filer_public/9c/f3/9cf3db44-b703-4cd0-98c5-28413f272aac/2015_sustainability_progress_report.pdf

38 2019 Environmental, Social & Governance Report. https://corporate.walmart.com/media-library/document/2019-environmental-social-governance-report/_proxyDocument?id=0000016a-9485-d766-abfb-fd8d84300000

39 Nestlé's human rights framework and roadmap. https://www.nestle.com/sites/default/files/2021-12/nestle-human-rights-framework-roadmap.pdf

40 Human Rights report 2020. https://www.unilever.com/files/origin/1c684e01e7fd1f5e9a9a9142ce34801136320eba.pdf/unilever-human-rights-report-2020-supplier-audit-update.pdf

41 https://www.debeersgroup.com/sustainability-and-ethics/leading-ethical-practices-across-the-industry/tracr

42 https://www.forbes.com/sites/amazonwebservices/2019/12/12/nestles-chain-of-origin-coffee-brings-supply-chain-transparency-with-amazon-managed-blockchain/?sh=70d4b33f193b

43 https://www.supplieriq.us/

44 In an IBM survey in the U.S., 94% of consumers surveyed said they would be more loyal to a brand that offered full transparency, and 63% said they would pay up to 36% more for products that were responsibly made and sourced transparently. https://www.ibm.com/products/supply-chain-intelligence-suite/food-trust)

45 https://www.sap.com/products/spend-management/supplier-risk.html

Section 4
Resilience, Sustainability, and Strategic Integration of AI

Chapter 15
Transformative Artificial Intelligence for Sustainable Supply Chains:
Optimizing Green Logistics and Circular Economy

Ananya Pandey
https://orcid.org/0000-0002-2419-6314
Christ University, Bangalore, India

ABSTRACT

Artificial intelligence (AI) is revolutionizing supply chain management by providing ways to improve operational effectiveness and sustainability. In supply chain operations, businesses can decrease waste, and lower carbon footprints by utilizing machine learning, predictive analytics, and decision-making. As environmental concerns grow, industries are using AI technologies more and more to improve supply chains' sustainability, efficiency, and transparency. AI greatly enhances distribution and transportation networks by assisting with fuel efficiency, route planning, and emission monitoring via green logistics. Furthermore, by making it easier to reuse, recycle, and remanufacture things, AI advances circular economy models. It helps companies make the shift from linear to circular production systems by forecasting product lifecycle stages and controlling material flows. Keeping in view the above, this chapter analyzes the critical role of AI in shaping future supply chains, where economic performance aligns with environmental stewardship, fostering a more sustainable global economy.

DOI: 10.4018/979-8-3373-0923-1.ch015

INTRODUCTION

Across all industries, sustainability has become a top corporate objective, making it difficult for businesses to compete globally on sustainability. Sustainability was defined as "meeting the needs of the present without compromising the ability of future generations to meet their own needs" by the United Nations Brundtland Commission in 1987. Nearly 140 developing nations are currently looking for solutions to meet their development needs, but given the growing threat posed by climate change, significant efforts must be made to guarantee that current progress does not have an adverse effect on future generations (Luther, 2021). A supply chain that successfully and competitively incorporates moral and ecologically conscious behaviour is said to be sustainable. Transparency in the whole supply chain is essential; sustainability efforts must cover everything from the procurement of raw materials to last-mile logistics, as well as product returns and recycling procedures (Jadhav et al., 2019). The development of supply chain sustainability is being significantly influenced by digital transformation and the increasing complexity of digital supply chain technologies. Artificial intelligence (AI), big data management, advanced analytics, and security solutions like blockchain and RFID sensors have given contemporary supply chains previously unheard-of visibility and responsibility (Closs et al., 2011). Businesses are now far more able—and obligated—to share best practices for sustainable logistics and green supply chains, as well as to exhibit corporate social responsibility (Sanchez-Flores et al., 2020). In addition to promoting green operations, supply chain management sustainability initiatives within an organization's Corporate Social Responsibility (CSR) initiatives also save money and enhance the supply chain over time (Osei et al., 2023). Artificial Intelligence (AI) is used by businesses to improve worker safety, estimate demand for parts and components, track inventory, manage warehouse capacity, optimize shipping and delivery, and help maintain the integrity of transaction records across international supply chains (Boute & Udenio, 2022). Workflow management and optimization across practically every supply chain link is being greatly aided by these kinds of capabilities. For instance, supply chain systems that use machine learning algorithms can predict consumer demand more precisely, which results in more cost-effective inventory management, by identifying patterns and linkages in data sets that are frequently invisible to humans or non-AI systems. In order to suggest alternate shipping routes and lower the possibility of unforeseen delays, AI can also evaluate variables like traffic and weather (Islam et al., 2024). This improves delivery times. In order to identify inadequate quality control practices and health and safety infractions, it can monitor work environments. As supply chain experts continue to test the system, new use cases are continually being developed. Although AI has the potential to significantly increase supply chain productivity and reduce operating expenses, putting the technology into practice can be challenging and costly, particularly when it comes to training proprietary data to create custom machine learning models (Madancian et al., 2023). In order to prepare their supply chains for the integration of AI systems and the way these technologies can revolutionize the administration and operation of their logistics networks, manufacturers and logistics providers can take certain actions. In the light of the above perspective, this chapter aims to explain the context of sustainability in supply chain management with the use of AI. It further explores the need of management and enhancement in the supply chain with green technology, green logistics and integrated circular economy practices. Also, a need towards collaboration across industries for global impact and scaling AI solutions for long-term sustainability is analyzed.

FOUNDATIONS OF SUSTAINABLE SUPPLY CHAINS

Governments, investors, workers, and consumers have all increased pressure on businesses to act more socially and environmentally responsible in recent years. The business case for sustainable operations is becoming stronger every year at the same time (Rafi, 2022). Since supply chains consume a lot of money and resources and are often a source of needless waste, they have gained attention from many businesses. Sustainability of the supply chain has therefore become a major corporate objective. Businesses are now measuring how their products and services affect society and the environment at every stage of their life cycles (Mefford, 2011). The objective is to have a beneficial influence on the people and communities in and around their operations while minimizing environmental harm from things like waste creation, water use, and energy usage. These worries are on top of the standard business supply chain worries about profit and revenue (Abubakar et al., 2022). Globally, businesses have taken action to reduce waste, enhance working conditions, and reduce carbon emissions. Through monitoring sustainability metrics in supply chain management systems, they keep an eye on complex initiatives that, for instance, promote greater social responsibility among suppliers, recycle materials and goods, or give priority to renewable energy (Fritz, 2022). According to Scientific American, Subaru's Indiana auto production—the first zero-waste facility in the United States—is a striking illustration of a sustainable supply chain (Frohnweiser, 2023). To make sure that things aren't being transported needlessly, businesses can also employ intelligence and pre-established guidelines. For instance, they can make sure that products are shipped from the closest distribution center rather than one located across the nation.

Core Principles of Sustainable Supply Chain

Taking into account social, economic, and environmental aspects, sustainable supply chain management is a comprehensive approach to supply chain management. While reducing adverse effects on the environment and society, it seeks to generate value for all parties involved. The following highlights some of the fundamentals of supply chain management.

Transparency and Traceability

Businesses and consumers can learn about the production and distribution processes of items through supply chain transparency. This entails being aware of the production processes, labour practices, the path taken by products from the point of origin to the end user, and any environmental effects that may arise (Blowfield, 2000). Businesses and consumers may act ethically and make decisions based on their beliefs and objectives when there is transparency throughout the whole supply chain (Hastig & Sodhi, 2020). Transparency in the supply chain provides consumers with information that is pertinent to their consumption and purchase decisions. According to a 2022 study, nearly half of participants stated they paid more for products labelled as socially or environmentally conscious, and over half of respondents stated that environmental sustainability was more important to them now than it was a year ago (Gardner et al., 2019). Additionally, transparency provides a means to show that commitment as more customers look for firms that follow sustainable practices. Businesses can take action to mitigate these risks and guarantee long-term operations by recognizing them (Brammer & Walker, 2011).

Environmental Sustainability

Companies face sustainability challenges in nearly every industry, including the depletion of natural resources, the end of fossil fuels, and climate change. The so-called triple bottom line, or sustainability management, often aims to balance environmental, social, and economic performance (e.g. CO 2, waste, or resource use) (Miller, 2020). Measures like price and customer service have always fueled the growth of supply chains. Environmental concerns have recently come into greater focus due to the sustainability challenge. For example, supply chain models now incorporate environmental constraints, carbon taxes and emission trading schemes are taken into account, and the impact of greenhouse gas emissions is taken into account when choosing a mode of transportation (Sherafati et al., 2020). The analysis of the trade-off between economic and environmental performance criteria inevitably involves multi-objective concerns.

Furthermore, in terms of mitigating and reducing the environmental impact, any business strategy that reduces the environmental impact of the distribution and logistics network is referred to as "green logistics" (Gruchmann, 2019). Green logistics, also known as sustainable logistics, ensure a healthy profit margin without compromising the welfare of the environment or consumer pleasure. Using cutting-edge technology like AI, machine learning, and advanced analytics, astute companies are racing to comprehend and adopt sustainable logistics management.Businesses see a range of advantages as they transition to more sustainable logistics, such as increased profitability and better corporate citizenship (Rodrique et al., 2017). Customers are rapidly switching allegiance to enterprises that show substantial, long-term progress toward a sustainable future as they witness the actual effects of climate change on a daily basis on newsfeeds and streaming channels. Consumers (and shareholders) are not satisfied with or influenced by "greenwashing," and they support a circular supply chain that includes reverse logistics (Bailey et al., 2016).

Social Responsibility

Businesses have enormous opportunities to manufacture affordable goods and services at scale because of globalization, but there is also an increasing demand for worker safety and dignity from consumers, shareholders, governments, and employees. Although labor exploitation is a complex, ever-changing, worldwide socio-economic issue that affects many industries, there are encouraging new approaches to lessen it (Hamann & Bertels, 2018). Human rights (including working conditions, child labor, and slave labor), occupational health and safety, sustainable production, and environmental practices are all aspects of social responsibility that businesses must be mindful of when it comes to the supply chain (Ramasastry, 2015). Businesses must manage the ethical, legal, and financial issues and hazards that may emerge if they select a supplier who, for instance, uses child or slave labor, conducts animal research, or has subpar working conditions for its employees (Winstanley et al., 2022). For all parties involved in a company's value chain, socially conscious supply chain management can contribute to the creation, preservation, and expansion of long-term environmental, social, and financial value. Businesses can safeguard their long-term survival and obtain a social license to operate by putting socially conscious supply chain procedures into place (Kuwornu et al., 2023).

ARTIFICIAL INTELLIGENCE IN SUPPLY CHAIN MANAGEMENT

AI in logistics is changing how businesses manage intricate, expensive procedures. Logistics companies are under increasing pressure to adopt digital transformation due to growing operating costs and enduring inefficiencies (Lieder & Rashid, 2016). As an example, AI-driven solutions, such as warehouse automation, are currently increasing safety by 90% and reducing operating costs by up to 50%. AI has a quantifiable effect on the industry in this way (De Angelis et al., 2018; Dash et al., 2019). AI in logistics software development turns laborious, manual procedures into a data-driven, efficient environment (Santibanez Gonzalez et al., 2023). AI's automated and predictive skills are causing a significant change toward efficiency and precision in an industry that was previously dominated by static planning and erratic delays (El Makhloufi, 2023). Data becomes the lifeblood of contemporary businesses in the ever-changing world of trade. It serves as the foundation for wise decision-making, and data gives firms the ability to access a wealth of information (Chauhan et al., 2022). By carefully examining the abundance of information, businesses may turn raw data into a treasure trove for strategic expansion (Marr, 2023).

Data Analytics

Data becomes the cornerstone of success in the intricately linked field of supply chain management. Supply chain businesses may simplify inventory management, anticipate disruptions, and solve the mystery of variable demand by leveraging data (Long, 2018). By employing these tactical strategies, data-driven supply chain companies achieve unprecedented success, increasing productivity, cutting expenses, and strengthening their competitive advantage in a constantly changing market (Vidal et al., 2024). By giving decision-makers useful insights from examining large data sets, data analytics improves supply chain planning and forecasting (Yu et al., 2018). A more effective supply chain results from the informed decisions made possible by these insights. Additionally, proactive decision-making based on data-driven forecasts is made possible by predictive analytics. Data analytics uses sophisticated methods that take into account a number of variables to enhance demand forecasts in supply chain planning. Stockouts and overstocking are less common when forecasts are accurate (Karki et al., 2024). Additionally, customized projections adapt to changing market circumstances, guaranteeing that supply chain planning stays flexible and responsive.

Machine Learning

Machine learning for supply chain optimization can help businesses estimate demand more accurately. Large volumes of data from multiple sources can be analyzed by machine learning algorithms to generate more precise forecasts of client requirements. By assisting companies in maintaining ideal stock levels, machine learning may greatly enhance inventory management (Dalal et al., 2024). Because fewer stockouts and overstocks occur, carrying and warehousing costs are reduced. Additionally, automated replenishment systems can be implemented more easily with machine learning, guaranteeing timely product supply and effective stock control. Simplified supplier management is made possible by the use of machine learning in supply chain optimization (Tirkolaee et al., 2021). Businesses may proactively handle any supplier risks and disruptions and preserve a stable supply chain by using algorithms to detect them. Additionally, machine learning may help with supplier selection and management to guarantee optimal performance and dependability, as well as enhance supplier performance evaluation. Furthermore, tracking and monitoring shipments in real time can assist in spotting possible problems and offering preventative fixes (Maheshwari et al., 2021). By reducing repairs and downtime, predictive maintenance can guarantee the supply chain runs smoothly. Supply chain optimization with machine learning can boost productivity and cut expenses. Businesses can find areas for cost reduction and improve many parts of their supply chain operations by using data-driven decision-making. Increased efficiency results from better resource allocation and waste reduction, which improves supply chain performance as a whole (Koot et al., 2021).

Automated Decision Support Systems

In order to optimize operations, boost efficiency, and enable predictive maintenance, AI-based decision support systems are essential to this paradigm because they facilitate the integration and processing of sensor and Internet of Things data. AI-capable robots are very accurate and efficient at difficult jobs (Gupta et al., 2022). Robots with AI capabilities may select and pack orders, manage inventory, and even manage shipping operations in warehouses. This degree of automation can boost operational effectiveness and drastically save labor expenses (Braun et al., 2021). One of the main technologies driving this change is AI in decision support systems. The rapid development of Industry 4.0, which is defined by the integration of digital and physical systems, has increased the need for making wise decisions (Borangiu et al., 2020). AI-Based decision support systems have become essential instruments that help businesses make strategic and well-informed decisions. By processing vast amounts of data, identifying patterns, and producing actionable insights, these systems use AI to revolutionize decision-making in a variety of industrial areas (Soori et al., 2024). A key component of this change is the incorporation of AI into the decision support system, which offers hitherto unseen capabilities for data analysis, important insight extraction, and the support of informed decision-making processes (Perifanis & Kitsios, 2023). As businesses manage difficult operational issues and want to seize new opportunities to improve competitiveness, efficacy, and flexibility, using AI-based decision support systems becomes strategically essential (Soori et al., 2024).

ARTIFICIAL INTELLIGENCE DRIVEN GREEN LOGISTICS

AI reduces emissions and fuel consumption by optimizing routes, and predictive maintenance makes sure cars run as efficiently as possible, which further lowers their carbon impact. AI-powered inventory control also lowers waste and energy consumption in storage facilities. A package will take up more needless space during transit and emit more carbon dioxide if it contains more empty space. The growth of e-commerce has made this problem worse. Businesses must maximize space when packaging individual products, as well as pallets and cubes, in order to lower their carbon emission footprint (Ahmad et al., 2022).

Smart Warehousing: Energy Efficiency and Resource Optimization

Digital transformation and environmental trends are driving advancements in warehousing. Legacy companies can enter a new era of energy efficiency and savings with the help of smart systems and assets (Javaid et al., 2022; Ercan et al., 2022). Despite costly connections, warehouses that deploy energy-efficient technology continue to have a competitive edge (Marchet et al., 2014). In order to prevent smart technology from using more energy than it saves, warehouse energy efficiency requires corporate goals to frame integrations (Coelho et al., 2020). Data collection and equipment installation come with hefty upfront expenses (Marchi & Zanoni, 2017). Buildings are becoming larger, and operating costs for warehousing are currently between $2 and $3 per square foot. As industries like e-commerce grow faster than anticipated and consume a lot of electricity, the required square footage contracts will also increase dramatically (Shaheen & Lipman, 2007). As a result, any smart energy gadget in a warehouse needs to be considerate of and appropriate for the various climate objectives covered by any contract (Del Rio, 2021).

Greener power use goals need to strengthen a company's core as climate concerns continue to put pressure on businesses. Thought leaders in the industry are very concerned about future-proofing warehouses because of the rapidly evolving and complex trends, such as nearshoring, modular design, and legislatively prompted regulatory changes (Ivanov, 2022). All of these could have an impact on energy through asset consolidation or environmental certifications. Due to significant obstacles that hinder the easy integration of new technology, energy-efficient activities have escaped storage (McKinnon, 2012). Misconceptions about return on investment are the first (Lachhab et al., 2017). 40% of businesses do not use automation solutions, which could improve energy efficiency, due to cost and return on investment concerns (Lim, 2017). Making a distinction between short- and long-term ROIs is a clever, pragmatic way to change this thinking. Although initial implementation and training may be expensive, the brand loyalty that results from growing reputations in the sustainable field among business-to-business clients is invaluable (Agu et al., 2024).

Furthermore, strengthening energy independence protects against fluctuating energy prices and the negative effects that go along with it. Warehouses prepare for these losses as though they were necessary expenses, factoring them into their annual budgets. However, warehouses shouldn't be exposed to the fossil fuel industry's instability, which will only worsen as prices fluctuate due to laws, inflation, shortages, and geopolitical unrest (Perotti & Colicchia, 2023). The boundaries of warehouses are already being reached. While shelf space is limited and manufacturers face a manpower scarcity, the volume of pallets that must be packed and carried every day is increasing. Increasing energy utilization through the addition of additional equipment and tools would help solve these issues (Adeodu et al., 2023). Nonetheless, avoiding this temptation is a component of a conscientious warehouse optimization and discovery process. Making poor decisions is avoided by being aware of the obstacles to real efficiency in a warehouse (Karásek, 2013).

Dynamic Routing and Real-Time Freight Optimization

Logistics services must be economical, safe, and quick to provide to clients if a business is to thrive in these rapidly evolving times. Using a route optimization technique, which assigns delivery fleets the most effective routes, is essential to a successful logistics operation. In logistics, dynamic route optimization entails starting from the beginning with a predetermined set of orders and allowing for modifications in response to weather or traffic conditions (Min & Zhou, 2002).

Scalability and adaptability are dynamic route planning primarily benefits. As the business expands, this kind of platform may adjust and make adjustments.

Dynamic route planning is now possible because of technological improvements that give businesses access to a variety of data collection methods, including wireless technologies, RFID, real-time location services, GPS navigation systems, and many more (Tan & Sidhu, 2022). The fleet's present location, traffic, weather, fuel consumption, and many other logistics-related factors are all revealed by this data collection, which may be used to modify the delivery route to accommodate customers' demands and delivery timetables. Delivery errors may be decreased, on-road efficiency could be improved, and last-mile issues could be avoided with the help of dynamic route optimization software. Delivery executives can be tracked in real time by businesses using a dynamic route planning tool (Nguyen et al., 2020). Delivery operations can be streamlined by making the most use of available resources thanks to this fleet visibility. Businesses might assign more deliveries, decrease idle time, and enhance delivery dispersion with the aid of such a platform. Increased productivity will boost the company's overall earnings (Watkins et al., 2013). When weighed against the advantages of implementing a dynamic route planning platform, the cost is negligible. While giving customers a faster delivery, a platform such as this will assist businesses in managing their deliveries, increasing efficiency, reducing fuel expenses, and adding more stops to their delivery route (Maestro et al., 2021).

ENABLING CIRCULAR ECONOMY WITH ARTIFICIAL INTELLIGENCE

In the years to come, supply chain sustainability will be driven by innovation. The circular economy and data-driven supply chains are two developments that will maintain the pace in this field (Montag, 2023). A circular economy aims to eliminate waste and pollution from systems and products, such as supply chains. Products in this system are designed to endure longer, have a little environmental impact, and be readily disassembled and reassembled or changed for future use. Cloud-based supply chain execution solutions that offer comprehensive analytics and can even extract data from equipment sensors and other Internet of Things devices are used by businesses in data-driven supply chains (Khan et al., 2022). Businesses can then identify, put into practice, and track plans to become more sustainable since they have a better understanding of their operations.

Reverse Logistics and Product Recovery

One intricate and frequently disregarded aspect of logistics is the reverse supply chain. It entails moving materials and products in the opposite direction of their initial flow. Product returns throughout the supply chain have been on the rise in recent years (Jenkins, 2021). Shorter product life cycles, greater consumer choice, and globalization are some of the causes of this. As the globe continues to enter the eCommerce era, the issue will only worsen. As the name suggests, reverse logistics flips the order of operations (Kim & Gupta, 2012). In a reverse supply chain, the products are reused in various ways after making the journey from the consumer to the manufacturer (or, less frequently, from the subsequent links in the chain, such as the stores or wholesalers) (Guide & Van Wassenhove, 2002). One type of AI-based program that lets one choose how to allocate returns based on real-time data is an AI disposition engine. In order to filter returns for the maximum recovery rate, they employ AI algorithms to evaluate product quality, resale price, processing expenses, future touch points, transportation fees, and storage requirements. AI can reduce returns processing time by 75% and decide the optimal course of action for every return case by automatically calculating the entire cost of returns management (Yang et al., 2022).

Material Recycling and Reuse with AI

Waste is made up of many different components, including paper, aluminum, and various polymers, but recycling each waste stream requires a particular kind of processing. As a result, before materials can be completely recycled, they need to be sorted and divided (Ragaert et al., 2017). In order to identify materials in a waste stream based on a number of criteria, computer vision scans those materials. In addition to recognizing an infinite number of material classifications, Recycleye Vision technology can distinguish between materials that are packaged and those that are not, as well as between materials that are of food grade and those that are not, as well as between colors and shapes (Chertow et al., 2024). This sorting procedure may be finished swiftly, precisely, and safely with AI computer vision, which boosts productivity in materials recovery facilities (MRFs). More waste can be processed in a given amount of time because of this efficiency boost, which boosts recycling outputs and speeds up the recycling process. Additionally, by decreasing or doing away with the requirement for manual material sorting, switching to AI-powered sorting can save money (Fang et al., 2023). Sorting is accelerated and accuracy is increased when robotic technologies are incorporated into the recycling process. As a result, recycling is more effectively divided into waste streams. Consequently, this increases cost-effectiveness and makes it possible for MRFs to produce more. An AI robot can choose materials and sort them into the proper streams, functioning as a sophisticated recycling sorter. After that, recyclables are compacted using additional recycling equipment, like a baler, before being moved on to the next phase of the recycling procedure (Bogue, 2019).

MEASURING IMPACT AND PERFORMANCE

Measuring the impact and performance of AI in a supply chain requires a multi-faceted approach. It includes the Key Performance Indicators (KPIs), AI tools and several ethical and societal implications. Brands utilize sustainability KPIs, which are precise and quantifiable measurements, to assess their economic, social, and environmental impact. These KPIs offer a framework for establishing and accomplishing sustainability goals and assist companies in understanding how their activities affect the environment and society (Hristov & Chirico, 2019). Since many nations and states have made ESG reporting required, it is crucial that businesses gather their own data on their sustainability initiatives to make sure they are accomplishing specific objectives. ESG ratings are crucial; low ratings could cost a company clients and investors, as well as result in a fine (Clément et al., 2022). Sustainability KPIs are characterized by unambiguous measurements that quantify many aspects such as energy use, water usage, recycling rates, carbon dioxide emissions, and more. The largest areas of influence in e-commerce are transportation and packaging waste-related carbon emissions. Also, Business success in our fast-paced, cutthroat environment depends on excellent supply chain management and logistics. These fields are changing as a result of AI-powered applications, which provide fresh approaches to improving efficiency, streamlining processes, and optimizing resources (Shobhana, 2024). From route optimization and real-time monitoring to automated inventory management and predictive analytics, AI enables businesses to make better decisions more quickly. To guarantee that AI is applied properly and ethically, businesses must be watchful in addressing concerns including job displacement, data privacy, bias, environmental effect, and transparency (Konidena et al., 2024).

CHALLENGES AND BARRIERS

Although the technology has enormous potential to cut expenses and streamline procedures, its deployment can occasionally be costly and challenging. When integrating intelligence into supply chain processes, businesses frequently encounter certain difficulties. Firstly, data quality and authenticity is a major concern. Data is the holy grail of supply chains, serving as the foundation for important decisions (Ronchini et al., 2024). To assist in the creation of strategic plans, historical and contemporary data, as well as internal and external data, are all gathered and examined. Depending entirely on AI for information may seem like a risky move. Right now, the best way to tackle this problem would be to use AI's skills to gather data while allowing for some human involvement to verify the results and make judgments based on final judgment (Spangler, 1991). AI researchers are hopeful that accuracy and quality will increase with advancement, even though supply chain professionals continue to express concerns about data accuracy. Secondly, high investment cost is another challenge. AI implementation requires a significant time and financial commitment. Because supply chain ecosystems are frequently complicated, partners may need specialist hardware in order to apply AI (Sgantzos & Grigg, 2019). As IT integrates apps and data sources and trains AI models, among other necessary duties, AI may also initially demand a large amount of maintenance. To use AI, employees need to be properly trained; else, issues could arise. Among other problems, inaccurate data interpretations and inputs can lead to mistakes across the supply chain (Sarker, 2022). Because AI is developing so quickly, it could be challenging to find workers with the necessary AI knowledge. One option is to train current staff to use AI, but this will cost money and time (McKinnon et al., 2015; Ogbuke et al., 2022).

CONCLUSION

In the complex and interconnected global environment of today, it is critical for enterprises to achieve sustainable supply chain performance. Effective supply chain management in this context is fuelled by the dynamic capability and flexibility of information systems. Furthermore, supply chains must adhere to a wide range of regulations in order to produce sustainable results. Due to a mix of growing environmental, social, and economic pressures as well as technical advancements, the significance of sustainable supply chain management has grown dramatically in recent years. Carbon emissions linked to supply chains are frequently caused by the extraction of raw materials, manufacturing procedures, and transportation. To properly prevent climate change, we must address them. Stricter environmental and social regulations are being enforced by governments and international organizations. Companies with sustainable supply chains are in a better position to fulfil these responsibilities without facing penalties or major interruptions. Businesses that have sustainable supply chain management have the opportunity to stand out in the marketplace in the current business period, where sustainability has been regarded as a differentiator. Because of this differentiation, these businesses are in a better position to take a bigger chunk of the market, which will guarantee their long-term success and survival. Because business operations are intertwined with environmental, social, and economic frameworks, sustainable supply chain management is significant. Additionally, given the difficulties of these systems, it is critical that businesses assume responsibility and show that they are interested in sustaining long-term, sustainable operations.

REFERENCES

Abubakar, I. R., Maniruzzaman, K. M., Dano, U. L., AlShihri, F. S., AlShammari, M. S., Ahmed, S. M. S., & Alrawaf, T. I. (2022). Environmental sustainability impacts of solid waste management practices in the Global South. *International Journal of Environmental Research and Public Health, 19*(19), 12717. DOI: 10.3390/ijerph191912717 PMID: 36232017

Adeodu, A., Maladzhi, R., Katumba, M. G. K. K., & Daniyan, I. (2023). Development of an improvement framework for warehouse processes using lean six sigma (DMAIC) approach: A case of third-party logistics (3PL) services. *Heliyon, 9*(4), e15034. DOI: 10.1016/j.heliyon.2023.e14915 PMID: 37082643

Agu, E. E., Iyelolu, T. V., Idemudia, C., & Ijomah, T. I. (2024). Exploring the relationship between sustainable business practices and increased brand loyalty. *International Journal of Management & Entrepreneurship Research, 6*(8), 2463–2475. DOI: 10.51594/ijmer.v6i8.1365

Ahmad, S., Utomo, D. S., Dadhich, P., & Greening, P. (2022). Packaging design, fill rate and road freight decarbonisation: A literature review and a future research agenda. *Cleaner Logistics and Supply Chain, 4*, 100066. DOI: 10.1016/j.clscn.2022.100066

Bailey, A. A., Mishra, A., & Tiamiyu, M. F. (2016). Green advertising receptivity: An initial scale development process. *Journal of Marketing Communications, 22*(3), 327–345. DOI: 10.1080/13527266.2014.904812

Blowfield, M. (2000). Ethical sourcing: A contribution to sustainability or a diversion? *Sustainable Development (Bradford), 8*(4), 191–200. DOI: 10.1002/1099-1719(200011)8:4<191::AID-SD146>3.0.CO;2-E

Bogue, R. (2019). Robots in recycling and disassembly. *The Industrial Robot, 46*(4), 461–466. DOI: 10.1108/IR-03-2019-0053

Borangiu, T., Morariu, O., Răileanu, S., Trentesaux, D., Leitão, P., & Barata, J. (2020). Digital transformation of manufacturing: Industry of the future with cyber-physical production systems. *Romanian Journal of Information Science and Technology, 23*(1), 3–37.

Boute, R. N., & Udenio, M. (2022). AI in logistics and supply chain management. In Dolgui, A., Ivanov, D., & Rozhkov, M. (Eds.), *Global logistics and supply chain strategies for the 2020s: Vital skills for the next generation* (pp. 49–65). Springer., DOI: 10.1007/978-3-030-95764-3_3

Brammer, S., & Walker, H. (2011). Sustainable procurement in the public sector: An international comparative study. *International Journal of Operations & Production Management, 31*(4), 452–476. DOI: 10.1108/01443571111119551

Braun, M., Hummel, P., Beck, S., & Dabrock, P. (2021). Primer on the ethics of AI-based decision support systems in the clinic. *Journal of Medical Ethics, 47*(12), e3. DOI: 10.1136/medethics-2019-105860 PMID: 32245804

Chauhan, C., Kaur, P., Arrawatia, R., Ractham, P., & Dhir, A. (2022). Supply chain collaboration and sustainable development goals (SDGs): Teamwork makes achieving SDGs dream work. *Journal of Business Research, 147*, 290–307. DOI: 10.1016/j.jbusres.2022.03.044

Chertow, M., Reck, B. K., Wrzesniewski, A., & Calli, B. (2024). Outlook on the future role of robots and AI in material recovery facilities: Implications for US recycling and the workforce. *Journal of Cleaner Production, 470*, 143234. DOI: 10.1016/j.jclepro.2024.143234

Clément, A., Robinot, É., & Trespeuch, L. (2022). Improving ESG scores with sustainability concepts. *Sustainability (Basel), 14*(20), 13154. DOI: 10.3390/su142013154

Closs, D. J., Speier, C., & Meacham, N. (2011). Sustainability to support end-to-end value chains: The role of supply chain management. *Journal of the Academy of Marketing Science, 39*(1), 101–116. DOI: 10.1007/s11747-010-0207-4

Coelho, P. M., Corona, B., ten Klooster, R., & Worrell, E. (2020). Sustainability of reusable packaging—Current situation and trends. *Resources, Conservation and Recycling. X, 6*, 100037. DOI: 10.1016/j.rcrx.2020.100037

Dalal, S., Lilhore, U. K., Simaiya, S., Radulescu, M., & Belascu, L. (2024). Improving efficiency and sustainability via supply chain optimization through CNNs and BiLSTM. *Technological Forecasting and Social Change, 209*, 123841. DOI: 10.1016/j.techfore.2024.123841

Dash, R., McMurtrey, M., Rebman, C., & Kar, U. K. (2019). Application of artificial intelligence in automation of supply chain management. *Journal of Strategic Innovation and Sustainability, 14*(3), 43–53. DOI: 10.33423/jsis.v14i3.2105

De Angelis, R., Howard, M., & Miemczyk, J. (2018). Supply chain management and the circular economy: Towards the circular supply chain. *Production Planning and Control, 29*(6), 425–437. DOI: 10.1080/09537287.2018.1449244

Del Rio, D. D. F., Sovacool, B. K., & Griffiths, S. (2021). Culture, energy and climate sustainability, and smart home technologies: A mixed methods comparison of four countries. *Energy and Climate Change*, *2*, 100035. DOI: 10.1016/j.egycc.2021.100035

El Makhloufi, A. (2023). *AI application in transport and logistics: Opportunities and challenges (An exploratory study).*

Ercan, T., Onat, N. C., Keya, N., Tatari, O., Eluru, N., & Kucukvar, M. (2022). Autonomous electric vehicles can reduce carbon emissions and air pollution in cities. *Transportation Research Part D, Transport and Environment*, *112*, 103472. DOI: 10.1016/j.trd.2022.103472

Fang, B., Yu, J., Chen, Z., Osman, A. I., Farghali, M., Ihara, I., Hamza, E. H., Rooney, D. W., & Yap, P.-S. (2023). Artificial intelligence for waste management in smart cities: A review. *Environmental Chemistry Letters*, *21*(4), 1959–1989. DOI: 10.1007/s10311-023-01604-3 PMID: 37362015

Fritz, M. M. (2022). A supply chain view of sustainability management. *Cleaner Production Letters*, *3*, 100023. DOI: 10.1016/j.clpl.2022.100023

Frohnwieser, S. M. (2023). *Lunawood C grade: What do we do with it?* https://urn.fi/URN:NBN:fi:amk-2023100426864

Gardner, T. A., Benzie, M., Börner, J., Dawkins, E., Fick, S., Garrett, R., Godar, J., Grimard, A., Lake, S., Larsen, R. K., Mardas, N., McDermott, C. L., Meyfroidt, P., Osbeck, M., Persson, M., Sembres, T., Suavet, C., Strassburg, B., Trevisan, A., & Wolvekamp, P. (2019). Transparency and sustainability in global commodity supply chains. *World Development*, *121*, 163–177. DOI: 10.1016/j.worlddev.2018.05.025 PMID: 31481824

Gruchmann, T. (2019). Advanced green logistics strategies and technologies. In Piotrowicz, W., & Cuthbertson, R. (Eds.), *Operations, logistics and supply chain management* (pp. 663–686). Springer., DOI: 10.1007/978-3-319-92447-2_29

Guide, V. D. R., & Van Wassenhove, L. N. (2002, February 1). *The reverse supply chain*. Harvard Business Review. https://hbr.org/2002/02/the-reverse-supply-chain

Gupta, S., Modgil, S., Bhattacharyya, S., & Bose, I. (2022). Artificial intelligence for decision support systems in the field of operations research: Review and future scope of research. *Annals of Operations Research*, *308*(1), 215–274. https://link.springer.com/article/10.1007/s10479-020-03856-6. DOI: 10.1007/s10479-020-03856-6

Hamann, R., & Bertels, S. (2018). The institutional work of exploitation: Employers' work to create and perpetuate inequality. *Journal of Management Studies, 55*(3), 394–423. DOI: 10.1111/joms.12325

Hastig, G. M., & Sodhi, M. S. (2020). Blockchain for supply chain traceability: Business requirements and critical success factors. *Production and Operations Management, 29*(4), 935–954. DOI: 10.1111/poms.13147

Hristov, I., & Chirico, A. (2019). The role of sustainability key performance indicators (KPIs) in implementing sustainable strategies. *Sustainability (Basel), 11*(20), 5742. DOI: 10.3390/su11205742

Islam, M. S., Suad, S. F. R., & Rahman, A. (2024). Leveraging AI to overcome key challenges in last-mile delivery: Enhancing customer experience and operational efficiency in e-commerce. *Supply Chain Insider, 14*(1).

Ivanov, D. (2022). Viable supply chain model: Integrating agility, resilience and sustainability perspectives—Lessons from and thinking beyond the COVID-19 pandemic. *Annals of Operations Research, 319*(1), 1411–1431. DOI: 10.1007/s10479-020-03640-6 PMID: 32836614

Jadhav, A., Orr, S., & Malik, M. (2019). The role of supply chain orientation in achieving supply chain sustainability. *International Journal of Production Economics, 217*, 112–125. DOI: 10.1016/j.ijpe.2018.07.031

Jenkins, A. (2021). *A guide to reverse logistics: How it works, types and strategies*. Oracle NetSuite. https://www.netsuite.com/portal/resource/articles/inventory-management/reverse-logistics.shtml

Karki, R., Shrestha, N., & Adhikari, P. (2024). *Data analytics to enhance supply chain decision-making, inventory management, and logistic optimization.*

Khan, Y., Su'ud, M. B. M., Alam, M. M., Ahmad, S. F., Ahmad, A. Y. B., & Khan, N. (2023). Application of Internet of Things (IoT) in sustainable supply chain management. *Sustainability, 15*(1), 694. DOI: 10.3390/su15010694

Kim, J., & Gupta, P. (2012). Emotional expressions in online user reviews: How they influence consumers' product evaluations. *Journal of Business Research, 65*(7), 985–992. DOI: 10.1016/j.jbusres.2011.04.013

Konidena, B. K., Malaiyappan, J. N. A., & Tadimarri, A. (2024). Ethical considerations in the development and deployment of AI systems. *European Journal of Technology, 8*(2), 41–53. DOI: 10.47672/ejt.1890

Koot, M., Mes, M. R. K., & Iacob, M. E. (2021). A systematic literature review of supply chain decision making supported by the Internet of Things and Big Data Analytics. *Computers & Industrial Engineering*, *154*, 107076. DOI: 10.1016/j.cie.2020.107076

Kuwornu, J. K. M., Khaipetch, J., Gunawan, E., Bannor, R. K., & Ho, T. D. (2023). The adoption of sustainable supply chain management practices on performance and quality assurance of food companies. *Sustainable Futures : An Applied Journal of Technology, Environment and Society*, *5*, 100103. DOI: 10.1016/j.sftr.2022.100103

Lachhab, F., Bakhouya, M., Ouladsine, R., & Essaaidi, M. (2017). Energy-efficient buildings as complex socio-technical systems: Approaches and challenges. In Nemiche, M., & Essaaidi, M. (Eds.), *Advances in complex societal, environmental and engineered systems* (pp. 247–265). Springer., DOI: 10.1007/978-3-319-46164-9_12

Lieder, M., & Rashid, A. (2016). Towards circular economy implementation: A comprehensive review in context of manufacturing industry. *Journal of Cleaner Production*, *115*, 36–51. DOI: 10.1016/j.jclepro.2015.12.042

Lim, W. M. (2017). Online group buying: Some insights from the business-to-business perspective. *Industrial Marketing Management*, *65*, 182–193. DOI: 10.1016/j.indmarman.2017.03.011

Long, Q. (2018). Data-driven decision making for supply chain networks with agent-based computational experiment. *Knowledge-Based Systems*, *141*, 55–66. DOI: 10.1016/j.knosys.2017.11.006

Luther, D. (2021, December 18). *Supply chain sustainability: Why it is important & best practices*. Oracle NetSuite. https://www.netsuite.com/portal/resource/articles/erp/supply-chain-sustainability.shtml

Madancian, M., Taherdoost, H., Javadi, M., Khan, I. U., Kalantari, A., & Kumar, D. (2023). The impact of artificial intelligence on supply chain management in modern business. In Alnoor, A., Sharaf, A. A. A., & Al-Fatlawi, K. A. A. (Eds.), *The international conference on artificial intelligence and smart environment* (pp. 566–573). Springer.

Maestro, J. A., Rodríguez, S., Casado, R., Prieto, J., & Corchado, J. M. (2021). Comparison of efficient planning and optimization methods of last mile delivery resources. In Q. Tang (Ed.), *Broadband communications, networks, and systems: 11th EAI International Conference, BROADNETS 2020, Qingdao, China, December 11–12, 2020, Proceedings* (pp. 163–173). Springer. DOI: 10.1007/978-3-030-68737-3_11

Maheshwari, S., Gautam, P., & Jaggi, C. K. (2021). Role of big data analytics in supply chain management: Current trends and future perspectives. *International Journal of Production Research, 59*(6), 1875–1900. DOI: 10.1080/00207543.2020.1793011

Marchet, G., Melacini, M., & Perotti, S. (2014). Environmental sustainability in logistics and freight transportation: A literature review and research agenda. *Journal of Manufacturing Technology Management, 25*(6), 775–811. DOI: 10.1108/JMTM-06-2012-0065

Marchi, B., & Zanoni, S. (2017). Supply chain management for improved energy efficiency: Review and opportunities. *Energies, 10*(10), 1618. DOI: 10.3390/en10101618

Marr, B. (2022, June 29). *Why data is the lifeblood of modern organizations*. Forbes. https://www.forbes.com/sites/bernardmarr/2022/06/29/why-data-is-the-lifeblood-of-modern-organizations/

McKinnon, A. C. (2012). Reducing energy consumption and emissions in the logistics sector. In McKinnon, A., Browne, M., Whiteing, A., & Piecyk, M. (Eds.), *Energy, transport, & the environment: Addressing the sustainable mobility paradigm* (pp. 521–537). Springer., DOI: 10.1007/978-1-4471-2717-8_29

Mefford, R. N. (2011). The economic value of a sustainable supply chain. *Business and Society Review, 116*(1), 109–143. DOI: 10.1111/j.1467-8594.2011.00379.x

Miller, K. (2020, December 8). *The triple bottom line: What it is & why it's important.* Harvard Business School Online. https://online.hbs.edu/blog/post/what-is-the-triple-bottom-line

Min, H., & Zhou, G. (2002). Supply chain modeling: Past, present and future. *Computers & Industrial Engineering, 43*(1–2), 231–249. DOI: 10.1016/S0360-8352(02)00066-9

Montag, L. (2023). Circular economy and supply chains: Definitions, conceptualizations, and research agenda of the circular supply chain framework. *Circular Economy and Sustainability, 3*(1), 35–75. DOI: 10.1007/s43615-022-00172-y PMID: 35582650

Nguyen Duc, D., Tran Huu, T., & Nananukul, N. (2020). A dynamic route-planning system based on Industry 4.0 technology. *Algorithms, 13*(12), 308. DOI: 10.3390/a13120308

Ogbuke, N. J., Yusuf, Y. Y., Dharma, K., & Mercangoz, B. A. (2022). Big data supply chain analytics: Ethical, privacy and security challenges posed to business, industries and society. *Production Planning and Control, 33*(2–3), 123–137. DOI: 10.1080/09537287.2020.1810764

Osei, M. B., Papadopoulos, T., Acquaye, A., & Stamati, T. (2023). Improving sustainable supply chain performance through organisational culture: A competing values framework approach. *Journal of Purchasing and Supply Management, 29*(2), 100821. DOI: 10.1016/j.pursup.2023.100821

Perifanis, N.-A., & Kitsios, F. (2023). Investigating the influence of artificial intelligence on business value in the digital era of strategy: A literature review. *Information (Basel), 14*(2), 85. DOI: 10.3390/info14020085

Perotti, S., & Colicchia, C. (2023). Greening warehouses through energy efficiency and environmental impact reduction: A conceptual framework based on a systematic literature review. *International Journal of Logistics Management, 34*(7), 199–234. DOI: 10.1108/IJLM-02-2022-0086

Rafi, T. (2022, June 7). *Why sustainability is crucial for corporate strategy.* World Economic Forum. https://www.weforum.org/agenda/2022/06/why-sustainability-is-crucial-for-corporate-strategy/

Ragaert, K., Delva, L., & Van Geem, K. (2017). Mechanical and chemical recycling of solid plastic waste. *Waste Management (New York, N.Y.), 69*, 24–58. DOI: 10.1016/j.wasman.2017.07.044 PMID: 28823699

Ramasastry, A. (2015). Corporate social responsibility versus business and human rights: Bridging the gap between responsibility and accountability. *Journal of Human Rights, 14*(2), 237–259. DOI: 10.1080/14754835.2015.1037953

Rodrigue, J.-P., Slack, B., & Comtois, C. (2017). Green logistics. In Brewer, B. S., Button, G., & Hensher, D. A. (Eds.), *Handbook of logistics and supply-chain management* (Vol. 2, pp. 339–350). Emerald., DOI: 10.1108/9780080435930-021

Ronchini, A., Guida, M., Moretto, A., & Caniato, F. (2024). The role of artificial intelligence in the supply chain finance innovation process. *Operations Management Research.* DOI: 10.1007/s12063-024-00492-2

Sánchez-Flores, R. B., Cruz-Sotelo, S. E., Ojeda-Benitez, S., & Ramírez-Barreto, M. E. (2020). Sustainable supply chain management—A literature review on emerging economies. *Sustainability (Basel), 12*(17), 6972. DOI: 10.3390/su12176972

Santibanez Gonzalez, E. D., Kandpal, V., Machado, M., Martens, M. L., & Majumdar, S. (2023). A bibliometric analysis of circular economies through sustainable smart cities. *Sustainability (Basel), 15*(22), 15892. DOI: 10.3390/su152215892

Sarker, I. H. (2022). AI-based modeling: Techniques, applications and research issues towards automation, intelligent and smart systems. *SN Computer Science, 3*(2), 158. DOI: 10.1007/s42979-022-01043-x PMID: 35194580

Sgantzos, K., & Grigg, I. (2019). Artificial intelligence implementations on the blockchain: Use cases and future applications. *Future Internet, 11*(8), 170. DOI: 10.3390/fi11080170

Shaheen, S. A., & Lipman, T. E. (2007). Reducing greenhouse emissions and fuel consumption: Sustainable approaches for surface transportation. *IATSS Research, 31*(1), 6–20. DOI: 10.1016/S0386-1112(14)60179-5

Sherafati, M., Bashiri, M., Tavakkoli-Moghaddam, R., & Pishvaee, M. S. (2020). Achieving sustainable development of supply chain by incorporating various carbon regulatory mechanisms. *Transportation Research Part D, Transport and Environment, 81*, 102253. DOI: 10.1016/j.trd.2020.102253

Shobhana, N. (2024). AI-powered supply chains towards greater efficiency. In Mangla, S. K., Tyagi, A. K., & Luthra, S. (Eds.), *Complex AI dynamics and interactions in management* (pp. 229–249). IGI Global., DOI: 10.4018/979-8-3693-0712-0.ch011

Soori, M., Jough, F. K. G., Dastres, R., & Arezoo, B. (2024). AI-based decision support systems in Industry 4.0: A review. *Journal of Economy and Technology.* DOI: 10.1016/j.ject.2024.08.005

Spangler, W. E. (1991). The role of artificial intelligence in understanding the strategic decision-making process. *IEEE Transactions on Knowledge and Data Engineering, 3*(2), 149–159. DOI: 10.1109/69.87995

Tan, W. C., & Sidhu, M. S. (2022). Review of RFID and IoT integration in supply chain management. *Operations Research Perspectives, 9*, 100229. DOI: 10.1016/j.orp.2022.100229

Tirkolaee, E. B., Sadeghi, S., Mooseloo, F. M., Vandchali, H. R., & Aeini, S. (2021). Application of machine learning in supply chain management: A comprehensive overview of the main areas. *Mathematical Problems in Engineering, 2021*, 1476043. DOI: 10.1155/2021/1476043

Vidal, U., Obregon, M., Ramos, E., Verma, R., & Coles, P. S. (2024). Sustainable and risk-resilient circular supply chain: A Peruvian paint manufacturing supply chain model. *Sustainable Futures : An Applied Journal of Technology, Environment and Society*, *7*, 100207. DOI: 10.1016/j.sftr.2024.100207

Watkins, S., Battles, J., & Vacek, R. (2013). Streamlining data for cross-platform web delivery. *Journal of Web Librarianship*, *7*(1), 95–108. DOI: 10.1080/19322909.2013.748393

Winstanley, D., Clark, J., & Leeson, H. (2002). Approaches to child labour in the supply chain. *Business Ethics (Oxford, England)*, *11*(3), 210–223. DOI: 10.1111/1467-8608.00279

Yang, G., Ji, G., & Tan, K. H. (2022). Impact of artificial intelligence adoption on online returns policies. *Annals of Operations Research*, *308*(1), 703–726. DOI: 10.1007/s10479-020-03602-y

Yu, W., Chavez, R., Jacobs, M. A., & Feng, M. (2018). Data-driven supply chain capabilities and performance: A resource-based view. *Transportation Research Part E, Logistics and Transportation Review*, *114*, 371–385. DOI: 10.1016/j.tre.2017.04.002

Zainal, F., Baharudin, H., Khalid, A., Karim, N. H., Ramli, S., Batan, A., & Mustapha, L. (2019). *Applying artificial intelligence in e-commerce reverse logistics: Enhancing returns management, supply chain efficiency, and sustainability through advanced technologies.*

Compilation of References

Abdel-Basset, M., Mohamed, R., & Chang, V. (2024). A Multi-Criteria Decision-Making Framework to Evaluate the Impact of Industry 5.0 Technologies: Case Study, Lessons Learned, Challenges and Future Directions. *Information Systems Frontiers*, 1–31.

Abe, M., & Ye, L. (2013). Building Resilient Supply Chains against Natural Disasters: The Cases of Japan and Thailand. *Global Business Review*, *14*(4), 567–586. DOI: 10.1177/0972150913501606

Abubakar, I. R., Maniruzzaman, K. M., Dano, U. L., AlShihri, F. S., AlShammari, M. S., Ahmed, S. M. S., & Alrawaf, T. I. (2022). Environmental sustainability impacts of solid waste management practices in the Global South. *International Journal of Environmental Research and Public Health*, *19*(19), 12717. DOI: 10.3390/ijerph191912717 PMID: 36232017

Adeodu, A., Maladzhi, R., Katumba, M. G. K. K., & Daniyan, I. (2023). Development of an improvement framework for warehouse processes using lean six sigma (DMAIC) approach: A case of third-party logistics (3PL) services. *Heliyon*, *9*(4), e15034. DOI: 10.1016/j.heliyon.2023.e14915 PMID: 37082643

Adepoju, O., Akinyomi, O., & Esan, O. (2023). Integrating Human-Computer Interactions in Nigerian Energy System: A Skills Requirement Analysis. *Journal of Digital Food, Energy & Water Systems*, *4*(2).

Agu, E. E., Iyelolu, T. V., Idemudia, C., & Ijomah, T. I. (2024). Exploring the relationship between sustainable business practices and increased brand loyalty. *International Journal of Management & Entrepreneurship Research*, *6*(8), 2463–2475. DOI: 10.51594/ijmer.v6i8.1365

Ahmad, S., Utomo, D. S., Dadhich, P., & Greening, P. (2022). Packaging design, fill rate and road freight decarbonisation: A literature review and a future research agenda. *Cleaner Logistics and Supply Chain*, *4*, 100066. DOI: 10.1016/j.clscn.2022.100066

Ahmed, I., Jeon, G., & Piccialli, F. (2022). From Artificial Intelligence to Explainable Artificial Intelligence in Industry 4.0: A Survey on What, How, and Where. *IEEE Transactions on Industrial Informatics, 18*(8), 5031-5042. *IEEE Transactions on Industrial Informatics.* DOI: 10.1109/TII.2022.3146552

Ahmed, Z., Mohamed, K., Zeeshan, S., & Dong, X. (2020). Artificial intelligence with multi-functional machine learning platform development for better healthcare and precision medicine. *Database : The Journal of Biological Databases and Curation, 2020,* baaa010. DOI: 10.1093/database/baaa010 PMID: 32185396

Akbari, M., & Do, T. N. A. (2021). A systematic review of machine learning in logistics and supply chain management: current trends and future directions. In Benchmarking (Vol. 28, Issue 10). DOI: 10.1108/BIJ-10-2020-0514

Akbari, M., & Hopkins, J. L. (2022). Digital technologies as enablers of supply chain sustainability in an emerging economy. *Operations Management Research: Advancing Practice Through Research, 15*(3), 689–710. DOI: 10.1007/s12063-021-00226-8

Akhil, B., & Madhuri, P. (2020). Machine learning in supply chain management: A systematic review. *The Journal of Supply Chain Management, 56*(3), 45–58. DOI: 10.1111/jscm.2020.10

Akter, S., Michael, K., Uddin, M. R., McCarthy, G., & Rahman, M. (2022). Transforming business using digital innovations: The application of AI, blockchain, cloud and data analytics. *Annals of Operations Research, 308*(1–2), 7–39. DOI: 10.1007/s10479-020-03620-w

Alayón, Claudia, Kristina Säfsten, and G. J. (2017). Conceptual sustainable production principles in practice: Do they reflect what companies do? *Journal of Cleaner Production,* 693–701.

Al-Dmour, A., Al-Dmour, R., Al-Dmour, H., & Al-Adwan, A. (2024). Blockchain applications and commercial bank performance: The mediating role of AIS quality. *Journal of Open Innovation, 10*(2), 100302. DOI: 10.1016/j.joitmc.2024.100302

Aldoseri, A., Al-Khalifa, K. N., & Hamouda, A. M. (2024). AI-Powered Innovation in Digital Transformation: Key Pillars and Industry Impact. *Sustainability (Switzerland), 16*(5). *Sustainability (Basel), 16*(5), 1790. DOI: 10.3390/su16051790

Ali, A., Mahfouz, A., & Arisha, A. (2017). Analysing supply chain resilience: integrating the constructs in a concept mapping framework via a systematic literature review. In Supply Chain Management (Vol. 22, Issue 1). DOI: 10.1108/SCM-06-2016-0197

Aljuneidi, T., Bhat, S. A., & Boulaksil, Y. (2023). A comprehensive systematic review of the literature on the impact of the COVID-19 pandemic on supply chains. *Supply Chain Analytics*, *3*, 100025. DOI: 10.1016/j.sca.2023.100025

Alloghani, M., Al-Jumeily, D., Mustafina, J., Hussain, A., & Aljaaf, A. J. (2020). A Systematic Review on Supervised and Unsupervised Machine Learning Algorithms for Data Science. DOI: 10.1007/978-3-030-22475-2_1

Almeida Teixeira, G., Mira da Silva, M., & Pereira, R. (2021). The Critical Success Factors of GDPR Implementation: a Delphi Study.

Alomar, M. A. (2022). Performance Optimization of Industrial Supply Chain Using Artificial Intelligence. *Computational Intelligence and Neuroscience*, *2022*, 1–10. DOI: 10.1155/2022/9306265 PMID: 35942447

Alzarooni, A. M., Khan, S. A., Gunasekaran, A., & Mubarik, M. S. (2022). Enablers for digital supply chain transformation in the service industry. *Annals of Operations Research*. DOI: 10.1007/s10479-022-05047-x

Ambhika, C., Gayathri, S., & Sheena, B. G. (2024, August). Enhancing Predictive Modeling in High Dimensional Data Using Hybrid Feature Selection. In *2024 5th International Conference on Electronics and Sustainable Communication Systems (ICESC)* (pp. 873-879). IEEE. DOI: 10.1109/ICESC60852.2024.10690153

Amejwal, M., El Jaouhari, A., Arif, J., Fellaki, S., & Jawab, F. (2022, May). Production flow management based on Industry 4.0 technologies. In 2022 14th International Colloquium of Logistics and Supply Chain Management (LOGISTIQUA) (pp. 1-7). IEEE.

Amini, M., & Jahanbakhsh Javid, N. (2023). A multi-perspective framework established on diffusion of innovation (DOI) theory and technology, organization and environment (TOE) framework toward supply chain management system based on cloud computing technology for small and medium enterprises. Organization and Environment (TOE) Framework Toward Supply Chain Management System Based on Cloud Computing Technology for Small and Medium Enterprises (January 2023). *International Journal of Information Technology and Innovation Adoption*, *11*, 1217–1234.

Antipov, E. A., & Pokryshevskaya, E. B. (2020). Interpretable machine learning for demand modelling with high-dimensional data using Gradient Boosting Machines and Shapley values. *Journal of Revenue and Pricing Management*, *19*(5), 355–364. DOI: 10.1057/s41272-020-00236-4

Anusha, S., Ezhilvandan, M., Gayathri, S., & Sivaraman, V. T. P., A., & R., S. S. (2024). Emerging Trends in Edge AI for Industry 4.0 and 5.0: Technologies, Applications, and Challenges. In V. Nadda, P. Tyagi, A. Singh, & V. Singh (Eds.), *AI Innovations in Service and Tourism Marketing* (pp. 211-228). IGI Global Scientific Publishing. DOI: 10.4018/979-8-3693-7909-7.ch010

Arif, J., & Jawab, F. (2011, May). Outsourcing logistics: strategic tools for decision to outsource logistic activities. In 2011 4th International Conference on Logistics (pp. 104-108). IEEE. DOI: 10.1109/LOGISTIQUA.2011.5939410

Arif, J., Azzouz, K., Mouzouna, Y., & Jawab, F. (2020). Design on improvement of traceability process in the outsourcing of logistics' activities using the internet of things (IoT) applications. *International Journal of Advanced Science and Technology*, *29*(1), 1093–1108.

Arif, J., El Farouk, I. I., Mouzouna, Y., & Jawab, F. (2019, March). The use of internet of things (IoT) applications in the logistics outsourcing: Smart RFID tag as an example. In *Proceedings of the International Conference on Industrial Engineering and Operations Management* (pp. 5-7).

Arif, J., Samadhiya, A., & Kumar, A. (2023). Net zero supply chain performance and industry 4.0 technologies: Past review and present introspective analysis for future research directions. *Heliyon*, *9*(11). PMID: 38027710

Ashton, K. (2009). "That 'internet of things' thing." *RFID Journal*, 4986.

Asilian, A., Shahinzadeh, H., Zanjani, S. M., Gharehpetian, G. B., Abdelaziz, A. Y., & Tanwar, S. (2023). The Role of Microelectronics for Smart Cities, Smart Grids and Industry 5.0: Challenges, Solutions, and Opportunities. *2023 13th Smart Grid Conference (SGC)*, 1–12. https://ieeexplore.ieee.org/abstract/document/10459310/

Aslam, H., Khan, A. Q., Rashid, K., & Rehman, S. (2020). Achieving supply chain resilience: The role of supply chain ambidexterity and supply chain agility. *Journal of Manufacturing Technology Management*, *31*(6), 1185–1204. DOI: 10.1108/JMTM-07-2019-0263

Azari, M., Arif, J., Jawab, F., & Moustabchir, H. (2024). Smart city implementation of electric vehicles: Challenges and Opportunities. *2024 IEEE 15th International Colloquium on Logistics and Supply Chain Management (LOGISTIQUA)*, 1–6. https://ieeexplore.ieee.org/abstract/document/10571532/

Azari, M., Jawab, F., Arif, J., Khaoua, Y., El Jaouhari, A., & Moustabchir, H. (2022). From city logistics to a merger of smart cities and smart logistics. *2022 14th International Colloquium of Logistics and Supply Chain Management (LOGISTIQUA)*, 1–5. https://ieeexplore.ieee.org/abstract/document/9938020/

Azari, M., Arif, J., Moustabchir, H., & Jawab, F. (2025). Navigating Challenges and Leveraging Future Trends in AI and Machine Learning for Supply Chains. In *AI and Machine Learning Applications in Supply Chains and Marketing* (pp. 257–282). IGI Global.

Azzouz, K., Arif, J., & Benboubker, M. B. (2021). Exploratory study of the role of logistics service providers in terms of traceability in the process of outsourcing of logistics' activities: Case of moroccan LSP. *International Journal of Engineering Research in Africa*, *54*, 187–208. DOI: 10.4028/www.scientific.net/JERA.54.187

Babai, M. Z., Ali, M. M., & Boylan, J. E. (2020). Forecasting and inventory control with machine learning techniques. *International Journal of Production Economics*, *223*, 107533. DOI: 10.1016/j.ijpe.2020.107533

Badri Ahmadi, H., Kusi-Sarpong, S., & Rezaei, J. (2017). Assessing the social sustainability of supply chains using Best Worst Method. *Resources, Conservation and Recycling*, *126*, 99–106. DOI: 10.1016/j.resconrec.2017.07.020

Bag, S. (2023). From resources to sustainability: A practice-based view of net zero economy implementation in small and medium business-to-business firms. *Benchmarking*, *31*(6), 1876–1894. DOI: 10.1108/BIJ-01-2023-0056

Bag, S., Pretorius, J. H. C., Gupta, S., & Dwivedi, Y. K. (2021). Role of institutional pressures and resources in the adoption of big data analytics powered artificial intelligence, sustainable manufacturing practices and circular economy capabilities. *Technological Forecasting and Social Change*, *163*, 120420. DOI: 10.1016/j.techfore.2020.120420

Baier, M., & Strohhecker, J. (2022). AI-driven demand forecasting in retail. *Decision Sciences*, *53*(2), 331–354. DOI: 10.1111/deci.12345

Bailey, A. A., Mishra, A., & Tiamiyu, M. F. (2016). Green advertising receptivity: An initial scale development process. *Journal of Marketing Communications*, *22*(3), 327–345. DOI: 10.1080/13527266.2014.904812

Bailey, B. C., & Peck, S. I. (2013). Boardroom Strategic Decision-Making Style: Understanding the Antecedents. *Corporate Governance*, *21*(2), 131–146. DOI: 10.1111/corg.12008

Balci, G., & Surucu-Balci, E. (2021). Blockchain adoption in the maritime supply chain: Examining barriers and salient stakeholders in containerized international trade. *Transportation Research Part E, Logistics and Transportation Review, 156*, 102539. DOI: 10.1016/j.tre.2021.102539

Balla, M., Haffner, O., Kučera, E., & Cigánek, J. (2023). Educational Case Studies: Creating a Digital Twin of the Production Line in TIA Portal, Unity, and Game4Automation Framework. *Sensors (Basel), 23*(10), 4977. DOI: 10.3390/s23104977 PMID: 37430895

Ball, P. (2021). What the COVID-19 pandemic reveals about science, policy and society. *Interface Focus, 11*(6), 20210022. DOI: 10.1098/rsfs.2021.0022 PMID: 34956594

Bansal, K., Anjimoon, S., Revathi, V., Gupta, M., & Sharma, A. (2024). The Evolution from Digital Production to Digital Society in Industry 4.0 towards Industry 5.0. In *Powering Industry 5.0 and Sustainable Development Through Innovation* (pp. 27–42). IGI Global.

Barata, J., & Kayser, I. (2023). Industry 5.0–past, present, and near future. *Procedia Computer Science, 219*, 778–788. DOI: 10.1016/j.procs.2023.01.351

Barnard, H. (2023). *Developing a managerial framework for digital manufacturing in the new normal era* (Doctoral dissertation, North-West University (South Africa)).

Basole, R. C., & Bellamy, M. A. (2014). Supply Network Structure, Visibility, and Risk Diffusion: A Computational Approach. *Decision Sciences, 45*(4), 753–789. DOI: 10.1111/deci.12099

Bedi, T., Rana, V., & Gautam, N. (2021). Changing Face Of The Apparel Industry By Incorporating Industry 4.0 And Paving Way For Industry 5.0. *Turkish Online Journal of Qualitative Inquiry, 12*(3).

Behera, R. K., Bala, P. K., & Rana, N. P. (2023). Creation of sustainable growth with explainable artificial intelligence: An empirical insight from consumer packaged goods retailers. *Journal of Cleaner Production, 399*, 136605. DOI: 10.1016/j.jclepro.2023.136605

Belhadi, A., Kamble, S. S., Mani, V., Venkatesh, V. G., & Shi, Y. (2021). Behavioral mechanisms influencing sustainable supply chain governance decision-making from a dyadic buyer-supplier perspective'. *International Journal of Production Economics, 236*, 108136. DOI: 10.1016/j.ijpe.2021.108136

Benabed, A., & Boeru, A. C. (2023). Globalization beyond Business Sustainability, Energy and the Economy of the Future. In *Proceedings of the International Conference on Business Excellence* (Vol. 17, No. 1, pp. 1569-1583). Sciendo. DOI: 10.2478/picbe-2023-0141

Bergmeir, C., & Benítez, J. M. (2012). Neural networks in demand forecasting: An empirical study. *Computers & Industrial Engineering*, *63*(3), 705–717. DOI: 10.1016/j.cie.2012.05.011

Bhamra, R., Small, A., Hicks, C., & Pilch, O. (2025). Impact pathways: Geopolitics, risk and ethics in critical minerals supply chains. *International Journal of Operations & Production Management*, *45*(5), 985–994. DOI: 10.1108/IJOPM-03-2024-0228

Bhatia, S., & Albarrak, A. S. (2023). A Blockchain-Driven Food Supply Chain Management Using QR Code and XAI-Faster RCNN Architecture. *Sustainability (Basel)*, *15*(3), 3. DOI: 10.3390/su15032579

Bhatnagar, R., & Dey, L. (2021). Demand forecasting techniques and applications in supply chain management: A review. *International Journal of Production Research*, *59*(17), 5120–5145. DOI: 10.1080/00207543.2020.1845483

Bhattamisra, , Banerjee, P., Gupta, P., Mayuren, J., Patra, S., & Candasamy, M. (2023). Artificial Intelligence in Pharmaceutical and Healthcare Research. *Big Data and Cognitive Computing*, *7*(1), 10. DOI: 10.3390/bdcc7010010

Bhatti, M. R. A. (2021). *Light-driven Actuation In Ultra-drawn Chain-oriented Polymers* (Doctoral dissertation, Queen Mary University of London).

Bittencourt, V. L., Alves, A. C., & Leão, C. P. (2021). Industry 4.0 triggered by Lean Thinking: Insights from a systematic literature review. *International Journal of Production Research*, *59*(5), 1496–1510. *Scopus*. DOI: 10.1080/00207543.2020.1832274

Blowfield, M. (2000). Ethical sourcing: A contribution to sustainability or a diversion? *Sustainable Development (Bradford)*, *8*(4), 191–200. DOI: 10.1002/1099-1719(200011)8:4<191::AID-SD146>3.0.CO;2-E

Boden, M. A. (2018). Artificial intelligence. In Routledge Encyclopedia of Philosophy. DOI: 10.4324/9780415249126-W001-1

Bogue, R. (2019). Robots in recycling and disassembly. *The Industrial Robot*, *46*(4), 461–466. DOI: 10.1108/IR-03-2019-0053

Borangiu, T., Morariu, O., Răileanu, S., Trentesaux, D., Leitão, P., & Barata, J. (2020). Digital transformation of manufacturing: Industry of the future with cyber-physical production systems. *Romanian Journal of Information Science and Technology*, *23*(1), 3–37.

Boruchowitch, F., & Fritz, M. M. C. (2022). Who in the firm can create sustainable value and for whom? A single case-study on sustainable procurement and supply chain stakeholders. *Journal of Cleaner Production*, *363*, 132619. DOI: 10.1016/j.jclepro.2022.132619

Bottani, E., Centobelli, P., Gallo, M., Kaviani, M. A., Jain, V., & Murino, T. (2019). Modelling wholesale distribution operations: An artificial intelligence framework. *Industrial Management & Data Systems*, *119*(4), 698–718. DOI: 10.1108/IMDS-04-2018-0164

Bouguerra, A., Hughes, M., Cakir, M. S., & Tatoglu, E. (2022). Linking entrepreneurial orientation to environmental collaboration: A stakeholder theory and evidence from multinational companies in an emerging market. *British Journal of Management*.

Boute, R. N., & Udenio, M. (2022). AI in logistics and supply chain management. In Dolgui, A., Ivanov, D., & Rozhkov, M. (Eds.), *Global logistics and supply chain strategies for the 2020s: Vital skills for the next generation* (pp. 49–65). Springer., DOI: 10.1007/978-3-030-95764-3_3

Brammer, S., & Walker, H. (2011). Sustainable procurement in the public sector: An international comparative study. *International Journal of Operations & Production Management*, *31*(4), 452–476. DOI: 10.1108/01443571111119551

Braun, M., Hummel, P., Beck, S., & Dabrock, P. (2021). Primer on the ethics of AI-based decision support systems in the clinic. *Journal of Medical Ethics*, *47*(12), e3. DOI: 10.1136/medethics-2019-105860 PMID: 32245804

Breque, M., De Nul, L. and Petridis, A. (2021). Industry 5.0 – Towards a Sustainable, Human-Centric and Resilient European Industry, in European Commission, .DOI: 10.1002/9781119865216.ch2

Brintrup, A., Kosasih, E., Schaffer, P., Zheng, G., Demirel, G., & MacCarthy, B. L. (2024). Digital supply chain surveillance using artificial intelligence: Definitions, opportunities and risks. *International Journal of Production Research*, *62*(13), 4674–4695. DOI: 10.1080/00207543.2023.2270719

Buck, L. E. (2019). Modern Slavery in the Global Supply Chain: An Analysis of Published Preventative Statements and Frameworks to Protect Businesses and Individuals. *The Boller Review*, *4*. DOI: 10.18776/tcu/br/4/115

Bulanon, D. M., & Kataoka, T. (2010). Fruit detection system and an end effector for robotic harvesting of Fuji apples. *Agricultural Engineering International: CIGR Journal, 12*(1), 203–210.

Bulanon, D. M., Kataoka, T., Okamoto, H., & Hata, S. (2004). Development of a real-time machine vision system for the apple harvesting robot. In *Proceedings of the SICE 2004 Annual Conference* (Vol. 1, pp. 595–598). IEEE.

Bulanon, D. M., Kataoka, T., Ota, Y., & Hiroma, T. (2002). A segmentation algorithm for the automatic recognition of Fuji apples at harvest. *Biosystems Engineering, 83*(4), 405–412. DOI: 10.1006/bioe.2002.0132

Buranasiri, B., Lai, P.-L., Woo, S., & Piboonrungroj, P. (2024). Impact of sustainable development goal orientation on supply chain collaboration and sustained competitive advantage: Evidence from the tea and coffee industry'. *The Asian Journal of Shipping and Logistics, 40*(2), 83–88. DOI: 10.1016/j.ajsl.2024.01.004

Burgess, P., Sunmola, F., & Wertheim-Heck, S. (2024). Information needs for transparency in blockchain-enabled sustainable food supply chains. *International Journal of Information Management Data Insights, 4*(2), 100262. DOI: 10.1016/j.jjimei.2024.100262

Buzzao, G., & Rizzi, F. (2021). On the conceptualization and measurement of dynamic capabilities for sustainability: Building theory through a systematic literature review. *Business Strategy and the Environment, 30*(1), 135–175. DOI: 10.1002/bse.2614

Cai, Y. J., & Lo, C. K. Y. (2020). Omni-channel management in the new retailing era: A systematic review and future research agenda. *International Journal of Production Economics, 229*, 107729. DOI: 10.1016/j.ijpe.2020.107729

Camarinha-Matos, L. M., Rocha, A. D., & Graça, P. (2024). Collaborative approaches in sustainable and resilient manufacturing. *Journal of Intelligent Manufacturing, 35*(2), 499–519. DOI: 10.1007/s10845-022-02060-6 PMID: 36532704

Camilleri, M. A. (2024). Artificial intelligence governance: Ethical considerations and implications for social responsibility. *Expert Systems: International Journal of Knowledge Engineering and Neural Networks, 41*(7), 1–15. DOI: 10.1111/exsy.13406

Cannas, V. G., Ciano, M. P., Saltalamacchia, M., & Secchi, R. (2024). Artificial intelligence in supply chain and operations management: A multiple case study research. *International Journal of Production Research, 62*(9), 3333–3360. DOI: 10.1080/00207543.2023.2232050

Cantini, A., Peron, M., De Carlo, F., & Sgarbossa, F. (2024). A decision support system for configuring spare parts supply chains considering different manufacturing technologies. *International Journal of Production Research*, *62*(8), 3023–3043. DOI: 10.1080/00207543.2022.2041757

Carbonneau, R., Laframboise, K., & Vahidov, R. (2008). Application of machine learning techniques for supply chain demand forecasting. *European Journal of Operational Research*, *184*(3), 1140–1154. DOI: 10.1016/j.ejor.2006.12.004

Cayre, R. (2022). *Offensive and defensive approaches for wireless communication protocols security in IoT* (Doctoral dissertation, Toulouse, INSA).

Chang, T.-S., & Bau, D.-Y. (2024). eXplainable artificial intelligence (XAI) in business management research: A success/failure system perspective. *Journal of Electronic Business & Digital Economics*. DOI: 10.1108/JEBDE-07-2024-0019

Chan, S., & Amling, W. (2019). Does orchestration in the global climate action agenda effectively prioritize and mobilize transnational climate adaptation action?'. *International Environmental Agreement: Politics, Law and Economics*, *19*(4–5), 429–446. DOI: 10.1007/s10784-019-09444-9

Chauhan, C., Kaur, P., Arrawatia, R., Ractham, P., & Dhir, A. (2022). Supply chain collaboration and sustainable development goals (SDGs): Teamwork makes achieving SDGs dream work. *Journal of Business Research*, *147*, 290–307. DOI: 10.1016/j.jbusres.2022.03.044

Chedrawi, C., & Haddad, G. (2022). The rise of quasi-humans in AI fueled organizations, an ultimate socio-materiality approach to the lens of Michel Serres. *Pacific Asia Journal of the Association for Information Systems*, *14*(2), 2. DOI: 10.17705/1pais.14202

Chen, B., Chao, X., & Ahn, H. S. (2019). Coordinating pricing and inventory replenishment with nonparametric demand learning. *Operations Research*, *67*(4), opre.2018.1808. DOI: 10.1287/opre.2018.1808

Chen, J., Sohal, A. S., & Prajogo, D. I. (2013). Supply chain operational risk mitigation: A collaborative approach. *International Journal of Production Research*, *51*(7), 2186–2199. DOI: 10.1080/00207543.2012.727490

Chen, L., Wu, H., & Das, A. (2025). Artificial intelligence for fostering sustainable agriculture. *Computers and Electronics in Agriculture*, *210*, 107620. DOI: 10.1016/j.compag.2025.107620

Chen, P.-K., Ye, Y., & Huang, X. (2023). The metaverse in supply chain knowledge sharing and resilience contexts: An empirical investigation of factors affecting adoption and acceptance. *Journal of Innovation & Knowledge*, *8*(4), 100446. DOI: 10.1016/j.jik.2023.100446

Chen, Q., Peng, Y., & Lu, Z. (2019). BioSentVec: creating sentence embeddings for biomedical texts. In *2019 IEEE International Conference on Healthcare Informatics (ICHI)* (pp. 1-5). IEEE. DOI: 10.1109/ICHI.2019.8904728

Chen, X., & Wang, Y. (2023). Robust Dynamic Pricing with Demand Learning in the Presence of Outlier Customers. *Operations Research*, *71*(4), 1362–1386. DOI: 10.1287/opre.2022.2280

Chen, Y., Kang, Y., Chen, Y., & Wang, Z. (2020). Probabilistic forecasting with temporal convolutional neural network. *Neurocomputing*, *399*, 491–501. DOI: 10.1016/j.neucom.2020.03.011

Chertow, M., Reck, B. K., Wrzesniewski, A., & Calli, B. (2024). Outlook on the future role of robots and AI in material recovery facilities: Implications for US recycling and the workforce. *Journal of Cleaner Production*, *470*, 143234. DOI: 10.1016/j.jclepro.2024.143234

Chien, C. F., & Wei, C. K. (2022). A hybrid demand forecasting model for managing supply chain risk. *International Journal of Forecasting*, *38*(3), 762–777. DOI: 10.1016/j.ijforecast.2021.10.008

Chi, T., Li, J., Trigeorgis, L. G., & Tsekrekos, A. E. (2019). Real options theory in international business. *Journal of International Business Studies*, *50*(4), 525–553. DOI: 10.1057/s41267-019-00222-y

Choi, T. M., Wallace, S. W., & Wang, Y. (2018). Big data analytics in operations management. *Production and Operations Management*, *27*(10), 1868–1881. DOI: 10.1111/poms.12838

Chołodowicz, E., & Orłowski, P. (2024). Neural Network Control of Perishable Inventory with Fixed Shelf Life Products and Fuzzy Order Refinement under Time-Varying Uncertain Demand. *Energies*, *17*(4), 849. DOI: 10.3390/en17040849

Chopra, S. & Meindl, P. (2020). Supply Chain Management: Strategy, Planning, and Operation.

Chopra, S., & Meindl, P. (2021). Supply chain management: Strategy, planning, and operation. Pearson.

Chopra, S., & Meindl, P. (2004). *Supply Chain Management: Strategy, Planning, and Operation* (2nd ed.). Person and Prentice Hall.

Christopher, M. (2005). *Logistics and Supply Chain Management – Creating Value-Added Networks* (3rd ed.). Pearson Education.

Christopher, M., & Peck, H. (2004). Building the Resilient Supply Chain. *International Journal of Logistics Management, 15*(2), 1–14. DOI: 10.1108/09574090410700275

Chu, T. T., & Pham, T. T. T. (2024). Vertical coordination in agri-food supply chain and blockchain: A proposed framework solution for Vietnamese cashew nut business. *Regional Science Policy & Practice, 16*(3), 12576. DOI: 10.1111/rsp3.12576

Clément, A., Robinot, É., & Trespeuch, L. (2022). Improving ESG scores with sustainability concepts. *Sustainability (Basel), 14*(20), 13154. DOI: 10.3390/su142013154

Closs, D., Speier, C., & Meacham, N. (2011). Sustainability to support end-to-end value chains: The role of supply chain management'. *Journal of the Academy of Marketing Science, 39*(1), 101–116. DOI: 10.1007/s11747-010-0207-4

Coelho, L., & Reis, S. S. (2023). Enhancing learning experiences through artificial intelligence: Classroom 5.0. In *Fostering pedagogy through micro and adaptive learning in higher education: Trends, tools, and applications* (pp. 169–191). IGI Global.

Coelho, P. M., Corona, B., ten Klooster, R., & Worrell, E. (2020). Sustainability of reusable packaging—Current situation and trends. *Resources, Conservation and Recycling. X, 6*, 100037. DOI: 10.1016/j.rcrx.2020.100037

Cohen, O., Linker, R., & Naor, A. (2010). Estimation of the number of apples in color images recorded in orchards. In *Computer and Computing Technologies in Agriculture III* (pp. 630–642). Springer.

Colin, J. (2005). Le supply chain management existe-t-il réellement? *Revue française de gestion, 31*(156), 135–149. DOI: 10.3166/rfg.156.135-149

Compagnucci, L., Lepore, D., Spigarelli, F., Frontoni, E., Baldi, M., & Di Berardino, L. (2022). Uncovering the potential of blockchain in the agri-food supply chain: An interdisciplinary case study. *Journal of Engineering and Technology Management, 65*, 101700. DOI: 10.1016/j.jengtecman.2022.101700

Cordell, G. A. (2024). The contemporary nexus of medicines security and bioprospecting: A future perspective for prioritizing the patient. *Natural Products and Bioprospecting, 14*(1), 1–32. DOI: 10.1007/s13659-024-00431-5 PMID: 38270809

Culot, G., Podrecca, M., & Nassimbeni, G. (2024). Artificial intelligence in supply chain management: A systematic literature review of empirical studies and research directions. *Computers in Industry*, *162*, 104132. DOI: 10.1016/j.compind.2024.104132

Dalal, S., Lilhore, U. K., Simaiya, S., Radulescu, M., & Belascu, L. (2024). Improving efficiency and sustainability via supply chain optimization through CNNs and BiLSTM. *Technological Forecasting and Social Change*, *209*, 123841. DOI: 10.1016/j.techfore.2024.123841

Darom, N. A., Hishamuddin, H., Ramli, R., & Mat Nopiah, Z. (2018). An inventory model of supply chain disruption recovery with safety stock and carbon emission consideration. *Journal of Cleaner Production*, *197*, 1011–1021. DOI: 10.1016/j.jclepro.2018.06.246

Dash, R., McMurtrey, M., Rebman, C., & Kar, U. K. (2019). Application of artificial intelligence in automation of supply chain management. *Journal of Strategic Innovation and Sustainability*, *14*(3), 26–37. DOI: 10.33423/jsis.v14i3.2105

Davis, J., Mengersen, K., Bennett, S., & Mazerolle, L. (2014). Viewing systematic reviews and meta-analysis in social research through different lenses. *SpringerPlus*, *3*(1), 511. DOI: 10.1186/2193-1801-3-511 PMID: 25279303

De Angelis, R., Howard, M., & Miemczyk, J. (2018). Supply chain management and the circular economy: Towards the circular supply chain. *Production Planning and Control*, *29*(6), 425–437. DOI: 10.1080/09537287.2018.1449244

de Cock, Michaëlle, and M. W. (2014). "Profits and poverty: The economics of forced labour." In *International Labour Organization*. https://www.ilo.org/wcmsp5/groups/public/---ed_norm/---declaration/documents/publication/wcms_243391.pdf

De Giovanni, P. (2023). Sustainability of the Metaverse: A Transition to Industry 5.0. *Sustainability (Basel)*, *15*(7), 6079. DOI: 10.3390/su15076079

De Leeuw, S., & Van der Meer, R. (2020). A systematic review of forecasting methods for short-term demand in retail. *European Journal of Operational Research*, *284*(3), 739–754. DOI: 10.1016/j.ejor.2019.12.036

Deif, A., & Vivek, T. (2022). Understanding AI Application Dynamics in Oil and Gas Supply Chain Management and Development: A Location Perspective. *HighTech and Innovation Journal*, *3*(0), 0. DOI: 10.28991/HIJ-SP2022-03-01

del Carmen Sandoval Madrid, A. (2023). *The nexus of sustainability and industry 5.0: Assessing Canadian organizations': Readiness for the next technological revolution* (Doctoral dissertation, University Canada West).

Del Rio, D. D. F., Sovacool, B. K., & Griffiths, S. (2021). Culture, energy and climate sustainability, and smart home technologies: A mixed methods comparison of four countries. *Energy and Climate Change*, *2*, 100035. DOI: 10.1016/j.egycc.2021.100035

Demizu, T., Fukazawa, Y., & Morita, H. (2023). Inventory management of new products in retailers using model-based deep reinforcement learning. *Expert Systems with Applications*, *229*, 120256. DOI: 10.1016/j.eswa.2023.120256

Deng, Y., Zhang, X., Wang, T., Wang, L., Zhang, Y., Wang, X., Zhao, S., Qi, Y., Yang, G., & Peng, X. (2023). Alibaba Realizes Millions in Cost Savings Through Integrated Demand Forecasting, Inventory Management, Price Optimization, and Product Recommendations. *INFORMS Journal on Applied Analytics*, *53*(1), 32–46. DOI: 10.1287/inte.2022.1145

Dereci, U., & Tuzkaya, G. (2024). An explainable artificial intelligence model for predictive maintenance and spare parts optimization. *Supply Chain Analytics*, *8*, 100078. DOI: 10.1016/j.sca.2024.100078

Dey, K., & Shekhawat, U. (2021). Blockchain for sustainable e-agriculture: Literature review, architecture for data management, and implications. *Journal of Cleaner Production*, *316*(June), 128254. DOI: 10.1016/j.jclepro.2021.128254

Dey, P. K., Chowdhury, S., Abadie, A., Vann Yaroson, E., & Sarkar, S. (2024). Artificial intelligence-driven supply chain resilience in Vietnamese manufacturing small- and medium-sized enterprises. *International Journal of Production Research*, *62*(15), 5417–5456. DOI: 10.1080/00207543.2023.2179859

Dillard-Wright, J., & Shields-Haas, V. (2021). Nursing with the people: Reimagining futures for nursing. *Advances in Nursing Science*, *44*(3), 195–209. DOI: 10.1097/ANS.0000000000000361 PMID: 33624989

Ding, Y., Tu, Y., Pu, J., & Qiu, L. (2021). Environmental Factors in Operations Management: The Impact of Air Quality on Product Demand. *Production and Operations Management*, *30*(9), 2910–2924. DOI: 10.1111/poms.13410

Dmitrieva, E., Balmiki, V., Lakhanpal, S., Lavanya, G., & Bhandari, P. (2024). AI Evolution in Industry 4.0 and Industry 5.0: An Experimental Comparative Assessment. In *BIO Web of Conferences* (Vol. 86, p. 01069). EDP Sciences.

Dolgui, A., & Ivanov, D. (2023). Metaverse supply chain and operations management. *International Journal of Production Research*, *61*(23), 8179–8191. DOI: 10.1080/00207543.2023.2240900 du Plessis, M. J., Gerber, R., Goedhals-Gerber, L. L., & van Eeden, J. (2025). Shaping the Future of Freight Logistics: Use Cases of Artificial Intelligence. *Sustainability (Basel), 17*(4), 4. DOI: 10.3390/su17041355

Duan, K., Onyeaka, H., Pang, G., & Meng, Z. (2024). Pioneering food safety: Blockchain's integration in supply chain surveillance. *Journal of Agriculture and Food Research, 18*, 101281. DOI: 10.1016/j.jafr.2024.101281

Dubey, R., Bryde, D. J., Blome, C., Roubaud, D., & Giannakis, M. (2021). Facilitating artificial intelligence powered supply chain analytics through alliance management during the pandemic crises in the B2B context. *Industrial Marketing Management, 96*, 135–146. DOI: 10.1016/j.indmarman.2021.05.003

Dubey, R., Gunasekaran, A., & Papadopoulos, T. (2024). Benchmarking operations and supply chain management practices using Generative AI: Towards a theoretical framework. *Transportation Research Part E, Logistics and Transportation Review, 189*, 103689. DOI: 10.1016/j.tre.2024.103689

Durai, S. S., & Sundaram, D. (2020). Traditional forecasting models and their application in demand management: A review and comparative analysis. *Computers & Industrial Engineering, 141*, 106332. DOI: 10.1016/j.cie.2020.106332

DUTTA. P. (2020). *Occupancy Based Load Switching using Microcontroller* (Doctoral dissertation, University of Technology).

Dutta, P., Choi, T.-M., Somani, S., & Butala, R. (2020). Blockchain technology in supply chain operations: Applications, challenges and research opportunities. *Transportation Research Part E, Logistics and Transportation Review, 142*, 102067. DOI: 10.1016/j.tre.2020.102067 PMID: 33013183

Dutta, P., & Kumar, S. (2021). Artificial intelligence in inventory and demand forecasting. *Journal of Retailing and Consumer Services, 62*, 102610. DOI: 10.1016/j.jretconser.2021.102610

EBSCO Information Services. (2024). EBSCOhost research databases.

Eiglsperger, J., Haselbeck, F., Stiele, V., Serrano, C. G., Lim-Trinh, K., Menrad, K., Hannus, T., & Grimm, D. G. (2024). Forecasting seasonally fluctuating sales of perishable products in the horticultural industry. *Expert Systems with Applications, 249*, 123438. DOI: 10.1016/j.eswa.2024.123438

El Asri, A., El Farouk, I. I., Jawab, F., Arif, J., & Moufad, I. (2022, May). The drug supply chain at the public hospital in Morocco: a literature review. In *2022 14th International Colloquium of Logistics and Supply Chain Management (LOGISTIQUA)* (pp. 1-5). IEEE. DOI: 10.1109/LOGISTIQUA55056.2022.9938022

El Jaouhari, A., Arif, J., & Jawab, F. (2024). Mediating the role of Internet of Things in Sustainable Automotive Supply Chain: Practical Evidence from a Delphi Analysis. In *2024 IEEE 15th International Colloquium on Logistics and Supply Chain Management (LOGISTIQUA)* (pp. 1-6). IEEE.

El Jaouhari, A., Azari, M., Arif, J., El Farouk, I. I., Jawab, F., & Moufad, I. (2022). IoT for the future of sustainable supply chain management in Industry 4.0: A Systematic Literature Review. *2022 14th International Colloquium of Logistics and Supply Chain Management (LOGISTIQUA)*, 1–6. https://ieeexplore.ieee.org/abstract/document/9938123/

El Jaouhari, A., Azari, M., Arif, J., El Farouk, I. I., Jawab, F., & Moufad, I. (2022, May). IoT for the future of sustainable supply chain management in Industry 4.0: A Systematic Literature Review. In 2022 14th International Colloquium of Logistics and Supply Chain Management (LOGISTIQUA) (pp. 1-6). IEEE.

El Jaouhari, A., Alhilali, Z., Arif, J., Fellaki, S., Amejwal, M., & Azzouz, K. (2022). Demand forecasting application with regression and IoT based inventory management system: A case study of a semiconductor manufacturing company. *International Journal of Engineering Research in Africa*, *60*, 189–210. DOI: 10.4028/p-8ntq24

El Jaouhari, A., Arif, J., Jawab, F., Samadhiya, A., & Kumar, A. (2024). Unfolding the role of metaverse in agri-food supply chain security: Current scenario and future perspectives. *International Journal of Food Science & Technology*, *59*(5), 3451–3460. DOI: 10.1111/ijfs.16972

El Jaouhari, A., Arif, J., Samadhiya, A., Dhayal, K. S., Luthra, S., & Singh, S. (2025). From Automation to Augmentation: Exploring the Role of Industry 5.0 Advanced Technologies for Developing Countries. *Engineering Management Journal*, *37*(3), 306–323. DOI: 10.1080/10429247.2024.2407254

El Jaouhari, A., Arif, J., Samadhiya, A., Kumar, A., Jain, V., & Agrawal, R. (2024). Are metaverse applications in quality 4.0 enablers of manufacturing resiliency? An exploratory review under disruption impressions and future research. *The TQM Journal*, *36*(6), 1486–1525. DOI: 10.1108/TQM-06-2023-0181

El Jaouhari, A., Samadhiya, A., Benbrahim, F. Z., Kumar, A., & Luthra, S. (2024). Forging a green future: Synergizing industry 4.0 technologies and circular economy tactics to achieve net-zero in sustainable supply chains. *Computers & Industrial Engineering, 110691*. DOI: 10.1016/j.cie.2024.110691

El Jaouhari, A., Samadhiya, A., Kumar, A., Šešplaukis, A., & Raslanas, S. (2024). Mapping the landscape: A systematic literature review on automated valuation models and strategic applications in real estate. *International Journal of Strategic Property Management, 28*(5), 286–301. DOI: 10.3846/ijspm.2024.22251

El Makhloufi, A. (2023). *AI application in transport and logistics: Opportunities and challenges (An exploratory study).*

El Yadari, M., Moufad, I., Jawab, F., & Arif, J. (2024). Logistic 4.0 Implementation For Efficient Urban Freight Transport: A Systematic Literature Review. In *2024 IEEE 15th International Colloquium on Logistics and Supply Chain Management (LOGISTIQUA)* (pp. 1-8). IEEE.

ElBaih, M. (2023). The Role of Privacy Regulations in AI Development (A Discussion of the Ways in Which Privacy Regulations Can Shape the Development of AI). *SSRN* 4589207. DOI: 10.2139/ssrn.4589207

Elbegzaya, T. (2020). *Application AI in Traditional Supply Chain Management Decision-Making*. http://dspace.unive.it/handle/10579/17733

Elkington, J. (1994). Towards the sustainable corporation: Win-win-win business strategies for sustainable development'. *California Management Review, 36*(2), 90–100. DOI: 10.2307/41165746

Elorza, M., Castellano, E., & Segura, S. (2024). Prediction of customer demand for perishable products in retail inventory management, using the hybrid prophet-XGBoost model during the post-COVID-19 period. *Applied Economics Letters*, •••, 1–7. DOI: 10.1080/13504851.2024.2333995

Ercan, T., Onat, N. C., Keya, N., Tatari, O., Eluru, N., & Kucukvar, M. (2022). Autonomous electric vehicles can reduce carbon emissions and air pollution in cities. *Transportation Research Part D, Transport and Environment, 112*, 103472. DOI: 10.1016/j.trd.2022.103472

Esmaeilian, B., Sarkis, J., Lewis, K., & Behdad, S. (2020). Blockchain for the future of sustainable supply chain management in Industry 4.0. *Resources, Conservation and Recycling, 2020*(163), 105064. DOI: 10.1016/j.resconrec.2020.105064

Esmaeili-Najafabadi, E., Azad, N., & Saber Fallah Nezhad, M. (2021). Risk-averse supplier selection and order allocation in the centralized supply chains under disruption risks. *Expert Systems with Applications, 175*, 114691. DOI: 10.1016/j.eswa.2021.114691

Fang, B., Yu, J., Chen, Z., Osman, A. I., Farghali, M., Ihara, I., Hamza, E. H., Rooney, D. W., & Yap, P.-S. (2023). Artificial intelligence for waste management in smart cities: A review. *Environmental Chemistry Letters*, *21*(4), 1959–1989. DOI: 10.1007/s10311-023-01604-3 PMID: 37362015

Fanoro, M., Božanić, M., & Sinha, S. (2021). A review of 4IR/5IR enabling technologies and their linkage to manufacturing supply chain. *Technologies*, *9*(4), 77. DOI: 10.3390/technologies9040077

Fawehinmi, O., Aigbogun, O., & Tanveer, M. I. (2024). The Role of Industrial Revolution 5.0 in Actualizing the Effectiveness of Green Human Resource Management. In *Green Human Resource Management: A View from Global South Countries* (pp. 291–312). Springer Nature Singapore. DOI: 10.1007/978-981-99-7104-6_17

Fernández-Miguel, A., García-Muiña, F. E., Jiménez-Calzado, M., Melara San Román, P., Fernández Del Hoyo, A. P., & Settembre-Blundo, D. (2024). Boosting business agility with additive digital molding: An Industry 5.0 approach to sustainable supply chains'. *Computers & Industrial Engineering*, *192*, 110222. DOI: 10.1016/j.cie.2024.110222

Ferreira, K. J., Lee, B. H. A., & Simchi-Levi, D. (2016). Analytics for an online retailer: Demand forecasting and price optimization. *Manufacturing & Service Operations Management*, *18*(1), 69–88. DOI: 10.1287/msom.2015.0561

Fildes, R., Goodwin, P., & Lawrence, M. (2019). The impact of forecasting methods on inventory performance. *International Journal of Forecasting*, *35*(4), 1221–1235. DOI: 10.1016/j.ijforecast.2019.01.001

Fildes, R., Kolassa, S., & Ma, S. (2022). Post-script—Retail forecasting: Research and practice. *International Journal of Forecasting*, *38*(4), 1319–1324. DOI: 10.1016/j.ijforecast.2021.09.012 PMID: 36217499

Fisher, M. (2018). The new science of retailing: How analytics and machine learning are transforming demand forecasting. *Journal of Business Logistics*, *39*(3), 231–249. DOI: 10.1111/jbl.12159

Flanigen, P. (2023). *Algorithms and Visualizations to Support Airborne Detection of Vertical Obstacles* (Doctoral dissertation).

Ford, D. R. (2020). *Review of Mike Davis (2020). The Monster Enters : COVID 19, Avian Flu, and the Plagues of Capitalism*. Postdigital Science and Education.

Formen, J. S., Hassan, D. S., & Wolf, C. (2024). Chemometric sensing of stereoisomeric compound mixtures with a redox-responsive optical probe. *Chemical Science (Cambridge)*, *15*(4), 1498–1504. DOI: 10.1039/D3SC05706B PMID: 38274061

Fowler, A., & Biekart, K. (2017). Multi-Stakeholder Initiatives for Sustainable Development Goals: The Importance of Interlocutors. *Public Administration and Development, 37*(2), 81–93. DOI: 10.1002/pad.1795

Friedman, B., & Hendry, D. G. (2019). *Value Sensitive Design: Shaping Technology with Moral Imagination.* MIT Press. DOI: 10.7551/mitpress/7585.001.0001

Fritz, M. M. (2022). A supply chain view of sustainability management. *Cleaner Production Letters, 3*, 100023. DOI: 10.1016/j.clpl.2022.100023

Fritz, M. M. C., & Cordova, M. (2023). 'Developing managers' mindset to lead more sustainable supply chains'. *Cleaner Logistics and Supply Chain, 7*, 100108. DOI: 10.1016/j.clscn.2023.100108

Frohnwieser, S. M. (2023). *Lunawood C grade: What do we do with it?* https://urn.fi/URN:NBN:fi:amk-2023100426864

Fujimaki, R., Muraoka, Y., Ito, S., & Yabe, A. (2016). From prediction to decision making - Predictive optimization technology. NEC Technical Journal, 11(1).

Gallego, G., & Ryzin, G. J. (2020). Revenue management with machine learning. *Management Science, 66*(8), 3485–3500. DOI: 10.1287/mnsc.2020.3771

Gao, Y., & Zhang, Y. (2021). Combining traditional and machine learning approaches for demand forecasting. *Journal of Business Research, 126*, 79–89. DOI: 10.1016/j.jbusres.2020.12.015

Gardner, T. A., Benzie, M., Börner, J., Dawkins, E., Fick, S., Garrett, R., Godar, J., Grimard, A., Lake, S., Larsen, R. K., Mardas, N., McDermott, C. L., Meyfroidt, P., Osbeck, M., Persson, M., Sembres, T., Suavet, C., Strassburg, B., Trevisan, A., & Wolvekamp, P. (2019). Transparency and sustainability in global commodity supply chains. *World Development, 121*, 163–177. DOI: 10.1016/j.worlddev.2018.05.025 PMID: 31481824

Garrido, S., Muniz, J.Jr, & Batista Ribeiro, V. (2024). Operations management, sustainability & Industry 5.0: A critical analysis and future agenda. *Cleaner Logistics and Supply Chain, 10*, 100141. DOI: 10.1016/j.clscn.2024.100141

Garti, M. O., Arif, J., & Jawab, F. (2024). Sustainable supply chain management: Past evaluation and present analysis for future research perspectives. In *2024 IEEE 15th International Colloquium on Logistics and Supply Chain Management (LOGISTIQUA)* (pp. 1-7). IEEE.

Ge, D., Pan, Y., Shen, Z.-J., Wu, D., Yuan, R., & Zhang, C. (2019). Retail supply chain management: A review of theories and practices. *Journal of Data, Information and Management, 1*(1–2), 45–64. DOI: 10.1007/s42488-019-00004-z

Gedam, V., Pimplapure, A., Sen, P., Pandey, S., Namdeo, Y., & Atkare, S. (2023). The transformative impact of artificial intelligence on supply chain management. *Journal of Survey in Fisheries Sciences, 10*(4), 3562–3573.

Geissdoerfer, M., Savaget, P., Bocken, N. M. P., & Hultink, E. J. (2017). The Circular Economy – A new sustainability paradigm? *Journal of Cleaner Production, 143*(0), 757–768. DOI: 10.1016/j.jclepro.2016.12.048

Ghadge, A., Kara, M. E., Moradlou, H., & Goswami, M. (2020). The impact of Industry 4.0 implementation on supply chains. *Journal of Manufacturing Technology Management, 31*(4), 669–686. DOI: 10.1108/JMTM-10-2019-0368

Ghobakhloo, M., Iranmanesh, M., Foroughi, B., Babaee Tirkolaee, E., Asadi, S. and Amran, A. (2023) 'Industry 5.0 implications for inclusive sustainable manufacturing: an evidence-knowledge-based strategic roadmap', Journal of Cleaner Production, June, Vol. 417, p.138023, .DOI: 10.1016/j.jclepro.2023.138023

Ghosh, S., Hughes, M., Hughes, P., & Hodgkinson, I. (2021). Corporate digital entrepreneurship: Leveraging industrial internet of things and emerging technologies. Digital Entrepreneurship, 183.

Goh, M., & Koon, M. (2023). Demand forecasting for inventory management in uncertain supply chains. *International Journal of Production Economics, 246*, 108376. DOI: 10.1016/j.ijpe.2022.108376

Goka, S., Moinuddin, S. Q., Cheepu, M., & Dewangan, A. K. (2024). Welding Practices in Industry 5.0: Opportunities, Challenges, and Applications. *Automation in Welding Industry: Incorporating Artificial Intelligence, Machine Learning and Other Technologies*, 263-279.

Gongal, A., Amatya, S., Karkee, M., Zhang, Q., & Lewis, K. (2015). Sensors and systems for fruit detection and localization: A review. *Computers and Electronics in Agriculture, 116*, 8–19. DOI: 10.1016/j.compag.2015.05.021

Gonzalez-Manzano, L., Fuentes, J. M. D., & Ribagorda, A. (2019). Leveraging user-related internet of things for continuous authentication: A survey. *ACM Computing Surveys, 52*(3), 1–38. DOI: 10.1145/3314023

Goodfellow, I., Bengio, Y., & Courville, A. (2016). *Deep learning*. MIT Press.

Govindan, K., Jain, P., Kr. Singh, R., & Mishra, R. (2024). Blockchain technology as a strategic weapon to bring procurement 4.0 truly alive: Literature review and future research agenda. *Transportation Research Part E, Logistics and Transportation Review*, *181*, 103352. DOI: 10.1016/j.tre.2023.103352

Gregori, F., Papetti, A., Pandolfi, M., Peruzzini, M., & Germani, M. (2018). Improving a production site from a social point of view: An IoT infrastructure to monitor workers condition. *Procedia CIRP*, *72*(March), 886–891. DOI: 10.1016/j.procir.2018.03.057

Greyson, D., Rafferty, E., Slater, L., MacDonald, N., Bettinger, J. A., Dubé, È., & MacDonald, S. E. (2019). Systematic review searches must be systematic, comprehensive, and transparent: A critique of Perman et al. *BMC Public Health*, *19*(1), 153. DOI: 10.1186/s12889-018-6275-y PMID: 30717742

Gruchmann, T. (2019). Advanced green logistics strategies and technologies. In Piotrowicz, W., & Cuthbertson, R. (Eds.), *Operations, logistics and supply chain management* (pp. 663–686). Springer., DOI: 10.1007/978-3-319-92447-2_29

Gružauskas, V., Gimžauskienė, E., & Navickas, V. (2019). Forecasting accuracy influence on logistics clusters activities: The case of the food industry. *Journal of Cleaner Production*, *240*, 118225. DOI: 10.1016/j.jclepro.2019.118225

Guan, Y., Yan, J., Shan, Y., Zhou, Y., Hang, Y., Li, R., Liu, Y., Liu, B., Nie, Q., Bruckner, B., Feng, K., & Hubacek, K. (2023). Burden of the global energy price crisis on households. *Nature Energy*, *8*(3), 304–316. DOI: 10.1038/s41560-023-01209-8

Guidani, B., Ronzoni, M., & Accorsi, R. (2024). Virtual agri-food supply chains: A holistic digital twin for sustainable food ecosystem design, control and transparency. *Sustainable Production and Consumption*, *46*, 161–179. DOI: 10.1016/j.spc.2024.01.016

Guide, V. D. R., & Van Wassenhove, L. N. (2002, February 1). *The reverse supply chain*. Harvard Business Review. https://hbr.org/2002/02/the-reverse-supply-chain

Gumbo, S., Twinomurinzi, H., Bwalya, K., & Wamba, S. F. (2023). Skills provisioning for the Fourth Industrial Revolution: A Bibliometric Analysis. *Procedia Computer Science*, *219*, 924–932. DOI: 10.1016/j.procs.2023.01.368

Gupta, S., Modgil, S., Bhattacharyya, S., & Bose, I. (2022). Artificial intelligence for decision support systems in the field of operations research: Review and future scope of research. *Annals of Operations Research*, *308*(1), 215–274. https://link.springer.com/article/10.1007/s10479-020-03856-6. DOI: 10.1007/s10479-020-03856-6

Gupta, S., Modgil, S., Meissonier, R., & Dwivedi, Y. K. (2024). Artificial Intelligence and Information System Resilience to Cope With Supply Chain Disruption. *IEEE Transactions on Engineering Management, 71*, 10496-10506. *IEEE Transactions on Engineering Management*. DOI: 10.1109/TEM.2021.3116770

Gu, Q., & Yang, Y. (2019). Ensemble methods for demand forecasting. *Annals of Operations Research, 271*(2), 123–138. DOI: 10.1007/s10479-018-3012-7

Gwala, R. S., & Mashau, P. (2024). Equality, Diversity, and Access in Digitalized Teaching in Higher Education. In *Accessibility of Digital Higher Education in the Global South* (pp. 105–131). IGI Global.

Haider Sayma, M., Hasan, M. R., Khatun, M., Rajee, A., & Begum, A. (2024a). Detecting the provenance of price hike in agri-food supply chain using private Ethereum blockchain network. *Heliyon, 10*(11), e30972. DOI: 10.1016/j.heliyon.2024.e30972 PMID: 38832272

Haleem, A., & Javaid, M. (2019). Additive manufacturing applications in industry 4.0: A review. *Journal of Industrial Integration and Management, 4*(04), 1930001. DOI: 10.1142/S2424862219300011

Haleem, A., Javaid, M., Singh, R. P., & Suman, R. (2022). Medical 4.0 technologies for healthcare: Features, capabilities, and applications. *Internet of Things and Cyber-Physical Systems, 2*, 12–30. DOI: 10.1016/j.iotcps.2022.04.001

Hamann, R., & Bertels, S. (2018). The institutional work of exploitation: Employers' work to create and perpetuate inequality. *Journal of Management Studies, 55*(3), 394–423. DOI: 10.1111/joms.12325

Han, B., Jiang, W., Habibi, M. A., & Schotten, H. D. (2021). *An Abstracted Survey on 6G : Drivers, Requirements, Efforts, and Enablers* (arXiv:2101.01062). arXiv. /arXiv.2101.01062DOI: 10.48550

Handfield, R. B., Graham, G., & Burns, L. (2020). Corona virus, tariffs, trade wars and supply chain evolutionary design. *International Journal of Operations & Production Management, 40*(10), 1649–1660. DOI: 10.1108/IJOPM-03-2020-0171

Hangl, J., Behrens, V. J., & Krause, S. (2022). Barriers, Drivers, and Social Considerations for AI Adoption in Supply Chain Management: A Tertiary Study. *Logistics (Basel), 6*(3), 3. DOI: 10.3390/logistics6030063

Han, Y., Chong, W. K., & Li, D. (2020). A systematic literature review of the capabilities and performance metrics of supply chain resilience. *International Journal of Production Research, 58*(15), 4541–4566. DOI: 10.1080/00207543.2020.1785034

Hasan, K., & Ahmed, T. (2017). *Applications of Internet of Things (IoT) Towards Smart Home Automation* (Doctoral dissertation, Stamford University Bangladesh).

Hasan, A. S. M. T., Sabah, S., Daria, A., & Haque, R. U. (2023). A peer-to-peer blockchain-based architecture for trusted and reliable agricultural product traceability. *Decision Analytics Journal, 9*, 100363. DOI: 10.1016/j.dajour.2023.100363

Hashim, M. A. M., Tlemsani, I., Mason-Jones, R., Matthews, R., & Ndrecaj, V. (2024). Higher education via the lens of industry 5.0: Strategy and perspective. *Social Sciences & Humanities Open, 9*, 100828. DOI: 10.1016/j.ssaho.2024.100828

Hassan, A., Dutta, P. K., Gupta, S., Mattar, E., & Singh, S. (Eds.). (2024). *Human-Centered Approaches in Industry 5.0: Human-Machine Interaction, Virtual Reality Training, and Customer Sentiment Analysis: Human-Machine Interaction, Virtual Reality Training, and Customer Sentiment Analysis*. IGI Global.

Hastig, G. M., & Sodhi, M. S. (2020). Blockchain for supply chain traceability: Business requirements and critical success factors. *Production and Operations Management, 29*(4), 935–954. DOI: 10.1111/poms.13147

Helo, P., & Hao, Y. (2022). Artificial intelligence in operations management and supply chain management: An exploratory case study. *Production Planning and Control, 33*(16), 1573–1590. DOI: 10.1080/09537287.2021.1882690

Henrysson, M., Papageorgiou, A., Björklund, A., Vanhuyse, F., & Sinha, R. (2022). Monitoring progress towards a circular economy in urban areas: An application of the European Union circular economy monitoring framework in Umeå municipality. *Sustainable Cities and Society, 87*, 104245. DOI: 10.1016/j.scs.2022.104245

He, P., Wen, J., Ye, S., & Li, Z. (2020). Logistics service sharing and competition in a dual-channel e-commerce supply chain. *Computers & Industrial Engineering, 149*, 106849. DOI: 10.1016/j.cie.2020.106849

Hermann, M., Pentek, T., and Otto, B. (2016). Design principles for industrie 4.0 scenarios. *In 2016 49th Hawaii International Conference on System Sciences (HICSS), 01*. DOI: 10.13140/RG.2.2.29269.22248

Hoeltgebaum, H., Borenstein, D., Fernandes, C., & Veiga, Á. (2021). A score-driven model of short-term demand forecasting for retail distribution centers. *Journal of Retailing, 97*(4), 715–725. DOI: 10.1016/j.jretai.2021.05.003

Hofmann, P., Samp, C., & Urbach, N. (2020). Robotic process automation. *Electronic Markets, 30*(1), 99–106. DOI: 10.1007/s12525-019-00365-8

Hopp, W. J., & Spearman, M. L. (2021). *Factory physics: Foundations of manufacturing management*. McGraw-Hill Education.

Hristov, I., & Chirico, A. (2019). The role of sustainability key performance indicators (KPIs) in implementing sustainable strategies. *Sustainability (Basel), 11*(20), 5742. DOI: 10.3390/su11205742

Huang, H., Zheng, O., Wang, D., Yin, J., Wang, Z., Ding, S., Yin, H., Xu, C., Yang, R., Zheng, Q., & Shi, B. (2023). ChatGPT for shaping the future of dentistry: The potential of multi-modal large language model. *International Journal of Oral Science, 15*(1), 29. DOI: 10.1038/s41368-023-00239-y PMID: 37507396

Huang, X., & Kechadi, M. T. (2020). AI-driven predictive models in supply chain management. *Expert Systems with Applications, 150*, 113239. DOI: 10.1016/j.eswa.2020.113239

Huber, J., & Stuckenschmidt, H. (2020). Daily retail demand forecasting using machine learning with emphasis on calendric special days. *International Journal of Forecasting, 36*(4), 1420–1438. DOI: 10.1016/j.ijforecast.2020.02.005

Huerta-Soto, R., Ramirez-Asis, E., Tarazona-Jiménez, J., Nivin-Vargas, L., Norabuena-Figueroa, R., Guzman-Avalos, M., & Reyes-Reyes, C. (2023). Predictable inventory management within dairy supply chain operations. *International Journal of Retail & Distribution Management*. DOI: 10.1108/IJRDM-01-2023-0051

Hu, H., Qi, Y., Lee, H. L., Shen, Z.-J. M., Liu, C., Zhu, W., & Kang, N. (2024). Supercharged by Advanced Analytics, JD.com Attains Agility, Resilience, and Shared Value Across Its Supply Chain. *INFORMS Journal on Applied Analytics, 54*(1), 54–70. DOI: 10.1287/inte.2023.0078

Hussain, A., Ansari, H. W. A., Nasir, H., & Maqbool, M. Q. (2023). Developing a Model for the Adoption of Industrial Revolution 5.0 Among Malaysian Manufacturing SMEs for Sustainable Growth. In *Opportunities and Challenges of Business 5.0 in Emerging Markets* (pp. 40–57). IGI Global. DOI: 10.4018/978-1-6684-6403-8.ch003

Hutchins, M. J., & Sutherland, J. W. (2008). An exploration of measures of social sustainability and their application to supply chain decisions. *Journal of Cleaner Production, 16*(15), 1688–1698. DOI: 10.1016/j.jclepro.2008.06.001

Hyndman, R. J., & Athanasopoulos, G. (2021). *Forecasting: Principles and practice*. OTexts.

Imran, M. A., & Hyun, K. (2024). In-store shopping trip predictions and impact factors during COVID-19 emergencies. *Transportation Planning and Technology, 47*(4), 540–565. DOI: 10.1080/03081060.2023.2282059

Irpan, M., & Shaddiq, S. (2024). Industry 4.0 and Industry 5.0—Inception, Conception, Perception, and Rethinking Loyalty Employment. *INTERNATIONAL JOURNAL OF ECONOMICS, MANAGEMENT* [IJEMBIS]. *BUSINESS, AND SOCIAL SCIENCE, 4*(1), 95–114.

Islam, M. S., Amin, S., Arifuzzaman, M., Rahman, M. H., & Hossain, R. (2023). *Automatic Train Wash Plant on Metro System* (Doctoral dissertation, Sonargoan University (SU)).

Islam, M. S., Suad, S. F. R., & Rahman, A. (2024). Leveraging AI to overcome key challenges in last-mile delivery: Enhancing customer experience and operational efficiency in e-commerce. *Supply Chain Insider, 14*(1).

Islam, H. (2025). Nexus of economic, social, and environmental factors on sustainable development goals: The moderating role of technological advancement and green innovation. *Innovation and Green Development, 4*(1), 100183. DOI: 10.1016/j.igd.2024.100183

Ismaeil, M. K., & Lalla, A. F. (2024). The role and impact of artificial intelligence on supply chain management: Efficiency, challenges, and strategic implementation. *Journal of Ecohumanism, 3*(4), 89–106. DOI: 10.62754/joe.v3i4.3461

Ismail, M. M., Ahmed, Z., Abdel-Gawad, A. F., & Mohamed, M. (2024). Toward Supply Chain 5.0: An Integrated Multi-Criteria Decision-Making Models for Sustainable and Resilience Enterprise. *Decision making: applications in management and engineering, 7*(1), 160-186.

Issaoui, Y., Khiat, A., Bahnasse, A., & Ouajji, H. (2019). Smart logistics: Study of the application of blockchain technology. *Procedia Computer Science, 160*, 266–271. DOI: 10.1016/j.procs.2019.09.467

Ivanov, D. (2022). Viable supply chain model: Integrating agility, resilience and sustainability perspectives—Lessons from and thinking beyond the COVID-19 pandemic. *Annals of Operations Research, 319*(1), 1411–1431. DOI: 10.1007/s10479-020-03640-6 PMID: 32836614

Ivanov, D. (2025, June 19). A survey of system-cybernetic principles in supply chain resilience: Viability, artificial intelligence, digital twins, and ecosystems. *International Journal of Systems Science, 0*(0), 1–16. DOI: 10.1080/00207721.2025.2519204

J. Murrey Atkins Library. (2021). *Web of Science*. University of North Carolina at Charlotte.

Jackson, I. (2022). AutoML Approach to Stock Keeping Units Segmentation. *Journal of Theoretical and Applied Electronic Commerce Research, 17*(4), 1512–1528. DOI: 10.3390/jtaer17040076

Jadhav, A., Orr, S., & Malik, M. (2019). The role of supply chain orientation in achieving supply chain sustainability. *International Journal of Production Economics, 217*, 112–125. DOI: 10.1016/j.ijpe.2018.07.031

Jagtap, S., Trollman, H., Trollman, F., Garcia-Garcia, G., Parra-López, C., Duong, L., Martindale, W., Munekata, P. E. S., Lorenzo, J. M., Hdaifeh, A., Hassoun, A., Salonitis, K., & Afy-Shararah, M. (2022). The Russia-Ukraine Conflict: Its Implications for the Global Food Supply Chains. *Foods, 11*(14), 2098. DOI: 10.3390/foods11142098 PMID: 35885340

Jahanbin, P., Wingreen, S. C., Sharma, R., Ijadi, B., & Reis, M. M. (2023a). Enabling affordances of blockchain in agri-food supply chains: A value-driver framework using Q-methodology. *International Journal of Innovation Studies, 7*(4), 307–325. DOI: 10.1016/j.ijis.2023.08.001

Jahin, M. A., Shahriar, A., & Amin, M. A. (2024). MCDFN: Supply Chain Demand Forecasting via an Explainable Multi-Channel Data Fusion Network Model.

Jaouhari, A. E., Bhilat, E. M. E., & Arif, J. (2023). Scrutinizing IoT applicability in green warehouse inventory management system based on Mamdani fuzzy inference system: A case study of an automotive semiconductors industrial firm. *Journal of Industrial and Production Engineering*. https://www.tandfonline.com/doi/abs/10.1080/21681015.2022.2142303

Jaouhari, A. E., & Arif, J. (2024). Artificial intelligence of things and circular warehouse process management of automotive parts: Conceptual framework and practice review. *International Journal of Process Management and Benchmarking, 17*(1), 109–135. DOI: 10.1504/IJPMB.2024.137789

Jaouhari, A. E., Arif, J., Fellaki, S., Amejwal, M., & Azzouz, K. (2022). Lean supply chain management and Industry 4.0 interrelationships: The status quo and future perspectives. *International Journal of Lean Six Sigma, 14*(2), 335–367. DOI: 10.1108/IJLSS-11-2021-0192

Jaouhari, A. E., Arif, J., Jawab, F., Samadhiya, A., & Kumar, A. (2024). In Jawab, F. (Ed.), *Leveraging the role of blockchain technology in the hospital supply chain: A systematic literature review and future trends* (Vol. 27, pp. 587–617). Springer., DOI: 10.1007/978-3-031-70292-1_28

Jaouhari, A. E., Arif, J., Samadhiya, A., Kumar, A., & Garza-Reyes, J. A. (2023). An environmental-based perspective framework: Integrating IoT technology into a sustainable automotive supply chain. *Benchmarking*, *31*(10), 3655–3689. DOI: 10.1108/BIJ-05-2023-0322

Jaouhari, A. E., Arif, J., Samadhiya, A., Kumar, A., & Trinkūnas, V. (2023). Are we there or do we have more to do? Metaverse in facility management and future prospects. *International Journal of Strategic Property Management*, *27*(3), 3. DOI: 10.3846/ijspm.2023.19516

Jasrotia, S. S., Rai, S. S., Rai, S., & Giri, S. (2024). Stage-wise green supply chain management and environmental performance: Impact of blockchain technology. *International Journal of Information Management Data Insights*, *4*(2), 100241. DOI: 10.1016/j.jjimei.2024.100241

Jauhar, S. K., Harinath, S., Krishnaswamy, V., & Paul, S. K. (2024). Explainable artificial intelligence to improve the resilience of perishable product supply chains by leveraging customer characteristics. *Annals of Operations Research*. DOI: 10.1007/s10479-024-06348-z

Jauhar, S. K., Jani, S. M., Kamble, S. S., Pratap, S., Belhadi, A., & Gupta, S. (2023). How to use no-code artificial intelligence to predict and minimize the inventory distortions for resilient supply chains. *International Journal of Production Research*. DOI: 10.1080/00207543.2023.2166139

Javaid, M., Haleem, A., Pratap Singh, R., Khan, S., & Suman, R. (2021). Blockchain technology applications for Industry 4.0: A literature-based review. *Blockchain: Research and Applications*, *2*(4), 100027. DOI: 10.1016/j.bcra.2021.100027

Javaid, M., Haleem, A., & Singh, R. P. (2023). ChatGPT for healthcare services: An emerging stage for an innovative perspective. BenchCouncil Transactions on Benchmarks. *Standards and Evaluations*, *3*(1), 100105.

Jena, S. K., & Sarmah, S. P. (2016). Future aspect of acquisition management in closed-loop supply chain. *International Journal of Sustainable Engineering*, *9*(4), 266–276. DOI: 10.1080/19397038.2016.1181120

Jenkins, A. (2021). *A guide to reverse logistics: How it works, types and strategies*. Oracle NetSuite. https://www.netsuite.com/portal/resource/articles/inventory-management/reverse-logistics.shtml

Jha, A., Rani, S., & Sharma, P. (2024). Sustainable AI-based production agriculture. *Sustainable Computing : Informatics and Systems*, *36*, 100987. DOI: 10.1016/j.suscom.2024.100987

Jiang, H., & Tian, C. (2019). Optimizing supply chain networks with AI-driven insights. *The Journal of Supply Chain Management*, *54*(4), 32–45. DOI: 10.1111/jscm.2019.19

Jokubauskis, D. (2020). *Development and applications of compact spectroscopic terahertz imaging systems using principles of optical beam engineering* (Doctoral dissertation, Vilniaus universitetas).

Jordan, A. A., Pegatoquet, A., Castagnetti, A., Raybaut, J., & Le Coz, P. (2020). Deep learning for eye blink detection implemented at the edge. *IEEE Embedded Systems Letters*, *13*(3), 130–133. DOI: 10.1109/LES.2020.3029313

Journal Ranking Portal. (2021). ABS Journal Ranking 2021.

Junhyeok, L., Youngchul, S., & Ilkyeong, M. (2024). A hybrid deep reinforcement learning approach for a proactive transshipment of fresh food in the online–offline channel system. *Transportation Research Part E, Logistics and Transportation Review*, •••, 187.

Jüttner, U., & Maklan, S. (2011). Supply chain resilience in the global financial crisis: An empirical study. *Supply Chain Management*, *16*(4), 246–259. DOI: 10.1108/13598541111139062

Kamal, S. A., Shafiq, M., & Kakria, P. (2020). Investigating acceptance of telemedicine services through an extended technology acceptance model (TAM). *Technology in Society*, *60*, 101212. DOI: 10.1016/j.techsoc.2019.101212

Kamble, S. S., Gunasekaran, A., Kumar, V., Belhadi, A., & Foropon, C. (2021). A machine learning based approach for predicting blockchain adoption in the supply Chain. *Technological Forecasting and Social Change*, *2021*(163), 120465. DOI: 10.1016/j.techfore.2020.120465

Kämpe, I. (2023). *Bringing human rights due diligence into law:Addressing modern slavery or business as usual?* Kirchherr, J., Reike, D., & Hekkert, M. (2017). Conceptualizing the circular economy: An analysis of 114 definitions. *Resources, Conservation and Recycling*, *127*(September), 221–232. DOI: 10.1016/j.resconrec.2017.09.005

Kandula, S., Krishnamoorthy, S., & Roy, D. (2021). A prescriptive analytics framework for efficient E-commerce order delivery. *Decision Support Systems*, *147*, 113584. DOI: 10.1016/j.dss.2021.113584

Kaplan, R. M., & Hays, R. D. (2022). Health-related quality of life measurement in public health. *Annual Review of Public Health*, *43*(1), 355–373. DOI: 10.1146/annurev-publhealth-052120-012811 PMID: 34882431

Karki, R., Shrestha, N., & Adhikari, P. (2024). *Data analytics to enhance supply chain decision-making, inventory management, and logistic optimization.*

Kar, S., Kar, A. K., & Gupta, M. P. (2021). Modeling Drivers and Barriers of Artificial Intelligence Adoption: Insights from a Strategic Management Perspective. *Intelligent Systems in Accounting, Finance & Management*, *28*(4), 217–238. DOI: 10.1002/isaf.1503

Kashem, M. A., Shamsuddoha, M., Nasir, T., & Chowdhury, A. A. (2023). Supply Chain Disruption Versus Optimization: A Review on Artificial Intelligence and Blockchain. *Knowledge (Beverly Hills, Calif.)*, *2023*(3), 80–96. DOI: 10.3390/knowledge3010007

Kassa, A., Kitaw, D., Stache, U., Beshah, B., & Degefu, G. (2023). Artificial intelligence techniques for enhancing supply chain resilience: A systematic literature review, holistic framework, and future research. *Computers & Industrial Engineering*, *186*, 109714. DOI: 10.1016/j.cie.2023.109714

Kassel, K., & Rimanoczy, I. (Eds.). (2018). *Developing a Sustainability Mindset in Management Education*. Routledge. DOI: 10.4324/9781351063340

Kelly, J. T., Campbell, K. L., Gong, E., & Scuffham, P. (2020). The Internet of Things: Impact and implications for health care delivery. *Journal of Medical Internet Research*, *22*(11), e20135. DOI: 10.2196/20135 PMID: 33170132

Kelso, C. R. (2009). *Direct occlusion handling for high-level image processing algorithms* (Master's thesis). Rochester Institute of Technology.

Kendzerska, T., Zhu, D. T., Gershon, A. S., Edwards, J. D., Peixoto, C., Robillard, R., & Kendall, C. E. (2021). The effects of the health system response to the COVID-19 pandemic on chronic disease management: A narrative review. *Risk Management and Healthcare Policy*, *14*, 575–584. DOI: 10.2147/RMHP.S293471 PMID: 33623448

Khaira, A. (2024). From 3D to 4D: The Evolution of Additive Manufacturing and Its Implications for Industry 5.0. In *Emerging Technologies in Digital Manufacturing and Smart Factories* (pp. 39-53). IGI Global.

Khalifa, N., Abd Elghany, M., & Abd Elghany, M. (2021). Exploratory research on digitalization transformation practices within supply chain management context in developing countries specifically Egypt in the MENA region. *Cogent Business & Management*, *8*(1), 1965459. DOI: 10.1080/23311975.2021.1965459

Khalil, S., & Belitski, M. (2020). Dynamic capabilities for firm performance under the information technology governance framework. *European Business Review*, *32*(2), 129–157. DOI: 10.1108/EBR-05-2018-0102

Khan, M. A., Khan, R., Praveen, P., Verma, A. R., & Panda, M. K. (2024). *Infrastructure possibilities and human-centered approaches with Industry 5.0*. IGI Global.

Khan, M. A., Khan, R., Praveen, P., Verma, A. R., & Panda, M. K. (Eds.). (2024). *Infrastructure Possibilities and Human-Centered Approaches With Industry 5.0*. IGI Global. DOI: 10.4018/979-8-3693-0782-3

Khan, Y., Su'ud, M. B. M., Alam, M. M., Ahmad, S. F., Ahmad, A. Y. B., & Khan, N. (2023). Application of Internet of Things (IoT) in sustainable supply chain management. *Sustainability*, *15*(1), 694. DOI: 10.3390/su15010694

Khaoua, Y., Mouzouna, Y., Arif, J., Jawab, F., & Azari, M. (2022). The contribution of blockchain technology in the supply chain management: The shipping industry as an example. In 2022 14th International Colloquium of Logistics and Supply Chain Management (LOGISTIQUA) (pp. 1-6). IEEE.

Khaoua, Y., Mouzouna, Y., Arif, J., Jawab, F., & Azari, M. (2022, May). The contribution of blockchain technology in the supply chain management: The shipping industry as an example. In 2022 14th International Colloquium of Logistics and Supply Chain Management (LOGISTIQUA) (pp. 1-6). IEEE.

Kholaif, M. M. N. H. K., Xiao, M., & Hamdy, A. (2023). 'Covid-19's effect on green supply chains and environmental sustainability; innovative technologies moderation'. *Journal of Cleaner Production*, *406*, 137083. DOI: 10.1016/j.jclepro.2023.137083

Khosrowabadi, N., Hoberg, K., & Imdahl, C. (2022). Evaluating human behaviour in response to AI recommendations for judgemental forecasting. *European Journal of Operational Research*, *303*(3), 1151–1167. DOI: 10.1016/j.ejor.2022.03.017

Kim, H., & Lee, Y. (2020). Review and improvement of demand forecasting techniques for supply chain management. *Journal of Manufacturing Science and Engineering*, *142*(5), 051006. DOI: 10.1115/1.4046892

Kim, J., & Gupta, P. (2012). Emotional expressions in online user reviews: How they influence consumers' product evaluations. *Journal of Business Research*, *65*(7), 985–992. DOI: 10.1016/j.jbusres.2011.04.013

Koh, L., Dolgui, A., & Sarkis, J. (2020). Blockchain in transport and logistics—Paradigms and transitions. *International Journal of Production Research*, *2020*(7), 58, 2054, 2062. DOI: 10.1080/00207543.2020.1736428

Ko, J. C., & Kim, K. H. (2021). Evaluating traditional forecasting methods for high-demand product categories in the retail industry. *Expert Systems with Applications*, *167*, 114276. DOI: 10.1016/j.eswa.2020.114276

Konidena, B. K., Malaiyappan, J. N. A., & Tadimarri, A. (2024). Ethical considerations in the development and deployment of AI systems. *European Journal of Technology*, *8*(2), 41–53. DOI: 10.47672/ejt.1890

Koot, M., Mes, M. R. K., & Iacob, M. E. (2021). A systematic literature review of supply chain decision making supported by the Internet of Things and Big Data Analytics. *Computers & Industrial Engineering*, *154*, 107076. DOI: 10.1016/j.cie.2020.107076

Kosasih, E. E., Papadakis, E., Baryannis, G., & Brintrup, A. (2024). A review of explainable artificial intelligence in supply chain management using neurosymbolic approaches. *International Journal of Production Research*, *62*(4), 1510–1540. DOI: 10.1080/00207543.2023.2281663

Kostopoulos, G., Davrazos, G., & Kotsiantis, S. (2024). Explainable Artificial Intelligence-Based Decision Support Systems: A Recent Review. *Electronics (Basel)*, *13*(14), 14. DOI: 10.3390/electronics13142842

Kotikangas, M. (2023). Utilization of digital twin for customer tailored variable speed drive.

Kouba, P., Kohout, P., Haddadi, F., Bushuiev, A., Samusevich, R., Sedlar, J., Damborsky, J., Pluskal, T., Sivic, J., & Mazurenko, S. (2023). Machine Learning-Guided Protein Engineering. *ACS Catalysis*, *13*(21), 13863–13895. DOI: 10.1021/acscatal.3c02743 PMID: 37942269

Kouhizadeh, M., Saberi, S., & Sarkis, J. (2021). Blockchain technology and the sustainable supply chain: Theoretically exploring adoption barriers'. *International Journal of Production Economics*, *231*, 107831. DOI: 10.1016/j.ijpe.2020.107831

Kourentzes, N., & Athanasopoulos, G. (2021). Elucidate structure in intermittent demand series. *European Journal of Operational Research*, *288*(1), 141–152. DOI: 10.1016/j.ejor.2020.05.046

Kralj, D., & Aralica, K. (2022, September). Industry 5.0 from the Perspective of Safety at Work. In *Occupational Safety and Health, Proceedings of the 8th International Professional and Scientific Conference, Zadar, Croatia* (pp. 21-24).

Kralj, D., & Aralica, K. (2023). Safety at work within industry 5.0-quo vadis. *Sigurnost: časopis za sigurnost u radnoj i životnoj okolini, 65*(3), 317-324.

Kumar, R. (2018). Bilingual Domain-Independent Natural Language Interface to Database.

Kumar, A., & Mishra, S. (2020). A review of AI techniques in demand forecasting. *Computers in Industry, 118*, 103213. DOI: 10.1016/j.compind.2020.103213

Kumar, G., Singh, R. K., Arya, V., & Mishra, S. K. (2024). Analyzing Barriers in Adoption of Artificial Intelligence for Resilient Health Care Services to Society. *Global Journal of Flexible Systems Managment, 25*(1), 179–197. DOI: 10.1007/s40171-024-00373-4

Kumari, P., Anand, A., Praveen, P., Verma, A. R., & Godiyal, A. (2024). Infrastructure Potential and Human-Centric Strategies in the Context of Industry 5.0. In *Infrastructure Possibilities and Human-Centered Approaches With Industry 5.0* (pp. 199-214). IGI Global.

Kumar, R., Singh, D., & Verma, A. (2025). AI-powered autonomous farming: The future of sustainable agriculture. *International Journal of Agricultural Robotics, 12*(1), 45–63.

Kurian, D. S., Pillai, V. M., Gautham, J., & Raut, A. (2023). Data-driven imitation learning-based approach for order size determination in supply chains. *European Journal of Industrial Engineering, 17*(3), 379. DOI: 10.1504/EJIE.2023.130601

Kurtulmus, F., Lee, W. S., & Vardar, A. (2014). Immature peach detection in color images acquired in natural illumination conditions using statistical classifiers and neural networks. *Precision Agriculture, 15*(1), 57–79. DOI: 10.1007/s11119-013-9323-8

Kusiak, A. (2024). Federated explainable artificial intelligence (fXAI): A digital manufacturing perspective. *International Journal of Production Research, 62*(1-2), 171–182. DOI: 10.1080/00207543.2023.2238083

Kuwornu, J. K. M., Khaipetch, J., Gunawan, E., Bannor, R. K., & Ho, T. D. (2023). The adoption of sustainable supply chain management practices on performance and quality assurance of food companies. *Sustainable Futures : An Applied Journal of Technology, Environment and Society, 5*, 100103. DOI: 10.1016/j.sftr.2022.100103

Kwilinski, A., Lyulyov, O., & Pimonenko, T. (2023). Environmental Sustainability within Attaining Sustainable Development Goals: The Role of Digitalization and the Transport Sector. *Sustainability (Basel), 15*(14), 11282. DOI: 10.3390/su151411282

Lachhab, F., Bakhouya, M., Ouladsine, R., & Essaaidi, M. (2017). Energy-efficient buildings as complex socio-technical systems: Approaches and challenges. In Nemiche, M., & Essaaidi, M. (Eds.), *Advances in complex societal, environmental and engineered systems* (pp. 247–265). Springer., DOI: 10.1007/978-3-319-46164-9_12

Lambert, D. M., & Cooper, M. C. (2000). Issues in Supply Chain Management. *Industrial Marketing Management*, *29*(1), 65–83. DOI: 10.1016/S0019-8501(99)00113-3

Lame, G. (2019). Systematic literature reviews: An introduction. *Proceedings of the Design Society: International Conference on Engineering Design*, *1*(1), 1633–1642. DOI: 10.1017/dsi.2019.169

Lam, H. Y., Tsang, Y. P., Wu, C. H., & Chan, C. Y. (2021). Intelligent e-vendor relationship management for enhancing global b2c e-commerce ecosystems. *Journal of Global Information Management*, *29*(3), 1–25. DOI: 10.4018/JGIM.2021050101

Landman, T. (2020). Measuring Modern Slavery: Law, Human Rights, and New Forms of Data. *Human Rights Quarterly*, *42*(2), 303–331. DOI: 10.1353/hrq.2020.0019

Lăzăroiu, G., Gedeon, T., Rogalska, E., Valaskova, K., Nagy, M., Musa, H., Zvarikova, K., Poliak, M., Horak, J., Cre oiu, R. I., Krulicky, T., Ionescu, L., Popa, C., Hurloiu, L. R., Nistor, F., Avram, L. G., & Braga, V. (2024). Digital twin-based cyber-physical manufacturing systems, extended reality metaverse enterprise and production management algorithms, and Internet of Things financial and labor market technologies in generative artificial intelligence economics. *Oeconomia Copernicana, 15*(3), 837–870. *Scopus*. DOI: 10.24136/oc.3183

LeCun, Y., Bengio, Y., & Hinton, G. (2015). Deep learning. *Nature*, *521*(7553), 436–444. DOI: 10.1038/nature14539 PMID: 26017442

Lee, H. L., & Billington, C. (1993). Material management in decentralized supply chains. *Operations Research*, *41*(5), 835–847. DOI: 10.1287/opre.41.5.835

Leung, K. H., Mo, D. Y., Ho, G. T. S., Wu, C. H., & Huang, G. Q. (2020). Modelling near-real-time order arrival demand in e-commerce context: A machine learning predictive methodology. *Industrial Management & Data Systems*, *120*(6), 1149–1174. DOI: 10.1108/IMDS-12-2019-0646

Leung, P. M. (2022). Trends in Sustainable and Ethical Consumption. *International Journal of Business Management and Visuals*, *5*(2), 30–36.

Liang, D., Cao, W., Zhang, Y., & Xu, Z. (2024). A two-stage classification approach for AI technical service supplier selection based on multi-stakeholder concern. *Information Sciences*, *652*, 119762. DOI: 10.1016/j.ins.2023.119762

Lieder, M., & Rashid, A. (2016). Towards circular economy implementation: A comprehensive review in context of manufacturing industry. *Journal of Cleaner Production*, *115*, 36–51. DOI: 10.1016/j.jclepro.2015.12.042

Li, L., Zhu, W., Chen, L., & Liu, Y. (2024). Generative AI usage and sustainable supply chain performance : A practice-based view. *Transportation Research Part E, Logistics and Transportation Review*, *192*, 103761. DOI: 10.1016/j.tre.2024.103761

Lima, F. A., & Seuring, S. (2023). A Delphi study examining risk and uncertainty management in circular supply chains'. *International Journal of Production Economics*, *258*, 108810. DOI: 10.1016/j.ijpe.2023.108810

Lim, W. M. (2017). Online group buying: Some insights from the business-to-business perspective. *Industrial Marketing Management*, *65*, 182–193. DOI: 10.1016/j.indmarman.2017.03.011

Lindsay, R., Kirkpatrick, A., Low, J. E., & Lindsay, R. (2017). Hardly Soft Law: The Modern Slavery Act 2015 and the Trend towards Mandatory Reporting on Human Rights. *Business Law International*, *18*(1), 18. https://heinonline.org/HOL/License

Linker, R., Cohen, O., & Naor, A. (2012). Determination of the number of green apples in RGB images recorded in orchards. *Computers and Electronics in Agriculture*, *81*, 45–57. DOI: 10.1016/j.compag.2011.11.007

Lin, X., Zhou, Y. W., Xie, W., Zhong, Y., & Cao, B. (2020). Pricing and Product-bundling Strategies for E-commerce Platforms with Competition. *European Journal of Operational Research*, *283*(3), 1026–1039. DOI: 10.1016/j.ejor.2019.11.066

Liu, K. S., & Lin, M. H. (2021). Performance Assessment on the Application of Artificial Intelligence to Sustainable Supply Chain Management in the Construction Material Industry. *Sustainability (Basel)*, *2021*(13), 12767. DOI: 10.3390/su132212767

Liu, Y., Han, T., Ma, S., Zhang, J., Yang, Y., Tian, J., He, H., Li, A., He, M., Liu, Z., Wu, Z., Zhao, L., Zhu, D., Li, X., Qiang, N., Shen, D., Liu, T., & Ge, B. (2023). Summary of ChatGPT-related research and perspective towards the future of large language models. *Meta-Radiology*, *1*(2), 100017. DOI: 10.1016/j.metrad.2023.100017

Li, Z. (2021). Consumer behavior analysis model based on machine learning. *Journal of Intelligent & Fuzzy Systems*, *40*(4), 6433–6443. DOI: 10.3233/JIFS-189483

Lo, H. W., Chan, H. W., Lin, J. W., & Lin, S. W. (2024). Evaluating the interrelationships of industrial 5.0 development factors using an integration approach of Fermatean fuzzy logic. *Journal of Operations Intelligence*, *2*(1), 95–113. DOI: 10.31181/jopi21202416

Long, L. N. B., Kim, H. S., Cuong, T. N., & You, S. S. (2023). Intelligent decision support system for optimizing inventory management under stochastic events. *Applied Intelligence*, *53*(20), 23675–23697. DOI: 10.1007/s10489-023-04801-3

Long, Q. (2018). Data-driven decision making for supply chain networks with agent-based computational experiment. *Knowledge-Based Systems, 141*, 55–66. DOI: 10.1016/j.knosys.2017.11.006

Loveridge, D., & Wilson, N. (2017). *"Engaging with the private sector through multi-stakeholder platforms* (Issue January 2017).

Lundberg, S. M., Erion, G., Chen, H., DeGrave, A., Prutkin, J. M., Nair, B., Katz, R., Himmelfarb, J., Bansal, N., & Lee, S.-I. (2019). Explainable AI for Trees: From Local Explanations to Global Understanding.

Luther, D. (2021, December 18). *Supply chain sustainability: Why it is important & best practices*. Oracle NetSuite. https://www.netsuite.com/portal/resource/articles/erp/supply-chain-sustainability.shtml

Lv, Z. (2023). Digital Twins in Industry 5.0. *Research, 6*, 0071.

Machado, N. T., & Rodriguez, C. M. T. (2025). A Logistics 5.0 maturity model: A human-centric and sustainable approach for the supply chain of the future. *ITEGAM-JETIA, 11*(51), Article 51.

Madakam, S., Holmukhe, R. M., & Jaiswal, D. K. (2019). The future digital workforce: Robotic process automation (RPA). *JISTEM-Journal of Information Systems and Technology Management, 16*, e201916001.

Madancian, M., Taherdoost, H., Javadi, M., Khan, I. U., Kalantari, A., & Kumar, D. (2023). The impact of artificial intelligence on supply chain management in modern business. In Alnoor, A., Sharaf, A. A. A., & Al-Fatlawi, K. A. A. (Eds.), *The international conference on artificial intelligence and smart environment* (pp. 566–573). Springer.

Madhav, V. V., Deekshith, A., Sai, K. N., Ramesh, M., & Reddy, S. S. (2023). Research on impact of artificial intelligence on logistics and supply chain management. *Journal of Emerging Technologies and Innovative Research, 10*(12). https://www.jetir.org

Maestro, J. A., Rodríguez, S., Casado, R., Prieto, J., & Corchado, J. M. (2021). Comparison of efficient planning and optimization methods of last mile delivery resources. In Q. Tang (Ed.), *Broadband communications, networks, and systems: 11th EAI International Conference, BROADNETS 2020, Qingdao, China, December 11–12, 2020, Proceedings* (pp. 163–173). Springer. DOI: 10.1007/978-3-030-68737-3_11

Magas, M., & Kiritsis, D. (2022). Industry Commons: An ecosystem approach to horizontal enablers for sustainable cross-domain industrial innovation (a positioning paper). *International Journal of Production Research*, *60*(2), 479–492. DOI: 10.1080/00207543.2021.1989514

Mahdikhani, M., & Meena, P. (2024). Metaverse applications and supply chain innovation: Insights from text mining. *Journal of Innovation & Knowledge*, *9*(4), 100591. DOI: 10.1016/j.jik.2024.100591

Maheshwaran, T., & Muthumarilakshmi, S. N. A. S., V., Suganya, K., Maheswari, B., Girija, P., & R., S. S. (2024). Securing E-Commerce Strategies With Cloud, Blockchain, AI, and ML. In P. Goel (Ed.), *Strategies for E-Commerce Data Security: Cloud, Blockchain, AI, and Machine Learning* (pp. 470-500). IGI Global Scientific Publishing. DOI: 10.4018/979-8-3693-6557-1.ch019

Maheshwari, S., Gautam, P., & Jaggi, C. K. (2021). Role of big data analytics in supply chain management: Current trends and future perspectives. *International Journal of Production Research*, *59*(6), 1875–1900. DOI: 10.1080/00207543.2020.1793011

Makridakis, S., Spiliotis, E., & Assimakopoulos, V. (2018). Statistical and machine learning forecasting methods. *International Journal of Forecasting*, *34*(3), 773–802. DOI: 10.1016/j.ijforecast.2018.01.008 PMID: 29584784

Malhotra, G., & Kharub, M. (2025). Elevating logistics performance: Harnessing the power of artificial intelligence in e-commerce. *International Journal of Logistics Management*, *36*(1), 290–321. DOI: 10.1108/IJLM-01-2024-0046

Manning, L., Brewer, S., Craigon, P. J., Frey, J., Gutierrez, A., Jacobs, N., Kanza, S., Munday, S., Sacks, J., & Pearson, S. (2022). Artificial intelligence and ethics within the food sector: Developing a common language for technology adoption across the supply chain. *Trends in Food Science & Technology*, *125*, 33–42. DOI: 10.1016/j.tifs.2022.04.025

Marchet, G., Melacini, M., & Perotti, S. (2014). Environmental sustainability in logistics and freight transportation: A literature review and research agenda. *Journal of Manufacturing Technology Management*, *25*(6), 775–811. DOI: 10.1108/JMTM-06-2012-0065

Marchi, B., & Zanoni, S. (2017). Supply chain management for improved energy efficiency: Review and opportunities. *Energies*, *10*(10), 1618. DOI: 10.3390/en10101618

Maroof, M. A., & Kapate, S. (2023). *Exploring Dynamics of Industry 5.0*. World Journal of Management and Economics.

Marr, B. (2022, June 29). *Why data is the lifeblood of modern organizations*. Forbes. https://www.forbes.com/sites/bernardmarr/2022/06/29/why-data-is-the-lifeblood-of-modern-organizations/

Marshall, D., McCarthy, L., McGrath, P., & Claudy, M. (2015). Going above and beyond: How sustainability culture and entrepreneurial orientation drive social sustainability supply chain practice adoption. *Supply Chain Management, 20*(4), 434–454. DOI: 10.1108/SCM-08-2014-0267

Martínez-Castañeda, M., & Feijoo, C. (2023). Use of blockchain in the agri-food value chain: State of the art in Spain and some lessons from the perspective of public support. *Telecommunications Policy, 47*(6), 102574. DOI: 10.1016/j.telpol.2023.102574

Masenya, T. M., & Chisita, C. T. (2022). Futurizing library services in a technology-driven dispensation: Reflections on selected academic libraries in Zimbabwe and South Africa. In *Innovative technologies for enhancing knowledge access in academic libraries* (pp. 1–21). IGI Global. DOI: 10.4018/978-1-6684-3364-5.ch001

Mat Ishah, N. S., Lee, K. L., & Nawanir, G. (2023). Educational supply chain sustainability'. *Asian Education and Development Studies, 12*(2/3), 137–149. DOI: 10.1108/AEDS-09-2022-0123

Ma, X., Zhang, J., & Zeng, Q. (2022). Forecasting seasonal demand using machine learning models. *Expert Systems with Applications, 203*, 117352. DOI: 10.1016/j.eswa.2022.117352

Mazar, M. (2023). Strategies for Improving Supply Chain Management in United Nations Peacekeeping Missions (Doctoral dissertation, Walden University).

McKinnon, A. C. (2012). Reducing energy consumption and emissions in the logistics sector. In McKinnon, A., Browne, M., Whiteing, A., & Piecyk, M. (Eds.), *Energy, transport, & the environment: Addressing the sustainable mobility paradigm* (pp. 521–537). Springer., DOI: 10.1007/978-1-4471-2717-8_29

Mediavilla, M. A., Dietrich, F., & Palm, D. (2022). Review and analysis of artificial intelligence methods for demand forecasting in supply chain management. *Procedia CIRP, 107*, 1126–1131. DOI: 10.1016/j.procir.2022.05.119

Mefford, R. N. (2011). The economic value of a sustainable supply chain. *Business and Society Review, 116*(1), 109–143. DOI: 10.1111/j.1467-8594.2011.00379.x

Meissner, J., & Montag, S. (2021). AI for adaptive supply chains. *Production and Operations Management, 30*(9), 2950–2973. DOI: 10.1111/poms.13454

Melnyk, O., Onishchenko, O., Fomin, O., Yarovenko, V., Pavlova, N., Drozhzhyn, O., & Vyshnevsky, D. (2025). Smart Port Concept: A Case Study Of Port-Integrated Autonomous Networks. *Journal for Maritime Research, 22*(1), 315–323.

Mentzer, J., Dewitt, W., Keebler, J., Min, S., Nix, N., Smith, C., & Zacharia, Z. (2001). Defining Supply Chain Management. *Journal of Business Logistics, 22*(2), 1–25. DOI: 10.1002/j.2158-1592.2001.tb00001.x

Merhi, M. I. (2023). An Assessment of the Barriers Impacting Responsible Artificial Intelligence. *Information Systems Frontiers, 25*(3), 1147–1160. DOI: 10.1007/s10796-022-10276-3

Miguéis, V. L., Pereira, A., Pereira, J., & Figueira, G. (2022). Reducing fresh fish waste while ensuring availability: Demand forecast using censored data and machine learning. *Journal of Cleaner Production, 359*, 131852. DOI: 10.1016/j.jclepro.2022.131852

Millard, J. (2023). Exploring the impact of digital transformation on public governance.

Millard, J. (2023). Impact of digital transformation on public governance. *Joint Research Centre (Seville site).*

Miller, K. (2020, December 8). *The triple bottom line: What it is & why it's important.* Harvard Business School Online. https://online.hbs.edu/blog/post/what-is-the-triple-bottom-line

Min, H. (2010). Artificial intelligence in supply chain management: Theory and applications. *International Journal of Logistics, 13*(1), 13–39. DOI: 10.1080/13675560902736537

Min, H. (2019). Blockchain technology for enhancing supply chain resilience. *Business Horizons, 62*(1), 35–45. DOI: 10.1016/j.bushor.2018.08.012

Min, H., & Zhou, G. (2002). Supply chain modeling: Past, present and future. *Computers & Industrial Engineering, 43*(1–2), 231–249. DOI: 10.1016/S0360-8352(02)00066-9

Mladineo, M., Celent, L., Milković, V., & Veža, I. (2024). Current State Analysis of Croatian Manufacturing Industry with Regard to Industry 4.0/5.0. *Machines (Basel), 12*(2), 87. DOI: 10.3390/machines12020087

Modaresi, R. (2024). *AI-Based Explainable Classification Of News Articles For Supply Chain Risk Management.* https://urn.kb.se/resolve?urn=urn:nbn:se:uu:diva-546454

Modgil, S., Singh, R. K., & Hannibal, C. (2022). Artificial intelligence for supply chain resilience: Learning from Covid-19. *International Journal of Logistics Management, 33*(4), 1246–1268. DOI: 10.1108/IJLM-02-2021-0094

Mohapatra, S., & Giri, A. (2017). Neural network-based forecasting for supply chain optimization. *Computers & Industrial Engineering, 113*, 393–403. DOI: 10.1016/j.cie.2017.09.024

Mohd Yamin, M. N., Ab. Aziz, K., Gek Siang, T., & Ab. Aziz, N. A. (2023). Determinants of Emotion Recognition System Adoption: Empirical Evidence from Malaysia. *Applied Sciences (Basel, Switzerland), 13*(21), 11854. DOI: 10.3390/app132111854

Moher, D., Liberati, A., Tetzlaff, J., & Altman, D. G.The PRISMA Group. (2009). Preferred Reporting Items for Systematic Reviews and Meta-Analyses: The PRISMA Statement. *PLoS Medicine, 6*(7), e1000097. DOI: 10.1371/journal.pmed.1000097 PMID: 19621072

Mohsen, B. M. (2023). Impact of artificial intelligence on supply chain management performance. *Journal of Service Science and Management, 16*(1), 44–58. DOI: 10.4236/jssm.2023.161004

Mokgomola, F., Telukdarie, A., Munien, I., Onkonkwo, U., & Vermeulen, A. (2024). Blockchain and Smart Contracts Based Agricultural Supply Chain. *Procedia Computer Science, 237*, 637–644. DOI: 10.1016/j.procs.2024.05.149

Mollenkopf, D. A., Ozanne, L. K., & Stolze, H. J. (2021). A transformative supply chain response to COVID-19′. *Journal of Service Management, 32*(2), 190–202. DOI: 10.1108/JOSM-05-2020-0143

Monczka, R. M., Handfield, R. B., Giunipero, L. C., & Patterson, J. L. (2020). Purchasing and supply chain management. Cengage Learning.

Montag, L. (2023). Circular economy and supply chains: Definitions, conceptualizations, and research agenda of the circular supply chain framework. *Circular Economy and Sustainability, 3*(1), 35–75. DOI: 10.1007/s43615-022-00172-y PMID: 35582650

Moore, S., Bulmer, S., & Elms, J. (2022). The social significance of AI in retail on customer experience and shopping practices. *Journal of Retailing and Consumer Services, 64*, 102755. DOI: 10.1016/j.jretconser.2021.102755

Morales-Contreras, M. F., Leporati, M., & Fratocchi, L. (2021). The impact of COVID-19 on supply decision-makers: The case of personal protective equipment in Spanish hospitals. *BMC Health Services Research, 21*(1), 1170. DOI: 10.1186/s12913-021-07202-9 PMID: 34711231

Mostafiz, M. I., Musteen, M., Saiyed, A., & Ahsan, M. (2022). COVID-19 and the global value chain: Immediate dynamics and long-term restructuring in the garment industry. *Journal of Business Research, 139*, 1588–1603. DOI: 10.1016/j.jbusres.2021.10.078

Moufad, I., & Jawab, F. (2017). Conception and validation of a decision support model for Urban Freight Transport. In 2017 International Colloquium on Logistics and Supply Chain Management (LOGISTIQUA) (pp. 94-99). IEEE. DOI: 10.1109/LOGISTIQUA.2017.7962880

Moyaux, T., Chaib-draa, B., & D'Amours, S. (2006). Supply Chain Management and Multiagent Systems: An Overview. In Chaib-draa, B., & Müller, J. P. (Eds.), *Multiagent based Supply Chain Management* (Vol. 28, pp. 1–27). Springer Berlin Heidelberg., DOI: 10.1007/978-3-540-33876-5_1

Mugurusi, G., & Oluka, P. N. (2021). Towards Explainable Artificial Intelligence (XAI) in Supply Chain Management: A Typology and Research Agenda. In Dolgui, A., Bernard, A., Lemoine, D., von Cieminski, G., & Romero, D. (Eds.), *Advances in Production Management Systems. Artificial Intelligence for Sustainable and Resilient Production Systems* (pp. 32–38). Springer International Publishing., DOI: 10.1007/978-3-030-85910-7_4

Mullan, P. (2020). *Beyond Confrontation: Globalists, nationalists and their discontents*. Emerald Publishing Limited. DOI: 10.1108/9781839825606

Munn, Z., Tufanaru, C., & Aromataris, E. (2014). JBI's Systematic Reviews: Data Extraction and Synthesis. *The American Journal of Nursing, 114*(7), 49–54. DOI: 10.1097/01.NAJ.0000451683.66447.89 PMID: 25742352

Muñoz-Villamizar, A., Piatti, M., Mejia-Argueta, C., Pirabe, L. F., Namdar, J., & Gomez, J. F. (2024). Navigating retail inflation in Brazil: A machine learning and web scraping approach to the basic food basket. *Journal of Retailing and Consumer Services, 79*, 103875. DOI: 10.1016/j.jretconser.2024.103875

Musani, P. (2023, October 25). *Decking the aisles with data: How Walmart's AI-powered inventory system brightens the holidays*. Walmart Global Tech. https://tech.walmart.com/content/walmart-global-tech/en_us/blog/post/walmarts-ai-powered-inventory-system-brightens-the-holidays.html

Mustapić, M., Trstenjak, M., Greguric, P., & Opetuk, T. (2023). Implementation and use of digital, green and sustainable technologies in internal and external transport of manufacturing companies. *Sustainability (Basel)*, *15*(12), 12. DOI: 10.3390/su15129557

Muthuswamy, M., & Ali, M., A. (. (2023). Sustainable Supply Chain Management in the Age of Machine Intelligence: Addressing Challenges, Capitalizing on Opportunities, and Shaping the Future Landscape. *Sustainable Machine Intelligence Journal*, *3*, 1–14. DOI: 10.61185/SMIJ.2023.33103

Mystakidis, S. (2022a). Metaverse. *Encyclopedia*, *2*(1), 486–497. DOI: 10.3390/encyclopedia2010031

Nadella, G. S., Nadella, G. S., Satish, S., Meduri, K., & Meduri, S. S. (2023). A Systematic Literature Review of Advancements, Challenges and Future Directions of AI And ML in Healthcare. *International Journal of Machine Learning for Sustainable Development*, *5*(3), 115–130. https://www.ijsdcs.com/index.php/IJMLSD/article/view/519

Naim, A., Alqahtani, H., Fatima, S., & Khan, M. F. (2023). Applications of Artificial Intelligence of Things in Green Supply Chain Management: Challenges and Future Directions. In *Blockchain, IoT, and AI Technologies for Supply Chain Management*. CRC Press. DOI: 10.1201/9781003264521-5

Nair, A., Pillai, S. V., & Senthil Kumar, S. A. (2024). Towards emerging Industry 5.0–a review-based framework. *Journal of Strategy and Management*. DOI: 10.1108/JSMA-04-2023-0067

Narkhede, G. B., Pasi, B. N., Rajhans, N., & Kulkarni, A. (2024). Industry 5.0 and sustainable manufacturing: A systematic literature review. *Benchmarking*.

Narkhede, G., Pasi, B., Rajhans, N., & Kulkarni, A. (2023). Industry 5.0 and the future of sustainable manufacturing: A systematic literature review'. *Business Strategy & Development*, *6*(4), 704–723. DOI: 10.1002/bsd2.272

Nascimento, D. L. M., Alencastro, V., Quelhas, O. L. G., Caiado, R. G. G., Garza-Reyes, J. A., Rocha-Lona, L., & Tortorella, G. (2019). Exploring Industry 4.0 technologies to enable circular economy practices in a manufacturing context: A business model proposal. *Journal of Manufacturing Technology Management*, *30*(3), 607–627. DOI: 10.1108/JMTM-03-2018-0071

Natalia, T., Pathani, A., Dhaliwal, N., Rajasekhar, N., & Khatkar, M. (2024). Blockchain Integration in Industry 5.0: A Security Experiment for Resilience Assessment. In *BIO Web of Conferences* (Vol. 86, p. 01070). EDP Sciences.

Natalia, V., Bisht, Y. S., Prabhakar, P. K., Arora, R., Mishra, S. K., & Rajasekhar, N. (2024). AI and Autonomous Systems: An Experiment in Industry 5.0 Transformation. In *BIO Web of Conferences* (Vol. 86, p. 01094). EDP Sciences.

Nazari, M. (2017). *Infrared Matrix-Assisted Laser Desorption Electrospray Ionization (IR-MALDESI): Development and Applications in Metabolomics, Mass Spectrometry Imaging, and Direct Analysis*. North Carolina State University.

Naz, F., Kumar, A., Majumdar, A., & Agrawal, R. (2022). Is artificial intelligence an enabler of supply chain resiliency post COVID-19? An exploratory state-of-the-art review for future research. *Operations Management Research : Advancing Practice Through Research*, *15*(1), 378–398. DOI: 10.1007/s12063-021-00208-w

Nel-Sanders, D. (2023). Revolutionising Public Private Partnerships: A Transition to the Fifth Industrial Revolution. *International Journal of Innovation in Management. Economics and Social Sciences*, *3*(1), 12–29.

Netherton, T., & Netherton, T. J. (2021). A Fully-Automated, Deep Learning-Based Framework For Ct-Based Localization, Segmentation, Verification And Planning Of Metastatic Vertebrae.

Nguyen Duc, D., Tran Huu, T., & Nananukul, N. (2020). A dynamic route-planning system based on Industry 4.0 technology. *Algorithms*, *13*(12), 308. DOI: 10.3390/a13120308

Nicoletti, B., & Appolloni, A. (2024a). Green Logistics 5.0: A review of sustainability-oriented innovation with foundation models in logistics. *European Journal of Innovation Management*, *27*(9), 9. DOI: 10.1108/EJIM-07-2024-0787

Nicoletti, B., & Appolloni, A. (2024b). Green Warehouse 5.0. In Appolloni, A., Kumar, V., Kuzmin, E., & Akberdina, V. (Eds.), *The Future of Industry* (Vol. 70, pp. 303–320). Springer Nature Switzerland., DOI: 10.1007/978-3-031-66801-2_20

Ni, D., Xiao, Z., & Lim, M. K. (2020). A systematic review of the research trends of machine learning in supply chain management. *International Journal of Machine Learning and Cybernetics*, *11*(7), 1463–1482. DOI: 10.1007/s13042-019-01050-0

Nimmy, S. F. (2024). *Explainable Artificial Intelligence in Supply Chain Operational Risk Management (XAI-SCORM): A Comprehensive Approach towards Interpretability, Transparency, and Trustworthiness* [Thesis, UNSW Sydney]. DOI: 10.26190/unsworks/30133

Ning, H., Wang, H., Lin, Y., Wang, W., Dhelim, S., Farha, F., Ding, J., & Daneshmand, M. (n.d.). *A Survey on Metaverse: The State-of-the-art*. Technologies, Applications, and Challenges.

Noori, S. F., Yuvaraj, D., Abas, S. M., Sivaram, M., & Porkodi, V. (2024). Multifaceted Interplay between Mobile Edge Computing based on Industry 5.0 in Transportation. *International Journal of Intelligent Systems and Applications in Engineering*, *12*(15s), 106–114.

Nozari, H., Szmelter-jarosz, A., & Ghahremani-nahr, J. (2022). Analysis of the Challenges of Artificial Intelligence of Things (AIoT) for the Smart Supply Chain (Case Study: FMCG Industries). *Sensors (Basel)*, *22*(8), 2931. DOI: 10.3390/s22082931 PMID: 35458916

Nyemba, W. R., Chikuku, T., Chiroodza, J. R., Dube, B., Carter, K. F., Mbohwa, C., & Magombo, L. (2020). Industrial design thinking and innovations propelled by the Royal Academy of Engineering in Sub-Saharan Africa for capacity building. *Procedia CIRP*, *91*, 770–775. DOI: 10.1016/j.procir.2020.02.233

O'Neil, S., Zhao, X., Sun, D., & Wei, J. C. (2016). Newsvendor Problems with Demand Shocks and Unknown Demand Distributions. *Decision Sciences*, *47*(1), 125–156. DOI: 10.1111/deci.12187

Ogbuke, N. J., Yusuf, Y. Y., Dharma, K., & Mercangoz, B. A. (2022). Big data supply chain analytics: Ethical, privacy and security challenges posed to business, industries and society. *Production Planning and Control*, *33*(2–3), 123–137. DOI: 10.1080/09537287.2020.1810764

Okamoto, H., & Lee, W. S. (2009). Green citrus detection using hyperspectral imaging. *Computers and Electronics in Agriculture*, *66*(2), 201–208. DOI: 10.1016/j.compag.2009.02.004

Okorie, O., Russell, J., Jin, Y., Turner, C., Wang, Y., & Charnley, F. (2022). Removing barriers to Blockchain use in circular food supply chains: Practitioner views on achieving operational effectiveness. *Cleaner Logistics and Supply Chain*, *5*, 100087. DOI: 10.1016/j.clscn.2022.100087

Omar, H., Klibi, W., Babai, M. Z., & Ducq, Y. (2023). Basket data-driven approach for omnichannel demand forecasting. *International Journal of Production Economics*, *257*, 108748. DOI: 10.1016/j.ijpe.2022.108748

Onishi, Y., Yoshida, T., Kurita, H., Fukao, T., Arihara, H., & Iwai, A. (2019). An automated fruit harvesting robot by using deep learning. *Robomech Journal*, *6*(1), 13. DOI: 10.1186/s40648-019-0141-2

Onu, P., Mbohwa, C., & Pradhan, A. (2024). Blockchain-Powered Traceability Solutions: Pioneering Transparency to Eradicate Counterfeit Products and Revolutionize Supply Chain Integrity. *Procedia Computer Science, 232*, 1420–1427. DOI: 10.1016/j.procs.2024.01.140

Oran, I. B., & Cezayirlioglu, H. R. (2021). AI-Robotic applications in logistics industry and savings calculation. *Journal of Organizational Behavior Research, 6*(1–2021), Article 1–2021.

Osei, M. B., Papadopoulos, T., Acquaye, A., & Stamati, T. (2023). Improving sustainable supply chain performance through organisational culture: A competing values framework approach. *Journal of Purchasing and Supply Management, 29*(2), 100821. DOI: 10.1016/j.pursup.2023.100821

Owusu, P. K., Nortey, D. N. N., Koffie-Ocloo, D., & Afriyie, G. O. (2023, December). Evaluating customer satisfaction with AI chatbot interactions in the Ghanaian insurance industry: Focusing on Star Assurance Ltd. In *Conference proceedings edited by* (p. 43).

Pakseresht, A., Ahmadi Kaliji, S., & Hakelius, K. (2024a). Blockchain technology characteristics essential for the agri-food sector: A systematic review. *Food Control, 165*, 110661. DOI: 10.1016/j.foodcont.2024.110661

Pakseresht, A., Yavari, A., Kaliji, S. A., & Hakelius, K. (2023a). The intersection of blockchain technology and circular economy in the agri-food sector. *Sustainable Production and Consumption, 35*, 260–274. DOI: 10.1016/j.spc.2022.11.002

Pang, T. Y., Lee, T. K., & Murshed, M. (2023). Towards a New Paradigm for Digital Health Training and Education in Australia: Exploring the Implication of the Fifth Industrial Revolution. *Applied Sciences (Basel, Switzerland), 13*(11), 6854. DOI: 10.3390/app13116854

Papadopoulos, T., Singh, S. P., Spanaki, K., Gunasekaran, A., & Dubey, R. (2022). Towards the next generation of manufacturing: Implications of big data and digitalization in the context of industry 4.0. *Production Planning and Control, 33*(2–3), 101–104. DOI: 10.1080/09537287.2020.1810767

Paramasivam, B. (2020). Investigation on the effects of damping over the temperature distribution on internal turning bar using Infrared fusion thermal imager analysis via SmartView software. *Measurement, 162*, 107938. DOI: 10.1016/j.measurement.2020.107938

Park, K., & Jiang, H. (2023). Signaling, Verification, and Identification: The Way Corporate Social Advocacy Generates Brand Loyalty on Social Media. *International Journal of Business Communication, 60*(2), 439–463. DOI: 10.1177/2329488420907121

Patel, M., Gupta, V., & Zhang, X. (2022). *Towards on-device AI and blockchain for 6G enabled agricultural supply-chain management*. arXiv Preprint arXiv:2203.06465. https://arxiv.org/abs/2203.06465

Patel, K. (2023). Revolutionizing Consumer Data Analysis: The Development and Impact of a Unique Customer Identifier. *International Journal of Computer Trends and Technology*, *71*(12), 61–74. DOI: 10.14445/22312803/IJCTT-V71I12P111

Patil, et al. (2022). "Utilization of Artificial Intelligence in Healthcare System, Pharmaceutical Industry & Education". International Journal of Advanced Research in Science, Communication and Technology.

Patnaik, D., Pradhan, B. B., & Barik, T. R. (2024). *Optimization Potential Using AI and Metaverse In Supply Chain Management: A Forward-Looking Perspective. 22*(1).

Pattnaik, S., Liew, N., Kures, A. O., Pinsky, E., & Park, K. (2024). Catalyzing Supply Chain Evolution: A Comprehensive Examination of Artificial Intelligence Integration in Supply Chain Management. *Engineering Proceedings*, *68*(1), 1. DOI: 10.3390/engproc2024068057

Pellegrino, R., Russo, F., & Basile, L. J. (2024). The role of supply chain integration in the risk management of circular economy: A multiple case study in the furniture industry. *Procedia Computer Science*, *232*, 2933–2940. DOI: 10.1016/j.procs.2024.02.109

Pereira Perdigao, G. (2018). Internship and master thesis: Concept of Operation: Unmanned Maintenance Dredging.

Pereira, M. M., & Frazzon, E. M. (2021). A data-driv en approach to adaptive synchronization of demand and supply in omni-channel retail supply chains. *International Journal of Information Management*, *57*, 102165. DOI: 10.1016/j.ijinfomgt.2020.102165

Perifanis, N.-A., & Kitsios, F. (2023). Investigating the influence of artificial intelligence on business value in the digital era of strategy: A literature review. *Information (Basel)*, *14*(2), 85. DOI: 10.3390/info14020085

Perotti, S., & Colicchia, C. (2023). Greening warehouses through energy efficiency and environmental impact reduction: A conceptual framework based on a systematic literature review. *International Journal of Logistics Management*, *34*(7), 199–234. DOI: 10.1108/IJLM-02-2022-0086

Pesqueira, A., & Sousa, M. J. (2022). Life Sciences Industry Blockchain Value Management, Investments, and Finance Impact Assessment: Global Questionnaire Survey of 1524 Industry Professionals and Executives. In Incorporating AI Technology in the Service Sector (pp. 67-107). Apple Academic Press.

Pesqueira, A., Bolog, S., Sousa, M. J., & Almeida, D. (2023). Impact of Decentralized and Agile Digital Transformational Programs on the Pharmaceutical Industry, Including an Assessment of Digital Activity Metrics and Commercial Digital. In Proceedings of International Conference on Information Technology and Applications: ICITA 2022 (Vol. 614, p. 341). Springer Nature. DOI: 10.1007/978-981-19-9331-2_29

Pesqueira, A. (2023). Blockchain and Pharmaceuticals: A Bibliometric and Systematic Literature Review of Scientific Publications Between 2000 and 2021. *Technology, Business, Innovation, and Entrepreneurship in Industry*, *4*(0), 25–48. DOI: 10.1007/978-3-031-17960-0_2

Pesqueira, A., & Bolog, S. (2023). Patient empowerment with direct insights from healthcare professionals questionnaires. In *Internet of Things in Biomedical Sciences: Challenges and applications* (pp. 12–1). IOP Publishing. DOI: 10.1088/978-0-7503-5311-3ch12

Pesqueira, A., Sousa, M. J., & Pereira, R. (2025). Individual Dynamic Capabilities and Artificial Intelligence in Health Operations: Exploration of Innovation Diffusion. *Intelligence-Based Medicine*, *11*, 100239. DOI: 10.1016/j.ibmed.2025.100239

Pettersen, I. J., Nyland, K., & Robbins, G. (2020). Public procurement performance and the challenge of service complexity–the case of pre-hospital healthcare. *Journal of Public Procurement*, *20*(4), 403–421. DOI: 10.1108/JOPP-01-2020-0002

Phillips, W., Lee, H., Ghobadian, A., O'Regan, N., & James, P. (2015). Social Innovation and Social Entrepreneurship. *Group & Organization Management*, *40*(3), 428–461. DOI: 10.1177/1059601114560063

Piccarozzi, M., Silvestri, C., Fici, L., & Silvestri, L. (2024). Metaverse: A possible sustainability enabler in the transition from Industry 4.0 to 5.0′. *Procedia Computer Science*, *232*, 1839–1848. DOI: 10.1016/j.procs.2024.02.006

Plebe, A., & Grasso, G. (2001). Localization of spherical fruits for robotic harvesting. *Machine Vision and Applications*, *13*(2), 70–79. DOI: 10.1007/PL00013271

Polas, M. R. H., Afshar Jahanshahi, A., Kabir, A. I., Sohel-Uz-Zaman, A. S., Osman, A. R., & Karim, R. (2022). Artificial Intelligence, Blockchain Technology, and Risk-Taking Behavior in the 4.0IR Metaverse Era: Evidence from Bangladesh-Based SMEs. *Journal of Open Innovation, 8*(3), 168. DOI: 10.3390/joitmc8030168

Ponomarov, S. Y., & Holcomb, M. C. (2009). Understanding the concept of supply chain resilience. *International Journal of Logistics Management, 20*(1), 124–143. DOI: 10.1108/09574090910954873

Pournader, M., Ghaderi, H., Hassanzadegan, A., & Fahimnia, B. (2021). Artificial intelligence applications in supply chain management. *International Journal of Production Economics, 241*, 108250. DOI: 10.1016/j.ijpe.2021.108250

Pramanik, P., Jana, R. K., & Ghosh, I. (2024). AI readiness enablers in developed and developing economies: Findings from the XGBoost regression and explainable AI framework. *Technological Forecasting and Social Change, 205*, 123482. DOI: 10.1016/j.techfore.2024.123482

Priyadarshi, R., Panigrahi, A., Routroy, S., & Garg, G. K. (2019). Demand forecasting at retail stage for selected vegetables: A performance analysis. *Journal of Modelling in Management, 14*(4), 1042–1063. DOI: 10.1108/JM2-11-2018-0192

ProQuest LLC. (2024). ProQuest databases.

Pundziene, A., Heaton, S., & Teece, D. J. (2019). 5G, dynamic capabilities and business models innovation in healthcare industry. In 2019 IEEE International Symposium on Innovation and Entrepreneurship (TEMS-ISIE) (pp. 1-8). IEEE. 24 DOI: 10.1109/TEMS-ISIE46312.2019.9074330

Punia, S., Nikolopoulos, K., Singh, S. P., Madaan, J. K., & Litsiou, K. (2020). Deep learning with long short-term memory networks and random forests for demand forecasting in multi-channel retail. *International Journal of Production Research, 58*(16), 4964–4979. DOI: 10.1080/00207543.2020.1735666

Punia, S., Singh, S. P., & Madaan, J. K. (2020). From predictive to prescriptive analytics: A data-driven multi-item newsvendor model. *Decision Support Systems, 136*, 113340. DOI: 10.1016/j.dss.2020.113340

Qaffas, A. A., Ben HajKacem, M.-A., Ben Ncir, C.-E., & Nasraoui, O. (2023). An Explainable Artificial Intelligence Approach for Multi-Criteria ABC Item Classification. *Journal of Theoretical and Applied Electronic Commerce Research, 18*(2), 848–866. DOI: 10.3390/jtaer18020044

Qiang, L., Jianrong, C., Bin, L., Lie, D., & Yajing, Z. (2014). Identification of fruit and branch in natural scenes for citrus harvesting robot using machine vision and support vector machine. *International Journal of Agricultural and Biological Engineering*, *7*(2), 115–121.

Qi, M., Mak, H. Y., & Shen, Z. J. M. (2020). Data-driven research in retail operations—A review. *Naval Research Logistics*, *67*(8), 595–616. DOI: 10.1002/nav.21949

Rafi, T. (2022, June 7). *Why sustainability is crucial for corporate strategy*. World Economic Forum. https://www.weforum.org/agenda/2022/06/why-sustainability-is-crucial-for-corporate-strategy/

Ragaert, K., Delva, L., & Van Geem, K. (2017). Mechanical and chemical recycling of solid plastic waste. *Waste Management (New York, N.Y.)*, *69*, 24–58. DOI: 10.1016/j.wasman.2017.07.044 PMID: 28823699

Raheman, F. (2022). Sharonomics: A Radical Economic Theory for the Next Industrial Revolution and Beyond. *Theoretical Economics Letters*, *12*(6), 1710–1748. DOI: 10.4236/tel.2022.126094

Rahman, N. A. A., Abdullah, M. A., Hassan, A., & Mahroof, K. (2023). *17 Hard Hit by Halal Meat Cartel Controversy*. Technologies and Trends in the Halal Industry.

Rakholia, R., Suárez-Cetrulo, A. L., Singh, M., & Simón Carbajo, R. (2024). Advancing Manufacturing Through Artificial Intelligence: Current Landscape, Perspectives, Best Practices, Challenges, and Future Direction. *IEEE Access, 12*, 131621-131637. IEEE Access. DOI: 10.1109/ACCESS.2024.3458830

Rakun, J., Stajnko, D., & Zazula, D. (2011). Detecting fruits in natural scenes by using spatial-frequency-based texture analysis and multiview geometry. *Computers and Electronics in Agriculture*, *76*(1), 80–88. DOI: 10.1016/j.compag.2011.01.007

Ralston, P., & Blackhurst, J. (2020). Industry 4.0 and resilience in the supply chain: A driver of capability enhancement or capability loss? *International Journal of Production Research*, *58*(16), 5006–5019. DOI: 10.1080/00207543.2020.1736724

Ramanathan, R., & Ramanathan, U. (2018). Supply chain forecasting with neural networks. *Decision Support Systems*, *117*, 68–78. DOI: 10.1016/j.dss.2018.11.003

Ramasastry, A. (2015). Corporate social responsibility versus business and human rights: Bridging the gap between responsibility and accountability. *Journal of Human Rights*, *14*(2), 237–259. DOI: 10.1080/14754835.2015.1037953

Ramkumar, G., Kasat, K., Khader, P. R. A., Muhammed, P. K. N., Raghu, T., & Chhabra, S. (2022). Quality enhanced framework through integration of blockchain with supply chain management. *Measurement. Sensors*, *24*, 100462. DOI: 10.1016/j.measen.2022.100462

Rane, N. L. (2023). Integrating Leading-Edge Artificial Intelligence (AI), Internet of Things (IoT), and Big Data Technologies for Smart and Sustainable Architecture, Engineering and Construction (AEC) Industry: Challenges and Future Directions. *International Journal of Data Science and Big Data Analytics*, *3*(2), 73–95. DOI: 10.51483/IJDSBDA.3.2.2023.73-95

Rani, S., & Srivastava, G. (2024). Secure hierarchical fog computing-based architecture for industry 5.0 using an attribute-based encryption scheme. *Expert Systems with Applications*, *235*, 121180. DOI: 10.1016/j.eswa.2023.121180

Rashid, A. B., & Kausik, A. K. (2024). AI revolutionizing industries worldwide: A comprehensive overview of its diverse applications. *Hybrid Advances*, 100277.

Rashid, M. R. A., Hasan, M., Islam, M. A., Tasnim, S. T., Taifa, R. J., Mahbub, S., Mansoor, N., Ali, M. S., Jabid, T., Islam, M., & Islam, M. M. (2024a). Transforming agri-food value chains in Bangladesh: A practical application of blockchain for traceability and fair pricing. *Heliyon*, *10*(21), e40091. DOI: 10.1016/j.heliyon.2024.e40091 PMID: 39583833

Rashid, S., & Ratten, V. (2021). Entrepreneurial ecosystems during [the survival of small businesses using dynamic capabilities. World Journal of Entrepreneurship, Management and Sustainable Development.]. *COVID*, 19.

Reddy, P. K., & Thomas, B. (2022). *Towards technological adaptation of advanced farming through AI, IoT, and robotics: A comprehensive overview*. arXiv Preprint arXiv:2202.10459. https://arxiv.org/abs/2202.10459

Revilla, E., & Sáenz, M. J. (2014). Supply chain disruption management: Global convergence vs national specificity. *Journal of Business Research*, *67*(6), 1123–1135. DOI: 10.1016/j.jbusres.2013.05.021

Revilla, E., Saenz, M. J., Seifert, M., & Ma, Y. (2023). Human–Artificial Intelligence Collaboration in Prediction: A Field Experiment in the Retail Industry. *Journal of Management Information Systems*, *40*(4), 1071–1098. DOI: 10.1080/07421222.2023.2267317

Riaz, M., Kausar, R., Jameel, T., & Pamucar, D. (2024). Cubic picture fuzzy topological data analysis with integrating blockchain and the metaverse for uncertain supply chain management. *Engineering Applications of Artificial Intelligence, 131*, 107827. DOI: 10.1016/j.engappai.2023.107827

Richey, R. G., Chowdhury, S., Davis-Sramek, B., Giannakis, M., & Dwivedi, Y. K. (2023). Artificial intelligence in logistics and supply chain management: A primer and roadmap for research. In Journal of Business Logistics (Vol. 44, Issue 4). DOI: 10.1111/jbl.12364

Rieder, E., & Schmuck, M. (2024). Will Industry 5.0 have a serious impact on processes in companies? A scientific look at the changes that could accompany Industry 5.0′. *Procedia Computer Science, 237*, 742–750. DOI: 10.1016/j.procs.2024.05.161

Rinat, K., Thakur, G., Gupta, M., Madhuri, T. N. P., & Bansal, S. (2024). Comparative Analysis of Big Data Computing in Industry 4.0 and Industry 5.0: An Experimental Study. In *BIO Web of Conferences* (Vol. 86, p. 01068). EDP Sciences.

Robert, F., Shaohui, M., & Stephan, K. (2022). Retail forecasting: Research and practice. *International Journal of Forecasting*, *38*(4). PMID: 36217499

Robson, I., Ojiako, U., & Maguire, S. (2022). A complexity perspective of dynamic capabilities in enterprise project organizations. *Production Planning and Control*, 1–25.

Rocha, F., Garcia, G., Pereira, R. F. S., Faria, H. D., Silva, T. H., Andrade, R. H. R., Barbosa, E. S., Almeida, A., Cruz, E., Andrade, W., Serrantola, W. G., Moura, L., Azpúrua, H., Franca, A., Pessin, G., Freitas, G. M., Costa, R. R., & Lizarralde, F. (2021). ROSI: A robotic system for harsh outdoor industrial inspection – System design and applications. *Journal of Intelligent & Robotic Systems*, *103*(2), 30. DOI: 10.1007/s10846-021-01459-2

Rodrigue, J.-P., Slack, B., & Comtois, C. (2017). Green logistics. In Brewer, B. S., Button, G., & Hensher, D. A. (Eds.), *Handbook of logistics and supply-chain management* (Vol. 2, pp. 339–350). Emerald., DOI: 10.1108/9780080435930-021

Romao, M., Costa, J., & Costa, C. J. (2019). Robotic process automation: A case study in the banking industry. In *2019 14th Iberian Conference on Information Systems and Technologies (CISTI)* (pp. 1–6). IEEE. DOI: 10.23919/CISTI.2019.8760733

Ronaghi, M. H. (2021). A blockchain maturity model in agricultural supply chain. *Information Processing in Agriculture*, *8*(3), 398–408. DOI: 10.1016/j.inpa.2020.10.004

Ronchini, A., Guida, M., Moretto, A., & Caniato, F. (2024). The role of artificial intelligence in the supply chain finance innovation process. *Operations Management Research*. DOI: 10.1007/s12063-024-00492-2

Saberi, S., Kouhizadeh, M., Sarkis, J., & Shen, L. (2019). Blockchain technology and its relationships to sustainable supply chain management. *International Journal of Production Research*, *57*(7), 2117–2135. DOI: 10.1080/00207543.2018.1533261

Sadeghi, R. K., Ojha, D., Kaur, P., Mahto, R. V., & Dhir, A. (2024). Explainable artificial intelligence and agile decision-making in supply chain cyber resilience. *Decision Support Systems*, *180*, 114194. DOI: 10.1016/j.dss.2024.114194

Saen, R. F., Yousefi, F., & Azadi, M. (2024). Artificial intelligence powered predictions: Enhancing supply chain sustainability. *Annals of Operations Research*. DOI: 10.1007/s10479-024-06088-0

Sánchez-Flores, R. B., Cruz-Sotelo, S. E., Ojeda-Benitez, S., & Ramírez-Barreto, M. E. (2020). Sustainable supply chain management—A literature review on emerging economies. *Sustainability (Basel)*, *12*(17), 6972. DOI: 10.3390/su12176972

Sandanayake, Y. G., & Perera, A. T. D. (2021). Impact of ML algorithms in e-commerce supply chains. *Journal of Business Research*, *123*, 375–385. DOI: 10.1016/j.jbusres.2021.01.067

Sandhu, R. K., Thomas, M. A., & Osei-Bryson, K. M. (2024). Supporting Secure and Efficient Collaborative Health Information Exchange: A Hybrid Blockchain and Ontology based Approach. *Blockchain: Research and Applications*, *100248*. DOI: 10.1016/j.bcra.2024.100248

Santibanez Gonzalez, E. D., Kandpal, V., Machado, M., Martens, M. L., & Majumdar, S. (2023). A bibliometric analysis of circular economies through sustainable smart cities. *Sustainability (Basel)*, *15*(22), 15892. DOI: 10.3390/su152215892

Saputro, E. P. (2024). Kolaborasi Manusia Dan Sumber Daya Robotik Menuju Masa Depan Manufaktur Berkelanjutan Industri 5.0. *Innovative: Journal Of Social Science Research*, *4*(1), 2504–2516.

Sarfaraz, A., Chakrabortty, R. K., & Essam, D. L. (2023). The implications of blockchain-coordinated information sharing within a supply chain: A simulation study. *Blockchain: Research and Applications*, *4*(1), 100110. DOI: 10.1016/j.bcra.2022.100110

Sarker, I. H. (2022). AI-based modeling: Techniques, applications and research issues towards automation, intelligent and smart systems. *SN Computer Science*, *3*(2), 158. DOI: 10.1007/s42979-022-01043-x PMID: 35194580

Schinckus, C. (2020). The good, the bad and the ugly: An overview of the sustainability of blockchain technology'. *Energy Research & Social Science*, *69*, 101614. DOI: 10.1016/j.erss.2020.101614

Schlosser, R., Walther, C., Boissier, M., & Uflacker, M. (2019). Automated repricing and ordering strategies in competitive markets. *AI Communications*, *32*(1), 15–29. DOI: 10.3233/AIC-180603

Schoepf, S., Foster, J., & Brintrup, A. (2024). Identifying Contributors to Supply Chain Outcomes in a Multiechelon Setting: A Decentralised Approach. *IEEE Transactions on Industrial Informatics, 20*(12), 13811-13819. *IEEE Transactions on Industrial Informatics*. DOI: 10.1109/TII.2024.3435431

Scholten, K., Scott, P. S., & Fynes, B. (2014). Mitigation processes - antecedents for building supply chain resilience. *Supply Chain Management*, *19*(2), 211–228. DOI: 10.1108/SCM-06-2013-0191

Scholten, K., Sharkey Scott, P., & Fynes, B. (2019). Building routines for non-routine events: Supply chain resilience learning mechanisms and their antecedents. *Supply Chain Management*, *24*(3), 430–442. DOI: 10.1108/SCM-05-2018-0186

Schröder, A. J., Cuypers, M., & Götting, A. (2024). From Industry 4.0 to Industry 5.0: The Triple Transition Digital, Green and Social. In *Industry 4.0 and the Road to Sustainable Steelmaking in Europe: Recasting the Future* (pp. 35–51). Springer International Publishing. DOI: 10.1007/978-3-031-35479-3_3

Scopus. (2024). Scopus: Content coverage guide.

Scuotto, V., Magni, D., Theofilos, T., & Del Giudice, M. (2022). Chief digital officer and organizational creativity toward digitalization. *IEEE Transactions on Engineering Management.*

Secinaro, , Calandra, D., Secinaro, A., Muthurangu, V., & Biancone, P. (2021). The role of artificial intelligence in healthcare: A structured literature review. *BMC Medical Informatics and Decision Making*, *21*(1), 125. DOI: 10.1186/s12911-021-01488-9 PMID: 33836752

Segato, , Marzullo, A., Calimeri, F., & De Momi, E. (2020). Artificial intelligence for brain diseases: A systematic review. *APL Bioengineering*, *4*(4), 041503. DOI: 10.1063/5.0011697 PMID: 33094213

Seiti, H., Shabani, M., Ghanbari, H., Ben-Amor, S., & Hameed, A. I. (2024). *Toward a Human-Centric Metaverse: Novel Causal Decision Models for Supply Chain Risk Management* (SSRN Scholarly Paper 5007940). Social Science Research Network. DOI: 10.2139/ssrn.5007940

Selvarajan, S., Manoharan, H., & Shankar, A. (2024). SL-RI: Integration of supervised learning in robots for industry 5.0 automated application monitoring. *Measurement. Sensors, 31*, 100972. DOI: 10.1016/j.measen.2023.100972

Senoner, J., Netland, T., & Feuerriegel, S. (2022). Using Explainable Artificial Intelligence to Improve Process Quality: Evidence from Semiconductor Manufacturing. *Management Science, 68*(8), 5704–5723. DOI: 10.1287/mnsc.2021.4190

Sezer, O. B., & Gudelek, M. U. (2019). Financial and operational forecasting using deep learning. *Applied Soft Computing, 83*, 105628. DOI: 10.1016/j.asoc.2019.105628

Sgantzos, K., & Grigg, I. (2019). Artificial intelligence implementations on the blockchain: Use cases and future applications. *Future Internet, 11*(8), 170. DOI: 10.3390/fi11080170

Shaheen, S. A., & Lipman, T. E. (2007). Reducing greenhouse emissions and fuel consumption: Sustainable approaches for surface transportation. *IATSS Research, 31*(1), 6–20. DOI: 10.1016/S0386-1112(14)60179-5

Sharma, A. J., & Rathore, B. (s. d.). Examine the enablers of generative artificial intelligence adoption in supply chain: A mixed method study. *Journal of Decision Systems, 0*(0), 1-33. DOI: 10.1080/12460125.2024.2410030

Sharma, A., & Singh, B. (2022). Measuring Impact of E-commerce on Small Scale Business: A Systematic Review. *Journal of Corporate Governance and International Business Law, 5*(1).

Sharma, R., & Gupta, H. (2024). Leveraging cognitive digital twins in Industry 5.0 for achieving strategies'. *Journal of Cleaner Production, 448*, 141364. DOI: 10.1016/j.jclepro.2024.141364

Sharma, R., Shishodia, A., Gunasekaran, A., Min, H., & Munim, Z. H. (2022). The role of artificial intelligence in supply chain management: Mapping the territory. *International Journal of Production Research, 60*(24), 7527–7550. DOI: 10.1080/00207543.2022.2029611

Sharma, S. K., Chakraborti, S., & Jha, T. (2019). Analysis of book sales prediction at Amazon marketplace in India: A machine learning approach. *Information Systems and e-Business Management, 17*(2–4), 261–284. DOI: 10.1007/s10257-019-00438-3

Sharma, V. K., & Kumar, H. (2024). Enablers Driving Success of Artificial Intelligence in Business Performance: A TISM-MICMAC Approach. *IEEE Transactions on Engineering Management, 71*, 4665-4675. *IEEE Transactions on Engineering Management*. DOI: 10.1109/TEM.2023.3236768

Sherafati, M., Bashiri, M., Tavakkoli-Moghaddam, R., & Pishvaee, M. S. (2020). Achieving sustainable development of supply chain by incorporating various carbon regulatory mechanisms. *Transportation Research Part D, Transport and Environment, 81*, 102253. DOI: 10.1016/j.trd.2020.102253

Shiraishi, C. S. H., Roriz, C. L., Carocho, M., Prieto, M. A., Abreu, R. M. V., Barros, L., & Heleno, S. A. (2025). Blockchain revolution in food supply chains: A positive impact on global food loss and waste. *Food Chemistry, 467*, 142331. DOI: 10.1016/j.foodchem.2024.142331 PMID: 39644658

Shivendra, C., K., Tripathi, M. K., & Maktedar, D. D. (2021). Block chain Technology in Agriculture Product Supply Chain. *2021 International Conference on Artificial Intelligence and Smart Systems (ICAIS), December 2021*, 1325–1329. DOI: 10.1109/ICAIS50930.2021.9395886

Shiwlani, A., Khan, M., Sherani, A. M. K., & Qayyum, M. U. (2023). Synergies of AI and Smart Technology: Revolutionizing Cancer Medicine, Vaccine Development, and Patient Care. International Journal of Social. *Humanities and Life Sciences, 1*(1), 10–18.

Shi, Y., Wang, T., & Alwan, L. C. (2020). Analytics for Cross-Border E-Commerce: Inventory Risk Management of an Online Fashion Retailer. *Decision Sciences, 51*(6), 1347–1376. DOI: 10.1111/deci.12429

Shobhana, N. (2024). AI-powered supply chains towards greater efficiency. In Mangla, S. K., Tyagi, A. K., & Luthra, S. (Eds.), *Complex AI dynamics and interactions in management* (pp. 229–249). IGI Global., DOI: 10.4018/979-8-3693-0712-0.ch011

Shojaeinasab, A., Charter, T., Jalayer, M., Khadivi, M., Ogunfowora, O., Raiyani, N., Yaghoubi, M., & Najjaran, H. (2022). Intelligent manufacturing execution systems: A systematic review. *Journal of Manufacturing Systems, 62*, 503–522. DOI: 10.1016/j.jmsy.2022.01.004

Shoushtari, F., Ghafourian, E., & Talebi, M. (2021). Improving performance of supply chain by applying artificial intelligence. *International journal of industrial engineering and operational research, 3*(1), 14-23.

Shrestha, A., & Mahmood, A. (2019). Review of deep learning algorithms and architectures. In IEEE Access (Vol. 7). DOI: 10.1109/ACCESS.2019.2912200

Shujahat, M., Sousa, M. J., Hussain, S., Nawaz, F., Wang, M., & Umer, M. (2019). Translating the impact of knowledge management processes into knowledge-based innovation: The neglected and mediating role of knowledge-worker productivity. *Journal of Business Research, 94*, 442–450. DOI: 10.1016/j.jbusres.2017.11.001

Silveira Ramalho, T., & De Fátima Martins, M. (2022). Sustainable human resource management in the supply chain: A new framework'. *Cleaner Logistics and Supply Chain, 5*, 100075. DOI: 10.1016/j.clscn.2022.100075

Silvestri, R., Carloni, E., Morrone, D., & Santovito, S. (2024). The role of blockchain technology in supply chain relationships: Balancing efficiency and relational dynamics. *Journal of Purchasing and Supply Management, 100967*. DOI: 10.1016/j.pursup.2024.100967

Simchi-Levi, D., Trichakis, N., & Zhang, P. Y. (2019). Designing response supply chain against bioattacks. *Operations Research, 67*(5), 1246–1268. DOI: 10.1287/opre.2019.1862

Singh, A., & Agrawal, N. (2018). Demand forecasting with machine learning in manufacturing. *Manufacturing & Service Operations Management, 20*(3), 339–351. DOI: 10.1287/msom.2018.0705

Sinha, S., & Modak, N. M. (2021). A systematic review in recycling/reusing/remanufacturing supply chain research: A tertiary study. *International Journal of Sustainable Engineering, 14*(6), 1411–1432. DOI: 10.1080/19397038.2021.1986594

Skipper, J. B., & Hanna, J. B. (2009). Minimizing supply chain disruption risk through enhanced flexibility. *International Journal of Physical Distribution & Logistics Management, 39*(5), 404–427. DOI: 10.1108/09600030910973742

Śledziewska, K., & Włoch, R. (2021). The Economics of Digital Transformation. *The disruption of.*

Śledziewska, K., & Włoch, R. (2021). The foundations of the digital economy. In *The Economics of Digital Transformation*. Taylor & Francis. DOI: 10.4324/9781003144359-1

Smart, P. (2022). Minds in the Metaverse: Extended Cognition Meets Mixed Reality. *Philosophy & Technology, 35*(4), 87. DOI: 10.1007/s13347-022-00580-w

Sodiya, E. O., Jacks, B. S., Ugwuanyi, E. D., Adeyinka, M. A., Umoga, U. J., Daraojimba, A. I., Lottu, O. A., Sodiya, E. O., Jacks, B. S., Ugwuanyi, E. D., Adeyinka, M. A., Umoga, U. J., Daraojimba, A. I., & Lottu, O. A.Enoch Oluwademilade SodiyaBoma Sonimitiem JacksEjike David UgwuanyiMojisola Abimbola AdeyinkaUchenna Joseph UmogaAndrew Ifesinachi DaraojimbaOluwaseun Augustine Lottu. (2024). Reviewing the role of AI and machine learning in supply chain analytics. *GSC Advanced Research and Reviews, 18*(2), 2. DOI: 10.30574/gscarr.2024.18.2.0069

Soluk, J., Decker-Lange, C., & Hack, A. (2023). Small steps for the big hit: A dynamic capabilities perspective on business networks and non-disruptive digital technologies in SMEs. *Technological Forecasting and Social Change*, *191*, 122490. DOI: 10.1016/j.techfore.2023.122490

Sombultawee, K., Lenuwat, P., Aleenajitpong, N., & Boon-Itt, S. (2022). COVID-19 and Supply Chain Management: A Review with Bibliometric. *Sustainability (Basel)*, *14*(6), 3538. DOI: 10.3390/su14063538

Soori, M., Jough, F. K. G., Dastres, R., & Arezoo, B. (2024). AI-based decision support systems in Industry 4.0: A review. *Journal of Economy and Technology*. DOI: 10.1016/j.ject.2024.08.005

Soori, M., Dastres, R., & Arezoo, B. (2023). AI-powered blockchain technology in industry 4.0, a review. *Journal of Economy and Technology*, *1*, 222–241. DOI: 10.1016/j.ject.2024.01.001

Soumaya, F., Jabir, A., & Fouad, J. (2024). Transport 4.0 tools opportunities and benefits in last mile logistics: Past review and future perspectives. *2024 IEEE 15th International Colloquium on Logistics and Supply Chain Management (LOGISTIQUA)*, 1–6. https://ieeexplore.ieee.org/abstract/document/10571462/

Spangler, W. E. (1991). The role of artificial intelligence in understanding the strategic decision-making process. *IEEE Transactions on Knowledge and Data Engineering*, *3*(2), 149–159. DOI: 10.1109/69.87995

Speringer, M., & Schnelzer, J. (2019). Differentiation of industry 4.0 models. *Vienna, Austria.*

Sreelakshmi, S., Babu, A. A., Lakshmipriya, C., Gracious, L. A., Nalini, M., & Subramanian, R. S. (2024, October). Enhancing Intrusion Detection Systems with Machine Learning. In *2024 2nd International Conference on Self Sustainable Artificial Intelligence Systems (ICSSAS)* (pp. 557-564). IEEE. DOI: 10.1109/ICSSAS64001.2024.10760341

Srinivasan, S., Hema, D. D., Singaram, B., Praveena, D., Mohan, K. K., & Preetha, M. (2024). Decision Support System based on Industry 5.0 in Artificial Intelligence. *International Journal of Intelligent Systems and Applications in Engineering*, *12*(15s), 172–178.

Srivastava, V., Mahara, T., & Yadav, P. (2021). An analysis of the ethical challenges of blockchain-enabled E-healthcare applications in 6G networks. *International Journal of Cognitive Computing in Engineering*, *2*, 171–179. DOI: 10.1016/j.ijcce.2021.10.002

Sroginis, A., Fildes, R., & Kourentzes, N. (2023). Use of contextual and model-based information in adjusting promotional forecasts. *European Journal of Operational Research, 307*(3), 1177–1191. DOI: 10.1016/j.ejor.2022.10.005

Stadtler, H., & Kilger, C. (Eds.). (2005). *Supply chain management and advanced planning: Concepts, models, software and case studies* (3rd ed.). Springer. DOI: 10.1007/b106298

Stajnko, D., Lakota, M., & Hočevar, M. (2004). Estimation of number and diameter of apple fruits in an orchard during the growing season by thermal imaging. *Computers and Electronics in Agriculture, 42*(1), 31–42. DOI: 10.1016/S0168-1699(03)00086-3

Statista (2022). Artificial Intelligence (AI) Adoption Rate in Supply Chain and Manufacturing Businesses Worldwide in 2022 and 2025.

Stevenson, M., & Spring, M. (2007). Flexibility from a supply chain perspective: Definition and review. In International Journal of Operations and Production Management (Vol. 27, Issue 7). DOI: 10.1108/01443570710756956

Strand, V., Lotfi, M., Flynn, A., & Walker, H. (2024). A systematic literature review of modern slavery in supply chain management: State of the art, framework development and research opportunities'. *Journal of Cleaner Production, 435*, 140301. DOI: 10.1016/j.jclepro.2023.140301

Sturm, N., Mayr, A., Le Van, T., Chupakhin, V., Ceulemans, H., Wegner, J., Golib-Dzib, J.-F., Jeliazkova, N., Vandriessche, Y., Böhm, S., Cima, V., Martinovic, J., Greene, N., Vander Aa, T., Ashby, T. J., Hochreiter, S., Engkvist, O., Klambauer, G., & Chen, H. (2020). Industry-scale application and evaluation of deep learning for drug target prediction. *Journal of Cheminformatics, 12*(1), 1–13. DOI: 10.1186/s13321-020-00428-5 PMID: 33430964

Subramanian, R. S., Yamini, B., Sudha, K., & Sivakumar, S. (2024). Ensemble-based deep learning techniques for customer churn prediction model. *Kybernetes*. DOI: 10.1108/K-08-2023-1516

Suganya, G., Selvakumar, J. J., Varadharajan, P., & Pachiyappan, S. (2024). Skill Sets Required to Meet a Human-Centered Industry 5.0: A Systematic Literature Review and Bibliometric Analysis. *Advances in Web Technologies and Engineering, 5*(0), 231–252. DOI: 10.4018/979-8-3693-0782-3.ch014

Sundarakani, B., Pereira, V., & Ishizaka, A. (2020). Robust facility location decisions for resilient sustainable supply chain performance in the face of disruptions. *International Journal of Logistics Management, 32*(2), 357–385. DOI: 10.1108/IJLM-12-2019-0333

Sunmola, F. T., Burgess, P., & Tan, A. (2021). Building Blocks for Blockchain Adoption in Digital Transformation of Sustainable Supply Chains. *Procedia Manufacturing*, *55*(C), 513–520. DOI: 10.1016/j.promfg.2021.10.070

Sunmola, F., Baryannis, G., Tan, A., Co, K., & Papadakis, E. (2025). Holistic Framework for Blockchain-Based Halal Compliance in Supply Chains Enabled by Artificial Intelligence. *Systems*, *13*(1), 1. DOI: 10.3390/systems13010021

Sunmola, F., & Burgess, P. (2023). Transparency by Design for Blockchain-Based Supply Chains. *Procedia Computer Science*, *217*, 1256–1265. DOI: 10.1016/j.procs.2022.12.324

Suri, G. S., Kaur, G., & Shinde, D. (2024). Beyond boundaries: Exploring the transformative power of AI in pharmaceuticals. *Discover Artificial Intelligence*, *4*(1), 82. DOI: 10.1007/s44163-024-00192-7

Swim, J. K., Clayton, S., & Howard, G. S. (2011). Human behavioral contributions to climate change: Psychological and contextual drivers. *The American Psychologist*, *66*(4), 251–264. DOI: 10.1037/a0023472 PMID: 21553951

Takahashi, H., & Yamada, K. (2021). When the Japanese stock market meets [Impact of ownership, China and US exposure, and ESG channels. *International Review of Financial Analysis*]. *COVID*, 19.

Talha, S. E., Arif, J., & Jawab, F. (2024, May). Resilience Championship: Innovative Strategies for Supply Chain Management in the Face of Global Storms. In 2024 IEEE 15th International Colloquium on Logistics and Supply Chain Management (LOGISTIQUA) (pp. 1-8). IEEE.

Tang, A., Tchao, E. T., Agbemenu, A. S., Keelson, E., Klogo, G. S., & Kponyo, J. J. (2024). Assessing blockchain and IoT technologies for agricultural food supply chains in Africa: A feasibility analysis. *Heliyon*, *10*(15), e34584. DOI: 10.1016/j.heliyon.2024.e34584 PMID: 39170464

Tan, W. C., & Sidhu, M. S. (2022). Review of RFID and IoT integration in supply chain management. *Operations Research Perspectives*, *9*, 100229. DOI: 10.1016/j.orp.2022.100229

Tarihal, B., Kaliwal, R., & Ammanagi, A. (2024). The transformative influence of artificial intelligence on supply chain management. *ITM Web of Conferences, 68*, 01016. DOI: 10.1051/itmconf/20246801016

Tariq, , Awan, M. J., Alshudukhi, J., Alam, T. M., Alhamazani, K. T., & Meraf, Z. (2022). Software Measurement by Using Artificial Intelligence. *Journal of Nanomaterials*, *2022*(1), 7283171. DOI: 10.1155/2022/7283171

Taylor, A. (2025, March 4). *How Procter & Gamble and Unilever use AI for smarter manufacturing and supply chains.* Cleverence. https://www.cleverence.com/articles/business-blogs/how-procter-and-gamble-and-unilever-use-ai-for-smarter-manufacturing-and-supply-chains/

Taylor, C. L. (2024a). *"Corporate Social Advocacy:A Study of Brand and Consumer Activism in the Era of Social Media.*

Taylor, C. L. (2024b). Corporate Social Advocacy. *A Study of Brand and Consumer Activism in the Era of Social Media.*

Taylor, J. W., & Letham, B. (2021). Forecasting supply chain disruptions using ML models. *International Journal of Forecasting*, *37*(1), 69–82. DOI: 10.1016/j.ijforecast.2020.06.008

Tchuente, D., Lonlac, J., & Kamsu-Foguem, B. (2024). A methodological and theoretical framework for implementing explainable artificial intelligence (XAI) in business applications. *Computers in Industry*, *155*, 104044. DOI: 10.1016/j.compind.2023.104044

Teece, D. J., Pisano, G., & Shuen, A. (1997). Dynamic capabilities and strategic management. *Strategic Management Journal*, *18*(7), 509–533. DOI: 10.1002/(SICI)1097-0266(199708)18:7<509::AID-SMJ882>3.0.CO;2-Z

Tian, K., Zhu, Z., Mbachu, J., Ghanbaripour, A., & Moorhead, M. (2025). Artificial intelligence in risk management within the realm of construction projects: A bibliometric analysis and systematic literature review. *Journal of Innovation & Knowledge*, *10*(3), 100711. DOI: 10.1016/j.jik.2025.100711

Tirkolaee, E. B., Sadeghi, S., Mooseloo, F. M., Vandchali, H. R., & Aeini, S. (2021). Application of machine learning in supply chain management: A comprehensive overview of the main areas. *Mathematical Problems in Engineering*, *2021*, 1476043. DOI: 10.1155/2021/1476043

Todo, Y., Nakajima, K., & Matous, P. (2015). How do supply chain networks affect the resilience of firms to natural disasters? Evidence from the great east Japan Earthquake. *Journal of Regional Science*, *55*(2), 209–229. DOI: 10.1111/jors.12119

Toorajipour, R., Sohrabpour, V., Nazarpour, A., Oghazi, P., & Fischl, M. (2021). Artificial intelligence in supply chain management: A systematic literature review. *Journal of Business Research*, *122*, 502–517. DOI: 10.1016/j.jbusres.2020.09.009

Tran, Y., Zahra, S., & Hughes, M. (2019). A process model of the maturation of a new dynamic capability. *Industrial Marketing Management*, *83*, 115–127. DOI: 10.1016/j.indmarman.2018.11.009

Tronnebati, I., & Jawab, F. (2020, December). The similarities and differences between the green and sustainable supply chain management definitions and factors: A literature review. In 2020 IEEE 13th International Colloquium of Logistics and Supply Chain Management (LOGISTIQUA) (pp. 1-6). IEEE. DOI: 10.1109/LOGISTIQUA49782.2020.9353939

Tronnebati, I., & Jawab, F. (2024). The impact of green and sustainable supply chain management practices on sustainable performance: A comparative analysis. *International Journal of Logistics Systems and Management*, *47*(3), 267–294. DOI: 10.1504/IJLSM.2024.136855

Tronnebati, I., Jawab, F., Frichi, Y., & Arif, J. (2024). Green supplier selection using fuzzy ahp, fuzzy tosis, and fuzzy waspas: A case study of the moroccan automotive industry. *Sustainability (Basel)*, *16*(11), 4580. DOI: 10.3390/su16114580

Trstenjak, M., Mustapić, M., Gregurić, P., & Opetuk, T. (2023). Use of green industry 5.0 technologies in logistics activities. *Tehnički Glasnik*, *17*(3), Article 3.

Trstenjak, M., Opetuk, T., Đukić, G., & Cajner, H. (2022). Logistics 5.0 implementation model based on decision support systems. *Sustainability (Basel)*, *14*(11), 11. DOI: 10.3390/su14116514

Tsang, Y. P., Fan, Y., Lee, C. K. M., & Lau, H. C. W. (2024). Blockchain sharding for e-commerce supply chain performance analytics towards Industry 5.0. *Enterprise Information Systems*, *18*(4), 2311807. DOI: 10.1080/17517575.2024.2311807

Ullah, H., Manickam, S., Obaidat, M., Laghari, S. U. A., & Uddin, M. (2023). Exploring the Potential of Metaverse Technology in Healthcare: Applications, Challenges, and Future Directions. *IEEE Access: Practical Innovations, Open Solutions*, *11*, 69686–69707. DOI: 10.1109/ACCESS.2023.3286696

Ulrich, M., Jahnke, H., Langrock, R., Pesch, R., & Senge, R. (2021). Distributional regression for demand forecasting in e-grocery. *European Journal of Operational Research*, *294*(3), 831–842. DOI: 10.1016/j.ejor.2019.11.029

Utchay, H. U. (2005). Convergence and divergence in global economy and social development: global perspectives on the contents of economic and soical development policy and its effects on rich and poor countries. Diss. Åbo Akademis förlag-Åbo Akademi University Press, In *Journal GEEJ* (Vol. 7, Issue 2).

Vacchi, M., Siligardi, C., & Settembre-Blundo, D. (2024). Driving Manufacturing Companies toward Industry 5.0: A Strategic Framework for Process Technological Sustainability Assessment (P-TSA). *Sustainability (Basel)*, *16*(2), 695. DOI: 10.3390/su16020695

Vaishya, , Javaid, M., Khan, I. H., & Haleem, A. (2020). Artificial Intelligence (AI) applications for COVID-19 pandemic. *Diabetes & Metabolic Syndrome, 14*(4), 337–339. DOI: 10.1016/j.dsx.2020.04.012 PMID: 32305024

Valeriya, G., Kirola, M., Gupta, M., Bharathi, P., & Acharya, P. (2024). Evaluating the Impact of AI-Based Sustainability Measures in Industry 5.0: A Longitudinal Study. In *BIO Web of Conferences* (Vol. 86, p. 01058). EDP Sciences.

Valle, F. D., & Oliver, M. (2020). Blockchain Enablers for Supply Chains: How to Boost Implementation in Industry. *IEEE Access, 8*, 209699-209716. IEEE Access. DOI: 10.1109/ACCESS.2020.3038463

Vallentin, A., Thórisson, K. R., & Latapie, H. (2023). Addressing the Unsustainability of Deep Neural Networks with Next-Gen AI. In International Conference on Artificial General Intelligence (pp. 296-306). Cham: Springer Nature Switzerland. DOI: 10.1007/978-3-031-33469-6_30

Van Belle, J., Guns, T., & Verbeke, W. (2021). Using shared sell-through data to forecast wholesaler demand in multi-echelon supply chains. *European Journal of Operational Research, 288*(2), 466–479. DOI: 10.1016/j.ejor.2020.05.059

Van der Poll, J. A. (2022). Problematizing the Adoption of Formal Methods in the 4IR–5IR Transition. *Applied System Innovation, 5*(6), 127. DOI: 10.3390/asi5060127

Van Engelenburg, S., Janssen, M., & Klievink, B. (2018). A blockchain architecture for reducing the bullwhip effect. In Shishkov, B. (Ed.), *Business Modeling and Software Design. BMSD 2018. Lecture Notes in Business Information Processing* (Vol. 319). Springer., DOI: 10.1007/978-3-319-94214-8_5

Van Hoek, R. (2019). Unblocking the chain–findings from an executive workshop on blockchain in the supply chain. *Supply Chain Management, 25*(2), 255–261. DOI: 10.1108/SCM-11-2018-0383

van Hoek, R. (2024). Insight from industry-early lessons learned about AI adoption in core procurement processes, directions for managers and researchers. *Supply Chain Management, 29*(4), 794–803. DOI: 10.1108/SCM-02-2024-0143

van Wynsberghe, A. (2021). Sustainable AI: AI for sustainability and the sustainability of AI. *AI and Ethics, 1*(3), 213–218. DOI: 10.1007/s43681-021-00043-6

Vatin, N. I., Negi, G. S., Yellanki, V. S., Mohan, C., & Singla, N. (2024). Sustainability Measures: An Experimental Analysis of AI and Big Data Insights in Industry 5.0. In *BIO Web of Conferences* (Vol. 86, p. 01072). EDP Sciences.

Venkatesh, R., & Rathi, S. (2019). Application of AI in demand planning. *Operations Research Letters*, *47*(4), 197–205. DOI: 10.1016/j.orl.2019.04.010

Venketbabu, T., Aswathy, M. P., Sangeetha, J., Anish, T. P., Nalini, M., & Subramanian, R. S. (2024, October). Revolutionizing Image Processing: Innovations Impacts and Future Trends. In *2024 2nd International Conference on Self Sustainable Artificial Intelligence Systems (ICSSAS)* (pp. 901-907). IEEE.

Verstraete, G., Aghezzaf, E. H., & Desmet, B. (2019). A data-driven framework for predicting weather impact on high-volume low-margin retail products. *Journal of Retailing and Consumer Services*, *48*, 169–177. DOI: 10.1016/j.jretconser.2019.02.019

Veselovská, L. (2020). Supply chain disruptions in the context of early stages of the global COVID-19 outbreak. *Problems and Perspectives in Management*, *18*(2), 490–500. DOI: 10.21511/ppm.18(2).2020.40

Vidal, U., Obregon, M., Ramos, E., Verma, R., & Coles, P. S. (2024). Sustainable and risk-resilient circular supply chain: A Peruvian paint manufacturing supply chain model. *Sustainable Futures : An Applied Journal of Technology, Environment and Society*, *7*, 100207. DOI: 10.1016/j.sftr.2024.100207

Villar, A., Paladini, S., & Buckley, O. (2023, July). Towards Supply Chain 5.0: Redesigning Supply Chains as Resilient, Sustainable, and Human-Centric Systems in a Post-pandemic World. In *Operations* []. Cham: Springer International Publishing.]. *Research Forum*, *4*(3), 60. DOI: 10.1007/s43069-023-00234-3

Vlachos, I. (2023). Implementation of an intelligent supply chain control tower: A socio-technical systems case study. *Production Planning and Control*, *34*(15), 1415–1431. DOI: 10.1080/09537287.2021.2015805

Vlasta, M. (2023). Methodological framework for European regulation of (artificial) intelligence and its limits.

Vyas, N., Beije, A., & Krishnamachari, B. (2019). *Blockchain and the supply chain: concepts, strategies and practical applications*. Kogan Page Publishers.

Wallacei. (n.d.). *Wallacei evolutionary optimization engine*. https://www.wallacei.com/

Waller, M. A., Van Hoek, R., Davletshin, M., & Fugate, B. (2019). *Integrating blockchain into supply chain management: a toolkit for practical implementation*. Kogan Page Publishers.

Walmsley, T. G., Ong, B. H. Y., Klemeš, J. J., Tan, R. R., & Varbanov, P. S. (2019). Circular Integration of processes, industries, and economies. *Renewable & Sustainable Energy Reviews, 107*(March), 507–515. DOI: 10.1016/j.rser.2019.03.039

Wamba, S. F., & Queiroz, M. M. (2020). Blockchain in the operations and supply chain management: Benefits, challenges and future research opportunities. *International Journal of Information Management, 52*, 102064. DOI: 10.1016/j.ijinfomgt.2019.102064

Wamba, S. F., Queiroz, M. M., Jabbour, C. J. C., & Shi, C. V. (2023). Are both generative AI and ChatGPT game changers for 21st-Century operations and supply chain excellence? *International Journal of Production Economics, 265*, 109015. DOI: 10.1016/j.ijpe.2023.109015

Wamba, S. F., Queiroz, M. M., Trinchera, L., & Fia, M. (2021). Big data analytics-enabled sensing capability and organizational outcomes: Assessing the mediating effects of business analytics culture. *Annals of Operations Research, 299*(1-2), 289–314. DOI: 10.1007/s10479-020-03812-4

Wang, B., Zhou, H., Li, X., Yang, G., Zheng, P., Song, C., Yuan, Y., Wuest, T., Yang, H., & Wang, L. (2024). Human Digital Twin in the context of Industry 5.0. *Robotics and Computer-integrated Manufacturing, 85*, 102626. DOI: 10.1016/j.rcim.2023.102626

Wang, J., Chong, W. K., Lin, J., & Hedenstierna, C. P. T. (2023). Retail Demand Forecasting Using Spatial-Temporal Gradient Boosting Methods. *Journal of Computer Information Systems*. DOI: 10.1080/08874417.2023.2240753

Wang, S., & Yang, Y. (2021). M-GAN-XGBOOST model for sales prediction and precision marketing strategy making of each product in online stores. *Data Technologies and Applications, 55*(5), 749–770. DOI: 10.1108/DTA-11-2020-0286

Wang, S., Zhang, J., Wang, P., Law, J., Calinescu, R., & Mihaylova, L. (2024). A deep learning-enhanced Digital Twin framework for improving safety and reliability in human–robot collaborative manufacturing. *Robotics and Computer-integrated Manufacturing, 85*, 102608. DOI: 10.1016/j.rcim.2023.102608

Wang, X., & Wei, W. (2022). Traditional vs. advanced forecasting models: A comparative study in demand prediction for manufacturing systems. *Journal of Industrial Engineering and Management, 15*(1), 121–134. DOI: 10.3926/jiem.3402

Wang, Y., Su, Z., Zhang, N., Xing, R., Liu, D., Luan, T. H., & Shen, X. (2023). A Survey on Metaverse: Fundamentals, Security, and Privacy. *IEEE Communications Surveys and Tutorials, 25*(1), 319–352. DOI: 10.1109/COMST.2022.3202047

Wani, . (2022). Utilization of Artificial Intelligence in Disease Prevention: Diagnosis, Treatment, and Implications for the Healthcare Workforce. *Health Care*. PMID: 35455786

Wan, X., Zhang, G., Yuan, Y., & Chai, S. (2023). How to drive the participation willingness of supply chain members in metaverse technology adoption? *Applied Soft Computing*, *145*, 110611. DOI: 10.1016/j.asoc.2023.110611

Watkins, S., Battles, J., & Vacek, R. (2013). Streamlining data for cross-platform web delivery. *Journal of Web Librarianship*, *7*(1), 95–108. DOI: 10.1080/19322909.2013.748393

Wen, L. (2024). Design automation system synchronization for cyber physical system with dynamic voltage and frequency scaling in industry 5.0. *Measurement. Sensors*, *31*, 100981. DOI: 10.1016/j.measen.2023.100981

Wenzel, H., Smit, D., & Sardesai, S. (2019). A Literature Review on Machine Learning in Supply Chain Management Supply Chain Management," in Proceedings of the Hamburg International Conference of Logistics (HICL) - 27, 2019, no. September, p. 30.

Wenzel, H., Smit, D., & Sardesai, S. (2019). A literature review on machine learning in supply chain management. Artificial Intelligence and Digital Transformation in Supply Chain Management, September.

Whig, P., & Adusumilli, S. B. K. (2023). Enhancing Healthcare Delivery Through AI-Driven Supply Chain Innovations: A Case Study Perspective. *International Transactions in Artificial Intelligence, 7*(7), Article 7. https://isjr.co.in/index.php/ITAI/article/view/313

White, K., Habib, R., & Hardisty, D. J. (2019). How to SHIFT Consumer Behaviors to be More Sustainable: A Literature Review and Guiding Framework. *Journal of Marketing*, *83*(3), 22–49. DOI: 10.1177/0022242919825649

Widiawati, H. S., Ramadhani, R. A., & Sumantri, B. A. (2025). The role of eco-digital learning in enhancing the impact of IoT, blockchain, and artificial intelligence on green supply chain for SME internationalization. *Problems and Perspectives in Management*, *23*(1), 76–89. DOI: 10.21511/ppm.23(1).2025.06

Winstanley, D., Clark, J., & Leeson, H. (2002). Approaches to child labour in the supply chain. *Business Ethics (Oxford, England)*, *11*(3), 210–223. DOI: 10.1111/1467-8608.00279

Wolf, J. (2014). The relationship between sustainable supply chain management, stakeholder pressure and corporate sustainability performance. *Journal of Business Ethics, 119*(3), 317–328. DOI: 10.1007/s10551-012-1603-0

Xu, H., Lee, E., & Rim, H. (2022). Should businesses take a stand? Effects of perceived psychological distance on consumers' expectation and evaluation of corporate social advocacy. *Journal of Marketing Communications, 28*(8), 840–863. DOI: 10.1080/13527266.2021.1969588

Yadav, A., Garg, R. K., & Sachdeva, A. (2024). Artificial intelligence applications for information management in sustainable supply chain management: A systematic review and future research agenda. *International Journal of Information Management Data Insights, 4*(2), 100292. DOI: 10.1016/j.jjimei.2024.100292

Yadav, R., & Mahara, T. (2019). Factors Affecting E-Commerce Adoption by Handicraft SMEs of India. *Journal of Electronic Commerce in Organizations, 17*(4), 44–57. DOI: 10.4018/JECO.2019100104

Yamini, B., Ramana, K. V., Nalini, M., Devi, D. C., Maheswari, B., & Siva, S. R. (2024). Customer churn prediction model in enterprises using machine learning. *International Journal of Advanced Technology and Engineering Exploration, 11*(110), 94.

Yang, B., Xu, X., Gong, Y., & Rekik, Y. (2023). Data-driven optimization models for inventory and financing decisions in online retailing platforms. *Annals of Operations Research*. DOI: 10.1007/s10479-023-05234-4

Yang, G., Ji, G., & Tan, K. H. (2022). Impact of artificial intelligence adoption on online returns policies. *Annals of Operations Research, 308*(1), 703–726. DOI: 10.1007/s10479-020-03602-y

Yang, J., Blount, Y., & Amrollahi, A. (2024). Artificial intelligence adoption in a professional service industry: A multiple case study. *Technological Forecasting and Social Change, 201*, 123251. DOI: 10.1016/j.techfore.2024.123251

Yao, X., & Askin, R. (2019). Review of supply chain configuration and design decision-making for new product. *International Journal of Production Research, 57*(7), 2226–2246. DOI: 10.1080/00207543.2019.1567954

Yao, X., Sanl, T., & Gulcu, A. (2015). Markdown optimization for multiple products with a common markdown budget constraint. *Journal of Revenue and Pricing Management, 14*(6), 442–450. DOI: 10.1057/rpm.2015.4

Yontar, E. (2023). The role of blockchain technology in the sustainability of supply chain management: Grey based Dematel implementation. *Cleaner Logistics and Supply Chain, 8*, 100113. DOI: 10.1016/j.clscn.2023.100113

Younis, H., Sundarakani, B., & Alsharairi, M. (2022). Applications of artificial intelligence and machine learning within supply chains: Systematic review and future research directions. *Journal of Modelling in Management, 17*(3), 916–940. DOI: 10.1108/JM2-12-2020-0322

Yu, W., Chavez, R., Jacobs, M. A., & Feng, M. (2018). Data-driven supply chain capabilities and performance: A resource-based view. *Transportation Research Part E, Logistics and Transportation Review, 114*, 371–385. DOI: 10.1016/j.tre.2017.04.002

Zaalouk, A., Moon, S., & Han, S. (2023). Operations planning and scheduling in off-site construction supply chain management: Scope definition and future directions'. *Automation in Construction, 153*, 104952. DOI: 10.1016/j.autcon.2023.104952

Zaid, O., Arif, J., & Jawab, F. (2024, May). Human-centric supply chain management towards industry 5.0. In 2024 IEEE 15th International Colloquium on Logistics and Supply Chain Management (LOGISTIQUA) (pp. 1-7). IEEE.

Zainal, F., Baharudin, H., Khalid, A., Karim, N. H., Ramli, S., Batan, A., & Mustapha, L. (2019). *Applying artificial intelligence in e-commerce reverse logistics: Enhancing returns management, supply chain efficiency, and sustainability through advanced technologies.*

Zamani, E. D., Smyth, C., Gupta, S., & Dennehy, D. (2023). Artificial intelligence and big data analytics for supply chain resilience: A systematic literature review. *Annals of Operations Research, 327*(2), 605–632. DOI: 10.1007/s10479-022-04983-y PMID: 36212520

Zarbà, C., Chinnici, G., Matarazzo, A., Privitera, D., & Scuderi, A. (2024). The innovative role of blockchain in agri-food systems: A literature analysis. *Food Control, 164*, 110603. DOI: 10.1016/j.foodcont.2024.110603

Zatsu, V., Shine, A. E., Tharakan, J. M., Peter, D., Ranganathan, T. V., Alotaibi, S. S., Mugabi, R., Bin Muhsinah, A., Waseem, M., & Nayik, G. A. (2024). Revolutionizing the food industry: The transformative power of artificial intelligence—A review. *Food Chemistry: X, 24*, 101867. DOI: 10.1016/j.fochx.2024.101867 PMID: 39431210

Zhang, C., Cho, S., & Vasarhelyi, M. (2022). Explainable Artificial Intelligence (XAI) in auditing. *International Journal of Accounting Information Systems, 46*, 100572. DOI: 10.1016/j.accinf.2022.100572

Zhang, L., & Yao, Y. (2024). Demand forecasting in retail: An empirical evaluation of traditional methods. *Journal of Retailing and Consumer Services, 68*, 103017. DOI: 10.1016/j.jretconser.2023.103017

Zhang, L., Zhang, M., Mujumdar, A. S., & Chen, Y. (2024). From farm to market : Research progress and application prospects of artificial intelligence in the frozen fruits and vegetables supply chain. *Trends in Food Science & Technology, 153*, 104730. DOI: 10.1016/j.tifs.2024.104730

Zhao, G., Ye, C., Zubairu, N., Mathiyazhagan, K., & Zhou, X. (2025a). Deployment of Industry 4.0 technologies to achieve a circular economy in agri-food supply chains: A thorough analysis of enablers. *Journal of Environmental Management, 373*, 123856. DOI: 10.1016/j.jenvman.2024.123856 PMID: 39740446

Zhao, J., & Gómez Fariñas, B. (2023). Artificial Intelligence and Sustainable Decisions. *European Business Organization Law Review, 24*(1), 1–39. DOI: 10.1007/s40804-022-00262-2

Zheng, J., Zhang, J. Z., Kamal, M. M., Liang, X., & Alzeiby, E. A. (2025). Unpacking human-AI interaction: Exploring unintended consequences on employee Well-being in entrepreneurial firms through an in-depth analysis. *Journal of Business Research, 196*, 115406. DOI: 10.1016/j.jbusres.2025.115406

Zhou, Q., Yang, Y., & Fu, S. (2022). Deep reinforcement learning approach for solving joint pricing and inventory problem with reference price effects. *Expert Systems with Applications, 195*, 116564. DOI: 10.1016/j.eswa.2022.116564

Ziatdinov, R., Atteraya, M. S., & Nabiyev, R. (2024). The Fifth Industrial Revolution as a Transformative Step towards Society 5.0. *Societies (Basel, Switzerland), 14*(2), 19. DOI: 10.3390/soc14020019

Zore, Ž., Čuček, L., & Kravanja, Z. (2018). Synthesis of sustainable production systems using an upgraded concept of sustainability profit and circularity. *Journal of Cleaner Production, 201*, 1138–1154. DOI: 10.1016/j.jclepro.2018.07.150

Zreik, M. (2023). Sustainable and smart supply chains in China: A multidimensional approach. In *Integrating intelligence and sustainability in supply chains* (pp. 179–197). IGI Global. DOI: 10.4018/979-8-3693-0225-5.ch010

Zrelli, I., & Rejeb, A. (2024). A bibliometric analysis of IoT applications in logistics and supply chain management. *Heliyon, 10*(16), 16. DOI: 10.1016/j.heliyon.2024.e36578 PMID: 39262942

Zwanka, R. J., & Buff, C. (2021). COVID-19 Generation: A Conceptual Framework of the Consumer Behavioral Shifts to Be Caused by the COVID-19 Pandemic. *Journal of International Consumer Marketing*, *33*(1), 58–67. DOI: 10.1080/08961530.2020.1771646

About the Contributors

Jabir Arif is an Associate Professor at Sidi Mohamed Ben Abdellah University, Morocco. He holds an M.Sc., Engineering, Ph.D., and HdR degrees in Industrial Engineering and Logistics from the National School of Applied Sciences Tangier and the Faculty of Sciences and Technologies Fez. Before transitioning to academia, he worked as a Production Planner in the automotive industry and later as a Senior Engineer at the Ministry of Public Services and Modernization of Administration, managing national major projects. His research focuses on Supply Chain Management & Logistics, Outsourcing of Logistic Activities, Risk Assessment, IoT, Artificial Intelligence, and Industrial Engineering. His recent publications emphasize operational efficiency, sustainability, green warehouse inventory management, and logistics traceability. Pr. Arif is a regular reviewer for Q1-Q2 journals in his field, including Cleaner Logistics and Supply Chain, Computers & Industrial Engineering, Digital Engineering, and International Journal of Production Research. He has served on the Technical and Scientific Committees of multiple international conferences and workshops. Pr. Jabir Arif has been recognized among the Top 15 Moroccan Researchers in Decision Sciences over the last decade by the National Center for Scientific and Technical Research (CNRST). His expertise has been showcased as a Distinguished Speaker at IEOM Society events on Global Supply Chain and Logistics in 2022 and 2023. In addition to his research contributions, he serves as a Faculty Advisor for IEOM Student Chapters and is an active member of the Industrial Engineering and Operations Management Society (IEOM). His commitment to advancing logistics and supply chain knowledge extends to his role in the scientific and organizing committees of major international conferences, including LOGISTIQUA, MITA, GOL, and CPI. Beyond academia, Pr. Arif actively engages in professional forums as a moderator and speaker on topics related to logistics, supply chain, and foreign trade. He also contributes to social and educational initiatives as a member of the Moroccan Student Foundation, supporting scholarship recipients.

With extensive academic and industry experience, he continues to make significant contributions through teaching, publishing, and international collaborations.

Fouad Jawab is a Full Professor at the Higher School of Technology of Sidi Mohamed Ben Abdellah University in Fez, Morocco. He is a recognized academic and researcher in the fields of logistics, supply chain management, and industrial engineering. Prof. Jawab currently leads the research team "Industrial Management and Logistics" (MILOG) and serves as Vice-Director of the "Industrial Technologies and Services" (IST) research laboratory. He is also the former Director of the "International Management, Decision Techniques and Logistics" (MIDLOG) laboratory. Over the years, he has played a central role in the development and management of academic and professional training programs. He previously headed the Department of Science and Management Techniques (STG) and the University Diploma of Technology (DUT) in Logistics and Transport Management (GLT). He currently serves as the Program Director of the Professional Bachelor's Degree in Logistics, which trains future professionals in logistics strategy, operations, and innovation. A pioneer in the academic logistics field in Morocco, Prof. Jawab is the Founder of the International Conference on Logistics and Supply Chain Management (LOGISTIQUA)—a leading scientific event that brings together international scholars, researchers, and practitioners to discuss emerging trends, challenges, and innovations in supply chain and logistics management. In addition to his academic and administrative roles, Prof. Jawab is deeply involved in research collaboration, doctoral supervision, and scientific dissemination. His work contributes significantly to the advancement of knowledge and practice in industrial logistics, supply chain optimization, and decision-making tools in industrial contexts.

***

Kuldeep Agnihotri is a Director/ Principal at ISBA Group of Institutes, Indore (MP). His area of expertise is Accounting, Finance, Corporate Law and Taxation. He is having more than 18 Years of work Experience including 16 years of Academics in Postgraduate and Undergraduate courses and 02 years of corporate experience as well. He has done his Ph.D. in Commerce from Devi Ahilya Vishwavidyalaya, Indore (MP), MBA with specialisation in finance and marketing, M.Com with specialisation in accounting from Dr. H.S. Gour Central University Sagar, B.Ed, COA from ICWAI Kolkata, Faculty Development Programme from IIT Mumbai. He has participated and presented research papers in many National and International Conferences/ Seminars. He has more than 45 Publication to his credit and his research paper published in research Journals of national and international repute (Including UGC Care, Scopus & ABDC Indexed Journals). He has Authored of 13

Text Books and Editor of 09 Edited Books. He has 27 Indian Patents published in his credit including a UK (International) Design Patent granted and earned a copyright from the Govt. of India for his research work. He is a Registered Ph.D. Research Supervisor (Guide) at Devi Ahilya Vishwavidyalaya, Indore (A State University of Madhya Pradesh) and under his guidance many students are doing Ph.D.

Nittan Arora is working as an Associate Professor in the Department of Business Management, CT Institute of Engineering, Management and Technology. He has recieved his Ph.D and MBA degree from I.K Gujral Punjab Technical University and B.Com from Guru Nanak Dev University. He has also qualify JRF and UGC NET. He has total work experience of 13 years including industry. His research interests are related to the field of finance and financial services. He has presented and published different research papers in national, international conferences and journals.

V V S Murty Bolla working as the faculty in the Department of Artificial Intelligence and Data Science, Faculty of Science and Technology at ICFAI Foundation for Higher Education (IFHE), Hyderabad. He has 14 years of teaching experience, having previously served at institutions such as Institute of Advanced Research University Gujarat, VSM Autonomous Engineering College, and Sir C R Reddy College. He is pursuing a Ph.D. at RTM Nagpur University, Nagpur. He completed M.Tech in Computer Science from Jawaharlal Nehru Technological University, Kakinada, and M.Sc. in Statistics from Andhra University, Visakhapatnam, and Andhra Pradesh. His research contributions include publications in national and international journals. He has actively participated in national and international conferences, Faculty Development programs, and Workshops

Saurabh Chandra is an accomplished legal scholar and currently serves as an Associate Professor & Assistant Dean at the School of Law, Bennett University, India. With a robust academic foundation, he earned his Bachelor of Arts and Bachelor of Laws (B.A. LL.B.) from the prestigious Aligarh Muslim University (A.M.U.). He further specialized in Business Laws, completing his Master of Laws (LL.M.) at the renowned National Law School of India University (NLSIU), Bangalore. Dr. Chandra's academic journey culminated in a Doctorate in Law (Ph.D.) from the esteemed National Law University (NLU) Delhi. In addition to his impressive legal education from some of India's most prestigious institutions, Dr. Chandra also holds a master's degree in management with specialization in Human Resources in Management and another in Journalism and Mass Communication. With almost two decades of teaching experience, he has numerous publications to his credit. His expertise is complemented by a robust portfolio of scholarly publications.

By bridging the gap between theoretical insights and real-world applications, Dr. Chandra's work serves as a valuable resource for academics, legal practitioners, and industry professionals alike. Dr. Chandra brings a wealth of experience in Academic Administration, having successfully held various key administrative positions. His diverse qualifications and extensive experience make him a distinguished figure in the academic and legal communities.

Mohd. Asif Gandhi is working as Associate Professor in Department of Mechanical Engineering at Anjuman-I-Islam's Kalsekar Technical Campus, Panvel, India; with additional charge as Controller of CIRDPI Cell (Centre of IPR; R&D Projects; Publications and Internal Revenue Generation) for the entire campus. He was formerly the HoD of Mechanical Engineering Department. He is a B.E. (Production Engineering) from M.H. Saboo Siddik College of Engineering; a M.E. (Production Engineering)(Specialization in Manufacturing Engineering) from Fr. Conceicao Rodrigues College of Engineering both affiliated to University of Mumbai; and a Ph.D. in Industrial Engineering from NITIE (now called IIM Mumbai), Mumbai, India. He has worked 10 years in the industry and 17 years in academia.

J. Elavarasi is an Assistant Professor in the Department of Artificial Intelligence and Data Science at Vel Tech High Tech Dr. Rangarajan Dr. Sakunthala Engineering College. She specializes in machine learning, deep learning, and intelligent systems. She is dedicated to guiding students in innovative AI-based projects and research initiatives. Her academic involvement includes publishing papers and participating in technical workshops and FDPs. Ms. Elavarasi strives to create an engaging learning environment that nurtures technical excellence and creativity.

Eti Khatri is working as an Associate Professor at Department of Management Studies, Nitte Meenakshi Institute of Technology, Bangalore. She is having 15 years of academic and research experience in finance, economics and supply chain management. She has worked for various institutions across India. She has earned her PhD from University of Rajasthan, Jaipur. She is guiding three scholars under Visvesvaraya Technological University, Belgaum, Karnataka. She has published several research papers in National and International Journals indexed by Scopus and Web of Science. She edited five books and contributed various chapters for knowledge books. She has three funded projects in her account sponsored by Karnataka State Council for Science and Technology. She has conducted various workshops and delivered guest talks in various academic institutions and organizations. She is working as a youth service director in Rotary and takes active participation in social activities.

L. A. Anto Gracious is an accomplished academic professional in Information Technology and Computer Science, known for his dedication to education, technology, and research. He holds a B.Tech in IT from C.S.I Institute of Technology (2006), an MBA in Technology Management, and an M.Tech in IT from Francis Xavier Engineering College (2011). He began his career as a Programmer at Software Solutions Integrated Limited, later transitioning to academia in 2011 as an Assistant Professor at Marthandam College of Engineering and Technology. Over eight years, he excelled in teaching, led the Software Development Cell, and earned multiple awards for his contributions. He later served at St. Xavier's Catholic College of Engineering and currently holds a position at R.M.K. College of Engineering and Technology. A prolific researcher, Anto focuses on machine learning, wireless sensor networks, and healthcare technologies. His work is widely published, and he has received accolades such as the Best Paper Award and multiple Best Faculty Awards.

P. Girija is working with the Department of IT at Panimalar Engineering College, Chennai. She is actively involved in research activities and academic writing under the aegis of Panimalar Engineering College. Her work focuses on emerging technologies and innovative practices in her field of expertise. Ms. Girija contributes to the academic community through publications, conferences, and collaborative research initiatives. She is committed to fostering academic excellence and continuous professional growth.

P. Suganya is an Assistant Professor in the Department of Computer Science and Engineering at Manakula Vinayagar Institute of Technology, Puducherry. She is dedicated to teaching and mentoring students in core areas of computer science. Her professional interests include software development, data structures, and emerging technologies in computing.

Nandana P Pillai is a dedicated second-year student at RV College of Engineering, specializing in Electronics and Communication. With a passion for exploring cutting-edge technologies, she constantly seeks to push the boundaries of innovation within her field. Her drive for continuous learning and growth fuels her ambition to make a lasting impact on the rapidly evolving world of technology, where she aims to contribute meaningfully through her expertise and creativity.

Ananya Pandey is a Research Scholar in School of Law at Christ University, Bangalore. She has her research interests in the field of Constitutional Law, Environment Law, Human Rights, Food Security, Intellectual Property Law and Jurisprudence.

Antonio Pesqueira is a healthcare and pharmaceutical commercial and supply chain management leader, with an emphasis on technological advancements and process improvement. Concurrently, he holds esteemed academic positions as a professor and research fellow at ISCTE/IUL. Within the Technology and Architecture Research Department, he contributes to the Ph.D. program, focusing his research on digital technologies, healthcare data management, blockchain, and the nexus of innovation and business management. He has notably chaired the Pharmaceutical Supply Chain & Security World Forum and is often invited as a keynote speaker at events such as the Pharma Track & Trace, and Serialization & Labeling Summit. Co-authored more than 20 scholarly articles and book chapters that have been featured in prestigious scientific journals. These include the Journal of Business Research, Future Generations Computer Systems, Journal of Medical Systems, Knowledge Management, WSEAS Transactions on Business and Economics, and Information Systems Frontiers, to name a few. Moreover, his outstanding contributions have been acknowledged at various peer-reviewed international conferences.

Ananthi S.N is an Assistant Professor in the Department of Computer Science and Engineering at S.A. Engineering College, Chennai. She is committed to delivering quality education in core computing disciplines. Her areas of interest include software engineering, database systems, and data analytics.

Jayashree Shivakumar is a student at RV College of Engineering, specializing in Electronics and Communications. With an unwavering passion for technology, she actively seeks to explore cutting-edge innovations and expand her expertise. Driven by a strong desire to tackle real-world challenges, Jayashree is committed to applying her knowledge to develop impactful solutions that contribute to the ever-evolving tech landscape. Her enthusiasm for learning and problem-solving fuels her ambition to make a meaningful difference in the field of electronics and beyond.

Bhupinder Singh working as Professor at Sharda University, India. His areas of publications as Smart Healthcare, Medicines, fuzzy logics, artificial intelligence, robotics, machine learning, deep learning, federated learning, IoT, PV Glasses, metaverse and many more. He has 3 books, 139 paper publications, 163 paper presentations in international/national conferences and seminars, participated in more than 40 workshops/FDP's/QIP's, 25 courses from international universities of repute, organized more than 59 events with international and national academicians and industry people's, editor-in-chief and co-editor in journals, developed new courses. He has given talks at international universities, resource person in international conferences such as in Nanyang Technological University Singapore, Tashkent State University of Law Uzbekistan; KIMEP University Kazakhstan, All'ah meh Tabatabi University Iran, the Iranian Association of International Criminal law, Iran and Hague Center for International Law and Investment, The Netherlands, Northumbria University Newcastle UK.

Siva Subramanian R is an faculty member in the Department of Computer Science and Engineering at SRM Institute of Science and Technology. He is engaged in academic research and teaching in the field of computer science. His interests include programming, data science, and emerging technologies.

T. Thilagam is an Assistant Professor (Senior Grade) in the Department of Computer Science and Engineering at Vel Tech Rangarajan Dr. Sagunthala R&D Institute of Science and Technology, Chennai. Her research interests include network security, cloud computing, and cryptography.

A. Thangam is currently an Assistant Professor in the Department of Mathematics at Pondicherry University – Community College, Pondicherry. His current area of research is Optimization and its applications in Inventory, Logistics, Supply chain, and Fuzzy Mathematics. He has published 25 papers in National and International Journals and he is guiding candidates for Ph.D in Mathematics. He has 13 years of teaching experience, He has published 9 patents.

Varadharajan Bhoopathy is a Professor at Sree Rama Engineering College. He holds a Ph.D. in Information and Communication Engineering from Anna University and has over 16 years of academic experience. Specializing in wireless sensor networks and IoT, he has published numerous research papers and holds several international patents. Dr. Bhoopathy is a recipient of prestigious awards for his contributions to education and research. His commitment to academia continues to drive innovation and excellence in the field of computer science.

Index

A

B

C

D

E

H

I

L

M

N

P

R

S

T

V

www.ingramcontent.com/pod-product-compliance
Lightning Source LLC
LaVergne TN
LVHW080612300926
849162LV00005B/1131

* 9 7 9 8 3 3 7 3 0 9 2 3 1 *